VERMONT ~~~~ C~ P9-CDS-232
MO~~~ELIER, VT.
WITHDRAWN

ESSENTIALS OF PSYCHOLOGICAL TESTING

UNDER THE EDITORSHIP
OF
GARDNER MURPHY

ESSENTIALS OF
PSYCHOLOGICAL TESTING

SECOND EDITION

WITHDRAWN

LEE J. CRONBACH
University of Illinois

HARPER & BROTHERS, PUBLISHERS, NEW YORK

Essentials of Psychological Testing, Second Edition

Copyright 1949 by Harper & Brothers
Copyright © 1960 by Lee J. Cronbach

Printed in the United States of America

All rights in this book are reserved.
No part of the book may be used or reproduced
in any manner whatsoever without written per-
mission except in the case of brief quotations
embodied in critical articles and reviews. For
information address Harper & Brothers
49 East 33rd Street, New York 16, N.Y.

D-L

Library of Congress catalog card number: 59–13919

151.2
C947e

TO MY PARENTS

11623

Contents

PART THREE. TESTING OF TYPICAL PERFORMANCE

Figures

Tables

COMPUTING GUIDES

Preface

THE purposes stated for this book in the original edition have also guided its revision. The basic course in testing should present the principles of testing in such a way that the student will learn to choose tests wisely for particular needs, and will be aware of the potentialities and limitations of the tests he chooses. We now have a large number of general principles of testing to aid in such evaluation and interpretation.

Psychological testing has been advanced chiefly by two lines of work: one, the practical and clinical application of instruments; the other, the theoretical and mathematical analysis of testing problems. These two lines of thought have often remained independent, so that test interpretations employed by clinicians and counselors frequently appear untrustworthy when judged by psychometric standards. Conversely, the clinician often finds the precisely designed and narrowly focused tests that come from the psychometric specialist unsatisfactory because they do not serve his practical needs. The cleavage between these two schools of thought has been reduced during the past decade, on the one hand by the increased concern of clinicians for the rigorous specification of hypotheses and validation, on the other hand by the broadening of psychometric theory to make a place for tests designed for purposes other than prediction of a specific criterion. This book views tests from both the practical and technical perspectives, so that the industrial, clinical, educational, or military psychologist will learn how the psychometric specialist evaluates tests and the psychometric specialist will understand the practical requirements which tests must meet.

The book is intended to serve the needs of undergraduates and beginning graduate students in psychology and counseling. It makes no attempt to exhaust any one of the fields of testing; rather, it covers those essentials on which later study of such specialties as industrial selection, clinical case interpretation, or test theory may be based.

There has been substantial change from the first edition of the book, though the broad outline and aims remain the same and most of the basic principles stand unchanged. The past decade has seen notable advances in testing and test theory, including the *Technical Recommendations* for psychological and achievement tests and the associated reformulation of concepts of validity, the extensive validation of differential aptitude batteries, and the decline of diagnostic pattern interpretation of the Wechsler intelligence scale from a widely accepted practice to a discredited hypothesis. One of the most striking changes in this period has been the improved quality of the information supplied by test publishers. For many tests, flimsy and inadequate manuals have been replaced by technical handbooks of monograph length, thereby increasing the importance of skill in interpreting information about reliability, validity, and norms.

In my teaching, I place particular emphasis upon this skill, the principal assignments being concerned with reviewing of tests and selecting tests for particular programs (e.g., guidance of freshmen in a described liberal arts college). The presentation of specific tests in this book is designed to assist in this function and not to substitute for it. Tests selected for extended description have wide application, illustrate important techniques and types of evidence, or illustrate significant principles. The space given to a test is by no means an indication of its merit; perhaps the prime determiner of inclusion has been the amount and variety of relevant information available, which biases the selection toward older tests. In order to introduce the student to a wider range of tests, a summary listing is given in many chapters. This summary is primarily a set of suggestions for further study. The annotation is too brief to serve as a critical review, and perhaps carries favorable or unfavorable connotations which I did not intend. I have accepted this risk in order to provide a preliminary guide to the beginner lost in the morass of test titles. It is urged that the reader use the summaries only to prepare a list of tests to be studied further, bearing in mind that even this summary covers only a fraction of the tests on the market. A decision about the merit of a test must come after a study of the test manual and accompanying information, the Buros yearbook reviews, and other sources. A word about the restriction of the listings to tests used in the United States is in order. So far as the principles which constitute the main content of the book are concerned, there is no such restriction. The principles of testing are universal, as can be seen by comparing this book to such sources in the bibliography as Meili, Vernon, Laugier, and Piéron, and by the international status of such tests as the Binet, the GATB, the MMPI, and the TAT. The differences between the psychometric and impressionistic testers within each country are far greater than any national differences. On the other hand, the summary of specific instruments is confined entirely to tests and editions on the American market. This neglect of tests developed in other countries is made necessary both by the facts of test distribution abroad, which limit the use of any one test, and by the inability of a reviewer to comment fairly on tests with which his acquaintance is remote.

The questions which stud the book are part of the text, capitalizing on the fact that the mind profits most when it works as it reads. By thinking through the questions on each section, the reader sees how the principles apply and becomes aware of topics which require further thought. The questions do not always have specific answers. Frequently they are deliberately controversial, or can be answered only by a qualified "Yes, but—." The student who sees two sides to any of the questions can have considerable confidence that he is doing good thinking.

In accomplishing my purposes, I have been greatly aided by my professional associations of the past ten years. Particularly broadening were the intimate association over a five-year period with the Committees on Test Standards of APA and other associations, the opportunity to pursue research in test theory made possible by the Bureau of Educational Research of the University of Illinois and the Office of Naval Research, and the opportunity given me by the Office of Naval Research and the National Institutes of Health to become acquainted with test research and applications at home and abroad. My colleagues in these ventures taught me much about tests. Howard B. Lyman, Russell P. Kropp, and Andrew Baggaley gave suggestions for the revision, and Jean W. Macfarlane's criticisms of this manuscript led to many improvements. I wish also to give special thanks to the representatives of various test publishing houses, all of whom have been most coöperative in supplying information about their tests and in helping me to clarify my ideas. As always, the students on whom these ideas have been tried were a major source of motivation and insight. Mrs. Lester M. Friend's services as typist of many drafts of the manuscript are acknowledged with appreciation.

LEE J. CRONBACH

September, 1959

PART ONE

BASIC CONCEPTS

Who Uses Tests?

THE testing movement stands as a prime example of social science in action, since it touches on vital questions in all phases of our life. What is character, and what sorts of children have good character? What personality make-up promises that an adolescent will be a stable, effective adult? How can we tell which 6-year-olds are ready to begin learning to read? Is this young man a good prospect for training in watchmaking, or should he go into a different vocation—say steamfitting or patternmaking? Such are the problems toward which testing and research on individual differences are directed. In this book, we will survey the methods which have been and are being developed to solve these problems.

TYPICAL TEST USERS

One way to get a quick overview of the region we are to explore is to find out what testers do. By meeting a few of the people who work with tests we can get an impression of the variety of services tests perform and of the way they fit into a psychological career. The people to be described are imaginary, each one being a composite portrait of many psychologists such as can be found in every part of the country.

Let's begin by calling on Helen Kimball. At about eleven on a January morning, we find her at her desk in the central administration building of the school system of Riverton, population 17,000. Miss Kimball is dark, attractive, 35ish. Her position bears the title School Psychologist. The office in which we find her is unusually bright, with decorative pictures, drapes, and a table low enough to accommodate a child. On the table are spread several objects: blocks, a cutout puzzle, a folder of pictures.

Miss Kimball apologizes for the disorder of the table as she greets us. "I just finished testing a boy and haven't had time to clean up the materials. Usually I keep just a toy or two on the table, to attract the interest of any child sent down to see me. These test materials are from the Wechsler intelligence scale and a picture test for studying personality called the The-matic Apperception Test." When we express interest in her case, and inquire about the reason for testing the boy, she outlines his background as follows.

Charles is a boy from a foreign home, middle-to-low economic status, who in the fourth grade suddenly is causing trouble after having been known as a friendly, successful pupil in other grades. His teacher reports that he has made almost no progress in school subjects since the start of the year, that he refuses her attempts to give him extra help, and that he has begun to disturb the class by hitting other boys, taking objects from the girls to annoy them, and similar misdemeanors. A check with the files showed that his previous teachers had made many favorable reports: "A fine worker. Does everything a little better than most other boys." "Learns new ideas quickly. Good at number work." But the objective tests given at the end of the third grade showed that he was not superior. In fact, in reading comprehension Charles was two months behind the average pupil of his class, and in arithmetic, his best score, he just reached the average. Probably the teachers were misled by his cheerfulness and industry into overrating his past learning.

"Now," says Miss Kimball, "they asked me to try to determine the causes of his problem. Teachers in each school check most of the cases; for instance, they give intelligence tests and reading tests, and make studies of the children the school needs to know more about. Charles was sent to me because the teacher felt his behavior presented an especially serious problem. The school did have a mental-test record, because Charles' class took the Kuhlmann-Anderson group intelligence test two months ago. Charles' IQ was only 65. But his teacher said Charles wouldn't work on the test. He did a few items, then stopped and looked out the window; when she urged him to go ahead, he worked slowly, and seemed not to be trying.

"So my first problem was to try to find out how bright Charles is, to learn what to expect of him. The Wechsler or the Stanford-Binet is our usual measure. Since we give these tests individually, most children coöperate well. When I gave the Wechsler this morning, Charles did about as well as most 10-year-olds; I haven't computed his IQ yet, but from the impression I formed as I gave the test, it will come out about 90 to 100—just a trifle below average. The score might be affected by his schooling, as many of the questions use language. The Performance section of the test, though, uses blocks, picture puzzles, and other tasks not likely to be affected by schooling, and he did about the same as on the Verbal section; apparently language difficulties aren't his big problem. I was pleased that he coöperated, since he'd had trouble before. He was eager to work, cheerful, and seemed pleased with his accomplishment. But of course we started out slowly, and I made a great effort to interest him in the 'games.'

"I did two other things with Charles. Usually we don't test so much in one day, but the school wants to make some decisions about Charles at midyear. So we broke off the testing and chatted awhile; then I gave him a vision test. I chose that because I noticed some squinting during the intelligence test, and the teacher had noted a few complaints of headaches. My vision tests aren't as precise as an oculist's, but they showed a little deficiency in one eye. Worse, though, is his coördination; the eyes don't work together, but instead look at slightly different parts of the page when he is reading. This probably can be corrected, but we'll need further visual tests to be sure. Poor visual coördination would cause trouble in reading and lead to fatigue.

"Since the emotional problem seemed to be severe, judging from the reports of Charles' social behavior, I used my picture test. The child makes up stories about each picture, and the stories often reveal his worries and wishes. Here's one picture, for example, showing a boy huddled up in a corner. Charles made up a story that the boy was playing with the others and they made him stop and go home. The other boys said he had a different way of playing that wasn't right. Several stories like that suggest that Charles is greatly worried about losing his friends, and about 'being different.' The test gives many other suggestions about Charles' problems, but I need to study the record before I form definite conclusions.

"Our next steps will be to check on the vision problem and to clarify the emotional difficulties. I'll have several conferences with Charles, helping him talk out his difficulties. Then we will see what can be done to help him solve them. The fact that he has normal mental ability is encouraging, since we know he can do well if his adjustment improves. It will help to know that he is average rather than superior, as past teachers suggested. Perhaps he's had to live up to too high a reputation. We may use further tests later; the ones used so far have narrowed our field of investigation, so that my conferences with Charles will be effective."

This sample gives some idea of Miss Kimball's work. No two cases are just alike, nor are the same tests appropriate for every case. In contrast to this "clinical" approach is the work of a personnel manager for a department store. This is a store with about 350 employees, ranging from roustabouts to buyers and office personnel. Edward Blake, the personnel manager, is a heavy-set, graying man of 45, who seems interested in whatever we have to say. But there is also a briskness, a sticking-to-a-schedule. "The routines of the job? I don't do much testing myself; but I do interview everybody we hire. That helps the store, because every employee knows there's someone here in the office who has met him and to whom he can take his problems.

"When an applicant comes in, he fills out a personal-history blank, and my assistant, Miss Field, gives him a set of tests. The tests aren't quite the same for everybody. We give all applicants a short multiple-choice intelligence test, since different jobs in the store call for employees of different caliber. Most applicants get a test of simple arithmetic—addition, percentages, discounts, and so on. For package wrappers and merchandise handlers, we use a simple test of motor ability in which they place wooden cubes in a box as rapidly as possible. It doesn't predict who'll be the best employee, but it saves us from some lemons. For a few departments, we have trade tests, tests of information about the job. Some men claim to be shoe salesmen when they don't know a last from a counter. These tests check on the experience the applicant claims in his application blank.

"Whatever tests Miss Field gives are scored and recorded on the application blank. Then, when there is a vacancy, we pull out the names of people who have the qualifications that job requires. I call in one or more of these people, interview them, and if I think they'll do, I hire them. The tests are most useful to sort out the good from the poor prospects. Miss Field can give the tests very easily, and it saves us a lot of time we'd spend interviewing people who wouldn't be good workers. Of course, Miss Field does a nice job, making sure each person knows we're interested in him, and sending each one away with a feeling that he's had fair consideration."

Mr. Blake, of course, is a little different from some other personnel manager we might have talked to. But his work is fairly typical of that in businesses having substantial turnover.

Unlike Miss Kimball and Mr. Blake, Max Samuels and Paul Sheridan are using tests for research which will have only distant practical applications. We find them in the Psychology Laboratory of Atherton University on a July day, surrounded by piles of test booklets. Samuels gets up from a tape recorder to which he has been listening and offers to show us around the project.

"We're studying how people solve problems. When we give an ordinary intelligence test, we see that people have many difficulties that seem to have nothing to do with their brightness. Sometimes a person becomes confused and makes the same mistake three or four times, even though he has already done harder problems. Another person may plan a solution to a problem and carry out several steps in an orderly way, but when he makes one error he loses his sense of direction and slips back into random trial and error. We are trying to develop exact methods of measuring these habitual ways of reacting to difficulties. They are important elements in problem solving, affecting scores on mental tests and also performance in practical situations. Intelligence tests, which measure the person's general level of success, do not give accurate measures of his manner of problem solving.

"Sheridan and I are just beginning to explore what the important variables in problem solving may be. We will spend a couple of years refining our observation techniques before we are ready to carry out formal studies. Both of us teach during the school year, but we spend about a quarter of our time giving tests to students. During the summer we analyze the records, revise the tests for the next tryout, and take a few more steps toward a theory of problem solving."

The first test Samuels shows us uses the same blocks Miss Kimball had on her table. The person tested is shown a mosaic design and asked to make the same design out of blocks. "In the intelligence test," Samuels says, "the score reports the number of designs completed within certain time limits. The tester may note casual observations of the kinds of error the person makes, but he does not score them. We are trying to obtain dependable scores indicating how systematically the person attacks the problem, how often he repeats a mistake, and how long a time passes before he notices a mistake. Sheridan gives the test in a room with a large mirror set in the wall. The mirror is fixed so that one can see through from the back; I sit on that side and observe every detail of what the subject does. I dictate a record into the tape recorder. We can listen to the tapes whenever we wish, and work out the nature and time of each error. We have developed new designs which make certain types of error more likely, and later we hope to develop a simpler scoring method which will not require a tape recorder."

Samuels shows several other tests using mazes, anagrams, and designs made by building up layers of cutout colored stencils. "Our main purpose," he says, "is to identify consistent patterns which the person shows on many different problems. These patterns are the ones we expect him to carry over when he writes a theme in English or tries to identify an unknown substance in chemistry."

We inquire about a piece of apparatus with a ring of lights and a few pushbuttons. "This," he says, "is an experimental test which permits us to present much longer and more complex tasks than the usual puzzle. It is used to measure abilities of high-level scientific and technical workers; one needs very difficult tasks to separate the best men in such a group. We are using it with average students because they make many errors, and our main concern is to study the types of error made by different persons. The apparatus is wired so that it follows some simple rules. These rules change with every problem. There are three pushbuttons which turn on and off various combinations of lights. The person's task may be to turn on light number 3 only. He presses the buttons in turn to find out what lights each button controls. For instance, when he presses button 1, lights 3, 4, and 5 go on. When he has all the information, he must find a sequence of actions which will leave only light 3 lit. A problem of this type can be made very complicated; even a bright person takes thirty minutes on some of our problems. One interesting feature of this apparatus is its automatic recording. Every time the person presses a button, a record is punched on a teletype tape. This tape can later be decoded to show just what the person did and when."[1]

Sheridan comes in at this moment with an armload of boxes that turn out to contain cards for use in computing machines. His role in the project, he explains, is to analyze the data after all the tests and records have been scored. "The electronic computer has been a blessing to research like this. We obtain about 200 scores on every student we test, and it would take forever to work out the relations on an ordinary calculator. But the electronic machine gives us the answers in just a few hours. The catch is that sometimes it takes a month to put all the records onto these cards. Every observation has to be reduced to numerical form before it can be treated statistically.

"Our main statistical method is factor analysis. This helps us to separate the variables which affect only a single task from the ones which show up consistently throughout the person's performance. We also find out which test scores give the best measures of each variable. The results so far suggest that we will eventually have dependable measures of how persistent, how systematic, and how adaptable the person is.

"We are not primarily interested in practical applications of the test. If we can classify people according to the way they solve problems, then we want to study how they get that way. Probably anxiety is an important cause of many of these errors, but we want to learn why one anxious person's errors habitually differ from those of another. We will eventually do experiments in which we frustrate people in various ways to see if different kinds of emotional stress produce different sorts of errors. But before we can do such research we have to be able to distinguish and measure these errors."

It is easy to think of applications for such tests as Sheridan and Samuels are developing. The tests might be useful in diagnosing mental patients, in selecting students for specialized training, or in analyzing students whose school performance is below their ability level. Very often, tests that are developed for laboratory investigations are put to practical use by applied psychologists.

Our three examples represent only a few of the many ways in which tests are used. We might also describe the clinical psychologist in a hospital, the tester preparing standardized tests for school use, the vocational counselor, and many others. In addition to these highly qualified investigators, we might pay more attention to the Miss Fields who give most of the tests in offices, clinics, schools, and industries. From the portraits presented we can draw these generalizations which warrant learning about tests:

Tests play an important part in making decisions about people and in

[1] For a technical description of research using a machine of this type, see John, 1957.

psychological research. There are a great variety of tests, covering many sorts of characteristics. Even for a single characteristic such as mental ability, there are many tests which have different uses. The significance of test scores is greatest when they are combined with a full study of the person by means of interview, case-history records, application blanks, and other methods. Tests provide facts which help us understand people; they almost never are a mechanical tool which can render decisions automatically.

PURCHASING TESTS

Who May Obtain Tests?

Tests are useful to many professions, but in the hands of persons with inadequate training they do a great deal of harm. An untrained user may administer a test incorrectly. He may place undue reliance on inaccurate measurements. He may misunderstand what the test measures and reach unsound conclusions. It is therefore important for the user to confine himself to tests that he can handle properly.

To see the implications of this remark, consider industrial personnel testing as an example. To a manager it may appear simple to give a group intelligence test, score it with a punched-out key, tabulate the scores, and hire the best man. A personnel psychologist, however, knows that on some routine jobs average men make better employees than highly intelligent men, who become bored and quit. He knows that a general mental test does not measure the abilities most important in many factory jobs. He knows that even experts make errors when they try to guess which tests will predict success in a given job; a scientifically designed tryout is essential to make sure that the tests actually pick better employees.

Introducing and operating an industrial testing program requires many different abilities:

1. Analyzing the job to identify abilities which could be relevant.
2. Selecting promising tests for tryout.
3. Constructing new tests when no published test is suitable.
4. Planning and carrying out an experimental trial; choosing the final set of tests.
5. Deciding how test results are to be used in selection.
6. Routinely administering tests to applicants.
7. Scoring.
8. Interpreting the test and making hiring decisions within the general plan.

A great deal of training is required to perform steps 1 through 5. For most tests used in industry, steps 6 and 7 can be performed by an intelligent clerical worker under proper supervision. Step 8 may be a routine operation or may call for a decision by an executive who considers a psychologist's recommendation along with other facts.

Industrial personnel workers in the United States are qualified at various levels:

● Diploma in industrial psychology. A diploma is given by the American Board of Examiners in Professional Psychology to an industrial psychologist who possesses (among other qualifications) the training and experience required for carrying out all phases of a testing program.[2] A person holding this diploma is called a diplomate.

● Ph.D. in personnel psychology. A psychologist at this level (who may have received his training in a university department of psychology, education, or business management) should be able to perform all the functions listed above. If he has limited experience, he may need to consult a better-qualified person, especially in planning the program. Numerous consulting firms provide assistance of this type.

● Limited specialized training. Workers who have training in personnel methods equivalent to a master's degree can carry out specialized functions within a general plan. They can administer complicated tests, collect data on the performance of employees, and make some decisions about individuals. A psychologist can train an intelligent assistant to perform such functions, although he must then provide close supervision.[3]

● Intelligent workers without psychological training. A person without psychological training can learn to administer many group tests, take charge of the scoring of objective tests, and apply mechanical rules for selection on the basis of scores.

● Ordinary clerical workers. Workers at this level should be used only for routine scoring under competent supervision, and for assisting in test administration.

If we were to consider some other use of tests such as a vocational counseling service, a school testing program, or a diagnostic service in a mental hospital, we would observe similar needs. In each of these services there is need for some routine handling of tests and test data, for responsible supervision, and for high-level planning of the total program. A testing program involves far more than buying a package of tests and going to work.

The amount of specialized training required depends upon the tests to be used. Some tests can be administered and interpreted by responsible persons who have no specialized training. Other tests serving the same general

---

[2] The Board also grants diplomas in clinical psychology and in counseling. For further information on diploma requirements see Daniel and Louttit, 1953.

[3] One psychologist (Wilson, 1951) has described how he trained convicts (including a safecracker, a dope peddler, and a counterfeiter) to give even fairly complicated tests to other prisoners.

purpose can be used only by well-qualified psychologists. For example, two tests which might have some value in selecting men for training as junior executives are the *Ohio State Psychological Examination* and the *Thematic Apperception Test* (TAT). The former is a precise, and fairly difficult test of vocabulary knowledge and verbal reasoning ability. The directions and scoring procedure are so simple that a careful high-school graduate can follow them. An employer with no psychological training can easily understand what the results mean. To administer and interpret the TAT, a person must have graduate training in the psychology of personality and should have additional supervised experience with this particular test. It is used to investigate the drives and creative abilities of the applicant, and the conclusions it suggests are not highly dependable. Serious errors in judgment would result if the test were interpreted by anyone save a cautious and able psychologist.

The APA Code for Test Distribution.   Distributors of tests try to restrict sales to qualified persons, just as the sale of medicines is restricted. Test distributors check the qualifications of purchasers to determine whether they are able to use whatever tests they order. Severe restrictions are placed on the tests which are most difficult to interpret and the misinterpretation of which would be most serious.

A further reason for restriction is to prevent copies of questions from falling into the hands of persons who will later take the test. Students would like to become familiar with a college entrance examination in advance, but this knowledge would give them an unfair advantage over other applicants. Parents sometimes try to help their child by coaching him on intelligence test items, but to the extent that their coaching succeeds, it prevents the psychologist from making sound decisions. The control system protects all legitimate users of published tests.

The guiding principles of the control system are set down in the *Ethical Standards of Psychologists*. This important statement was officially adopted by the American Psychological Association in 1950. The following paragraphs abstract and paraphrase the formal statement, omitting legalistic details applying only to borderline problems (*Ethical Standards*, 1953, pp. 146–148):

> Tests and diagnostic aids should be released only to persons who can demonstrate that they have the knowledge and skill necessary for their effective use and interpretation. Tests can be classified in the following categories:
>
> *Level A.* Tests or aids which can be adequately administered, scored and interpreted with the aid of the manual and a general orientation to the kind of organization in which one is working. (Examples: educational achievement, trade, and vocational proficiency tests.) Such tests

and aids may be given and interpreted by responsible nonpsychologists such as school principals and business executives.

Level B. Tests or aids which require some technical knowledge of test construction and use, and of supporting subjects such as statistics, individual differences, the psychology of adjustment, personnel psychology, and guidance. (Examples: general intelligence and special aptitude tests, interest inventories and personality screening inventories.)

These tests and aids can be used by persons who have had suitable psychological training; or are employed and authorized to use them in their employment by an established school, government agency, or business enterprise; or use them in connection with a course for the study of such instruments.

Level C. Tests and aids which require substantial understanding of testing and supporting psychological topics, together with supervised experience in the use of these devices. (Examples: clinical tests of intelligence, and personality tests.)

Such tests and aids should be used only by Diplomates of the American Board of Examiners in Professional Psychology; or persons with at least a master's degree in psychology and at least one year of properly supervised experience; or other psychologists who are using tests for research or self-training purposes *with suitable precautions;* or graduate students enrolled in courses requiring the use of such devices under the supervision of a qualified psychologist; or members of kindred professions with adequate training in clinical psychological testing; or graduate students and other professional persons who have had training and supervised experience in administering and scoring the test in question, and who are working with a person who is qualified to interpret the test results.

Being a trained psychologist does not automatically make one a qualified user of all types of psychological tests. Being qualified as a user of tests in a specialty such as personnel selection, remedial reading, vocational and educational counseling, or psychodiagnosis does not necessarily qualify one in other specialties. Being a psychiatrist, social worker, teacher, or school administrator does not *ipso facto* qualify one to use projective techniques, intelligence tests, standardized achievement tests, etc.

The system for controlling distribution varies somewhat with the publisher. The major distributing firms check the name of each purchaser against the directory of diplomates and similar sources to determine whether his qualifications are sufficient for the tests he has ordered. If there is doubt, the purchaser is asked to give information about his training. The distributor may ask some qualified psychologist who knows the purchaser (e.g., one of his former professors, or his clinical supervisor) to endorse his request. The publisher evaluates this information and authorizes the person to purchase tests up to a certain level. Because such investigations are costly, some of the smaller publishers have made no effective effort to control sales of their tests.

The ethical responsibility for restricting tests rests on the purchaser as much as on the distributor. A person who uses a test for which his training is insufficient runs the risk of making serious errors. It is essential that every tester evaluate his own qualifications (discussing them with a better-trained person if he is in doubt) and decide what tests he is ready to use. Ideally, professional workers would restrict their own testing by self-control, so that the publisher would have to concern himself only with nonprofessionals such as employers who believe that anyone can apply personality tests, parents who want to test their children's intelligence, or job applicants who want to practice for tests they may be asked to take.

1. Sometimes a tester relies on the distributor's judgment, thinking like this: "I'm not sure whether I'm qualified to use this test. I'll order it, describing my training honestly; then if the publisher sells it to me, I will know that I'm qualified." What is wrong with this attitude?
2. An employer without psychological training decides to buy personality tests and use them on applicants. What is gained by refusing to sell him the tests, in view of the fact that without them he will base his judgments entirely on superficial impressions gained through an interview?
3. Examine two or three publishers' catalogs to see what statements are made about restriction of sale. Are the restrictions uniform? Do they follow the APA code exactly?
4. Classify the following tests according to the levels of the APA code:
    a. A mechanical aptitude test requires the person to assemble simple objects (e.g., a mousetrap) as fast as possible.
    b. The Strong Vocational Interest Blank is an objectively scored questionnaire.
    c. A test of arithmetic computation is intended for screening store clerks, cashiers, and similar employees.
    d. A diagnostic oral reading test calls for careful observation of the pupil's errors, self-confidence, method of attacking unfamiliar words, etc.
5. What is meant in the code by the phrase "with suitable precautions"?
6. The code does not authorize distribution of tests to people who wish to assess their own aptitudes, skills, or personality characteristics. What are the reasons for this policy?
7. Most American tests are distributed through publishers to anyone who is qualified and wishes to buy them. Another system is found in various national employment services and youth agencies, especially in Europe. Each counseling service devises a special set of aptitude tests for its own use. Only the counselors employed by this agency are allowed to use the tests. What are the advantages and disadvantages of this type of control, compared with the usual type of distribution?

Sources of Information About Tests

A first step in looking for tests is to consult the catalogs of major test publishers. Except for a few tests obtainable only from smaller firms, the important tests are distributed in the United States by five companies: California Test Bureau, Educational Testing Service, Psychological Corporation, Science Research Associates, and World Book Company. The person need-

---

(a) ● **Mechanical Comprehension Tests**

GEORGE K. BENNETT, *et al.*

Designed to measure ability to understand mechanical relationships, these tests. consist of drawings with simply phrased questions about them. The effects of special environment and of rote memory of physical laws are minimized. Useful in selecting personnel for mechanical work and for selection of students for technical and engineering training.

FORM AA has norms for a large variety of school and industrial groups. Appropriate for general population testing; for more highly selected groups, use Forms BB or CC.

FORM AA-F is identical with Form AA except that instructions and questions are in *both* English and French, for use with French-Canadians.

FORM AA-S is the Spanish language edition of Form AA; preliminary norms from Cuba.

FORM BB is more difficult than Form AA. Norms based on ten groups of students, applicants, and employed technicians and engineers.

FORM BB-S is identical with Form BB except that instructions and questions are in Spanish; preliminary norms from Venezuela.

FORM CC (Owens-Bennett) is more difficult than Form BB and yields a wider range of scores at high ability levels. Norms are based on engineering students.

FORM W1 (Bennett-Fry) is the women's form of this series. Norms are based on high school freshmen and senior girls and several occupational groups of women. Difficulty level is between AA and BB.

High school and above. Time: no limit, about 30 min. Arranged with the test in reusable booklets and with separate IBM answer sheets, which may be scored either by hand or by machine.

Order booklets *and* answer sheets *separately, specifying* form *and* quantity *of each.*

Booklets, sold in packages of 25 with manual and scoring stencils.

1-9 packages	$4.50 each
10 or more packages	4.00 each
Single copies	25 cents each

Answer Sheets. Specify Form AA, BB, CC, W1, AA-S or BB-S (AA-F uses regular AA answer sheet.) Sold *only* in packages of 50, $1.90 each, and packages of 500, $16.00 each.

Specimen Set, 50 cents. *Specify form desired.*

Spanish forms AA-S and BB-S together in one specimen set, $1.00.

---

ing to purchase tests should therefore obtain the current catalogs of these firms, and of other publishers likely to have tests in his field of interest.[4]

The catalog lists and describes tests. Most of the catalogs indicate clearly what level of training is required to use each test, and who may purchase it. The publisher's recommendation should be viewed conservatively; in some instances the publisher indicates that a test can be used by a purchaser with limited training, even though testing authorities would favor a stricter standard.

Just what information the catalog itself can provide is illustrated by the excerpt above describing the Bennett tests, which we shall discuss fully in

---

[4] Addresses of publishers are given in the Appendix.

Chapter 3 and subsequently.[5] (The first symbol in the excerpt is a code letter
—a—indicating that this falls in the least restricted category of tests. Any
recognized business or industrial firm may purchase this test for use in personnel selection, even if there is no qualified psychologist on its staff.)

Tests may be suggested by several additional sources, particularly the
Mental Measurements Yearbooks (see p. 101).

Before a decision to purchase the test for use is made, a detailed study of
its manual is needed. Whereas the catalog description is only a paragraph
long, the manual offers several pages of information on the purposes to
which the test is best suited, methods of administering and interpreting it,
and its limitations. Sometimes the part of this information which describes
the research basis of the test is placed in a technical handbook, leaving the
less technical description for the examiner's manual. If the manual is divided
in this way, both parts should be consulted. A "specimen set" of a test is a
package including a manual, test booklet, and scoring key. Most universities
and many school systems and counseling centers maintain collections of
specimen sets for the use of students and professional staff. In addition, specimen sets may be purchased directly from the publisher.

Suggested Readings

Benton, Arthur L. Cerebral disease in a child. In Arthur Burton & Robert E. Harris,
Clinical studies of personality. New York: Harper, 1955. Pp. 600–611.
  A difficult problem in psychodiagnostics is simply presented. A 9-year-old
  was referred because of emotional and school problems. Test performance on
  the Stanford-Binet scale and on special drawing tests showed great variability in mental functioning. Interpretation of the performance led to a
  diagnosis of brain disease, subsequently confirmed by an operation.
Crutchfield, Richard S. Conformity and character. *Amer. Psychologist,* 1955, **10,**
  191–198. (Reprinted in Don E. Dulany, Jr., & others, *Contributions to modern
  psychology.* New York: Oxford University Press, 1958. Pp. 293–307.)
  In an illustration of the use of test procedures to advance scientific knowledge,
  an experimental test of readiness to conform to the opinion of one's group is
  described. Results show the relation of this tendency to personality and to
  the nature of the group.
Lawson, Douglas E. Need for safeguarding the field of intelligence testing.
  J. educ. Psychol., 1944, **35,** 240–247.
  Errors are made when teachers with inadequate training administer or
  interpret tests of mental ability.
Ogg, Elizabeth. *Psychologists in action.* Public Affairs Pamphlet No. 229, 1955.
  This description of the roles psychologists play is written for laymen and for
  those considering careers in the field.
Super, Donald B. A case study in exploration: curricular and occupational. *The
  psychology of careers.* New York: Harper, 1957. Pp. 92–100.

[5] From the 1959–1960 catalog of the Psychological Corporation.

A typical problem in counseling an adolescent girl who is uncertain about possible careers is described. Information from aptitude, interest, and achievement tests is combined with the girl's own statements and her school record to help her to a greater degree of self-understanding.

Swanson, Wendell M., & Lindgren, Eugene. The use of psychological tests in industry. *Personnel Psychol.*, 1952, **5**, 19–23.

A questionnaire survey of firms in Minneapolis and St. Paul gives a realistic summary of the testing programs in use for selecting employees.

Purposes and Types of Tests

DECISIONS FOR WHICH TESTS ARE USED

ANYONE who works with people is continually making decisions. A personnel manager decides whom to hire; a teacher decides whether each pupil is ready for long division; a physician decides how a patient should be treated. If the decision maker obtains better information before making his decision he will have a better chance of attaining the results he desires.

All decisions involve prediction. Any test tells about some difference among people's performances at this moment. That fact would not be worth knowing if one could not then predict that these people will differ in some other performance or in the same performance at some other time.

Consider a test of visual recognition. We flash a row of letters on the screen for an instant, and the person reports what he has seen. Some people recognize four letters; others grasp seven in the same brief interval. This difference is intriguing, but it is unimportant until it can be related to some other behavior. The applied psychologist sees that this task possibly has something in common with airplane recognition and with perception in reading. He investigates whether the flash-recognition test will predict success in these practical activities. If so, it can assist the armed forces to select lookouts, or help the primary grade teacher to plan reading instruction.

Prediction is involved in clinical use of tests also. A clinician might use the flash technique to see whether a person has especial difficulty in perceiving emotionally toned words like *guilt* and *failure*, that being a possible indicator of emotional disturbance. Such a test is useful only if the unusual score foreshadows deviant behavior at some time in the future. The clinician would not need to detect emotional maladjustment if that were only an internal condition which could never crop out. The significance of the clinical test hinges on the fact that certain responses permit one to predict behavior which should be forestalled or encouraged.

The scientific investigator may not care whether the tests he uses have value for practical decisions. He may not even be interested in individual differences. But he too must have tests which predict. The flash test is a good laboratory measuring instrument because its scores are stable. If conditions are not altered, a person makes about the same score each time he is tested; thus today's test predicts tomorrow's score. If the score changes when the experimenter changes the illumination, we know that the change resulted from the illumination and not from chance variation. The experimenter therefore can study systematically how flash perception is related to illumination. When this relation is fully understood, he has a general law which predicts what changes in perception will accompany changes in illumination. If the test were not able to predict tomorrow's performance from today's (other things being equal), it would be of no use to the experimental psychologist.

1. Demonstrate that prediction is intended in each of the following situations:
    a. A foreman is asked to rate his workers on quality of work.
    b. Airlines require a periodic physical examination of pilots.
    c. A psychologist investigates whether students are more "liberal" in their attitudes toward birth control after two years of college study.
    d. A teacher gives James a grade of C in algebra and Harry a grade of A.
2. Tests are used to obtain information which will permit sounder decisions. Does this statement apply to the Gallup public opinion poll?

Selection

Tests aid in making many sorts of decisions, including selection and classification of individuals, evaluation of educational or treatment procedures, and acceptance or rejection of scientific hypotheses. We shall consider briefly each of these types of decision, beginning with selection.

In a selection decision, an institution decides to accept some men and to reject others. Hiring an employee is such a selection decision. The distinguishing feature of the selection decision is that some men are rejected, and their future performance is of no concern to the institution. A person may be "selected" and "classified" at the same time.

Classification

In classification, we decide which of many possible assignments or treatments a person shall receive. Examples: The college student asks a counselor to help him choose the best curriculum. The Navy tests each recruit to determine whether he should be assigned to the engine room, the chartroom, or the gun turret. The schoolboy who reads poorly is given a series of tests to determine what method of remedial instruction he needs, and whether he should first have some other treatment (eyeglasses, psychotherapy, etc.).

One important classification problem is diagnosis of mental patients. This may seem like an attempt merely to find the right name for a patient's disorder, but it really is a choice among treatments, since the patient's label determines what treatment he gets.

Where people are assigned to different levels of work (rather than to distinctly different types of work) we have a placement decision. Placement is a special case of classification. "Placement tests" are used to allocate college freshmen to the proper section of English, i.e., to the appropriate treatment. Choosing officer candidates from among enlisted men is a placement decision rather than a selection decision, since the men not chosen as officers remain in the army and are used in a different way.

A sharp distinction between classification decisions and selection decisions is required because a test which is useful in making one type of decision may not help with the other (Cronbach and Gleser, 1957). A test which detects serious emotional disturbances would be very useful in keeping unstable men out of the Army (selection). The test might not help at all, on the other hand, in deciding how to treat men who break down in the service (classification). As we shall see in Chapter 12, one interprets validity data quite differently for classification and selection purposes.

Testing often leads to a description of the person, which can be far more individualized than a simpler classification. For instance, a test battery plus other facts might classify a student as a promising engineer, and this would lead him to a decision to enroll in engineering. A description would report in addition the many particular assets and liabilities that distinguish this student from other prospective engineers. He is especially interested in aviation; he has a rather immature and uncoöperative attitude toward superiors; he works energetically in short bursts, with no long-range scheduling. All these facts are useful to the counselor. Each one bears on a different decision about course planning, about disciplinary treatment, about advice on study, and so on.

When a test is used descriptively, we do not confine ourselves to one definite question. Rather, we try to record all important facts so that they will be available when questions about treatment arise. A description may catalog a student's interests, describe his personality pattern, or give an inventory of his knowledge about his major field. The description is multidimensional and helps us resolve many different questions about how to treat the person.

Evaluation of Treatments

So far we have considered only decisions about individuals. Tests are equally important as an aid in evaluating treatments. When the teacher gives an arithmetic test, he is testing his instruction as much as he is testing the students' effort and ability. If the results are poor, he should probably alter his method. When more than one instructional method is under consideration, an experimental comparison can be made; a test shows which method gives the best results and should be used hereafter.

In industry, questions about treatment or management can be decided by suitable tests. The effectiveness of training is judged by performance tests. Supervision and personnel policies can be judged by tests of attitudes and morale.

Verification of Scientific Hypotheses

The functions discussed above illustrate the usefulness of tests in making decisions of immediate practical importance. Tests are also used extensively to measure outcomes of scientific experiments, as was illustrated in our earlier discussion of the measurement of flash perception. The experimenter is not making decisions about particular individuals. He is trying to decide whether to accept or reject a particular hypothesis (such as, "The change of perceptual span with change in illumination is greater when a subject is under stress"). Tests provide a more objective and dependable basis for comparisons than do rough impressions.

Sometimes the investigator uses tests published for practical purposes, but a test tailor-made to fit the experiment will often work better. In one study, for example, the experimenter played phonograph recordings of words backwards, in order to study how people learn to recognize strange stimuli (Lewis, 1946). Such a task, just because it is novel, makes a very good experimental test.

3. Show that a reading test might sometimes be used by college counselors or administrators for each of the four types of decision listed above.
4. Classify each of the following according to the type of decision represented:
    a. A foundling home measures intelligence of a child and uses this as a basis for deciding which home to place the child in.
    b. An instructor rides with a pilot at the end of his training, and fills out a checklist to show which maneuvers he performs correctly.
    c. A psychologist compares the average intelligence of only children with that of children from larger families of similar social background.
    d. All applicants for a driver's license are tested.
    e. A test is given in a junior high school for the purpose of identifying adolescents likely to become delinquent.
    f. A university class is divided in two parts, one of which sees the lectures and demonstrations by television, while the other hears and sees the instructor directly. Both groups are given the same examination.
5. Education and psychotherapy are both learning experiences, yet tests are used much more often for routine evaluation in school than in therapy. What reasons can you suggest?

6. Describe one circumstance where tests might be used descriptively by:
    a. An employment manager.
    b. A social worker dealing with children.
    c. A teacher of typewriting.
7. When tests are used to obtain a description, it can be said that a classification decision is being made. Explain.

WHAT IS A TEST?

The layman is likely to think of a test as a series of questions requiring a written or oral answer. Psychological tests are, however, extremely varied, and the variety is steadily growing. Perhaps the best definition to cover the range of tests described in this book is as follows: *a test is a systematic procedure for comparing the behavior of two or more persons*. We shall not give attention to unsystematic, spur-of-the-moment procedures for sizing up a person —casual conversation, for example.

We shall examine a large number of principles regarding tests, and a large number of criteria for deciding whether a test is satisfactory. Perhaps we should define *test* so as to include all the procedures to which these criteria and principles apply. If we did this, however, we would have to extend the definition to cover measures of animal behavior and measures of nonbehaviorial characteristics. For example, to determine how atomic radiation affects behavior of animals, it is necessary to measure their activity before-and-after, and the procedure has to satisfy the same logical requirements as does any test of human behavior. In one study (Isaac and Ruch, 1956), the investigators believed that spontaneous movement of monkeys would be affected by radiation. To measure this effect, they tried four techniques: rating by an observer, recording from a photocell pointed across the cage, and two methods of recording the movements of the cage floor, which was suspended so that it vibrated when the animal moved. Determining the best technique is just like choosing among educational and clinical tests; the experimenters had to apply the very indices of reliability and test intercorrelation which we shall study in later chapters. Thus, while this book is most concerned with tests used to study differences between people, much of the material is significant for the animal experimenter, for the sociologist comparing communities, or for any other behavioral scientist.

Our definition includes measurements using apparatus, laboratory procedures for observation of social responses, questionnaires for obtaining reports on personality, and systematic records collected on an industrial production line. The reader is warned, however, that many definitions of *test* are in current use, varying with the writer's purpose. Some writers restrict the word *test* to measuring instruments, but we shall not. A true measuring instrument is supposed to assign to every person a number which locates him on a scale of equal units, as we do when we report height in inches. Not only do psychological tests give less perfect measurements, in this sense, than do instruments used in other sciences, but many useful devices do not "measure" at all. In particular, some personality tests yield a verbal description instead of summing up the person by means of scores.

Standardization

A distinction between standardized and unstandardized procedures grew up in the early days of testing. Every laboratory in those days had its own method of measuring memory span, reaction time, and so on, and it was difficult to compare results from different laboratories. It was likewise difficult for school officials to answer such practical questions as whether pupils were learning to spell as well as could be expected, when every teacher used a different test. Standardized tests were designed to overcome these problems. A *standardized test* is one in which the procedure, apparatus, and scoring have been fixed so that precisely the same test can be given at different times and places.

Some tests are provided with tables of norms stating what scores are usually earned by representative subjects. Tests having such norms are sometimes called "standardized tests," and the process of gathering norm data is called "standardization." We are not using the word *standardized* in that sense, because we wish to emphasize standardization *of procedure*. A test may have a table of norms even though its procedures are not clearly specified, and a test with well-standardized procedures may not have norms. Obviously, collecting norms is not profitable until procedures are well standardized.

The first major step toward standardization of psychological testing came in 1905, when a committee of the American Psychological Association defined procedures (e.g., for testing memory) which could be followed in all laboratories. Today, most of the published tests with which American applied psychologists and teachers operate are carefully standardized. In personality assessment, however, a number of quite unstandardized procedures are in general use.

Standardization has a place in all research. In experimental psychology, standardization is not yet as well accepted as in testing, but the need for standardized procedures is much the same. These remarks of Underwood and Richardson (1956, p. 84) regarding concept-formation experiments give arguments for standardization which apply equally well to tests:

> . . . tasks or materials which have been used are quite diverse in nature. With few exceptions (e.g., Weigl-type card sorting) no systematic series of experiments has been built around a single task. While this lack

of task standardization attests to the ingenuity of individual workers in constructing new materials, the situation may not be entirely satisfactory for efficient development of laws and theories. In the more highly-developed areas in psychology only a few basic tasks, procedures, or materials have been used. Thus, classical conditioning, the Skinner box, nonsense syllables, the pursuit rotor (to mention a few) all have had widespread use. While some may justifiably raise questions concerning generality of findings based on such a limited number of procedures and tasks, it cannot be doubted that interlaboratory communication and continuity is greatly facilitated by the use of common basic tasks and procedures.

Tests vary in the completeness with which they are standardized. Printing the questions and mass-producing the equipment assures uniformity in those respects, but the directions to the subject are not always worked out in complete detail. Every condition which affects performance must be specified if the test is to be regarded as truly standardized. Thus for a test of color-matching ability, one needs to use uniform color specimens, to follow uniform directions for administration and scoring, and also to use precisely the right amount and kind of illumination. If standardization of the test were fully effective, a man would earn very nearly the same score no matter who tested him or where. There are, however, many difficulties in completely standardizing the tester's procedure and the subject's attitude, some of which will be discussed in Chapter 3.

Objectivity

Tests vary in their degree of objectivity. A fully *objective* test is one in which every observer or judge seeing a performance arrives at precisely the same report. To do this, he must pay attention to the same aspects of the performance, record his observations to eliminate errors of recall, and score the record by the same rules. The objectivity of the procedure may be judged by the degree of agreement between the final scores assigned by two independent observers. The more *subjective* the observation and evaluation, the less the two judges agree.

Tests in which the subject selects the best of several alternative answers (e.g., true-false, multiple-choice) are referred to as "objective tests," because all scorers can apply a scoring key and agree perfectly on the result. In contrast, an ordinary essay test allows room for great disagreement among scorers. By careful instructions to the observer or scorer, free-response tests and observations can be made fairly objective.

8. Judge each of these statements true or false and defend your answer:
   a. Batting averages are *objectively* determined.

   b. The 220-yard low hurdle race is a *standardized* test.
   c. A teacher has each member of the class read the same article in a current magazine. Time is called at the end of three minutes, and each pupil marks the place where he is reading. He then counts the number of words read and computes his reading rate in words-per-minute. This score is compared with a table of average reading speeds for typical magazine articles. This test is highly *objective*.
   d. The test described in **c** is *standardized*.
9. Psychological tests often start from very crude procedures. Psychologist X thinks that he obtains useful information by laying a sheet of paper on the table at arm's length from his subject and asking him to touch with his pencil exactly in the center of a circle printed on the paper. The subject is told to withdraw his hand and repeat the movement, as rapidly and accurately as possible, until he is told to stop. Psychologist X gives the man a mark from 1 to 10 on each of the following qualities: speed, carefulness, and persistence.
   a. What changes would improve the objectivity of the test?
   b. What aspects of the procedure would need to be taken into account in standardizing the test?
10. Industrial morale surveys often use questions made up by the plant personnel office or its consultants. What advantages and disadvantages would there be in using the same standardized questions in many different plants?
11. The Kohs Block Design Test (see Figure 5, p. 42) is one of the most popular testing procedures. The subject is required to construct a pattern from colored blocks to match a printed sample. The test is chiefly used in child guidance, clinical diagnosis, and measurement of intelligence of persons who do poorly on verbal tests. It is also used for research on frustration and on cultural differences. At least twenty versions of the test (different items, different scoring rules, etc.) are used in different clinics and different countries. What are the possible advantages and disadvantages of this diversity?
12. The Kohs test was first published as a long series of carefully chosen items. Why do you think so many different versions now exist in different countries, even though the test is used for the same purpose in these places?

Psychometric and Impressionistic Testing

There are two philosophies of testing, growing from different historical roots and fostering different types of test procedure and interpretation; both are mingled in contemporary practice. While we cannot discuss these different approaches exhaustively, especially in this introductory chapter, we can survey the main characteristics of each.

Psychometric testing obtains numerical estimates of single aspects of performance. Its ideal is expressed in the famous dicta of E. L. Thorndike that "If a thing exists, it exists in some amount," and "If it exists in some amount, it can be measured." One can observe in this statement a hidden assumption that the psychologist is concerned with "things," i.e., with distinct elements or traits which have a real existence. All people are considered to possess the same traits (e.g., intelligence, or mechanical experience), but in different amounts. This view of psychological investigation takes its cue from physical science, which identifies common aspects of dissimilar objects and describes any object by numbers representing such abstract dimensions as weight, volume, and intensity of energy of a certain wave length.

The second approach leads to a comprehensive descriptive picture of the individual. We shall refer to this style of investigation as impressionistic. Impressionistic psychologists think that understanding another person requires a sensitive observer who looks for significant cues by any available means and integrates them into a total impression. Studying one trait or element at a time is, in their view, no substitute for considering the person as a whole. The impressionist is not satisfied with knowing "how much" of some ability the person has; he asks how the subject expresses his ability, what kinds of errors he makes, and why (see Barron, 1957).

To evaluate a subject's background, for example, a psychometric tester would have him respond to a biographical checklist covering experiences which many people have and which are likely to be important in their development. (For example: "Were you a Boy Scout patrol leader?") He would score responses objectively by counting the number of items checked in such categories as "Interest in sports" and "Leadership experience." The impressionist, on the other hand, would ask for an autobiographical essay, perhaps setting no more definite task than "Please write your life story on these pages." From the response, he could see what the subject considers important about himself, what emotional tone he uses to describe his past, and what unique experiences he has had—experiences the checklist would not cover. The free response may give little information on important areas covered thoroughly by the checklist, but it covers matters the checklist ignores.

Each approach has merit, and each has its special limitations. Both have contributed to the development of present practice, and neither style can be adopted to the exclusion of the other. The measurer must fall back upon judgment whenever he applies information from scores in teaching, therapy, or supervision of employees, and the portraitist cannot ignore the accurate facts psychometric instruments provide. There are several differences between the psychometric and impressionistic schools; a particular testing procedure may follow one school on one point and another on the next. The styles differ with respect to definiteness of tasks employed, control of response, objective recording of basic data, formal numerical scoring and numerical combination of data to reach decisions, and critical validation of interpretations.

Definiteness of Task. The test designer decides how definitely the task is to be explained to the subject. In some tests, such as the biographical essay mentioned above, the subject is free to employ any style and any content he chooses. On the other hand, a questionnaire in which the subject is to check each activity he has engaged in during the past five years leaves little or no room for individual interpretation.

A test is said to be *structured* when all subjects interpret the task in the same way. The more latitude allowed, the less structured the test is. Of special interest are *projective* tests, which ask the subject to interpret a stimulus that has no obvious meaning. For instance, he may be shown an inkblot and told to report what it looks like to him. If he asks how many ideas to report, whether to use the same portion of the blot in two ideas, or any other such question, he is told, "That's up to you."

Structuring the task controls the performance so that all subjects are judged on very much the same basis. It therefore permits a definite answer to a question formulated in advance (e.g., how much experience with small boats has the subject had?). The less structured technique allows greater variation in responses and in that sense reveals more individualized response patterns. (The subject's essay may, for example, give information on some unusual interest, such as training dogs for show, but may tell nothing about boating experience.)

Recognition vs. Free Response.   Most tests can be designed either in a free-response or in a recognition form, which allows greater control of responses and makes scoring less impressionistic. In a mental test, series-completion items (7 5 8 6 9 . . .) and verbal analogies (wolf is to cub as cat is to ————) may be left in free-response form, or the subject may be offered alternative answers from which to choose.

The psychometric tester generally prefers the recognition test because it can be more objectively scored, does not depend on fluency or expressive skill, and is less subject to misinterpretation of questions than the free-response form. Many testers, however, prefer the free-response form. The most important reason is that the free response permits observations which illuminate the scored aspect of performance. If a student writes out a long-division problem, for example, the tester can judge his neatness and his organization of work, and perhaps can base diagnostic conclusions on the errors he commits.

Product vs. Process.   A principal difference between psychometric and impressionistic testing is that the former concerns itself with the tangible product of the performance—the answer given, the block tower constructed, or the essay written. When a psychometric tester does pay attention to the process of performance, he arms himself with a record sheet for tabulating what the subject does. The impressionistic tester, however, watches the subject at work in order to form a general opinion; this general impression is indeed the basic datum with which the psychologist works. In describing their military testing during World War II, "German psychologists [who carry the impressionistic style to extremes] stated repeatedly that observations of the candidate's behavior during a test were more important than the actual score which he earned. . . . One man . . . said that the chief fault of inexperienced military psychologists was that they attached too much weight to objective scores and did not pay enough attention to the formation of an intuitive impression from observation of the candidate's reactions and expressions. Individual examiners were permitted and often encouraged to vary testing procedures and to emphasize their favorite tests" (Fitts, 1946).

Analysis of Results. It follows that formal scoring plays a large part in the psychometric test and a very minor part in the work of the impressionistic tester. American devotion to the numerical score sometimes goes to such extremes that a tester reports nothing about a child but the IQ calculated for him, discarding all the other information obtained in an hour of close observation. The thoroughly impressionistic tester may in his turn translate a test performance into a character description without ever counting up a score. Preferably, in individual testing, both scores and descriptive information are taken into account.

When a decision is to be made, one can apply some formal rule to the various facts or can combine them impressionistically. For example, a teacher may assign a course grade by strictly averaging the tests, or may form an overall impression that this student is "doing B work even if he did slump at the end" and that one is "not really as good as his tests suggest." The psychometric tester tends to prefer the impersonal procedure, while the impressionist thinks an informal method is more flexible and realistic.

The psychometric tester's insistence on numerical scores influences his choice of tests. Some testers bombard the subject with one test after another, seeming to have almost a mystical faith that the accumulation of numbers will provide all the information needed to solve his problems. In this concentration on measurable variables the tester may ignore equally pertinent aspects of the individual for which no scorable instruments have been developed. It is easy, in child guidance, to obtain measures of ability, and fairly adequate instruments exist for obtaining an "emotional adjustment" score. These scores, however, tell only a small part of the story, and the psychologist should certainly go on to investigate the child's image of his mother, his father, and his teacher, and what activities in his life give him the greatest satisfaction, even if none of these questions can be answered by a number on a scale, or taken into a statistical formula.

Emphasis on Critical Validation. Finally, we come to the question of critical validation. Psychometric testers are taught to distrust judgments based on tests and observations. Ideally, a psychometric tester accompanies every numerical score with a warning regarding the error of measurement, and every prediction with an index showing the probability of its coming true. The impressionist is less likely to carry out formal validation studies, often being satisfied to compare impressions based on one procedure with impressions gained from another. Validation of qualitative interpretations and "portraits" is much more difficult than validation of scores and requires a greater readiness for self-criticism on the part of the psychologist.

The most critical issue, indeed, between psychometric and impressionistic testing is that of confidence in the psychologist. Those who develop and advocate rigorous psychometric procedures regard the tester as a source of bias tending to obscure the truth. Those who prefer less structured procedures regard the observer as a sensitive and even indispensable instrument. The impressionist does not deny the danger of bias and random error in judgment. He, however, fears that narrowing one's focus to what can be represented in a numerical score on a standard procedure throws away most of the psychologically important information. The gains from intuitive observation and interpretation, he believes, more than offset the errors it introduces.

Most testers occupy an intermediate position—intermediate between obsession with scores and unrestrained use of intuition. Formal, strictly objective procedures are normally combined in some manner with judgment, everywhere save in mass classification programs such as military processing.

The impressionistic style assigns great responsibility to the test interpreter. He must be an artist, sensitive to observe and skillful to convey his impressions. Some psychologists are presumably much better judges of personality than others. The psychometric method seeks procedures which everyone can use equally well. The objective test is a camera pointed in a fixed direction; every competent photographer should get the same picture with it. Thus psychometric testing aims to reduce analysis of individual differences to a routine technical procedure. To the extent that it succeeds, it reduces the need for an authoritative, "wise" professional psychologist. A similar conflict between the technical and the artistic ideal is found in medicine. Laboratory tests assume more and more of the burden of medical diagnosis, yet doctors have great respect for the legendary genius who diagnoses unerringly the malady overlooked by the tests.

13. "Psychometric testing trusts the judgment of the test constructor, where it is unwilling to trust the tester." Is this a defensible statement?
14. Distinguish between *structured* and *standardized*.
15. In what respects are the following procedures unstructured?
    a. In the Ayres handwriting test, pupils are told to write the Gettysburg Address neatly, doing as much as they can in a fixed time.
    b. In the Draw-a-Man test of mental development, the child is told to "draw the best man you can."
    c. In a recorded pitch-discrimination test, the subject hears two tones and responds H, L, or N, according as the second tone appears higher than, lower than, or no different from the first.
16. What are the advantages and disadvantages of the biographical checklist as compared to the essay?

17. Is the issue between psychometric and impressionistic testers one that can be settled by suitable factual research?

CLASSIFICATION OF TESTS

Tests might be classified in many ways—according to form, purpose, content, and other characteristics. We shall place tests in two classes, the first being those which seek to measure the *maximum* performance of the subject. We use these when we wish to know how well the person can perform at his best; they may be referred to as tests of ability. The second category includes those tests which seek to determine his *typical* performance, i.e., what he is likely to do in a given situation or in a broad class of situations. Tests of personality, habits, interests, and character fall in this category, because characterizations like "shy," "interested in art," and "anxious when in disagreement with a superior" describe the individual's typical behavior.

Tests of Ability

The distinguishing feature of a test of ability is that the subject is encouraged to earn the best score he can. An ability is a response subject to

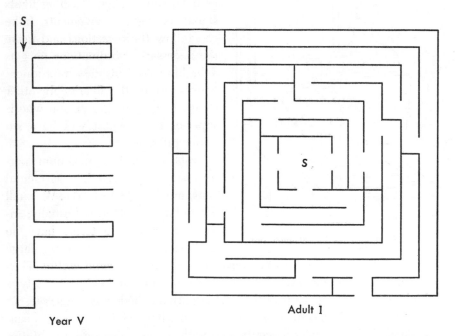

Year V

Adult 1

FIG. 1. Two of the Porteus mazes. The subject is required to trace the correct path through a maze. A failure is judged whenever his pencil enters a blind alley. He is then given further trials on the same maze. When he gets one maze correct he goes on to a more difficult one, continuing until he fails several trials at a particular level. (Copyright 1933, The Psychological Corporation. Reproduced by permission.)

voluntary control (McClelland *et al.*, 1958, p. 206). Naturally, the adequacy of the test depends upon the degree to which the person is motivated, i.e., upon his willingness to demonstrate his ability. The goal of the tester is to bring out the person's best possible performance.

Notice that we define ability tests in terms of what the tester is trying to learn rather than by describing the test itself. A test intended to reveal maximum performance sometimes fails to do so (for example, when the subject becomes too tense to perform well). Moreover, the same testing procedure can be used either to measure ability or to study typical performance. For example, although the Porteus maze (Figure 1) can be scored solely in terms of speed and correctness, it also permits the tester to observe how much foresight and planning the subject uses. Since any test performance depends on both ability and personality, our classification is somewhat arbitrary.

Some ability tests measure performance on familiar tasks: for example, a road test for a driver's license. Others require the person to do something completely unfamiliar. The Complex Coördination Test requires a person who has never flown a plane to operate a "stick" and "rudder bar" just as if he were flying. Flashing lights signal for certain movements. If he can follow the directions and make the necessary coördinations he gets a high score. This task reproduces one aspect of the flyer's job; other things being equal, a person who is superior on this test will be a superior pilot.

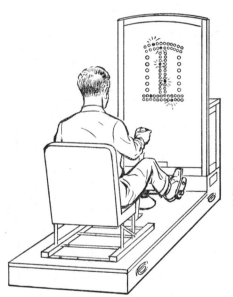

FIG. 2.   The Complex Coördination Test.

Tests measuring maximum performance are referred to as mental tests, intelligence tests, etc. We shall not define these terms formally; indeed, most of the terms have no well-established definition. One large group of tests we shall refer to as *measures of general mental ability*. They seek to measure those mental abilities which are valuable in almost any type of thinking or learning. Tests of this sort are often called "intelligence tests," but that name leads to controversy because "intelligence" has so many meanings. General abilities may be contrasted with the more specialized abilities which are of value only in a limited range of tasks. Among the specialized abilities are mechanical comprehension, sense of pitch, and finger dexterity.

There is no widely used name for tests of this sort; we shall refer to them as *measures of special abilities*. While a test for a single specialized ability may be used by itself, it is more common to test several such abilities at once so as to study the person's ability profile.

A *proficiency test* measures ability to perform some task which is significant in its own right: reading French, playing a piano, trouble-shooting an airplane engine. Since one of the principal uses of such a test is to evaluate performance of persons who have been given training in the task, these tests are often referred to as *achievement tests*.

An *aptitude test* is one used to predict success in some occupation or training course—there are tests of engineering aptitude, musical aptitude, aptitude for algebra, and so on. In form, these tests are not distinctly different from other types. An engineering aptitude test may include sections measuring general mental ability, mechanical and spatial reasoning (special abilities), and proficiency in mathematics. The test is referred to as an achievement test when it is used primarily to examine the person's success in past study, and as an aptitude test when it is used to forecast his success in some future course or assignment.

Tests of Typical Performance

Tests of typical performance are used to investigate not what the person can do but what he does. There is little value in determining how courteous a girl applying for store employment can be when she tries; almost anyone of normal upbringing has the ability to be polite. The test of a suitable employee is whether she maintains that courtesy in her daily work, even when she is not "on her best behavior." To take another example, any inspector with proper vision and training should be able to detect defective parts. A test which determines how well he spots defects when trying especially hard would measure vision rather than carefulness. The chief difference between the good and the poor inspector is that the latter permits himself to be distracted and careless in run-of-the-mill duty.

For cheerfulness, honesty, open-mindedness, and many other aspects of behavior, a test of ability has almost no practical value. Most people can produce a show of the behavior when it is demanded of them. But those who act cheerfully, honestly, or impartially when they know they are being tested may not do so in other situations. Typical performance is important even when we are concerned with aptitude for success. If we are hiring an executive whose past success guarantees his ability, we also wish to know *how* he usually operates. Does he supervise closely, down to the last detail? Or does he outline a general task and turn his subordinates loose? Is he equally concerned with production, human problems, and finances? Does he prefer long-range planning or quick adaptation? Knowing his pattern is necessary to place him properly in the organization.

In tests of ability a high score is desirable, but in most tests of typical performance no particular response can be singled out as "good." For example, there is nothing good or bad about interest in engineering. One who has this interest can use it, but one who does not finds other worth-while activities. Likewise, people show wide variation in dominance-submission in social relations. We cannot say that any certain degree of dominance is best, since our world has places for persons of all types.

The person's characteristic behavior is our best clue to his personality. Habits have predictive value in themselves; what a person does once he is likely to do again. Most psychologists would object, however, to assuming that a person's observable habits *are* his personality. New situations continually arise, and a description of his customary behavior does not directly indicate what he will do in a new situation. A boy may have a reputation as a womanhater, but some girl will come along who arouses a quite different response. A clinician who establishes warm relations with most clients will encounter some who arose only hostile feelings in him. Because we do not wish to regard these exceptional reactions as capricious and unexplainable, we interpret reactions in various situations as reflections of a more basic and consistent "personality structure." This structure has to be inferred from behavior. The psychologist hopes that when he understands the structure he will be able to predict the person's responses even to new situations.

Testing of typical performance is difficult. It has been accomplished, with greater or less success, in a variety of ways. These methods may be divided into behavior observations and self-report devices.

Behavior Observations. Behavior observations are attempts to study the subject when he is "acting naturally." Observations are made both in standardized test situations and in unstandardized or "natural" conditions.

The standardized observation requires that each subject be placed in essentially the same situation. Personality may be observed during a mental test, during a group discussion, or while the subject is walking a rail blindfolded. Special tasks are often devised which give an especially good opportunity for observation. These tasks may be referred to as *performance tests of personality*.

The standardized observation permits relatively exact comparison of persons who are not normally seen in similar circumstances. Moreover, it reveals characteristics which could be seen only occasionally in everyday life. Such procedures have been used, for example, to observe typical reactions to frustration. The person commences a task and is prevented in some way from attaining his goal. The way he reacts gives insight into his emotional control. In one famous study, preschool children were given the opportunity to play with ordinary, reasonably interesting toys. Then they were allowed into an adjoining room with extremely attractive toys. After a period of play in this room, they were herded back into the first room, and a wire screen was placed between them and the attractive toys.

As the artist's representation of this experiment shows (Figure 3), the children reacted in many ways: pounding on the fence, regressing to simple play with rocks, trying to pry under the fence, or going off to take a pretended nap. The observers recorded the children's behavior, finding that

FIG. 3. Varied behavior among children subjected to experimental frustration. (After a study by Barker and others, 1941; drawing reproduced from Morgan, 1942, p. 249.)

after frustration their games were less mature and less constructive than before.

If an observation is to bring to light typical behavior, the subject must not know what characteristic is being observed. The observer may be concealed, or the subject may be led to believe that he is being tested on one behavior when something else is being observed. Thus when reaction to frustration is being studied, the subject may be told that his mental ability is being tested. His responses when he is frustrated by difficult questions are usually genuine and little disguised.

Data on typical behavior may also be gathered by observing samples of the person's ordinary daily activities, "in the field," as it were. Children on the playground reveal a good deal about their habits and personality; so do noncoms leading platoons, and workers in the office. Field observations may use elaborately standardized recording procedures—even sound-motion pictures—or may, on the contrary, consist merely of an impressionistic judgment. The baseball batting average is a summary of systematically recorded field observations. The industrial supervisor's merit ratings are also based on observation, but the judgments are almost completely unsystematic.

Self-Report Devices.   The subject has had much opportunity to observe himself. If he is willing, he can give a helpful report of his own typical behavior. Questionnaires are used to obtain such reports. The crucial problem in self-report, if it is to be interpreted as a picture of typical behavior, is honesty. If the person tries to give the best possible picture of himself instead of a true description, the test will fail of its purpose. Even when he tries to be truthful, we cannot hope that he is a really detached and impartial observer of himself. His report is certain to be distorted to some degree.

Most self-report inventories offer a fairly comprehensive picture of personality. Some of them, however, are specialized in their coverage. There are study-habit inventories, interest inventories, social attitude inventories, and so on. Other tests are designated as "adjustment inventories," "character tests," etc.; such a name suggests the way in which the score is to be interpreted but does not identify a distinctive form of test.

It is generally agreed that personality questionnaires should not use the word *test* in their titles (*Technical Recommendations*, 1954, p. 10). If an instrument is marketed under the title "The Jones Dominance-Submission Test," employers, teachers, or others with limited psychological training may think that a person's dominance is being directly measured. If the instrument merely asks the subject a series of questions about himself, he can describe himself in any way he likes. A title such as "The Jones Dominance Questionnaire" or "The Jones Dominance Inventory" is less likely to give an impression of trustworthiness than "The Jones Dominance Test." It is desirable to use some term such as *questionnaire* whenever the word *test* might be misinterpreted.

18. Classify each of the following procedures as a test of ability, a self-report test, observation in a standardized situation, or observation in an unstandardized situation:
    a. An interviewer from the Gallup poll asks a citizen how he will vote in a coming election.
    b. A television producer wishes to know what program features appeal to different types of listeners. He presents a show to a small audience, who press signal buttons to indicate whether they enjoy or dislike what they are seeing at each moment.
    c. A test of "vocational aptitude" asks the subject how well he likes such activities as selling, woodworking, and chess.
    d. A spelling test is given to applicants for a clerical job.
    e. Inspectors in plain clothes ride buses to determine whether operators are obeying the company rules.

f. During an intelligence test, the examiner watches for evidence of self-confidence or its absence.

g. In a test of "application of principles in social studies," students are told of a conflict about admitting Negroes to a housing project. They are asked what the city council should do and to give reasons to support the choice.

h. An inspector in a stocking factory is supposed to detect all stockings with knitting faults. To check her efficiency, at certain times a number of faulty stockings which have been marked with fluorescent dye are mixed into the batch for inspection. The dye is invisible to the worker, but by turning an ultraviolet lamp onto the stockings after inspection the supervisor can readily locate the faulty stockings which the inspector missed.

Procedural Terms

There are a number of miscellaneous terms designating tests according to their procedure. The meaning of such terms as *pencil-and-paper test, apparatus test, oral test,* and so on should be obvious. Although all tests call for performance of some sort, the name *performance test* is usually applied to tests requiring a nonverbal response. Among the performance tests which have been used for various purposes are repairing a piece of electronic apparatus, drawing a picture of a man, stringing beads, and "inventing" a hatrack when given two long sticks and a C-clamp.

Group tests differ from *individual* tests in that the former permit many subjects to be tested at once. Group tests can be given to a single individual if that is desirable. Many individual tests require careful oral questioning or observation of reactions. Some individual tests can be modified and simplified to permit group administration. An example is the Rorschach test of personality. In the individual form of that test, a subject looks at a card bearing an inkblot and tells what he thinks the blot looks like. He is questioned about each response until the tester is sure just what the subject sees. In the group form, the blots are projected onto a screen. Subjects write their responses, and individual questioning is omitted.

Another meaning for *group test* has developed in recent years. The term now often refers to procedures for studying the behavior of the individual in a group. To observe leadership, initiative, and reaction to opposition, six persons may be asked to work together to solve a problem. The behavior of each person is observed.

19. Classify each of the following tests, using as many of the descriptive terms discussed in the text as are clearly applicable.

a. The Study of Values consists of printed questions, such as

In your opinion, can a man who works in business all the week best spend Sunday in
a. trying to educate himself by reading serious books

   b. *trying to win at golf, or racing*
   c. *going to an orchestral concert*
   d. *hearing a really good sermon*

The subject answers each question by checking whichever answer he prefers. Answers are scored by a numerical key to determine how important "aesthetic," "religious," and other values are for him.
   b. In the Stenquist Mechanical Aptitude Test, the subject marks illustrations of tools and other objects to show which go together (e.g., hammer and anvil).
   c. A Picture Arrangement Test item presents a set of four pictures which, arranged in the correct order, tell a story in the manner of a cartoon strip (see Figure 33). Each picture is on a separate card. The cards are presented in a random arrangement and the subject arranges them to make an intelligible story.
   d. In a finger dexterity test the subject mounts washers on rivets and places each one in a hole on a special board, working as rapidly as possible.
20. Classify the procedures used by Miss Kimball, the school psychologist described in Chapter 1, according to the terms used in this chapter.

Suggested Readings

Baldwin, Alfred L. The role of an "ability" construct in a theory of behavior. In David C. McClelland & others, *Talent and society*. New York: Van Nostrand, 1958. Pp. 195–233.
   Baldwin discusses the nature of ability and the theoretical requirements of ability tests. His argument that only voluntary behavior shows ability, as distinguished from habit, amplifies our distinction between maximum performance and typical performance.
Bingham, Walter V. On getting rattled. *Personnel Psychol.*, 1950, 3, 105–111.
   This article describes some apparatus tests for measuring coördination which, with slight modification, can be used to observe temperament.
Melton, Arthur W. (ed.). Problems and techniques of mass testing with apparatus. In *Apparatus Tests*. Washington: Government Printing Office, 1947. Pp. 22–53.
   The aptitude testing program discussed in these reports was the most elaborate one ever conducted. This chapter shows what had to be taken into account in standardizing procedures so that men tested in California could be compared precisely with men tested in Texas.
Munn, Norman L. Intelligence, and The assessment of personality. *Psychology.* (3rd ed.) Boston: Houghton Mifflin, 1956. Pp. 48–81, 170–181.
   An introductory textbook describes a great variety of prominent tests, giving drawings or photographs of most of them. The chapter on intelligence also provides considerable information on the nature and growth of intelligence.

Administering Tests

SOME tests are sufficiently simple for any intelligent adult to give success-fully; others are so subtle that months of special training are required before the tester can do a fully effective job. In general, group tests require less training to administer than individual tests, although there are some excep-tions. If the tester has no responsibility save to read a set of printed direc-tions, any conscientious, nonthreatening person should be successful. Where it is necessary to question the subject individually and to use follow-up questions if the first answer is unclear, great skill and experience are re-quired.

The tester must take pains to give every subject a chance to exhibit his ability, and to obtain results comparable to those of other testers. The im-portance of rigorous adherence to prescribed testing procedure is especially obvious in the great competitive testing programs for scholarship awards and college admissions. The Scholastic Aptitude Test of the College En-trance Examination Board, the most prominent example, is given in 1000 American centers and 40 foreign ones. At 9 A.M. on a particular Saturday in January, the seal is broken on the test package in each center: in Bronxville and Berkeley and Bell Buckle, Tennessee, in Beirut and Kubasaki and Kodaikanal. The completed papers pour into the scoring centers and reports go out to the colleges. A boy tested in Beirut may be in competition with one from Berkeley for admission to the same college, and the selection procedure is unfair unless the two are tested in an identical manner.

To assure fair testing, the tester must become thoroughly familiar with the test. Even a simple test usually presents one or two stumbling blocks which can be anticipated if the tester studies the manual in advance.

The tester must maintain an impartial and scientific attitude. Testers are usually keenly interested in the persons they test, and desire to see them do well. As a result, the beginning tester is tempted to give hints to the subject or to coax him toward greater effort. It is the duty of the tester to obtain from each subject the best record he can produce; but he must produce this by his own efforts, without unfair aid. The tester must learn to suppress not only direct hints but also those unconscious acts which serve as cues to the subject.

This is especially a problem in individual testing, where each question is given orally. On a mental-test item where the child is supposed to receive only one trial, his answer may show that he did not comprehend the question. The tester will often be tempted to repeat the question "since the child could certainly have answered correctly if he had understood what was wanted"; this must not be done, since the test directions permit only one trial. Adjustments are sometimes warranted, however; for example, the result might be discarded (rather than scored as wrong) if an outside disturbance caused the child's failure.

Unintended help can be given by facial expression or words of encouragement. The person taking a test is always concerned to know how well he is doing, and watches the examiner for indications of his success. Suppose he is given the task: "Repeat backward, 2–7–5–1–4." He may begin "4–1–7 . . ."; if the examiner, on hearing the "7," permits his facial expression to change, the subject may take the hint and catch his own mistake. The examiner must maintain a completely unrevealing expression, while at the same time silently assuring the subject of his interest in what he says.

Maintaining rapport is necessary if the subject is to do well. That is, the subject must feel that he wants to coöperate with the tester. A teacher who knows and likes a child, or a counselor who has worked with an adult, can often secure more spontaneous and representative performance than a stranger called in to administer tests. Those who are acquainted with the subject, however, will be less impartial and must be unusually circumspect in following procedures. No rules can be given for the establishment of rapport, but the tester who likes people will develop many techniques. The person who proceeds coldly and "scientifically" to administer the test, without convincing the subject that he regards him as an important human being, will frequently find it difficult to maintain coöperation. Poor rapport is evidenced by inattention during directions, giving up before time is called, restlessness, or finding fault with the test.

This chapter gives a general introduction to test administration. It cannot, of course, make the reader into a skilled tester; that comes only with practice. To clarify our discussion in this and the next three chapters, we digress here to describe the Bennett Test of Mechanical Comprehension and the Block Design test in some detail. These tests are important in themselves, but we present them here so that we can refer to them to illustrate general principles of testing. If possible, the reader should take each of these tests himself.

TWO SPECIMEN TESTS

Test of Mechanical Comprehension

The Test of Mechanical Comprehension (TMC) originated by George K. Bennett is one of the most widely used tests in the "special ability" group. The first form appeared in 1940. Four forms were published under Bennett's name, other versions have been included in military classification batteries and vocational aptitude tests, and a recent version is contained in the important DAT battery for high-school guidance. A list of the forms and their purposes was given in the catalog excerpt in Chapter 1 (p. 14).

The test manual (Bennett, 1947) begins with this description of purpose:[1]

The Test of Mechanical Comprehension measures the ability to perceive and understand the relationship of physical forces and mechanical elements in practical situations. This type of aptitude is important for a wide variety of jobs and for engineering and many trade school courses.

. . . .

Mechanical comprehension may be regarded as one aspect of intelligence if intelligence is broadly defined. The person who scores high in this trait tends to learn readily the principles of operation and repair of complex devices. Like other aptitude tests, it is influenced by environmental factors, but not to an extent that introduces important difficulties in interpretation. Formal training in physics appears to increase the score by not more than 4 points. Care has been taken to present items in terms of simple, frequently encountered mechanisms that do not resemble textbook illustrations or require special knowledge.

The test booklet carries instructions to the student and draws his attention to two specimen items (Figure 4). The manual carries the following directions to the tester:

This test has no time limit. Ordinarily, a great majority complete the test in twenty to twenty-five minutes; little is gained by allowing more than thirty minutes.

After distributing the booklets and answer sheets, say: *You have been given a test booklet containing questions and a separate sheet for your answers. Be sure to write on only the answer sheet. Make no marks on the booklet itself.*

Now look at the directions printed on the cover of your test booklet while I read them aloud to you.

Fill in the requested information on your ANSWER SHEET. [E.g., name, age, sex, date, last grade completed.] . . .

Now line up your answer sheet with the test booklet so that the "Page 1" arrow on the booklet meets the "Page 1" arrow on the answer sheet. Demonstrate. *Then look at Sample X on this page. It shows pictures of two rooms and asks, "Which room has more of an echo?" Because it has neither rugs nor curtains, there*

[1] Directions, norms, and specimen items reproduced by permission. Items copyright 1941, 1947, by The Psychological Corporation.

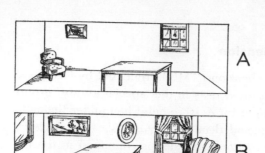

X

Which room has more of an echo?

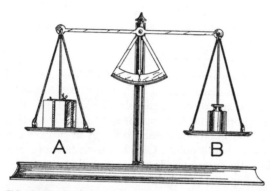

Y

Which weighs more?
(If equal, mark C.)

FIG. 4. Mechanical Comprehension Test items. (Sample X is from Form AA of the Bennett test, and Sample Y from Form A of the DAT Mechanical Reasoning Test. Both items used by permission of The Psychological Corporation. Bennett item copyright 1940, 1941, 1955; DAT item copyright 1947.)

is more of an echo in room "A," so blacken the space under "A" on your answer sheet. Now look at Sample Y and answer it yourself. Fill in the space under the correct answer on your answer sheet. Are there any questions? If the answers on the answer sheet are not directly opposite the questions, raise your hand.

After Sample Y has been answered, say: On the following pages there are more pictures and questions. Read each question carefully, look at the picture, and fill in the space under the best answer on the answer sheet. Make sure that your marks are heavy and black. Erase completely any answer you wish to change. Be certain that you use the right column on the answer sheet for each page. The arrow on the page should meet the arrow on the answer sheet. These arrows are at a different place on each page to help you.

Now open your booklets and fold back the cover so that only Page 2 shows, like this. Demonstrate. Then slip your answer sheet under the booklet and line it up so that the arrows for "Page 2" meet, like this. Demonstrate. When you finish a page, go right on to the next. Now begin the test. Answer all the questions; you will probably have plenty of time to finish. If you have any questions, raise your hand. The examiner should make sure that everyone understands how to use the answer sheet.

If the answer sheets are to be machine scored, the examiner should include appropriate directions regarding the special pencils.

The answer sheet is similar to that illustrated on page 67.

Block Design Test

The history of the Block Design test illustrates the way in which tests develop. S. C. Kohs was a clinical psychologist who invented the procedure and made up a set of items (Kohs, 1923). It was only one among a large number of mental tests invented during the 1920's, when applied psychology first came into prominence. As schools began to hire psychologists to examine children, a demand arose for well-standardized collections of tests. A psychologist acting as editor collected tests by various authors, improved the directions, materials, and scoring procedures, and applied the whole set to a large group of typical pupils to obtain standards of comparison. Several such collections were made, including those of Grace Arthur and Pintner and Paterson, each being designed to fill slightly different needs. The Block Design procedure was used in many of these collections, being a good nonverbal measure of analytic and synthetic reasoning with a wide range of difficulty. Revision and restandardization has continued down to the present day. Each modification alters the number of items or the directions, or introduces new designs. We shall describe the test in the recent WAIS version (Wechsler, 1955, p. 47).

The test makes use of a set of colored one-inch cubes originally sold for children's play. The test instructions begin as follows:

Start with Design 1 for all subjects. Take four blocks and say *You see these blocks. They are all alike. On some sides they are all red; on some, all white; and on some, half red and half white.* Turn the blocks to show the different sides. Then say *I am going to put them together to make a design. Watch me.* Arrange the four blocks slowly into the design shown on Card 1, *without* exposing Card 1 to the subject. Then, leaving the model intact, give four *other* blocks to the subject and say *Now make one just like this.* If the subject successfully completes the design within the time limit, score 4 points and proceed to Design 2.

If the subject fails to complete the design within the time limit or arranges the blocks incorrectly, pick up his blocks, leaving the examiner's model intact, and say *Watch me again.* Demonstrate a second time using subject's blocks, then mix them up, still leaving the examiner's model intact, and say *Now you try it and be sure to make it just like mine.* Whether subject succeeds or fails on this trial, proceed to Design 2.

Occasionally a subject will try to duplicate the examiner's model exactly, including the sides. When this occurs on Design 1, tell the subject that only the top needs to be duplicated.

A second sample is then administered in a similar manner. The test proper begins with Design 3. The directions are:

Designs 3–10. Place the card for Design 3 before the subject and provide him with four blocks. Say *Now make one like this. Tell me when you have finished.* When the subject indicates he has finished or at the end of the time limit, mix up his blocks and present Design 4 with the remark *Now make one like this. Go*

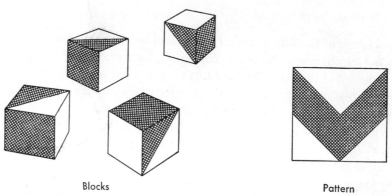

Blocks   Pattern

FIG. 5. Block Design test materials. (Pattern copyright 1940, © 1955 by The Psychological Corporation. Reproduced by permission.)

ahead; let me know when you have finished. Follow this procedure for all succeeding designs.

When Design 7 is reached, take out the five other blocks and say *Now make one like this, using nine blocks. Be sure to tell me when you have finished.* For Design 10 [which has an irregular outline], do not permit the subject to rotate the card to give the design a flat base. However, give full credit if his reproduction of the design is rotated not more than 45°.

> *Time Limits*   Designs 1–2   60 seconds (Time each trial separately)
> Designs 3–6   60 seconds
> Designs 7–10   120 seconds

Record time taken for the subject to complete each design if it is done correctly within the time limit; bonuses are given for rapid performances on Designs 7–10.

Discontinue   After 3 consecutive failures. Failure on both trials of either Design 1 or Design 2 is considered one failure.

As in other individual tests, the tester observes the subject's performance with care. He notes the time required to complete each task, and any errors. In addition, he watches for any revealing remark, any emotional reaction or blocking, and any unusual method of attacking the task. Some persons are cautious and some are impulsive. Some deal with the pattern as a whole and some must consider each tiny section in turn. Some give up when they face difficulty, some become erratic and make the same error repeatedly, and others show increased interest under the greater challenge.

1. If the TMC were administered individually, could profitable observations be made?
2. Can you think of any questions a subject might ask which the TMC directions do not cover?

3. Wechsler's directions specify only that the blocks are to be "mixed up" after each trial. Could this procedure be standardized more exactly? Should it?
4. Wechsler prescribes that each sample should be demonstrated only twice. Even if the subject is unable to do the task on the second sample, the tester proceeds to the next design. Is this a wise procedure?
5. The manual is not regarded as sufficient to prepare one to give the Wechsler test. The tester learns by observing an experienced tester and discussing procedures with him. What do you think you could learn about giving the Block Design test that the manual did not tell you?

PROCEDURE FOR TEST ADMINISTRATION

Conditions of Testing

Certain general problems of administration are common to all tests. The first of these is the physical situation where the test is given. If ventilation and lighting are poor, subjects will be handicapped. On speed tests particularly, their scores will be lower than they deserve if they do not have a convenient place to write, including sufficient space to spread out materials. Subjects must be placed so that they can hear directions and see demonstrations clearly. Very large rooms are generally bad for group testing, unless proctors are stationed to watch subjects closely. The large room has the disadvantage that a person may hesitate to ask a question about unclear directions which he would raise before a smaller audience. This may be solved by having him raise his hand so that a proctor will come to his seat and answer his question.

The state of the person tested affects the results. If the test is given when he is fatigued, when his mind is on other problems, or when he is emotionally disturbed, results will not be a fair sample of his behavior. Occasionally it is necessary to test a person at an unfavorable time, as when psychological examinations must be given to a criminal at the time of his trial. Tests to be used in classification and guidance of college freshmen are frequently given in the midst of a hectic week of orientation, college activities, establishment of new friends and living arrangements, and adjustment to a semiadult world. Sometimes a freshman who later proves to be normally intelligent does very badly on placement tests because of homesickness, distraction, emotional exhaustion, or unidentified causes. While tests given under these conditions do have predictive value for most of the group, some individual scores are misleading. If a test must be given at a psychologically inopportune time, the only correct procedure is to maintain an adequately critical attitude toward results. Conditions can often be improved by spacing tests to avoid cumulative fatigue, providing for adequate rest on the night before tests, and administering the program with a minimum of bustle and confusion.

During World War II, the General Classification Test was often given to soldiers just after induction when they lacked sleep, were recovering from a farewell party, or felt ill from inoculations. In one study men who took a second form of the test after becoming stabilized in Army routines raised their scores 11.25 points on the average. This is a large enough shift to raise a man from the category of potential noncom to that of potential officer (Duncan, 1947).

Time of day may influence scores, but it is rarely important. Alert subjects are more likely to give their best than subjects who are tired and dispirited. Equally good results can be produced at any hour, however, if the subjects want to do well. In most instances, fatigue apparently affects motivation rather than the ability one can summon up. The most thorough examination of hour-by-hour variation was conducted by Air Force psychologists (Melton, 1947, pp. 49–51). In one study of 2500 cadets being classified at Buckley Field, Colorado, they found striking and significant differences in psychomotor test performance (finger dexterity, rudder control, discrimination reaction time, etc.). In general, performance was at its peak between 10 A.M. and 3 P.M. In an attempt to confirm and interpret this difference with further tests of nearly 9000 cadets at other places, negligible differences were found. The inconsistency has not been explained, but it appears that under most operating conditions fluctuations during the day can be avoided. The experience at Buckley Field warns the tester never to close his mind to the possibility that error may enter his tests from unexpected sources.

Control of the Group

Group tests are given only to reasonably mature and coöperative subjects who expect to do as the tester requests. Group testing, then, is essentially a problem in command. For efficient testing, subjects must follow instructions promptly and all must do the same thing. This attitude must be maintained without interfering with the opportunity of individuals to ask questions. One person should be in charge, standing in front of the group where he can see all members. He will find helpful the adage "Never give an order unless you expect it to be obeyed." False starts, preliminary attempts to call the group to order while late-comers are finding seats, and ineffectual rapping for attention make it more difficult to secure real conformity when work begins. The tester should have full attention when he starts to talk, so that repetition will not be necessary.

Directions should be given simply, clearly, and singly. A complex instruction: "Take your booklet, turn it face down, and then write your name on the answer sheet," will lead to misunderstanding and confusion. It is better to break the instruction into unmistakable simple units: "Take your booklet." (Hold a sample up, and watch the group to be sure everyone has taken his booklet before proceeding.) "Turn it face down." (Demonstrate and wait until everyone has complied.) "Now take your answer sheet." (Exhibit a sample, and wait for compliance.) "Write your name on the blank at the top, last name first." The subjects have a chance to ask questions whenever they are necessary, but the examiner attempts to anticipate all reasonable questions by full directions.

Military techniques are effective for control of a group. When a military manner is assumed, however, it may enhance the "inhuman" character of the test situation and give some people the feeling that the examiner is not interested in their welfare. Effective control may be combined with good rapport if the examiner is friendly, avoids an antagonistic, overbearing, or fault-finding attitude, and is informal when formal control is not called for. After establishing control, for example, he may often relax his "command manner" and make informal comments about the test and its purpose; this does not interfere with his resuming formal control for the test proper.

Emergencies arise which prevent uniform testing of all persons. Occasionally, for example, a person becomes ill during the test and must leave the room. Usually it will be possible to collect his materials, indicate that the test is invalidated, and provide for a make-up on another occasion, perhaps with a different form of the test. The goal of the tester is to obtain useful information about people. There is no value in adhering rigidly to a testing schedule if that schedule will not give true information. Common sense is the only safe guide in the exceptional situation.

6. An employment office gives all applicants an intelligence test when their applications are filed. One man takes the test, together with several friends, and the group leave together. Ten minutes later he returns, greatly agitated: "Was I supposed to turn over the last page? I thought I had finished when I got to the bottom of page 9, so I looked back over my answers. I had plenty of time, and I'm sure I could have done well on the last page—my friends say the questions there were easy." What should be done in this case, if at the bottom of page 9 the booklet carried the printed statement "Go on to the next page"?

7. In testing a group of college freshmen to obtain information for use in guidance, the examiner finds that a student newly arrived from Latin America is having great difficulty following directions because of unfamiliarity with English. The student asks many questions, requests repetitions, and seems unable to comprehend what is desired. What should the examiner do?

8. In the course of a clinical analysis of a preschool child who is believed to be poorly adjusted, a report on a series of tests is requested. The psychometrist who gives the tests finds the child is negativistic. After coöperating reluctantly on two tests he becomes inattentive and careless on the third. Assuming that the test results are needed as soon as possible, what should the tester do?

Directions to the Subject

The most important responsibility of the test administrator is giving directions. The purpose of standardized tests is to obtain measurements which may be compared with measurements made at other times; *it is therefore imperative that the tester give the directions exactly as provided in the manual.* If the tester understands the importance of this responsibility, it is simple to follow the printed directions, reading them word for word, adding nothing and changing nothing.

The standard directions usually invite the subject to ask questions after the directions have been read. In answering such questions, the tester must not add to the ideas expressed in the standard directions, since such supplementation might give this subject an advantage over those not having such aid. The directions are part of the test situation; in some intelligence and personality tests the way the subject follows directions is intended to influence his score.

The most troublesome questions concern matters not discussed in the standard directions. Examples are: "Should we guess if we are not certain?" "How much is taken off for a wrong answer?" "Are there any catch questions?" "If I find a hard question, should I skip it and go on, or should I answer every question as I go?" The published directions to the test were evidently not adequate if they ignored these topics. When the tester refuses to give an answer to the questions about guessing—and he must refuse if the scores are to be compared with norms—some subjects will guess and some will not. Therefore, while the directions are superficially standard, the procedure becomes unstandardized because subjects interpret indefinite instructions, each in his own way.

Attempts to test skill in flying have shown the crucial importance of defining the task clearly for the subject. In making a check test on ability to execute a maneuver, testers found it necessary to tell the pilot exactly how the performance would be scored. When they omitted this, one pilot kept his attention on maintaining altitude perfectly, whereas another of equal ability earned a different score because he concentrated on holding the plane's heading steady. Tests should be provided with directions which leave no ambiguities for variable interpretation. When the tester must use a standard test for which directions are imperfect, he faces a difficulty for which there is no ideal solution.

9. The Bennett TMC directions are printed in the student's test booklet, and also read word for word by the examiner. (The only difference is the sentence in which the examiner asks if there are any questions.) Why is it desirable to read the directions aloud instead of allowing the student to read to himself?

10. How would you answer the following questions raised by students after hearing the TMC directions?

    a. Is this a speed test?
    b. If I am not sure of the answer should I mark what I think is best?
11. The California Test of Mental Maturity consists of twelve sections, each containing a different type of item. The sections are separately timed, each requiring 3–10 minutes. Is there any reason why a high school seeking data for guidance should not give pupils one or two sections of the test each day until all of it is taken, rather than giving it in one or two sittings as the manual suggests?

Judgments Left to the Examiner

While the directions will be standardized in many respects, it is unwise to standardize the tester's procedures too rigidly. Precisely the same action or remark by the examiner can have a different significance for different subjects, and if so, rigid procedure itself introduces an unstandardized element into the testing. This may be illustrated first with regard to the problem of terminating a test.

Directions for most tests place some limit on the time allowed to solve any problem or to work on any subtest (see the Block Design directions, for example). To conform to the directions, the tester need only use his stop watch attentively. Where no time limit is stated, it is still necessary to stop the painfully conscientious subject who works long after he has done his best.

Sometimes an individual test allows credit only when a task is done in (say) two minutes, but does not tell the examiner to stop the subject at that time. The tester must decide whether to let the subject work after he has passed the credit limit or to interrupt him. This is one of the situations where the art of testing comes into play; no rules can prescribe how to terminate an unsuccessful trial.

In an ability test like Block Design, success on one problem has an encouraging effect during the next, but the effect of failure depends on the tester. In the tester's eyes, the subject fails when he does not complete the task within the time limit. If the subject is allowed to continue without interruption, however, he may finish the task and think that he has succeeded. This of course tends to help his subsequent performance. On the other hand, even in extra time the subject may be unable to solve the problem. When he appears to be getting confused and upset, it may be best to terminate the problem and give him a fresh start. To let him continue might make him hopelessly discouraged. In the absence of definite instructions on procedure, the tester should observe the subject's attitudes carefully and choose whatever course seems likely to have the best effect on his subsequent performance.

Terman and Merrill (1937, pp. 55–58), in their advice to examiners giving the Stanford-Binet mental test, give further illustrations of the necessity for variation in tactics:

The tests of each year group should be given in the order in which they appear in the manual. . . . In order to secure the child's best effort, however, it is sometimes necessary to change the test sequence. For example, if the child shows resistance toward a certain type of test, such as repeating digits, drawing, etc., it is better to shift temporarily to a more agreeable task. When the subject is at his ease again, it is usually possible to return to the troublesome tests with better success. Such difficulties are particularly likely to be encountered in the testing of pre-school children. This group presents so many special problems that we have felt it necessary to give a separate discussion of the techniques of pre-school testing.

The examiner's first task is to win the confidence of the child and to overcome any timidity he may feel in the presence of a stranger. Unless rapport has first been established, the results of the first tests are likely to be misleading. The time and effort necessary for accomplishing this are variable factors, depending upon the personality of both the examiner and the subject. It is impossible to give specific rules for the guidance of the examiner in establishing rapport. The address which flatters and pleases one child may excite disgust in another. The examiner must himself be genuinely interested and friendly or no amount of skilled technique will enable him to establish a sympathetic, understanding relationship with children. There are people who lack personal adaptability to an extent that makes success in this field for them impossible. Such a person has no place in a psychological clinic.

Nothing contributes more to satisfactory rapport than keeping the child encouraged. This can be done in many subtle, friendly ways; by an understanding smile, a spontaneous exclamation of pleasure, an appreciative comment, or just the air of quiet understanding between equals that carries assurance and appreciation. Any stereotyped comment following each test becomes perfunctory and serves no purpose other than to punctuate the tests. In general it is wise to praise frequently and generously, but if this is done in too lavish and stilted a fashion it is likely to defeat its purpose. The examiner should remember that he is giving approval primarily for effort rather than for success on a particular response. To praise only the successful responses may influence effort in the succeeding tests. Praise should never be given between the items of a particular test, but should be reserved until the end of that test [i.e., subtest]. Under no circumstances should the examiner permit himself to show dissatisfaction with a response, however absurd it may be. With younger children, especially, praise should not be limited to tests on which the child has done well. Young children are characteristically uncritical and are often enormously pleased with very inferior responses.

In praising poor performances of older subjects, the examiner should remember that the purpose of commendation is to insure confidence and not to reconcile the subject to an inferior level of response. In the case of a failure that is embarrassingly evident to the child himself, the examiner will do well to make some excuse for it. Expressions of commendation should be varied and should fit naturally into the conversation.

Although the examiner should always encourage the child to believe that he can answer correctly if he will only try, he must avoid the common practice of dragging out responses by too much urging and cross-questioning. To do so often robs the response of significance and is likely to interfere with the maintenance of rapport. While the examiner must be on his guard against mistaking exceptional timidity for inability to respond, he must also be able to recognize the silence of incapacity or the genuineness of an "I don't know."

The competent examiner must possess in a high degree judgment, intelligence, sensitivity to the reactions of others, and penetration, as well as knowledge of and regard for scientific methods and experience in the use of psychometric techniques. No degree of mechanical perfection of the tests themselves can ever take the place of good judgment and psychological insight of the examiner.

12. The Bennett directions are vague as regards timing: "Little is gained by allowing more than thirty minutes." The DAT form of the test is definite. "At the end of 30 minutes, say 'Stop!'" What are the advantages and disadvantages of the two procedures?

Guessing

At the start of an objective ability test, some subject is likely to ask, "Should I guess if I am not certain?" Sometimes the test directions include an answer to this question, but even where such advice is given, some ambiguity remains. It is against the rules for the tester to give supplementary advice; he must retreat to such a formula as "Use your own judgment." The discussion which follows is intended to clarify the guessing problem for the tester but should not influence his procedure in giving tests.

To simplify the discussion, we can speak as if items fall into two categories: those for which the subject knows the answer, and those for which he does not know it. If the item calls for a choice of alternatives, the subject has a chance of picking the correct response even on the items he does not know. If there are two alternatives, as in true-false items, he will succeed by chance alone on 50 percent of his guesses. In scoring a two-choice test, we assume that any wrong choice represents an unlucky guess, and that the number of lucky guesses is equal to the number of wrong guesses. The final score on a true-false test is counted as "number of items right minus number marked wrong," i.e., total number of items marked correctly less the number thought to have been marked correctly by guessing. If there are n choices per item, the chance probability of a correct guess is $\dfrac{1}{n}$ and that of an unlucky guess is $\dfrac{n-1}{n}$. For every $n-1$ incorrect guesses, we expect 1 correct guess. Hence the scoring formula most often used is "Right minus $\dfrac{\text{Wrong}}{n-1}$." Other scoring formulas have been developed, some of which are probably superior to this one, but none of them is much used. In a test with a liberal time allowance and comparatively easy items, subjects usually mark every item. When that happens, the rank order of the scores remains the same whether the score used is "number right" or $R - \dfrac{W}{n-1}$.

A correction formula is desired because some people guess more freely than others. The guessers would mark many right answers by chance alone. The scoring formulas attempt to wipe out gains due to guessing. Unfortunately, the basic logic described above does not describe the situation fairly, and the formula does not truly "correct for guessing." The basic assumption is incorrect. You cannot divide items into those the subject knows perfectly and those he does not know at all. There are items he knows fairly well but is not positive of, and other items where he has hazy knowledge. "Guessing" is not a matter of pure chance. Even on the items he knows least about, the guesser's experience and common sense should permit him to choose correctly more often than he would if he selected answers by rolling dice. A person who guesses *intelligently* on ten five-choice items can expect to get perhaps four items right, instead of the two items expected from chance guessing. By formula, four right answers would give him a score of 2½ points. Since a person who does not guess receives a score of zero on the same 10 items, the score is raised by willingness to gamble.

The subject decides what risk he is willing to run. Some people mark only the items they are very sure of. Others mark any item they think they understand, and still others mark absolutely every item. This difference in tendency to gamble is not eliminated by any change of directions or penalties. As the penalty becomes more severe, guessing diminishes, but the bold still take more chances than the timid (Swineford, 1941; Torrance and Ziller, 1957).

Even if the standard "correction for chance" is used, the person who gambles on every doubtful item is likely to gain more than he loses. The only exception is where the test constructor is so skillful in writing misleading alternatives that the guesser is likely to pick them in preference to the right answer. Therefore the person taking a test is usually wise to guess freely. (But remember that the tester is not to give his group an advantage by telling them this trade secret!)

From the point of view of the tester, tendency to guess is an unstandardized aspect of the situation which interferes with accurate measurement. Most European group tests remove the opportunity for blind guessing by presenting items in "open end" form, where the subject must write or draw the answer. American group tests, however, are almost always in multiple-choice form because these items require less time and can be scored mechanically.

The systematic advantage of the guesser is eliminated if the test manual directs everyone to guess, but guessing introduces large chance errors. Statistical comparison of "do not guess" instructions and "do guess" instructions shows that with "do not guess" instructions the tests have slightly greater predictive power (Greene, 1952, pp. 73–75; see also Lindquist, 1951, pp. 347 ff.). Chance errors multiply when everyone guesses, and their cumulative influence on accuracy of measurement outweighs the advantage of "do not guess" instructions. The most widely accepted practice now is to educate students that wild guessing is to their disadvantage, but to encourage them to respond when they can make an informed judgment as to the most reasonable answer even if they are uncertain. The following advice given to College Board applicants is much fairer than strict instructions not to guess:

> When the test is scored, a percentage of the wrong answers is subtracted from the number of right answers as a correction for haphazard guessing. It is improbable, therefore, that mere guessing will improve your score significantly; it may even lower your score. If, however, you are not sure of the correct answer but have some knowledge of the question and are able to eliminate one or more of the answer choices as wrong, your chance of getting the right answer is improved, and it will be to your advantage to answer such a question.

13. Bennett Form AA items (with very few exceptions) have two alternatives. The test is scored $R - \frac{1}{2}W$, for no stated reason. What effect will this formula have as compared to $R - W$? Whom does it favor?
14. In the difficult Form CC of the TMC, items have five alternatives. What is the corresponding scoring formula?
15. When scores are "corrected for guessing," some person may receive a negative score. What does this mean? Is he less able than a person scoring zero?
16. Compute scores for each of the following persons by the usual correction formula:

Test, 1, true-false.　　　A has 20 right, 6 wrong, 7 omitted.
　　　　　　　　　　　　B has 22 right, 8 wrong, 3 omitted.

Test 2, three-choice.   C has 15 right, 6 wrong, 4 omitted.
                                    D has 18 right, 3 wrong, 4 omitted.

Test 3, five-choice.   E has 20 right, 6 wrong, 9 omitted.
                                    F has 6 right, 6 wrong, 23 omitted.

17. Give a difficult five-choice test (untimed) to a friend with instructions to answer items only when fairly certain of the correct answer. When he has finished the test, provide a pencil of another color and direct him to answer all the remaining items, making the best guess he can. Determine his raw score on each trial with and without correction for chance. If the test manual included "do not guess" directions, how much would he gain or lose by guessing despite the directions?

18. If you were taking a five-choice test of professional knowledge in psychology as a requirement for a diploma, would you mark items of which you were uncertain? Assume that the test is scored $R - \frac{1}{4}W$.

19. In a time-limit test of mental ability using multiple-choice items, how rapidly should the subject work, in view of the fact that higher speed leads to more errors?

20. Some instructors advocate scoring achievement tests by formulas which penalize guessing very heavily, such as "Number right minus twice number wrong." What effect would this have on validity of measurement? (Cronbach, 1941; Etoxinod, 1940).

21. Should test directions tell what scoring formula will be used?

MOTIVATION FOR TAKING A TEST

In making a physical measurement—for instance, weighing a truckload of wheat—there is no problem of motivation. Even in weighing a person, when we put him on the scale we get a rather good measure no matter how he feels about the operation. But in a psychological test the subject must place himself on the scale, and unless he cares about the result he cannot be measured.

Incentives That Raise Scores

In an ability test, our problem is like that of the industrial manager who wants a high rate of production. Effort and productivity depend on the reward the person foresees. The most direct reward for good test performance is being hired for a job or being given a desirable assignment. Equally powerful and more universally available as a source of motivation is "ego involvement," that is, the desire to maintain self-respect and the respect of others. Effort is stimulated also by sheer interest in the task and by the habit of conforming to authority.

The test score is not readily altered by simple incentives. There have been many attempts to raise test performance by prizes, pep talks, and monetary payments for increases in score. Almost invariably, such attempts fail to produce appreciable improvement on ability tests over the scores earned under the regular conditions of administration. (See, for example, Benton, 1936; Ferguson, 1937.) These incentive studies generally offered rewards for compliance with the demand of an authority who wanted the test scores. When the motivational pattern is shifted to arouse the subject's own concern over his test score, we find that scores can be improved. Flanagan (1955), in a study of a large number of aviation cadets and high-school students, compared evidence of careless and unmotivated performance under various conditions. His evidence was obtained by counting, first, the number of cadets who used stereotyped patterns of marking the answer sheet, such as the sequence A B A B A B, and second, the number earning chance scores on easy items. Even though the tests affected the cadets' duty assignments, a few of these completely meaningless responses were found. On a memory test, which was fairly typical of the entire series of tests, two cadets per thousand showed stereotyped patterns, and five obtained chance scores. High-school students were given a similar test with no particular incentive, merely being told that research data were being collected. Here there were four stereotyped-response papers per thousand, and 21 chance scores. But in another school where the students expected that they would receive a full report on the tests together with counseling, there were no stereotyped responses, and only three chance patterns per thousand. It is evident that research employing tests has little meaning unless the subject is given a personal reason for taking the test. If he is merely asked to cooperate in an experiment, his responses may be casual or even careless.

Motivation to do a task well or to make a good impression on an adult is learned. During his early years, the child develops attitudes toward himself and toward task performance which have a profound influence on his response to tests and to school assignments. The typical middle-class child learns to work hard because he obtains praise, tangible rewards, and special opportunities when he achieves well. The lower-class child very often learns to take assignments less seriously and to work barely enough to keep out of trouble. His self-respect depends most on his relations with his classmates outside of school, and relatively little on obtaining approval from adult authorities (Eells et al., 1951).

Motives That Reduce Scores

The subject may frankly wish to do poorly on a test (see Pollaczek, 1952). There are times when pupils try to limit their scores on mental tests because a school has a classification plan in which, it is rumored, the better students will be required to do extra work. If, in military classification, men suspect that passing certain tests qualifies one for an unpopular assignment, there is a temptation to fail deliberately. Another instance is the boy who deliberately failed his school subjects so that instead of being promoted he would be kept in the grade where his less intelligent friends were to remain.

When the subject wishes to earn the best score he can, his very desire to do well may interfere with good performance. When one is tense, he commits errors that he would readily detect as such otherwise. In psychomotor tests, tension leads to poor coördination and erratic movements. In a verbal test, the subject who fears criticism of his answers may attempt to escape it by being overcritical of himself. In clinical mental testing, anxious patients frequently find fault with their own answers or elaborate them to include all possible variations and qualifications. In doing this they may spoil an answer that would have received credit. Anxiety over tests is generated at an early age by the attitudes of teachers, parents, and other children. Sarason and his associates developed a special questionnaire to measure "test anxiety," using such items as "When the teacher says she is going to give the class a test, do you get a nervous (or funny) feeling?" (Sarason *et al.*, 1958). Substantial individual differences were found which are fairly stable, as shown by retests at a later date. The median elementary-school child admits to 12 anxiety symptoms on the list of 43 covered by the test. Anxiety increases gradually through the school years. It is especially interesting to note that the anxiety scores have only very slight negative correlations with ability. Evidently, test anxiety is about as common among the very able pupils as among the dull ones.

The detrimental effects of anxiety may be increased by the very tactics the tester uses to elicit the subject's best efforts. Sarason and his associates (1952) used his questionnaire to identify Yale freshmen with high and low anxiety (HA and LA groups, respectively). These groups were divided. Half the students received "ego-involving" (EI) instructions which stressed that these were intelligence tests and would be used to assist in interpreting freshman entrance tests. The NEI ("not ego-involved") group, on the contrary, was told that the examiner was standardizing some tasks and that no one would examine individual standings. The test was a stylus maze, and five trials were given. Error scores are shown in Figure 6. We find that the NEI groups had intermediate scores, there being little difference between the HA-NEI and LA-NEI subgroups. In the low-anxiety group, EI instructions had a small, generally helpful effect. The subjects with high anxiety about tests, however, did much worse when threatened by the importance of doing well than they did under emotionally neutral conditions.

That anxious and defensive reactions interfere with test efficiency is also shown in a study of student nurses (G. Wiener, 1957). Student nurses at the top and bottom extremes on "distrustfulness" were selected by a questionnaire. Each student took sections of the Wechsler intelligence scale. The

Picture Completion test asks the subject what is missing in a picture (e.g., one eyebrow in a sketch of a face). Distrustful subjects were inclined to deny that anything was missing when the answer did not come to them immediately. Likewise, on a test of similarities ("How are praise and punishment alike?") the distrustful students were more inclined to deny that the words were alike. The difference, though significant, was small; distrustful students averaged 2.7 suspicious comments on the two tests compared to 0.9 for the trustful students. To measure the effect of suspiciousness on scores, Wiener compared scores on the PC and Similarities tests with a vocabulary score that presumably is not affected by suspiciousness. This comparison

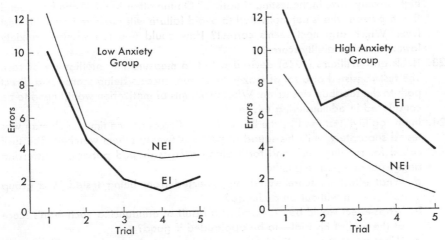

FIG. 6. Maze performance under ego-involving (EI) and neutral (NEI) instructions (Sarason et al., 1952).

shows that extreme suspiciousness lowers the IQ by about three or four points. As Wiener says, "People who say, 'There is nothing missing in that picture!' are responding to internal needs rather than to the testing situation." This is a maladaptive response, and necessarily lowers scores.

Threats are ever present in testing: a delinquent fears that his punishment will depend on the test results; a child fears that a poor intelligence rating will disappoint his parents and diminish their affection; a college girl fears that failure will force her to leave her campus friends and return to the farm; an anxious patient fears that a test will prove him insane. Fears such as these can be listed without end. A striking example is the case of the young reserve officer, extremely eager to serve in time of war, who failed his physical examination twice because the importance of passing made him emotional— and the emotion always brought his blood pressure over the acceptable limit. A series of "reconditioning" treatments eventually made it possible for him to take the test calmly. High blood pressure is more directly an emotional concomitant than is poor thinking, but the disrupting physiological responses have their mental counterparts.

Insofar as the tester can convince the subject that the tests will be used to help him, not to harm him, the validity of scores will be increased. Emphasis must be placed on the positive use of results. A job applicant fearful of failing an aptitude test can be given to understand that test scores may indicate a field where he will succeed. A patient fearing the verdict of a diagnostic test should understand that it will point the way to a cure.

22. Mandler and Sarason (1952) comment, "It is questionable whether intelligence test scores adequately describe the underlying abilities of individuals with a high anxiety drive in the testing situation." On the other hand, it can be argued that a person who is not motivated to avoid failure will perform below his best level. Which argument seems correct? How could you test whether anxiety lowers or raises ability scores?

23. Hebb and Williams (1946) devised a test to measure the intelligence of rats. The test consisted of a set of mazes to be run, success being scored if a direct path to the foodbox was taken. What problems of motivation would need to be considered in administering this test?

24. In an "agility" test used by the British Armed Forces at one time, each man was tested separately while his squad of perhaps twenty others watched. The task called for running back and forth along a cross-shaped pattern, transferring rings from one post to another.
    a. What effect on score would be expected from being tested in a group rather than without an audience?
    b. What effect would be expected as a result of announcing each man's score at the end of his trial—to be applauded if good?
    c. What advantage or disadvantage would a man have who came last in the group?

25. If, on a personality test, a person reveals something discreditable about himself, can one suggest any reason other than a strong desire to be honest?

Preparing the Subject for the Test

The motivation most helpful to valid testing is a desire on the part of the subject that the score be valid. This is not the normal competitive set where one desires a high score whether it is true for him or not. It is a scientific set, a desire to find out the truth even if the truth is unpalatable. Ideally, the subject actually becomes a partner in testing himself.

Too often an autocratic approach is followed, something like "Take this test and I shall decide what is to be done with you." Most testers would disclaim any intention of dictating, yet it is true that tests have most often been used for the private information of the tester, who then bases recommendations on them.

Coöperation between tester and subject is not an impossible goal. Psychotherapy is based on diagnostic testing; decisions of school administrators depend on standard tests; the employment manager must take responsibility for hiring the best-qualified applicants. Responsibility cannot ordinarily be transferred to the person tested, but the subject can be made a member of the tester's team. The tester can take him into confidence as to the purpose of the testing and portray the test as an opportunity to find out about himself, just as the physician often tells the patient what medicine is being given and what good results are to be expected from it. If the subject knows what a test is measuring and why a fair measurement is to his advantage, he will have little motive to provide an untruthful picture. Perhaps the most "autocratic" of the current uses of testing is in industrial hiring—necessarily so, since the goal of testing is profit to the firm. Yet the tests given in the hiring line are to the advantage of the person tested, and it will build good will if he knows it. The very facts regarding turnover that lead the employer to screen applicants are facts which would reassure the worker if he knew them. If he does well on the test, he can have confidence that he will make good on the job. If he does badly, he is unlikely to last on the job. The failure on the tests saves him from wasting time in a dead end; he can begin instead to accumulate experience and seniority in another job for which he is fitted.

The desirability of preparing the subject for the test by appropriate advance information is increasingly recognized. It was formerly the common practice in counseling centers to administer a test battery routinely to every person coming in, and to use the test results as a basis for the first counseling interview. Now counseling more often commences with one or two interviews which help the person define his problem. The interview gives him a more realistic understanding of what tests can do, reduces anxiety about the test results, and helps in the choice of tests. Another type of indoctrination is found in some of the great nation-wide testing programs like that of the College Entrance Examination Board. Booklets have been prepared for both the Scholastic Aptitude Test and the subject proficiency tests. The booklet describes the test, gives advice on efficient work procedures, and provides specimen items. This information increases the applicant's confidence and reduces the disadvantage which an applicant inexperienced in taking standard tests might otherwise have.

26. How could a "coöperative" point of view in testing be adopted:
    a. By a school principal who wishes to divide his eighth grade into sections on the basis of intelligence?
    b. By a veteran's counselor who must approve the plan of a handicapped veteran to go to college and prepare for dentistry?
    c. By a consulting psychologist who is asked by a social agency to diagnose and report on a potential delinquent?
27. What explanation would you give the subject in each of the following cases?
    a. College freshmen are to be tested to determine which ones may fail because of reading deficiency.

b. At the end of a course in industrial relations for foremen, an examination on judgment in grievance cases is to be given.

28. Is it ethical, in a test of emotional adjustment, to phrase directions so that the subject believes his imaginative ability is being tested?

Coaching and Test Sophistication. Preparation may be carried to extreme lengths. In Great Britain, a test given near the age of 11 determines what type of secondary education a child will receive. This is a fateful decision, opening or closing the gate to most professions and to financial and social status. Parents, concerned to help their children, often pay private tutors to prepare the child for the examination by special after-school lessons. Indeed, it has been said that in some districts two-thirds of the candidates receive such "black-market" coaching. The school system, unwilling that these children should have an advantage, then may introduce a special "coaching class" during the term preceding the examinations. Coaching for the arithmetic and language tests consists chiefly of additional drill. The third portion of the examination is a test of general mental ability. Coaching may include study of tests used in past years, practice on reasoning problems used in typical mental tests, and instruction on how to solve test problems rapidly.

Preparation of this sort guarantees that the coached pupils perform at their best, but perhaps spoils the test by giving them an improper advantage over uncoached pupils. To evaluate any such procedure, it is necessary to consider the distinction between intrinsic and extrinsic aspects of the test performance (Gulliksen, 1950). The test is used to decide which pupils will profit most from a later educational program. Any ability which aids performance on the test and in the later instruction also may be called *intrinsic,* whereas an ability useful only in the test is *extrinsic* to the decision being made. Coaching which improves the performance intrinsically is fair, and does not spoil the test. Teaching extra arithmetic gives the pupil an advantage on the test, but this extra training presumably will also make him a better student. Teaching him how to solve mazes, however, is beneficial only in tests presenting maze items; it cannot help his later schoolwork.

There have been many studies to measure the effects of coaching, and the studies differ in procedure and results. Some very large gains in score were found in studies where subjects were initially almost completely unfamiliar with objective speeded tests. Recent British results (Alfred Yates *et al.,* 1953, 1954) show what can be expected among reasonably well-educated pupils today. Gains are measured by repeating the same test after the experimental interval. According to these studies,

"Control" groups gain (on the average) about 2–3 points in IQ, merely as a result of taking the first test.

"Coached" groups gain about 5–6 points, after having been told about tests and having had numerous representative items explained by the teacher.

"Practiced, uncoached" groups gain about 6 points, after taking from four to eight tests without special explanation.

"Practiced and coached" groups may gain 8–10 points.

It is noted in all these studies that a very extended period of practice or coaching is no more helpful than a few sessions. Gains such as those shown in these studies, and in the corresponding American studies (Dear, 1958), are relatively small. While they might make the difference between success and failure in obtaining admission to a higher school, for a pupil near the borderline, coaching will not raise a poor college prospect sufficiently to help him over the examination hurdle.

29. What implications does the British investigation of coaching have for Americans who use mental tests to select scholarship winners?
30. In Japan a young man's career opportunities depend very much on his ability to capture one of the limited number of openings in the University. Vacancies are filled on the basis of entrance examinations and school records. Magazines bearing such titles as *Student Days, Examiners' Circle,* and *Period of Diligent Study* have large circulations. These magazines deal with topics of interest to candidates including information about typical test materials (though the actual test questions are of course guarded). Would such magazines increase or decrease the validity of the tests?
31. In planning a competitive mental test to be given all Japanese youth applying for higher schools, two policies appeared possible. One was to devise new types of test items each year, so that knowledge about previous examinations would be of no help. The other proposal favored using the same types of questions every year (for example, number series) but changing the items used. Compare the plans from the point of view of the test maker, the student, and the person interpreting the results.
32. Which of these types of preparation for a scholastic aptitude test leads to changes in intrinsic ability?
   a. Vocabulary-building exercises.
   b. Advice about whether to guess when in doubt.
   c. Therapeutic counseling to reduce fear of failure and feelings of inadequacy.
33. In some college residence halls, students file questions from past examinations. From the point of view of the professor teaching the course year after year, does this increase or decrease the validity of measurement?

Testing Procedure as Standardization of Behavior

We may understand better the problem of framing directions and arousing proper motivation if we realize that the psychometric tester tries to standardize the behavior of the subject, as well as the test stimuli. Even though he is measuring individual differences, his procedures are designed to *eliminate* individual differences—to eliminate, that is, variation in every characteristic save the one that his test is supposed to measure.

To clarify this, consider the physiological measure of basal metabolism rate. If a doctor wants a BMR measure, he requires his patient to fast for eight hours before the test. This eliminates differences in eating habits which would affect oxygen utilization. For the test itself, it is necessary to reduce the patient's bodily activity to an absolute minimum by putting him into bed; every patient is, in effect, reduced to a standard activity level. The BMR, calculated from the oxygen intake and the carbon dioxide exhaled, is a useful measure of the patient's physiological state. This measure is taken in an artificial "standard condition" which almost never occurs in real life. The person's metabolism rate as he goes about his daily affairs is not much like his BMR, since it is affected by his eating, activity, and other variables.

Psychological tests are similarly designed to extract one variable, purified as much as possible, from the total life activity. The psychologist is concerned if some students fail to understand his directions because this irrelevant difference will affect his results. He is concerned if some students receive coaching, if some are especially anxious about the test, if some interpret the test as a speed test while others think carefulness counts most. All these sources of variation blur his measurement. He tries, in setting the stage for a test, to reduce all his subjects to a "standard state" of motivation, expectation, and interpretation of the task.

An example of such standardization is found in certain tests intended to measure personality traits. One might evaluate these qualities by observing behavior in everyday affairs. The meaning of this behavior is uncertain, however, since different subjects may be trying to do quite different things. If the situation is more definitely structured so that all subjects have the same goal in mind, differences are more certainly attributable to personality. For this reason, many tests of persistence, reaction to frustration, flexibility, and other traits are disguised as measures of ability. The subject is given a definite task and motivated just as for an ability test. He does not realize that the tester will pay attention chiefly to how he goes about the task.

TESTING AS A SOCIAL RELATIONSHIP

The tester has been accustomed to think of himself as an unemotional, impartial task-setter. His traditions encourage the idea that he, like the physical scientist or engineer, is "measuring an object" with a technical tool. But the "object" before him is a person, and testing involves a complex psychological relationship. The traditional concern with motivation and rapport recognizes this fact but, as illustrated in the foregoing sections, leads to little more than a recommendation that the tester be pleasant and encouraging, and help the subject understand the value of the test. This, we are beginning to suspect, barely touches the real social-psychological complexities of testing. As Schafer (1954, p. 6) says,

> The clinical testing situation has a complex psychological structure. It is not an impersonal getting-together of two people in order that one, with the help of a little "rapport," may obtain some "objective" test responses from the other. The psychiatric patient is in some acute or chronic life crisis. He cannot but bring many hopes, fears, assumptions, demands and expectations into the test situation. He cannot but respond intensely to certain real as well as fantasied attributes of that situation. Being human and having to make a living—facts often ignored —the tester too brings hopes, fears, assumptions, demands and expectations into the test situation. He too responds personally and often intensely to what goes on—in reality and in fantasy—in that situation, however well he may conceal his personal response from the patient, from himself, and from his colleagues.

The subject coming for an individual test almost invariably is in difficulties. He may have been referred by some authority who demands that he be tested; if so, the tester may be simply another authority to rebel against. Other subjects are self-referred. One might expect coöperation in such a case because the subject is asking for help, but he too may come with motives which conflict with the tester's objectives. The very fact that he has had to seek psychological help may disturb the person who wants to be independent. He may have doubts regarding his own adequacy which he attempts to suppress by every available strategy. It is commonplace to discover, behind a college student's self-referral for remedial reading or vocational counseling, a problem of sexual adjustment or emotional conflict with parents. The student, by focusing his attention and that of the psychologist on a superficial or nonexistent problem, is using an unconscious sleight-of-hand to conceal the problems he does not want to face.

Instead of being hostile and resistant, the subject may present himself as friendly and totally submissive. This can go far beyond the normal, mature fact-giving which the tester wishes for. Some subjects "turn themselves over" to the psychologist, thereby avoiding responsibility for their own problems.

None of us is willing to expose himself completely, or even to learn the whole truth about himself, yet the job of the tester is to penetrate personal secrets. In clinical testing and interviewing particularly, the psychologist really tries to bring to the surface the whole personality—sexual attitudes, feelings of inadequacy, hostilities and wishes the patient is ashamed of, and so on. Even when the tester has a much more limited aim, the patient may believe that his intimate desires and anxieties will be exposed by the tests. The popular literature on psychology and psychiatry being what it is, the subject may expect the psychologist to be almost pruriently concerned with tabooed areas. Or he may view the tester as a modern magician from whom no truth can be hidden and whose every judgment is beyond question.

These attitudes define a role which the tester is expected to play, and the tester's own self-conceptions define another. When tester and subject meet, therefore, their mutual demands may support each other, or they may pull in opposite directions. A client who wants to escape responsibility may fall into the hands of a tester who likes to pose as infallible and to dominate others. This tester is unlikely to sense that the client's seeming passivity is just a strategy adopted to keep the tester from probing into an unstated problem. The situation is little better if the tester is one who, because of self-doubt, cannot comfortably take responsibility. Pressed by the client to make a definite recommendation, this insecure tester will retreat from responsibility. He will pile test upon test, so that the mass of data will relieve him of the burden of judgment. He will qualify his interpretations and obscure them in technical jargon to frustrate the client's unacceptable demand. Finally, he terminates the counseling with "All tests can do is give you a basis for making your own decision." By this he avoids a counseling relation—longer, more intimate, but uncomfortable—in which he could bring the client to understand his passivity and hesitancy.

Schafer points out that the tester chooses his profession because it satisfies his needs. The tester may be one who feels inadequate in social relations, but who can obtain reassurance from seemingly objective instruments. He may prefer the brief and distant contact of objective testing to the demanding personal relations that teachers and therapists have. He may be answering doubts about himself by comparing himself favorably at every turn with those he tests. On the contrary, instead of having these remote and competitive attitudes, he may be one who seeks grateful and dependent reactions from subjects.

All these patterns can distort testing procedures and test interpretations. The overly "objective" tester may be unwilling to give the subject the emotional support required to reduce resistance and elicit his best performance. He may overemphasize difficulties that can be treated unemotionally (limited vocabulary, for example) but overlook emotional needs. The competitive tester may be too ready to identify weaknesses, or to describe subjects he admires as having virtues he hopefully sees in himself. (Wilson tells us that, when he trained a group of intelligent convicts to give a performance test to new inmates, he had to supervise constantly to prevent their making procedural errors to reduce the subject's score and so magnify their own superiority.) The tester who seeks emotional support from patients may be too lenient and encouraging, and all too willing to overlook weaknesses in the record.

Granting that both tester and subject come to the situation with a full complement of human motives, some of which they are not aware of, what should the tester do about it? At this point, with research on these motives almost entirely lacking, we can make only common-sense suggestions. The first of these is "Know thyself." The more the tester knows of his own personality, of his preferences for different types of subject, and of the biases he brings to test interpretation, the greater the chance that he can meet each situation properly. The second suggestion is Schafer's recommendation that the social situation itself be considered an important way of understanding the subject, and that his strategies, demands, and resistances themselves be taken into account in interpreting scores. His view, which is the only thorough statement on the problem yet attempted, is well summarized in this paragraph (1954, pp. 72–73):

> There are those who would object that this total-situation approach violates the objectivity of test interpretation. Only in the narrow and false sense in which objectivity has been usually conceived is this true. The ideal of objectivity requires that we recognize as much as possible what is going on in the situation we are studying. It requires in particular that we remember the tester and his patient are both human and alive and therefore inevitably interacting in the test situation. True, the further we move away from mechanized interpretation or comparison of formal scores and averages, the more subjective variables we may introduce into the interpretive process. The personality and personal limitations of the tester may be brought into the thick of the interpretive problem. But while we thereby increase the likelihood of personalized interpretation and variation among testers, we are at the same time in a position to enrich our understanding and our test reports significantly. The more data we use, after all, the greater the richness and specificity of our analyses—and in the long run the more accurate we become.

Schafer's view obviously demands impressionistic interpretation, and is not fully acceptable to psychometric testers. His view need not be accepted, since no evidence is offered that these complex interpretations can indeed be made accurately. Those who reject Schafer's recommendation must, however, face the problem of interpersonal dynamics and find their own solution. Even a strictly poker-faced administration of an individual mental test is an hour-long stress situation, every moment of which involves emotional interaction between tester and subject.

From a psychometric viewpoint, it has been suggested that the effect of tester personality is merely that different testers obtain different average results. IQs obtained by one tester average a few points higher than those of another. Rorschachs given by tester X contain more "movement" responses than those of tester Y. Why not, then, "calibrate" each tester as a laboratory thermometer is calibrated, so that his errors can be compensated for? If we know that, on the average, his Wechsler IQs average 2.3 points higher than those of other testers, we can adjust his reports. This is not a realistic suggestion. Calibration requires an overwhelming amount of research, and at best such a correction deals with the average error rather than the errors which vary from case to case. Individual tests cannot be standardized well enough so that all testers will obtain identical results; the best hope is that careful training of testers can remove most of their consistent errors.

34. In what way could sympathy and love for children bias a tester? What parts of the testing process would be affected by this bias?
35. If social factors and examiner differences affect individual tests more than group tests, does this imply that group tests are better measuring instruments?
36. Does a formal and impersonal attitude toward all subjects standardize the testing relationship?

Suggested Readings

Biber, Barbara, & others. Stenographic record of psychological examination. *Life and ways of the seven-year-old.* New York: Basic Books, 1952. Pp. 631–639.
> This is a record of remarks made by both examiner and subject before and during a series of performance tests of mental ability, including the Porteus maze and several formboards. Note the many places where the examiner is willing to digress from the test into other conversation in order to maintain rapport.

Bingham, Walter V. Administration of tests, and Giving group tests. *Aptitudes and aptitude testing.* New York: Harper, 1937. Pp. 224–244.
> These common-sense suggestions, based on long experience, will be of great value to beginning testers. A translation of a German checklist for observing behavior during the test, used for an impressionistic evaluation of performance, is included.

Schafer, Roy. Interpersonal dynamics in the test situation. *Psychoanalytic interpretation in Rorschach testing.* New York: Grune & Stratton, 1954. Pp. 6–73.
> In a thought-provoking discussion of the motives with which the tester and subject approach each other, Schafer speculates regarding defenses in the tester's personality (dependence, overintellectualization, sadism, etc.) which may reduce his effectiveness.

Thompson, Anton. Test-giver's self-inventory. *Calif. J. educ. Res.,* 1956, **7,** 67–71.
> A checklist pointing out nearly fifty specific practices that characterize good test administration includes numerous techniques that practical experience shows to be advisable, which inexperienced group testers tend to overlook.

Wilson, Donald Powell. *My six convicts.* New York: Rinehart, 1951.
> A best-seller describes the experiences of a psychologist doing research on drug addiction in a prison, using convicts as testing assistants. Of special value are Chapters III and IV, describing how the team overcame reluctance of convicts to take tests. See also, on p. 235, the explanation in convict language of "the coefficient of correlation."

4

Scoring

SCORING PROCEDURES

ANY student who has tried to understand why he received a low score on some essay examination must realize how difficult it is to define a good answer and to determine the proper credit for a partially correct response. Starch and Elliott (1912, 1913) provided conclusive evidence on the faults of impressionistic scoring as long ago as 1912. They presented a pupil's English composition to a convention of teachers and asked a number of volunteers to grade it. On a percentage scale, the grades assigned ranged from 50 to 98. This evidence of disagreement could perhaps be dismissed, since judging a composition is influenced by preferences for various styles. To drive home their point, however, they had a geometry paper graded in the same way. The scores ranged from 28 to 92, presumably because of variation in the credit given to neatness, partial solutions, etc.

No scientific research on behavior can be done nor can we hope to reach sound practical decisions if scoring standards vary erratically. One solution is to develop rules for judgment which all scorers will follow. The other possibility is to use recognition items where the subject is to choose the right answer; this eliminates all judgment from scoring, once the initial key is agreed upon by competent persons.

Scoring of Free Responses

Individual testing continues to use problems calling for some degree of judgment in scoring, but methods can be devised which permit fairly objective scoring of the important features of behavior. Ayres, for example, produced a guide for scoring pupil handwriting (Figure 7). Samples of handwriting representing various levels of quality are given; the teacher locates the sample most similar to the pupil's work in order to determine his score. Product-rating scales can be developed for judging quality of sewing, shopwork, etc. Objective methods have not been completely successful in scoring verbal tests, but variation among scorers is reduced by guides which show the approved scoring for representative answers. Noteworthy examples are the scoring manual for the Stanford-Binet test of intelligence (Terman

60	90
Four score and seven years ago our fathers brought for theupon thes continent a new nation, conceived in liberty, and dedicated to the proposition that all	*Fourscore and seven years ago our fathers brought forth upon this continent a new nation, conceived in liberty*

FIG. 7. Part of Ayres' scale for scoring handwriting samples. (Copyright 1912, Russell Sage Foundation. Reproduced by permission of the present publisher, Educational Testing Service.)

and Merrill, 1959) and the volume by Beck (1944) on the Rorschach test of personality.

While the scoring guide is adequate for most testing of individuals, special precautions must be taken when free-response tests are used to compare experimental treatments. The scorer who believes or wishes to prove that one treatment is superior may unconsciously tend to give higher scores to the subjects who had that treatment (Goodenough, 1940). To prevent such bias, it is necessary to mix all records together before presenting them to a scorer who does not know which group any person belongs to. This procedure is called "blind" scoring.

1. The question "Why should people wash their clothing?" is to be used in an oral intelligence test for adults, to test comprehension of common situations. Prepare a set of standards for judging correctness of answers. Make your rules so clear that scorers would be able to agree in scoring new answers.

Scoring of Recognition Items

The scoring guide for a recognition test consists of a list of the correct answers and a scoring key which a clerk can use. Several efficient procedures for obtaining and scoring responses have been devised, including the carbon booklet, the pinprick booklet, and the separate answer sheet. One common form of the separate answer sheet is shown in Figure 8. With the separate answer sheet, costs are reduced because the same booklet can be used repeatedly, and the answers can easily be scored by a punched key or by machine. The carbon booklet consists of a face-page backed with carbon paper and a hidden under-page printed with an answer key. The pages are sealed together, and the subject marks his choices on the face-page. His marks are traced by the carbon onto the bottom page. The scorer tears open a perforated edge of the booklet to reveal the bottom page on which printed squares show where the correct answers should appear. It is a simple matter

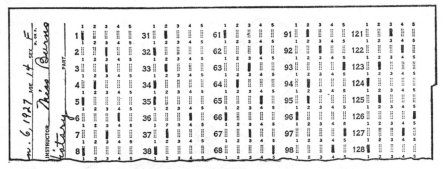

FIG. 8. Portion of answer sheet for machine scoring. (Courtesy International Business Machines Corporation.)

to count the number of carbon marks falling within the squares. The pin-prick method is similar to the carbon booklet. Instead of checking his answer with a pencil, the subject sticks in a pin at that point. Squares are printed on the back of the page so that when the booklet is torn open the number of holes falling within squares indicates the score.

Machine Scoring. The scoring machine most widely known is that developed by International Business Machines in the late 1930's. The subject blackens an answer space with a soft pencil. Electrified "fingers" in the machine sense where pencil marks appear, since the graphite in the marks carries current. A meter shows the total number of properly placed marks. The machine will report number of errors, rights-minus-wrongs, and other types of scores. Under ideal conditions, it can score as many as 500 papers per hour accurately (Traxler, 1954; Lindquist, 1951, pp. 408 ff.). Military classification centers rely on the machines to process recruits. Large school systems operate such machines to score tests for the entire system. In most sections of the country, a test-scoring service is available where tests from scattered schools may be machine-scored for a moderate fee.

The main difficulty with the IBM machine, and one which concerns test administrators, is that it cannot score accurately unless answer spaces are neatly blackened by the student. While the machine is supposed to deliver one unit of credit whenever a mark appears in the right space, whether the mark is light or heavy, wide or narrow, in practice this cannot be expected. The mark must be made with the proper sort of soft pencil, and to be sure of being counted must fill completely the space between the dotted lines on the answer sheet. Furthermore, stray pencil marks and smudges due to untidy erasure register and are counted as errors. The number of improperly blackened or untidy papers is so great that scoring agencies have clerks examine each paper before feeding it to the machine; if necessary, the clerk blackens more heavily where the student used a faint mark to indicate his answer, and erases stray marks. This adds appreciably to the cost of scoring.

FIG. 9.   IBM test-scoring machine. (Courtesy International Business Machines Corporation.)

The need for such re-marking can be almost entirely eliminated by proper test administration and proctoring.

Newer electronic scoring machines are becoming available. One developed by the University of Iowa for its high-school testing program combines a photoelectric "reading" device with an electronic computer (Lindquist, 1954). Responses to as many as 960 items (i.e., an entire battery of tests) can be put on a single answer sheet. The student records his name in a special "name grid." (If his name is Jones, he blackens *J* in the first column, *O* in the second, etc.). It is estimated that this machine is able to score 6000 answer sheets per hour and print both raw scores and converted scores on a summary sheet. Part scores and weighted composites can be obtained, and many computations desired for research can also be carried out at the same time.

We are beginning to see automation in testing itself, as well as in scoring. This is particularly demonstrated in the application of "Skinner box" techniques to human subjects. As used in the psychological laboratory the Skinner box has taken the form of a cage in which the rat, pigeon, or other animal activates a mechanism by making a particular response: striking a lever, tapping a spot on the cage wall, etc. Rewards for correct performance can be administered automatically according to any desired schedule—for example, by dropping a food pellet into the tray at the end of one minute if the lever has been struck during that minute. Skinner (1958) is now adapting the same principle to the study of arithmetic performance of children. The child responds to problems presented by the machine, pushing a button to indicate his answer; a correct response is rewarded by a signal. The machine puts the child through an automatic drill, and at the end delivers a record showing the child's rate of response and his accuracy.

In a mental hospital, Skinner and Lindsley arranged a room where patients receive rewards for pulling a lever (Lindsley, 1956). The rewards include cigarettes, a brief look at an entertaining picture, or (as a social reward) the opening of a window where they can watch one of the doctors working at his desk. In this device also, an automatic recording machine traces the rate of response and thus provides a performance record which might have diagnostic significance. One of the most striking features of the method is that it provides a completely nonverbal test. The subject can be introduced into the test room with no instructions whatsoever and left to discover for himself what happens when he pulls the lever and to respond to the reward in his own manner.

2. If Skinner's procedures yield interpretable information, it will be possible to administer the "test" automatically to mental-hospital patients. Disregarding questions of cost, what are the advantages and disadvantages of automatic testing, as compared with face-to-face testing by a clinical psychologist?

3. Reëxamine the directions for the TMC (Chapter 3). How would you alter those directions to make sure that students blacken answer sheets satisfactorily?

4. What effects upon the character of tests and their use might be expected to follow from the availability of a machine which makes it possible to obtain virtually an unlimited number of scores from a single answer sheet, at negligible cost?

INTERPRETATION OF SCORES

Raw Scores

Most tests yield a direct numerical report of a person's performance called his *raw score*. This may be the number of questions he answered, the time he required for the task, or some similar number. Because raw scores are readily available, and familiar from long experience in classroom examinations, many people interpret them without realizing their limitations. An example from the old-fashioned report card will demonstrate the problem.

Willie brings home a report showing that his average in arithmetic is 75, and his average in spelling is 90. His parents can be counted on to praise the latter and disapprove the former. Willie might quite properly protest, "But you should see what the other kids get in arithmetic. Lots of them get 60 and 65." The parents, who know a good grade when they see one, refuse to be sidetracked by such irrelevance. But what do Willie's grades mean? It might appear that he has mastered three-fourths of the course work in arithmetic, and nine-tenths in spelling. But Willie objects to that, too. "I learned all my combinations, but he doesn't ask much about those. The tests are full of word problems, and we only studied them a little." Willie evidently gets 75 percent of the questions asked, but since the questions may be easy or hard, the percentage itself is meaningless. We cannot compare Willie with his sister Sue, whose teacher in another grade gives much easier tests so that Sue brings home a proud 88 in arithmetic. It could be, too, that Willie's shining 90 in spelling is misleading, if the spelling tests deal with the very words assigned for study.

A raw score on a psychological test, taken by itself, has no significance. It can be interpreted only by comparing it to some standard. Stoddard's remarks (1943, p. 83) illustrate this point: "In American college circles, the statement that John Smith has run 100 yards in $9\%_{10}$ seconds reveals an extraordinary accomplishment. On a priori grounds there is no occasion for knowing whether a man should run 100 yards in 8 seconds or 20 seconds. But Smith is immediately placed against the background of the thousands of men who, having run their best, could not get under 10 seconds."

It is especially important to realize that we cannot interpret psychological test scores as we do physical measures. Physical measuring scales generally have a true zero and equal units along the scale; this permits us to say, for example, that one boy is twice as tall as another, or has attained 60 percent of his probable adult height. We cannot make statements like this about psychological measures. Suppose Willie had earned a score of 10 percent in spelling. Would this mean that he knows only one-tenth of the words he should? No, for the teacher probably did not ask about easy words that Willie was sure to know. Even a score of zero on the test would not mean zero ability to spell. The difference between Willie with a score of zero and the model pupil who earns 100 is perhaps a difference in ability to spell only twenty words out of an active vocabulary of several thousand—if those twenty constituted the test. The same argument applies to tests of reasoning ability. A raw score of 80 may appear to represent ability twice as great as a raw score of 40. The test does not include the problems everyone can solve, however; if people were tested on every possible problem calling for reasoning, the true ratio might be 140 to 180, or 1040 to 1080. Even an infant, looking toward the door when he hears his mother's footstep, shows some degree of ability to reason. Absolute zero in any ability is "just no ability at all."

Differences in raw scores do not ordinarily represent "true" distances between individuals. Suppose, on DAT Mechanical Reasoning Form A, Adam gets 53 points, Bill gets 56, and Charles gets 59. The raw-score differences are equal. Is Charles truly as different from Bill as Bill is from Adam? We cannot be sure, since the score difference depends on the items used. Judging from the published norm tables for twelfth-graders, if these same boys took the Bennett Form AA the "equal differences" would be replaced by unequal ones: Adam would get 44 points, Bill would get 45, and Charles 48.

The only way one can meaningfully talk about "equal differences" is to bring in some practical criterion which provides a standard of value. Different standards will lead to different numerical scales for the same test. On the DAT the three boys' raw scores are equally spaced. Their probabilities of passing a college engineering course may be .70, .90, and .96, respectively. Their most likely freshman grade averages may be D, C+, and B−. And their respective probabilities of later success in a very demanding engineering firm may be .0001, .05, and .50. "Equal intervals" on one of these scales are quite unequal on the other.

Having scored a test, the tester has four alternatives:

● He may compare the score directly to some accepted standard of performance. For example, a school may admit to the first grade all children who earn a certain predetermined score on a readiness test.

● He may compare the score to other scores in the group tested.

● He may compare the score to scores in a reference group by means of a table of norms.

● He may use an expectancy table to estimate the individual's probable subsequent performance.

Of these methods, the most common is to compare the individual with a reference group. The tester refers to a table in the manual to learn what the normal range of performance is. More than that, he converts the raw score into some type of *derived score* which is a permanent record of the individual's relative position. The most common types of derived score are percentiles and standard scores.

Many statistical methods used by the test developer are simple enough to be followed by the test user, who can prepare norm tables or expectancy tables for his own group. Expectancy tables, which we consider first, require no more than simple tabulation, and calculation of percentages.

5. Decide whether an absolute zero exists for each of the following variables and, where possible, define it:
   a. Height.
   b. Ability to discriminate between the pitches of tones.
   c. Speed of tapping.
   d. Gregariousness, seeking the companionship of others.
   e. Rifle aiming.
6. If several pupils in Willie's class move away and are replaced by newcomers, will his raw score in arithmetic probably change? His rank in his class?
7. If a different set of test questions were used in arithmetic, would Willie's raw score change? His rank?
8. Alfred, a college freshman, is to receive guidance on his academic plans, and is given four tests of ability. Scores are presented in four different ways. Interpret separately each row of scores.

	Vocabu-lary	Verbal Reasoning	Nonverbal Reasoning	Mechanical Compre-hension
Raw score	116	32	44	48
Percent of possible points	77	73	80	71
Points above average	24	10	20	0
Rank among 260 freshmen	104	113	161	136

9. Two runners train for the mile. One, between his junior and senior years, reduces his time from 4:16 to 4:04. The other starts with a time of 5:16. What time must he achieve for us to say that he has made as much improvement as the first runner?

Expectancy Tables

The expectancy table is a useful device for interpreting performance. The test developer or test user administers the test to a large number of persons and subsequently observes their success; these results can be tabulated to form an experience table such as Table 1. This table is based on application of a general scholastic aptitude test (the Ohio State University Psychological Examination) to 920 freshmen at Ohio State. To interpret a student's score, the counselor need only direct attention to the row of the table corresponding to the score; the entries show how likely the student is to attain any particular grade average. This explanation is more definite and more complete than can be offered by any other system of norms. As Bingham says (1951, p. 552), "The counselor of an entering student who has scored in the lowest decile range (lowest tenth) on this test can now show him these expectancies, and point out, if it seems advisable, that his chances of keeping off probation (Point-Hour Ratio = 1.50) are a little better than even; that he has one chance in a hundred of earning high honors; and that in any event much depends on the persistence and strength of his own determination, a powerful factor not measured by this or any other psychological test."

Expectancy data may also be presented in charts like Figure 10. The

TABLE 1.   Expectancy Table for First-Semester Freshman Achievement

Score on OSU Psychological Test		Probability of Earning a Point-Hour Ratio of at Least				
Raw Score	Percentile Rank	1.00 (D av.)	1.50 (Proba- tion)	2.00 (C av.)	2.50	3.00 (B av.)
114–150	90–	100	99	93	80	56
102–113	80–89	100	96	91	60	30
92–101	70–79	100	95	90	60	29
83–91	60–69	99	90	78	41	27
75–82	50–59	98	87	74	25	13
66–74	40–49	97	80	62	25	13
56–65	30–39	96	79	61	17	5
48–55	20–29	95	75	47	13	4
39–47	10–19	95	63	33	7	2
0–39	–9	87	58	29	3	1

Source: Bingham, 1951, based on data from G. B. Paulsen.

chart gives less precise interpretations than the table but is especially useful for explaining scores to laymen. The charts illustrated are based on three different tests; it can be seen that the dexterity test is a much less accurate predictor than the other two. Besides interpreting scores for individuals, the expectancy table gives information on the validity of a test (see Chapter 5).

10. Expectancy tables prepared for local use are clearly meaningful. Can expectancy tables profitably be included in test manuals, in view of the fact that probability of success on a job depends on local conditions?
11. Interpret this information about scores of a prospective aircraft armorer, prior to training: mechanical aptitude, 120; trade information, 140; nut-and-bolt test, 100.

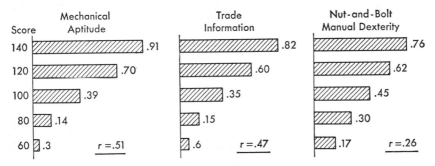

FIG. 10.   Expectancy charts showing probability of earning at least an average grade in training as an aircraft armorer (*Personnel Classification Tests*, 1946).

Percentile Scores

The easiest way to make comparisons is to rank the scores from highest to lowest. Reporting that a person stands third out of forty conveniently states his position relative to others. Ranks, however, depend on the number of persons in the group. If we wish to examine change in standing from one occasion to another we have difficulty because the size of the group changes. To avoid this difficulty, ranks are changed to percentile scores (also called percentile ranks and centile ranks). A *percentile score* is the rank expressed in percentage terms. A person's percentile score tells what proportion of the group falls below him. Suppose there are 40 persons, 27 superior to A and 12 poorer. Then we arbitrarily divide case A (and all persons tied with him,

1. Begin with the raw scores (these are scores of 75 ninth-grade boys on Bennett Form AA).	37 43 27 44 27 27 26 31 35 42 50 35 43 36 26 50 47 36 26 32 32 38 36 21 24 40 39 35 38 36 38 21 17 26 35 22 18 50 30 38 50 16 45 8 34 26 34 28 41 27 39 41 30 23 33 22 31 36 40 54 24 22 8 33 42 41 41 31 34 36 32 20 22 34 41
2. Identify the highest score and the lowest score. If there is a wide range, choose a class interval of 1, 2, 5, 10, 20, etc., and divide the range into classes of equal width. Fifteen or more classes are desirable.	Highest score = 54; lowest score = 8; range = 46. Class interval of 5 will be used. (A smaller interval, such as 2, would be preferable but would be inconvenient in this computing guide.)

			Fre-quency (f)	Cumu-lative Fre-quency	Cumu-lative Per-cent
Scores	Tallies				
50–54	⁄⁄⁄⁄⁄		5	75	100
45–49	⁄⁄		2	70	93
40–44	⁄⁄⁄⁄⁄ ⁄⁄⁄⁄⁄ ⁄⁄		12	68	90
35–39	⁄⁄⁄⁄⁄ ⁄⁄⁄⁄⁄ ⁄⁄⁄⁄⁄ ⁄⁄		17	56	75
30–34	⁄⁄⁄⁄⁄ ⁄⁄⁄⁄⁄ ⁄⁄⁄⁄		14	39	52
25–29	⁄⁄⁄⁄⁄ ⁄⁄⁄⁄⁄		10	25	33
20–24	⁄⁄⁄⁄⁄ ⁄⁄⁄⁄⁄		10	← 15	20[b]
15–19	⁄⁄⁄		3	5[a]	7
10–14			0	2	3
5– 9	⁄⁄		2	2	3
				0	0
			75		
			N		

3. Tally the number of cases with each score.
4. Write the number of tallies in the Frequency (f) column. Add this column to get N, the number of cases.
5. Begin at the bottom of the column and add frequencies one at a time to determine the cumulative frequency, the number of cases below each division point.
6. Divide the cumulative frequencies by N to determine cumulative percentages.

[a] 5 cases fall below 19.5; 15 below 24.5; etc.
[b] 20 percent of the cases fall below 24.5; 20 is the cumulative percentage corresponding to a raw score of 24.5.

if any) between the two groups, saying that 27½ cases are above him and 12½ cases below. Since 12½ is 31 percent of 40, his percentile score is 31.

By this method of computation, the person exactly in the middle of the group is at the 50th percentile. The 50th percentile is called the *median*. The median indicates the performance of the most typical member of the group.

A graphic procedure is often used to compute percentiles. The graphic method disregards irregularities in the distribution of scores in a particular sample and therefore gives a better estimate of what may be expected when further groups are tested. Computing Guide 1 demonstrates this method, using a set of Bennett TMC scores for a ninth-grade class.

Transforming raw scores to percentile scores changes the shape of the dis-

7. Plot cumulative percentage against score. (In practice, a large sheet of graph paper would be used.)

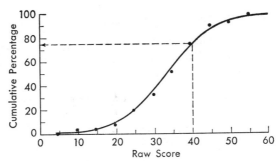

8. Draw the smooth curve which best fits the points plotted.

9. Determine the percentile equivalent of a score by reading from the curve. (The lines on the chart show how one finds that the percentile equivalent of a raw score of 40 is 74.)

Percentile Equivalents

Raw	%ile	Raw	%ile	Raw	%ile
12	2	24	17	36	60
13	2	25	20	37	64
14	3	26	22	38	67
15	3	27	26	39	71
16	4	28	29	40	74
17	5	29	33	41	77

COMPUTING GUIDE 1.   DETERMINING PERCENTILE EQUIVALENTS

tribution. In Figure 11, raw scores for the same ninth-grade class have been plotted. The distribution is high at the center and tapers away at each end. When each score is changed to a percentile equivalent in the lower part of the figure, the distribution is nearly rectangular. With larger samples the percentile distribution becomes almost perfectly rectangular. Persons near

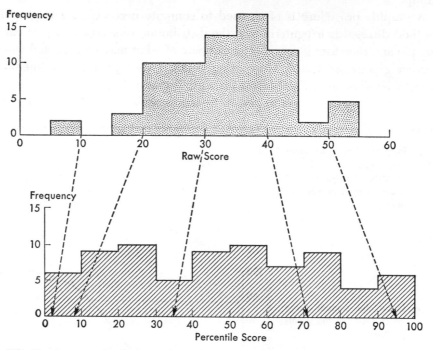

FIG. 11.   Raw-score distribution and distribution of percentile equivalents for same group.

the middle of the raw-score scale are spread apart; persons at the end are squeezed together. It is important to realize that a rather large percentile difference near the median often represents a small difference in perform-ance. Conversely, the difference between the 90th and the 99th percentiles, though it looks small on this scale, may be as great as the difference between a five-minute and a four-minute mile.

Averaging two percentile scores gives a result different from what would be obtained if the average of the corresponding raw scores were changed to a percentile score. Raw scores of 14 and 22 average 18, which has a percen-tile equivalent of 6. The percentile equivalent of 14 is 4, and that of 22 is 13. If we had made the mistake of averaging percentiles, our answer would have been 8½ instead of 6. While one rarely makes a huge error by averaging per-centiles, the cumulation of such errors can distort statistical findings, and therefore percentiles should not be averaged. The median is the proper measure of central tendency in analyzing percentile scores.

Percentile scores must not be compared unless the groups on which they are based are comparable. Published norms for tests may be based on dissimilar groups. Purdue Pegboard norms are based on industrial trainees; Form AA of the TMC gives norms for engineering freshmen. A person at the 75th percentile on both tests according to these norms does not have equally high standing in these two abilities. For the TMC, separate tables for industrial trainees are available, and we find that a score which is at the 73rd percentile among freshmen is at the 90th percentile among trainees. Wherever percentiles are used, the norm group involved must be kept in mind.

TABLE 2.   Bennett TMC Norms for Boys in Grade 9

Percentile	Score
99	54
95	47
90	44
85	41
80	39
75	38
70	36
65	35
60	33
55	32
50	31
45	30
40	29
35	27
30	26
25	23
20	22
15	20
10	17
5	14
1	5
Number of cases	833
Mean	30.8
s.d.	10.4

SOURCE: Bennett, 1947.

In the manual for the Bennett TMC, the user finds a collection of percentile conversion tables permitting him to compare his subject with various reference groups. One such table is reproduced here. This can be used like the table prepared in Computing Guide 1, although the tables are arranged differently.

A score of 39 falls at the 80th percentile in the norm table, even though it was nearer the median (68th percentile) of the small class (Computing

Guide 1). The median of the small class (34) is higher than the median of the standardization group; the class is evidently a superior group. This demonstrates the value of carefully collected norms. A person who is just average in mechanical comprehension would not be especially encouraged to choose a mechanical field. The average student within this class, however, proves to be superior (63rd percentile), compared to students generally. It is this larger group with whom he will compete after high school.

12. Interpret the following record of ability test scores for one person, where all scores are percentile scores based on a random sample of adults: Verbal, 54; Number, 46; Spatial, 87; Reasoning, 40.
13. Estimate Alfred's percentile score in each of the four tests he took (question 8, p. 72).
14. Why does the table of Bennett norms begin at 1 and stop at 99, instead of ranging from 0 to 100? What percentile score corresponds to a raw score of 60 (perfect)?
15. Scores usually change when a test is repeated, because of chance errors of measurement. If each of the following persons changes two points up or down in raw score on the TMC, how much would his percentile score change?
    a. A person with a percentile score of 55 on the first test.
    b. A person at the 95th percentile on the first test.
16. The scores below are the times, in seconds, required by a group of persons to perform an easy Block Design problem. Prepare a table of percentile equivalents for this group:

    52 34 41 42 46 45 27 48 35 35 38 29 54 36 33 30
    48 39 44 36 36 34 51 40 30 33 37 41 56 32 48 35
    37 28 28 45 31 39 31 27 35 36 34 42 38 33 33 31
    39 28 36 33 37 36 34 54 34 32 33 38
17. According to the table prepared in problem 16, how much difference in seconds does a difference of 10 percentile points represent?

Standard Scores

Mean and Standard Deviation.   The second common way to summarize the performance of a group is to use the mean and standard deviation. The *mean* (M) is the arithmetical average obtained when we add all scores and divide by the number of scores. The *standard deviation* (s.d., or s) is a measure of the spread of scores. The variation of two sets of scores may be different even though the averages are the same. Figure 12 shows the smoothed distribution of scores of two classes taking the same test. Even though the groups are similar in mean ability, the distributions are not at all alike. Group B contains far more very superior and inferior cases and therefore has a larger standard deviation.

One method of computing the mean and standard deviation is outlined in Computing Guide 2. The complicated formula makes it hard to see just what the standard deviation means, but in effect it is an average of the deviations

1. Begin with the raw scores (these are scores of 75 ninth-grade boys on Bennett Form AA).	37 43 27 44 27 27 26 31 35 42 50

1. Begin with the raw scores (these are scores of 75 ninth-grade boys on Bennett Form AA).

37	43	27	44	27	27	26	31	35	42	50
35	43	36	26	50	47	36	26	32	32	38
36	21	24	40	39	35	38	36	38	21	17
26	35	22	18	50	30	38	50	16	45	8
34	26	34	28	41	27	39	41	30	23	33
22	31	36	40	54	24	22	8	33	42	41
41	31	34	36	32	20	22	34	41		

2. Identify the highest score and the lowest score. If there is a wide range, choose a class interval of 1, 2, 5, 10, 20, etc., and divide the range into classes of equal width. Fifteen or more classes are desirable.

Highest score = 54; lowest score = 8; range = 46. Class interval of 5 will be used. (A smaller interval, such as 2, would be preferable but would be inconvenient in this computing guide.)

3. Tally the number of cases with each score.

4. Write the number of tallies in the Frequency (f) column. Add this column to get N, the number of cases.

Scores	Tallies	Frequency (f)	d	fd	fd²
50–54	///	5	4	20	80
45–49	//	2	3	6	18
40–44	/// /// //	12	2	24	48
35–39	/// /// /// //	17	1	17	17
30–34	/// /// ////	14	0	0	0
25–29	/// ///	10	−1	−10	10
20–24	/// ///	10	−2	−20	40
15–19	///	3	−3	− 9	27
10–14		0	−4	− 0	0
5– 9	//	2	−5	−10	50
		75 N		+18 Σfd	290 Σfd²

5. Select any interval, usually near the middle of the distribution. Call this the arbitrary origin. (Here, the 30–34 interval is used.) Determine the deviation d of each interval from the arbitrary origin.

6. Multiply in each row the entries in the f and d columns, and enter in the fd column.

7. Multiply the entries in the d and fd columns, and enter in the fd² column. Add the fd and fd² columns. (Σ is a symbol meaning "sum of.")

$$c = \frac{18}{75} = .24$$

$$M = 32.0 + 5\,(0.24)$$
$$M = 32.0 + 1.20 = 33.20$$

8. Substitute in the following formulas:

$$c \text{ (correction)} = \frac{\Sigma fd}{N}$$

$$M \text{ (mean)} = A.O. + i \times c$$

$$s.d. = i \times \sqrt{\frac{\Sigma fd^2 - Nc^2}{N-1}}$$

$$s.d. = 5 \times \sqrt{\frac{290 - 75\,(0.24)^2}{74}}$$

$$s.d. = 5 \times \sqrt{\frac{290 - 75\,(.058)}{74}}$$

$$s.d. = 5 \times \sqrt{\frac{290 - 4.3}{74}} = 5 \times \sqrt{\frac{285.7}{74}}$$

$$s.d. = 5 \times \sqrt{3.86} = 5\,(1.96)$$
$$s.d. = 9.80$$

A.O. is the midpoint of the score-interval selected as arbitrary origin, and i is the width of the interval.

COMPUTING GUIDE 2. DETERMINING THE MEAN AND STANDARD DEVIATION of persons' scores from the group mean. We might measure the spread of scores by finding how far each person is from the mean and averaging (ignoring the direction of deviation). For mathematical reasons, the standard deviation formula takes the average of the squares of the deviations

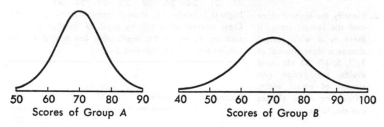

FIG. 12.   Distributions of scores of two classes on the same test.

rather than of the deviations directly, and then takes the square root of the result.

The standard deviation indicates how much variation there is within a group. In much statistical analysis the square of the standard deviation, called the *variance* of the distribution, is used as an index of variation.

18. a. Compute the mean and standard deviation for the Block Design scores given in problem 16, p. 78.
   b. How does the mean compare with the median computed previously?
   c. What is the approximate percentile rank for a score 2 s.d. above the mean in this distribution?

Conversion Scales.   We can replace the person's raw score with a derived score showing his position relative to the mean. To say how far above or below he is, we use the standard deviation as a unit. We can say that one person is 2.5 s.d. above the mean and another is at -1 s.d. (i.e., is 1 s.d. below the mean). From Computing Guide 2, we see that a score of 43 is about 1 s.d. above the mean, for example. Derived scores based on standard deviation units are called *standard scores*.

Computing Guide 3 shows how to convert raw scores to a standard-score scale with a mean of zero and each s.d. above the mean counted as one unit. One can also convert scores to the "T-score" system which sets the mean at 50 (to avoid negative scores) and each s.d. equal to 10 points. As Figure 13 shows, changing raw scores into standard scores does not alter the form of the distribution (except for slight changes due to regrouping).

Whereas the Bennett TMC presents norms in percentile form, the Wechsler Block Design norms are in standard-score form (called "scaled scores" by Wechsler). As an example, Table 3 gives the norms for people aged 20–24. The range of converted scores is from 0 to 19, because Wechsler chose to set the mean equal to a standard score of 10, and to count each s.d. above or below the mean as 3 standard-score points.

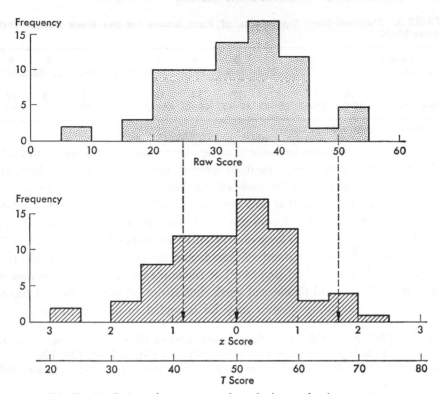

FIG. 13. Distributions of raw scores and standard scores for the same group.

1. Begin with the raw scores to be converted, and find the mean and s.d. as in Computing Guide 2.

For the data in Computing Guide 2,

$$M = 33.2, \text{ s.d.} = 9.80$$

2. To obtain z-scores, express each raw score as a deviation from the mean. Divide by the s.d.

$$z \text{ score} = \frac{\text{raw score} - \text{mean}}{\text{standard deviation}}$$

For raw score 50:

$$z = \frac{50 - 33.2}{9.80} = \frac{16.8}{9.80} = 1.7$$

For raw score 25:

$$z = \frac{25 - 33.2}{9.80} = \frac{-8.2}{9.80} = -.8$$

3. To obtain T scores, multiply the z score by 10 and add to 50.

$$T \text{ score} = 50 + \frac{10 \text{ (raw score} - \text{mean)}}{\text{standard deviation}}$$

For raw score 50, z = 1.7

$$T = 50 + 10 \,(1.7) = 67$$

For raw score 25, z = −.8

$$T = 50 + 10 \,(-.8) = 42$$

COMPUTING GUIDE 3. CALCULATION OF STANDARD SCORES

TABLE 3. Standard-Score Equivalents of Raw Scores for the Block Design Test, Ages 20–24

Scaled score	0	1	2	3	4	5	6	7	8	9
Raw score	0	1	2	3–8	9–12	13–16	17–20	21–24	25–28	29–31

Scaled score	10	11	12	13	14	15	16	17	18	19
Raw score	32–34	35–37	38–40	41–43	44–45	46–47	—	48	—	—

SOURCE: Wechsler, 1955, p. 103.

One can develop standard scores using other values for the mean and s.d. Table 4 summarizes several standard-score systems now in use. While there have been logical reasons for many of the variations, only confusion results from so large a variety. It is now recommended (*Technical Recommendations,* 1954) that test developers use the *T*-score system, with mean 50 and s.d. 10. If it is desirable to keep converted scores below 10 so that they will fit into one column of a standard punchcard for statistical operations, the stanine scale (pronounced *stay-nine*) is recommended. The *z* conversion is used in statistical and theoretical work, but is not often used by test interpreters. The remaining systems may be expected to die out in time.

19. The 1959 Stanford-Binet test fixes the mean IQ at 100 and the standard deviation at 16. Express in *T*-score form the following IQs: 100, 84, 132, 150.
20. In Computing Guide 2, what standard score corresponds to a raw score of 40? 48? 4?
21. Draw a figure to show the relation between raw scores and *T* scores in Computing Guide 3.

Smoothed Score Distributions.   The frequency distribution shown at the top of Figures 11 and 13 is jagged, but if more cases were added and smaller class intervals were used it would become relatively smooth. We can estimate the most likely shape of that distribution by drawing a smooth curve as shown in the top portion of Figure 14. This distribution is not perfectly

TABLE 4.   Standard-Score Systems

Mean Set Equal to	s.d. Set Equal to	Standard Score Corresponding to 1 s.d. Above Mean	Standard Score Corresponding to 2 s.d. Below Mean	Name of System, Remarks
0	1	1	−2	z scores, prominent in mathematical theory of testing
5	2	7	1	Stanine scores
10	3	13	4	Used for Wechsler subtests
50	10	60	30	T scores; most widely used system
100	15 or 16	115 or 116	70 or 68	Deviation IQ used by many mental tests
100	20	120	60	Used for aptitude tests of U.S. Employment Service

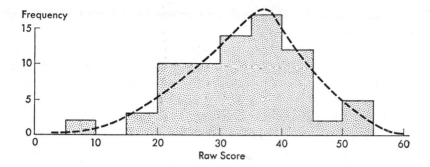

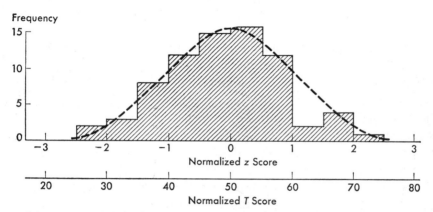

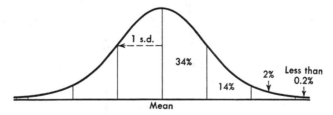

FIG. 14. Smoothed distribution of raw scores and distribution of normalized scores.

symmetrical, but it tails off on both sides. Most tests yield distributions of this general character. Since every distribution has its own shape, there is some advantage in converting the score scale so that every test has the same distribution form. The normal probability curve is used for this.

The Normal Probability Curve. The normal curve (Figure 15) is a smooth, symmetric frequency curve which has important mathematical properties.

FIG. 15. Percentage of cases falling in each portion of a normal distribution.

The standard deviation is the distance from the mean to the "point of inflection" on the shoulder of the normal curve. This, as shown in Figure 15, is the point which separates the convex, hill-like portion from the concave tail. The normal curve is important in the theory of probability and is used in statistical analysis to determine whether a particular experimental result may be a chance occurrence.

Many biological measures such as heights of American men fall into a nearly normal distribution, perhaps because chance combinations of chromosomes determine the variable. In psychological tests also, it is very common to obtain normal distributions of scores. Early investigators thought it a natural law that abilities are normally distributed. It is now realized that such a statement is meaningless, since the shape of the distribution depends on the scale of measurement. The distributions of actual test scores depend on the way the test is constructed. By selecting items suitably, we can change the score distributions to U-shaped, flat, skewed to one side, etc. (F. M. Lord, 1952; Cronbach and Warrington, 1952). The use of normal curves in test scaling is therefore merely a convenience and is not based on any "normal distribution of behavior" in nature.

If we slice a normal distribution into bands one standard deviation wide, a fixed percentage of the cases always falls in each band. As Figure 15 shows, 34 percent of the cases fall between the mean and +1 s.d. In the next interval are 14 percent, and in the third 2 percent. Since 99.6 percent of the cases fall between +3 s.d. and −3 s.d., the whole range of test scores is somewhere near 6 standard deviations (less, when the group is small). These facts are handy for interpreting standard scores and for roughly reconstructing the score distribution if the mean and s.d. are known.

Whenever we have, or assume, a normal distribution, we can quickly convert standard scores to percentile scores, and vice versa. Below the mean (z score of zero, or T score of 50) are 50 percent of the cases. Below +1 s.d. are $50 + 34$ or 84 percent of the cases; hence a T score of 60 equals a percentile score of 84.

22. What percentile rank corresponds to a score of 2 s.d. above the mean? To a score 1 s.d. below the mean?
23. In a normal distribution, what is the relation of the mean and median?
24. Assuming that scores are normally distributed on a test where the mean is 60 and s.d. is 8, interpret the following scores: Sara, 64; Harriet, 68; Charles, 87; Bob, 48.
25. Using Figure 15, interpret each of the following in percentile terms: a z score of 3.0; a z score of −2.0; a T score of 40; a T score of 65.

Normalized Scores.   Scores are somewhat easier to interpret if all tests are reduced to a scale having a known distribution. For this purpose, testers most commonly employ *normalized standard scores*. These scores are obtained by stretching a distribution to make it nearly normal, and then changing it to standard-score form. One procedure which accomplishes this result is to compute percentiles by the method of Computing Guide 1, and then

TABLE 5.   Relations Between Standard Scores and Percentile Scores, When Raw Scores Are Normally Distributed

Distance from Mean in s.d. (z Score)	T Score	Percentile Score	Percent of Cases in "Tail" of Curve	Percentile Score	T Score	Distance from Mean in s.d. (z Score)
3.0	80	99.9	0.1	0.1	20	−3.0
2.9	79	99.8	0.2	0.2	21	−2.9
2.8	78	99.7	0.3	0.3	22	−2.8
2.7	77	99.6	0.4	0.4	23	−2.7
2.6	76	99.5	0.5	0.5	24	−2.6
2.5	75	99.4	0.6	0.6	25	−2.5
2.4	74	99.2	0.8	0.8	26	−2.4
2.3	73	99	1	1	27	−2.3
2.2	72	99	1	1	28	−2.2
2.1	71	98	2	2	29	−2.1
2.0	70	98	2	2	30	−2.0
1.9	69	97	3	3	31	−1.9
1.8	68	96	4	4	32	−1.8
1.7	67	96	4	4	33	−1.7
1.6	66	95	5	5	34	−1.6
1.5	65	93	7	7	35	−1.5
1.4	64	92	8	8	36	−1.4
1.3	63	90	10	10	37	−1.3
1.2	62	88	12	12	38	−1.2
1.1	61	86	14	14	39	−1.1
1.0	60	84	16	16	40	−1.0
0.9	59	82	18	18	41	−0.9
0.8	58	79	21	21	42	−0.8
0.7	57	76	24	24	43	−0.7
0.6	56	73	27	27	44	−0.6
0.5	55	69	31	31	45	−0.5
0.4	54	66	34	34	46	−0.4
0.3	53	62	38	38	47	−0.3
0.2	52	58	42	42	48	−0.2
0.1	51	54	46	46	49	−0.1
0.0	50	50	50	50	50	0.0

to read from Table 5 the standard score corresponding to that percentile value.

In our illustrative distribution of ninth-grade TMC scores, 95 is the percentile equivalent of a raw score of 50, and Table 5 indicates that the corresponding normalized T score is 66. This compares with a T score of 67 (not normalized) obtained in Computing Guide 3. Such small changes, stretching out the scale at the upper end and compressing it at the lower end, produces the distribution shown at the bottom of Figure 14. This distribution is more symmetric than the raw-score distribution. If more cases had been used, the smoothed distribution would be completely normal.

Profiles

With derived scores, it is possible to compare performance on one test with that on another. This is illustrated in the Differential Aptitude Tests, a set of eight tests for different abilities. One section is a new form of the Ben-

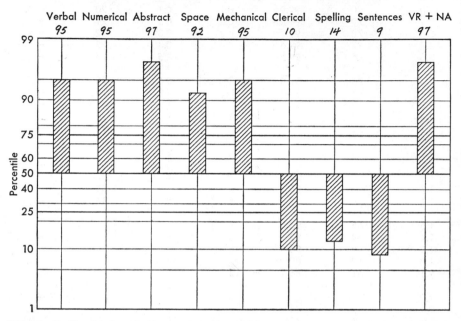

FIG. 16. Profile of Robert Finchley on the Differential Aptitude Tests (Bennett, Seashore, and Wesman, 1951).

nett TMC. The tests vary in length and in difficulty, so that from the raw scores alone one cannot judge the person's greatest ability. After raw scores are changed to percentiles or normalized standard scores, one can plot a profile showing his relative standing in all fields. The profile shown in Figure 16 is that of a high-school junior; the norms for junior boys were used to convert his scores. Robert is highly superior in the various reasoning tests, and is almost equally outstanding in all of them. His last three scores are quite poor.

Comparison of Systems

Since the manual sometimes offers more than one type of conversion table and since the user often has to develop local norms for tests, he needs some basis for deciding which system of scores is preferable.

The percentile score has these advantages: it is readily understood, which makes it especially satisfactory for reporting data to persons without statistical training; it is easily computed; it may be interpreted exactly even when the distribution of test scores is nonnormal. The disadvantages of the percentile score are these: it magnifies small differences in score near the mean which may not be significant, and it reduces the apparent size of large differences in score near the tails of the distributions; it may not be used in many statistical computations.

The advantages of standard scores are as follows: Differences in standard score are proportional to differences in raw score; use of standard scores in averages and correlations gives the same result as would come from use of the raw scores. The disadvantages are that standard scores cannot be interpreted readily when distributions are skewed, and that untrained persons generally find them difficult to understand. In general, statisticians prefer standard scores while those who interpret tests directly to laymen prefer percentiles.

Normalized standard scores have become increasingly popular and are generally suitable. The normalized scores spread out cases in both tails of the distribution and yet can readily be translated into percentiles. The DAT profile form shown in Figure 16 illustrates typical current practice. One can read off standard scores (normalized) when they are needed for statistical comparisons but can talk to the subject in terms of percentiles.

26. A teacher wishes to convert scores on class examinations so that he can tell at a glance how well a person is doing and can average all tests equally in the final grade. Should he use raw, percentile, or standard scores?

27. In a certain college, all freshmen are given a "scholastic aptitude test." The results are to be mimeographed and confidential copies given to all professors. Should the report use raw scores, standard scores, or percentiles?

28. The psychometrist gives a wide variety of tests to veterans needing counseling. After each man has taken from four to eight tests, results are to be placed on a standard report form so that performance on all tests can be compared by the counselor, in conference with the veteran. What problems will be encountered if all results are reported in percentiles? If all results are reported as standard scores?

NORMS

The test manual assists the user to interpret scores by presenting information regarding "normal" performance. This information takes the form of one or more tables. The user should have no difficulty in interpreting the information provided in the manual, although every manual organizes its tables a bit differently. For example, the Bennett test manual provides tables of percentile equivalents (cf. Table 2) so that the user may compare an individual with any one of the following groups: 833 ninth-grade boys, 370 tenth-grade boys, 613 engineering-school freshmen, 1836 candidates for policeman and fireman positions, 548 candidates for apprentice training, 145 candidates for engineering positions, 1637 workers in a paper factory, 226 trainees in an airplane factory, and fifteen other groups. The DAT form has separate norms for boys and girls, for each grade from 8 through 12. This battery is primarily used in high-school guidance.

No detailed information about the Bennett norm groups is given; hence a user of the test can only guess whether his situation resembles that of the tenth grade or of the "engineering positions" in the table. These norms were published in 1940. They may be contrasted with the more modern description given in the manual for the DAT Mechanical Reasoning Test (Bennett *et al.*, 1959):

> Over one hundred school systems from all major geographic areas contributed to the normative sampling. In some cities the whole school population in five grades (eight through twelve) was tested; in some, all pupils in one to four grades were tested; in some larger cities, classes in representative schools (as judged by the local research director) were examined. A complete listing of the normative sample showing the number of students in each grade in each community is [obtainable]. . . . The total number of students included in the present norms (1952) is over 47,000.
>
> The states which contributed to the normative study . . . and the number of communities in each were: Arizona, 1; California, 5; Colorado, 1; . . . West Virginia, 2. The testing of the normative sample was done throughout the school year. It is appropriate to assume that the norms represent mid-year performance.

Some testers attach too much importance to norms, either when they select tests or when they interpret scores. Others, recognizing that norms are helpful, are unduly impressed by the number of cases used in compiling the norm tables. We shall see, however, that the size of the standardizing sample alone does not indicate how satisfactory the norms are.

Norms are unimportant in many uses of tests, particularly when one intends only to identify individual differences within a group. For example, norms are of little use to the employment manager who wishes to hire the brightest ten persons in a group of applicants. Norms are also of little value where a critical score is used. If a personnel manager knows from actual trial that persons with scores of 72 on test A make satisfactory punch-press operators, it is not necessary for him to compare applicants with national norms.

In guidance and clinical work, it is extremely important to use norms in interpreting scores. The person's position relative to his group has to be fixed as definitely as possible. A child who scores at the 20th percentile on a test of readiness for first grade will have difficulties in school, but he is by no means a rare exception. If our norms placed him at the 2nd percentile instead, we would not expect him to fit into the regular program at all.

For many test interpretations, local norms are far more important than large-group norms. Classes differ so much that a child who is at the 20th percentile in the typical first grade would be at the 2nd percentile in some other school which enrolls pupils from a select neighborhood. One example of such school-to-school differences is given in Table 6.

TABLE 6. School-to-School Differences in Mechanical Reasoning Scores of Ninth-Grade Boys

City	Name of School	Approximate Number of Cases	Mean	s.d.
Worcester, Mass.	Commerce	60	28.3	12.7
Worcester, Mass.	Five other schools	190	29.4	11.9
St. Joseph, Mo.	Benton	70	30.3	11.7
St. Joseph, Mo.	Lafayette	70	35.8	10.7
St. Paul, Minn.	Wilson	50	34.0	10.3
Independence, Mo.	Chrisman	175	37.6	12.4

SOURCE: Bennett *et al.*, 1947.

Norms, to be useful, must permit the tester to compare the subject with his prospective companions and competitors. The manual for the Wechsler intelligence scale gives norms based on adults in general. But a boy who is above the average for his age, compared to people in general, may be below average among college freshmen. If we wish to predict whether he can succeed in college, we need Wechsler norms based on college students alone. More than that, we need to know the norms for the particular college he plans to attend.

Sections of the country, occupational groups, and schools vary widely in America. One example of the geographical differences to be expected is given in Table 7. The SSCQT was given for several years to young men who might wish to attend college; those earning scores of 70 and over were

TABLE 7. Geographical Differences in Selective Service College Qualification Test Scores

Residence	Percentage of Freshmen Registrants Scoring Below				
	50	60	70	75	80
New England	1	4	44	71	92
Middle Atlantic	1	3	40	69	92
East North Central	2	4	45	74	94
West North Central	1	5	44	73	93
South Atlantic	6	11	57	78	94
East South Central	7	15	66	85	97
West South Central	9	16	63	84	95
Mountain	2	4	46	75	94
Pacific	2	5	45	72	93

SOURCE: *Statistical Studies*, 1955, p. 89.

generally allowed to postpone their military service until completion of college. The test, designed to be as fair a measure of scholastic aptitude as possible, called for verbal and quantitative reasoning. There are large differences among regions: in the Midwest and East the average registrant was at a high enough level to be exempt from immediate draft, whereas in the South only 40 percent of the registrants have performed at this level.

Whenever he can, the test interpreter should prepare norms for the groups with which he deals directly. A high-school counselor could profitably use information about the score distribution for all boys in his high school, for boys in the shop curriculum, for boys who later attend the local college, and for workers in certain large local industries. He uses published norms because it takes time and effort to accumulate local norms or because, as is often the case, he cannot possibly accumulate local norms. A clinician, for example, has no chance to prepare norms for a random sample of 60-year-old men, yet he needs to compare the men he tests with a community average.

> Except where the primary use of a test is to compare individuals with their own local group, norms should be published at the time of release of the test for operational use. Norms should refer to defined and clearly described populations. These populations should be the groups to whom users of the test will ordinarily wish to compare the persons tested. If appreciable differences between groups exist (e.g., groups differing in age, sex, amount of training, etc.), and if a person would ordinarily be compared with a subgroup rather than with a random sample of persons, then separate norm tables should be provided in the manual for each group. [*Technical Recommendations,* 1954.]

These are official recommendations (see p. 101) regarding test norms. All these principles have been violated at times in the past. Tests have been published with no norms. Others have offered norms based on inadequate samples, and often the samples are improperly described. The difficulties in this aspect of test interpretation are pointed out forcibly in these remarks by a test publisher (H. G. Seashore and J. H. Ricks, Jr., 1950):

> Legitimate and illegitimate general norms abound in current test manuals. People-in-general norms are legitimate only if they are based upon careful field studies with appropriate controls of regional, socioeconomic, educational, and other factors—and even then only if the sampling is carefully described so that the test user may be fully aware of its inevitable limitations and deficiencies. The millions entering the armed forces during World War II provided the basis of some fairly good norms on young adult men, though mainly on tests not available to the public. The standardization of the Wechsler Intelligence Scale for

Children is a recent attempt to secure a representative smaller sample of children aged 5–15 for setting up tables of intelligence quotients which may be considered generalized norms for children. The earlier work of Terman's group to set up good national norms on a small, well-chosen sample is well known. In the standardizing of some educational achievement tests, nationwide samplings of children of each appropriate grade or age and from different types of schools in all parts of the country are sought in an effort to produce norms that are truly general for a given span of grades or ages.

Unfortunately, many alleged general norms reported in test manuals are not backed even by an honest effort to secure representative samples of people-in-general. Even tens or hundreds of thousands of cases can fall woefully short of defining people-in-general. Inspection of test manuals will show (or would show if information about the norms were given completely) that many such massed norms are merely collections of all the scores that opportunity has permitted the author or publisher to gather easily. Lumping together all the samples secured more by chance than by plan makes for impressively large numbers; but while seeming to simplify interpretation, the norms may dim or actually distort the counseling, employment, or diagnostic significance of a score.

With or without a plan, everyone of course obtains data where and how he can. Since the standardization of a test is always dependent on the cooperation of educators, psychologists and personnel men, the foregoing comments are not a plea for the rejection of available samples but for their correct labeling. If a manual shows "general" norms for a vocabulary test based on a sample two-thirds of which consists of women office workers, one can properly raise his test-wise eyebrows. There is no reason to accept such norms as a good generalization of adult—or even of employed-adult—vocabulary. It is better to set up norms on the occupationally homogeneous two-thirds of the group and frankly call them norms on female office workers. Adding a few more miscellaneous cases does not make the sample a truly general one.

As a rule, then, in reading a test manual we should reject as treacherous any alleged national or general norms whose generality is not supported by a clear, complete report on the sample of people they represent, or norms which are obviously opportunistic accumulations of samples weighted by their size according to chance rather than logic.

If the manual describes the norm sample adequately, the user can judge the norms by these questions:

● Does the standard group consist of the sort of person with whom my subjects should be compared?

- Is the sample representative of this group?
- Does the sample include enough cases?
- Is the sample appropriately subdivided?

Norms for any group must be a fair description of that group. A fair sample is assured when the test maker takes an exactly random sample of the population (e.g., of all American college freshmen). Since this is difficult, the test maker usually tries to obtain a mixture of cases from all segments of the population; for college students, he would draw on large and small colleges, private and public, from all sections of the country. If any segment is too heavily represented, the norms will be biased.

In a small sample, accidental inclusion of a few additional good or poor cases will make the norms unrepresentative. In large samples, such variations should cancel out. No fixed number of cases is required for dependable norms. It is better to keep the sample strictly representative, and small, than to accumulate large numbers of cases which may not be representative. The most unsatisfactory norms are those based on whatever cases happen to be conveniently available. A manual may report, "The norms are based on scores of 2700 sophomores taking general psychology at four Western colleges." Norms such as these are useless unless the tester wishes to know how his cases compare with sophomore psychology students at western colleges.

Even when the norm sample is large and representative, it should ordinarily be subdivided if important, clearly identifiable subgroups earn different average scores. On the DAT Mechanical Reasoning Test, the Grade 9 median is 32 while that for girls is only 19. As Wesman (1949, p. 227) points out:

> Counseling would be very different if one had only the single sex scores [in the norm table]. For example, a boy with a Mechanical Reasoning score of 40 (in Grade 10) would be close to the 75th percentile on a combined distribution scale. With only that information, the counselor would be compelled to consider him as having enough ability to compete favorably in a curriculum or occupation requiring mechanical understanding. If he entered such a curriculum, however, his competition would be almost entirely male. Compared with boys only, his score of 40 leaves him at the 50th percentile, a ranking not at all superior.

A new method of developing test norms may become prominent shortly. This method involves *calibrating* a new test (or a test needing new norms) against another well-standardized test. This is similar to the procedure the maker of an aneroid barometer uses when he places marks on its dial so that readings agree with an accurate mercury barometer. The method has not been useful in psychology because no instrument has had norms sufficiently perfect to be taken as a standard for other tests. It has been proposed, however, to administer an experimental set of tests of various abilities and personality characteristics to a strictly representative sample of 500,000 high-school students. The proposed sample would constitute perhaps 5 percent of the entire age group (ignoring the rather small fraction not in school).

The developer of a new test for high-school ages could use these data as a basis for standardizing. To do so, he would select whichever of the experimental tests measures about the same thing as his test does. For example, a new Form DD of the TMC could be calibrated against whatever test of mechanical comprehension is in the experimental battery. Call this test X. The test developer would apply both test X and Form DD to the same sample. This sample should be reasonably representative of high-school students (for example, it should not be restricted to boys in a technical high school), but it can be fairly small and need not be exactly representative. The *equipercentile* method is then used to establish what scores on test X and Form DD represent the same level of ability. Scores falling at the same percentile in the calibration sample are taken as equivalent. Suppose we have the following information:

Raw Score on Test X	Percentile Rank in National Sample for Grade 9	Percentile Rank in Calibration Sample	Raw Score on Form DD Having Same Percentile Rank in Calibration Sample
80	98	99	60
60	82	88	52
40	63	70	43

One would conclude, for example, that a score of 60 on Form DD is equivalent to a score of 80 on test X. We therefore would expect it to fall at the 98th percentile if it were standardized on a national sample of ninth-graders. Similarly, one can use the data for test X to establish norms for other grades, students in technical curricula, girls in vocational courses, etc. Once Form DD scores are matched to scores on test X, any norms, expectancy tables, or other research on test X can be used to interpret Form DD. Certain statistical corrections may be necessary, however, unless Form DD and test X are highly correlated (Lindquist, 1951, pp. 750–760).

Test norms become obsolete and need to be checked periodically. Research on the Wechsler intelligence tests, for example, suggests that the scores of adults are, on the average, higher than those for similar age groups a decade ago. These changes may be attributed to an increasing level of education.

It is essential that norms be verified whenever a test is altered. Changes of items or format make the test easier or harder and can even alter its meaning. The Crawford Structural Visualization test is made by cutting a circular disk into nine pieces of irregular shape. The score is the time the subject takes in fitting the pieces together. Originally this test was made of heavy aluminum. After it had been in use for some years, the manufacturer began to use wood instead of metal. Psychologists who applied both old and new versions found that the mean time for the wooden test was 182 seconds, whereas the original test had a mean of 140 seconds (J. W. Wilson and K. E. Carpenter, 1948). The publisher had altered the test so that the published norms were now meaningless; it was a serious error not to revise the manual.

29. It might be appropriate to compare a high-school girl's performance on the Mechanical Reasoning test with girls' norms, boys' norms, or the combined norms, depending on the decision to be made. Illustrate.

30. How do you explain the geographical differences on the SSCQT? Is it sound national policy to encourage more students from one region to attend college than from another?

31. Assuming a normal distribution, what standard score corresponds to a raw score of 40 in each of the schools in Table 6?

32. For Form CC, the difficult version of TMC intended for use in engineering schools, separate norms are reported for 148 engineering freshmen at Princeton, and for four groups at Iowa State College: 325 engineering freshmen, 175 agricultural engineering freshmen, 121 sophomores in architectural engineering, and all engineering seniors (108). It is reported that the subgroups of senior engineers were so similar that separate norms were not required. How adequate are these norms? What other tables, if any, would be desirable?

33. In a particular college which admits all high-school graduates who apply, the median score of the freshman class is at the 65th percentile of the published norms for freshmen for the Henmon-Nelson test. What factors might account for this deviation?

34. A psychologist standardizes a primary intelligence test by testing every child entering the first grade in San Francisco during a particular year.
    a. For what purposes would these norms be valuable?
    b. Could equally satisfactory norms be obtained without testing every first-grader?
    c. In what way would these norms be biased, as a sample of all 6-year-old children in San Francisco?

35. A "music aptitude" test measures such factors as tone discrimination. There is evidence that scores are increased by musical training. If the test is to be used for advising college freshmen whether to study music, what sort of cases should be used to establish national norms?

36. How would you proceed to get an extremely representative sample of adult men in Chicago to use as a standardizing group for a mental test? Assume that you have sufficient research funds to pay each man $2.00 for taking the test.

37. Would local norms or national norms be most useful in interpreting each of the following?
    a. A personality test given to indicate whether a prisoner is psychotic.
    b. An intelligence test given to an infant considered for adoption.
    c. A reading test given to determine if a high-school boy needs individual remedial instruction.

Suggested Readings

Bauernfeind, Robert H. Are sex norms necessary? *J. counsel. Psychol.*, 1956, 3, 57–63. Wesman, Alexander G. Separation of sex groups in test reporting. *J. educ. Psychol.*, 1949, **40**, 223–229.

These authors argue as to whether one should present separate norms for each sex in test manuals. The two articles should be compared to note the points where the writers agree, and to determine why they come to different conclusions.

Froehlich, Clifford P., & Darley, John G. Statistical methods of summarizing the results of a single test or measuring device. *Studying students*. Chicago: Science Research Associates, 1952. Pp. 12–38.

In extremely simple language the authors explain the computation of standard deviations, percentiles, and other statistics, and also discuss desirable qualities of test norms.

Lorge, Irving, & Thorndike, Robert L. Procedures for establishing norms. *Technical manual, Lorge-Thorndike Intelligence Tests.* Boston: Houghton Mifflin, 1957. Pp. 4–6.

This compressed summary describes the extensive research conducted to establish norms for one of the prominent modern mental tests. The procedures used to select communities for testing are unusually well designed. Results show how norms depend on the socioeconomic level of the community tested.

Seashore, Harold G. Methods of expressing test scores. *Test Serv. Bull.*, 1955, No. 45. (Available on request from the Psychological Corporation.)

A dozen scales for reporting test scores are compared, including stanines, percentiles, College Board scores, and so on.

Traxler, Arthur E. Administering and scoring the objective test. In E. F. Lindquist (ed.), *Educational measurement.* Washington: American Council on Education, 1951. Pp. 329–416.

Besides describing, with excellent illustrations, all the major techniques used for efficient scoring of tests both by hand and by machine, the chapter discusses procedures for assuring that standard instructions are followed.

Traxler, Arthur E. The IBM test scoring machine: an evaluation. *Proceedings, 1953 Invitational Conference on Testing Problems.* Princeton: Educational Testing Service, 1954. Pp. 139–146.

Traxler discusses the history and contribution of these machines, raising incidental questions as to the possible harm done by forcing all large-scale testing into the mold of five-choice multiple-choice items which fit the machine efficiently. Gives a realistic picture of the practical limitations of automatic test scoring. Other papers in the same symposium describe superdevices some of which are still in the drawing-board stage.

5

Validity

NEED FOR CRITICAL EVALUATION OF TESTS

WHEN a teacher investigates the mental ability of his pupils, he looks for the best mental test available. An industrial psychologist selecting workers for a factory wishes to try the best possible test of mental ability. The clinical psychologist studying a child who may be feeble-minded needs the mental test which will give the most accurate results. Each of these users therefore asks, "What is the best test of mental ability?" But the test which best serves one of these testers is probably not the best for either of the others.

The purchaser of tests has a confusing problem. He is faced with long tests and short tests, famous tests and unfamiliar tests, old tests and new tests, ordinary tests and novel tests. The catalog of a leading test distributor offers 33 tests of general mental ability and 19 tests of personality. Each of these tests was produced by a psychologist who thinks his test is in some way superior to the others on the market. He is frequently correct.

Different tests have different virtues; no one test in any field is "the best" for all purposes. No test maker can put into his test all desirable qualities. A change in design improves the test in one respect only by sacrificing something else. Some tests work well with children but not with adults; some give precise measures but require a long time; some give satisfactory general measures but are inferior for detailed diagnosis.

Tests must always be selected for the particular purpose for which they are to be used. Even in similar situations the same tests may not be appropriate. Readiness of a child for first grade must be measured by different tests, depending on the instructional plan. Tests which select supervisors well in one plant prove valueless in another. And clinicians may have to choose different tests for each patient. No list of "recommended tests" can eliminate the necessity for carefully choosing tests to suit each situation.

The user of tests has constantly to evaluate new developments. New tests are produced, new uses of tests are discovered, and new findings about old tests are brought to light. Any list of superior tests, therefore, soon becomes outdated. Of the nine psychological tests most used in clinics in 1935 only two remained in the top nine in 1946. Only two of the newcomers to the list were published later than 1935; the other five were available in 1935 but their usefulness was overlooked at that time (Louttit and Browne, 1946). Buros (1941, p. 11) made the following comment in selecting tests for discussion in his yearbook:

> The decision was made to include old as well as new tests. Reviews of old tests may prove effective in eliminating from use many tests which were among the best in their day but are now outmoded and inferior to recently constructed tests. On the other hand, such reviews may result in increasing the use of old tests and testing techniques which compare very favorably with tests being currently published. The sale of outmoded and ever-decreasingly valid tests persists far beyond the sale of textbooks published in the same years.

Prominence and popularity are not necessarily signs of quality. In clinical psychology and counseling particularly, fads in testing flourish. As Schafer says (1954, p. 6), "Because of its rapid growth, a boom town excitement has characterized clinical psychology until very recently. News of a 'good' test, like news of striking oil, has brought a rush of diagnostic drillers from the old wells to the new and has quickly led to the formation of a new elite" of persons specializing in that test. Techniques rushed into application far in advance of adequate research include projective tests such as the Rorschach, formulas for detecting brain damage from intelligence tests, and questionnaires such as the Taylor anxiety scale. The last-named, indeed, is a set of questions which the author developed for use only in laboratory research on learning, but clinical investigators seized the scale for diagnostic use without any evidence that the scale was superior for that purpose. Many of the fads in testing wane quickly, but some invalid tests hold their "bestseller" status for a generation.

The testing "industry" of today had informal, even casual, beginnings. A psychologist or physician wanted to observe some type of motor, intellectual, or emotional behavior and chose a stimulus or task which he thought gave a good opportunity for observation. As he mentioned his findings to others, they copied his technique in their own clinics and laboratories. Soon there was a small market for equipment (tachistoscopes for studying flash perception, blocks for tests like Kohs', etc.). A few books were written between 1910 and 1915, each describing one investigator's procedures, but there was no large-scale manufacture of tests. Test publication in the modern sense resulted from the great interest in clinical and educational testing after World War I, and particularly from the popularity of standardized group tests. The view then prevalent was that a test score could be interpreted adequately only by comparison to national norms based on thousands of cases. Users all over the country wished to purchase the same tests, packaged in a form which ensured uniform procedure, and accompanied by national norms.

One of the forces creating the American testing industry of today is the decentralization of schools, clinics, and guidance services. Every school system is free to adopt tests or not, and to choose whichever ones it prefers. Each counseling agency can purchase a different set of tests, and sometimes each psychologist within the agency chooses tests for himself. This decentralization, combined with a demand for carefully developed instruments, provides a competitive market which encourages publication of tests in great number and great variety. With these tests available, an industrial psychologist rarely thinks it necessary to make up new tests for his own factory. Even a great national agency such as the Veterans Administration relies on published tests for its clinical program.

In Europe, competitive publication is almost unknown. There is, on the one hand, a tendency for each clinical psychologist or each industrial psychologist to develop his own testing procedures—that is, to modify the methods his colleagues have used. School systems and guidance services, on the other hand, are generally under centralized national control. Each service therefore develops its own series of standardized tests, and the counselor or local school administrator has no choice. A certain amount of test publication is now beginning in Europe, the stock consisting largely of translated American and British tests. There are also books by clinicians describing diagnostic procedures. Procedures are not fully standardized, and little test research is published; this means that the person responsible for a testing program in Europe must take on even greater responsibility than his American counterpart.

American test publication began in a small way. A psychologist who had prepared a test printed copies for general sale, perhaps through a firm selling apparatus to psychology laboratories. As the demand for tests grew, particularly after World War I, some textbook publishers began to handle tests, and some firms specializing in school tests were established. Until about 1945, the typical test was developed by an author or team of authors who completed the test and then offered it to the publisher. The publisher gave some assistance in the final stages of research and in editing the test manual, but the main scientific responsibility was the author's.

In recent years, this situation has changed. Experience made clear that satisfactory tests require long periods of development, following the best technical research design. Publishers and consumers began to examine more critically the quality of test material and the technical information regarding the effectiveness of the test. Today, authors are often discouraged from releasing new tests on which research is inadequate, even though tests of similar quality would have been accepted by most publishers twenty years ago. Test construction has increasingly been taken over by the test publishers, who have added technical staffs for this purpose.

In addition to tests on the open market, Americans are making increasing use of so-called "program" tests. These are tests developed to fit the needs of a particular large program. Examples are an aptitude test developed for medical-college admission, another for awarding college scholarships on a competitive basis, and a battery of aptitude and achievement measures used in schools throughout a state for guidance purposes. These programs often require "secure" tests whose questions can be kept secret from persons to be tested. Tests for the programs are sometimes developed by professional persons employed by the testing agency. More often, the tests are developed by the staff of a test publisher. Many of the tests are constructed to resemble published tests which have already been standardized and validated. Program tests should be developed as carefully as tests published to be used by the whole profession. Technical information about the quality of the tests is not readily available to the general student of testing, which sometimes interferes with the evaluation of research using program tests.

Though there has been an increasing concentration of responsibility in the hands of persons well trained in test construction, even the newer tests have marked limitations. Some of these limitations result only from the fact that no one test can do everything, but some tests still are published without adequate research and refinement. Some, even popular ones, do not succeed in measuring what they were intended to measure, and some measure characteristics other than what their titles suggest. Furthermore, the author's description of a test understandably advertises its favorable features. Even today, some test manuals seriously mislead the uncritical reader. One recent aptitude battery for vocational guidance was published with what seemed at first glance to be impressive evidence of validity; but nearly all the "evidence" consisted of validity coefficients for an entirely different set of tests used in military selection. The only connection between the two batteries was a vague resemblance in plan. Since some published tests are nearly worthless, and since others extremely useful for one purpose will not perform well in another situation, the user must be able to choose among tests intelligently.

Ability to judge tests is important for many people who will never choose tests themselves. The business executive may turn his selection and promotion problems over to psychological consultants. The psychiatrist or juvenile-court judge may place full responsibility for choice and interpretation of tests on clinical psychologists. Nonetheless, such consumers of test results must know how tests are evaluated and be aware of the common weaknesses of tests. Some industrial consultants recommend testing programs which other psychologists regard as overelaborate or inadequately validated; the executive needs to know something about testing if he is to ask the right questions regarding their proposals. There is an understandable tendency for the clinical tester to become overenthusiastic about the procedures in which he is expert, and to make his recommendations too confidently.

On the other hand, executives, psychiatrists, judges, and others who receive reports from psychologists frequently depart from the recommendations made. Such departures, insofar as they take into account facts not available to the tester, are necessary and justified. But giving great weight to supplementary impressions and little weight to objectively observed behavior spoils more decisions than it helps. If the user of test information knows how tests are validated, he can decide when his own impressions are substantial enough to be given comparable weight.

1. "Improving a test in one way weakens it in another." What advantage, and what disadvantage, comes from each of the following changes?
   a. Lengthening a test.
   b. Making it interesting to children.
   c. Making it more diagnostic of strong and weak points.
   d. Giving it as an individual test instead of as a group test.
2. This is a letter received by a psychologist from an industrial personnel manager hiring office and factory workers. How would you answer it on the basis of the paragraphs above, knowing that the tests mentioned are representative of their type?

   ". . . Just now we are planning the use of the following tests: Otis intelligence and Minnesota Multiphasic Personality Inventory, and aptitude tests related to our openings, such as the Bennett test. Does this seem to be a well-balanced testing schedule for industry? Are there tests that you think preferable to these?"

3. It has been suggested that the American Psychological Association set up a committee to award a Seal of Approval to all well-prepared tests. Discuss the advantages and disadvantages of such a system. Would this plan eliminate the need for critical judgment by users?

The Test Manual

The manual (sometimes supplemented by a technical handbook) is the principal source of information about the technical quality of a published test. The manual is sold with the tests and provides detailed directions, scoring procedures, and research findings.

Manuals are not always as useful as they should be. Some manuals omit facts which users need to judge the test, or gloss over unfavorable evidence. Even a generally excellent manual may have some inadequate sections.

Faults are particularly frequent in tests issued before 1945, because authors of older tests rarely prepared complete manuals or brought their manuals up-to-date.

Preparing a good manual is difficult. The more research there is on the test, the harder it is to summarize properly into a manual. The manual must be clear enough so that any qualified user can comprehend it—and so that the reader who is not qualified will realize that he is not. Yet the material must be precise enough to satisfy specialists in test research.

The Technical Recommendations. A major aid in the preparation and use of test manuals is the *Technical Recommendations* published in 1954. Committees of national organizations interested in measurement studied the problem of improving information about tests and prepared a lengthy set of *Technical Recommendations for Psychological Tests and Diagnostic Techniques* (1954). A supplementary statement dealing with problems of achievement testing was also prepared (*Technical Recommendations,* 1955).

The *Technical Recommendations* indicate what the manual should contain. Many of the recommendations are accompanied by examples illustrating good or poor procedure. Figure 17 gives an extract from the *Technical Recommendations* to illustrate their form and content. This chapter and the next, on judging the quality of tests, discuss the aspects of tests with which the *Technical Recommendations* are concerned.

The recommendations are used in several ways. Authors use them as a guide in writing manuals, and publishers use them in deciding when a test is ready for release. The recommendations draw the attention of test purchasers to points to consider in evaluating a test.

Test Reviews. The trend toward improved test construction and manuals was accelerated by the work of Professor O. K. Buros, who began to release critical reviews of tests in 1934. These critical listings now take the form of *Mental Measurements Yearbooks,* the most recent of which appeared in 1950, 1953, and 1959.

Nearly all tests currently on the market, and some program tests, are reviewed in the Buros series. Each test is examined by two or more specialists chosen because of their practical experience and technical knowledge. Reviewers discuss what each test may best be used for, and draw attention to any questionable claims made in the test manual. Test reviews may also be found in several journals, particularly *Educational and Psychological Measurement* and *Journal of Consulting Psychology.* Although these reviews are an aid to the purchaser of tests, he must still judge tests for himself. He will find that reviewers sometimes disagree in judging a test, particularly when they approach it from different points of view. Sometimes a reviewer gives much attention to rather petty faults, and the reader must weigh these criticisms against the merits of the test. On the other hand, reviewers fail occasionally to notice faults. Even with a well-balanced review of a particular test, the final decision to use it or not to use it depends on the specific situation, which only the prospective user knows.

We have already discussed some of the qualities which make a test suita-

---

F. Scales and Norms

F 1. Scales used for reporting scores should be such as to increase the likelihood of accurate interpretation and emphasis by test interpreter and subject. ESSENTIAL

[Comment: Scales in which test scores are reported are extremely varied. Raw scores are used. Relative scores are used. Scales purporting to represent equal intervals with respect to some external dimension (such as age) are used. And so on. It is unwise to discourage the development of new scaling methods by insisting on one form of reporting. On the other hand, many different systems are now used which have no logical advantage, one over the other. Recommendations below that the number of systems now used be reduced to a few with which testers can become familiar, are not intended to discourage the use of unique scales for special problems. Suggestions as to preferable scales for general reporting are not intended to restrict use of other scales in research studies.]

F 2. Where there is no compelling advantage to be obtained by reporting scores in some other form, the manual should suggest reporting scores in terms of percentile equivalents or standard scores. VERY DESIRABLE

[Comment: Professional opinion is divided on the question whether mental test scores should be reported in terms of some theoretical growth scale, such as the intelligence quotient or the Heinis index. Thus, a test developer who has rationale for such scales as these should use them if he regards them as especially adequate.

On the other hand, there is no theoretical justification for scoring mental tests in terms of an "IQ" which is not derived in terms of the theory underlying the Binet IQ and which has different statistical properties than the IQ does. Standard or percentile scores would be preferable to arbitrarily defined IQ scales such as are used in the Otis Gamma and Wechsler-Bellevue tests.

Strong recommends that Vocational Interest Blank scores be converted into letter grades where "A" indicates that at least two-thirds of the criterion group equaled or exceeded a given score, etc. He bases this recommendation on the ground that finer score discriminations would lead only to unwarranted attempts at finer interpretative discrimination.]

F 2.1 If grade norms are provided, tables for converting scores to percentiles (or standard scores) within each grade should also be provided. ESSENTIAL

[Comment: At the high school level, norms within courses (e.g., second year Spanish) may be more appropriate than norms within grades.]

F 3. Standard scores obtained by transforming scores so that they have a normal distribution and a fixed mean and standard deviation should in general be used in preference to other derived scores. For some tests, there may be a substantial reason to choose some other type of derived score. VERY DESIRABLE

FIG 17. A section from the *Technical Recommendations* (1954).

---

ble or unsuitable. In Chapter 1 attention was drawn to the necessity of selecting tests which the user is competent to give and interpret. Chapters 3 and 4 introduced other considerations, including clarity of directions, freedom from coachability, convenience of scoring, objectivity, and adequacy of norms. All these are important because they affect directly or indirectly the power of the test to improve decisions.

The quality which most affects the value of the test, however, is its validity. Validity is high if a test measures the right thing, i.e., if it gives the information the decision maker needs. No matter how satisfactory it is in other respects, a test which measures the wrong thing is worthless. We shall devote the remainder of this chapter to validity. Other relatively less important factors in choosing a test will be treated in the next chapter, after which we shall consider as a whole the problem of choosing a test.

TYPES OF VALIDITY

A test which helps in making one decision may have no value at all for another. This means that we cannot ask the general question "Is this a valid test?" The question to ask is "How valid is this test for the decision I wish to make?" or more generally, "For what decisions is this test valid?"

Very often, especially in selection or classification, the decision is based on a person's expected future performance as predicted from the test score. If these expectations are confirmed, the test has given highly useful information, but if the predictions do not correspond to what happens later, the test was worthless. To know how validly the test predicts, a follow-up study is required.

In selection or classification, the psychologist wants to maximize some outcome: job success, amount learned, obedience to law, etc. He gives a test, makes his predictions, tries the treatment suggested by these predictions, and waits to see what happens. He obtains a record of the outcome (foreman's rating, school grade, or number of court appearances, for example). This record, which we speak of as a *criterion,* he compares to the prediction. This is a straightforward empirical[1] check on the value of the test. The psychologist has determined what we call its *predictive validity.*

In many situations for which tests are developed, some more cumbersome method of collecting information is already in use. If the existing method is considered useful for decision making, the first question in validation is whether the new test agrees with the present source of information. If they disagree, the test may have value of its own, but it is certainly not a substitute for the original method. Validation again requires an empirical comparison. Both the test and the original procedure are applied to the same subjects, and the results are compared. For example, tests intended for clinical diagnosis are compared with the judgments made by a psychiatrist who interviews each patient. A test of proficiency in radar maintenance may be

---

[1] An *empirical* method involves collection and analysis of data. It is contrasted with purely logical methods of arriving at conclusions.

compared with ratings given by an instructor who watches each man in the shop. This type of empirical check on agreement is called *concurrent validation,* because the two sources of information are obtained at very nearly the same time (Figure 18).

When tests are used to evaluate educational or therapeutic programs, a

 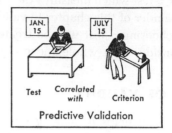

FIG. 18.   Predictive and concurrent validation compared.

different kind of validation may be needed. The program is trying to produce a certain change in behavior, and therefore, to evaluate the effectiveness of the program, the tester needs to measure just that type of behavior. If a course is supposed to teach American geography, it would not be fair to measure its effectiveness by a test on the geography of New England. The tester interested in evaluation needs to ask, "Does this test represent the content or activities I am trying to measure?" Instead of comparing scores on the test with some other measure or judgment, as in empirical validation, he must examine the items themselves and compare them with the content he wishes to include. This process is called *content validation.* Thus the content validity of the geography test would have to be studied by checking the items against the course of study the students have followed.

The aforementioned types of validity are examined when a test is intended for a specific practical use. Sometimes, however, the test is used to arrive at a description of the individual which will be used for many purposes, or the test may measure outcomes for scientific rather than immediately practical purposes. In these applications, the test results are likely to be translated into general psychological terms. Instead of reporting that an experimental treatment "has increased the score on the Jones test," the psychologist wants to make the broader interpretation that "anxiety" has increased. The concept *anxiety* is part of a psychological theory which tells what behavior to expect from a person with great anxiety, under various conditions. Whenever a tester asks what a score means psychologically or what causes a person to get a certain test score, he is asking what concepts may properly be used to interpret the test performance. This type of theoretical concept is called a *construct,* and the process of validating such an interpretation is called *construct validation*. In order to show that a given construct applies to a test, it is necessary to derive hypotheses about test behavior from the theory related to the construct and to verify them experimentally. The theory of "anxiety" accepted by the tester might include such expectations as the following: if persons are exposed to a threat of electric shock, their anxiety will increase; neurotics are more anxious than nonneurotics; anxiety is lowered by administration of a certain drug; anxious persons have a high level of aspiration. Each of these expectations can be tested by an experiment or a statistical study of group differences. Determining construct validity is much more complex than the other types of validation, as our later discussion will show.

Table 8 summarizes the statements made to this point.

With so many different ways to examine validity, each one applying to a particular use of the test, it is apparent that no test developer can validate his test exhaustively. The test user cannot expect the manual to provide complete evidence on validity, yet he does not wish to use a test whose validity is uncertain. What can we legitimately demand of the test developer? The *Technical Recommendations* indicate that he must assume the burden of proof whenever he recommends the test for a certain use. "The manual should report the validity of each type of inference for which the test is recommended." Most tests have a few principal uses for which their validity has been thoroughly studied, and this research answers the questions of most test users. The user who wishes to apply the test in any other way may have to make his own validity studies.

No matter how complete the test author's research, the person who is developing a selection or classification program must, in the end, confirm for himself the validity of the tests in his particular situation. And the person who is evaluating a training program must determine the content validity of the tests for this program. In this chapter we shall concentrate on understanding the material presented in test manuals. Later (Chapter 12), it will be necessary to examine how the tester can conduct validation studies in his own situation.

The Bennett TMC manual (Form AA) is fairly typical, though less extensive than many recent manuals. It summarizes studies of predictive and concurrent validity made in industry and military training. This information indicates that the test has considerable predictive value for mechanical trades and engineering. In the manual there is no information on the test as a predictor of school and college grades—a serious omission. Concurrent correlations of the TMC with several intelligence tests and with other mechanical aptitude tests are reported. This feature informs the tester about the possibility of substituting the TMC for one of the other tests, and also aids in inter-

TABLE 8. Four Types of Validation

	Question Asked	Procedure	Principal Use	Examples
Predictive validity	Do test scores predict a certain important future performance?	Give test and use it to predict the outcome. Some time later obtain a measure of the outcome. Compare the prediction with the outcome.	Tests used in selection and classification decisions.	Admission test for medical students is compared with later marks. Mental test given infants at time of adoption is compared to test of school readiness at age 6.
Concurrent validity	Do test scores permit an estimate of a certain present performance?	Give test. Obtain a direct measure of the other performance. Compare the two.	Tests intended as a substitute for a less convenient procedure.	Group mental test is compared to an individual test. Diagnosis of brain damage based on Block Design test is compared with neurological evidence.
Content validity	Does this test give a fair measure of performance on some important set of tasks?	Compare the items logically to the content supposed to be measured.	Achievement tests.	A test of shorthand ability is examined to see whether the content is typical of office correspondence. Tasks in a sewing proficiency test are compared with the course of study pupils have followed.
Construct validity	How can scores on this test be explained psychologically?	Set up hypotheses. Test them experimentally by any suitable procedure.	Tests used for description or in scientific research.	A test of art aptitude is studied to determine how largely scores depend on art training, on experience in Western culture, etc.

preting the construct "mechanical comprehension." Content validation is not required for the TMC.

How well does this information fill the counselor's needs? Counselors need to advise students regarding many questions of vocational specialization, yet only scattered validity studies are available. Indeed it would be impossible to conduct separate validations for all the vocations counselees will wish to consider. The list would have to cover architecture, aeronautics and hydraulics, metalworking and woodworking, design, construction, maintenance, and so on *ad infinitum*. Even where a predictive study has been made for a specific occupation, one must recognize that not all jobs within the occupation make the same demands. The counselor therefore cannot hope to make definite predictions.

The counselor can interpret the score only by knowing what "mechanical comprehension" signifies, as here measured. How much does it depend on specific training? This can be determined by learning how much scores increase during a shop course or a physics course. Does it apply solely to mechanical-manipulative occupations, or to all work that requires reasoning about forces and motion? This is answered by intergrating the available prediction studies. Are individual differences stable enough to justify long-range predictions? This calls for a long-term follow-up. Does mechanical comprehension promise skill in handling tools and machines? The answer comes from the comparison of TMC scores to scores on apparatus tests.

The Bennett manual does not include all this information. Older tests, in general, were published without comprehensive validation, and even the best manual must leave some questions unanswered. The modern DAT manual, after 35 pages of validity data, concludes with a statement urging the counselor to prepare expectancy tables for courses in his own school and for jobs in his own community. The test constructor is not expected to answer every last question about validity before publishing his test, but he is expected to give the test user a fair impression of its validity.

4. Would predictive or concurrent validity be studied in these situations?
    a. The U.S. Employment Service wishes to test men to determine which ones have had enough experience to be referred to contractors who have vacancies for electricians.
    b. A medical school wishes to test the personalities of its applicants to determine which ones are best suited to a physician's responsibilities.
    c. A pencil-paper test is used to identify students entering junior high school who have emotional difficulties and should be singled out for counseling.
5. A typing test which has excellent content validity for the original user may have poor content validity for some other user. Illustrate this statement.
6. Why would it be valuable to find out "what a test of pharmacy aptitude measures," if we already know that it predicts success in pharmacy school?

PREDICTIVE AND CONCURRENT VALIDITY

The Criterion

An investigator studies predictive validity when his primary interest is in some outcome. The outcome is what we want to improve by our professional decisions: it is the employee's production on a job, the patient's response to therapy, the counselee's satisfaction with his life after counseling. The *criterion* is a record of the outcome.

For example, suppose a wholesale hardware concern wants to hire good salesmen and is trying a test to predict sales ability. The outcome that interests the firm is the sales each man will make. For research, this outcome has to be expressed in terms of some definite index of success. Perhaps "amount sold in six months" will serve as a criterion measure. This result must be compared to test scores recorded before the men were hired, to learn how much predictive validity the test has. If the test is unrelated to the criterion, it is invalid for selecting salesmen for this firm. A single predictive study does little to clarify what psychological factors are represented in a test, but it does establish the test's usefulness and limitations for one practical situation.

The greatest difficulty in empirical studies is to obtain a suitable criterion measure. If the index does not really represent "selling success," the test has not been given a fair trial. Let us look at the weaknesses of the criterion suggested for validating the salesmanship test. In the first place, it represents only the wholesale hardware business, so that at best we can judge the test for only this one use; additional predictive studies will be required if the test is considered for hiring men to sell insurance or machine-tools. Although "amount sold" appears to be a fair basis for judging success, some men were assigned more desirable territory than others, so that sales do not reflect ability alone. Suppose we control this by comparing each man's sales with normal sales in his territory. We still have not considered the possible effect on business of variable factors, such as poor crops in one region. Still another problem is that sales alone may not be what we desire from a salesman. A high-pressure salesman may build up high total sales on a first trip but, by overselling, create problems which will eventually harm the firm's business.

A common type of criterion is the rating or grade. Aptitude tests are validated against marks earned in school. Industrial predictors are validated against ratings by supervisors. These ratings are rather poor criteria because the judge often does not know the facts about the person and because judges disagree. When a test fails to predict a rating, it is hard to say whether this is the fault of the test or of the rating.

Concurrent validity is investigated when the test is proposed as a substitute for some other information; this information is then the criterion. Designers of new tests frequently establish concurrent validity for their instruments by comparing them to established tests. New tests of intelligence, for example, have frequently been correlated with the Stanford-Binet intelligence test, whose predictive and construct validity have been studied extensively. A test which agrees with the Binet test measures "whatever the Binet test measures" and may be relied upon for the same purposes. This procedure is helpful only if the test used as criterion is meaningful and important. There is little value in knowing that three questionnaires of "neurotic tendency" agree if none of the tests measures anything save ability to see through the test and give "desirable" answers. Likewise, a psychologist who distrusts psychiatric diagnoses would be hesitant to use them as a criterion for a personality test.

7. Criticize each of the following criteria:
   a. Ratings of student teachers by their supervisors, as an index of teaching ability.
   b. Number of accidents a driver has per year, as an index of driver safety.
   c. Number of accidents a driver has per thousand miles, as an index of driver safety.
8. A test of preschool children is validated in three ways: (1) Intelligence is defined as ability to learn responses with which one has had no previous experience. The test items are examined and found to fit this definition. (2) Scores on the test, given at age 3, are found to be related to reading skill and vocabulary knowledge at the end of the first grade. (3) Scores on the test, given at age 3, are found to be related to scores on the Stanford-Binet test given at age 16.
   a. What possible uses of the test are warranted, on the basis of each of these studies?
   b. Would it be possible for a test to show high validity by method (2) and to lack validity according to the other two procedures?
9. A study-habits inventory asks such questions as "Do you daydream when you should be studying?"
   a. What criterion would you use to determine empirically whether the inventory really measures study habits?
   b. What criterion would you use to determine whether the inventory predicts success in college?
   c. Which study would be best to show that the test is valid?
10. Criticize the procedure indicated in the following report of a study of success of teachers college students (cited by Eckelberry, 1947):

    "The correlation between all thirty of the [predictor] variables and the [school] superintendents' ratings was only .17, but that between the variables and marks earned during four years of college was .79. Since college marks were predictable on the basis of the thirty variables and . . . the superintendents' ratings were not, the marks were substituted for the ratings as a criterion of success."

Correlation Coefficients

A study of predictive or concurrent validity is nearly always reported in terms of a correlation coefficient. This is a statistical summary of the relationship between two variables, and it plays a fundamental part in test research. It is the most common method for reporting the answer to such questions as the following: Does this test predict performance on the job? Do these two tests measure the same thing? Do scores people made on this test a year ago agree with the scores they make now?

To illustrate correlation, let us consider ten hardware salesmen who were given three tests when hired. After six months, when the criterion records are in, we have the information in the left portion of Table 9. The problem is

TABLE 9.   Data on Ten Hardware Salesmen

Salesman	Test Scores Test 1	Test 2	Test 3	Criterion Measure	Criterion Rank	Test Rank 1	2	3
A	30	45	34	$25,000	6	4	7	7
B	34	64	35	38,000	2	2	3	5½
C	32	32	35	30,000	4	3	9	5½
D	47	52	31	40,000	1	1	5	9
E	20	74	36	7,000	10	9	1	4
F	24	50	40	10,000	9	7	6	1
G	27	53	37	22,000	7	5	4	3
H	25	36	30	35,000	3	6	8	10
I	22	71	32	28,000	5	8	2	8
J	16	28	39	12,000	8	10	10	2

to judge which test is the best predictor. The test scores are hard to examine in "raw" form, since each test has a different average.

One way to simplify the data is to change them to ranks, as in the right portion of Table 9. (Note that when two men tie on test 3, we give them the rank halfway between the positions which the pair occupies.) Now we see that E, poorest on the criterion, has very low rank on test 1, high on 2, average on 3. Man F, also poor as a salesman, is below the median on 1 and 2, but at the top in 3. Before reading ahead, study Table 9 to decide how valid each test is for selecting hardware salesmen.

Rank Correlation.   To obtain a single estimate of the goodness of each test, we compute a correlation. A simple procedure, useful for studies involving few cases, is the rank-difference correlation. (Below, we shall show the product-moment technique, the more complicated computation that is most used in test research.) The symbol ρ (the Greek letter rho) is used for a rank-difference correlation coefficient. In Computing Guide 4, we show the steps in determining ρ_{1c} comparing test 1 with the criterion c.

When the computations for all three tests are performed, we have these correlations between test and criterion:

$$\rho_{1c} = \quad .782$$
$$\rho_{2c} = -.090$$
$$\rho_{3c} = -.754$$

A positive coefficient shows that high standing on the test goes with high standing on the criterion. A negative coefficient shows that high standing on the test goes with *low* standing on the criterion.

Example

1. Begin with the pairs of scores to be studied.
2. Rank men from 1 to N (number of men) in each set of scores. (Note that the lowest man must have rank N, unless he ties with someone.)
3. Subtract the rank in the right-hand column from the one in the left-hand column. This gives the difference D. (As a check, make sure that this column adds to zero.)
4. Square each difference to get D^2
5. Sum this column to get ΣD^2
6. Apply the formula:

Man A ($x = 30$; $c = 25,000$)
Man A has ranks 4, 6
$N = 10$

Man A: $4-6 = -2$

Man A: $(-2)^2 = -2 \times -2 = 4$

$$\rho \text{ (rho)} = 1 - \frac{6(\Sigma D^2)}{N(N^2 - 1)}$$

$$\rho = 1 - \frac{6(36)}{10(100 - 1)}$$

$$= 1 - \frac{216}{990}$$

$$= 1 - .218$$

$$\rho = .782$$

| Man | Scores | | Ranks | | Rank Differ-ence(D) | Squared Differ-ence(D²) |
	Test	Criterion(c)	Test	Criterion		
A	30	$25,000	4	6	−2	4
B	34	38,000	2	2	0	0
C	32	30,000	3	4	−1	1
D	47	40,000	1	1	0	0
E	20	7,000	9	10	−1	1
F	24	10,000	7	9	−2	4
G	27	22,000	5	7	−2	4
H	25	35,000	6	3	3	9
I	22	28,000	8	5	3	9
J	16	12,000	10	8	2	4
					$\Sigma D = 0$	$\Sigma D^2 = 36$

COMPUTING GUIDE 4.   RANK-DIFFERENCE CORRELATION

A zero coefficient means that one cannot predict the criterion from the test. A correlation of 1.00 or −1.00 shows perfect relationship; when this occurs, the criterion score (or rank) can be predicted exactly. Test 1 identified the best salesman and the second-best accurately, but the third-best salesman ranked sixth on the test, which lowered the correlation. The larger the correlation, whether positive or negative, the more accurate the prediction. On test 3, a low score picks out a superior salesman. From these data we conclude that either test 1 or test 3 is a good predictor for this firm.

11. Compute ρ_{2c} and ρ_{3c}.
12. Obtain a combined score by subtracting score 3 from score 1 for each man. Correlate this with the criterion. Would it improve prediction to use both tests?

Product-Moment Correlation. Although harder to learn, the product-moment technique for computing correlation is easier to apply to large groups than the rank method. The rank formula is equivalent to computing the product-moment correlation between ranks.

A product-moment correlation (r) may be determined from a "scatter diagram" obtained by plotting pairs of scores. The scores of Table 9 can be put in this form. We set up a chart, with the first variable (test score) along the horizontal axis and the second variable (sales) along the other (see Figure 19). Man A is plotted above 30 on the x-axis (test 1), and opposite $25,-

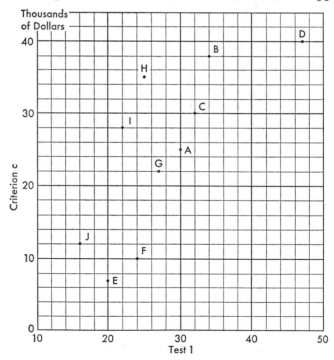

FIG. 19. Scatter diagram for test 1 and criterion c.

000 on the y-axis (criterion). We can observe how criterion scores correspond to test scores. As score 1 rises, c tends to rise.

At the end of the chapter is a computing guide showing how one obtains a product-moment correlation from the scatter diagram. It is not necessary to learn this procedure in order to interpret coefficients.

Any statistic has a certain variation from one sample to another. Even if groups of subjects are drawn at random from the same population, the correlation coefficients between two variables will differ from sample to sample. Using a large sample of course makes the correlation more dependable. The fluctuation of correlations from sample to sample may be considerable. If the correlation of two scores in a large population is .30, in ten random samples of 100 cases each the product-moment correlations would vary thus: .17, .47, .34, .31, .24, .39, .20, .25, .28, .45. If samples are not random, but come from different firms or communities, the fluctuation of coefficients will be even greater.

13. Prepare scatter diagrams relating tests 2 and 3 to the criterion.
14. How much would the rank correlation in Computing Guide 4 change if person J had been replaced by a person with score 21 and criterion $26,000?

Meaning of Correlations. How well one variable predicts another is shown by the scatter diagram. Figure 20 shows scatter diagrams corresponding to various sizes of coefficient. When $r = 1.00$, one variable is predicted perfectly from the other. With $r = .60$, prediction is only approximate. People who stand at 8 on X average near 7 on Y, but they spread from 3 to 9. An employer wishing not to lose any applicant whose Y score is 8 or better would have to hire everyone with an X score of 4 or better. Prediction becomes progressively poorer as the scatter diagram becomes "fatter."

Another way of considering the meaning of correlation is to translate the scatter diagram into an expectancy chart. The expectancy charts shown in Figure 10 (p. 73) correspond to test-criterion correlations of .51 for mechanical aptitude, .47 for trade information, and .26 for the nut-and-bolt test.

When the correlation is less than 1.00, one measure is influenced by some factor not found in the other measure. Random errors of measurement lower correlation. So do causal factors not involved equally in both variables. For example, the correlation between intelligence and school marks is only moderate because many factors besides mental ability influence the marks: pupil effort, teacher bias, previous school learning, health, and so on.

It is incorrect to interpret high correlation as showing that one variable "causes" the other. There are at least three possible explanations for a high correlation between variables A and B. A may cause or influence the size of B, B may cause A, or both A and B may be influenced by some common factor or factors. The correlation between vocabulary and reading may be

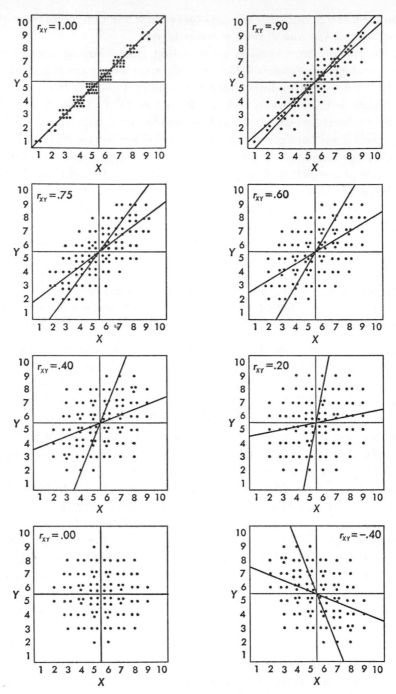

FIG. 20. Scatter diagrams yielding correlations of various sizes.

taken as an example. Does good vocabulary cause one to be a good reader? Possibly. Or does ability to read well cause one to acquire a good vocabulary? An equally likely explanation. But to some extent both scores result from high intelligence, a home in which books and serious conversation abound, or superior teaching in the elementary schools. Only a theoretical understanding of the processes involved, or controlled experiments, permits us to state what causes underlie a particular correlation. Without this, the only safe conclusion is that correlated measures are influenced by a common factor.

15. How large a correlation would you anticipate between the following pairs of variables?
   a. Age and annual income of men aged 20 to 50.
   b. Age in January, 1930, and age in March, 1950.
   c. Scores on two intelligence tests, given the same week.
   d. Annual income and number of children, among married urban men.
   e. Maximum and minimum temperature in Wichita, each day for a year.
16. What is the expectancy of earning above average on Y, if a person has a score of 8 on X? Determine this for each value of r in Figure 20.
17. What possible causal relations might underlie each of the following correlations?
   a. Between amount of education and annual income of adults (assume that r is positive).
   b. Between average intelligence of children and size of family (assume that r is negative).
   c. Between Sunday-school attendance and honesty of behavior (assume that r is positive).
18. Beginning with the information in Figure 20, prepare an "expectancy table" similar to Table 1, corresponding to each of the following values of r: 1.00, .90, .40, .20.

Typical Validity Coefficients

Correlations between test and criterion are called validity coefficients. Table 10 lists some fairly typical coefficients of predictive and concurrent validity, taken, in each case, from the test manual. Some test-criterion combinations yield much greater validity than others. The variation in results for the Short Employment Tests should be particularly noted in Table 10. It is very unusual for a validity coefficient to rise above .60, which is far from perfect prediction.

Although we would like higher coefficients, any positive correlation indicates that predictions from the test will be more accurate than guesses. Whether a validity coefficient is high enough to warrant use of the test as a predictor depends on such practical considerations as the urgency of improved prediction, the cost of testing, and the cost and validity of the selection methods already in use. To the question "What is a good validity coefficient?" the only sensible answer is, "The best you can get." If a criterion can be predicted only with validity .20, the test may still make an appreciable practical contribution. Naturally, a greater contribution is required to justify an expensive, inconvenient procedure than an inexpensive one.

In interpreting any correlation coefficient, the range of the group studied

TABLE 10.   Illustrative Validity Coefficients

Test	Sample	Criterion	Type of Validity	Coefficient
California Short-Form Test of Mental Maturity	100 children referred to a guidance department	Wechsler individual test	Concurrent	.77 for total score
Gordon Personal Profile	122 college students	Ratings of personality by dormitory mates	Concurrent	.49 to .73 for four subscores
Iowa Tests of Educational Development	634 students in six Iowa colleges tested in grade 9	Grade point averages as college freshmen	Predictive	.58
Short Employment Tests: Verbal Number Clerical	51 operators of proof machines in a large bank	Supervisor's merit ratings of job performance	Concurrent	.15 .25 .37
Short Employment Tests: Verbal Number Clerical	80 skilled operators of bookkeeping machines in a bank	Records of production on ten days	Not stated	.10 .26 .34
Short Employment Tests: Verbal Number Clerical	262 students in a one-year secretarial training course	Satisfactory completion of course vs. noncompletion or noncertification	Predictive	.15 .48 .47
Short Employment Tests: Verbal Number Clerical	52 stenographers and clerks in an industrial concern	Ratings of job performance	Predictive	.45 .08 .31

must be considered. The correlation is smaller in a select group than in a group containing a wide range of ability. High-school achievement would predict college marks with a validity much above .60 if all those with poor records went on to college. The validity of the Iowa Tests for advising pupils whether to plan on going to college is higher than their validity for selecting among the high-school graduates who apply for college admission, because the latter group is already restricted. (For further discussion of this point, see p. 351.)

Relation of Concurrent Validity to Predictive Validity.   If a user needs a test badly, he may want to employ it for prediction even before the evidence on its predictive validity has been accumulated. Indeed, when a test such as the Strong Vocational Interest Blank is invented to predict whether an adolescent will enjoy a career as a physician, the criterion data cannot be obtained for some twenty years. This would sometimes mean a very long delay between the invention of a test and its practical use, if we insisted on waiting for the predictive coefficient before applying the test predictively.

Concurrent validity can be determined at once, and may shed some light on the probable predictive validity of the test. Strong published his test in 1928, offering as evidence of validity the fact that interest scores distinguished men of different occupations from each other. For instance, the Physician scores of doctors averaged much higher than those of nondoctors. The purpose of the test is not to find out whether a man is at present a doctor; it is to find out if a young man will, as he grows older, be satisfied with that career. If the direction of a man's interests at age 40 is the same as at 20, then the concurrent validation based on older men does show that the test can safely be used to give vocational advice at age 20. Until long-term follow-up studies were made, users of the Strong test had to assume stability of interests. After publication of the test, Strong continued to accumulate evidence by following adolescents for twenty years or more and by 1954 was able to verify that the test indeed predicts vocational status over a long period.

A concurrent-validation procedure may be employed for almost any predictive test, by administering it to persons whose criterion performance can be observed immediately. An aptitude test for medical students may be given at the time of graduation from medical school, grades being used as a criterion. A test intended to identify potential neurotics may be evaluated by determining whether it distinguishes present neurotic cases from some nonneurotic group such as medical patients coming to the same clinic. Kohs (1923, p. 182) offered a concurrent validation when he reported a correlation of .80 between Block Design IQs and Stanford-Binet IQs at the time he released his test. Almost never do we find research reports in which concurrent and predictive validities are determined under the same conditions, so that we cannot say just how much they are likely to differ. A reasonably close comparison may be made between the following correlations of educational proficiency tests with college grades in corresponding courses (Dressel and Schmid, 1951):

	Concurrent	Predictive
English	.61	.55
Social Studies	.79	.30
Science	.68	.49

The concurrent correlations were obtained at Michigan State University and the predictive correlations at Dartmouth, and it may be that the smaller range of ability at Dartmouth accounts for part of the decline in the validity coefficients.

19. Which of the following describes concurrent validity, and which describes predictive validity? In which instances has concurrent validity been measured even though the test appears to be intended for predictive purposes?
   a. The Short Employment Tests are found to correlate .91 with the General Clerical Test, which has been used for some time as a predictor of job success.
   b. The manual for the Henmon-Nelson Test of Mental Ability reports correlations with school grades assigned one month later.
   c. A correlation is calculated to determine how well a certain test distinguishes patients diagnosed as schizophrenic from those diagnosed as brain-damaged.
   d. School records of delinquents and nondelinquents in high school are searched to learn what scores collected in the elementary grades correlate with delinquent status.

20. A test of ability to understand spoken words is validated by administering it to first-graders at the end of the year, and correlating it with their present reading ability. The coefficient is fairly high. Would you expect a similarly high predictive-validity coefficient
   a. if the test is used at the start of the first grade to predict end-of-year reading?
   b. if the test is used at the end of the first grade to predict response of poor readers to a special remedial reading program?
   c. if the test is used with 4-year-olds, to predict later success in Grade 1 reading?

21. Would the attitude of present employees, taking a test in a concurrent-validation experiment, be the same as the attitude of applicants taking the test?

Example of Validity Information.   Let us now examine some of the data on validity given in the DAT manual, for that version of the TMC. The data offered include correlations with subsequent course grades, a four-year follow-up of school achievement, and a follow-up of post-high-school careers. Only a brief extract can be considered here.

Table 11 gives some of the coefficients relating mechanical comprehension to course grades in science and shop. It is obvious that one cannot speak of "the validity" of a test for a certain field, save as a shorthand expression for a general trend. The variation of coefficients is great, even from group to group in the same school. There are many explanations for this: sampling fluctuations, differences in course content, differences in reliability of grading, differences in level of ability, etc. Ghiselli (1955, p. 112) reports similar radical fluctuations among validity coefficients for tests of mechanical comprehension against training criteria for repairmen in industry. He tabulated over 100 coefficients from various studies, finding a range from −.30 to +.60. Eleven studies reported validity coefficients above .50, and fourteen found coefficients below .20. This finding is not peculiar to the mechanical reasoning test. Whenever numerous coefficients are obtained for the same test and the same type of criterion, variation such as this is found. Only where conditions are highly standardized is a second validity coefficient likely to dupli-

TABLE 11. Validity of the TMC as a Predictor of Course Grades for Boys

Course	Grade	Location	Time Between Test and Marks	Number of Cases	Validity Coefficient
Industrial Arts	9	Mt. Vernon, N.Y.	1 year	67	.39
	9	Worcester, Mass.	4 months	89	.20
	9	Worcester, Mass.	1 year	79	.05
Woodworking	10	Independence, Mo.	3 months	42	.30
General Science	9	Mt. Vernon, N.Y.	1 year	84	.19
	9	Columbia, Mo.	8 months	88	.50
Physics	11	Schenectady, N.Y.	$3\frac{1}{2}$ years	42	.47
	—	White Plains, N.Y.	1–2 years	41	.41

SOURCE: Bennett *et al.*, 1959, pp. 44 ff.

cate a first. Where training follows a uniform plan, where the level of ability is held constant by selection, and where the criterion is based on objectively measured performance, validity coefficients are as stable as the size of the sample allows. Such a coefficient, however, may not confidently be assumed to apply to another setting.

In most predictive uses of tests, the published validity coefficient is no more than a hint as to whether the test is relevant to the tester's decision. He must validate the test in his own school or factory, and even then he can expect coefficients to fluctuate. For this reason, testers are usually forced back upon a psychological rather than a purely statistical use of scores.

While a test publisher may be expected to include representative validity studies in the manual, much further evidence accumulates after the test is distributed. Only a thorough search of professional journals can locate all this information. The industrial psychologist can find many of the studies relevant to his selection problems in the "Validity Information Exchange" published quarterly in *Personnel Psychology*. One particular issue (Autumn, 1954), for example, presents thirteen different studies, among which three use the Bennett test. We learn that among policemen in St. Louis, Du Bois and Watson obtained correlations for Form BB of about .28 with training grades and marksmanship, .20 with an achievement test, and .10 with rating on duty. (No other test was better able to predict the rating.) Bruce found no useful relation between Form AA and ratings of foremen in a tobacco plant, and McCarthy a correlation of −.10 with ratings of foremen in a factory which makes electrical equipment. Another useful source is the Dorcus-Jones *Handbook* (1950), which abstracts 426 studies on employee selection published prior to 1949. It is evident that the test manual can never exhaustively summarize or integrate such a varied literature.

22. How can the negative correlation of Bennett scores and foremanship ratings be explained?
23. The mechanical reasoning test yields coefficients as high as .50. With this validity, what is the likelihood that a person who is above average on the test will be above average on the criterion? (Use Figure 20.)
24. How do you account for the fact that the validity of the TMC as a predictor in physics is not higher than .50?
25. What facts might the principal of the school in Schenectady obtain to determine why the TMC predicted shop grades poorly, as compared to results in some other schools? Should these facts be included in the test manual?
26. What factors account for the variation in validity coefficients for industrial repairmen found by Ghiselli?

CONSTRUCT VALIDITY

Every test is to some degree impure, and very rarely does it measure exactly what its name implies. Yet the test cannot be interpreted until we know what factors determine scores. As Kent says (1937, pp. 422–423),

> When a child of reading age is referred to the clinic because of his failure to learn to read, it is of the first importance to ascertain whether his mental capacity is or is not within normal limits. A composite test which contains reading matter . . . discriminates against the subject whose inability to read is due to any cause other than mental retardation. A test which calls for oral response discriminates very seriously against the child who by reason of speech defect or impediment is unable to make himself understood. It is little more than a farce to use a timed test or a test containing timed items for a psychotic subject whose mental processes are pathologically slowed up. What we measure by the test may be significant, but it is something quite other than what the test is intended to measure.

Such items as Kent criticizes would probably correlate with criteria of school success, and would probably be judged to have "content validity" as a sample of significant adaptive performances. The difficulty is that the test cannot be interpreted as a measure of a single psychological quality.

Construct validation is an analysis of the meaning of test scores in terms of psychological concepts (Cronbach and Meehl, 1955).

Sometimes the tester starts with a test which he wishes to understand better. Sometimes he starts with a concept for which he wishes a measuring instrument. The interpretation of a test is built up very gradually, and probably is never complete. As knowledge develops, we arrive at a more complete listing of the influences that affect the test score, and may be able to estimate the strength and character of each influence. At present, the interpretation of even the best-established psychological tests falls far short of the ideal.

While predictive validity is examined in a single experiment, construct validity is established through a long-continued interplay between observation, reasoning, and imagination. First, perhaps, imagination suggests that construct A accounts for the test performance. The investigator reasons, "If that is so, then people with a high score should have characteristic X." An experiment is performed, and if this expectation is confirmed, the interpretation is supported. But as various deductions are tested, some of them prove to be inaccurate. The proposed interpretation must be altered either by invoking a different concept, by introducing an additional concept, or by altering the theory of the concept itself. The process of construct validation is the same as that by which scientific theories are developed (Spence, 1958). Some constructs are "young" and not much theory has developed around them. Mechanical comprehension is an example. Older concepts (for example, intelligence and ego-strength) are imbedded in elaborate theories.

There are three parts to construct validation:

> Suggesting what constructs might account for test performance. This is an act of imagination based on observation or logical study of the test.
> Deriving testable hypotheses from the theory surrounding the construct. This is a purely logical operation.
> Carrying out an empirical study to test this hypothesis.

The actual sequence of operations need not be so neatly ordered. Often one accumulates much experience with a test before offering an interpretation. Sometimes the test is used for a long time before any theory is developed around it. This was true, indeed, for the TMC.

What do we mean when we talk of explaining performance on the TMC? Essentially, we mean being able to state what influences affect the score and what influences do not. Once it was thought that there were three "intelligences"—verbal, mechanical, and social. To test the interpretation that the TMC measures "mechanical intelligence," we would have to know what this is. If it is said that mechanical intelligence is an inborn ability to perform all tasks involving apparatus, we can begin research. We find that the TMC correlates .68 with a pencil-and-paper test of reasoning with forms, but only .08 to .39 with various dexterity tests. We are inclined, therefore, to interpret it as a measure of problem solving rather than of mechanical performance. When we find that boys do much better than girls, we become very suspicious of the view that the aptitude is inborn. Perhaps it represents experience with mechanics, or even knowledge acquired in school. Research on that point shows that scores do increase after a course in physics, but only by a small amount. Differences between persons are much the same before and after the course.

It is necessary not merely to identify an influence but to find out how strong it is. The writer once suspected that much of the TMC score depended on knowledge of a few specific principles (e.g., gears, levers), each of which was involved in several items. But when separate scores were obtained on each type of item, these scores correlated highly. Since a person high on gear problems was high on other items, it was unnecessary to introduce the concept of specific subtypes of mechanical comprehension. Such specific knowledge could account for only a small amount of the difference among persons.

It is already evident that no single type of research is used in construct validation. We can give a brief tabulation of procedures merely to indicate the diversity of methods and describe the relevance of each method to the TMC.

● Examination of items. This is sufficient to rule out some explanations; thus it is easily seen that neither arithmetic nor verbal reasoning affects scores. But it is also seen that the machines used are those common in Western culture, not in primitive Africa; this reminds us to consider cultural background in interpreting the test outside industrial nations.

● Administration of test to individuals who "think aloud." This may show that in some items quite irrelevant features of the test (e.g., an obscure drawing) affect the score. It may show that some people succeed by an intuitive perception of answers which others reach by painstaking logic. This would suggest that the score means different things for different persons.

● Correlation with practical criteria. Learning what courses or jobs the TMC predicts clarifies what types of mechanical work it applies to.

● Correlation with other tests (and factor analysis). If the TMC correlates highly with a general intelligence test, it need not be interpreted in terms of a special mechanical aptitude. As a matter of fact, it does depend to a substantial degree, but by no means entirely, on general mental ability.

● Internal correlations. The study of separate types of items described above is of this type.

● Studies of group differences. The comparison of boys and girls is an example.

● Studies of the effect of treatment on scores. Training in physics proved not to affect the TMC greatly.

● Stability of scores on retest. If scores are unstable, one could not interpret mechanical comprehension as a lasting, vocationally significant aptitude. An obtained correlation of .69 between ninth- and twelfth-grade scores for boys promises a reasonable degree of stability, but also shows that this aptitude is far from a fixed quantity.

The user of the test wants to know how the test can be interpreted, and how confidently. The manual should indicate what interpretation the author advises, and should summarize the available evidence from all types of studies relevant to this interpretation. If the user wishes to make some other interpretation, he must examine all the evidence on the test in the light of his own theory.

27. Kohs (1923, pp. 168 ff.) wished to argue that the Block Design test measured "intelligence," defined as "ability to analyze and synthesize." He then offered the following types of evidence (plus others) for his claim. How does each of these bear on construct validity? (The Stanford-Binet test was at that time recognized as the best available measure of intelligence but was thought possibly to depend too heavily on verbal ability and school training.)
    a. Logical analysis of the "mental processes" required by the items.
    b. Increase in average score with each year of age.
    c. Correlations as follows:

Binet score with age	.80
BD score with age	.66
BD score with Binet score	.81

    d. Correlations:

Binet score with teachers' estimates of intelligence	.47
BD score with teachers' estimates of intelligence	.23

    e. Correlations:

Binet score with vocabulary	.91
BD score with vocabulary	.77

    f. Correlations between successive trials:
        on Binet, .91; on BD, .84
28. Which of the variables in Kohs' study are acceptable as criteria of pure intelligence?

Suggested Readings

French, John W. Validation of new item types against four-year academic criteria. *J. educ. Psychol.*, 1958, 49, 67–76.
    This predictive study compares different types of tests for college applicants in terms of their power to predict grades and successful completion of college work. The study is unusual because of the large number of measures used, the large sample in each college, and the repetition of the experiment in many colleges. Note particularly the degree to which results differ for different criteria and different colleges.
Peak, Helen. Problems of objective observation. In Leon Festinger & Daniel Katz (eds.), *Research methods in the behavioral sciences.* New York: Dryden, 1953. Pp. 243–299.
    This chapter, directed toward the social scientist choosing a measurement procedure for a research project, discusses the qualities which make a proce-

dure satisfactory. Dr. Peak outlines many methods used in establishing construct validity.

Thorndike, Robert L. The estimation of test validity: criteria of proficiency. *Personnel selection.* New York: Wiley, 1949. Pp. 119–159.

Thorndike describes the various types of measures that may be used as criteria, particularly in industrial applications of tests.

Validity. *Technical recommendations for psychological tests and diagnostic tech-*

---

1. Begin with the pairs of raw scores to be studied.

2. Tabulate the points in a scatter diagram, entering one tally for each pair of scores. (The first pair [24–35] is tabulated in the cell above 24 on the X scale, and opposite 35 on the Y scale. This cell is outlined in the illustration.)

X	Y	X	Y	X	Y	X	Y	X	Y
24	35	27	38	26	39	29	35	30	42
25	39	28	37	30	39	24	38	28	37
24	39	29	36	32	40	17	24	30	39
25	36	19	34	30	42	29	38	26	37
31	43	28	37	25	38	29	38	26	39
22	38	27	32	32	43	27	36	23	37
30	43	25	38	26	37	30	39	20	29
24	35	30	41	24	36	26	40	25	38
25	40	31	41	21	32	25	33	15	31

	f_y	d_y	$f_y d_y$	$f_y d_y^2$	$\Sigma f_y d_x$	$\Sigma f d_x d_y$
43	3	6	18	108	15	90
42	2	5	10	50	8	40
41	2	4	8	32	9	36
40	3	3	9	27	5	15
39	7	2	14	28	9	18
38	8	1	8	8	−2	−2
37	6	0			3	
36	4	−1	−4	4	1	−1
35	3	−2	−6	12	−1	2
34	1	−3	−3	9	−7	21
33	1	−4	−4	16	−1	4
32	2	−5	−10	50	−4	20
31	1	−6	−6	36	−11	66
30		−7				
29	1	−8	−8	64	−6	48
28		−9				
27		−10				
26		−11				
25		−12				
24	1	−13	−13	169	−9	117

X: 15 16 17 18 19 20 21 22 23 24 25 26 27 28 29 30 31 32

f_x	1		1		1	1	1	1	1	5	7	5	3	3	4	7	2	2	45	13	613	9	473
d_x	−11	−10	−9	−8	−7	−6	−5	−4	−3	−2	−1	0	1	2	3	4	5	6	N	$\Sigma f_y d_y$	$\Sigma f_y d_y^2$		$\Sigma f d_x d_y$
$f_x d_x$	−11		−9		−7	−6	−5	−4	−3	−10	−7		3	6	12	28	10	12		9 $\Sigma f_x d_x$			
$f_x d_x^2$	121		81		49	36	25	16	9	20	7		3	12	36	112	50	72		649 $\Sigma f_x d_x^2$			

niques. Washington: American Psychological Association, 1954. Pp. 13–28. (*Psychol. Bull.*, 1954, **51**, Supplement.)

This section of the recommendations introduces the four types of validity, recommends types of information about validity to be included in test manuals, and gives specific examples of good and bad practice. It is suggested that the reader compare the manual of some recent test with these recommendations.

---

3. Count the number of tallies in each column, and write it below the diagram in a row labeled f_x. Count the number in each row, and write it beside the diagram in a column labeled f_y.

4. Select an arbitrary origin for X and for Y, and determine the mean and standard deviation for each as in Computing Guide 2 (computation not shown).

$$A.O._x = 26.0 \quad A.O._y = 37.0$$
$$c_x = .20 \quad c_y = .29$$
$$M_x = 26.2 \quad M_y = 37.3$$
$$s_x = 3.83 \quad s_y = 3.72$$

5. In each cell of the scatter diagram, multiply the number of tallies by the value of d_x written below that column, and write the product in the cell. (In the outlined cell, for instance, there are two tallies, and d_x is -2; the product is -4.)

In each row, add the numbers written in the cells, and place in a column labeled $f_y d_x$.

Multiply each entry in this column by d_y and enter in a column labeled $f d_x d_y$.

Add the column $f d_x d_y$.

Substitute the numbers in the following formula:

$$r_{xy} = \frac{\frac{\Sigma f d_x d_y}{N} - c_x \cdot c_y}{s_x \cdot s_y}$$

$$r_{xy} = \frac{\frac{473}{45} - .06}{3.83 \cdot 3.72}$$
$$r_{xy} = \frac{10.51 - .06}{14.24} = \frac{10.45}{14.24}$$
$$r_{xy} = .73$$

COMPUTING GUIDE 5. COMPUTING THE PRODUCT-MOMENT CORRELATION COEFFICIENT

6

How to Choose Tests

THE first important consideration in choosing a test is its validity. As we have seen in the preceding chapter, validity information permits us to judge whether the test measures the right thing for our purposes. Validity is examined by comparing scores to an external criterion, by comparing items to a specified body of content, or by establishing an explanation of scores in terms of general constructs. There are many additional qualities to consider in choosing a test, some related to its statistical properties and some to its practical features.

RELIABILITY

Reliability studies give information about the consistency of a person's scores on a series of measurements. For example, Bennett reports that on the TMC for ninth-graders "the standard error of a score is 3.7." If a boy were tested many times on a series of equivalent mechanical comprehension tests, his scores would vary; the *standard error* is a calculated estimate of the amount of this variation. It says that the series of raw scores for this one boy would have a standard deviation of about 3.7. Since the standard deviation of scores of *different* persons is 10.4 points, a standard error of 3.7 allows the boy's position within the group to shift over an appreciable range, as Figure 21 shows. When we test the boy only once, he earns just one of his many possible scores. We do not know in which part of his range we happened to catch him.

Since scores vary from one trial to another, no one measure can be trusted absolutely. The obtained score indicates only roughly the level of the person's ability or typical behavior. The smaller the standard error, the more precisely his level can be judged. Reliability information tells how much confidence we can place in a measurement.

Reliability always refers to consistency throughout a series of measurements. There are various ways to observe such a series—for example, by using the same test repeatedly or by using a series of "parallel" forms. Different experimental procedures measure the effect of different types of variation, and therefore different reliability coefficients mean different things.

Test scores vary over time. Attention and effort change from moment to moment. Over longer periods, further shifts in score are created by physical

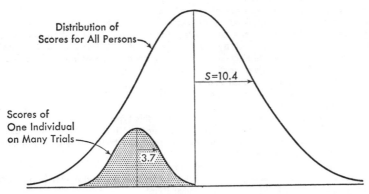

Distribution of
Scores for All Persons

$S=10.4$

Scores of
One Individual
on Many Trials

3.7

FIG. 21. Variation in standing of a single person.

growth, learning, changes in health, and personality change. If we employ different test items for each measurement, another type of variation is introduced. The person who is lucky on one trial, finding items that are easy for him, will encounter unfamiliar items on some other trial and earn a lower score. To these variations must be added the unaccountable "chance" effects. Chance effects enter even when we use the same procedure twice in rapid succession; the two scores differ to some extent because of guessing, instantaneous lapses of attention, and so on. Table 12 lists the sources of variation in test scores.

A judgment that a student has completed a course or that a patient is ready for release from therapy must not be seriously influenced by chance errors, temporary variations in performance, or the tester's choice of questions. An erroneous favorable decision may be irreversible. An erroneous unfavorable decision, though reversible, is unjust, disrupts the person's morale, and retards his development. Unless the tester and subject recognize how fallible a measure is, they are likely to rely on it more than is justified.

Research likewise requires reliable measurement. In most experimental designs a test of significance is used to learn whether an observed difference results from the experimental treatment or could be accounted for by chance variation. The larger the chance variation in the test employed, the harder it is to find a significant difference between groups. Large error variance masks scientifically important variations created by the experimental conditions. Making a test more reliable improves the efficiency of an experiment in the same way that increasing the number of subjects does.

TABLE 12.   Possible Sources of Variance in a Test Score

I. Lasting and general characteristics of the individual
   1. General skills (e.g., reading)
   2. General ability to comprehend instructions, testwiseness, techniques of taking tests
   3. Ability to solve problems of the general type presented in this test
   4. Attitudes, emotional reactions, or habits generally operating in situations like the test situation (e.g., self-confidence)
II. Lasting and specific characteristics of the individual
   1. Knowledge and skills required by particular problems in the test
   2. Attitudes, emotional reactions, or habits related to particular test stimuli (e.g., fear of high places brought to mind by an inquiry about such fears on a personality test)
III. Temporary and general characteristics of the individual (systematically affecting performance on various tests at a particular time)
   1. Health, fatigue, and emotional strain
   2. Motivation, rapport with examiner
   3. Effects of heat, light, ventilation, etc.
   4. Level of practice on skills required by tests of this type
   5. Present attitudes, emotional reactions, or strength of habits (insofar as these are departures from the person's average or lasting characteristics—e.g., political attitudes during an election campaign)
IV. Temporary and specific characteristics of the individual
   1. Changes in fatigue or motivation developed by this particular test (e.g., discouragement resulting from failure on a particular item)
   2. Fluctuations in attention, coördination, or standards of judgment
   3. Fluctuations in memory for particular facts
   4. Level of practice on skills or knowledge required by this particular test (e.g., effects of special coaching)
   5. Temporary emotional states, strength of habits, etc., related to particular test stimuli (e.g., a question calls to mind a recent bad dream)
   6. Luck in the selection of answers by "guessing"

SOURCE: After R. L. Thorndike, 1949, p. 73.

In a test intended for predicting a definite criterion, reliability is less important than predictive validity. If predictive validity is satisfactory, low reliability does not discourage us from using the test. In comparing two tests which measure the same thing, however, the more accurate test will have the higher validity coefficient.

1. Locate each of the following sources of variance in Table 12:
   a. During a speeded test a student breaks his pencil and loses time while obtaining another.
   b. An industrial worker who has been in this country for a short time misunderstands an important phrase in the instructions for a performance test.
   c. A "hillbilly" is unable to answer correctly a question from an intelligence test about the purchase of a railroad ticket.
   d. A suspicious patient refuses to coöperate and gives perfunctory answers.
   e. A student guesses at every item of which he is uncertain.
2. Give an example of each source of variance in Table 12 which might affect performance on the Block Design test.
3. Which types of variation in Table 12 would lower the correlation between test and criterion in each of the following situations?
   a. A test of high-jumping ability is used to select finalists in a track meet. The criterion is performance in the meet, two weeks after the trials.

b. A pencil-and paper test of mechanical ability is used to predict performance of mechanical trainees. Piecework earnings after training are used as the criterion.

Interpretation of Coefficients

Reliability is usually expressed in terms of a "reliability coefficient," i.e., the correlation between two measurements obtained in the same manner, or in terms of the standard error of measurement which we have already described. Before considering the procedures used to estimate reliability, we can discuss general principles applying to all such coefficients. The principles are as follows:

- A reliability coefficient tells what proportion of the test variance is nonerror variance.
- The reliability coefficient depends on the length of the test.
- The reliability coefficient depends on the spread of scores in the group studied.
- A test may measure reliably at one level of ability and unreliably at another level.
- The validity coefficient cannot exceed the square root of the reliability coefficient.

Reliability and Error of Measurement. Variation between persons is described by the standard deviation s, or by the score variance s^2. This variation represents a combination of the differences that we wish to measure (e.g., true ability in spelling) and the variation associated with a particular measurement (e.g., words used in the test, fatigue of some persons on the day of testing). The true ability of any person would remain constant from one measure to another, but obtained scores would vary to some extent.

This conception of a "true score" assumes that we would really like to determine the person's score on a very large sample of behavior. For employment purposes, we would like to know what proportion of words the stenographer will spell correctly during the next several years. We test performance on only one day and on only one set of words; this is a small sample of the total performance which we wish to estimate. In a school spelling test, the teacher may want to estimate performance on a particular assigned test of words on a particular day. But this estimate should ideally cover the pupil's "true" knowledge on that day, as observed on many, many trials. Any one trial on a particular word is a small sample of his performance on that word. The *true score* is the average score the person would obtain if the performance were observed by a very long series of samples or trials (assuming no practice effect from the testing). *Error* is defined as the variation or fluctuation of the person's scores within the series. It is a sampling error arising because any one trial exposes only a portion of the behavior that interests us.

The size of these sampling errors is described by the standard error of measurement (s_e), or by the "error variance" (s_e^2). The obtained score is a combination of the true score and the error on a particular trial. The variance of obtained scores is the total of the error variance and the variance of true scores.

These variances have a direct relation to the correlation between scores from two samples of behavior. If we let r_{11} stand for the reliability coefficient (correlation between scores),

$$r_{11} = 1 - \frac{s_e^2}{s^2} = \frac{s^2 - s_e^2}{s^2} = \frac{\text{True variance}}{\text{Total variance}}$$

From the data for the TMC, we find

$$\begin{array}{llll} \text{Total} & s = & 10.4 & s^2 = 108.2 \\ \text{Error} & s_e = & 3.7 & s_e^2 = 13.7 \\ \text{True} & & & s^2 = 94.5 \text{ (by subtraction)} \end{array}$$

$$r_{11} = \frac{94.5}{108.2} = .87$$

The reliability coefficient tells what proportion of the test variance is due to "true" individual differences, and not to sampling error. In this example, 87 percent of the variance is "true" and therefore 13 percent is "error." Just what we mean by "error" is defined in part by the experimental procedure, as we shall see later.

Reliability and Test Length. The importance of lengthening tests is that with every question added, the sample of performance becomes a more adequate index of performance on all possible questions. A single addition problem is a very poor sample of a person's ability, since we are quite likely to present a number combination that is particularly hard or easy for him. By asking more and more questions of the same general sort, we come closer to a good estimate of his general ability on addition problems.

Longer tests are also less influenced by other chance factors. If a test has only five multiple-choice items, a few people might get all the items correct just by guessing. In a fifty-item test, practically no one could do well by guessing. Variations due to guessing tend to cancel out. Three fifteen-minute observations of a child's social behavior provide a poor sample of his typical behavior; thirty observations, however, should give a dependable picture.

The Spearman-Brown formula (see Computing Guide 6) permits us to estimate what reliability the test would have if it were lengthened or shortened. The formula assumes that when we change the length of the test we do not change its nature. Extreme increases in test length, however, introduce boredom and may reduce reliability. Furthermore, unless one is careful, added items or added periods of observation may not cover the same behavior or ability as the original test.

One must examine the reliability of every score he intends to interpret. Some testers, knowing that a test as a whole is reliable, place faith in its part scores also. Since short tests are likely to be unreliable, a part score based on a few items is of limited value. The reliability of part scores as well as of total scores should be given in the test manual. If this reliability is low or unknown, the part scores cannot be relied upon.

While inaccuracy lowers validity, this does not necessarily argue for making predictor tests very long. An increase in test length has a great effect on reliability but a much smaller effect on validity. The following formula applies, where t_n represents a test n times as long as test t (Gulliksen, 1950b, pp. 88 ff.):

$$r_{t_n c} = r_{tc} \sqrt{\frac{r_{t_n t_n}}{r_{tt}}}$$

The observed test-criterion correlation is r_{tc}. Under the square root sign, r_{tt} is the observed reliability for test t and $r_{t_n t_n}$ is the reliability of the longer test, calculated by the Spearman-Brown formula. Figure 22, derived from the formula above, shows the effect of lengthening or shortening the TMC, using r_{tc} as .40 and r_{tt} as .87. As we lengthen the test, its reliability approaches 1.00 according to the Spearman-Brown formula (broken line). The increase in validity is expected to follow the solid line in the figure. As the test is made longer and longer, validity approaches .43 as a limit. Validity

---

1. Suppose that a test has a known reliability. The Spearman-Brown formula, given at right, estimates the reliability of the score from a similar test n times as long.

$$r_n = \frac{nr}{1 + (n-1)r}$$

where
r is the original reliability; r_n is the reliability of the test n times as long

2. To predict the reliability of a test twice as long as the original test, substitute in the formula $n = 2$.

$$\text{If } r = .40, \ r_2 = \frac{2(.40)}{1 + (1)\,.40}$$

$$= \frac{.80}{1.40} = .57$$

3. Suppose the original test is to be reduced to only half its original length. The reliability of the short test is estimated using $n = \frac{1}{2}$.

$$r_{1/2} = \frac{\frac{1}{2}(.40)}{1 + (\frac{1}{2} - 1)\,(.40)}$$

$$= \frac{.20}{1 - \frac{1}{2}(.40)} = \frac{.20}{.80} = .25$$

COMPUTING GUIDE 6. USE OF THE SPEARMAN-BROWN FORMULA

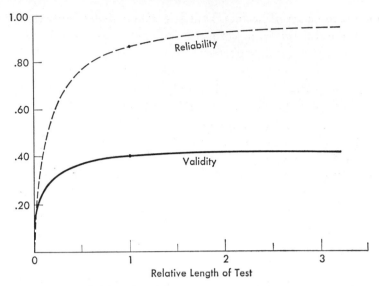

FIG. 22.   Reliability and validity of the TMC as its length is changed.

creeps up so slowly that lengthening a test beyond a certain point is un-profitable. Beyond that point it is better to use the extra time to measure some other aspect of behavior.

4. A spelling test of thirty words has a reliability coefficient of .80. What reliability would be expected if ninety words were used?
5. Which kinds of variation (Table 12) are reduced in influence when a test is lengthened?

Relation of Reliability to Validity.   An inaccurate test cannot be a good predictor. There is a rule which states how reliability limits validity: The correlation between the test and an independent criterion can never be higher than the square root of the correlation between two forms of the test. For example, if reliability is .64, validity cannot exceed .80. This con-clusion is derived from the formula relating test length to validity. Suppose the test is so closely related to the criterion that the two would be perfectly correlated if the test were free from error of measurement. That is, suppose that when n becomes extremely large, $r_{t_n t_n} = 1.00$ and $r_{t_n e} = 1.00$. Then, ac-cording to the formula given above, $r_{t_n c} = \sqrt{r_{t_n t_n}}$.

Why is it that a test can correlate higher with a different measure than it does with its own twin? To understand this, consider two short spelling tests, and a "criterion" based on exhaustive measurement over several weeks, with thousands of words. Each test score is much influenced by random error of sampling and guessing, but the criterion is not. The errors in the two tests lower the correlation between them. Just one such set of errors affects a test-criterion correlation, which therefore is higher than the test-test correlation which both sets of errors affect.

Reliability and Range of Scores.   Errors of measurement are most trouble-some when the differences in ability or personality among the subjects are small. When we are hiring one person out of a group of applicants, the final decision often hinges on a difference of a few points between the best and next-best man. Slight errors of measurement in such a case might result in hiring the poorer man. If one is screening applicants for factory work merely to rule out incompetents, however, a less-refined test will be satis-factory. Errors of a few points cannot conceal the gross deficiencies in ability which distinguish the "hopeless" from the average run of workers.

Assuming that error of measurement remains constant, we see from the formula given above that r_{11} decreases when the variance of true score decreases.

A test which has satisfactory reliability for use with a wide-range group may be unsatisfactory in a highly selected group. A rather crude mental test can be used to identify which pupils entering school have mental handi-caps; but to divide the handicapped group, determining who is to be placed in a special class, requires a much more accurate test. A criterion rating by a supervisor may be adequately reliable for distinguishing failures from acceptable men but is not so good for telling which men within the satis-factory group are truly best.

6. The reliability of a test is .95 in a group for which s is 20. What will the re-liability be in a group where s is 10? (Compute s_e for the wide-range group, and use this value to compute the reliability for the second group.)

Reliability at Different Score Levels.   When a single reliability coefficient is reported, we tend to assume that a test has the same accuracy for all types of people. This assumption is often incorrect. Many tests are reliable only at certain levels of performance. The Gates Reading Survey for Grades 3–10, for example, gives reliable estimates of reading skill for pupils in most grades. When third-graders take the test, they find it so difficult that they do a great deal of guessing. As a result, individual differences within the third grade are unreliably reported. Tests, no matter how reliable, are inac-curate for pupils whose scores are near the chance level. Easy tests give in-accurate measures of individual differences in the extremely high ranges of talent.

Figure 23 shows the scores of Navy recruits who took a pitch-discrimina-tion test twice. If the test were accurate, the two scores for each man would be nearly the same and all points would fall along the diagonal line. The test consists of 100 pairs of tones; in each pair, the man reported whether the second tone was higher or lower than the first. A score of 50 would be ob-tained by pure chance. According to the scatter diagram, high scores are fairly reliable. Men scoring 85 on the first test fell between 72 and 95 on re-

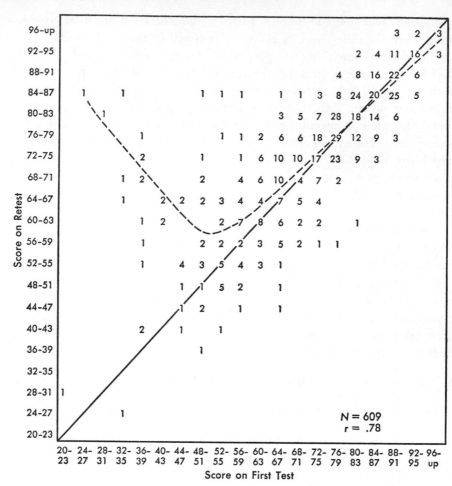

FIG. 23.   Test and retest scores on pitch discrimination (Ford et al., 1944).

test. But men scoring near the chance level (e.g., 55) scattered widely on the retest (40 to 87). It is evident that the standard error of low scores is great.

The broken line shows the average score, on the second test, of men in each column. The upcurve of this line at the left is especially interesting. Many men with very low scores in the first test did well on the retest. A score of 25 is too far below 50 to be a chance score. Probably men having such low scores on the first test misunderstood directions and judged the first tone instead of the second. Following directions correctly on the retest would shift their scores from seventy items wrong to seventy items right.

A test should be appropriate in difficulty for the decision to be made. Figure 24 shows distributions of scores on several tests given the same group. The very easy test A may be quite satisfactory for measuring differences at the lower end of the group. Test A is probably unreliable for the group as a whole, since variation of only a few points causes a subject to drop from the top of the group to the average. Furthermore, it does not distinguish between the persons tying at 100, even though they probably are not equally

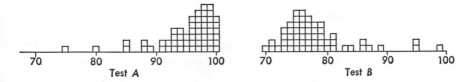

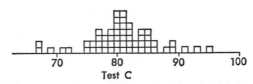

FIG. 24.   Distributions of scores for several tests given to the same group.

able. Test B is difficult. The distribution is skewed in the opposite direction from that for test A; high scores spread out, but differences at the low end of the scale are too small to distinguish individuals reliably. A normal distribution, such as that for test C, spreads out cases at both ends of the scale. With a symmetrical distribution, scores at the two ends are likely to be equally reliable. For this reason, tests yielding roughly normal distributions are preferred where it is necessary to distinguish equally well all along the scale. If our decision requires us only to distinguish the best men, test B is efficient. If we need only to eliminate the poorest men, we could use A.

7. Which distribution in Figure 24 would be most desirable in each of the following cases?
   a. A psychologist wishes to measure liberalness of attiudes, to study its relation to voting habits.
   b. A college wishes to pick out freshmen needing special training in reading.
   c. A test for college guidance measures interest in medicine.
   d. An employer wishes to select the best statistician from a group of applicants.
8. The California Test of Personality, Elementary, contains several subtests, one of which is Feeling of Belonging. A low score on this questionnaire is said to indicate maladjustment. According to the test manual, the percentile rank corresponding to each possible score is as follows:

Score	1	2	3	4	5	6	7	8	9	10	11	12
P.R.	1	1	1	1	1	5	10	15	25	40	65	90

   a. How would a boy's standing in the group change if his score changed two points?
   b. What is the shape of the raw-score distribution? What does this distribution imply regarding the usefulness of the test?

9. In World Series baseball, some pinch hitters reach batting averages as high as .750, whereas the best regular players rarely exceed .400 for seven games. How can this be explained? What principle regarding reliability does it illustrate?

Types of Coefficient

A person's scores vary from time to time and from form to form of the test. Some of these variations are regarded as a weakness in the measuring procedure, i.e., as "error." But the meaning of "error" depends on the purpose of testing. If a score is supposed to indicate a person's temporary condition at the time of testing, it is desirable for scores to vary from moment to moment. If the score is supposed to represent a lasting quality, moment-to-moment variation is undesirable. Consider, for example, a test purporting to measure rigidity of thinking. This might be used to predict performance as a scientist, to measure the level of adjustment of a patient during and after therapy, or to measure the effect of a particular stress applied during an experiment. Should variation of a person's score over time be regarded as true variance or as error variance? Stability would be a great advantage in predicting scientific success where we need to measure a lasting characteristic. Since we want an estimate of behavior over a long period, instability from occasion to occasion is error, for this use of the test. Likewise, we need a stable measure of rigidity to judge a patient's status after therapy; there is no point in knowing that he functions well today if he is likely to think rigidly next week. On the other hand, if the therapist wants a week-to-week barometer of the patient's temporary state, stability would be a disadvantage. Likewise, to measure outcomes in a stress experiment, the test must be sensitive to momentary states of the individual. Too stable an instrument would be of no value for these two purposes.

For a comprehensive understanding of the test, we would like to know what proportion of the variance can be ascribed to each of the four categories of Table 12. We obtain such estimates by making two or more measures of each person and then correlating the scores or performing a variance analysis. Different experiments have to be made to measure each type of variation. Figures 25 and 26 help to explain the various reliability coefficients. Each experiment treats some types of variation as "error"; in the diagrams these are left unshaded, while the nonerror variance is shaded.

The first procedure to be considered is the *retest* correlation obtained by administering the same test on two occasions. This is called a *coefficient of stability*, because it tells us how stable this particular performance is. General-lasting characteristics (e.g., in the TMC, general understanding of levers) enter both measures. A person high in this ability tends to be high on both trials. Specific-lasting characteristics also affect both measures similarly; knowledge of a particular fact about air pressure on an airplane rudder will help one on that particular item of both test and retest. This characteristic contributes to variation between persons, not to variation between trials for

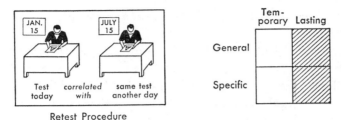

FIG. 25.   The coefficient of stability. Shading indicates the portion counted as true variance.

the same person. Temporary factors (e.g., health, or casual variation in memory) may help an individual on one occasion and lower his score on the other. They therefore lower the test-retest consistency and are counted as error in this type of reliability (Figure 25).

The *coefficient of equivalence* tells how well the test score agrees with other equivalent measures made at the same time. It is obtained by giving

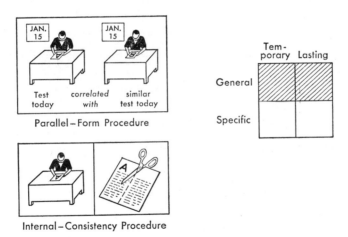

FIG. 26.   The coefficient of equivalence. Shading indicates the portion counted as true variance.

two forms (e.g., Form A and Form B of the TMC) in close succession. The two forms should be closely comparable, measuring the same general attributes at the same approximate level of difficulty. As Figure 26 shows, general attributes affect both tests the same way. But since the tests include different items, a specific attribute like knowledge about the airplane rudder helps on one form but not the other. It therefore lowers the correlation be-

tween forms. "Internal-consistency" procedures, which also lead to a coefficient of equivalence, are discussed below.

A third procedure, less commonly used, introduces an appreciable delay
between test and equivalent test. Now, both changes in the person and sub-
stitution of new items lower the correlation and are included in the error
variance. This coefficient reflects both the stability and the equivalence of
the measures.

If all three coefficients are obtained, we can determine how much of the
test variance is due to each type of variation, but such information is not
often available. For the Mechanical Reasoning Test of the DAT battery,
however, these correlations are reported (in various sources):

> Form A with Form B, immediate   .85
> Retest after three years, Form A   .73
> Form A with Form B, three-year interval   .65

These facts permit us to construct Figure 27 by subtracting the various estimates from 1.00 and from each other. As Figure 27 shows, only lasting-gen-

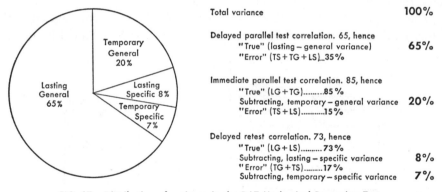

FIG. 27.   Distribution of variance in the DAT Mechanical Reasoning Test.

eral components count as true variance in the delayed between-forms correlation; therefore, 65 percent of the test variance is lasting and general. In the
immediate between-forms correlation, lasting-general and temporary-gen-
eral variance are both counted as nonerror. By subtraction, the temporary-
general variance must be 85 percent less 65 percent, or 20 percent. By further subtraction, we find that the temporary-specific and lasting-specific
components account for 7 percent and 8 percent, respectively. We conclude
that most of the score variance is due to general abilities and habits, rather
than to information specific to particular items. Quite a large proportion of
the variance is due to characteristics which remain stable over three years.

10. Prepare a diagram resembling Figure 26 for the delayed equivalent-forms coefficient.

11. A teacher gives a standardized test of knowledge of scientific facts to his class in chemistry. Several students make scores lower than he had expected.
   a. He asks, "Could it be that I gave a form of the test which included many questions these particular pupils happened not to know? Would their scores have changed much if they had been asked other questions of the same type?" What reliability coefficient answers this question?
   b. He asks, "Could the performance of these students be due to the fact that they were having an 'off' day? Does a pupil's score on tests of this type vary much from day to day?" Which coefficient is most helpful in answering this question?

12. Which types of variance are to be regarded as "error" when a questionnaire regarding emotional problems is used for this purpose:
   a. To select high-school pupils with whom the counselor should have an early conference.
   b. To identify recruits likely to break down in service.
   c. To identify the area within which a pupil has conflicts, as a preliminary to a counseling interview.

13. One favorite method of estimating reliability is to split a test in two parts, score them separately, and correlate. This correlation between half-tests is treated by the Spearman-Brown formula to obtain a coefficient for the full test. Show that this is properly considered a "coefficient of equivalence" even though only one form is used.

14. What can you say about the variance make-up of a test, knowing only that a delayed retest gives a coefficient of .70, and an immediate parallel test gives a coefficient of .80?

15. Given these facts about a test measuring "liberality" of political attitudes, prepare a diagram similar to Figure 27.

Between-forms correlation at same sitting	.90
Between-forms correlation, one year apart	.60
Retest correlation, one year apart	.65

16. In speaking about hearing tests for children a writer says: "Physical and psychological changes from day to day may make tests at two sittings less valid than a complete test at one sitting. We find that we get worse results on cloudy days than on sunny days."

   In what sense is the word *valid* used? Can you defend the contrary statement that scores at two sittings would be *more* valid than a complete test at one sitting?

Coefficients of Stability

Retest coefficients might be obtained with any interval between tests from a few minutes to several years. If the two tests are close together, the person will remember some of his former answers. This carry-over makes the retest correlation a little higher than the correlation between two independent measures.

There is no single coefficient of stability for a test; rather, there is one for each time interval. The longer the time between tests, the lower the coefficient of stability, as we shall see when we study results for the Stanford-

TABLE 13.   Illustrative Reliability Coefficients

Test	Sample	Procedure	Type of Reliability	Coefficient
School and College Ability Tests	370 high-school seniors	Kuder-Richardson formula 20	Equivalence	.93 (verbal) .91 (quantitative) .95 (total)
Pintner General Ability Test, Non Language, Intermediate, Form K	203 12-year-old boys in two communities	Odd-even correlation	Equivalence	.86
Short Employment Tests	About 230 candidates for nursing school	Testing with parallel forms on same occasion	Equivalence	.87 to .92 for three sections
Short Employment Tests	72 machine operators in a bank	Retest after two years	Stability	.71 to .84 for three sections
Allport-Vernon Study of Values	48 persons (not otherwise described)	Correlation between comparable half-tests	Equivalence	.49 to .84 for six scores
Allport-Vernon Study of Values	Not described	Retest after three months	Stability	.39 to .84 for six scores

Binet test. For 7-year-olds, the immediate retest correlation is about .90; it declines steadily, so that after four years the retest correlation is only .74, and after eleven years it is only .68 (see p. 176). From this we can estimate that at least 22 percent of the test variance at age 7 results from individual differences which are accurately measurable at the present moment but will be altered by time and experience.

The tester must interpret information on stability in the light of his purposes. If he intends to make long-range predictions or to measure a trait which is supposed to be constant, he wants stability over long periods. For other uses of tests, stability over a long time is of little importance.

Coefficients of Equivalence

The tester usually wants to know the person's standing on some general quality of which the test items are representative. Very rarely are the qualities to be measured so specific that they must be measured by just one set of items. In the TMC, for example, the aim is to measure the person's ability to solve virtually any mechanical problem. If scores depended very much on content of specific items, the test would be an unsatisfactory predictor except for criteria to which this specific knowledge is relevant. The correlation between equivalent forms is therefore likely to be the most useful index of test reliability.

Where only one form of a test can be given, an internal-consistency procedure is used as a substitute for a between-forms coefficient. In the *split-half method*, the test is given in the usual fashion but then is scored in two parts. It is necessary that the two halves be independent, so that success on an item in one half does not help with an item in the other half. Correlating the two parts gives a coefficient of equivalence for the half-tests, and the Spearman-Brown formula is often used (with $n = 2$) to obtain the coefficient for the full test. A better estimate is obtained by the formula

$$r_{tt} = 2\left(1 - \frac{s_a{}^2 + s_b{}^2}{s_t{}^2}\right)$$

where s_a and s_b are the standard deviations of the half-tests. The two formulas give very nearly the same result in most studies. The coefficient obtained is an estimate of the coefficient of equivalence between two full-length tests which are as similar as the two halves are.

Two internal-consistency formulas developed by Kuder and Richardson are often used to obtain coefficients of equivalence for tests where one point is given for every correct answer and zero for a wrong answer. "Kuder-Richardson Formula 20" gives a coefficient for any test which is equal to the average of all possible split-half coefficients. The KR20 coefficient may generally be taken as a good approximation to an equivalent-form correlation. Coefficient KR20 is computed from the proportion passing each item, and from the standard deviation of scores (Guilford, 1956, pp. 454–455).

The second formula, KR21, is less accurate but very simple to compute. This formula can be used by any tester to get quick estimates of the coefficient of equivalence in his group, if his test is scored by the "number right" formula. The quantities used in the formula are the mean (M), the number of items (k), and the standard deviation (s).

$$r_{KR21} = \frac{k}{k - 1}\left(1 - \frac{M(k - M)}{ks^2}\right)$$

For most tests this formula will give very nearly the same result as KR20, but sometimes it gives a much lower coefficient. When the two estimates differ by a large amount, the decision as to which coefficient is most relevant depends upon technical considerations which we cannot treat here.

Internal-consistency procedures cannot be used with speeded (time-limit) tests, because the parts of the test are not independent. A person who gets stuck on one item and spends extra time on it will fail to reach the items at the end of the test. The correlation of items within a trial is therefore higher than the correlation between items separately administered, and the split-half or Kuder-Richardson reliability is spuriously high. The Primary

Mental Abilities Tests for Ages 11 to 17 are given with short time limits, yet the manual reports only split-half reliabilities. Anastasi and Drake (1954) administered the half-tests with separate time limits in order to get a proper estimate of reliability, and compared these with reliabilities computed by the spurious single-administration method. The results are as follows for the four PMA tests:

Verbal: separately timed halves .90; single administration .94
Reasoning: .87;   .92
Space: .75;   .90
Number: .83;   .92

It is obvious that the split-half estimates from the single administration are inflated and give too favorable an impression of the test.

17. A classroom teacher gives a forty-item test with mean 34 and s.d. 3. What is the KR21 reliability?

APPEAL TO THE LAYMAN

When a patient loses faith in the medicine his doctor prescribes, it loses much of its power to improve his health. He may skip doses, and in the end he may decide doctors cannot help him and let treatment lapse altogether. For similar reasons, in selecting a test one must consider how worth while it will appear to the subject who takes it and to other laymen who will see the results.

If an applicant for a job is given an employment test which he considers silly or unrelated to the job, he is likely to be resentful. This will make it difficult to obtain valid scores. If he is not hired, he may excuse his failure by criticizing the test; what he says to his friends damages public relations and makes it harder to obtain job applicants. Even the successful man may feel that he was hired in spite of the test, and begin work with antagonism toward management. Some satisfactory workers have had little schooling and are distrustful of tests which probe their weaknesses; catch questions and questions which seem childish are especially likely to arouse criticism.

If a test is interesting and "sensible," taking it is likely to be a pleasant experience. This not only tends to make the scores valid but also helps to establish good relations between the personnel worker and the subject. An Italian bus company contracted with psychological laboratories in two cities to give tests to applicants for jobs as drivers. After a few months, it was found that most of the applicants were traveling to Rome—going as much as 100 miles farther than necessary—because the Rome center had elaborate testing apparatus while the second center used simple equipment to measure the same aptitudes. The applicants thought the elaborate tests fairer and more dependable.

British experience with War Office selection boards is a second case in point. The selection board observes candidates during several days of field testing, apparatus tests, discussions, etc. Before this system was established, men from the ranks rarely applied for commissions because they thought the tests then used gave an advantage to applicants from good homes and good schools. They think the selection board is a fairer system where a man can show his true ability, and this attitude has been of great assistance in recruitment of officers—so much so that, although the board system is costly, and very possibly less valid than objective tests could be, there is no thought of changing it.

The subject is not the only one who must be satisfied with the psychologist's tests. The British selection program has had to satisfy a Labor cabinet insistent that poor boys have a fair chance to become officers, the parents of the boys tested, and the old-line officers who train the accepted men. A psychologist who installs a highly valid industrial selection program will find it in the ashcan a year later unless he convinces both management and the union that the test is fair. Users of test results have strong prejudices. If a group of social workers is accustomed to mental test A, the psychologist who decides to substitute mental test B will encounter difficulty. Even if test B is more accurate than A, the social worker may disregard results from B because it does not have his confidence. So important is user acceptability that the psychologist working with teachers, industrial personnel men, or physicians must often use a test which would be his second or third choice on the basis of technical qualities alone.

A test which looks good for a particular purpose is said to have "face validity." Adopting a test just because it appears reasonable is contrary to scientific practice; many a "good-looking" test has failed as a predictor. Civil service examiners, for example, prepared two tests to measure ability in alphabetic filing. One gave five names per item—John Meeder, James Medway, Thomas Madow, Catherine Meagan, Eleanor Meehan—and asked which name would be *third* in alphabetic order. The other test required the subject to place a name in the proper place in a series; for example:

Robert Carstens	A_____
	Richard Carreton
	B_____
	Roland Casstar
	C_____
	Jack Corson
	D_____
	Edward Cranston

Though the makers were confident that the tests were representative of the same skill, and though both tests had reliabilities above .80, they correlated .01 (Mosier, 1947).

Such evidence as this (reinforced by the whole history of phrenology, graphology, and tests of witchcraft!) is strong warning against adopting a test solely because it is plausible. If one must choose between a test with "face validity" and no technically verified validity and one with technical validity and no appeal to the layman, he had better choose the latter. The job of the tester is, after all, to get information which improves decisions. The tester should seek and usually can find a test which has both face validity and technical validity.

18. If a clinical tester is examining a criminal to establish whether he is mentally responsible, he may have to present his results in court and stand cross-examination on them (I. Frank, 1956). In what ways might his choice of tests differ from those he would use in examining a similar case at the request of a hospital psychiatrist?

19. A certain examination for French secondary-school admission was deliberately made very difficult to obtain a skewed distribution, since only a small number of places was to be filled. When the children told of the questions at home, parents organized protest meetings which ultimately brought the problem to the attention of the Minister of Education, who decided to give a second test to those who had failed. Do you agree with this decision?

PRACTICAL CONSIDERATIONS

Ease of Application

In almost any field, one can choose between tests to be administered by untrained persons and tests which can be given only by an expert. The test which is simpler to apply will have more complete directions and simple objective scoring, and requires no observation or judgment by the tester. The more complex test offers more comprehensive findings, but only in the hands of a well-qualified tester. Attention should also be paid to the adequacy with which the manual assists the user in drawing conclusions from test results. This is especially important when a psychologist is choosing a test whose results many other persons will consult.

A test manual may present all the important information about the test and yet fail to communicate to the reader. Lennon found, indeed, that large numbers of schoolteachers fail to grasp even simple factual statements in an achievement test manual (Lennon, 1954, pp. 90–94). The implication is that a person in charge of a testing program must make a major effort to educate all those who will give or interpret tests, rather than to rely on the manual to convey the insights they need.

Equivalent or Comparable Forms

We have noted, in connection with reliability, that equivalent forms are often available. *Equivalent* or *parallel* forms are tests measuring the same thing at the same level of difficulty, so that equal raw scores have the same meaning on each form. They are especially valuable when each person is tested twice—for instance, before and after therapy. The use of new questions rules out the effect of memory. An equivalent form is useful also for checking a dubious score. A second test would be given, for example, when the tester suspects that emotional disturbance spoiled the first test.

Two tests are said to be *comparable* when their raw scores can be converted to the same derived-score scale. Some school achievement tests are organized in a series at different levels of difficulty so that the pupil may be tested each year. Although the tests are not equivalent, a scale is provided so that performances on the easier test and the harder test can be compared to determine the pupil's gain. Another type of comparability is seen in the DAT profile chart, which permits comparison of mechanical aptitude with other abilities. Such comparisons, based on the same norm group, have an obvious value for interpretation.

Time Required

Time available for testing is always limited, and therefore short tests are preferred, other things being equal. Too long a testing period bores the subject and makes him uncoöperative. Where morale is high, however, one can give very long testing batteries successfully. We have already seen that reliability, and to a lesser extent validity, depends on test length. Shortening tests to a few items will destroy their value, but not much is gained by lengthening tests beyond 100 items per score except in competitive examinations where a few points make a great difference. The Bennett TMC has sixty items and requires about thirty minutes for most adolescent subjects. This is a usual length for a test yielding a single score.

Multiscore vs. Single-Score Tests

A test or battery yielding several scores has to be longer than a single-score test, if its scores are to be reliable. It is difficult, however, to state whether a multiscore test is superior to a single-score test occupying the same time. The single score is likely to be much more reliable than the several scores of the other test. The tester who needs several facts about the individual may prefer to obtain somewhat unreliable answers to all these questions rather than to measure one dimension precisely and remain without information on the others. A high-school counselor would obviously prefer ten-minute tests of five specialized abilities to a fifty-minute test which measures mechanical reasoning very precisely and tells nothing about the other four. He probably should not go so far as to substitute ten three-minute tests for the thirty-minute TMC—but it is hard to define a perfect balance between breadth of coverage and precision.

When many decisions are to be made, each requiring a different sort of information, the best solution is to allow a large amount of time for gathering information. There are limits to this, however. In clinical diagnosis of children with behavior problems, for example, one could think of hundreds of tests and observations which might shed light on different aspects of development. An employer hiring an executive can likewise raise a very large number of questions. While no general rule can be given as to the best division of limited testing time, it is clear that the greatest amount of time should be given to the most important questions. Where there are several questions of about equal importance, it is definitely more profitable to use a brief test giving a rough answer to each one than to use a precise test which answers only one or two questions (Cronbach and Gleser, 1957).

The disadvantage of quick, crude measures disappears when we make them a first step in a sequential measuring program. In hiring employees, for example, the very poor prospects can be weeded out by a rather inaccurate pencil-and-paper test, and sometimes those who score very well on such a test can be hired at once. Then only the applicants near the borderline need be given an accurate and more costly test. In testing an individual for guidance or diagnosis, we can begin with a multiscore test covering many variables (a battery of short aptitude tests, or an interest measure covering all fields). A further, more precise test can then be used for any variable (e.g., clerical aptitude, or interest in speaking activities) which looks important on the basis of the first results.

Cost

The cost of the usual test is only a few cents, but when one is testing a large number of persons, a difference in cost may be worth some attention. Fortunately there is little relation between the cost of tests and their quality, so that even a limited budget permits the use of well-constructed tests. Cost is greatly reduced where it is possible to use an answer sheet and a reusable question booklet. The reusable TMC booklet costs about 18 cents per copy (in packages of 25). The answer sheets cost an additional 4 cents. In determining the cost of a test, one must consider not only the cost of the materials but also the cost of scoring.

A fairly representative figure on costs of testing is suggested by the charges of a nonprofit test scoring and rental service operated by a state university for the high schools it serves (Unit on Evaluation, 1955). Costs include shipping, handling, materials, scoring labor, and other items. A school can rent the typical test booklet for 3 cents and purchase the answer sheet for about 3 cents. The scoring charges vary with the number of scores obtained for each sheet, from about 4 cents per pupil up to 15 cents. This means that guidance testing for sixty pupils, measuring five aptitude and achievement areas, would cost the school under $30, including all costs except teacher time for administering the tests and time used to interpret results to students. Since the decisions for which the tests are used make a great difference in the educational efficiency of the school and the soundness of the pupil's life plans, concern about cost of testing should be given almost no weight in choice of tests.

EVALUATING A TEST

We have now introduced nearly every concept that is used in judging the adequacy of a test. Subsequent chapters will describe the various types of tests and apply these concepts. In that application, the concepts will be explained more completely. Even though those chapters need to be studied before attempting to draw conclusions about particular tests, we can here summarize the concepts and present a form useful in evaluating any test.

The development of a testing program requires, first of all, a clear purpose. As we pointed out earlier, one must search for a test that fits the decision to be made, not just for "a good test of reading" or "a good personality test." It is unrealistic for the student of testing to evaluate a test in the abstract, yet one cannot consider all possible applications simultaneously. For this reason, it is suggested that any test manual be approached with a definite measurement problem in mind. Our form carries a space for entering this purpose, which might be specific (selecting girls for training as punchcard clerks) or rather general (obtaining information for subsequent use in counseling high-school pupils as problems arise).

Ordinarily the tester's situation restricts the type of test that may be considered. It determines the choice between group and individual tests, the age or ability range, and the level of interpretative skill to be used. Thus a test to be given for later reference in high-school counseling will be a group test (since individual testing of a whole school is not practicable), will have to cover the whole range of a normal population, and will have to be suitable for interpretation by counselors and probably by all teachers and administrators. With such crude specifications in mind, one turns to publishers' catalogs, the Buros *Yearbooks,* texts on measurement or applied psychology, etc., and makes a list of tests to consider. The form presented in Table 14 is a convenient record of facts and opinions regarding tests examined in detail. We have numbered the entries to make it easier to connect our discussion with various entries.

The top section (entries 1–9) includes the simple descriptive facts which

TABLE 14.   A Form for Evaluating Tests

1. Title	16. Predictive validation (criterion, number and type of cases, result)
2. Author	17. Concurrent validation (criterion, number and type of cases, result)
3. Publisher	18. Other empirical evidence indicating what the test measures
4. Forms and groups to which applicable	19. Comments regarding validity for particular purposes
5. Practical features	
6. General type	20. Equivalence of forms or internal consistency (procedure, cases, result)
7. Date of publication	21. Stability over time (procedure, time interval, cases, result)
8. Cost, booklet; answer sheet	22. Norms (type of norms, cases)
9. Time required	23. Comments regarding adequacy of reliability and norms for particular purpose
10. Purpose for which evaluated	
11. Description of test, items, scoring	24. Comments of reviewers
12. Author's purpose and basis for selecting items	25. General evaluation
13. Adequacy of directions; training required to administer	26. References
14. Mental functions or traits represented in each score	
15. Comments regarding design of test	

can often be obtained from the catalog. They are for the most part self-explanatory. It is suggested that you enter (6) one or two words to describe the general type, so that completed analysis forms may be filed by categories. In the specimen form filled out for the Bennett TMC (Table 15), we have inserted simply the word *aptitude*. The date of publication (7) is not highly significant, since some older tests are excellent. An old test should ordinarily be scrutinized with special care, however, since some items may be obsolete, the norms may not be useful, and the manual is likely to be incomplete. One should give particular attention to the date of the last thorough revision of the manual.

(This is one of the places where publishers sometimes introduce misleading information to make a test more appealing. It is possible to copyright the test manual every year so that it looks up-to-date, even though no real change has been made. Such embellishments will not confuse the reader unless he gives undue weight to superficial values. There are many such half-truths or misleading claims in manuals. Some can be spotted by any alert reader, while others are identifiable only by an expert. If the reader finds that the manual or test advertising is untrustworthy in one respect, he must of course view all the remaining information with suspicion. The scientific and ethical quality of the manual, however, is not always a sign of the quality of the test. A few excellent tests have manuals which are open to severe criticism for exaggerated claims.)

The next step is to form an impression of the test by examining the items, the scoring principles, and the aims the author had in mind in preparing the test. It is this impression which largely determines the appeal of the test to the subject and to other laymen. In the form (11), one can describe the items superficially and should also list the titles of subtests to be separately scored. Attention should be given to the objectivity of scoring.

The author's stated intentions (12) help one to understand the nature of the test. One should be hesitant to use it for a quite different purpose, although this is sometimes defensible. The manual will usually indicate whether the author was interested in selection, guidance, clinical use, or classroom evaluation and will often tell what aptitudes or traits he had in mind in preparing items. The source of items is particularly important if the test is to be interpreted on the basis of content validity.

Many test manuals report statistical studies used in selecting items. The most common procedure is to correlate the item score with the total score on the test, discarding items which do not seem to measure the same thing as the rest. Though this procedure is likely to improve a test—particularly since it eliminates ambiguous items and makes the items more similar to each other—it does not necessarily improve validity. Indeed, narrowing the range of content (in a mechanical aptitude test, for example) can lower validity by covering the field less thoroughly. For this reason, item-test correlations should never be referred to as "item-validity coefficients." The consumer usually cannot evaluate the technical procedures used in test construction.

Directions (13) can be examined with regard to their clarity and the extent to which they standardize the test.

An armchair analysis of the test items should be made (14) to judge what abilities, experiences, work habits, or personality traits influence the score. Such an analysis is required for each of the subscores which is to be interpreted. One cannot hope to identify all the contributing variables, but the effort raises questions to be used in interpreting validity studies and helps in interpreting the test. The report should state what the score seems to indicate, whether this is what the author intended or not, and also list irrelevant variables which are likely to distort scores. As a part of this analysis it is usually desirable to take the test oneself or to administer it to a suitable subject and observe his performance.

Empirical evidence of validity (16–19) may be of various sorts. Spaces are provided for predictive and concurrent validation, and also for other studies bearing on construct validity. Some of these spaces may be irrelevant for a particular test or a particular purpose and if so would not be filled in. While

TABLE 15. Evaluation Form for the TMC

1. Title. Test of Mechanical Comprehension
2. Author. George K. Bennett (with Diana Fry, Wm. A. Owens in some forms)
3. Publisher. Psych. Corp.
4. Forms and groups to which applicable.
   AA: high-school boys, job applicants
   AA-F: French language form of AA; questions and directions in both languages
   BB: experienced workers, advanced students
   CC: engineering students, high-level job applicants
   W-1: high-school girls, female job applicants
5. Practical features. Can be machine-scored.
6. General type. Aptitude
7. Date of publication. 1940, 1947 (AA); 1941, 1951 (BB); 1947 (W-1); 1949 (CC).
8. Cost, booklet, 18¢; answer sheet, 4¢
9. Time required. 30 min.

10. Purpose for which evaluated. Vocational guidance of high-school pupils.

11. Description of test, items, scoring. Pictures of simple apparatus. Questions in 3-choice form (5-choice in CC) as to what will happen to an object when force is applied, which of two structures is most stable, etc. Objective scoring $(R - \frac{1}{2}W$; R in CC). Only one overall score obtained.
12. Author's purpose and basis for selecting items. Intended to measure an ability required in many jobs and training courses. Past experience is allowed to affect scores, but the items require understanding rather than rote knowledge. Items were put through various stages of criticism and tryout; items retained were those discriminating high scorers (on the total test or a pooled Mech. Comp. score) from low scorers.
13. Adequacy of directions; training required to administer. Directions are unusually clear and simple. Classroom teacher can handle. Answer sheet for all forms save CC involves awkward matching of arrows to line up with booklet.
14. Mental functions or traits represented in each score. General experience with machines common in Western world, understanding of simple principles of motion, energy. Formal physics helpful but not required. Solutions can be intuitive or deductive; more rigorous deduction required in CC. Unspeeded.
15. Comments regarding design of test. Highly efficient. Use of correction formula in scoring unnecessary but harmless. Note that no claim is made that the test measures an innate aptitude.

16. Predictive validation (criterion, number and type of cases, result). Manual gives reference to numerous military and industrial studies where TMC was correlated with grades in technical training or job ratings. Coefficients range from .30 to .60.
    Evidently generally useful, though the test usually must be supplemented by general mental or verbal measures. Information is lacking on usefulness of the test for prediction in high-school courses, or on long-range predictions from high-school testing. Such data are available for DAT version. Form CC has validities .28 to .50 for college freshmen, with performance in technical courses as criteria. Note that range is restricted, compared to h.s. group.
17. Concurrent validation (criterion, number and type of cases, result). Some of the "predictive" studies cited above may be concurrent; manual is not clear as to time separating test and criterion.
18. Other empirical evidence indicating what the test measures. Study of 1471 applicants for fireman-policeman jobs shows that high-school physics raises scores about $\frac{1}{2}$ s.d. on AA. (This information is needed—and not now available—for CC, where effect of physics or math might be greater.)
    Form AA correlates about .50 with general mental tests in wide-range groups; BB and CC correlate .20–.30 among applicants to engineering school. Considerable overlap with spatial tests (.50 with Minn. Paper Form Board in wide-range group, .66 with College

TABLE 15 *(Continued).*

Board spatial test among engineering-school applicants). Correlation of .30 with tool dexterity test. Factor-analytic studies[a] show a mechanical experience factor prominent in the test; there are also substantial loadings with general mental ability, and spatial or visualization ability.

19. Comments regarding validity for particular purposes. Test has predictive value for jobs or courses involving nonroutine machine operation. Overlaps general and spatial tests, so that its independent value would depend on the situation. Lack of data on predictive power in high school limits interpretability.

20. Equivalence of forms or internal consistency (procedure, cases, result). Split-half method, Form AA, 500 ninth-grade boys, $r = .84$. Similar coefficients for other forms, lower in groups of restricted range. Interform correlation about .80 for BB vs. CC; no others reported.
21. Stability over time (procedure, time interval, cases, result). No information presented.
22. Norms (type of norms, cases). Each manual offers several columns of percentile norms for various groups in schools and industry. Selection of groups is poorly described (e.g., "833 ninth-grade boys," "417 applicants for unskilled jobs"). For CC, tables are given separately for two specific engineering schools.
23. Comments regarding adequacy of reliability and norms for particular purpose. Reliability of .80 is satisfactory but low. A second test should be given if a few points' difference in score would alter a decision.

The norms presented have limited usefulness; the counselor would have to obtain norms for his school, for special courses in the school, and if possible for the local job market. Absence of information on stability prevents confident use of the test for long-range predictions earlier than twelfth grade.

24. Comments of reviewers

"The manuals of directions are models of conciseness and honesty. . . . There is little doubt that the test measures comprehension of many mechanical principles, but its value for prediction has been questioned on the ground that several items involve principles or facts which one is unlikely to encounter in everyday mechanical experience, outside of a physics course" (Charles M. Harsh, in Buros, 1949, p. 720).

"The *Test of Mechanical Comprehension* . . . should prove to be a useful tool especially to those persons engaged in educational and vocational guidance. It should also find increasing usage in the technical school and the industrial employment office. It is an attractive test; the items are intrinsically interesting; all the forms appear to have been well constructed; and they are easy to give. The range of usefulness of the test will undoubtedly increase as more validity data are made available" (George A. Satter, in Buros, 1949, p. 723). (Note: Considerably more evidence of validity has appeared since the date of this comment.)

25. General evaluation. This is an exceptionally popular test, various versions having been included in a large number of prediction batteries and having repeatedly shown value against mechanical criteria. The concreteness of the test makes it appealing to subjects and laymen; when used in guidance, it dramatizes the concept of special abilities.

Form AA could be used in ninth grade to explore aptitudes, and CC could be used with seniors considering engineering or technical courses. The DAT Mechanical Reasoning Test is a revision of the Bennett TMC which should be preferred in high-school guidance for numerous reasons: superior norms, more substantial validity information against high-school criteria, comparability to other tests of the DAT battery, more information on stability.

As compared to other mechanical aptitude tests, the Bennett and DAT are less dependent on either shop experience or dexterity. The test is a measure of understanding and intellectual trainability; it does not guarantee proficiency without training, nor skill in manual performance.

[a] The meaning of information of this sort will be considered in Chapters 9 and 10.

most users examine only the evidence presented in the test manual, one can evaluate the test better if he considers data published elsewhere. For some tests, the volume of research is so great that it can only be summarized or sampled. Under heading 18 any study might be listed that helps to establish what the score measures. One might list, for a mechanical aptitude test, evidence of its overlap with general intelligence, of its degree of speeding, or of the extent to which physics students earn better scores than those who have not studied physics. Factor analyses are often relevant to this question. Here specifically, it is necessary to select the most important information from that available.

The final evaluation of validity (19) is the most important single entry in the form. Does the test give the information needed to make the intended decision? What degree of confidence can be placed in it? What level of psychological training is required to interpret the test as proposed? To reach such an integrated conclusion, it is necessary to weigh positive and negative evidence, to decide which of several contradictory findings is most trustworthy, and to judge the adequacy of the body of evidence as a whole. It is especially important to note what necessary evidence on validity is lacking.

The next major section (20–23) considers reliability and norms. This information is usually presented in the manual and needs only to be summarized. The most common faults in reliability information are failure to report subtest reliability, and application of internal-consistency formulas to speeded tests. Norms must be examined critically for representativeness, and for relevance to the user's own situation.

It is of course important to examine whatever critical reviews are available, and the record form includes a space (24) for quotations which summarize the reviewer's evaluation. The general evaluation (25) is a final summary of the advantages and limitations of the test for the particular purpose, considering both its technical and its practical features. It is appropriate to compare the test with others having the same general function. One can also point to supplementary information which should be combined with the test. Special ways of applying the test, over and above its use as a measuring instrument, should be noted. These would include making supplementary observations during the test, examining responses to obtain cues for diagnosis, using test responses as a point of departure in a counseling interview, etc.

An analysis of this sort for every test under consideration (whether the analysis is put in writing or not) provides a basis for a total testing program. A program is more than a list of good tests. A program will be designed so as to minimize wasteful overlap and timed so as to get each piece of information when it will be most helpful. Testing cannot be planned by itself. In industry or the armed forces it must be dovetailed with recruiting, training, and assignment. In the clinic, testing must be considered as part of the whole therapeutic effort. The final program states what tests will be given and when, and how the results will be used in assigning the person or in helping him to understand himself.

Suggested Readings

Anastasi, Anne. Test reliability. *Psychological testing.* New York: Macmillan, 1954. Pp. 94–119.

This textbook chapter covers essentially the same principles and techniques about reliability as the present chapter includes.

Rothney, John W. M., & others. Test scores: etiology and interpretation. *Measurement for guidance.* New York: Harper, 1959. Pp. 116–150.

How to read a test manual and test advertising critically is discussed, with numerous examples. These authors maintain a severely critical attitude toward tests, demanding a closer approach to perfection than does the present text.

Wesman, Alexander G. Reliability and confidence. *Test Serv. Bull.,* 1952, No. 44. (Available on request from Psychological Corporation. Also reprinted in H. H. Remmers & others (eds.), *Growth, teaching, and learning.* New York: Harper, 1957. Pp. 449–457.)

In a simple presentation Wesman covers the major difficulties in the interpretation of reliability coefficients reported in test manuals.

PART TWO

TESTS OF ABILITY

7

Measurement of General Ability:
The Binet and Wechsler Scales

THE EMERGENCE OF MENTAL TESTING

Tests Before Binet

THE outstanding success of scientific measurement of individual differences in behavior has been that of the general mental test. Despite the overenthusiasm and occasional errors that have attended its development, the general mental test stands today as the most important single contribution of psychology to the practical guidance of human affairs. Among mental tests, none has been more influential than that fathered by Alfred Binet. A history of mental testing is in large part a history of the Binet test and its descendants.

The first systematic experimentation on individual differences in behavior arose from the accidental discovery of differences in reaction time among astronomers. In 1796, an assistant named Kinnebrook at Greenwich Observatory was engaged in recording, with great precision, the instant when certain stars crossed the field of the telescope. When Kinnebrook's results were found to be consistently eight-tenths of a second later than the observations of his superior the Astronomer Royal, he was thought incompetent in his work and was discharged. Not until twenty years later did more careful study show that the differences between observers were the result of the different speeds with which they could respond to stimuli. Only gradually did such differences come to be recognized as significant facts about human nature, rather than as annoying errors contaminating scientific work.

Physiologists, biologists, and anthropologists were stimulated by the scientific climate of the nineteenth century to make a great variety of measurements of human characteristics. Notable among these early workers was Sir Francis Galton, whose interest in differences among individuals developed from Darwin's newly published theory of differences among species.

During the latter half of the nineteenth century, Galton invented ways of measuring physical characteristics, keenness of the senses, and mental imagery. These methods, though not developed fully by Galton, served as models for later tests. In addition, Galton demonstrated that outstanding intellectual achievement tended to occur frequently in certain families. Genius, evidently, was not an accident or a gift of the gods, but a natural phenomenon to be investigated scientifically.

At this time, psychology was only beginning to emerge as an objective science. Mental processes, it was suggested, could be observed under standard conditions by an experimenter. Scientific observations, supplementing or even replacing philosophical speculation, could provide an exact description of the relation between the mental and physical worlds. This was the aim with which Wundt opened the first psychological laboratory in Leipzig, and he and his colleagues did triumphantly establish quantitative psychological laws comparable in form to those of physics. Believing that psychological research should analyze behavior into its simplest elements, he designed techniques for measuring very limited functions. Wundt, trying to establish the general laws governing all minds, was not concerned with individual differences. His laboratory procedures and particularly his interest in quantitative research, however, had a strong influence on early tests. In the United States as early as 1890, J. McKeen Cattell was using a mixture of procedures from Wundt's and Galton's laboratories to measure sensory acuity, strength of grip, sensitivity to pain from pressure on the forehead, and memory for dictated consonants. Cattell was first interested in the range of individual differences as a laboratory problem, but he quickly became excited about the practical value of identifying superior individuals by means of these procedures.

This line of effort unfortunately met an early debacle when it was discovered that the new tests measuring simple elements of behavior seemed to have no relation to significant practical affairs. The crucial study was Wissler's work on test scores of Columbia students (Wissler, 1901). He correlated college marks with the Cattell tests, finding such negligible correlations as the following: reaction time, $-.02$; canceling a's rapidly on a printed page, $-.09$; naming colors, $.08$; auditory memory (recall of digits), $.16$. We now recognize that low correlations were certain to result, no matter what mental functions were tested, because Wissler's brief tests were quite unreliable, especially in his highly selected group. The disappointment which followed the Wissler study, however, delayed attempts to base an applied psychology on the findings of the laboratory.

Wundt tested elements which could be precisely defined, using stimuli which could be accurately controlled in the laboratory. The tests had validity in the same way that a chemist's measure of the freezing point of a substance has validity; the result describes a clearly defined characteristic and is readily interpreted at a superficial level, no matter how much remains to be learned about the underlying process. Tests of this sort have an obvious content validity, and continued investigation in the laboratory spins an ever stronger web of theory between these measures and important constructs. Their validity for predicting practical criteria, however, has usually been negligible (except that color vision and other sensory qualities are important in some tasks).

For practical prediction, psychologists have relied on tests constructed on quite another principle. Whereas laboratory tests have mostly dealt with narrowly defined functions, most practical tests are complex worksamples. When a complex performance is to be predicted, a sample of that very performance will often prove to be a good predictor. To minimize effects of specific training and to obtain a test of wide applicability, the test may sample, not the criterion task exactly, but the general type of reasoning or motor performance required by the criterion. The Bennett TMC is of this nature. The Block Design test is not a sample of a real task but is an artificial task requiring complex reasoning similar to life problems without depending on special knowledge.

Practical testing came into psychology from medicine. Clinicians dealing with mental defectives and pathological cases needed diagnostic tests. Psychiatrists looked for tests which would distinguish normal from abnormal subjects, and distinguish among various types of mental disorders. Kraepelin and other nineteenth-century psychiatrists used reasoning problems and tests of performance in continuous work. These tests were comparable to requirements of life outside the laboratory. Though few of the tests of this period survive in present-day diagnosis, clinical tests still are chiefly concerned with complex processes. Alfred Binet, to whom we turn in a moment, was a physician by training and he chose tests which could distinguish between clinical groups—no matter how obscure or complex the "psychological meaning" of the tests.

The Binet tests did have practical value for the physician, the educator, the social worker, and, in modified form, for the employer. The practical tests of today are much closer to worksamples of life performance than to the psychophysical measures of Wundt. These complex tests will surely never be replaced, but neither have they shown much recent development. Ability tests have remained about the same since 1920, and personality tests since 1930. The practical tests of today differ from the tests of 1920 as today's automobiles differ from those of the same period: more efficient and more elegant, but operating on the same principles as before.

Instruments measuring relatively limited types of performance have undergone more radical changes. Factor analysis of ability tests is leading to a conception of abilities and their relations going far beyond that of 1920, and numerous tests have been prepared to measure elementary performances. The original suspicion that simple laboratory measures might have important relations to personality is now being substantiated; for example, whether a mental patient perceives an intermittent light as steady or flickering is related to his diagnosis. The simpler tests are (with rare exceptions) too inefficient for practical use, and in that sense they stand where Wissler's experiment left them. But these tests are better rooted in psychological theory than the complex tests which are most useful at the moment, and they should ultimately have practical value.

The Binet Tests

Alfred Binet, a French physician, became interested in studying judgment, attention, and reasoning about 1890. His interest in these complex mental processes led him to try a greater variety of tests than his predecessors had used. In studies published between 1893 and 1911, he tried to find out just how "bright" and "dull" children differed. Having little preconception regarding this difference, he tried all sorts of measures: recall of digits, suggestibility, size of cranium, moral judgment, tactile discrimination, mental addition, graphology—even palmistry! He found, as did other investigators, that the tests of sensory judgment and other simple functions had little relation to general mental functioning, and he gradually identified the essence of intelligence as "the tendency to take and maintain a definite direction; the capacity to make adaptations for the purpose of attaining a desired end; and the power of auto-criticism" (Terman, 1916, p. 45).

The stage was set, then, for the call in 1904 to produce the first practical mental test. Paris school officials became concerned about their many nonlearners and decided to remove the hopelessly feeble-minded to schools where they could be taught a simplified curriculum. The officials could not trust teachers to pick out the feeble-minded. They did not want to segregate the child of good potentiality who was making no effort and the troublemaking child the teacher wished to be rid of. Moreover, they wanted to identify all the dull from good families whom teachers might hesitate to rate low, and the dull with pleasant personalities who would be favored by the teacher. Therefore they asked Binet to assist in producing a method for distinguishing the genuinely dull. Binet's scale, which drew on his earlier studies, was published in collaboration with Simon in 1905. In 1908 a revision was published, and in 1911 another.

There was a great demand at this time, especially in America, for objective methods of investigating psychological development. Although Thorndike was using experimental tests on animals, American psychological research had been dominated by introspection, anecdotes, and questionnaires, all of which were as fallible as the person reporting. Binet's method, which was to a large degree impartial and independent of the preconceptions of the tester, was welcomed enthusiastically as a research technique and as a means of studying subnormal children.

In 1910, Lewis M. Terman began experimentation with the Binet tests. He produced the Stanford Revision of the Binet Scale in 1916. This revision extended application of Binet's method to normal and superior children. The Stanford-Binet had immediate popularity and became, rightly or wrongly, the yardstick by which other tests were judged. Although there had been various previous mental tests, the outstanding popularity of the Stanford test made its conception of mental ability the standard. The acceptance of the Stanford test was due to the care with which it had been prepared, its success in testing complex mental activities, the easily understood "IQ" it provided, and the important practical results which it quickly produced. Although many criticisms have been made of the test, it was and is an exceptionally useful instrument.

The 1916 Stanford-Binet was replaced in 1937 when Terman and Merrill published Forms L and M of the Stanford-Binet. These tests improved on the construction of the former edition and offered two comparable forms. The latest revision (1960) combines the best tests of the 1937 revision into a single Form L-M and improves and updates the scoring system. In all parts of the world there have been other versions taken directly from the Binet test or one of the Terman revisions.

More Recent Trends

Evolution of general mental tests since 1911 has taken two directions. On the one hand, individual tests have been increasingly designed to allow illuminating observation as a supplement to the accurate overall score. While the Binet items reveal considerable diagnostic information, they were not chosen for this purpose. We have already mentioned that much can be learned about the child's personality by watching him solve mazes, and the Binet scale includes a few maze items. Porteus, however, capitalizes on the special value of the maze by providing a whole series of mazes of graduated difficulty. The Kohs blocks have a similar advantage. The highest development of tests for observation and diagnosis are the popular Wechsler scales.

Whereas this trend led to more elaborate mental tests and gave great responsibility to the observer, the other line of evolution was toward simpler and more mechanical tests. Procedures which could be applied to large numbers of people at once and scored routinely were first demanded for military purposes. Several psychologists had devised experimental group tests prior to 1916. When it became necessary in World War I to expand the Army at an explosive rate, the Army requested psychologists to provide a group test so that inductees who were promising could be given officer training, those who were unfit could be rejected, and the remainder could be appropriately classified. In one of the major achievements of practical psychology, a group including Terman, Yerkes, and Bingham assembled a test whose final version became famous as Army Alpha. Alpha tested ability to follow directions, simple reasoning, arithmetic, and information. It was a practical test, easily administered and highly useful to the Army, as Figure

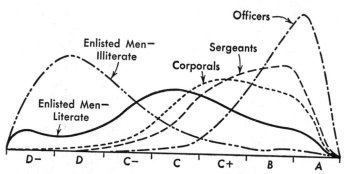

FIG. 28. Alpha scores of Army personnel of various ranks (Yoakum and Yerkes, 1920).

28 suggests. It convinced the nation that adequate prediction of success could be achieved through mass processing, and schools and industry were quick to demand tests of this type after the war. Alpha in a civilian revision and comparable group tests by Otis and others were extensively applied.

Since 1920 there have been changes in test design. For example, whereas the early tests were highly speeded, time limits are generous in recent American tests. The content of today's general mental tests is not, however, greatly different from that of Army Alpha. They are more efficient and have better norms, but they are not different in kind. The introduction of specialized tests such as the TMC has been the most important innovation in group testing since the 1920's. Recent research has increased the variety of things the psychologist finds it important to measure. Though specialized tests are being used more and more in guidance, clinical work, and educational and industrial selection, they are nearly always supplementary to general mental tests derived from Binet's work.

Do not assume that other lines of approach before and after Binet had no merit, merely because they failed to attain comparable prominence. Early workers explored many leads which appear to have been unduly neglected (Peterson, 1925). Binet himself (following still earlier workers) made use of inkblots to study imaginative and perceptual processes, but this technique fell into obscurity from which it emerged only because Rorschach independently revived the procedure twenty years later. In his monograph *The Experimental Study of Intelligence,* Binet described the application of inkblot and imagery tests to his daughters, arriving at qualitative descriptions of the way their intelligence functioned which read as if taken from the most modern results of projective techniques. The possibilities of improved impressionistic procedures, which psychologists are today examining, were neglected while Binet's psychometric strategy of summarizing all intelligence in a single score was adopted. The accidents of time and place play a large part in psychological history; there was, in 1905, a great practical need for a simple and objective way of summarizing a child's general level of mental development, but no popular demand for analysis of individual patterns of thought.

CHARACTERISTICS OF THE STANFORD-BINET SCALE

In the Stanford-Binet (SB) scale, as in every test to be studied, one can trace how the investigators solved four problems which face the test designer. First, he must decide what he intends to measure. Second, he must invent or select items which serve that purpose. Third, he must find a measuring unit in which to express results, since behavior rarely can be described in countable units like inches, pounds, or light-years. Fourth, he must show the validity of the test. Knowing how these were solved for the SB not only reveals wherein it made a contribution but also throws light on its limitations.

Assumptions About Intelligence

The person making the first mental test is in the position of the hunter going into the woods to find an animal no one has ever seen. Everyone is sure the beast exists, for he has been raiding the poultry coops, but no one can describe him. Since the forest contains many animals, the hunter is going to find a variety of tracks. The only way he can decide which one to follow is by using some preconception, however vague, about the nature of his quarry. If he seeks a large flat-footed creature he is more likely to bring back that sort of carcass. If he goes in convinced that the damage was done by a pack of small rodents, his bag will probably consist of whatever unlucky rodents show their heads.

Binet was in just this position. He knew there must be something like intelligence, since its everyday effects could be seen, but he could not describe what he wished to measure, as it had never been isolated. Some workers, then and now, have objected to this circular and tentative approach whereby mental ability can be defined only after the test has been made. Tests are much easier to interpret if the items conform perfectly to a definition laid down in advance. When faculty psychology was in vogue, many separate tests were designed for the separate mental faculties: reasoning, memory, attention, sensory discrimination, and so on. None of these tests used singly, however, was found to have predictive value. Terman (1916, p. 151) explained this as follows:

> The assumption that it is easier to measure a part, or one aspect, of intelligence than all of it, is fallacious in that the parts are not separate parts and can not be separated by any refinement of experiment. They are interwoven and intertwined. . . . Memory, for example, cannot be tested separately from attention, or sense discrimination separately from the associative processes. After vainly trying to disentangle the various intellective functions Binet decided to test their combined functional capacity without any pretense of measuring the exact contribution of each to the total product.

Modern diagnostic tests do obtain useful information about distinct aspects of ability. In Binet's time, though, one of his great contributions was to replace the idea of separate functions with the concept of general intelligence. Having started with the idea that some children were bright and some dull, he found quickly that those who were best on tests of judgment were also superior in attention, memory, vocabulary, etc. In other words, the tests were correlated. The correlation shows that there must be some underlying unity among these mental tests. When psychologists refer to *general mental ability*, they refer to the characteristic that accounts for the correlation among mental tests.

Binet refined his idea of intelligence by trial and error. If color matching does not correlate with other estimates of mental ability, it must not be influenced by the common factor. If knowing certain information correlates with the tests of reasoning, both must measure intelligence. Out of a study of his best test items, Binet came to his famous description quoted above.

The term *intelligence test* is being replaced by such terms as *test of general mental ability* or *test of general scholastic ability*. "Intelligence" often connotes some sort of inborn mental superiority. Performance on the tests is influenced by many things not included in this concept of "intelligence." The test calls for knowledge, skills, and attitudes developed in Western culture, and perhaps better developed in some environments than in others. An "intelligent" person will do badly if he lacks the background the test requires. A person is born with potentialities which may or may not be developed. The Binet scale gives only very indirect evidence on "potentialities"—we can observe potentiality only when it has been developed into performance.

1. What do the following definitions of "intelligence" include that Binet's definition does not, and vice versa?
   a. "The ability to do abstract thinking" (Terman).
   b. "The power of good responses from the point of view of truth or fact" (E. L. Thorndike).
   c. "The property of so recombining our behavior patterns as to act better in novel situations" (Wells).
2. Would the same sort of test items be called for by each of these definitions?
3. Is previous learning included in intelligence by these definitions? By Binet's?

Selection of Items

To test high-jumping ability, we would ask a boy to jump over standards of various heights, beginning with easy ones and increasing the height until we found the highest level at which he could succeed. The experimental psychologist uses the same device in measuring weight discrimination. The test begins with pairs of weights which are easily discriminated, and the difference within pairs is gradually reduced until the person can no longer tell which is heavier. The Binet scale sets up similar "hurdles." It begins with items the subject is expected to pass, but as the items become more difficult, the subject begins to fail. The test is continued until we have determined the most difficult mental hurdle he can get over.

Binet, studying bright and dull school children, realized that mental ability increases with age. The older child is superior in taking directions, making adaptations, and judging his own ideas. It follows, then, that a good mental-test item should be easier for older children than for younger ones. An item should not be used if just 25 percent of children of every age can pass it—such an item is difficult, but it does not reflect mental development. In selecting items for the Binet test and its revisions, preference was given to items on which success is markedly related to age. Binet further assumed that it was important to measure a general quality running through all mental tasks. Therefore, a good item should correlate with the rest of the scale.

Items are located in the scale according to their difficulty for children at each age. A test which about 60 percent of 13-year-old children can pass is placed at Year XIII.

4. When a Japanese investigator prepares a counterpart of the SB for Japanese children, would a direct translation of the scale be satisfactory?

Description of the Scale

The child is given the SB by an experienced examiner, who presents each item in the precise manner called for by the directions. The examiner begins by establishing rapport, aided by the high interest the "games" have for the younger children and the challenge of the test situation for the older child. The first items tried are those for a mental level below that expected

TABLE 16.   Representative Tasks from the Stanford-Binet Scale

Year	Task	Correlation with Whole Test	Nature of Stimulus	Nature of Response
II-6	Points to toy object "we drink out of"	.55	Verbal	Motor
	Shows doll's hair	.63	Verbal	Motor
	Names *chair, key*	.70	Object	Verbal
	Repeats "4–7"	.63	Verbal	Verbal, memory
IV	Names *gun, umbrella*	.79	Picture	Verbal
	Recalls name of object (dog) when covered by box	.53	Object	Verbal, memory
	"Brother is a boy; sister is a. . . ."	.56	Verbal	Verbal
	Matches circles, squares	.75	Picture	Motor
	"Why do we have houses?"	.70	Verbal	Verbal
VI	Defines *orange, envelope*	.67	Verbal	Verbal
	Gives examiner 9 blocks	.77	Verbal	Motor
	Maze	.69	Object	Motor
	"An inch is short; a mile is. . . ."	.67	Verbal	Verbal
IX	Examiner notches folded paper; child draws how it will look unfolded	.62	Object	Drawing
	Verbal absurdities	.83	Verbal	Verbal
	Reproduces design from memory	.60	Picture	Drawing, memory
	Repeats "8–5–2–6" backward	.52	Verbal	Verbal, memory
	Figures change from a purchase	.62	Verbal	Calculation
XII	Defines *skill, juggler*	.79	Verbal	Verbal
	Finds absurdity in picture	.51	Picture	Verbal
	Defines *constant, courage*	.85	Verbal	Verbal
	Completes "The streams are dry . . . there has been little rain."	.72	Verbal	Verbal
Average Adult	Defines *regard, disproportionate*	.86	Verbal	Verbal
	Explains how to measure 2 pints of water with a 5-pint and a 3-pint can	.70	Verbal	Verbal
	Explains a proverb	.73	Verbal	Verbal
	Compares *laziness* and *idleness*	.80	Verbal	Verbal

of the child; beginning with easy tasks builds confidence. First, the *basal age,* the scale level at which the child passes all the tests, is located. Tests for the higher levels are then given in order, usually six tests at each level. Testing continues until the child fails all tests at some level.

In Form L-M, tests cover levels of mental development from age 2 to Superior Adult III. From ages 2 to 5, there are six tests (plus one alternate) at each half-year of development. Above age 5, hurdles are spaced one year apart; and above age 14, the levels have even wider spacing. No child takes the entire set of tests. A 9-year-old would begin with tests at year VIII and, if he passed those, would continue until he reached his limit of ability. Some 9-year-olds would be unable to go beyond the 11-year level, whereas others would still be passing a few tests at the 14-year level. One hour, more or less, is required for the testing procedure, although there is great variation from child to child.

Administering the scale requires skill. The tester must exercise considerable judgment in obtaining from each child as clear answers as possible, without probing more than the standardized directions allow. Rapport is especially a problem with younger children, who are not accustomed to tests or to tasks calling for sustained attention.

The child's response to the test varies greatly with his motivation and security in the testing situation. The insecure child's performance in a strange task with a strange examiner may be far below his potential. McHugh (1943) gave the SB to pupils entering kindergarten and then retested them after two months. Their mental-age scores increased nearly six months during this period and their IQs by 6 points, on the average. Tasks requiring oral response showed twice as much change as tasks calling for manipulative responses. McHugh suggests that shyness in a new situation accounts for most of the difference between the first and second test.

The young child often refuses to try items he should be able to solve, as in this set of examiner's notes on a boy in kindergarten (Mayer, 1935, p. 325):

> Always smiled and gave a sort of laugh when refusing to respond, but was none the less determined. Same in school, according to teacher. Refused to do things, but always smilingly and pleasantly, but will not yield. School doctor was unable to give him physical examination "because he refuses to open his mouth or do anything asked." On Pictures he said, "no," and politely but conclusively turned the page. "I won't tell you" was his affable answer for Comprehension, Materials, Opposite Analogies. "No, I don't want to" disposed of all repetitions. He pushed away Buttoning, refused to attempt the Knot, didn't want to draw a triangle, but was prevailed upon to try. Even with the privilege of delivering a note to the teacher offered as a bribe, he would not complete the bird. "No," he said, "I'll make a pig." He didn't want to fold a square, but in marked contrast was his alacrity in responding to Paper Folding —Triangle: "I'm going to make one, too," and took the paper to start before the examiner could give it to him.

Rust (1931) found that a child often passes an item he has refused if it is presented again on another day. If credit were allowed for such passes-after-refusal, one-quarter of the 3-year-olds tested would raise their IQs by 15 points or more. The Merrill-Palmer scale for preschool children contains a correction procedure to take refusals into account, but the SB does not.

Only those persons should give the SB who have been trained in its use and scoring. Terman suggests that an adequate training program calls for a general course in mental-test theory, a practicum course during which the student tests at least 25 subjects, and further experience in clinical courses where he gives the test to various kinds of subjects. Training may be considered complete when the person has tested about 100 cases under supervision, beyond the 25 practice subjects.

The scale includes a great variety of tasks, as can be seen from Table 16. Verbal Absurdities (Form L, Year IX; Terman and Merrill, 1937) is a rather typical test:[1]

Procedure: Read each statement and, after each one, ask "What is foolish about that?" If the response is ambiguous, say, "Why is it (that) foolish?"

(a) Bill Jones' feet are so big that he has to pull his trousers on over his head.

(b) A man called one day at the post office and asked if there was a letter waiting for him. "What is your name?" asked the postmaster. "Why," said the man, "you will find my name on the envelope."

(c) The fireman hurried to the burning house, got his fire hose ready, and after smoking a cigar, put out the fire.

(d) In an old graveyard in Spain they have discovered a small skull which they believe to be that of Christopher Columbus when he was about ten years old.

(e) One day we saw several icebergs that had been entirely melted by the warmth of the Gulf Stream.

The child passes this at Year IX and receives two months' credit on his mental-age score if three responses are satisfactory. Four correct allows two more months' credit and counts as a pass at Year XII.

The various subtests call for verbal and nonverbal performances, simple memory and complex reasoning, learned answers to familiar questions, and solution of novel problems calling for ability to adapt. Tasks involving objects and pictures are used at younger ages, with an increasing reliance on verbal problems through the school ages, and more tests of abstract thinking at the upper end of the scale.

Scoring is made as objective as possible by means of a scoring guide which contains specimen acceptable and unacceptable answers. In an absurdities item, the subject is expected to recognize clearly the central absurdity, and not to bring in irrelevant matters.

5. Judge the following answers to the problem "Bill Jones' feet are so big . . ." (from Pintner et al., 1944, p. 60) as right or wrong:
   a. You can't put them on because his legs are joined together.
   b. You can't put your trousers over your head because your legs are in them.
   c. He's supposed to put the trousers over his feet.
   d. A man couldn't put his pants over his head.

Scoring System

Binet's plan of successive hurdles makes it possible to report mental development in a simple and easily comprehended score called the mental age.

[1] Copyright 1937, 1960, Houghton Mifflin Co., and used by permission.

The subject's *mental age* is the chronological age at which the average child does as well as the subject does. John, who is only 5, can earn a mental age of 8 if he does as well as the average 8-year-old. Scoring would be simple if the child passed all tests to a certain level and failed all tests after that level. Because the failures enter gradually, the mental age is determined by adding credits (usually two months per test) for each test passed. Where test levels are two years apart, and six tests compose each level, each test counts four months; where levels are six months apart, each test counts one month. The total credit in months is converted into a mental age in years and months (written thus: 5–8 for 5 years, 8 months).

Table 17 reports the performance of six children. The first one, Frank, shows uniform performance; when he begins to fail, he fails nearly all tests

TABLE 17.   Stanford-Binet Performance of Six Children

Child			Frank	Billy	Herbert	May	Bruce	Nancy
Age			6–4	6–2	8–0	5–3	8–6	10–3
Year	Number of Tests	Credit per Test (Months)	Number of Tests Passed by Child at Each Level					
V	6	2	6	—	—	6	—	—
VI	6	2	6	6	6	6	6	—
VII	6	2	4	4	4	5	3	—
VIII	6	2	1	4	6	2	4	—
IX	6	2	0	2	3	1	1	6
X	6	2		3	1	3	0	4
XI	6	2		0	1	0		4
XII	6	2			0			3
XIII	6	2						1
MA			6–10	8–2				

at that level. His basal level is VI, so he receives a base credit of 6 years of mental age. Four tests passed at Year VII add 8 months' credit; one at VIII adds 2 months. His mental age (MA) is 6 years, 10 months. Billy has greater "scatter" of successes and failures. His MA is figured as follows:

Basal Age VI			6 yrs.
VII	4 tests, 2 mo. each		8 mo.
VIII	4 tests, " " "		8 mo.
IX	2 tests, " " "		4 mo.
X	3 tests, " " "		6 mo.
Total			6 yrs., 26 mo.;
			8 yrs., 2 mo. = MA

Mental age measures the child's performance; it is in effect the raw score on the test. Obviously he is a bright child if his MA is greater than his life age. Two children of the same MA have the same average level of ability, but they may differ in pattern of development. Young superior children pass different tests than older subnormal children (Magaret and Thompson, 1950).

The MA is an estimate of present performance and of promise in the immediate future. In any classroom, young superior children are more nearly equal in performance to average children than to bright children of normal age. In making decisions within a group of varied age (e.g., in sectioning of classes) the mental age rather than the IQ gives the most relevant information. In research also, if it is desired to equate groups, to separate groups of unequal ability, or to correlate some other variable with mental ability, the mental age should be used rather than the IQ. This principle is often violated. The correlation of IQ with another variable is lower than that of MA with the same variable in a group of mixed age.

Mental growth is slow after age 15 or 16. The mental-age units employed for higher ages are not directly related to the average performance at these ages and therefore should be considered only as another form of raw score. The average 20-year-old has a mental age well below 20.

6. Compute the mental ages for the remaining four children in Table 17.
7. A 20-year-old passes the following tests: XIV, all; Average Adult, 7 tests out of 8, credit 2 months each; Superior Adult I, 2 tests out of 6, credit 4 months each; Superior Adult II, 1 test out of 6, credit 5 months each. Find his MA.

THE INTELLIGENCE QUOTIENT

The "intelligence quotient" in the 1960 Stanford-Binet and nearly every other current test is nothing more than a standard score. Instead of the common scale with a mean of 50 and a standard deviation of 10, the IQ conversion fixes the mean at 100 and the standard deviation at 16. Since the IQ distribution is nearly normal, the IQ can be interpreted as an indication of the child's position in the group. The mental-age score is converted into an IQ by referring to tables in the Stanford-Binet manual. Tables are provided for ages from 2 to 18. For adults, the 18-year-old norms can be used, although, as will be seen later, the average mental-test score is not strictly constant throughout maturity.

This IQ is not really a quotient at all, and if it were not for its long tradition there would be considerable advantage in employing a standard-score scale with mean 50, as in other ability tests. The IQ was originally introduced as a ratio or quotient representing the child's rate of mental development. Mental age was divided by actual age and multiplied by 100 to remove the decimal fraction. For Frank, whose age is 6 years and 4 months (6.33) and whose mental age is 6–10 (6.83), the ratio IQ is 108. Development more rapid than the average is indicated by a quotient over 100.

The calculation of ratio IQs fell into disrepute for several reasons. The quotient was originally thought of as representing a fixed rate of development which could not only express relative brightness today but also predict mental age at subsequent ages. Evidence to be discussed below indicates that the child's rate of mental development is not fixed. Moreover, the ratio depends upon technical characteristics of the scale as well as upon his mental growth. In the 1937 SB, the standard deviation of IQs was below 16 at ages 5 and 6, and much larger at ages 3 and 12. These variations resulted, not from changing rates of development, but from the distribution of item difficulties at the various ages. A third objection was that the ratio IQ could not be applied to persons beyond age 13, where mental-age units become arbitrary. Special corrections were introduced to obtain IQs on Forms L and M for older subjects. For the 1960 revision, the investigators calculated the standard deviation of mental age for a representative sample of persons at each age. Whatever MA fell one standard deviation above the mean for that age was converted into an IQ of 116. A standard-score IQ formed in this manner is often called a "deviation IQ."

During the interim while the 1960 revision is replacing the 1937 revision, there will be some confusion because IQs on the two scales are not strictly comparable. A 12-year-old who has a ratio IQ of 138 on the older scale would have a deviation IQ of 132. These differences probably do not distort greatly the mean IQs in typical groups or the correlations of IQ with other variables. Research results from Forms L and M may be used in interpreting Form L-M.

8. Compute ratio IQs for the remaining children in Table 17.
9. If for age 15 the standard deviation of mental ages is 2 years and 10 months, find the deviation IQ corresponding to an MA of 16.

Distribution of IQs

The distribution of IQs in the 1937 standardization sample is shown in Table 18. The change to deviation IQs is not expected to alter this distribution greatly. The other two columns give comparative data for high-school and college samples.

While comparison of any person or group with the total national population is of some value, practical decisions require us to estimate how a person will fit into a more selected group. Even when the child enters school, his companions are not representative of the total population, for some subnormal children are institutionalized or cared for in the home. Community and neighborhood differences also restrict the range of any class. Through the grades there is slow but continuous elimination, especially where children are permitted to leave school to work. The superior child is less likely to leave school than the child who is frustrated in schoolwork. The end result

TABLE 18.   Percentage Distribution of IQs

IQ	Standardizing Sample (N = 2,904)	High-School Graduates (N = 21,597)	College Entrants (N = 1,093)
140 and above	1.3 ⎫		
130–139	3.1 ⎬ 12.6	9.7	31.7
120–129	8.2 ⎭		
110–119	18.1	22.8	46.1
100–109	23.5	29.9	18.1
90–99	23.0	23.2	4.0
80–89	14.5 ⎫		
70–79	5.6 ⎬ 22.7	14.3	.1
Below 70	2.6 ⎭		

NOTE: The standardizing sample data are for ratio IQs on the 1937 Stanford-Binet (Terman and Merrill, 1959). High-school data are for group tests as recorded in school files (Semens *et al.*, 1956). College data are for Wechsler-Bellevue and WAIS administered to freshmen at San Jose State College (Plant, 1958).

is a gradual rise in the average level. A study of a representative sample of dropouts in five school systems, made in the 1940's, permits us to construct Table 19. The very dull tend to drop out as soon as they reach age 16; since

TABLE 19.   Educational Records of 2500 Seventh-Graders

	Below 85	Intelligence Quotient 85–94	95–104	105–114	115+
All cases in Grade 7	400	575	650	575	400
Dropouts in Grades 7 and 8	93	30	14	5	2
Remainder entering Grade 9	307	545	636	570	398
Dropouts in Grades 9 and 10	241	171	143	78	29
Remainder entering Grade 11	66	374	493	492	369
Dropouts in Grades 11 and 12	52	65	81	55	25
Remainder continuing to graduation	14	309	412	437	344

SOURCE: Dillon, 1949.

they are usually retarded one or two grades, they leave before the ninth grade. By the end of high school, almost no one with IQ below 85 is still in school. A few of the superior pupils drop out because of lack of interest, financial problems, and other difficulties. Because tests other than the Binet were used, these IQs are not precisely comparable to Binet IQs. The IQ range in high school is obviously unlike the representative sample studied by Terman and Merrill, and college groups are even more selected, as Table 18 shows.

Since the range of abilities varies from school to school and from class to class, a final judgment of the pupil's standing must be based on local norms. Local norms change from time to time owing to population migration and changing school policies. At the college level, Wolfle's report (1954, p. 147) provides an important warning against overgeneralizing in interpreting an IQ. He studied 41 representative colleges with the AGCT test, whose scale is roughly comparable to an IQ scale. In the highest of the 41 colleges, the middle 50 percent of the entering freshmen fell between 126 and 137; in the lowest, the middle range was from 99 to 117. Clearly, a student who would succeed readily in one college might be far below his competitors in another. Information about the competition to be expected is necessary in guiding potential college students, both to insure that they will consider colleges where they have a chance to be accepted and to increase their chance of survival in the college they choose. To assist counselors, many colleges now publish leaflets describing the ability distribution in their entering classes, usually based on the Scholastic Aptitude Test of the College Entrance Examination Board.

Meaning of Particular IQs

Some writers translate IQ levels into labels such as "normal," "near genius," "feeble-minded," etc. This is misleading, because there is no borderline at which genius, for example, suddenly appears. Some persons of IQ 110 make significant original contributions, and some of IQ 160 lead undistinguished adult lives. Some adults of IQ 80 are incapable of adjustment to the world, and some of IQ 60 support themselves and make an adequate home.

A classification of mental deficiency provides a starting point for thinking about the individual case. Persons with IQs from 40 to 59, for example, may be labeled morons (Bernreuter and Carr, 1938), but while these categories are convenient, it is wrong to think of them as pigeonholes. A quantitative standard might seem to be the most just procedure for determining admission to an institution for the mentally deficient, but this policy, tried in the earlier days of testing, led to some ludicrous results. The distinguished Czech statesman Jan Masaryk, during a childhood stay in America, was confined briefly in an institution which had such a policy, no doubt because having to use a strange language pulled down his Binet IQ (Porteus, 1950, p. 40). Clinical disposition of a case is always to be based on a combination of mental-test data with evidence on the person's functioning in social and practical situations.

The human meaning of the high IQ is shown in the research by Catherine Cox Miles, who estimated the IQs of famous persons from their childhood histories. "Voltaire wrote verses from his cradle; Coleridge at 3 could read a chapter from the Bible. Mozart composed a minuet at 5; Goethe, at 8, produced literary work of adult superiority" (Cox, 1926, p. 217). The minimum IQs which could account for the recorded facts about these men were estimated as: Voltaire, 180; Coleridge, 175; Mozart, 160; Goethe, 190. The true IQs might conceivably have been higher, but full evidence was not available.

Terman and Oden (1947) followed children with high IQs into adulthood. Considered as a group, these young adults were found to be in every way superior to average men and women of comparable age. Here are a few of the facts about their careers: 90 percent entered college and 70 percent graduated. At an average age of 40, the 800 men had published 67 books, over 1400 scientific and professional articles, and over 200 short stories and plays. They had more than 150 patents to their credit. As Terman says (1954), "nearly all the statistics of this group are from 10 to 30 times as large as would be expected for 800 men representative of the general population." (See also Terman and Oden, 1959.)

The meaning of the IQ is best understood by one who has observed many children of known IQ in particular situations. A partial substitute for such a background may be gathered from the research literature, where various writers have established the IQ requirements of particular tasks. The general trend of these results is indicated in Table 20 and Figure 38. These stand-

TABLE 20.   Expectancies at Various Levels of Mental Ability

IQ	
130	Mean of persons receiving Ph.D.
120	Mean of college graduates
115	Mean of freshmen in typical four-year college
	Mean of children from white-collar and skilled-labor homes
110	Mean of high-school graduates
	Has 50–50 chance of graduating from college
105	About 50–50 chance of passing in academic high-school curriculum
100	Average for total population
90	Mean of children from low-income city homes or rural homes
	Adult can perform jobs requiring some judgment (operate sewing machine, assemble parts)
75	About 50–50 chance of reaching high school
	Adult can keep small store, perform in orchestra
60	Adult can repair furniture, harvest vegetables, assist electrician
50	Adult can do simple carpentry, domestic work
40	Adult can mow lawns, do simple laundry

Sources: Beckham, 1930; Havighurst and Janke, 1944; Plant and Richardson, 1958; Wolfle, 1954; *Guide to the Use of GATB*, 1958; and others.

ards are not dependable guides for decisions in specific situations, but they are nevertheless worth study.

10. Why is the mean of college freshmen IQs higher than the level where there is a 50–50 chance of succeeding in college? Is this a desirable situation?
11. If the academic curriculum requires an IQ of 105, what does this imply regarding educational planning for below-average youth?

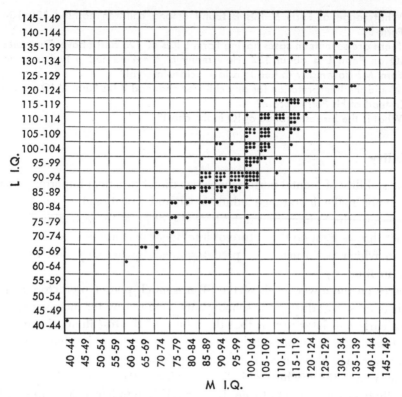

FIG. 29. IQs obtained by 7-year-olds when tested on two forms of the Stanford-Binet (Terman and Merrill, 1937, p. 45).

Error of Measurement

A coefficient of equivalence, telling how much the IQ is affected by short-term errors of measurement, has been obtained by administering Forms L and M a few days apart. The correlation is about .91 for unselected cases (Terman and Merrill, 1937, p. 47). This establishes the SB as one of the most reliable of all tests. Even so, the average shift of IQ from one measurement to another is substantial: 5.9 for IQ 130, 5.1 for IQ 100, 2.5 for IQs below 70. This means that an IQ of 130 may be 12 to 14 points from an estimate made for the same child a few days later, although such errors are infrequent. The best way to visualize the error of measurement is to study the scatter diagram for 7-year-olds, reproduced in Figure 29. We see that the test is more precise for low IQs; changes below IQ 80 are slight. Notice also the occasional large shifts, despite the general agreement between the two measures. For those with IQ 95–99 on Form L, the Form M estimates range from about 87 to about 112.

12. What range of Form M IQs is found among children earning 130–134 on Form L?
13. There are seventeen cases having Form L IQs of 125 and above. Their median IQ on Form L is about 134. How many of them earned a higher score on Form M? How many shifted to a lower class-interval?
14. Would the interpretation for any child be changed if his Form M IQ were used instead of his Form L score?
15. What is the largest change of IQ in the chart?

Stability

The stability of mental performance has direct practical importance, since we cannot make long-range educational and vocational plans if ability changes greatly. Evidence on stability is also of great theoretical importance, since it throws light on the nature of intelligent performance, and on the extent to which performance is predetermined by heredity and by events early in life.

Scores on the lower levels of the SB are much poorer predictors of later IQ than are scores during the school years. One reason for inconsistency between early and later tests is that the nature of the test items changes, and therefore different abilities are measured. Environmental influences during early years may also develop abilities not shown in early test performance, or may retard those which did show. Bayley (1949) retested children repeatedly from age 1 month to age 18 years. Although her results are based in part on special tests for infants and young children which we have not yet described (see pp. 208 ff.), the findings apply to any present mental tests. Table 21 gives correlations between earlier and later measures. In these re-

TABLE 21.   Correlation of Mental Test with Test at a Later Age

Approximate Age at First Test	Name of First Test	Years Elapsed Between First and Second Test			
		1	3	6	12
3 months	California First-Year	.10(CFY)	.05(CP)	—.13	.02
1 year	California First-Year	.47(CP)	.23	.13	.00
2 years	California Preschool	.74(CP)	.55	.50	.42
3 years	California Preschool	.64	—	.55	.33
4 years	Stanford-Binet	—	.71	.73	.70
6 years	Stanford-Binet	.86	.84	.81	.77(W)
7 years	Stanford-Binet	.88	.87	.73	.80(W)
9 years	Stanford-Binet	.88	.82	.87	—
11 years	Stanford-Binet	.93	.93	.92	—

SOURCE: Bayley, 1949. Some entries have been estimated from closely related data in Bayley's report. Initials indicate second test; W stands for Wechsler-Bellevue. Where no initial is given, the Stanford-Binet is the second test.

sults it is clearly seen that the later a test is given, the more stable the IQ is. Tests before age 2 are unstable even over short periods. Scores show a marked increase in long-range predictive power near age 6.

Figure 30 charts the change in scores found upon retesting of behavior-problem children with the 1916 revision. The average time between testings was 15 months, and the age at first test was generally between 7 and 14. A. W. Brown (1930) comments on these data as follows:

> Although the correlation . . . is high, a large number of cases make considerable change, and from the clinical point of view these are often

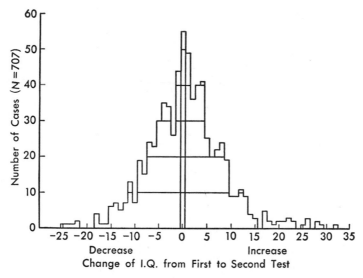

FIG. 30. Changes in IQ when 1916 Stanford-Binet is repeated after an average interval of fifteen months (A. W. Brown, 1930).

> the important cases. One hundred eight cases or 15.2 percent change eleven points or more. To say that the average change is about five points does not help a great deal, because in dealing with clinical cases one can never be sure that the particular case under observation may not be one that will show a large amount of change. It would seem advisable therefore to secure at least two ratings wherever an intelligence rating is especially important in disposing of the case or in making recommendations.

Another study of similar children over an even longer time (R. Brown, 1933) found that 3 percent changed more than 30 IQ points and 10 percent changed 21 to 30 points. It is unsound practice to rely on mental tests given several years previously. Extreme reversals, from IQ 70 to IQ 120, are rare, but some highly important shifts are found in most large groups.

The nature of IQ variation is seen most clearly in the records of individual children who have been tested repeatedly. No "typical" pattern can be shown, for the changes take many different forms. The three patterns in Figure 31, selected to show some of the possible trends, are by no means exceptional. (These records are plotted in terms of standard scores, with the mean for children in this study taken as zero.) Case 783 is a boy whose test performance did remain stable even though he had a poor health history, an insecure and underprivileged home background, poor grades, and emotional symptoms such as stammering and enuresis. "There never was a time in his

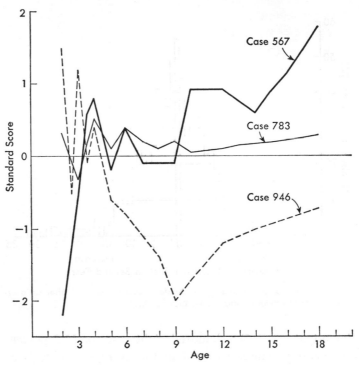

FIG. 31.   Records made by three children on successive mental tests (Honzik et al., 1948).

history when he was not confronted with extreme frustrations." The IQ nonetheless held to the same satisfactory level. Case 946 has had IQs as low as 87 and as high as 142. Her parents were immigrants, and unhappily married; their conflict led to a divorce when the girl was 7. At 9, with her mother remarried, the girl was insecure at home and excessively modest. Her later recovery perhaps reflects better adjustment to her family. The third case (567) shows consistent improvement. This girl's early years were marked by grave illnesses in the family, and the girl herself was sickly and shy. After age 10, her social life expanded and she developed rewarding interests in music and sports. This blossoming is paralleled in the test scores. Little is yet known about the causes of spurts of this kind.

Scores of emotionally disturbed or uncoöperative children are especially unstable. If maladjustment is continuous, the child's test score and his general performance may be constant, at an impaired level. But if the causes of emotional disturbance are remedied, drastic changes in IQ occur. Long-range planning on the basis of the IQ is justified so long as two precautions are observed: Interpretation must consider the elements in the child's background which would tend to raise or lower scores, and all judgments must be made tentatively, leaving the way open for a change of plans when change in development appears. The case of Danny (Lowell, 1941) should make clear the hazards that await the psychologist who treats every IQ as immutable.

Danny was born January 15, 1929. He entered kindergarten at the age of 5 years and was such a misfit that after a few weeks he was given a Binet test. The following are records of the four tests given before the end of Grade 6, with the date of test, chronological age, mental age, and IQ.

2–2–34	Age 5–0	MA 4–2	IQ 82
5–9–35	Age 6–4	MA 6–2	IQ 98
6–8–37	Age 8–5	MA 9–4	IQ 111
12–3–40	Age 11–11	MA 15–9	IQ 132

The first test showed such mental immaturity that Danny was excluded from kindergarten for a year. The next year he moved into another school district. This time his Binet score seemed normal; he was placed in the first grade in September in spite of his lack of social adjustment. The teachers complained that Danny seemed to live in a world of his own, was noticeably poor in motor coördination, and had a worried look on his face most of the time. The mother was called in, and only then was light thrown on his peculiarities.

The mother explained that while Danny was still a baby his father had developed encephalitis. In order for the mother to work, they lived in the grandparents' home where Danny could be cared for. Danny's grandfather was a high-strung, nervous old gentleman who was much annoyed by the child's noise and at times expostulated so violently that Danny became petrified with fear. The grandfather's chief aim was to keep things quiet and peaceful at any cost. When Danny was excluded from kindergarten the mother took him from the grandparents' home.

The next few years were a period of educational, social, and emotional growth for the starved child. He amazed his teachers with his achievement. He became an inveterate reader and could solve arithmetic problems far beyond his grade level. He was under a doctor's care much of the time and was also treated by a psychiatrist because of his marked fears. He made friends with boys in spite of physical inferiority.

VALIDITY OF THE STANFORD-BINET

Predictive Validity

The Binet test is generally used for prediction. It is employed in estimating the brightness of a child being considered for adoption, because prospective foster parents wish to be sure that the child has a good chance of equaling their own academic and business achievement. Another frequent application is in deciding how serious a case of mental deficiency or retardation is. Here again, both school performance and adjustment to the demands of normal living need to be predicted.

The stability of the IQ itself gives information on predictive validity. The adopting parent wants a child whose later IQ will be comparable to that of others in the family. Insofar as Binet performance at age 15 is accepted as a fair sample of intellectual performance, that test itself serves as a criterion for tests given in early years.

Interest in Binet performance, however, rests ultimately on its relevance to external criteria. You will recall that the Cattell-Wissler tests, for example, dropped from sight just because their predictive validity was disappointing. For the SB, there is rather little evidence to be cited in the form of up-to-date formal validation. For other tests, we will most often cite specific validity coefficients which permit us to compare quantitatively the efficiency of various devices used for making the same decision. The Binet test has been the patriarch of the tribe, standing without a rival until the Wechsler test recently became available. Many validity coefficients were calculated in the early days of the test, and these results were encouraging. Recent predictive studies have relied almost entirely on group tests, which were derived from the Binet scales. Since the individual test is nowadays reserved almost entirely for individual study of perplexing cases, data are not at hand for computing its predictive validity for representative samples.

We may not entertain serious questions about the relevance of the SB score to practical prediction. Studies of high-school dropouts, of job potentialities of the mentally retarded, and the like show that the test tells a great deal about the person's expected success. Terman's follow-up of gifted children is a particularly good long-range predictive validation against criteria of school performance, attainment in adult professional careers, financial success, marital success, and adult mental health.

When validity coefficients are calculated, the results are always much the same. Here, for example, are the correlations in one high school between SB IQ in Grade 9 and achievement tests one year later (E. A. Bond, 1940, p. 29):

With reading comprehension	.73
With reading speed	.43
With English usage	.59
With history	.59
With biology	.54
With geometry	.48

All studies show discrepancies between Binet performance and attainment, even though the predictions are right in the majority of cases. Some of Terman's bright boys—not very many—failed in college, or served a prison term, or had unhappy marriages and careers. Intelligence is only one facet of individuality to be considered in a practical decision about a child or adult. One can neither predict behavior of a person knowing only his IQ nor make a sound prediction without using a good estimate of his mental ability.

16. The correlation of SB IQs with grades of medical-school seniors was found to be only .15 in one study. The average IQ of these men was 131 (Mitchell, 1943). Explain why the correlation was so small.

Construct Validity: What the Test Measures

The most important questions to be asked about the test are: What variables affect performance? What does the construct "general mental ability" mean? Since most subsequent general mental tests have been made to have high correlations with the SB, statements about the meaning of general ability apply equally to these tests.

Looking at Table 16, we see that the test items do fit Binet's definition of intelligence, in that they call for ability to maintain a definite set, adaptation, and self-criticism. That the items all depend on some common element which we can call general ability is indicated by the fact that each item correlates with the total test. But a thoroughgoing analysis must do more than accept items because they include an element we wish to measure. An equally important question is : What elements affect the score that are not considered in the definition? Logical analysis plus experimental studies have led to several important conclusions.

● *The Stanford-Binet measures present ability, not inborn capacity.* Although it seems obvious that no test can measure anything but behavior here-and-now, there has been much confusion during the past forty years because to many people "intelligence" means inherited ability. While there is necessarily an inborn potentiality, the test measures only present ability which is affected both by innate factors and by experiences. Binet himself never considered that his tests measured innate capacity alone. If a user wishes to infer that a difference between SB scores of two children represents an innate difference, he must assume that the two children have had much the same experience during their lives. If a child has had the same opportunity as normal children to acquire skills, information concepts, and work attitudes called for by the tests, his failure to come up to normal performance can reasonably be interpreted as showing that he failed to profit from his opportunities. The ability level can be changed by radical changes in early environment (S. A. Kirk, 1958), although we have found no general techniques for "mental orthopedics" (Binet's phrase) which will accelerate significantly the mental development of normal children from normal homes.

We can list endless variations in experience that would make it easier for one child than another to perform the Binet tasks, even if the two have equal native ability. Freddie is only 5, but his father has played number games with him so that he can count and add very well. Harold's mother did not like having her walls marked, so she refused to let Harold use pencils or crayons except under her supervision; Harold, at 7, doesn't seem to enjoy drawing and is clumsy at it. Sarah lived in a remote rural area, where she never saw trains or telephones. Peter's parents are immigrants; although both parents can speak English, they find it difficult and use their native language at home. Frances has a set of books which include interesting puzzles, pictures containing absurdities, and pictures to compare for similarities and differences. Such variations in experience as these are common and may be counted on to modify both test performance and school performance.

17. List for each of these children some of the tests in Form L which they would find easier or harder than children with "normal" experiences.

● *Stanford-Binet scores are strongly weighted with verbal abilities.* The great majority of test items call for facility in using and understanding words. If the child does poorly at these tasks, he probably will do poorly in other verbal activities. He may do badly on the test because of poor schooling, but this will also cause him to do badly in school in the future. The Binet test is an excellent measure of scholastic aptitude, i.e., of readiness to do the sort of tasks required in school. Since Binet originally sought tests which would distinguish pupils judged superior in school performance from those judged inferior, it is not surprising that the final test measures an ability important in schoolwork. If one were to examine intelligent acts outside of school, verbal facility might be found less important. The test is not a measure of all types of mental ability; critics note that it underemphasizes insight, foresight, originality, organization of ideas, and so on. A high score on the test should not be interpreted as guaranteeing the qualities which the test does not measure.

Among the pupils for whom this verbal loading produces an unfair picture of overall intellectual performance are bilingual children, children from homes where English is little used, children with hearing deficiencies, and poor readers. The examiner can often identify such cases by their spread of successes and failures, with success on nonlanguage items at levels much beyond their first failure on verbal concepts. Table 22 compares children

TABLE 22. Mean IQ of Monolingual and Bilingual Children on the Binet Test and a Performance Test

Test	Mean IQ for Monolinguals (N = 106)	Mean IQ for Bilinguals (N = 106)	Difference[a]
Stanford-Binet	98.7	90.9	7.8
Atkins Object-Fitting	89.0	97.5	−8.5

[a] Significance tests show that neither difference could be due to chance.
SOURCE: Darcy, 1946.

who speak only English with bilinguals who speak a second language at home. Both groups were tested on the SB and the Atkins Object-Fitting Test, a performance test for preschool children which does not demand facility in English. It is evident that the bilingual group, superior on the nonverbal test, would be judged inferior on the SB.

18. Which items in Table 16 depend upon previous school learning?
19. Which items would offer an advantage to a child from an upper-class home compared to a child from an impoverished working-class home?
20. Suppose one is faced with Binet's original problem, of deciding whether a pupil failing in school could profit from the regular curriculum. If the pupil is bilingual, would the SB or a performance test serve better?

● *The Stanford-Binet score measures somewhat different mental abilities at different ages.* This shift of emphasis is apparent in Table 16. Early tests call for judgment, discrimination, and attention. Verbal tests and reasoning play a much greater part in later years. If all the tests measured general intelligence equally well, this would be no problem. But the simple mental developments of early childhood predict only roughly the later emergence of verbal and higher mental abilities. While the early levels of the scale are excellent for identifying children with abnormally slow development, they do not predict accurately the subject's later standing.

The clearest study on this comes from Maurer's work with the Minnesota preschool tests, which are similar to the early Binet levels. Maurer followed a group from preschool years to late adolescence and retested them to determine what preschool test items had best predicted intellect at maturity. At maturity she used a group test heavily weighted with verbal materials; this test is also highly correlated with both Binet scores and school success. She found that many items which correlated well with the rest of the preschool scale were poor predictors of later development. Among the poor predictors were pointing out parts of the body, obeying simple commands, comprehension, and paper folding (Maurer, 1946).

Measures of an ability made at the time when it is first being developed are generally poor predictors. How early a child learns to count, for example, depends upon accidental factors as well as upon his brightness. Many pupils who start later will overtake the one with the best early performance. Stable measures therefore must be based on abilities that are already well formed. Thus John E. Anderson (1944) argues that vocabulary is a good test for older children just because it is based on a long period of environmental stimulation. Maurer (p. 86) confirms this in her search for tests of young children which will predict later IQ.

> [Good] tests for younger children make only minimal demands on language. They require perception of form and spatial relationships and the ability to reproduce them. They do not demand complex motor coordinations. They require controlled attention and ability to persist to a goal. Many of them are comparatively independent of training. Tests for older children [4–5 years] involve use of language in relationships which are not often practiced and constitute problem-solving situations involving the use of well-developed tools.

● *The test requires experiences common to the U.S. urban culture and is of dubious value for comparing cultural groups.* The Zuñi Indians, for example, have a coöperative society most unlike the competitive attitudes we tend to encourage. Zuñi children have races. But a child who wins several races is censured for having made others lose face. He must learn to win some races to show he is capable, and then to hold back and give others an opportunity to win. In arithmetic, white teachers sent Zuñi children to the blackboard for arithmetic drills, with instructions to do a problem and turn their backs to the board when finished. Instead, the pupils faced the board until the slowest had finished; then all turned. This was to them simple courtesy; following the teacher's direction would have been exhibitionism. It is easy to see why the typical American speed test gives misleading results among the Zuñi. A Binet test fares no better; the first subject may fail some items deliberately, because he fears the next child will be unable to answer. All intelligence tests face the same problem; they are adequate only for comparing persons with similar experience. Anglo-Americans would perhaps do badly on a test developed by a Zuñi psychologist, using questions which differentiated between good and poor members of Zuñi culture.

● *The Binet test does not give a reliable measure of separate aspects of mentality.* Scores are influenced by specific as well as general abilities. It would be helpful in diagnosis if we could divide the Binet test into segments and obtain separate estimates of verbal ability, information, and so on. Any particular specialized ability is used in only a few items; therefore combining those items would not give a reliable measure of the ability. Binet and Terman deliberately sought a great variety of tests, so that no one subdivision of intelligence would have great weight in the final score. This feature makes the SB unsuitable for measuring the aspects of ability separately.

21. What sort of items have the greatest correlation with total test score at levels II-6 and IV (see Table 16)? What does this suggest regarding the meaning of "general mental ability" in preschool applications of the Stanford-Binet?

22. What items have the greatest correlation with total score at the upper end of the scale? What is the meaning of "general ability" at that level?

● *The Binet score is influenced by the subject's personality and emotional habits.* Binet's description of intelligence includes persistence, flexibility of mental approach, and criticalness, all of which are aspects of personality. Among the emotional habits which have an obvious effect on scores are shyness with strange adults, lack of self-confidence, and dislike for "schoolish" tasks. A self-critical person may say "I don't know" because he is dissatisfied with the best answer he can formulate; a person less sensitive to niceties may give an answer which is passable. A pedantic urge to accuracy may make it relatively easy to do memory tasks. Fear may cause a child to "freeze up" so that he cannot find a new mode of attack when his first one is blocked. No matter how careful a tester is, there is some danger that a child may fail an item that he could have passed if ability alone were required. One should therefore always bear in mind that the final test score shows how well the child functioned at this time; this score may be markedly affected by emotional complications.

Hutt (1947) points out that the child encounters considerable frustration from a succession of failures, and that this stress comes at different points for different children. He proposes to "standardize" this stress by alternating easy and hard items. In an experimental trial with comparable groups, he found that very well-adjusted children earned the same IQs on his "adaptive" procedure as on the usual test. The badly adjusted children, however, averaged 4.5 points higher in IQ with the adaptive method.

Any departure from standard administrative practice changes the meaning of scores. It can be readily seen that Hutt's method will yield a higher average IQ than the Terman-Merrill procedure. Many testers who are not willing to take the radical step Hutt proposes, which places a burden of judgment on the tester, are nonetheless distressed by the fact that the child encounters more and more failures, ending the test with no less than six failures in a row. This damages the clinical relationship and influences the subsequent tests. To avoid this outcome, and also to simplify administration, they favor "serial administration," in which all memory-for-digits items, for example, are presented together. Terman and Merrill arrange items by difficulty rather than content, and their directions insist that this order be followed. Nonetheless, a good many testers have changed over to the more convenient serial plan, pointing to the evidence of Frandsen and others (1950) that the mean IQ is the same for the two techniques.

23. In indicating the importance of objective mental testing, Terman says, "I believe it is possible for the psychologist to submit, after a forty-minute diagnostication, a more reliable and more enlightening estimate of the child's intelligence than most teachers can offer after a year of daily contact in the classroom." In which of the following features does the advantage of the test over the teacher's report lie?
   a. Freedom from personal prejudice.
   b. Considering more aspects of mental ability.
   c. Considering a basically different trait.
   d. Observing capacity rather than level of actual performance.
   e. Sampling behavior under a wide range of conditions.
   f. Permitting an exact comparison of the child with a standard of normality.
24. How could you decide whether Hutt's "adaptive" procedure is more valid than the standard method?

Diagnostic Interpretation

Children with the same MA are of course far from alike in mental development, as is shown by the fact that they pass quite different tests. The Stanford-Binet, as a standardized but complex situation, brings to light far more individual differences than the single score represents. Experienced testers always study such differences, and many have tried to develop supplementary systems of scoring to report this information. In particular, many have hoped that the scatter of performance would have diagnostic value. The *scatter* is the range from the child's earliest failure to his highest success; it suggests whether all aspects of ability have developed evenly. After many studies of scatter, investigators now agree that it has no value as a score. All other attempts to obtain diagnostic scores from the Stanford-Binet have similarly failed.

The SB test will not yield meaningful diagnostic scores because it was designed to prevent any factor save "general ability" from influencing scores to a measurable degree. We cannot trace accurately the child's development in simple recall, for example, because digit-span and other recall tests are not uniformly spaced at all levels of difficulty. Even within one year-scale, we cannot discuss the child's strengths and weaknesses with confidence, because tests grouped together do not have exactly the same difficulty.

Nevertheless, the psychologist ought to study the detailed pattern of test performance. If a child has an unusual handicap or facility in verbal tests, the examiner has an excellent opportunity to note it. Deficiencies in information, arithmetic skill, and reasoning may also be noted. A distinction should be made between the child successful because of coaching, who does well on such teachable items as counting to 13 or saying the days of the week in order, and the more genuinely intelligent child of the same age who can make up a coherent story about a picture and tell what day of the week comes before Tuesday. These indications, even if brought to light only in one or two subtests, provide profitable leads for further study. They should be confirmed by reliable tests of the separate abilities.

The SB affords an excellent opportunity to see how the child works. An impulsive child will be observed to use trial and error in an attempt to "force" a solution instead of reasoning. An inhibited child may refuse to take a chance on items where induction or imagination is called for and he cannot be positive that his answer is right. Others give answers even to questions about which they are ignorant.

The outcome of careful clinical study is illustrated by the tester's comments regarding John Sanders, a normal adolescent (age 12–8; IQ 109) (H. E. Jones *et al.*, 1943, pp. 91–92):

John showed a lively intellectual curiosity and was interested in a variety of things, but within each of these interests his attention seemed to be rigid and single-tracked. This lack of flexibility made it difficult for him to adapt to requirements when on unfamiliar ground. Upon encountering difficulties, he frequently demanded a pencil, because he could not "see" the words or numbers; I have never tested a more eye-minded person.

John's principal difficulties were on tests requiring precise operations, as in the use of numbers. With such tests he became insecure and often seemed confused, with slips of memory and errors in simple calculations. He asked to have instructions repeated, was dependent on the examiner, and easily discouraged. Although cooperative and anxious to do well, it was extremely hard for him to master a task (such as "memory span") in which he was required to be exact by fixed standards. If this is also true outside the testing situation, it is not surprising that in his school work he has found great difficulty in learning to spell, in mastering the mechanics of English, and in learning a foreign language. We cannot tell from this test *why* he has had such unusual difficulty in this kind of learning. However, the supposition can be offered that in tasks involving an imaginative and analytic approach he imposes form upon himself; in tasks of the type which he finds difficult, form is imposed upon him from without. Resistance to such controls may account in part for the discrepancies between John's actual intelligence and his achievement in certain fields.

Attempts have been made to identify emotionally disturbed persons by the pattern of their subtest scores, and abnormal groups do show some departure from normal averages. Myers and Gifford (1943), for example, find schizophrenics superior in vocabulary, abstract words, and dissected sentences, compared with normals of the same mental age, but much poorer on bead chains, picture absurdities, and memory for stories. Knowledge of such averages is useful background for the tester, but many normals show patterns which are just like those of typical patients. The SB pattern cannot be used to make a definite diagnosis.

Responses sometimes reveal disturbances of thinking. Feifel (1949) has found that mental patients and normals respond to vocabulary items in different ways. Normals tend to use synonyms, while abnormals give definitions by use and description, explanation, and illustration. Asked what an envelope is, normals said "a container," "a receptacle for paper," "something to put a letter in," etc. Typical patient responses were "a piece of paper you fold," "you write letters," "it's sticky on top so you can paste it down," and "to mail."

Responses may disclose values and attitudes. Strauss (1941) asked mentally defective delinquents, "What ought you to do before undertaking something very important?" (Year X). Their answers included: "Don't touch anything that doesn't belong to you," or "Run away from a guy who is going to take it. Go tell him nothing of the people that owns them." In defining *pity*, one of them answered, "Don't take pity on somebody, shoot them and kill them."

Essentially the SB is a standardized clinical observation. The fact that it yields an IQ should not blind the tester to his obligation to report everything he can observe. There is no adequate rationale for making and interpreting these observations, and the findings are necessarily tentative. But to avoid them because they are subjective is no more sound than if the psychologist were to refuse to have a conversation with the child because it would not lead to a statistically manageable and reliable score. The Binet tester with adequate experience has a great advantage over the clinical interviewer because he can observe the child in a standardized situation and can compare what he does with the behavior of other children. The fact that the child does not realize that the test situation reveals his emotions and habits of work is a further asset.

25. What sort of report should be placed in the school files for a child who has been given the SB?

General Evaluation

The Stanford-Binet scale is an instrument efficiently designed for one particular function, namely, providing a single score describing the child's present level of general intellectual ability. It is interesting to the child, precise, and well standardized. The large amount of research on the scale gives a basis for interpreting results which no newer test can offer. The 1960 revision makes an important improvement in discarding the conceptually and statistically unsatisfactory ratio IQ; on the new scale an IQ of a given size has the same interpretation at all childhood ages. The revision retains those items from Forms L and M which made the greatest contribution to the total score. The new scale places greater emphasis on word knowledge than the older forms. Items whose content is peripheral to scholastic aptitude were eliminated, to provide a more concentrated measure. The gain in accuracy is offset by some loss in variety of items and in opportunity for observation of mental processes. Although the revision eliminates the comparable forms of the 1937 version, this is a small loss. Few testers made use of Form M, and the Wechsler scale may be used for cases where a second measurement is required to confirm a doubtful Binet score.

The Stanford-Binet finds the Wechsler scale for children a strong competitor. The chief differences are in organization, in the greater precision of the Binet at low mental ages, and in the greater variety of tasks in the Wechsler scale. The difference in content of the two scales is magnified by the L-M revision, which narrows and focuses the SB. Deliberate concentration on verbal and educational abilities is an advantage for some purposes, a disadvantage for others, as is made apparent in E. L. Thorndike's comment (1921):

> If the boy has had ordinary American opportunities, this score [in standardized tests of the Binet or of the group test type] will prophesy rather accurately how well he will respond to intellectual demands in cases of "book-learning" at the time and for some time thereafter, and very possibly for all his life. It will prophesy less accurately how well he will respond in thinking about a machine that he tends, crops that he grows, merchandise that he sells, and other concrete realities that he encounters in the laboratory, field, shop, and office. It may prophesy still less accurately how well he will succeed in thinking about people and their passions and in responding to these.

Such objections as this have led clinicians to combine the SB with performance scales. The SB does not measure all aspects of mental ability, nor does it measure inborn capacity. It is properly interpreted as a measure of present status in one important type of mental development.

26. The Stanford-Binet has been criticized because it contains numerous items relating to death and other morbid subjects. What has this to do with the value of an intelligence test, so long as brighter pupils pass these items?
27. Terman, in revising the original Binet scale, discarded items which showed a consistent difference in favor of either sex. His argument was that a fair comparison could not be made if items favored one sex or the other. Did the elimination of such items raise or lower the validity of his scale?

PERFORMANCE SCALES

Individual tests owe their prominent place in testing of problem children, psychiatric patients, and the mentally retarded chiefly to their value as a situation for observing performance. Any individually administered test offers some opportunity to observe the nature of the subject's errors, habits of performance, and emotional reactions. Performance tests such as Block Design, however, permit especially revealing clinical observations. Moreover, they depend very little on language and schooling, which makes them suitable for evaluating young children, adults with limited schooling, and persons unfamiliar with the language of the tester.

The Stanford-Binet includes some performance tests: drawing, bead-stringing, fitting blocks into holes, etc. These tests are relatively few in number, are concentrated at the easier levels, and in general do not require complex reasoning. Terman equated intelligence to "the power of abstract thought," and therefore most of his items involved verbal or numerical concepts. While verbal items do have considerable predictive power, especially for educational criteria, clinical testers need more elaborate performance scales than the Binet offers.

Performance scales give somewhat different information from that yielded by the Stanford-Binet. Figure 32 shows a comparison of ten children on

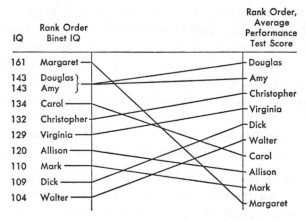

FIG. 32.   Rank of ten superior 7-year-olds on the Binet test and on a battery of performance tests (Biber *et al.*, 1952).

the Stanford-Binet and on a composite of three performance tests. There are several shifts in rank order, the most striking change being Margaret's. She is highly superior in schoolwork, but she has a heavy build, acts slowly, and is socially awkward with adults. Her difficulty in performance tests may therefore reflect personality problems that limit her effectiveness in many life situations.

A sample of the information the performance test yields to a skilled observer is indicated by the following record. Mark, 8 years old, had a Binet MA of 8-8. On some performance tests, however, he reached an MA of 9-6 (Biber *et al.*, 1952).

The most striking feature of Mark's examination was his extreme lack of confidence and his desire to do what was expected of him. This was manifested by his constant reference to the examiner. Throughout all of the tests, although he said little, it was evident that he was referring back to see whether the expression on the examiner's face indicated approval.

In the Healy Completion [fitting small blocks into holes to complete a picture] the examiner noticed that once when she gave him a friendly smile he was content to leave an inferior solution, as if he were guided much more by his wish to please than by his own good intelligence. Although she busied herself with papers and tried to pay as little attention as is compatible with a test situation, it was impossible to prevent this. The directions in the Healy Completion to look the work over carefully and see if there are any changes to make seemed to imply criticism to Mark, and he removed a block which was correctly placed and substituted a blank. His first responses were all good. In this test, he placed the first three accurately; then, apparently, he began feeling anxious or uncertain, and the last three he placed were blanks. It seemed that he was using the blanks as a way of avoiding committing himself to a mistake, and that he felt that he would rather do nothing than to get the wrong result. This test was the most plainly motivated by his desire for approval, although there were indications of it throughout the other tests as well.

In the Pintner-Paterson series, he seemed to be less conscious of the examiner, probably because he felt more sure of himself in these tests. When he was uncertain, as in the Ship and Triangle Tests [formboards], he would look up shyly as he worked. Several times he commented, "That's easy."

The first part of the [Porteus] maze series he enjoyed, working quickly, accurately, and with ease. After his first failure in Year VIII, he seemed much more uncertain and slow. After practically every one he said, "I'm not going to do any more of these." With constant encouragement, he went on and completed Years X, XI, and XII, although he had four trials on Year XII. Toward the end of the series, there was little evidence of real effort on his part, but rather he seemed to be going through the motions because the examiner urged him on.

Probably no test results on Mark are completely accurate because other factors besides ability are so definitely involved in his behavior. Difficulty did not stimulate him, as it did Douglas and Amy, for instance, but simply discouraged him and left him tense and uneasy. He was responsive to praise, but always with a questioning expression, as if he were trying to ferret out what one really thought of him. It was consistent with his total defensive attitude that he offered very little information during the test and several times he responded very shortly to questions that the examiner put to him.

28. What light do these observations throw on the interpretation of Mark's Binet IQ?
29. List several of the characteristics a tester should attempt to observe in giving an individual performance test.
30. In many clinical examinations, only part of a battery of performance tests is used, to save time. On what basis would you decide which subtests to retain?

THE WECHSLER SCALES

The most important performance tests today are those included in Wechsler's intelligence scales. His effort at test development began at the

Bellevue Hospital operated by the city of New York, where social derelicts of many sorts had to be tested. These persons might be feeble-minded, psychotic, or illiterate; estimation of the intellectual level of each case was important in determining his disposition. Wechsler prepared the Wechsler-Bellevue Scale Form I in 1939 to provide for such clinical evaluations. This scale was of great value in military hospitals during World War II and became one of the chief tools of the clinical psychologist after the war. A second form was published in 1946 but was never adequately standardized. The "Wechsler-Bellevue Scale" is now obsolete, having been replaced by better-constructed and better-standardized forms. Today's Wechsler series consists of WAIS, the Wechsler Adult Intelligence Scale (1955) for ages 16 and above, and WISC, the Wechsler Intelligence Scale for Children (1949) for ages 5–15.

Strange ironies attend the history of test development. Binet set out to identify mental defectives, yet the most famous piece of research with his scale was concerned with children of superior endowment. Wechsler tried to prepare a new type of mental test for adults, because adults and children differ in their interests and approach to work. Yet today his technique is popular as a children's test. His secondary hope in developing the test was that patterns of subtest scores would provide a ready means of clinical diagnosis. The hope was not realized, and this type of analysis is no longer depended upon because empirical checks show that pattern analysis has little validity. Wechsler's series is now of chief importance as a general individual test for all ages.

Test Materials and Procedure

Wechsler collected a variety of items, many of them from previously published tests. He subscribed to Binet's idea of a general mental ability, but his experience suggested that in the mental patient some types of performance or reasoning are more disturbed than others. Wechsler gave preference to items which he had found useful in understanding the intellectual functioning of patients. Wechsler sought items which, while falling within the area we identify as general mental ability, had sufficiently specific characteristics to silhouette different types of thinking or performance.

In contrast to the Terman-Binet plan of grouping items according to difficulty, mixing content randomly, Wechsler arranges them into subtests of various types. There are eleven scored subtests, grouped in a Verbal and a Performance scale. The Verbal scale includes tests of Information, Comprehension, Digit Span, Similarities, Arithmetic, and Vocabulary. The Performance scale includes Picture Arrangement, Picture Completion, Block Design, Object Assembly, and Digit Symbol tests.

We shall describe the Verbal scales only briefly and then turn to the Performance tests. Items are taken from the WAIS form (Wechsler, 1955).[2]

Information includes such items as "What is the population of the United States?" "What does rubber come from?" and "How many weeks are there in a year?" Comprehension questions include "Why should we keep away from bad company?" and "What does this saying mean? 'Shallow brooks are noisy.'" The subject is expected to give a generalized, fairly direct answer. In Digit Span, the subject is asked to repeat digits forward and backward. The Similarities scale asks the subject to tell how the following are alike: orange and banana, air and water, poem and statue, etc. Arithmetic is a test of numerical reasoning ability using simple verbal problems, such as "How many oranges can you buy for 36 cents if one orange costs four cents?" The subject is required to do the items mentally and receives no credit on an item where he uses more than a reasonable time (e.g., thirty seconds for the question about oranges). Vocabulary requires the subject to define or explain such words as "fabric," "conceal," and "tirade."

The Block Design test was described in Chapter 3. Materials used in several other Performance scales are illustrated in Figure 33. Whereas Block

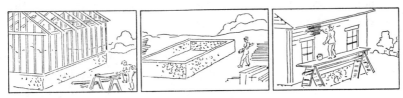

Picture Arrangement

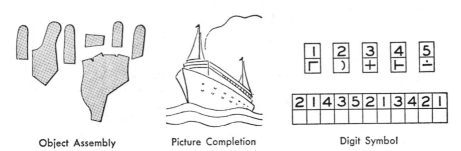

Object Assembly   Picture Completion   Digit Symbol

FIG. 33. Materials from Wechsler Performance tests. (Copyright ©, 1955, The Psychological Corporation. Reproduced by permission.)

Design requires analysis of a complex whole, breaking a pattern into elements, Object Assembly gives the parts and requires the person to discover how they go together. The four tasks are the profile, manikin, hand, and elephant. Time bonuses for rapid performance are allowed.

[2] Items quoted in this section copyright © 1955, The Psychological Corporation. Reproduced by permission.

Digit Symbol requires the person to fill in the proper code symbol under each number, doing as much as he can in a short time. Our illustration shows only five symbols; the actual test uses ten. The code remains in front of the subject as he works. Thus he can continually refer to the code, or he may carry it in his head. Learning the code is easy enough that for above-average adults the score becomes a measure of writing speed rather than mental ability.

There are two picture tests. Picture Completion uses items presented on cards, each showing a picture from which something is missing. The subject tells what is lacking. In Picture Arrangement, a story is told in three or more cartoon panels which are presented in random order; the subject must piece them together in the correct order. Here again, the subject must identify a complex whole from disorganized parts.

The WISC series is a downward extension using easier items than WAIS. The same subtests are used, but Digit Span is an optional test for children because it has a low correlation with overall performance. A Maze test is added as an optional performance test. Coding a simple message, a task used by Terman, is substituted for the more difficult Digit Symbol task.

The Wechsler scales are comparatively simple to administer, the full WAIS requiring about one hour. The directions are less complex than those for the Binet, and keeping similar items together reduces the task of the examiner. The skill of the examiner may influence the score greatly. In some of the verbal tests, the examiner must make rather sensitive judgments as to the correctness of an answer since it may be necessary to request the subject to elaborate his meaning. Answers that seem wrong may be correct when the subject explains himself. Subjectivity in scoring borderline answers is also a potential problem.

31. Does the Digit Symbol test call for the same mental processes when three digit-symbol pairs are used as when ten are used? Does Wechsler's Digit Symbol test call for the same processes from bright and dull subjects?
32. Which Wechsler subtests have the following characteristics?
   a. The score is affected by educational background.
   b. The test demands experiences found in the urban American culture.
   c. The test requires problem solving or reorganization of knowledge rather than mere recall.
   d. The test measures very simple mental processes such as Cattell and Wissler investigated.
33. How do the Wechsler test items differ from the higher levels of the Stanford-Binet?

Meaning of Wechsler IQs

The raw scores on the subtests are converted into scaled scores, i.e., normalized standard scores with a mean of 10 and s.d. of 3. This conversion for

WAIS is based on a reference group of adolescents and adults of each age, carefully chosen to match the census distribution on sex, geographical region, urban-rural residence, race, occupation, and education. A similar sample (restricted to white children) was used for the WISC.

Wechsler introduced standard-score IQs in his first edition, anticipating a practice which Terman and Merrill later accepted. He chose to fix the mean at 100 and the standard deviation at 15. The discrepancy between Wechsler standard scores and those developed with the Terman-Merrill s.d. of 16 is unfortunate, but should rarely be a source of serious confusion. Wechsler eliminated completely the mental-age conversion, which is a source of some misunderstanding in Binet interpretation.

Wechsler criticized sharply the original Stanford-Binet assumption that mental ability remains constant during adulthood. Mean scores on almost any mental test rise during early adulthood and decline later. Wechsler therefore developed separate standard-score conversions for adult age groups. In the Stanford-Binet system, where adult norms have not been developed, a given raw score yields the same IQ at all adult ages. In Wechsler's conversion tables, a raw score of 129 yields an IQ of 115 at age 16, 111 at age 20, 114 at age 40, 121 at age 60, and 136 at age 80. Wechsler's other major innovation in scoring was to provide separate standard-score conversions for the Verbal and Performance scales.

Wechsler and SB IQs are not interchangeable. When Bayley (1949) gave the 1937 SB and Wechsler-Bellevue tests to the same group of adolescents, the mean SB IQ was 132 and the mean Wechsler IQ only 122. The Wechsler s.d.'s were also lower. This is confirmed by the fact that in Wechsler's standardization for WISC only half as many children had IQs 130 and over as in the Terman-Merrill standardization. Even clearer evidence (Table 23)

TABLE 23. WISC and SB Results for Representative Children in New York City

	Mean	s.d.	Correlation with SB
Stanford-Binet Form L	108.4	15.8	—
WISC: Full scale	101.2	12.8	.82
Verbal scale	103.4	13.6	.74
Performance scale	98.3	15.0	.64

SOURCE: J. Krugman *et al.*, 1951.

comes from the New York City portion of the WISC standardization data, where 332 children drawn from eighteen schools were tested with both WISC and SB. The SB IQs ran substantially higher and their s.d. was greater (J. Krugman *et al.*, 1951). Since both the WISC and SB scales were standardized on carefully selected samples, it is hard to decide which set of norms is wrong. The best we can do without much more evidence is to recognize that SB IQs average some 7 points higher than Wechsler IQs during childhood and early adulthood.

Wechsler's WAIS standardization data are consistent with his belief that mental ability reaches its peak in early adulthood. In Figure 34, we see that

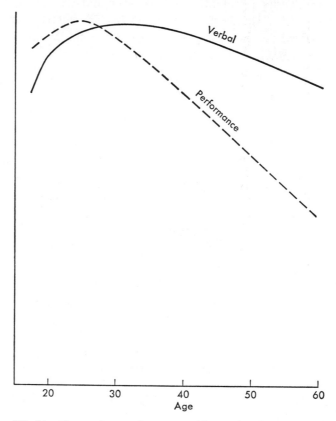

FIG. 34. Changes in mental-test score with age, based on cross-sectional samples for the WAIS (Wechsler, 1955). An arbitrary common scale has been used for plotting the two scores, since raw scores on one scale cannot be compared with raw scores of the other.

the average Performance score has its peak about age 22 and then drops very rapidly. The Verbal average rises until about age 30 and falls off more slowly. The Total score, not plotted, reaches its peak in the late 20's.

Although many other studies give similar curves, this result is no longer accepted as a true picture of the course of intellectual growth and decline. All the studies showing a drop in early adulthood are *cross sectional*, i.e., the average for each age is based on a different group of persons. This means that persons at the two ends of the chart belong to different generations and developed their ability under quite different social circumstances. Anastasi

(1956) points out that Wechsler's older groups have less education than his younger samples, which may account for much of their poorer performance. Bayley (1955) combined evidence from three longitudinal studies in which the same persons were tested on occasions as much as thirty years apart, and concludes that the test scores continue to rise at least until the age of 50. If her curve based on limited samples (and depending on a vocabulary test for many of its points) shows the true pattern of growth in mental ability, Wechsler's norms will soon be outdated (see also Bayley, 1957; Bradway et al. 1958). He proved that, in 1950, adults born in 1910 (age 40) performed worse than adults born in 1920 (age 30). But if Bayley is correct, this latter group will continue to grow, and in 1960 their scores will average much better than Wechsler's 40-year-old sample tested in 1950. Bayley's data suggest that cultural changes are year by year raising the mental ability of the nation.

34. A maze test is available in WISC but not in WAIS. What data would one obtain to decide whether the maze test should be made a part of the WAIS scale?

35. The age curve for the WAIS, based on data gathered in the 1950's, has its peak at a later point than the curve based on the Wechsler-Bellevue standardization in the late thirties. What does this fact imply?

36. Would a vocabulary score be more or less likely than a performance score to improve between ages 20 and 40?

Adequacy as a Measure of General Ability

The Wechsler test, taken as a whole, measures about the same ability as the Stanford-Binet. The correlation of .82 between the two tests reported in Table 23 is fairly representative of the concurrent validity of the Wechsler tests.

The correlations show that the Verbal scale is much more closely related to the SB than is the Performance scale, and in some studies the Verbal scale gives a significantly higher correlation with the SB than does the Full scale. There is, then, a real psychological difference between the Stanford-Binet and the broader Wechsler. In any composite score, however, elements present in only part of the test have far less influence on the total than do elements running all through the test. Abilities to comprehend directions, to concentrate, to criticize and correct one's responses, and to understand words and pictures referring to familiar experiences run through both the Verbal and the Performance scales. These general abilities therefore largely determine the total score on both the Wechsler and Binet tests; specific abilities found only in arithmetic items or performance items have some influence, but not very much.

The reliability of the Full scale of the WAIS is reported by Wechsler as .97

(Wechsler, 1958). This split-half coefficient based on persons of uniform age is spectacularly high; it is reasonable to expect a somewhat lower correlation between tests at two sittings. For the WISC, split-half coefficients are also above .90. There is as yet little evidence on the stability of Wechsler scores; we can expect the total score to be as stable as that from the Stanford-Binet, with the Verbal score more stable than the Performance score (Bayley, 1957). The subtests will probably show different degrees of stability, and such evidence may have important theoretical and practical implications.

37. Clinical psychologists frequently distinguish between a patient's "intellectual equipment" and his "functioning ability." Equipment is thought of, not as in-born capacity, but as the maximum intellectual power the person could sum-mon up at this time. The equipment often does not function at its best, how-ever, because of impulsiveness, inhibition due to anxiety, autistic thinking, and other limitations. This point of view argues that people fall below their true potential to varying degrees.
   a. In terms of these concepts, what does the Wechsler test reveal?
   b. In terms of these concepts, what does the Binet test reveal?
   c. Which of these concepts comes closest to "intelligence"?

The Verbal and Performance Scores

The separate IQs for Verbal and Performance tests measure different abil-ities. This is shown by their correlations with the Stanford-Binet, reported above, and by their correlation with each other. In various age groups Verbal IQ and Performance IQ correlate only .77 to .81, though their split-half re-liabilities are .93 or better.

Most performance tests, taken singly, are extremely unreliable, and even scales combining several tests may be undependable. The high reliability of Wechsler's Performance scale shows that he has done unusually fine test construction. Each performance item requires longer than a verbal item, and it is therefore difficult to obtain as good a sample of ability in limited time. Emotional blocking, carelessness, and undue haste often cause a person to fail a performance item which would otherwise be easy for him. Wechsler has overcome these adverse influences by writing clear directions, using a variety of tasks with several items of each type, and developing precise scor-ing standards. As a result, his Performance scale is probably the most de-pendable nonverbal measure ever developed.

Even though the two scales are highly reliable, the difference between them is less reliable (see p. 287). The Wechsler Verbal and Performance scores are quite accurate, and the difference between them has an estimated reliability of .74. This is high enough to justify drawing conclusions about the person whose Verbal and Performance IQs differ by 15 points or so. Small differences, however, cannot be taken seriously.

When a person does much better on performance tests than on verbal tests, we suspect him of having a language handicap. One who learned English late in life, who has had a very limited education, or who suffers from deafness will perform badly on tests of word knowledge and verbal reasoning, both because of difficulty in understanding the verbal test and because of limited ability to reason verbally. Since performance tasks depend very little on schooling and the directions use simple language, verbal handicaps reduce the score only slightly. Many adults who might be regarded as defective if judged only by their verbal comprehension are able to perform nonverbal tasks at an average level.

Behind this interpretation is the assumption that people who have developed normal performance ability would do equally well in verbal tasks if they had had normal experience. When one can identify restrictive factors in the person's past history, this interpretation can scarcely be denied. Poor verbal ability is easily understood in the case of the child from a bilingual home, the child who has had difficulty in learning to read, and the adult who dropped out of school at an early age. Many others, however, show Verbal-Performance differences where no handicap can be identified. The psychologist is unable to say whether such differences are due to unidentified background factors or to some innate lack of specialized verbal aptitudes.

While verbal handicaps are easily identified, there is rarely such an obvious handicap to explain the cases where Performance IQ is well below Verbal. Some poor performances are accounted for by emotional blocking. A performance test demands a longer period of steady work and sometimes a series of trial-and-error operations; the person who becomes upset will perform erratically. No comparable blocking occurs in short-answer verbal questions where the person's failures are less obvious to him, although it is sometimes observed in the Arithmetic subtest. A painstaking, cautious performance will lower the Performance score. Such undue caution is interpreted as having emotional origins.

Sometimes the verbal score is elevated by an artificially cultivated vocabulary. Some parents encourage children to build large vocabularies, and some students and adults make a great effort to learn new words. The tester sometimes observes in such subjects a love of big words and an effort to give impressively complicated answers to simple questions. The person who has a one-sided verbal development often does better on recall questions (Information, Vocabulary) than on items demanding independent thought (Comprehension, Similarities).

Since there is no single interpretation for any pattern of Verbal-Performance differences, such a difference is merely a signal to the tester that further data on the case are needed. A study of the test performance as observed, an inquiry into the person's background, and usually supplementary tests are required to arrive at a deeper understanding of the difference.

38. Digit Symbol is an exception to the finding that delinquents do better on Performance tests than nondelinquents. There is, in fact, a significant difference in the opposite direction. How can this be explained?
39. Wechsler deliberately included subtests which are susceptible to emotional influences in his measure of "intelligence." In your opinion, does this increase or decrease the usefulness of the test?
40. Bill and John, two 15-year-olds, are referred to the school psychologist because both are failing in ninth-grade work, their courses being social studies, English, general science, and art appreciation. Both have IQs of 93, but Bill has a Verbal IQ of 95 and a Performance IQ of 92, while John has a Verbal IQ of 87 and a Performance IQ of 106. How would the interpretations and suggestions for dealing with the two boys differ?
41. A relatively low Performance IQ suggests emotional disturbance. When Verbal IQ is lower than Performance IQ, can we conclude that the person is well adjusted? (Consider Mark, p. 191, in this connection.)

Interpretation of Subtests and Profiles

The Wechsler scale is neatly organized into subtests, and many attempts have been made to develop separate interpretations of the several subtests. The meaning of subtest scores is not reducible to such simple translations as "Low Vocabulary means poor ability to deal with symbols." Vocabulary is affected by the subject's acquaintance with our verbal culture, including schooling, and his ability to express himself, which may be impeded by emotion. It differs from Similarities in that Vocabulary can be passed on the basis of recall, whereas Similarities requires reorganizing information. The elements that influence each particular subtest can be known only through great experience with the test and study of the research literature.

Wechsler finds some association between patterns of subtest scores and particular types of mental disorder, and has recommended the test for clinical diagnosis. Many clinicians have developed special formulas of their own for combining subtest scores into indices supposedly characteristic of brain-damaged patients, schizophrenics, etc. As an illustration of these clinical hypotheses we may quote Schafer's description of the pattern found in psychopathic character disorder (1948, p. 54):

The characteristic pattern is a superiority of the Performance level over the Verbal, low scores on Comprehension and Similarities and high scores on the tests of visual-motor coordination and speed [Object Assembly, BD, Digit Symbol]. Often the Digit Span score does not drop, reflecting the characteristic blandness. Frequently Picture Arrangement is conspicuously high. This is especially true for shrewd "schemers." If Picture Completion is high, over-alertness or watchfulness is probably characteristic. . . .
Qualitatively the chief feature is usually blazing recklessness in guessing at

answers. . . . "George Bernard Shaw wrote Faust," "Magellan discovered the North Pole," "Chattel means a place to live (chateau)," "Ballast is a dance (ballet)," "Proselyte means prostitute," and so forth. . . . The over-all pattern will indicate that this is a bland, unreflective, action-oriented person whose judgment is poor, whose conceptual development is weak, but whose grasp of social situations may yet be quick and accurate.

Some of the proposals for diagnostic interpretation have been little more than plausible guesses or generalizations from small, unrepresentative samples. Even the suggestions based on sound research have limited practical value, primarily because they rest on unreliable difference scores. Only unusually large differences between subtests (greater than 3 scaled-score units) should be taken seriously (Wechsler, 1958, p. 164).

There is theoretical justification for expecting brain damage to impede one type of performance more than another, or for expecting psychopaths to suffer where pretentious, incautious responses are penalized. The effect of personality is masked, however, by the influence of general mental ability, other aptitudes and experience factors, attitudes in taking the test, and random errors. Many studies agree that on the average schizophrenics have Verbal IQs higher than Performance. But when we look at Rapaport's data (1945, Appendix II), we find that only 31 out of his 72 schizophrenics have Verbal IQs five points or more above the Performance IQ. Even among the highway patrolmen used as a comparison ("normal") group, 18 out of 54 showed this "sign."

Basing diagnosis on multiple signs reduces errors of classification, but rarely does a patient show all the signs of his class. At best, one can hope to find statistical trends which distinguish *groups* of psychopaths (for example) from other groups. No objective treatment of the Wechsler scores has proved able to classify individual patients with a useful degree of accuracy. Indices representing "scatter" of subtest scores—e.g., the range from highest to lowest subtest score—are worthless as diagnostic signs (Patterson, 1953, pp. 41–76).

It will be noted that Schafer did not propose to identify psychopaths by a numerical treatment of subtest scores. He examined the *nature* of the errors and successes to arrive at a qualitative picture of the personality. The Wechsler scale is in some ways superior to other tests or interview procedures as an aid in forming such impressions, because the questions are the same for all subjects, are varied, and elicit highly revealing responses. If the clinician wishes to describe the subject, he should consider the Wechsler subtests individually and qualitatively (with due awareness that he may be interpreting random variation). The clinician must not regard an impression formed in this manner as a diagnosis. The impression is useful, but it is not a scientific conclusion. The Wechsler yields a general measure of mental ability and a verbal-performance difference, and beyond that can offer hints leading to further study of the individual.

Before going on to a more general discussion of performance tests, we can summarize briefly the virtues and defects of the Wechsler scale. It is efficiently designed, interesting to most subjects, and at least as valid for predictive purposes as the Stanford-Binet. It covers a broader range of tasks and affords exceptionally good opportunities for qualitative observation of behavior and thought processes. The norms for the test, once a point of serious criticism, have been greatly improved. As a practical individual test, the Wechsler falls short in only one particular: the scale has insufficient range to measure very high and very low abilities dependably.

The test is, however, a distillation of clinical experience, and this contributes both to its strength and to its weakness. It is a useful sample of complex behavior in which emotional and intellectual factors are entwined. But it is based on no clear theory of intelligence and makes no serious effort to separate mental ability from other aspects of adaptation. The tasks are chosen from techniques invented thirty years or more ago, and there is no adequate rationale for interpreting the subtest scores. It is reasonable to hope that some future worker will start from a theory of mental processes, choose or design tests to measure those particular processes, and so arrive at a superior diagnostic device. The total score on such a test would almost certainly correlate substantially with Wechsler's.

42. Many clinicians have tried to select an abbreviated test from the Wechsler series so as to obtain a quick measure of ability, though one of inferior reliability (McNemar, 1950). What would you consider in deciding which three subtests to use? Which three subtests seem best to you for this purpose?

43. Is a high or a low correlation between subtests desirable in a general mental test?

44. What description of the patient's thought processes is suggested by each of these responses to "Why should we keep away from bad company?" (Schafer, 1948).
   a. Your friends will talk about you; if we want to live in a good environment we must choose good company. (IQ = 107)
   b. I don't know if that necessarily holds true. To prevent picking up their bad habits, I guess. (IQ = 123)
   c. It's a trend toward living the same kind of a life, get bad yourself. (IQ = 127)

45. Match the responses in the preceding question to these answers to "Why do we have laws?" given by the same set of patients.
   a. Govern the behavior of people. [E queries.] There has to be some maintenance of order by which government policies are carried out as well as personal behavior of individuals.
   b. To have a law-abiding group of people; otherwise they would corrupt the city.
   c. To make good citizens out of us; to keep the unruly under control.

46. Harper (1950), comparing 245 schizophrenics to 237 normals, established reliable differences between subtests. A formula for combining standard scores on subtests is offered: .28 Inf − .15 Comp + .17 DSp − .19 Pic Com + .25 BD − .35 DSym (+ other small terms). A "cutting score" halfway between the mean for normals and the mean for schizophrenics was used. In a new sample, 68 percent of schizophrenics fell beyond the cutting score. The formula is thus shown to be truly discriminating. In view of the large number of misclassifications, what value does the formula have in practice?

47. According to Harper's formula, schizophrenic profiles tend to have a high point on Block Design and a low point on Digit Symbol.
   a. Can you explain this?
   b. Could you give an equally convincing explanation if the opposite had been found?

48. What advantage would there be in using an "intelligence" test to diagnose abnormal personalities, over using a "personality" test having similar validity for that purpose? Would this argument hold if the "personality" test had definitely higher validity for diagnosing such cases?

WHAT PERFORMANCE TESTS MEASURE

There is no need to describe performance tests other than the Wechsler in detail. Some, like the Arthur scale, are collections of tests covering a variety of performances. Others, like the original Kohs Block Design Test (see p. 41) or the Porteus mazes (p. 29) are devoted to a single type of item.

Some performance tests are better measures of general ability than others, either because they are more reliable or because they make a greater intellectual demand. Simple timed formboards demand manipulative speed more than thought and have rather low correlation with general ability. In the WAIS the tests which correlate highest with the Performance IQ are Block Design and Picture Completion. Digit Symbol actually correlates higher with the Verbal IQ than with the Performance IQ (Wechsler, 1958, p. 255).

Cultural Influences

Frequently it has been claimed that performance tests are "culture free." A "culture-free" test is one on which scores are completely uninfluenced by experience in a particular environment. Such a test would give a fair comparison of mental abilities in different countries and across different social classes.

Educational handicaps show up directly in a verbal test. This is illustrated by tests on English "canal-boat children," who live a nomadic life and have an impoverished, unintellectual environment. Binet tests correlated .58 with educational level, but a performance test correlated only .26. The performance IQs were about 10 points higher (Gaw, 1925).

The skills involved in performance tests are developed through learning, and every culture provides some amount of training along the lines tested. Egyptian psychologists examined mental development in a primitive tribe living on the edge of the desert (Fahmy, 1954). They found that scores on most performance tests were quite a bit below the European average for children of the same age. On a test, however, which called for assembly of colored mosaics (similar to Block Design) these children averaged slightly above the European norms. Color plays a large part in the ceremonies of this culture and in the children's games. This evidently helps their test performance by giving them experience in examining patterns or by developing their interest in such tasks. (See also Havighurst et al., 1946.)

Training in particular types of discrimination and reasoning probably influences only a few performance measures. The subtle effects on attitude and motivation are likely to affect all tests. The educated classes in America, in Europe, and in nations influenced by Western civilization are taught from early childhood to take intellectual matters seriously. The child is rewarded for answering adults' seemingly pointless questions. He shares puzzles and word games with his playmates, and these experiences also cause him to take artificial problems seriously. These activities teach an attitude of self-criticalness and competitiveness.

There have been many attempts to compare the mental abilities of various nations and racial groups by means of performance tests or translated verbal tests. Differences in average performance are found in most studies, but the differences are fairly small. In every group tested a large proportion does better than the average of the white sample used in standardizing the tests. This is evidence in itself that no one racial group has a monopoly on talent. Precise comparisons of group averages have no practical importance, but they might be of great scientific importance if tests were equally fair to all groups. It is now generally agreed that no universal test for measuring mental ability can be developed. Any test calls for habits and attitudes which some cultures favor and other cultures inhibit. The test shows how well persons tested have developed *along those lines,* not how they rank on all tasks or how bright they are innately.[3]

49. In what ways, if any, might cultural differences affect performance on each of the following tests?
   a. Formboards (fitting blocks into variously shaped holes)
   b. Wechsler Picture Arrangement
   c. Porteus mazes

---

[3] Racial comparisons have frequently been misinterpreted because liberal writers want to prove that there are no innate differences in ability, and certain conservatives want to prove that nonwhite groups will not profit from improved educational opportunity. Balanced accounts of the many studies and of their possible interpretations are given in L. Tyler, 1956, pp. 276–309, and Anastasi, 1958, pp. 542–575.

Emotional Influences

Performance tests generally demand a longer period of sustained attention than the shorter items of individual verbal tests. This provides a greater opportunity for confusion or frustration to build up, and as a result the performance test is more likely to reflect emotional disturbance. Porteus (1950) discusses two studies of boys and girls in a reformatory, where maladjusted delinquents were compared with law-abiding, well-behaved inmates. In both studies, the adjusted and maladjusted groups had similar Binet IQs, but on the Porteus maze the maladjusted group dropped about 10 points below the others. Another study found that group psychotherapy raises the Porteus MA of schizophrenic patients by two years (H. N. Peters and F. D. Jones, 1951). This suggests that the psychotherapy releases ability previously suppressed by emotional conflicts.

Practical Correlates

The fact that performance tests are relatively independent of educational background raises their validity for some purposes and lowers it for others. When a tester is trying to predict subsequent educational achievement, the verbal test is likely to be more informative. Whatever handicaps depress the verbal score will also interfere with future attainment in most schooling, as was noted in E. L. Thorndike's comment (p. 189). He went on to voice the common expectation that a less verbal test would be a better predictor of practical adjustment. There is some evidence to support this view. In one study, the adjustment of borderline mental defectives in the community correlated .77 with their Porteus maze scores, but only .57 with Binet scores (Porteus, 1939). An earlier study used ratings of the efficiency of children in a school for the mentally retarded as criteria. There were separate ratings on "educational efficiency" and "industrial efficiency" (i.e., performance in occupational training). The Binet predicted the former much better than the maze (the respective correlations being .81 and .59 for girls). But the Binet predicted the trade-performance criterion less well (.66 vs. .75) (Berry and Porteus, 1920). One might expect the Wechsler Verbal score to correlate higher with school success than the Performance score. The only predictive correlations reported, however, show nearly equal correlations for the two scores (.62 and .65 respectively; Frandsen and Higginson, 1951. See also Mussen et al., 1952). Further investigations are needed to check and explain this finding.

The performance test has special importance in the clinic. Performance tests generally depend less on habit and more on ability to attack a new problem. They therefore are quicker to reflect the adverse effects of emotional disturbance or brain damage, and perhaps quicker to reveal the effects of therapeutic treatment. In cross-sectional studies of aging, for example, nonlanguage tests begin to decline in the 20's, whereas verbal ability holds almost constant until the mid-40's. When radical brain surgery is performed in an attempt to aid a psychotic, we might expect his intellectual performance to be affected. His MA on the Binet or Wechsler Full scale or on a group test will not be changed in any predictable way, the average change being negligible. His MA on the Porteus mazes will show an immediate drop of about 2 years, though it will ultimately recover and rise far above the original level (Mettler, 1949). This change is consistent with the clinical picture. The patient's personality shifts from a depressed, worried state to a carefree, adaptable state in which he gives little thought to the future. He then gradually stabilizes his behavior in a socially constructive pattern. The postoperative loss of planning and foresight is observed in his maze performance, and it of course leads to error. A similar decline appears in Object Assembly and Digit Symbol. No impairment is found in the Verbal tests or in Block Design, Picture Completion, and Digit Span.

Since performance tests involve spatial and perceptual abilities which predict success in certain types of jobs (see Chapter 10), they might have some significance for vocational guidance. As a factor analysis of the Wechsler to be reported later shows (p. 264), however, its subscores do not reveal these separate abilities clearly. Other general performance tests are even less satisfactory as measures of special ability. Tests which provide purer measures of specialized aptitudes will generally give better information for occupational choice.

50. If it were practical to use an individual test for selecting Army officers, would a verbal or a performance test be preferable?

51. Comment on this statement: "A person's true level of mental ability is shown by whichever IQ, verbal or performance, is higher."

52. Leona Tyler (1956, p. 10) makes this statement about performance tests and nonverbal tests: "If they are worth less to us than we expected as *substitutes* for the typical verbal intelligence test, they are worth more as supplements." What evidence justifies this statement? What implications does it have for planning a testing program?

NOTEWORTHY INDIVIDUAL TESTS

The Wechsler scale, combining as it does a good performance measure with a good verbal measure, has almost entirely replaced earlier performance batteries. Among general-purpose predictors, the Wechsler and the Stanford-Binet are equally prominent, with no other serious competitor. Our summary of important individual tests, then, would have few entries if the criterion for admission were wide use at the present time. Attention needs to be drawn, however, to some little-used tests of good quality, and to tests mentioned in the basic research studies of earlier days. Revisions of some of these tests are being made, and they may again become prominent.

Each listing below gives the title of the test, the authors, the publisher, and the date of major editions (including always the earliest and latest); ages or grades for which suited; remarks about nature, purpose, and quality. In preparing these statements, the writer has relied heavily but not exclusively on comments made by reviewers for the Buros yearbooks.

● Columbia Mental Maturity Scale; B. Burgomeister, L. H. Blum, Irving Lorge; World Book, 1953. Ages 3 to 12. Each item consists of three or more drawings printed on a large card. The child points to the one which does not belong with the others. Well suited to testing physically handicapped children. Though the test is brief, reliabilities near .90 are reported. Correlates about .75 with the Stanford-Binet.

● Draw-a-Man Test; Florence Goodenough; World Book, 1926. Ages 1 to 10. The child is asked to draw the best man he can. Scoring takes into account the basic structure of the drawing (e.g., are the arms attached to the trunk?) and details of features, clothing, etc. This is a simple test to administer, and scoring rules were carefully prepared. Though the Draw-a-Man can be applied in all cultures, it is dependent on cultural influences. Some comparable tests (e.g., House-Tree-Person) are used as a technique for examining personality, rather than as a measure of intellectual development alone.

● Leiter International Performance Scale; Russell G. Leiter; C. H. Stoelting, 1936, 1948. Ages 2 to 18. The tasks require perceptual matching, analogies, memory, and other varied items, many of them similar to verbal tests. The test is given with very simple directions (spoken or pantomime), and the items themselves require no language. The test has many excellent features, being especially suited to handicapped children. The IQ conversions are of questionable accuracy at preschool levels.

● Merrill-Palmer Scale; Rachel Stutsman; Stoelting, 1931. Ages 2 to 5. A scale for preschool children using interesting games, puzzles, pictures, etc. Language questions are simple tests of comprehension ("What cries?"). Some tests involve dexterity (cutting with scissors). Speed is heavily emphasized. The technical quality and content of the 1931 version compares unfavorably with the Stanford-Binet.

● Minnesota Preschool Scale; Florence Goodenough, Kathryn Maurer, M. J. van Wagenen; Educational Test Bureau, 1932, 1940. Ages 1½ to 6. Verbal comprehension and memory tests are used in a verbal score. A nonverbal scale includes form recognition, tracing, picture completion, block building, and simple puzzles. Some long-term follow-up studies of predictive validity have been made. This is an accurate test for ages 3 to 5, but not one with great appeal for the child.

- Pintner-Paterson Scale of Performance Tests; Rudolf Pintner and D. G. Paterson; Psychological Corporation, 1927. Ages 4 to 16. This was the first substantial performance battery. It included object assembly, formboards, and Healy Picture Completion (pictures to be completed by fitting in blocks). It played a major part in research and clinical work prior to the development of the Wechsler scale. Scores depend heavily on speed, and reliability is unsatisfactory.

- Point Scale of Performance Tests; Grace A. Arthur; Stoelting, Psychological Corporation, 1925, 1947. Ages 4½ years to adult. One of the best collections of performance tests standardized on the same sample. Includes formboards, maze, block design, etc. MAs tend to be lower than SB MAs owing to defects in the standardization.

- Stanford-Binet Scale; L. M. Terman and Maud A. Merrill; Houghton Mifflin, 1916, 1937, 1960. Ages 2½ years to adult. (See pp. 163 ff.)

- Valentine Intelligence Tests for Children; C. W. Valentine; Methuen, 1945, 1953. Ages 1½ to 15. A British scale combining items from well-tried sources (Gesell, Burt-Binet, Stanford-Binet, Merrill-Palmer, etc.). Generally regarded as a superior test for preschool ages, though its standardization is inadequate.

- Wechsler Intelligence Scales; David Wechsler; Psychological Corporation, 1940, 1955. WISC, 5–15 years; WAIS, 16 years to adult. (See pp. 191 ff.)

TESTS OF INFANT DEVELOPMENT

Tests such as we have discussed to this point set a task for the child and observe how well he can perform it. Such a method cannot be applied to the infant, who does not comprehend instructions and has not learned to do things on command. Tests of early development consist primarily of observations of the child's response to stimulation.

The basic aim of most of the scales has been to determine whether the child is showing the developments normal for his age, rather than to assess mental level specifically. We cannot test a 1-year-old on abstract thinking; we don't even know whether he is doing it at this age. We cannot test the 3-year-old on complex reasoning, because he has not developed adequate sustained attention and understanding of directions to attempt the problem. Investigators have concentrated on those aspects of behavior which can be identified objectively in the young child. Bayley, in her definitive study (1933), used a composite of 185 items from existing scales, of which the following are representative. The number in parentheses is the scale placement —the age in months at which the development is normally found.

(0.6) Lateral head movements, prone.
(1.4) Vertical eye coordination.

(3.0) Reaches for ring.
(3.6) Manipulates table edge.
(5.5) Discriminates strangers.
(5.9) Vocalizes pleasure.
(6.6) Lifts cup by handle.
(8.6) Says *da-da* or equivalent.
(9.3) Fine prehension.
(9.9) Rings bell purposefully.

(13.5) Makes tower of two cubes.
(16.6) Turns pages.
(20.1) Square or triangle in Gesell formboard, reversed.
(21.5) Names three objects.

(25.0) Understands two prepositions.
(28.4) Picture completion.
(34.6) Copies circle; one success on three trials required.
(35.6) Remembers one of four pictures.

The heavy emphasis on sensorimotor development in the infant tests makes it impossible to interpret them as measures of mental ability. As Boynton comments (Monroe, 1941, p. 629), "When the Linfert-Hierholzer Scale attempts to measure intelligence in terms of the child's ability to follow visually a ball or to use a spoon in eating, or when Charlotte Bühler looks for intelligence in a child's smile or in the fact that he seeks a lost toy, it is apparent that the procedure involves matters which neither the layman nor the psychologist would regard as integral aspects of intelligence at a later age." One way of meeting this objection is to regard the data as meaningful in their own right, as showing what the infant is doing. Information about the normal development of coördination, for example, may be important for the pediatrician who must recognize and diagnose disease, dietary deficiency, or abnormality. Data about development of sensorimotor behavior may be important for psychological theory also.

Most investigators, however, have wanted to forecast mental development. The psychologist dealing with placement of children for adoption, for example, desires a good early measure of mental ability. A good mental measure early in infancy might also be of value in identifying certain types of mental defect which can be overcome by early application of appropriate drugs. For such applications, the validity of the infant test as a mental test must be examined.

The correlations in Table 21 (p. 176) show that tests in the first two years, where the items are predominantly sensorimotor in type, have negligible correlations with tests at school age. A test at age 2 or 3, however, has fair ability to forecast school-age intelligence.

The rise in correlation is to some extent a reflection of increase in reliability with age. Tests for very young children are apt to be unreliable, in the first place, because the child's attentiveness and alertness fluctuate. Even if enough items are used to obtain a good estimate of his status in a given week, his standard score shifts markedly from month to month. All infants show unexplained spurts of development. The child may forge ahead rapidly in locomotor ability and then remain at the same level with no further change for weeks. Moreover, he may make progress in only one area at a time, improving his vocabulary while his coördination shows no further advance or vice versa.

Accuracy of measurement can be increased by using more items, or by combining estimates made in successive months. J. E. Anderson (1939, p. 376) suggests other precautions to increase the dependability of the measures:

> The earlier . . . the measurements are made, the less reliance can be placed on a single measurement or observation, if that measurement or observation is used for predicting subsequent development.
>
> The earlier . . . the measurements are made, the greater care should be taken to secure accuracy of observation and record and to follow standardized procedures.
>
> The earlier . . . the measurements are made, the more account should be taken of the possibility of disturbing factors, such as negativism and refusals, that operate as constant errors to reduce score.
>
> Since development is a timed series of relations or sequences, there are for many functions periods below which only a small portion of the function can be measured and above which a progressively larger portion can be measured. Hence, the possibilities of prediction are limited and progression with age is not an infallible indicator of the value of a measurement. Every effort should be expended to secure the most accurate and predictive tests by standardizing tests against multiple [criteria, particularly measures of ability in later life] rather than against single criteria.

This last point is at the heart of the difficulty. If the functions that constitute intelligence cannot be observed early in the child's life, substituting a measure of nonintellectual functions is no solution. We must wait until purposeful problem solving is present; more than that, we must wait until these types of behavior are reasonably well stabilized, since measures made while a type of behavior is just emerging are notoriously unreliable. This conclusion is supported by the results of Maurer, cited earlier, that observations of undirected behavior are not predictive of later IQ, but suitably chosen task performance is. Since tasks cannot be set for the child much below the age of 2, there is little hope of predicting the IQ from tests in infancy.

A much more optimistic but still cautious position on infant testing is taken by Escalona (1950). She regards the test as an opportunity to observe the functioning of the whole organism in "a situation which has structural and dynamic properties"; i.e., she turns away from an attempt at exact measurement of a single attribute and uses the test to enrich an impressionistic observation. Her position is influenced both by the field theory of Kurt Lewin and by the psychoanalytic approach to test interpretation represented by Rapaport and Schafer. She considers the child's total social response, management of his body, and attention pattern in Gesell's tests, and tries to judge his development qualitatively. One case she describes as follows:

An infant was first seen at the age of three months. At that time he gave every evidence of making unusually good developmental progress, earning test scores which placed him in the accelerated range. He was characterized by a very high activity level, bodily activity increased markedly in response to all stimulation. His capacity to tolerate delay or frustration seemed lower than that of most infants of the same age. At the three months age level, test performance reflects primarily gross motor coordination, vigorous responsiveness to stimulation and perceptual discrimination. At a later age, however, tests are designed so as to also elicit fine motor coordination which requires inhibition of impulse, as well as problem solving behavior which implies delay in attaining a goal.

A prediction was made that the child tended toward immediate discharge of tension, would probably find tasks calling for inhibition of impulses frustrating, and would be likely to earn only an average IQ on the later tests.

The child was retested at 9 months and at 22 months. On both occasions he was again noted to be a more than ordinarily active child. His total IQ dropped from the superior to the average range. Items requiring fine motor coördination and those requiring a playful and indirect approach to a goal were passed at a low level or were refused altogether. Verbal items and those requiring immediate grasp of a problem, however, were performed at high average and superior levels. Gross motor coördination remained outstandingly good.

In many instances the tester can judge whether a child has performed at his best. Escalona divides children into two categories in this respect. Those whose tests are judged "optimum" change their standing very little on tests a year or so later. No prediction can be made for those whose tests are judged nonoptimal. There are many large changes in this group.

Here we have a characteristic contrast between the psychometric and the impressionistic approach to testing. The psychometric criteria applied by Bayley indicate almost no predictive value in infant tests. Escalona's clinical method is said to give not only a statement of developmental level which is predictive in many cases but also a qualitative description of strong and weak points. There is no reason to question the correctness of either viewpoint. It is obvious, however, that not just any impressionistic interpretation can be depended upon. Until Escalona communicates the observational cues and the theory she uses to interpret tests, and until the various interpretations have been checked by systematic research, her method cannot be used by others.

53. Characterize the abilities used within each year level of Bayley's scale (assuming that the items listed are characteristic).
54. How do the abilities tested in her scale differ from those tested in the Stanford-Binet?
55. To what extent would differences in experience give some children an advantage on the tasks listed?

Important Infant Tests

● California First-Year Mental Scale; Nancy Bayley; University of California Press, 1933. Ages 1 to 18 months. A set of items chosen from other scales and standardized by retesting the same group of about fifty infants repeatedly. More data are available on this scale, taken as a whole, than on other infant tests.

● Cattell Infant Intelligence Scale; Psyche Cattell; Psychological Corporation, 1947. Ages 2 to 30 months. This is an attempt to extend the Stanford-Binet downward. Items are somewhat more complex than those in other schedules, but at the youngest ages simple perceptual responses (e.g., looking at a moving person) are counted. The test at age 1 correlates as high as .56 with SB IQ at age 3 but has very low correlations with school-age IQ (Cavanaugh *et al.*, 1957). It has no predictive value before the first birthday.

● Gesell Developmental Schedules; Arnold Gesell and others; Psychological Corporation, 1925, 1949. Ages 4 weeks to 6 years. A schedule of behaviors divided into four areas: motor, adaptive, language, and personal-social. The child is stimulated, e.g., by placing a block in front of him, and his reactions are compared with expectations for his age. The standardization, reliability, and interpretation of scores are open to question. As Anastasi says (1954, p. 283), "These schedules may be regarded as a refinement and elaboration of the qualitative observations routinely made by pediatricians."

● Griffiths Mental Development Scale; Ruth Griffiths; University of London Press, 1954. Ages 0–2 years. Five carefully prepared scales, using original items together with those of Gesell and others, measure locomotor, personal-social, hearing-speech, hand-eye, and performance developments. The total scale includes 260 items and permits more reliable measurement than any other instrument. Retest reliability with more than a six-month interval is .87 (Griffiths, 1954). Too little research is available to evaluate the scale at present.

Suggested Readings

Anastasi, Anne. Race differences: methodological problems. *Differential psychology.* (3rd ed.) New York: Macmillan, 1958. Pp. 542–575.

An authoritative discussion of the proper interpretation of studies comparing test scores of racial groups includes some representative findings. The subsequent chapters review several major investigations, particularly of differences between Negroes and whites.

Brown, Elinor W. Observing behavior during the intelligence test. In Eugene Lerner & Lois B. Murphy (eds.), Methods for the study of personality in young children. *Monogr., Soc. Res. in Child Developm.*, 1941, 6, (4), 268–283.

Responses of two 4-year-olds to the Stanford-Binet are presented to show that performance depends on personality and response to the examiner, as well as on intellect. Students should read this protocol if they have not seen a demonstration of individual mental testing.

Richards, T. W. Mental test performance as a reflection of the child's current life situation: a methodological study. *Child Developm.*, 1951, 22, 221–233. (Reprinted in Eugene L. Hartley & Ruth E. Hartley, eds., *Outside readings in psychology*, 2nd ed. New York: Crowell, 1958. Pp. 260–273.)

A child's Binet performance from age 3 to age 10 fluctuated from IQ 115 to IQ 140. Richards traces observation records, parent attitudes, and personality tests to show a correspondence between test changes and changes in the pressures and satisfactions in the child's life.

Schofield, William. Critique of scatter and profile analysis of psychometric data. *J. clin. Psychol.*, 1952, 8, 16–22.

Schofield reviews the studies claiming to find information in Wechsler profile shape that can be used for clinical diagnosis. Wishful thinking, accompanied by inadequate research design, is blamed for the widespread and unjustified faith in profile interpretation. The faults in this research should be noted in planning any validation study.

Terman, Lewis M. The discovery and encouragement of exceptional talent. *Amer. Psychologist*, 1954, 9, 221–230. (Reprinted in Don E. Dulany, Jr., & others, eds., *Contributions to modern psychology.* New York: Oxford University Press, 1958. Pp. 51–65. Also in H. H. Remmers & others, eds., *Growth, teaching, and learning.* New York: Harper, 1957. Pp. 63–77.)

This lecture surveys some of the principal American work with mental tests, including Terman's follow-up of exceptional children. Terman reviews the childhood differences between those who succeeded in later life and those whose careers were mediocre, emphasizing the cultural factors that bring talent to fruition.

8

Group Tests of General Ability

GROUP tests are used far more extensively than individual tests because of their economy and practicality. Particularly in dealing with masses of subjects, whether in the Army, industry, schools, or research, group tests are indispensable. The better group tests are as reliable as comparable individual tests, and for many objectives they have equally good predictive validity. Moreover, they do not require specially trained testers.

The group test is based on the assumption that subjects understand the nature and purpose of testing, and that each wants to do his best. Wherever these ideal conditions are not met, the scores of some individuals will be invalid. The individual test gives the examiner a good chance to note that the subject is ill, unduly tense, or confused by the directions, and thus the experienced examiner can recognize when the score is invalid. In the group test, a standard procedure is applied, and no special consideration can be given to individuals. The group test is the practical solution to the problem of obtaining information when large numbers of individuals must be considered at once—for example, in classifying recruits or identifying pupils who cannot keep up with the normal pace. Wherever the important objective is to make decisions which are correct on the average, the group test is suitable. Wherever the primary consideration is thorough understanding of the individual, the flexibility and intimacy of the individual test make it much more satisfactory. In schools, group tests are often used as a preliminary device to identify pupils to be studied individually.

REPRESENTATIVE INSTRUMENTS

Most of the early group tests were based on the "omnibus" or hodge podge principle of the Binet scale. The test mixed a great variety of problems so that specialized abilities called for by certain questions (e.g., arithmetic) had very little influence compared to the general ability required by all the problems. As the makers of the famous Army Alpha Examination put it, the ideal was to find tests all related to the criterion and having very little relation to each other. The omnibus test with items in haphazard order or with many short subtests was the most common type of group test until the 1940's. Such a test was used to obtain just one score, a measure of general ability. Many recent tests are designed so that sections can be scored and interpreted separately.

Instead of using the omnibus test where specific abilities tend to cancel each other, some British workers limited their group tests to items thought to be pure measures of general ability. Charles Spearman was the leading spirit in an attempt to isolate the essence of general ability by finding items which measured general ability and nothing else. In the course of this work he invented *factor analysis,* a statistical method which plays a large part in current test development (see Chapter 9). We need not at this point elaborate on Spearman's method beyond saying that, in effect, he looked for items which correlate with all other types of mental-test items. The best measures of "*g*" or general ability, according to Spearman's research, were abstract reasoning problems. Like Binet before him, Spearman studied his items in an attempt to formulate a definition of what his test measured. He concluded that g consists of facility in "apprehension of one's own experience, the eduction of relations, and the eduction of correlates"—i.e., in making observations and extracting general principles.

A Homogeneous Test: Matrices

The matrix item is the single most popular technique for measuring mental ability, although it is better known abroad than in the United States. This item was invented by L. S. Penrose and J. C. Raven in England and published as Raven's Progressive Matrices Test in 1938. Raven, following Spearman's theory, desired to measure the ability to perceive relationships. The matrix item is a "two-dimensional" analogies problem, as illustrated in Figure 35. The subject is directed only to select the design that completes the pattern. The figures are altered from left to right according to one principle, from top to bottom by another. The subject must identify these principles and apply them to determine the needed design.

The matrix principle is highly flexible. The possible range of difficulty is enormous, as can be seen in the examples given. The test may be administered individually or in groups, and may be speeded or given with liberal time allowance. For testing less mature subjects, the items can be presented as a series of formboards where the subject actually chooses a block and fits it into the blank space. The directions are very simple, so that verbal understanding plays little part. Indeed, with very easy initial items, the test can be administered in pantomime so that the verbal element is entirely eliminated.

No one form of the matrix test is used widely. Since items are rather easy to prepare, psychologists in all parts of the world have developed tests of their own. These versions can be used for hiring employees or selecting students for special courses, with little fear that the items will become known in advance. The disadvantage of this variation is the lack of comprehensive data on any one form. The published version of the Progressive Matrices is

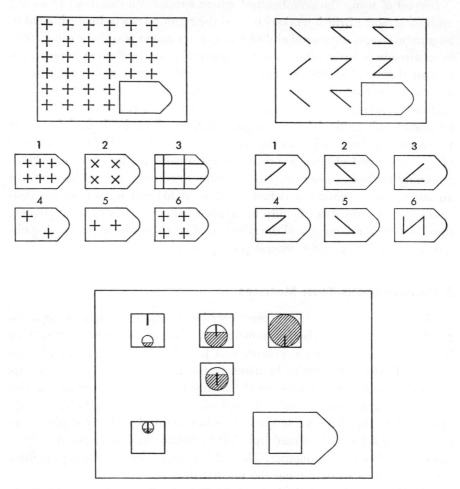

FIG. 35. Matrix items at three levels of difficulty. The first and second items are like those in the Progressive Matrices, being of the usual difficulty. The third item is a very difficult matrix in free-response form, designed for testing college graduates.

available in the United States, but its standardization is poor. The norms for the group test are based on 1407 children (in half-year age groups) and 3665 militiamen and 2192 civilians (in five-year groups). These are English cases, and no further description is given. For general clinical and educational testing, inability to compare a given case to acceptable American norms is a serious drawback. For selection within a group of job applicants, of course, norms are of very little importance.

The matrix test has a sizable correlation with individual tests. For children, the correlation with SB is about .60 (Keir, 1949). For an adult sample, Wechsler Performance correlates .70 and Wechsler Verbal .58 with Matrices (J. Hall, 1957; see also Martin and Weichers, 1954). The subtest having the highest correlation with Matrices is Block Design. Obviously, the matrix items are relatively independent of the educational attainments which affect the Binet and the Verbal score, though Ombredane *et al.* (1956), in studying underdeveloped African tribes, found that test scores were affected by level of education. Raven suggests that in practical testing the matrix measure of ability to solve new problems be supplemented by a measure of *past* attainment, such as vocabulary. This is especially important for persons whose efficiency is impaired by old age, emotional disturbance, etc.

The Raven Matrices were adopted as the principal test for military classification in Great Britain during World War II. This nonverbal test was chosen to make sure that normally intelligent recruits were not rejected because of poor education. The fact that the matrix is so nearly a pure test of one ability limited its military usefulness. Tests combining general, verbal, and numerical abilities proved to be better predictors of performance in training courses. Specialized spatial-mechanical tests such as the Bennett generally made a better contribution to prediction of success in mechanical jobs. The matrix test was most helpful in predicting performance in visual signalling and radar operating (Vernon and Parry, 1949, pp. 235, 244). Experience such as this has led the practical tester to give more attention to the specialized abilities than formerly. A relatively pure measure of *g* is not usually as good a predictor as a composite of *g* with verbal, spatial, or the other abilities required by the course or job to which the person is assigned. One of the reasons Binet's test was highly successful was that it called for the specialized abilities in about the same combination that schooling itself did. It is therefore a better predictor of school adjustment than a purer test might be.

The purely nonverbal score, however, has one special function in school testing. It calls attention to pupils who have good reasoning ability but who are below standard in reading and verbal development. Such cases are obscured by a test that mixes verbal and nonverbal components together, and thus the school overlooks children who could do much better work if given suitable help. The nonverbal test is also useful in employee selection where range of educational background is wide. Among African tribesmen trained to operate heavy mining machinery, the matrix test predicted performance ratings with validity .51. This coefficient was based on performance after two practice tests, which proved more valid than measurement without practice (Ombredane *et al.*, 1956).

An Omnibus Test: Kuhlmann-Anderson

American group tests have been influenced little by theories about intelligence. Instead, they have been developed pragmatically, by trying items and retaining those which correlate with such criteria as school success or job success.

One of the important American group tests is the Kuhlmann-Anderson Intelligence Test series. Most group tests are printed in a single booklet, with a different booklet for each three-grade range from kindergarten to adulthood. The Kuhlmann-Anderson, however, has nine different booklets, so that a class can be given a version of the test closely fitted to its ability. The pupils who do well on this booklet may then be given the next higher test, and those who do badly can be given the next easier test to obtain a more accurate measurement. Under this plan few pupils encounter items where they have to guess, and the test is shorter because unnecessary easy items are eliminated.

The development of this scale is characteristic of the procedures used in the older group tests of general ability. Beginning in 1916, Kuhlmann began a tryout of items for use in state institutions in Minnesota, and in 1919 began (with Dr. Rose G. Anderson) to prepare formal tests. In the next four years more than 100 varieties of items were tried out; 51 seemed promising enough for further use. Four more years of research led to a selection of 35 subtests for the published scale. The scale then passed through five further editions, sometimes with minor changes of content to replace unsatisfactory tests or to extend the range, sometimes with modification of norms or format. Authors of present-day tests often employ a similar procedure but use the experience of previous investigators to shorten the research.

The scale now contains 39 tests, organized in booklets which partly overlap each other. Thus booklet K (kindergarten) includes tests 1–10; A (Grade 1), tests 4–13; B (Grade 2), tests 8–17, and so on up to booklet G for Grades 7–8 and booklet H for Grades 9–12. Figure 36 shows representative test items. Many of these item types are used in other group tests. Each test consists of at least eight items. A time limit is set either for each item or for the subtest. These limits are liberal in the first two booklets, but later levels introduce a substantial degree of speeding.

Nearly all of the subtests require adaptation to new situations, yet they also depend on experience and many of them involve special abilities (verbal, spatial, etc.). Kuhlmann and Anderson followed Binet's principle of combining such a great variety of tests that no one specialized ability plays a large part in the score. Verbal ability is important because the pupil must comprehend directions, but the test designers use simple vocabulary, introduce reading only in the later tests, and even at advanced levels use only short and familiar words. An example of ingenious testing is test 8, Counting, which measures judgment and accuracy with numbers without using the formal number system or other school learning.

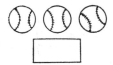

Test 2. Picture errors. "Put a dot on the part that is wrong."

Test 5. Pattern Completion. "Put in the stick that is left out of the second figure."

Test 8. Counting. "Put as many dots in the box as there are balls"

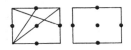

Test 10. Copying. (The square with lines is held up before the class for 10 seconds.)

top rattle doll
sled playing

Test 21. Classification. "Find the one that does not belong with the others."

old rich wide
poor green full

Test 23. Opposites. "Find the two opposites."

robin winter horse
song squirrel fence

Test 26. Similarities. "Find the three things which are alike."

N-B-U-M-E-R
N _____

Test 28. Anagrams. "You are given the first letter. Write the rest of the word."

inaudible distinct
deafening faint loud

Test 32. Arrangement. "If these were arranged in order, which would be the middle one?"

Basket
Picture

Test 34. Directions. "If the word contains E but not R nor I write 3 after it."

5 6 8 11 15

Test 39. Number series. "Write the two numbers which should come next."

FIG. 36. Representative Kuhlmann-Anderson items. The directions used in testing are much simpler and more complete than these abbreviated quotations suggest. (Copyright 1952, Personnel Press, Inc. Reproduced by permission.)

Subtests which have substantial correlation with age were selected in preference to subtests with low correlations. A second criterion was the correlation of subtests with each other. Those having low correlations with other subtests were preferred, so as to increase the comprehensiveness of the test by bringing in many aspects of ability. This, of course, is just the opposite of the procedure used in constructing a homogeneous test of a narrowly defined ability. The Kuhlmann-Anderson measures substantially the same thing as the Stanford-Binet. When errors of measurement are reduced by averaging three trials of each test, SB IQ and Kuhlmann-Anderson IQ correlate almost perfectly (Dearborn and Rothney, 1941).

1. What abilities does the Kuhlmann-Anderson test require that the Raven Matrices do not?
2. The Kuhlmann-Anderson norms are based on "15,000 cases from representative Minnesota, New York, New Jersey, and Pennsylvania communities . . . selected in consultation with State Departments of Education." What further information about the norm group would be desirable? How satisfactory is this sample?
3. In the normative sample, the standard deviation of the Kuhlmann IQ was about 11 points at ages 6–10. Why is this fact important to the test user?
4. The Kuhlmann-Anderson correlates higher with present achievement than does the Stanford-Binet. Why? Is this an advantage or a disadvantage?
5. Is it possible for a person to do consistently better on group mental tests than on individual tests?

PROBLEMS OF DESIGN AND VALIDITY

Dependence on Language

The matrix test is entirely free from verbal content, and the Kuhlmann-Anderson uses predominantly nonverbal items. Many other popular tests, however, are almost completely verbal. Vocabulary and verbal reasoning have always been found good predictors of school and college success, and arithmetic reasoning and number series are also popular item forms.

TABLE 24.   Approximate Level of Reading Ability Required to Comprehend Items of Group Mental Tests[a]

	First Items	Last Items
Kuhlmann-Anderson (booklets for Grade 6)	5.0	7.5
Otis (Higher, Form C)	7.0	13.0
Terman-McNemar		
a. Information	5.5	10.0
b. Logical selection	9.0	17.0
c. Analogies	6.0	7.0
d. Best answers	9.0	9.0
Henmon-Nelson (Form A, Grades 7–12, nonarithmetic items)	6.5	14.0

[a] The reading level is estimated by determining readability from sentence length. A reading level of 7.0 is the performance of the average seventh-grader. SOURCE: R. H. Johnson and G. L. Bond, 1950.

A test which is strictly verbal will be much influenced by the person's reading ability and familiarity with the language. While it may permit a useful prediction of his school success, where language is continually important, it would be wrong to interpret his low score as a sign of lack of mental ability.

To avoid such errors, most testers prefer to use a test which includes both verbal and nonverbal items. Sometimes the two types are included in a single score, as in the Kuhlmann-Anderson. Sometimes separate scores are obtained, as in the Raven Matrices and the vocabulary test recommended to accompany it.

It is wrong to assume that a test which requires no reading is independent of language abilities. The directions are almost always verbal, and not always easy to comprehend. Sometimes the solution to a problem such as figure analogies or matrices requires complex symbolic reasoning with abstract concepts. The person almost certainly relies on his vocabulary to arrive at the answer. A person whose language experience has been limited (e.g., a deaf child or a bilingual) is likely to be handicapped on some of the so-called nonlanguage tests.

Comparability of Scores

Each test maker develops norms for his tests using his own standardizing group. It is particularly important to realize than an IQ of a given size has a different meaning in different tests, or on the same test at different ages. In a recent study over 2200 9- and 10-year-olds took four prominent group tests. Where the Stanford-Binet distribution indicates that about 220 should have IQs 120 and over, the Kuhlmann-Anderson showed such IQs for 137 children, and the Henmon-Nelson for 524 children. At the low end of the scale, where 220 are expected to fall below IQ 80, Kuhlmann-Anderson reports 53 and Henmon-Nelson reports 119 such cases (Eells *et al.*, 1951).

In another study, Lennon compared three tests on equivalent samples and determined what raw scores on the three tests were comparable (Lennon, 1952). These scores were then converted to IQs and MAs, using the tables from the test manuals. He found, for example, that an IQ of 130 on the Terman-McNemar is earned by the same pupils who would earn 123 on Otis Gamma and 126 on the Pintner Verbal. An MA of 14 on the Terman corresponds to 12-9 on Otis and 13-6 on Pintner. Obviously differences in standardizing samples cause IQs on some tests to average higher or to spread out more than on others. Another source of variation is the use of now-obsolete statistical techniques intended to yield ratio IQs. As all testers shift to the use of standard scores or percentiles within age groups, comparability of tests will depend wholly on the adequacy of norming.

Degree of Speeding

Most group tests of ability are given with a time limit. Whether an ability test should be speeded is arguable. The time allowed for an ability test may be so short that standings are determined almost entirely by speed of work, or may be so liberal that everyone finishes. Most tests present items in order of difficulty so that each student encounters the items he can do, and only the best student is pinched by the time limit. Table 25 indicates the effect on score when pupils are given added time on three typical tests. Evidently, most pupils finish in the standard time all the items they can do. For occasional cases, of course, speed will still be the principal factor determining scores.

TABLE 25.   Effect of Giving Pupils Additional Time on Group Intelligence Tests

Age of Pupils	Number of Pupils	Test	Standard Time	Extra Time	Mean Points Earned in Standard Time	Mean Points Earned in Additional Time
9–10	223	Otis Alpha Non-Verbal	20 min.	30 min.	65.0	1.1
9–10	226	Henmon-Nelson	30 min.	20 min.	54.1	3.4
13–14	235	Otis Beta (verbal)	30 min.	15 min.	60.4	0.9

SOURCE: Eells, 1948.

Formerly a distinction was made between "speed tests" (time-limit tests) and "power tests" (work-limit tests). A test with a time limit, however, does not necessarily depend on speed. To decide whether a time-limit score depends on speed, we would need a special experiment. We would first give the test in the usual manner, obtaining score x, and then allow enough time for everyone to finish, obtaining the unspeeded score y. If most persons have the same relative standing on x and on y, the added time made little difference and the time-limit score depends on the same abilities as the untimed score (Helmstadter and Ortmeyer, 1953; Cronbach and Warrington, 1951). In the Kuhlmann-Anderson manual an experiment is reported in which children were allowed to complete the test after time had been called, using a second color of pencil so that both timed and untimed scores were available. The two sets of scores correlated as follows: in Grade 3, .74; Grade 5, .83; Grade 7, .87; Grade 9, .93. Perhaps it appears that these correlations are so high that the two tests measure the same thing; but making allowance for the nonindependence of the two measures, we estimate that in Grade 5, for example, at least 31 percent of the test variance is due to speed.

We cannot tell whether this is an advantage or a disadvantage in prediction without knowing whether the criterion task calls for speeded performance, and what type of speed it calls for. When the criterion task does not demand speed or demands a type of speed not involved in the test, speeding the test introduces an irrelevant variable. For general academic criteria, a measure of power independent of speed is more relevant than a speeded score. With a long testing time, an unspeeded test is more valid than a speed test covering the same material. If only a short time is available for testing, however, a speeded test will be more reliable than an unspeeded test containing very few items. As a result, the *short* speeded test has greater predictive validity than the even briefer test that everyone can finish in the same time (F. M. Lord, 1953).

The trend in recent American tests is to provide ample time for nearly everyone to finish. This point of view is not universally accepted. Eysenck (1953) and Furneaux, in England, argue that the speed with which the mind produces hypotheses is the essence of good problem solving, and that a speeded test is therefore the best measure of mental ability.

Stability

Test scores are unstable when behavior patterns are being acquired, and we would expect a pencil-and-paper test score to be unstable in the earliest school years. The reliability of the Detroit First-Grade Intelligence Test is .91 by a split-half method, indicating good accuracy, but is only .76 when a retest after four months is given. Seagoe (1934) gives data on repeated measurements of various groups after a two-year interval, as follows:

Detroit First Grade at age 6–4 with Detroit Primary at 8–8 $r = .64$
Detroit First Grade at age 6–3, with Haggerty Delta at 8–8 $r = .66$
Detroit Primary at age 8–9 with National Form B at 10–8 $r = .73$
National Form A at 10–4 with Terman at 12–5 $r = .80$
National Form B at 10–7 with Terman at 12–6 $r = .87$

Predictions of intellectual performance over short intervals of time can be made with substantial accuracy, but the mental test permits only approximate long-range predictions in the lower grades of school. Allen (1944b) reports, for example, that the Kuhlmann-Anderson IQ in the middle of Grade 1 predicts achievement early in Grade 4 with a validity of .52.

Once the initial development of reading and seatwork is past, group tests for successive ages measure about the same thing and do so with considerable stability, as Seagoe's data show. By adolescence, scores appear to be extremely stable. H. E. Jones reports that scores at age 17 on the Terman Group Test correlate .84–.90 with retests at age 33 (J. E. Anderson, 1956, p. 159). Despite this stability, the tester should not rely on an old mental-test score when a critical decision is being made. Some young people make substantial changes in mental performance over a three-year period.

Overlap with Achievement Tests

The Kuhlmann-Anderson, like most group tests of general ability, is closely related to educational status. According to the test manual the test distinguishes sharply between accelerated and retarded children in the same grade. The concurrent correlation of the test with total score on an educational achievement battery, with age held constant, is .84 in one study, .77 in another (Hilden and Skeels, 1935; Allen, 1944a). This correlation is higher than that of the Stanford-Binet with achievement.

Some experts argue that it is impossible to separate aptitude or intelligence from achievement. If intelligence and achievement tests measure the same things, we are only fooling ourselves by giving them different labels. We can examine this criticism by making use of two statistical principles: reliability is the proportion of test variance that is nonerror variance; the validity coefficient squared indicates what proportion of test variance measures the same attribute as the criterion. If the reliability is .86[1] for the Kuhlmann-Anderson, and the intercorrelation of test with achievement is .84, we arrive at Figure 37. The square of the intercorrelation indicates the overlap

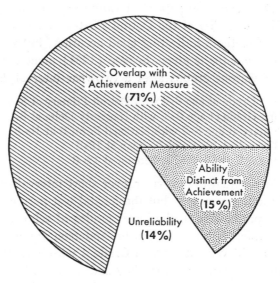

FIG. 37.   Overlap of the Kuhlmann-Anderson test with an achievement measure.

in variance. Seventy-one percent of the test variance represents what the achievement test measures; 14 percent is error. Therefore, 15 percent of the Kuhlmann-Anderson test variance is due to some reliably measured ability independent of achievement. The test would report some differences among children having identical school achievement, but among children with the same achievement *about half of the individual differences in IQ are due only to random errors.* A similar conclusion would hold for other heterogeneous group tests of mental ability (Coleman and Cureton, 1954). For most chil-

---

[1] A coefficient of equivalence computed from subtest intercorrelations for Grade 5, by a modified analysis-of-variance method. The coefficient reported in the manual, .94, is based on a split-half technique which should not be applied to speeded tests.

dren, a group mental test leads to the same prediction that a comprehensive achievement test would.

Ability to Predict Vocational Performance

The group mental test is clearly important to vocational guidance since it predicts success on a great many jobs. In some jobs, however, special abilities are much more important than general ability, and in some routine occupations workers with very high intelligence are less suitable than persons of mediocre ability.

The mental ability found in various occupations is shown in Figure 38, based on test scores of Army draftees. Though persons in higher-level occu-

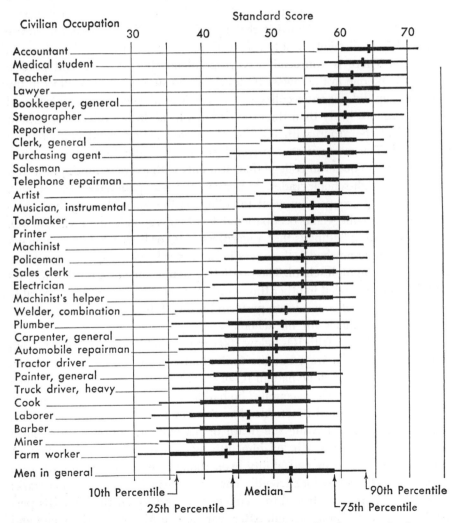

FIG. 38. Standard scores on the Army General Classification Test for occupational groups (Stewart, 1947).

pations have greater average ability, there is an extreme range within each occupation.

Just what will happen to a boy with a given IQ is difficult to predict. He may do well in school and college and enter a profession, or he may drop out of school and remain in an unskilled job. Figure 39 is based on unpublished data from a follow-up study of students who graduated from high school in Flint, Michigan, in 1943. Ten years later the investigator located and obtained information about the subsequent careers of 97 boys. The figure shows what happened to boys at each ability level.

The boys are divided into three levels according to Kuhlmann-Anderson IQ in Grade 9. For each group, the figure shows high-school grades, college history, and occupation ten years after graduation. The chart merits detailed study; it indicates the uncertain predictive value of high-school test scores, while at the same time showing that they have a definite relation to future success. We shall mention only a few of the relations that can be traced in the figure. There is appreciable correspondence between IQ and grades; practically no one in the lowest IQ level earned superior marks. Boys in the lowest group did not enter college unless their grades were exceptional, and they were more likely than the other groups to be in unskilled jobs. About one-third of the group with IQ 90–104 entered college, and half of them graduated. The group with superior IQs earned better high-school marks, but they did no better in college than students with average ninth-grade IQs and similar high-school grades. Moreover, the occupational status of high and middle IQ groups who went to college is the same. Among those who did not go to college the occupational level corresponds somewhat to IQ. The most striking finding is that, regardless of IQ or high-school average, every student who finished college was in an upper-level occupation ten years after completing high school. The predictive significance of a ninth-grade IQ would differ somewhat in other times and other places; it would be desirable for any high-school counselor to perform his own follow-up study in order to establish expectancies for his school.

The fact that boys with IQs below 100 can succeed in college is hard to explain in any general way, but the individual cases often are quite understandable. Alex, though he had an IQ of 93 in Grade 9, eventually became a lawyer. The IQ was not inaccurate: he had 93 on a retest some months later, and 113 on the Stanford-Binet. Alex had lived in a boarding home during his early school years following the death of his mother, and suffered from a sense of inadequacy which led him into aggressive, offensive behavior. A counselor felt that Alex had ability even though his tests and grades were poor. Under the counselor's friendly encouragement he improved his marks to the B level and transferred to a college-preparatory curriculum. His personal adjustment also improved. After war service Alex entered college and completed his law course successfully (Cantoni, 1954).

IQ 105 and Above (30 Cases)

High-school grade average:	Below 1.5		1.5–2.4			2.5+			Total 30		
	xxx		xxxxx xxxxx xxxxx xx			xxxxx xxxxx					
	No college xxx	Entered college	No college xxxx xxxx	Entered college xxxxx xxxx		No college xxxx	Entered college xxxx xx		No college	College, no degree	Degree
				No degree xxxx	Degree xxxxx		No degree x	Degree xxxxx			
Occupational status:											
Business, professional	0		2	2	5	2	1	5	4	3	10
Skilled	0		6	1	0	2	0	0	8	1	0
Unskilled or semi-skilled	3		0	1	0	0	0	0	3	1	0
									15	5	10

IQ 90–104 (49 Cases)

High-school grade average:	Below 1.5		1.5–2.4			2.5+			Total 49		
	xxxxxxxx		xxxxxxxxxx xxxxxxxxxx xxxxxxx			xxxx					
	No college xxxxxxxx	Entered college	No college xxxxxxxxxx xxxxxxxxxx x	Entered college xxxxxxxxxx xxxxxx		No college x	Entered college xxx		No college	College, no degree	Degree
				No degree xxxx xxxx	Degree xxxx xxxx		No degree x	Degree xx			
Occupational status:											
Business, professional	1		3	5	8			2	4	5	10
Skilled	6		9	2	0			0	15	2	0
Unskilled or semi-skilled	1		9	1	0	1	1	0	11	2	0
									30	9	10

IQ Below 90 (18 Cases)

High-school grade average:	Below 1.5		1.5–2.4			2.5+			Total 19		
	xxxxx		xxxxxxxxxx			xx					
	No college xxxxx	Entered college	No college xxxxxxxxxx	Entered college x		No college	Entered college xx		No college	College, no degree	Degree
				No degree	Degree x		No degree x	Degree x			
Occupational status:											
Business, professional	1		2		1		0	1	3	0	2
Skilled	2		4		0		1	0	6	1	0
Unskilled or semi-skilled	2		4		0		0	0	6	0	0
									15	2	2

FIG. 39. Educational and occupational history of 97 high-school boys. (Data supplied by Dr. Louis J. Cantoni; see Cantoni, 1955.)

The rather large number of "late bloomers" like Alex warns against making a definite and final separation between students with high and low ability at the start of high school. It is hard to teach complex ideas to dull pupils, and their presence in the mathematics or French class will impede the teaching of the ablest. Many potentially able students, though, will not be recognized in the ninth grade. Any grouping plan must make provision for the student whose ability is discovered midway through high school. He must be able to fulfill college requirements without too much loss of time; otherwise, much of his talent will be wasted.

The facts so far presented bear on differences between occupations but not on those within occupations. Many validation studies are available for specific vocations. One especially interesting result comes from a follow-up of workers in the home office of an insurance company. Nearly 700 workers hired between 1937 and 1949 were tested on a short general mental test at that time. New workers enter in the lower job categories and are promoted as their performance shows merit. The correlation between responsibility held in 1954 and score at time of hiring was .60. Fifty-four percent of those in "decision-making jobs" had had scores of 120 and over; only 5 percent with scores 0–99, and 19 percent in the 100–119 range, held these high-ranking jobs (Knauft, 1955).

Ghiselli (1955) reviewed the entire literature on prediction of success of workers and found that the group mental test predicts both training and performance criteria for many jobs. The coefficients for any job title range from very high to negligible, depending upon the range of ability in the group tested and the demands of the specific job. Average validities for group mental tests against job proficiency fall in the following ranges:

.00 to .19   Sales, service occupations, machining workers, packers and wrappers, repairmen
.20 to .34   Supervisors, clerks, assemblers
.35 to .47   Electrical workers, managerial and professional

Somewhat similar results are reported by the USES. Correlations for general mental ability are above .40 for success of automobile mechanics, key-punch operators, practical nurses, and bindery workers, for example. In contrast, correlations are below .15 for electronics parts assemblers, welders, pottery decorators, and meat-packing workers (*Guide to the Use of GATB*, 1958).

6. Characterize the occupations for which general ability is a good predictor.

NOTEWORTHY GROUP TESTS

The tests listed below are a representative sample including some of the good current tests, tests primarily of historical importance, and tests illustrating novel measurement techniques. The descriptions are designed to indicate some of the ways the tests differ rather than to provide a full review of important qualities, and the reader should obtain fuller information from the test manual and from reviews of any test that interests him.

• American Council Psychological Examination (ACE); L. L. and T. G. Thurstone; Educational Testing Service, 1924, frequent revisions. For college entrants; high-school form also available. This test was formerly the principal instrument used in testing college freshmen and in research on college success. The total score predicts grade averages, usually with validity about .45. There are two part scores: L (linguistic), based on vocabulary, verbal analogies, etc.; and Q (quantitative), based on number series, figure analogies, etc. No consistent evidence was found that the L and Q scores predicted success in verbal and scientific subjects, respectively, as intended (Berdie et al., 1951). Because the part scores were of little value and the many subtests awkward to administer, the test is now being supplanted.

• Army Alpha Examination; various authors, revisions, and publishers; currently distributed by Western Psychological Services, Psychological Corporation, 1916, 1939, et seq. For secondary school and adult use. Originally designed for Army group testing, the test has several speeded subtests calling for information, reasoning, and practical judgment. Has no advantage over more modern tests.

• California Test of Mental Maturity (CTMM); E. T. Sullivan, W. W. Clark, E. W. Tiegs; California Test Bureau, 1936, 1957. Levels from kindergarten to adult. One of the most widely accepted current tests, with unusual variety of items, good format and standardization, and a continuous series of levels. The full test requires over one and one-half hours at school ages. There is a Short Form for use where less reliable measurement is acceptable. Separate "Language" and "Non-Language" IQs are offered, but there is little evidence to indicate the practical significance of differences between the two IQs. Subscores for memory, logical reasoning, etc., attempt to provide a profile of abilities, but these subscores have dubious validity and should be given little attention. By standardizing CTMM along with the California Achievement Tests, the authors provide for comparison of the pupil's attainment scores with the expectancy for his IQ level (see p. 387).

• College Qualification Tests; George K. Bennett and others; Psychological Corporation, 1957. College and precollege. An eighty-minute test designed for measuring general scholastic promise of college applicants and students. In addition to the total, the part scores measure verbal ability, numerical reasoning, and information in three fields. This, like SCAT, is essentially a sample of educational attainments. Norms are provided for various types of college and also for upper years of high school. The total score predicts freshman grade average, validity often being above .60.

● Concept Mastery Test; Lewis M. Terman; Psychological Corporation, 1939, 1956. College juniors and above. An untimed test designed to measure the highest ranges of vocabulary and verbal reasoning.

● Cooperative School and College Ability Tests (SCAT); anon.;[2] ETS, 1955. Grade 4 to college. This test is offered to replace the ACE as a device primarily for predicting academic success. A Verbal score measures vocabulary and reading comprehension; a Quantitative score measures arithmetic reasoning and understanding of arithmetic operations. Both measure school-learned abilities. The tests are well prepared, but validity, stability, and discriminating power in exceptional groups have not yet been thoroughly investigated. They should serve well for selecting potential college-goers, and appear highly suitable for use by educators not psychologically trained.

● Culture-Free Intelligence Tests; R. B. Cattell; IPAT, 1933, 1944, 1950. Age 4 to adult, 3 levels. A nonverbal test including matrices and other reasoning tasks with geometric figures. The test is independent of language skill but is not truly free of cultural influences. Norms for the test are unsatisfactory; IQs have a very large s.d.

● Davis-Eells Games; Allison Davis and Kenneth Eells; World Book, 1953. Grades 1–2, 3–6. Items are designed to be interesting and fair to lower-class children (see below). Problems are presented pictorially rather than verbally, and the test is relatively difficult to administer. Though the test is long, the reliability is lower than that for competing tests. The test does not predict academic performance under present teaching methods as well as verbal tests do, but is designed to locate children for whom new teaching approaches are needed.

● Henmon-Nelson Tests of Mental Ability; Tom A. Lamke and M. J. Nelson; Houghton Mifflin, 1931, 1950, 1957. Grades 3–6, 6–9, 9–12, college. A thirty-minute test of the "spiral omnibus" pattern in which various item types are presented in rotated order with a steady rise in difficulty. Items include information, proverb interpretation, figure analogies, following directions, etc. Carbon-sheet method of quick scoring. The 1957 revision is well designed as a short measure of scholastic ability having reliability over .90, but considerable overlap with reading ability and no diagnostic features.

● Kuhlmann-Anderson Intelligence Tests; F. Kuhlmann and Rose G. Anderson; Personnel Press, 1927, 1952. Age 6 to maturity. (See pp. 218 ff.)

● Lorge-Thorndike Intelligence Tests; Irving Lorge and Robert L. Thorndike; Houghton Mifflin, 1954. Levels from kindergarten through high school. A well-constructed test. At the primary level, questions requiring verbal understanding and reasoning are read by the teacher, and the pupil responds

---

[2] An entry of "anon." indicates that the test was prepared by the staff of some organization—in this case, the Educational Testing Service. The responsibility for test design is shared so widely that listing the many coöperating authors would not be informative.

by marking pictures. In Grades 4 and above, nonverbal and verbal sections can be separately administered. The nonverbal items call mostly for general ability, independent of vocabulary and reading. Since the verbal and non-verbal scores correlate about .70, differences between the scores will not be significant for the majority of pupils.

• Miller Analogies Test; W. S. Miller; Psychological Corporation, 1926, 1950. Superior adults. A test of 100 very difficult verbal analogies items, administered only at licensed centers. Severe restrictions protect the security of items, since it is used by many graduate schools to test applicants. Sizable validity coefficients for predicting success in graduate study are reported, despite the narrow range of ability within which the test is designed to discriminate.

• Ohio State University Psychological Examination (OSPE); H. A. Toops; Ohio College Association, 1919, frequent revisions. SRA publishes Form 21 (1940); the Minnesota Scholastic Aptitude Test is a shortened version of Form 23. High school, college. By restricting items to vocabulary and reading ability, the author obtains a score which predicts college marks with unusual accuracy (coefficients of .60 are common). The test requires about two hours.

• Otis Quick-Scoring Mental Ability Tests; A. S. Otis; World Book, 1920, 1936, 1954. Forms for Grades 1 to college. Otis was one of the first to experiment with group measurement techniques. His tests generally combine verbal and nonverbal reasoning items to obtain a quick measure of general ability. IQs tend to be lower than for other tests. The technical development and the manuals for these tests are less adequate than for tests of recent origin, but predictive validities against school achievement compare favorably with other tests.

• Pintner General Ability Tests; Rudolf Pintner; World Book, 1931, 1945. Grades 4–9. There are separate language and nonlanguage tests, each requiring about 45 minutes. There are companion tests for lower grades, namely, the Pintner-Cunningham Primary Test and the Pintner-Durost Elementary Test. The latter contains two subscores, one being based on verbal reasoning items read by the pupil. The other measures vocabulary and verbal reasoning independent of reading skill by having the pupil mark pictures in response to questions read by the teacher. The two scores give significantly different information. The verbal test for intermediate grades is much like other older tests. The nonlanguage test contains six subtests, some of which are ingenious and taxing reasoning tests. The nonlanguage score adds more unique information to data normally available from achievement tests than does the verbal test or the usual omnibus intelligence test.

• Progressive Matrices; J. C. Raven; H. K. Lewis (London), Psychological Corporation, 1938, 1947, 1951 Ages 5½ to 11; age 9 upward. One of the best available techniques for obtaining a nonverbal measure of reasoning ability, though the single type of item places a possibly undesirable emphasis on spatial reasoning. The norms are based on poorly selected groups. Reliability of the scale in single age groups, especially young ones, is inadequate. An efficient, properly standardized form is badly needed.

• Scholastic Aptitude Test (SAT); anon.; College Entrance Examination Board, 1926 to date. This examination is administered in a controlled program to applicants for admission to affiliated colleges. Not sold for general use. Tests measure vocabulary, verbal reasoning, knowledge of high-school

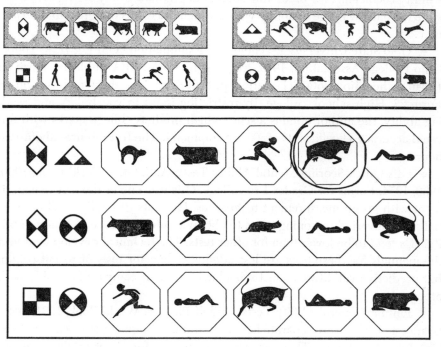

FIG. 40. Nonverbal item for the Semantic Test of Intelligence. (Rulon, 1952. Reproduced by permission of Dr. Phillip J. Rulon.)

mathematics, and quantitative reasoning, combining comprehension items with subtle reasoning in order to discriminate at high levels of ability. Within the group surviving to the fourth year of college, SAT-Verbal correlates .43 with grade average in the typical college, and SAT-M (Quantitative) correlates .27 (J. French, 1957).

• Semantic Test of Intelligence; P. J. Rulon; unpublished, 1952. Adult. A nonreading test for testing conceptual reasoning, designed to determine which illiterates in the Army should have literacy training. (This is part of an effort to utilize draftees who would otherwise have to be rejected.) The man is taught by pantomime the meaning of certain symbols, and works through a series of "decoding" problems, beginning with two-choice items.

In Figure 40, the upper panel shows that the first symbol stands for "cow"; the first phrase is "cow jumping," and the fourth picture should be circled. Correlations show that this worksample of learning is more a measure of ability to learn, and less a measure of attainment, than other mental tests (Rulon and Schweiker, 1953).

• Terman-McNemar Test of Mental Ability; L. M. Terman and Quinn McNemar; World Book, 1940, 1949. Grades 7–12. A well-constructed test, reliable and easily interpreted. Restricted to verbal reasoning and information in order to predict school marks.

7. In an adult counseling center, adults with varying educational backgrounds and vocational goals must be given advisement. Prepare what you consider a minimum list of intelligence tests (group and individual) needed to cope with all nonpsychiatric cases.

8. Prepare a minimum list of intelligence tests needed by a school psychologist who is expected to diagnose any pupil, age 6 to 16, whose behavior or school work is considered unsatisfactory.

9. Would a group or an individual test be preferable
   a. in screening applicants for teaching positions in a large city?
   b. in testing juvenile delinquents prior to decisions about probation?
   c. in research on trends in the intelligence of immigrants?
   d. in selecting secretarial employees for a university?

10. What interpretation would be made if a child has Non-Language IQ 120, Language IQ 90? What interpretation would be made if the Language IQ were 120, Non-Language 90?

11. In the CTMM (Elementary) test, pupils listen to a story about "The Pack Train." In the story, a man goes to a mining camp by pack train, passing a glacier and being threatened by a grizzly bear. After hearing the story, pupils go on to take other sections of the test. After an elapsed time of 25 minutes, the pupils are asked questions about the story. What does the test measure besides general ability in "delayed recall"?

USE AND FUTURE PROSPECTS OF ABILITY TESTS

After a generation of enthusiastic acceptance, group tests of ability have come under attack from many quarters. One challenge comes from the analytic measures of differentiated abilities, which hope to offer accurate descriptions of patterns of ability in place of the overall index of the omnibus test. The other principal challenge grows out of the recognition that the tests —at least from age 8 to 20—are strongly influenced by past school achievement.

Chief Functions of Group Mental Tests

If one is comparing students who have been in the same class, the high correlation between general ability tests and achievement batteries means that it makes little difference which we use, since they lead to similar decisions.

When one compares persons coming from *different* educational backgrounds, the general ability test is often much the more suitable because it is not matched to any particular educational experience. Among the important functions of the general mental test are these:

● Comparing pupils at the beginning of a school year. The mental test is fair to pupils coming from various schools, whereas an achievement battery might not be.

● Decisions regarding the admission of college students. High-school grades or rank in high-school class usually predict better than mental tests, but it is hard to compare grades from different schools, especially small ones. A combination of high-school grades with a group mental test commonly predicts college marks with a validity of .60 to .70 (D. Harris, 1940). Achievement batteries can be substituted for the mental test as a predictor. Several studies of the Iowa Tests of Educational Development find validities of .60–.70 for the test alone (*Using the Iowa Tests,* 1957), but this test requires several hours whereas the usual college-level mental test takes from 45 minutes to two hours.

● Selecting employees. The fact that persons have different school backgrounds makes an achievement battery unsuitable, especially where the job depends little on school learning. General mental tests are often more acceptable to adult job applicants than a test reminiscent of schoolwork would be.

● In research, for dividing subjects into groups of equal ability so as to compare different methods of instruction or to study effects of motivation, etc.

The Spectrum of Ability Tests

In the descriptions of tests labeled as measures of general mental ability, scholastic aptitude, or intelligence, it is apparent that that name covers a considerable variety of test content. Tests can be arranged in approximately the pattern shown in Figure 41, along a spectrum ranging from those which are strictly measures of outcomes of education to those which are most independent of specific instruction. For the sake of contrast, we anchor the scale at the educational end (A) with tests of subject-matter proficiency which measure how much the pupil knows about particular courses such as algebra and physics. A few tests (notably CQT) have measured information in subject fields as a part of "scholastic aptitude" tests. Tests of general educational development are next in order (B). These tests, to be described in Chapter 13, measure general abilities and study skills which might be acquired in many different courses such as ability to interpret graphs and charts, ability to comprehend and draw conclusions from scientific articles, etc. At C, the tests measure educational proficiencies such as size of vocabulary and arithmetic reasoning; these intellectual tools are even more fundamental to intellectual work than those at *B*. At *D* we begin to move away from things directly taught in school; the tests present puzzling verbal problems which

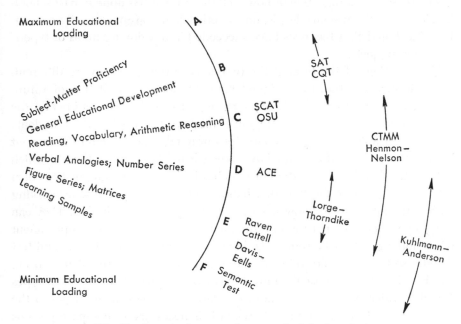

FIG. 41. Spectrum for comparing tests of scholastic aptitude.

require the student to reorganize knowledge. The distinction between *C* and *D* tasks may be illustrated by vocabulary items. A *C* item would ask the meaning of a fairly rare word—for example, requiring choice of the nearest synonym for the given word, as in this Lorge-Thorndike item:

> subvention   meeting   support   change   criminal   lessee

A *D* item uses words known to most pupils in the grade tested but requires a difficult comparison. For example, the DAT Verbal Reasoning Test (Bennett *et al.*, 1947) requires choice of two words to complete an analogy:

> . . . is to static as dynamic is to . . .
>   1. radio   2. politic   3. inert   4. air
>   A. speaker   B. motor   C. regal   D. active

At *E*, we come to tasks which require reasoning with abstract concepts but which require little if any familiarity with the examiner's language. As we move toward *F*, we attempt to emphasize concepts and experiences familiar to every subject, while still requiring careful reasoning.

Spearman's *g* seems to correspond closely to *E* on this spectrum; it is concerned with the ability of the individual to form or detect relationships and abstractions. Most group tests combine tasks at levels D and E, sometimes in separate verbal and nonverbal scores. Many recent tests, particularly for college-level students, move up the spectrum to B and C levels, thus becoming more directly a reflection of how well the student has done in past schooling. Tests for the primary levels, on the other hand, are necessarily concentrated at E and F. A few tests have succeeded in developing items of type F for older subjects.

The functions of the tests at the two ends of the spectrum are different. Those toward the top are designed for cold-blooded prediction of future school success. One who has done poorly in past schooling is a bad bet for the future, no matter what his "intelligence" may be. Those who admit students to college or award college scholarships rarely take a chance on the student "who would succeed *if* he turned over a new leaf." They prefer the test which deliberately handicaps the student who has had poor schooling or has taken little advantage of it. On the other hand, the teacher and counselor working with a student wants to know what undeveloped resources he has. They can rely on past achievement for an estimate of probable future accomplishment when nothing out-of-the-routine is done for the student, but the mental test ought also to locate undeveloped potential that novel treatment may bring out. For the latter purpose the most information is provided by tests of types E and F which have a minimum of overlap with achievement. Tests in the range from D to F are preferable when it is necessary to compare persons coming from different educational and cultural backgrounds. The more different the backgrounds, the farther toward F the test should be, unless the criterion task requires some particular background.

12. Classify the Kuhlmann-Anderson subtests illustrated in Figure 36 on the spectrum.

The Shift Toward Achievement Tests for Academic Prediction

It is evident that tests of types D and E have much overlap with tests at B and C, but the effort of test developers, beginning with Binet, was directed to measuring "mental ability" as distinct from achievement. Recently, many test developers have come to the conclusion that this is not a profitable endeavor when one's aim is to predict school success. These workers are now recommending tests of types B and C for this purpose. The ACE test, for example, was for a long time the principal instrument used by colleges for measuring scholastic aptitude of entering freshmen. In 1955 its publishers, acting on the advice of specialists in educational guidance, introduced in its place the School and College Ability Tests (SCAT).

The SCAT is a measure of verbal and arithmetic comprehension; these abilities played a large part also in the ACE, but that test included number series, figure analogies, and other reasoning tasks not directly taught in school. According to the manual (Cooperative Test Division, 1955, pp. 3–5):

> The tests in the SCAT series have been designed and developed for the principal purpose of helping teachers and counselors—and students themselves—to estimate the capacity of each *individual student* [in high school and college] to undertake the academic work of the next higher level of schooling. . . .

> In considering the general purposes for which the SCAT series was to be designed, and the continuity of measurement that was to be a principal objective in development of the series, the Advisory Committee recommended strongly that the new tests should measure "school-learned abilities" directly, rather than psychological characteristics or traits which afford indirect measurement of capacity for school learning. This recommendation was based on three general observations shared by all members of the committee: (a) that the best *single* predictor of how well a student is likely to succeed in his school work next year is "how well he is succeeding this year"; (b) that a certain few school-learned abilities appear to be critical prerequisites to next steps in learning throughout the range of general education—among them skills in reading and in handling quantitative information; and (c) that school-learned abilities usually can be discussed with students and parents in a more objective way than can such emotionally-loaded characteristics as "intelligence" or "mental ability."

Demand for Ability Tests Independent of Social and Educational Background

While one group of testers proposes to abandon general ability tests as unnecessary, many others have taken the position that the solution to the problem of overlap is to make general ability tests less dependent on background even if this reduces their correlation with subsequent school success.

There has been particular dissatisfaction with the tests for high levels of ability, most of which are measures of information at least as much as they are measures of thinking power. It is not a simple matter to invent unambiguous difficult items, and most testers raise difficulty by increasing the degree of speeding or by introducing items which depend on rare knowledge. The Concept Mastery Test and the Miller Analogies Test, for example, require the subject to have a very large vocabulary. The matrix test can be made very difficult, but no high-level version of it has been published.

A related defect is the failure of present tests, whether group or individual, to measure creative ability (Thurstone, 1951). Efforts to test types of thinking characterized by logic, accuracy, and knowledge have been very successful. There has been little success in identifying the types of thinking which distinguish the novelist from the engineer or the theorist from the museum curator. This is probably of minor importance at younger ages where all abilities seem to be highly correlated, although even here we perhaps occasionally overlook a child who has high potential along lines not stressed in our tests. In vocational guidance, we have little basis for judging which man will be most insightful, most creative, and most original.

A much more severe criticism is made by Allison Davis, who argues that use of tests dependent upon past schooling and school-related behavior denies many children a fair opportunity. Children who do well on mental tests are encouraged by teachers, and if they have trouble with school work a special study of their difficulties is made. If a child with a poor mental-test record, on the other hand, has trouble with schoolwork, the teacher is likely to accept this as natural and make no deeper inquiry. The child who could do better schoolwork than he has in the past is neglected just because the poor background lowers his mental-test score.

Davis (1951) and his associates believe that American society contains several cultural segments, of which the largest and most distinctive are the middle class and the lower or "working" class. The former group, consisting of professional, skilled, and white-collar workers, values education as a means of maintaining a desirable place in society. On mental tests, the average middle-class child does better than the average lower-class child. Davis thinks that this social-class difference results from the way the tests are constructed rather than from deficiencies in reasoning ability among the lower-class children. Tests, he says, are biased against the lower-class child (1951, p. 15):

> The type of problem in present tests, which is clearly biased, may be illustrated by the following:
>
> A symphony is to a composer as a book is to what?
>   ( )paper ( )sculptor ( )author ( )musician ( )man

On this problem 81 percent of the higher socio-economic groups marked the correct response, but only 51 percent of the lower socio-economic group did so. In an experiment designed by Professor Ernest Haggard we made a problem similar to that just read, but we used words and situations common to all social groups of children. This problem was read to the pupils:

> A baker goes with bread, like a carpenter goes with what?
>   ( )a saw ( )a house ( )a spoon ( )a nail ( )a man

On this culturally fair problem, 50 percent of each socioeconomic group gave the correct answer.

This criticism of test content implies that some types of reasoning tests handicap the lower-class child more than others. There are two major studies which bear on this contention, both of them carried out by associates of Davis. Havighurst and Janke applied individual tests to all the 10-year-olds and nearly all the 16-year-olds in a midwestern town. The average IQs are shown in Table 26. In this table, class C consists of families of white-collar

TABLE 26.   Average IQ of Middle- and Lower-Class Groups

Social Status	N		10-Year-Olds				N		16-Year-Olds	
		Stanford-Binet	Cornell-Coxe Performance Battery	Draw-a-Man	Porteus Maze (MA)			Stanford-Binet	Wechsler-Bellevue
C	26	114	116	107	12.8		44	112	109
D	68	110	110	102	12.8		49	104	102
E	16	91	96	91	10.4		13	98	103

Source: Havighurst and Janke, 1944, 1945.

workers and small businessmen, D, of semiskilled workers and laborers, and E, of the lowest occupational groups and the down-and-outers. All the tests except the Wechsler-Bellevue show about the same difference between classes. The performance tests do not give a substantially more favorable picture of the lower-class child than does the Stanford-Binet. Whatever cultural handicaps or hereditary handicaps there may be seem to be present in *both* verbal and performance measures. The difference between Binet and Wechsler results for 16-year-olds is not large enough to require explanation.

The second study (Eells *et al.*, 1951) involved the administration of numerous group tests to a very large number of pupils. As expected, the scores correlated with social status (.33 for the Kuhlmann-Anderson). This difference was found on all types of items. Ninety-one percent of the items for 16-year-olds, and 63 percent for 10-year-olds, were easier for the middle-class child. Although verbal items showed a slightly greater difference, this study also implies that the handicap of the lower class is not primarily a function of test content.

Eells made another observation, however, which points to differences in test motivation as a possible source of inaccurate comparison. High-status pupils tended consistently to select the most plausible incorrect choices ("distractors") whereas the low-status pupils scattered responses widely over all wrong choices. This seems to indicate that the lower group guesses more, and puts forth less effort on hard items. This problem of differential motivation is one already mentioned in connection with study of national and racial differences. Tests are constructed to predict readiness for academic schooling and therefore emphasize abstract ideas, careful self-criticism, and willingness to work at a task which offers no visible reward. Davis' case studies indicate that working-class children live in a world concerned with concrete problems where sound thinking and errors meet with tangible rewards and penalties. Havighurst comments as follows on the motivational differences between classes (Eells *et al.*, 1951, p. 21):

> The characteristic middle-class attitude toward education is taught by middle-class parents to their children. School is important for future success. One must do one's very best in school. Report cards are studied by the parents carefully, and the parents give rewards for good grades, warnings and penalties for poor grades. Lower-class parents, on the other hand, seldom push the children hard in school and do not show by example or by precept that they believe education is highly important. In fact, they usually show the opposite attitude. With the exception of a minority who urgently desire mobility for their children, lower-class parents tend to place little value on high achievement in school or on school attendance beyond minimum age.

> When the middle-class child comes to a test, he has been taught to do his very best on it. Life stretches ahead of him as a long series of tests, and he must always work himself to the very limit on them. To the average lower-class child, on the other hand, a test is just another place to be punished, to have one's weaknesses shown up, to be reminded that one is at the tail end of the procession. Hence this child soon learns to accept the inevitable and to get it over with as quickly as possible. Observation of the performance of lower-class children on speed tests leads one to suspect that such children often work very rapidly through a test, making responses more or less at random. Apparently they are convinced in advance that they cannot do well on the test, and they find that by getting through the test rapidly they can shorten the period of discomfort which it produces.

In an effort to provide a test which will not seem unduly abstract and schoolish to lower-class children, and which will not penalize them for past indifference to schooling, Davis and Eells developed a new group test. The "Davis-Eells Games" require reasoning, but they deal with everyday situations rather than abstractions (Figure 42). The items appear to be interesting to pupils, appealing to much the same motivation as a comic strip satisfies. Just how well the test achieves its aim is difficult to judge from present evidence. It is much less dependent on reading than the Kuhlmann-Anderson, which is itself less verbal than many group tests (Love and Beach, 1957). One study finds that lower-class children lag just as far behind the middle-class group on the Davis-Eells as on a conventional test, another finds a smaller correlation with social class for the Davis-Eells than for the conventional test, and a third finds just the opposite, the lower-class group having a relatively greater handicap on the Davis-Eells (Coleman and Ward, 1955; Noll, 1958; Fowler, 1957). These discrepancies may be due to community differences, but they make it clear that we have much to learn about the implications of social class for test interpretation.

"This picture shows a woman; it shows a man with a bump on his head; and it shows a broken window. A boy is outside the window. Look at the picture and find out the thing that is true.

No. 1. The man fell down and hit his head.

No. 2. The ball came through the window and hit the man's head.

No. 3. The picture does not show how the man got the bump on his head. Nobody can tell because the picture doesn't show how the man got the bump."

(No. 2 is scored as right)

"Each boy is trying to take three packages home. Which boy is starting to load the packages the best way so he can take all three home?"

(No. 3 is scored as right)

FIG. 42. Specimen items from the Davis-Eells Games. Questions below the figure are read aloud to the group by the tester. (Copyright 1953, World Book Company. Reproduced by permission.)

Placed alongside the arguments which led to the construction of SCAT, Davis' arguments bring out an issue hidden beneath previous testing practice. Ever since Binet, mental testers have tried to ride in two directions at once. They try to predict school success and therefore include measures of educational skill in their tests. But they also ask the same tests to measure a psychological attribute which is thought of as distinct from educational attainment. Most present tests are a muddled combination of predictive measures which rest upon past achievement, of measures unrelated to either past or future achievement, and of measures which predict future performance but do not depend on past schooling. Despite their ambiguity these tests serve many purposes fairly well, particularly when other dependable information is lacking, as is the case in employee selection and recruit classification. Other information is available in most school counseling, however; the potential user then ought to ask what the mental test offers that adds to the other data. This question forces the test developer to take a clear position. He can develop a superior measure of educated skills, or he can develop a superior measure of unschooled abilities. Either of these can add to the understanding of the pupil in a way that no poorly defined composite can.

The argument for basing educational decisions (selection, placement, guidance) on achievement tests expresses a conservative outlook (Cronbach, 1957). One who uses such tests takes as his task to predict who will do well in school and society as now constituted. In his eyes, the tests are unfair only if lower-class children do better in school than their test scores forecast. Investigations show just the contrary: when test scores are matched the middle-class children do somewhat better in school (Turnbull, 1951); if anything, the tests do not give the middle-class group enough advantage. Stroud (1942) concluded that "for purposes of prediction of success in schools *as now organized,* intelligence tests appraise the ability of unfavored groups as fairly as they appraise the ability of the average or the favored groups and . . . although the low average intelligence-quotient of the unfavored groups may be the fault of society or of biology, it is not due to unfairness inherent in the intelligence tests" (italics ours). The home, the school, and the world of business all demand working for remote goals by means of abstract ideas. The usual group mental tests show how well a pupil is likely to fit into that system.

Davis' position attacks this conservative philosophy. He believes that society should be fitted to the individual. If our schooling calls for thinking and motivational patterns that fit only the child of middle-class parents, we may be neglecting our responsibility to discover teaching methods that will bring out the ability of the lower-class child. Fundamental as this argument is, it has limited practical significance at this moment, because neither Davis nor anyone else has suggested what educational methods should be used with the lower class. When and if new methods for this purpose are found, the tests that predict success may be different from those now used by schools.

Much theoretical knowledge is required on the relation of ability patterns to choice of teaching method. Ideally one would like to put each person into that type of instruction where he will do best. There is a great need for studies of the correlation of tests with success under various methods of instruction. A test which correlates higher under one procedure than another is needed if we wish to allocate the pupil to the method best for him. There has been no systematic research on validity taking method of instruction into account.

13. In 1958, a committee of testing specialists made the following recommendations (among others) to state school officials regarding desirable testing programs (*Identification and Guidance of Able Students*, 1958). Classify the recommended tests on the spectrum and indicate what published tests seem to meet these specifications.
    a. For selecting college scholarship winners, if there is a state-wide competition, the final examination should measure use and comprehension of the English language, quantitative reasoning, and ability to handle problems of comprehension in basic fields of knowledge including the sciences.
    b. In Grade 6 or 7 there should be a scholastic aptitude test as little dependent on academic skills as possible—i.e., a reasoning test based on material not directly taught in school. In addition the test should probably yield a score based on verbal and quantitative material.
    c. In Grade 10 or 11 there should be a test oriented primarily toward predicting college success. Its content should probably be in the region where aptitude and achievement merge.
14. What reasons can you give for or against the above recommendations insofar as they concern type of test and placement?
15. Among college entrants, boys tend to surpass girls on tests of mathematical abilities and girls surpass boys in literary interpretation. How would you take these facts into account in planning a test to be used in a state-wide public competition for scholarships?
16. Travers says (Donahue *et al.*, 1949, pp. 148–149):

    "The most recent emphasis in testing children of elementary school age has been upon diagnosing the causes of difficulties in specific aspects of learning. The development of diagnostic tests in various subject matter fields has shifted attention from the problem of predicting over-all academic success to the problem of determining the causes of academic difficulties. The shift in emphasis is a fortunate one since it is doubtful whether over-all predictions of achievement in elementary school are particularly useful except where extreme deviates are being considered."

    Do you agree with the last statement? Can the classroom teacher use information about the pupil's MA, if it is within one year of the group average?

The Interpretation of "General Mental Ability"

The preceding section discussed the practical implications of mental tests, but before leaving the topic we should also consider the place of the concept of "general mental ability" in psychological science. You will recall that the original measures of individual differences, tried by Galton and J. McK. Cattell, isolated narrowly defined abilities such as speed of judgment. This work produced completely miscellaneous instruments and results and seemed to have no relevance to the general problem of human intelligence. Binet started a revolution with his hodgepodge, complex instrument, and all the more recent testers of general ability have followed his banner. Did he really hit on the essence of mental ability? Or can we hope for some radically different approach which will penetrate more deeply into the problem?

The efforts of many psychologists have been directed to attempts to understand general mental ability. From one side, they study the tests and their correlations and try to infer what the common ability running through the test depends upon. From the other side, they examine thinking processes and try to explain what differentiates the more successful from the less successful thinker.

The large amount of research based on tests has established a picture of the "general ability" of the tests. We see the tests as, first of all, a sample of performance in solving a standardized intellectual problem. While it is not a true sample of everyday life, it is nearly as complex as any practical task. Far more than the person's "intellect" is involved. His effort and his success depend on his self-concept, his feeling about the authority who gives the test, his ability to tolerate stress and frustration, and many other qualities. The test, then, gives a picture of the adjustment of the total person to a standardized situation making intellectual demands.

The adjustment which the test calls for seems to involve the ability to interpret a complicated stimulus situation, to test various possibilities mentally, and to carry out a response which in some way "completes" the situation. It is evident that such interpretations are dependent on past experience. Even in a strange problem like the matrix the person must select essential elements and bring to bear abstract concepts previously learned. At the same time, level of development no doubt depends on innate potential. The mental-test score reflects present proficiency, i.e., the structure of habits and behavior processes which experience has molded out of the raw material heredity provided.

The interpretations made of tests in practical work stem largely from a clinical orientation. It is not surprising that clinical workers should regard the test as a measure of the functioning of the total person rather than of intellect alone, and consider this an advantage rather than a disadvantage. General psychologists, on the contrary, have been asking just how man's mind is able to interpret his world, and they have therefore tried to isolate intellectual processes for separate examination. It is from such "pure" research on thinking processes that we today hear the strongest suggestions for new approaches to intellectual measurement.

The work of Piaget is representative of this trend. His work may be regarded as a direct continuation of the line of research Binet was engaged in before he turned to making mental tests for the Paris schools. Binet had been trying to understand how attention, memory, and other processes operate, and out of these experiments he drew his practical test procedures. Piaget has devoted his lifetime to the study of developmental changes. How, he asks, do perception and reasoning differ in the older and younger child? Do older children show different processes of thought, or merely superior speed and complexity? (Piaget, 1947).

Only a brief summary of his conclusions can be offered. He reports that the changes are qualitative, that the older child thinks in quite a different way from the younger. The child must first learn to make perceptual comparisons and to abstract from his sense impressions certain constructs or "schemata." His first schemata are merely the identifications of objects: for instance, the recognition of his mother as the same person no matter how her dress, posture, and other superficial appearances change. He gradually builds one schema upon another, thereby acquiring a repertoire of tools of thought. Once he realizes that "an object" exists, he can think of it as continuing to exist even when hidden; this stage is necessary before he can be expected to find a hidden object. He later develops ideas of shape (constant even though the retinal image changes), size, identity, order, etc. For example, the preschool child may be able to compare the size of two blocks, selecting the larger. There is a certain age where he can judge each pair correctly, and yet cannot arrange a whole series in order. He focuses on one pair at a time, and cannot think of the overall order. A schema or idea such as "order" may first appear in a concrete form; i.e., the child can compare two bead chains only when they are laid out side by side. Then he learns to hold the abstract order in mind so that he can compare, for example, a straight chain with one twisted in a "figure eight." When the idea of order is completely abstracted, he can solve logical problems such as "Town A is north of B, and C is south of B; what can you say about A and C?"

This type of research (see also Harlow, 1949) is beginning to isolate a strictly intellectual aspect of the person's reactions to the world. Solving any problem, it is argued, calls for the possession of certain schemata. The schematic interpretation replaces the immediate, Gestalt impression. To reproduce a Block Design pattern efficiently, for instance, the child must disregard the overall pattern and divide the figure mentally into equal squares.

The person does not perceive his world as a physical event. Rather, he creates a picture in his mind, building up that picture by using whatever schemata he knows and considers important. This abstract picture, being simpler than the world, lends itself to formal, accurate reasoning. Piaget and his associates, as well as workers in other centers, are now translating his experimental procedures into tests for individual measurement. The bead tests mentioned above are an example. Such tests will perhaps permit an inventory of the individual's equipment for thinking. It is too early to say whether these tests will have direct practical importance; it is a good bet that the total score on such a test will correlate highly with Binet's hodge-podge scale. Tests based on modern cognitive theory seem certain, however, to advance our understanding of thought processes and of the experiences which improve intelligence.

17. Investigators of the aged argue (J. Anderson, 1956, pp. 162, 170–172) that mental tests for the older adult should call for maturity of judgment, so that they would be similar to the intellectual requirements of the person's daily life. What sort of test items would meet this demand? Could such tests be applied to adolescents?

18. One of the subtests of the Tanaka group intelligence test requires the subject to cross slanting lines, making X's as rapidly as he can, thus: X X X X X / / / / / /. Such a subtest is rarely used in American intelligence tests. On what basis could the inclusion of such a test be criticized? What argument or evidence would justify including this subtest in a general mental test?

19. Tuddenham (1948) gave Army Alpha to a representative sample of soldiers drafted in World War II. Comparing these data with norms for white enlisted soldiers in World War I, he found that whereas only 17 percent of the World War I group had raw scores greater than 104, this score was the median of the World War II sample. How can this difference be explained?

Suggested Readings

Examiner's manual, Cooperative School and College Ability Tests. Princeton: Educational Testing Service, 1957 (or later edition).

    This is a good example of a modern manual. Study of all sections will be profitable. It explains the test maker's decisions about what to measure, how to report scores, etc., along with clear details of standardization research.

Hebb, D. O. The growth and decline of intelligence. *The organization of intelligence.* New York: Wiley, 1949. Pp. 274–303.

    Clinical studies after brain surgery and studies of animals are described which indicate that innate potential can be distinguished from comprehension developed in a particular culture. Hebb's theory emphasizes the importance of appropriate early experience to develop ability.

Heim, Alice W. Validating intelligence tests. *The appraisal of intelligence.* London: Methuen, 1954. Pp. 96–112.

    Heim describes five types of investigation which may be used to judge the adequacy of a general mental test and shows the way in which each type of study, considered alone, might be misleading.

Tyler, Ralph W. Can intelligence tests be used to predict educability? In Kenneth Eells & others, *Intelligence and cultural differences.* Chicago: University of Chicago Press, 1951. Pp. 39–47.

    Tyler distinguishes between tests designed to predict success in present educational treatments and tests which might be designed to select able persons who will not succeed in present treatments but might do well under other methods yet to be invented.

9

Factor Analysis:
The Sorting of Abilities

NEARLY all the tests considered to this point grew out of Binet's original discovery that complex problems measure general adaptive ability better than do simple tests of reaction and discrimination. Most innovations in ability testing since 1920 have been concerned with narrower abilities required in particular jobs or school subjects. Separate measures of verbal, mechanical, numerical aptitudes, etc., were designed, and many of them have proved valuable in guidance and personnel classification. We might merely describe these tests and summarize data on their validities, but such a catalog would be endless. It will be better to look first at the modern techniques of classifying abilities which guide the development of such tests.

Factor analysis is a systematic method for examining the meaning of a test by studying its correlations with other variables. The investigator gives a large collection of tests to the same persons. The analysis tries to determine how many distinct abilities are being measured reliably, to detect additional "trace" abilities which could be measured reliably by modifying the tests, and to reduce the confusion which results when the same ability is given different names in different tests. Factor analysis gives information about the nature and organization of individual characteristics and clarifies what any given test measures. It is used in studies of interests, attitudes, and personality as well as in studies of ability. The purpose of this chapter is to clarify what factor analysts are doing and to show how a factorial study is interpreted.

It is hard to gain even a partial understanding of factor analysis. The technique is complicated, though the basic idea is as simple as correlation itself. The results of investigations have often disagreed, perhaps chiefly because some of the older work used crude techniques and insufficient data. During those earlier days, substantial controversies developed whose echoes still confuse current discussion. Fortunately, these issues have largely been settled, and factorists agree on many basic facts.

Although factor analysis is mathematical, it involves considerable judgment. The investigator chooses whatever method of organizing his results makes the best sense to him, and the result is variation among studies. This is confusing, just as it confuses the beginning student of geography to find different maps picturing Greenland in different ways. These differences are of little concern to the nonspecialist; the important thing is that all maps agree that there is such a large island in the North Atlantic. In our discussion of factor analysis we shall concentrate on such major features of the landscape and omit technical details.

THEORY OF FACTORIAL ANALYSIS

Interpreting Sets of Correlations

Looking at a collection of scores such as the Wechsler subtests, we first face the question, Just how many different abilities are present? The word *ability* in such a question refers to a group of performances all of which correlate highly with one another, and which as a group are distinct from (have low correlations with) performances that do not belong to the group (Vernon, 1956). Vocabulary tasks perhaps define such a group. They hang together, but are they distinct from other types of items? To take a specific example, Wechsler Vocabulary items call for recall of word meanings. Wechsler Similarities items call for verbal comparison of concepts. Are these the same ability? Or can we interpret one as measuring word knowledge and the other as measuring verbal reasoning?

For a group of junior-high-school students,

reliability of Vocabulary $= .90$
reliability of Similarities $= .80$
correlation of Vocabulary and Similarities $= .52$.

The two tests evidently overlap. Squaring the correlation of .52 tells us that 27 percent of either test can be regarded as representing a common or overlapping "factor." The reliability indicates that 20 percent of the Similarities variance is due to error. This leaves 53 percent of the Similarities variance; this nonoverlapping remainder must be due to some distinct ability, not common to Vocabulary. Likewise, 43 percent of Vocabulary is due to an ability not involved in Similarities. There is a common factor of verbal facility or reasoning, but each test also involves something independent. Hence the two tests do involve distinct abilities.

Factor analysis works along these general lines, starting from correlations.

Correlation indicates whether tests possess a common element. Binet applied such reasoning when he decided that his tests, all having a substantial relation to each other, must be influenced by the same common factor, general intelligence. Wissler, whose tests had very small intercorrelations, concluded correctly that his tests had very little in common and therefore represented different abilities or, as we would now call them, factors.

TABLE 27. Intercorrelations of Three
Tests for Navy Recruits

	A	B	C
A		.81	.69
B			.69
C			

To simplify tables, each correlation is presented only once. The correlation of A with B (or B with A) is .81. Symmetrical entries could be made below the diagonal if desired.
SOURCE: Conrad, 1946.

The factor concept can be illustrated by means of a series of correlation tables. Table 27 gives correlations of three Navy classification tests with each other. These data suggest two conclusions:

Because the correlations are generally positive, the tests must be affected by some common characteristic.

Tests A and B have more in common than either has in common with test C.

The reasonableness of such a result is clear when we find that A is the General Classification test, B the Reading test, and C the Arithmetic Reasoning test. Probably the common element in all three tests is a composite of general reasoning ability and past learning. Two verbal tests may well have more in common than either has in common with a mathematical test.

TABLE 28. Intercorrelations of Four Measures for Adult Workers

	Arithmetic Reasoning	Turning	Assembly
Vocabulary	.66	.06	.14
Arithmetic Reasoning		.03	.16
Turning			.38
Assembly			

SOURCE: *Guide to the Use of GATB*, 1958, III, G-1.1.

Table 28 has a very different pattern of correlations which shows clearly the presence of two distinct abilities. A verbal-educational ability is found in the Vocabulary and Arithmetic tests. Some psychomotor ability affects both the Turning test (placing pegs in holes) and the Assembly test (assembling a rivet and washer).

A formal factor analysis goes beyond inspection and calculates how much each test is influenced by the various factors, as we did by a simple but inefficient method for the two Wechsler subtests. (For procedures see Thurstone, 1947.)

1. Table 29 presents correlations between six tests of the Navy classification battery. Does there appear to be a single common factor among all these tests? If so, what might be its psychological nature?

TABLE 29.   Intercorrelations of Six Navy Classification Tests

	General Classification Reading	Arithmetic Reasoning	Mechanical Aptitude	Electrical Knowledge	Mechanical Knowledge
General Classification Reading	.81	.69	.60	.53	.49
Arithmetic Reasoning		.69	.56	.51	.46
Mechanical Aptitude			.61	.47	.41
Electrical Knowledge				.53	.55
Mechanical Knowledge					.78

SOURCE: Conrad, 1946.

2. Which pairs of tests in Table 29 seem to have the greatest overlap?

The Three Types of Factors

Three types of factors are commonly distinguished: general, group, and specific. A *specific factor* is present in one test but not in any of the others under study. A *group factor* is present in more than one test. A *general factor* is a factor found in all the tests. If all the correlations among a set of tests are positive, one can find a general factor. If there are any zero or negative correlations, a general factor will ordinarily not be found (Figure 43). The mathematical methods of the factor analyst determine the correlation between each test and each factor. These correlations provide a table of "factor loadings." *The square of the factor loading tells how much each factor contributes to the variance of the test* (cf. Table 30).

Many factorial studies must be completed to arrive at psychological theory (Ahmavaara, 1957). Just what factors appear and what form they take depend on what tests are correlated. If we analyze only numerical tests, there will be a numerical general factor. Put two or three numerical tests into a mixed collection, and the same ability shows as a group factor. Use just one numerical test in the battery, and the factor will be specific.

Possible correlations among three variables:

	1	2	3		1	2	3		1	2	3		1	2	3
1		.0	.0	1		.7	.7	1		.5	.0	1		.6	6
2			.0	2			.7				.0	2			.4

Corresponding factor patterns
(general factor heavily shaded; group factor lightly shaded)

All factors specific	General and specific factors	Group and specific factors	General, group and specific factors

It is also possible to have general and group, but no specific factors;
group factors alone; or a general factor alone. These are unlikely.

FIG. 43.   Possible factorial relations among tests.

3. The Wechsler test can be scored to emphasize information about a general factor, about group factors, or about specific factors present in various subtests. Demonstrate the truth of this statement.
4. Confidence may be manifested in a variety of situations: making a speech to a woman's club, taking one's car apart to repair it, piloting a jet plane, or going to a show instead of cramming for a test. Give three alternative explanations of the nature of confidence: one in which it is considered as a general factor, one in which it is divided into group factors, and one in which it is considered as a number of highly specific factors. Which theory do you think is most adequate?
5. Confidence is to be considered in selecting future fighter pilots. How would a psychologist test confidence for this purpose if he believed it to be a broad general trait? How would he proceed if he considered confidence to be specific to a particular situation?

How Factor Analysis Groups Tests.   We shall now examine several illustrative results. Our first example treats the Navy classification tests whose correlations were presented in Table 29. These tests had various part scores. Peterson was asked to determine how many different abilities were being measured, so that testers could report to classification officers all the scores giving distinct information without reporting the same ability under different names.

To answer this question, Peterson chose to break up the general factor among the tests and subtests, and rotated to obtain the "simple structure" shown in Table 31. There are three group factors, which may be interpreted

TABLE 30. Approximate Factor Loadings and Factor Composition of the Navy Mechanical Comprehension Test

Factor	Factor Loading	Percentage of Variance
Verbal-educational	.35	12
Mechanical experience	.64	41
Quantitative reasoning	.10	01
Total common factors ("communality")		↳ 54
Error, if $r_{tt} = .79$		21
Unique	.50	25
		100

These values are presented solely to illustrate the form of a factorial result. Though they are derived from D. Peterson's (1943) findings (see text) they do not give an adequate analysis of the mechanical comprehension test. For more complete results, see Table 31.

TABLE 31. Factor Analysis of Navy Classification Test Scores

Test	Subdivision	I	II	III	Specific
		Factor Loading[a]			
Reading	Reading	.70	0	0	x
General Classification (GCT)	Opposites	.76	0	0	x
	Analogies	.73	0	0	x
	Series Completion	.68	0	x	x
Arithmetic Reasoning (AR)	Arithmetic Reasoning	.56	0	x	x
Mechanical Knowledge (MK)	Tool Relations	0	.69	0	x
	Mechanical Information	x	.59	0	x
	Electrical Comprehension	x	.67	0	x
	Mechanical Comprehension	x	.64	0	x
Mechanical Aptitude (MAT)	Block Counting	0	0	.61	.64
	Mechanical Comprehension	0	x	.52	x
	Surface Development	x	x	x	.65

[a] x indicates factor loading between .20 and .50; 0 represents negligible loading, below .20. In this analysis there are small correlations between factors which the discussion in the text ignores. SOURCE: D. Peterson, 1943.

by examining the tests where they appear. Factor I in this study might be given the name Verbal-Educational (frequently designated *v:ed* in British reports). Factor II can be called Mechanical Experience. Factor III cannot be named without more facts about the tests than we have given, though it seems to involve quantitative reasoning. Note that two tests named "Mechanical Comprehension" measure different factors.

Peterson found only three common factors in the twelve tests. In addition, each test measures some specific ability. Specific-factor loadings are fairly small except in Block Counting and Surface Development. Thus the analysis suggests that nearly all the information in the twelve scores can be reported in five scores: Factor I, Factor II, Factor III, and two specific factors. To simplify the record of the recruit, GCT, Reading, and AR could perhaps be combined into a verbal score. MK could be kept separate as a measure of mechanical experience. It would presumably be valuable to extend MAT to obtain better measures of the three factors it contains. By not scoring subtests of GCT and MK, and by pooling similar tests, the tester would eliminate seven scores from the record a classification interviewer has to interpret. This condensation, however, would be too drastic.

Factor analysts concentrate on large factor loadings and often ignore loadings below .50. Looking only at the larger factors would imply that GCT, Reading, and AR duplicate one another, and that since each test is reliable the Navy could drop two of them. Many factor analysts would have made precisely this drastic recommendation. But Peterson did not, and he was correct.

Specific factors and group factors with loadings below .50 may be of considerable importance to validity. Table 32 shows how the three tests predict

TABLE 32.   Validity of Tests Loaded on the v:ed Factor
for Predicting Service-School Grades

Training Course	Arithmetic Reasoning	GCT	Reading
Basic engineering	.38	.31	.30
Electrician's mate	.57	.55	.42
Fire control	.34	.25	.34
Quartermaster	.53	.37	.36
Cooks and bakers	.33	.54	.40
Storekeeper	.43	.16	.26

SOURCE: Frederiksen and Satter, 1953.

grades at Great Lakes Naval Training Center. In those training courses which require arithmetic ability, AR tends to be a better predictor than the other tests. It would have been a mistake to drop the AR test or to pool it with other measures of Factor I. Either Factor III or the specific factor in AR is making an important contribution to validity, even though the loadings are below .50. In general, while factor loadings suggest how tests may be grouped, final decisions on design of testing programs should rest on information about the validity of all factors including the specific ones.

In interpreting this example we may recall that a single factor analysis identifies the factors in a set of tests, taken as a set. If one of the same tests were included in a different collection, a somewhat different factor composition would be found. For example, if numerical tests were added to the battery, Factor III might divide into a numerical ability (in AR and Block Counting) and a geometric or spatial ability. We shall see later that the MK test performs rather differently when analyzed in other batteries.

How Factor Analysis Interprets Tests.   The most extensive factorial interpretation of tests has been done in Air Force research. Hundreds of tests of all sorts were used to select pilots, navigators, and bombardiers. Analyzing the correlations among many tests on large samples led to factorial interpretations such as those graphed in Figure 44.

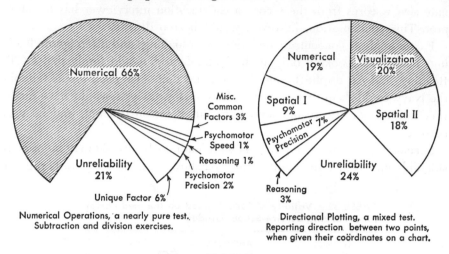

Numerical Operations, a nearly pure test.
Subtraction and division exercises.

Directional Plotting, a mixed test.
Reporting direction between two points,
when given their coördinates on a chart.

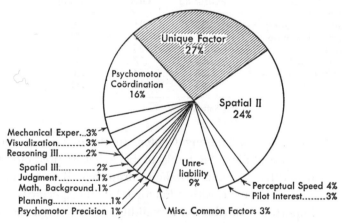

Complex Coördination, a highly complex test.
Job replica apparatus test.

FIG. 44.   Tests of different factorial purity. Factor loadings were determined by analysis of a complete battery of AAF classification tests (Guilford, 1947, pp. 828–831). The most prominent factor in each test is shaded.

The three tests are seen to be quite different in structure. Numerical Operations contains only one important factor, whereas Directional Plotting is influenced by four or five factors. Though Directional Plotting may predict some criterion that demands just this mixture of abilities, it is difficult to interpret psychologically. Complex Coördination is a test in which the person handles a stick and rudder in response to light signals. Its largest factor is one not found in other tests at all. The physical and psychological complexity of the test is reflected in the variety of factors it involves. This complexity evidently matches in some way the complexity of the pilot's job, for Complex Coördination is one of the best predictors of pilot success. (See also Figure 2 and pp. 303 ff.)

6. Compute the percentage contribution of each factor to the Reading test (Table 32), and make a composition diagram for it. Assume a reliability of .85.
7. Make a composition diagram for Block Counting.

"Simple Structure"

One important step in any factor analysis is that called "rotation." Rotation is a procedure for placing the factors so that the results will be most meaningful. Peterson, for example, decided to eliminate the general factor which his correlations indicated, breaking up the analysis to emphasize more diagnostic group factors.

A correlation table describes similarities between one test and all other tests. The factor analyst introduces artificial variables or "factors" which can be readily interpreted, and describes the test by its relations to these factors. The process is like that of describing the location of a home. Jones lives next to Smith and Adams, half a block from Brown and White, three blocks from James, Thomas, and Schultz. This description (which resembles a row in the correlation table) is useless if the person seeking Jones does not know where these others live, and inconvenient when he does know. So we introduce a reference system. We locate Jones as north of Main Street and west of State. Or we say he lives on this side of the highway, across the railroad tracks, and beyond the ice plant. We can place any home in relation to these reference lines. All the alternative descriptions are correct, differing only in completeness and communication value.

The principle of "simple structure" was suggested by L. L. Thurstone, the great American pioneer of factorial methods. His scientific aim was to describe complex performances as composites of simpler performances, i.e., to break test scores into more fundamental elements. For example, SB Memory for Sentences might be described as depending on verbal ability (three-tenths) and on memory ability (seven-tenths). Thurstone planned his factor analysis to find group factors having small loadings in some tasks and large loadings in others. A "simple structure" is one in which a large number of factor loadings are near zero, so that each test is described in terms of just a few factors. Thurstone aimed first to track down group factors, which would have zero loadings in some tests. Second, he aimed to discover or design "pure" tests each of which would have a high loading on just one factor. Numerical Operations is one such test. It measures a skill demanded by many tests and criteria, but it is almost entirely independent of verbal, reasoning, and other nonnumerical abilities.

British investigators have been less interested in pure measures of simple abilities. They, instead, rotate so as to identify broad factors present in a large number of tasks, $v{:}ed$ being one example.

THURSTONE'S "PRIMARY MENTAL ABILITIES"

The effort to isolate simple abilities is perhaps breaking down today, as we begin to suspect that no matter how far we advance the number of abilities still to be isolated always stretches far beyond the horizon. But the rather simple system of factors which Thurstone proposed in 1938 has had great influence on all subsequent classification of abilities.

Description of the Factors

Thurstone (1938) gave 56 tests to students at the University of Chicago and found six predominant factors: Verbal (V), Number (N), Spatial (S), Word fluency (W), Memory (M), and Reasoning (R). Subsequent studies also have found these factors to be useful reference axes, though Reasoning in particular is treated differently in recent work. Thurstone published a selected set of relatively pure tests to measure these "primary mental abilities." Items from the "PMA tests" are shown in Figure 45. To understand the Thurstone factors we can examine these items and also SB items known to have loadings on these factors.

The verbal factor V is found in vocabulary tests, and in tests of comprehension and reasoning. There are verbal loadings in SB vocabulary, comprehension, verbal absurdities, and other tests.

The number factor N appears in simple arithmetic tests. Tests of arithmetic skill are purer measures of N than are tests of arithmetic reasoning. Giving the number of fingers on one hand, and repeating digits backward are among the Binet items with loadings on N.

The spatial factor S deals with visual form relationships. Spatial loadings appear in picture absurdities, copying a diamond, drawing a design from memory, and paper cutting.

The memorizing factor M appears in tests which call for rapid rote learning, including memory for words, digits, and designs.

Reasoning, R, appears in tests requiring induction of a rule from several instances. Reasoning factors appear in the SB plan-of-search test, ingenuity (water-jar problems) and similarities between concepts.

The word-fluency factor W (which is clearly distinct from V) calls for

V

> Today much of our clothing is designed to make a fashionable appearance rather than for
>
> style   protection   children   sale   dresses
>
> *Synonyms:*   quiet   blue   still   tense   watery

N

> *Is this addition right or wrong?*   42
> 61
> 83
> ———
> 176
>
> *Mark every number that is exactly three more than the number just before it:*
>
> 4   11   14   10   9   12   16   8   10   3

S

> *Put a mark under every figure which is like the first figure in the row.*

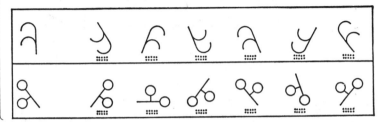

M

> *Study associations such as "chair-21" and "box-44." Mark the correct number on a later test.*

R

> *Letter series (Which letter comes next?)*
> abxcdxefxghx . . .
>
> *Letter groupings (Which group is different?)*
> AAAB   AAAM   AAAR   AATV

W

> *List as many four-letter words beginning with C as you can.*

FIG. 45. Items from the Chicago Tests of Primary Mental Abilities. (Copyright 1941 by L. L. and Thelma Gwinn Thurstone. Reproduced by permission of Mrs. Thurstone and Science Research Associates.)

ability to think of words rapidly, as in anagrams and rhyming. It is not found in the Stanford-Binet. The distinction between *V* and *W* is shown in two synonym tests tried by Thurstone. A test requiring the subject to select the correct synonym from several choices was saturated with *V* but not *W*; a test in which the subject rapidly supplies three synonyms for an easy word measured *W*, not *V*.

Thurstone's list of primary abilities is a convenient reference system. The word "primary," however, suggests that the list is more than a matter of convenience, that it represents something fundamental about the way the mind works. This implication raises questions which it has taken twenty years of research to answer:

Is general ability nothing but a mixture or average of the primary abilities?

Are these factors the only ones into which these tests could be divided?

Are these factors unitary and indivisible?

Is this a complete list of mental abilities?

Is this factor structure a reflection of innate human nature or of cultural influence?

To these might be added questions regarding predictive validity of the factors, but information on that subject will be accumulated through several succeeding chapters.

8. Do Thurstone's tests cover the same ground as the Kuhlmann-Anderson test? Can you find Kuhlmann-Anderson items which appear to represent each Thurstone factor?

9. Which Thurstone factors are most consistent with Binet's description of intelligence?

10. What factors would you expect to influence Wechsler Vocabulary scores? Digit Symbol?

The Status of General Ability

Thurstone intended by the name "primary abilities" to suggest that these abilities combine to produce aptitude for any complex intellectual performance, just as green, red, and blue spotlights can be mingled to produce any other hue, or white. If this is true, general mental ability is nothing but a mixture of primaries in some proportion. In sharp opposition is the view of Galton and Spearman that some persons are endowed with superior general adaptive ability which might be turned in various directions. This conflict of views was sharpened when Thurstone found no general intercorrelation among his Chicago tests. Since he found near-zero correlations between ability tests, he argued that no general factor exists.

Subsequent research has altered his argument. The low correlations proved to be due to the very restricted range of the University of Chicago sample. In less select groups, even Thurstone and his associates found general intercorrelations. As Burt (1958, p. 5) says:

In nearly every factorial study of cognitive ability, the general factor commonly accounts for quite 50% of the variance (rather more in the case of the young child, rather less with older age groups) while each of the minor factors accounts for only 10% or less. . . . For all practical purposes, almost every psychologist—even former opponents of the concept of general intelligence, like Thorndike, Brown, Thomson, and Thurstone—seems in the end to have come round to much the same conclusion, even though, for theoretical purposes, each tends to reword it in a modified terminology of his own.

The issue then reduces to how to take the general factor into account. Holzinger in America and Burt in England preferred to pay attention to the general factor first, and then to see what further information group factors add. Thurstone preferred to concentrate on group factors, and to account for the overall relation by identifying a "second-order" factor which unites the groups.

The Determinacy of Factors

Thurstone's list has often been regarded as a list of the basic elements of the human mind. Some persons have compared it to the chemist's list of elements. Others, critical of the approach, have condemned it as a new "faculty" psychology.

Factor analysis is in no sense comparable to the chemist's search for elements. There is only one answer to the question: What elements make up table salt? In factor analysis there are many answers, all equally true but not equally satisfactory (Guttman, 1955). The factor analyst may be compared to the photographer trying to picture a building as revealingly as possible. Wherever he sets his camera, he will lose some information, but by a skillful choice he will be able to show a large number of important features of the building.

The fact that many other investigators find similar factors has made it seem as if Thurstone's list did embody some fundamental truth. Yet his list does not include anything like the $v:ed$ factor of the British investigators, and his N factor is defined by simple arithmetic skill rather than by reasoning. Location of reference factors is a matter of judgment.

Thurstone's choice of his particular factors was dictated by a criterion of simplicity. He wanted irreducible factors and therefore matched his factors to very simple tests wherever he could. A test whose items seemed, on inspection, to involve many types of mental process would not satisfy him as a measure of a pure factor. This explains, for example, why N was defined in terms of elementary, overlearned computational skills.

The meanings of factors shift from time to time as new evidence and new criteria are introduced. As we shall see, N, R, and S have somewhat different meanings in current studies from the meanings they had in the 1938 list.

Divisibility of Factors

Thurstone and his students discarded the view that factors are irreducible. While verbal tests have enough in common to define a "verbal factor," they can be divided into several subgroups, thus establishing narrower factors within the verbal domain. One can divide a vocabulary test, for instance, into subgroups of words from different content areas. Within the subfactor of "science vocabulary," we would find that some students know more chemical terms than psychological ones. This could be pursued down to ridiculously fine detail. Other factors subdivide similarly.

Factor analysts now recognize that abilities are most clearly described by a hierarchy ranging from the very broad factors to those present only in very specific tests. One can plan his statistical analysis to find only the high-level factors, to find only factors of intermediate breadth, or to isolate dozens of detailed factors. Many investigators have suggested possible hierarchical arrangements, but all the proposals are tentative at present, subject to verification by further data. Vernon's diagram (Figure 46) is one

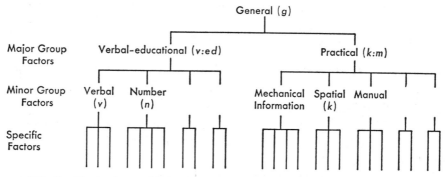

FIG. 46.   Sketch of a possible hierarchy of abilities. (After Vernon, 1950, pp. 22–23.)

such suggestion. (For an actual factor analysis deriving hierarchical factors at three levels, see Moursy, 1952, and Laugier, 1955, pp. 187–208.)

Completeness of the List

The preceding remarks have already indicated that the number of possible factors is inexhaustible, if we are willing to make the factors sufficiently trivial. The question remains, however, whether significant factors can be discovered beyond Thurstone's list. The answer is emphatically "yes." These remarks were written at the end of World War II (F. B. Davis, 1947, p. 59):

> The results of testing hundreds of thousands of men in the armed forces and of analyzing these data suggest to many psychologists that the number of basic mental abilities may often have been underesti-

mated. From factorial analyses of many different matrices of intercor-relations obtained as a result of testing aviation cadets in AAF classification centers, factors that have been mathematically determined have been named as indicated in the following list.

Carefulness	Perceptual speed
General reasoning I	Pilot interest
Integration I	Planning
Integration II	Psychomotor coordination
Integration III	Psychomotor precision
Judgment	Psychomotor speed
Kinesthetic motor	Reasoning II
Length estimation	Reasoning III
Mathematical background	Social science background
Mathematical reasoning	Spatial Relations I
Mechanical experience	Spatial Relations II
Memory I	Spatial Relations III
Memory II	Verbal
Memory III	Visualization
Numerical	

There is no objective method of determining whether the names attached to the factors discovered in the analyses are accurate descriptions of the mental abilities represented by the factors. In any case, . . . the number of basic mental abilities may be much larger than was formerly believed.

Some of these added factors came from the extension of factorial investigations to psychomotor tests. Some came from bringing new pencil-and-paper tests into the analysis. Some came as a result of subdivisions—but not trivial subdivisions—of the Thurstone factors.

One gets out of a factor analysis only what he puts in. This remark has become trite, but it is of basic importance. Factor analysis sorts the abilities present in the test battery; it does not unearth new ones. Thurstone identified the common elements in tests such as psychologists had been generally using. If psychologists had not yet designed tests covering some important ability, that ability could not show in Thurstone's list. The Air Force invented and tried out many additional possibilities but by no means covered the range of possible ability tests.

Origin of Factors

Many of those who believe that factor analysis is identifying "the way human abilities are organized" think that biological nature determines what factors are found. It is conceivable that perceptual speed and spatial judgment rely on different neural processes, and that a person could be superior on one process and not the other. It is equally possible to argue that correlations between abilities are produced by experience. Numerical performances develop together, presumably because they are taught together. A child who makes a bad start in arithmetic because of poor teaching will lag in all numerical tasks even though he may do well in verbal work. There is no need to conclude that the separation of numerical from verbal facility is inborn. On the other hand, we may yet find intellectual patterns of undeniable hereditary origin. Many sensory differences (e.g., color vision) are of this character.

11. One student says, "It seems to me the factor analysts are like astronomers trying to discover planets. The astronomer finds a new planet by detecting the pull it exerts on already known bodies. Then he makes more careful studies to check his conclusion and locate the planet exactly. The factor analyst locates one test against already established abilities." How satisfactory is this comparison?

12. Another student suggests that factors are comparable to constellations of stars, which the astronomer uses to label portions of the sky (e.g., "The nebula is in Orion"). How apt is this comparison?

THE PRESENT STATUS OF FACTOR ANALYSIS

From some points of view factor analysis has been a great success. It provides precise methods for handling large numbers of variables and for reducing them to a much smaller number of scores with little loss of information. Thus factor analysis is a highly important statistical method. Secondly, factor analysis has cut through a large amount of nonsensical interpretation which results from assuming that every test with a different name measures a different ability. Thirdly, factor analysis helps to describe what a test measures. It is gradually establishing a reference system that all psychologists can use to describe tests.

Some critics of factor studies were disappointed when they found that not all factors measured practically significant mental abilities. Even one of the pioneers in the field (Kelley, 1939) spoke of the discoveries as "mental factors of no importance." Probably the correct position to take is that factor studies clarify what present tests measure. They cannot identify factors not built into the original tests. They cannot guarantee to produce factors of practical importance. But by clarifying the content of tests they permit the psychologist to decide whether he is satisfied with them and help him to throw out the components that are useless. Furthermore, the sorting of abilities directs research to the question: For what is each of these human talents useful, and how can we capitalize on it?

The great goal of the factor analyst has been to discover a dependable list of the important abilities. Many abilities have been defined, and tests which give fairly pure measures for most of these factors are available. R. B. Cattell (Laugier, 1955, pp. 319–325) has proposed that an "international index" of well-established factors be prepared, but the other leading factor analysts argue that the definitions of factors are still shifting and that to "freeze" any present list would be premature. The difficulty is not that factor analysis fails to analyze data correctly. The problem is that, with so many different ways of placing reference factors, it is unlikely that the best possible system has been found.

Many investigators feel that factor analysis has paid undue attention to the content of the test item, i.e., to whether it deals with words, numbers, forms, or other symbols. Content groupings are of course to be found in tests using different content. A more fundamental problem, however, is the organization of mental *process*. Thurstone distinguished three such processes: memory, reasoning, and fluency. Meili (1946, 1955) found evidence for fluency, complexity (application of such ideas as *order*), plasticity (restructuring, as in Block Design or Hidden Figures), and integration (titling a picture). These may be subdivisions of Thurstone's reasoning factor. Attempts to study process are growing in number but are not near to final results.

A tentative three-way organization of intellectual tasks has recently been suggested by J. P. Guilford, as an outcome of a long series of studies of high-level intellectual performance. Guilford (1957) distinguishes five types of mental operation:

> Memory—retention of information
> Cognition—recognizing patterns, facts, etc.
> Convergent thinking—proceeding from information to a specific "right answer"
> Divergent thinking—proceeding from information to a variety of adequate solutions (as in finding titles to fit a plot)
> Evaluation—decisions concerning goodness or appropriateness of ideas (e.g., judging which problems are significant)

Tasks within each of these categories can be classified with respect to "content" and "product." The content categories are figural (directly perceived objects, events, drawings, etc.), symbolic (letters, numbers, etc.), semantic (verbal), and "behavioral" (interpretation of human behavior). The six kinds of "products" distinguished by Guilford are units of information, classes of units, relations between units, systems of information, transformations, and implications.

Since there are five operations, four content categories, and six products, there are 120 different combinations. Each combination represents a type of task which is or can be represented in an intellectual test, according to Guilford. For example, the common verbal comprehension tests fit into *cognition* of *semantic units of information*. A test which asks the subject to find the name of a sport concealed in the sentence "He chose a Mongol for his bride" is classified as *convergent thinking—symbolic—transformation*.

Guilford's system is still undergoing development, and it is not yet clear how well his categories reproduce the empirical relations found through factor analysis. The system emphasizes the distinction between test content and test process and is therefore an advance over the Thurstone explorations in which processes (fluency, reasoning) were mixed indiscriminately with content (verbal, spatial) factors.

The striking thing about Guilford's system, apart from its bold break with tradition, is the vast number of ability factors he requires. His system has over 120 cells, of which perhaps 50 have been matched with tests. It begins to be clear that we will never again have a list of a few simple primary abilities. According to Guilford (1957, p. 20):

> The obvious implication for intelligence testing is that the trend toward the multiple-score approach and the enlightened composite-score approach should be accelerated. The single, somewhat haphazardly composed, score has worked well; perhaps too well, hence the unwarranted complacency regarding it. It would seem that we now have information that should make possible a considerable advance in refinements of measurement of intelligence. If the apparent complexity implied is appalling, what seems to be needed is the courage to face reality. If the next steps do not seem to be clear, then the cure is more knowledge—knowledge concerning the whole list of intellectual factors, their relations to complex mental functioning, and their relations to everyday behavior.

13. Compare Meili's four factors to Guilford's major factors.
14. Where, in Guilford's system, do Thurstone's V, S, and W factors appear?

A FACTOR ANALYSIS OF THE WECHSLER SCALE

As a final example of factor analysis in test interpretation, we turn to a study of the Wechsler subtests (P. C. Davis, 1956). This analysis illustrates the modern technique of using "reference tests" to define factors.

Davis gave Form I of the Wechsler-Bellevue (very similar to WAIS) to 202 eighth-graders in Seattle. He wanted to learn as much as possible about subtest meanings and believed that group factors would be found if the obvious general factor among the subtests was broken up. He predicted the presence of particular factors, and for each such factor he introduced one or two reference tests into his battery to aid in rotation and interpretation. A reference test is one regarded as a fairly pure measure of a factor. The predicted factors and their reference tests were as follows:

Verbal comprehension. Two tests (Nos. 9 and 10 in Table 33). One called for choice of a correct synonym, one called for writing of definitions.

Numerical facility. Numerical Operations test (4; see Figure 44) calls for simple addition, division, etc., under time pressure.

Perceptual speed. Test (3) requires the pupil to match a figure of strange form with whichever of five other figures is exactly like it.

Visualization. Mechanical principles (6). This test adapted from Air Force research resembles the Bennett TMC. Visualization is a factor commonly identified in spatial tests (see p. 279), requiring understanding of movements of objects. Test 6 is influenced by both visualization and mechanical experience (Guilford, 1947, p. 894) and therefore is a rather poor reference test.

Arithmetic Reasoning (5). Verbally stated problems making little demand on computation are administered as a highly speeded test.

Mechanical information. The test (7) asks about a variety of tools and machinery.

In addition, Davis included other conveniently available scores: age, an Otis group test, and a test of current scientific information. Finally, he adapted parallel forms of three Wechsler subtests for group administration.

The correlations were almost all positive. Davis found ten factors, although he had suggested six initially. He rotated them to obtain a simple structure, that is, a pattern in which each test is loaded on few factors, and each factor is found in only a limited group of tests. The factors are listed in Table 33. (All loadings lower than .30 are omitted to reduce confusion.) Specific factor loadings for the Wechsler tests were calculated by the present writer, using a rough estimate of error variance. (For the other tests, error and specific factors cannot be separated because their reliabilities are unknown.)

Before going further, let us note that this is *a* factor analysis of the Wechsler, not the only possible analysis. A somewhat different structure would occur in a sample of a different kind. A different investigator might choose a slightly different rotation. Indeed, a different choice of reference tests would introduce some other factors. But these differences should be relatively minor in view of Davis' large sample and large number of measures. We would interpret factors as follows:[1]

[1] The writer has given some of the factors names different from Davis', for the sake of coördination with other analyses described in this book.

TABLE 33. Factor Analysis of Wechsler Scores with Reference Variables

Tests	Verbal Comprehension	Verbal Problem Solving	Nonverbal Reasoning	Numerical Speed	Information	Perceptual Speed	Visualization	Similarities	Fluency (?)	Unidentified	Unique and error
1. Age				−.32						−.40	
2. Otis Beta	.54			.30							.47
3. Perceptual Speed				.30		.52*					
4. Numerical Operations				.74*		.31					
5. Arithmetic Reasoning		.44*	.32								
6. Mechanical Principles			.39				.64*				
7. Mechanical Information			.44*								
8. Science Information	.57		.32								
9. Synonyms	.75*					.31					
10. Word Definition	.80*									.37	
11. Information—group	.61				.44						
12. Comprehension—group	.38								.62		
13. Similarities—group			.32		.44	.38		.65			
14. W Information	.42				.56						.46
15. W Comprehension		.33									.62
16. W Digit Span			.34						.37		.52
17. W Arithmetic		.57	.34	.36	.32						
18. W Similarities	.31							.65			.54
19. W Vocabulary	.60										.45
20. W Picture Arrangement										.49	.47
21. W Picture Completion						.38					.58
22. W Block Design			.41		.30	.38	.44				.40
23. W Object Assembly						.42	.34				.56
24. W Digit Symbol				.52		.37				.30	.61

SOURCE: Based on unpublished data supplied by Paul C. Davis. Asterisks indicate reference tests.

V—The first hypothesized factor, *verbal comprehension*, was defined by reference tests 9 and 10. Wechsler Vocabulary and Otis Beta are especially loaded with this factor. Three of the Wechsler "Verbal" tests, however, have loadings below .30.

VPS—This factor appears in both of the Arithmetic Reasoning tests, in Comprehension, and in Group Similarities. It might be titled *verbal problem solving*.

NV—Nearly all the tests requiring thinking about numbers or objects have moderate loadings on this factor. The common factor seems to involve some sort of *nonverbal reasoning*. This factor appeared instead of the hypothesized factor of mechanical information. The test of mechanical information did not have much in common with the Wechsler tests.

N—This factor has only small loadings on tests other than the reference test, Numerical Operations. The high loading of Digit Symbol must be due to the marked speeding of both tests, rather than to the fact that both tests involve numbers. We call the factor *numerical speed.*

I—This is an *information* or general education factor.

P—*Perceptual speed* is identified by the reference test. It appears in three of the Wechsler Performance tests. Loadings in two unspeeded verbal tests (9 and 13) seem to contradict the interpretation, but the loadings might result from sampling error.

Vz—This factor is present in the mechanical comprehension test, Picture Completion, Block Design, and Object Assembly. It can be only vaguely interpreted as some sort of *spatial* or *visualization* ability.

B—This is a factor defined only by *similarity* items. If only one of the two Similarities tests had been used, it would have been a specific factor. Here is an example of changing a specific factor to a "group factor" by bringing a similar test into the battery.

F—This is found in Group Comprehension, Digit Span, and Block Design. It is a minor factor having no reference test, and any interpretation of it is speculative.

?—This unanticipated factor links Picture Arrangement, Word Definition, Otis Beta, and Age. It is an uninterpretable factor having something to do with reasoning or education.

All Wechsler tests save Arithmetic have specific loadings over .30. The notable specific factors are found in Comprehension, Picture Completion, Object Assembly, and Digit Symbol.

What, now, have we learned about the Wechsler test?

• That if we break up the Verbal, Performance, and Full scale scores, we can find a large number of different abilities within the test. There is no reason to think that Davis' ten factors plus four unique factors constitute the most refined subdivision possible.

• That Wechsler subtests very rarely correspond to psychologically simple abilities. No Wechsler test is anywhere near to a pure measure of a commonly accepted reference factor.

• That it appears possible to estimate individual scores on some factors from appropriate combinations of Wechsler subtests. One could obtain moderately dependable measures of Verbal Comprehension, Visualization, Numerical Speed, Perceptual Speed, and Verbal Problem Solving as distinct abilities. The other factors are not reliably measured by the Wechsler subtests.

- That the Wechsler scores include a good deal of information about individual differences not observed in the group tests. The Performance subtests in particular resisted description in terms of factors common to other tests. Moreover, the subtests are to an appreciable degree distinct from each other.

What facts about factor analysis are illustrated in this study?

- That a good deal of variance, probably representing complex integrative processes, usually remains in specific factors.

- That different interpreters may disagree as to the psychological meaning of a factor, but that such disagreement is reduced when a factor is marked by a well-understood reference test.

- That the minor factors in a study are usually difficult to interpret. To delineate them clearly it is necessary to include reference variables for these factors in a further study.

15. What is the factorial composition of Otis Beta, assuming a reliability of .90?
16. What does the factor analysis suggest as to the best subtests to use in a short form of the Wechsler?
17. Davis suggests that if only five tests are used in the Verbal scale, Comprehension might well be omitted. His reason is that it has low loadings on numerous factors. What reasons might justify keeping it in the scale?
18. Davis names factor VPS "general reasoning." Why is this name open to question?

Suggested Readings

Schutz, Richard E. Patterns of personal problems of adolescent girls. *J. educ. Psychol.*, 1958, **49**, 1–5.

A factor analysis of a personality questionnaire shows how factorial results lead to a different organization of the scores from that arrived at by classifying items according to apparent content.

Vernon, Philip E. Mental faculties and factors, and Landmarks in the development of factor analysis. *The structure of human abilities.* New York: Wiley, 1950. Pp. 1–24.

Vernon shows by simple calculations how a factor analysis is performed, warns against common misinterpretations, and reviews several of the most important analyses of abilities.

10

Differential Abilities in Guidance

THURSTONE intended his Tests of Primary Mental Abilities to be used in guidance, hoping that the person's pattern of abilities would indicate the courses and jobs where he could expect greatest success. We are now ready to examine how validly such patterns can be interpreted, drawing on evidence regarding the differential batteries whose validity has been most thoroughly tested. We begin by describing two of them, the Differential Aptitude Tests (DAT) and the General Aptitude Test Battery (GATB).

THE DIFFERENTIAL APTITUDE TESTS

The DAT battery was published in 1947, primarily for high-school counseling. The eight tests measure aptitudes which previous research had suggested as important in guidance. Among the tests are a modification of the TMC, a clerical aptitude test, a spelling test, and a verbal reasoning test. This partial list makes it clear that the DAT is quite different from the PMA battery. No attempt is made to isolate simple, pure abilities. Instead, the tests aim to measure complex abilities which have a fairly direct relation to job families and curricula. Measures of proficiency are included because of their predictive value.

The tests require six to thirty minutes of working time. With the addition of time for directions, three sessions of eighty minutes each are required for the battery. Except for the Clerical test, the tests are essentially unspeeded. Items from each of the tests except Mechanical Reasoning and Verbal Reasoning are presented in Figure 47. (For MR and VR, see pp. 40, 235.)

The publication of this integrated collection marked an important forward step in aptitude testing. The counselor desiring tests of this nature previously had had to make up his own collection, using tests standardized and validated on different samples. Interpretation of profiles was therefore in-

NUMERICAL ABILITY.

1. Add

393
4658
3790
67
___

ANSWER

A 7908
B 8608
C 8898
D 8908
E **none of these**

ABSTRACT REASONING. Which figure is next in the series?

SPACE REASONING. Which figures can be made from the pattern?

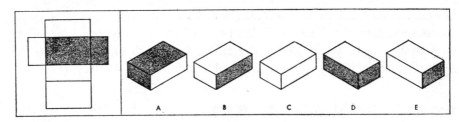

CLERICAL SPEED AND ACCURACY. Underline at right the symbol which is also underlined at left.

<u>AB</u>	AC	AD	AE	AF		AC	AE	AF	AB	AD
aA	aB	BA	Ba	<u>Bb</u>		BA	Ba	Bb	aA	aB
A7	7A	B7	<u>7B</u>	AB		7B	B7	AB	7A	A7

SPELLING. Which words are incorrectly spelled?

apointed
commission
visinity

SENTENCES. Which parts of the sentence are incorrect in grammar, punctuation, or spelling?

Ain't we / going to the / office / next week / at all.
  A   B   C   D   E

They / nearly were / starved / before they landed / somewheres in Florida.
  A   B   C   D   E

FIG. 47. Items from subtests of the Differential Aptitude Battery. (Items copyright 1947, The Psychological Corporation. Reproduced by permission.)

exact at best. Percentile conversions for all DAT scores have been calculated on the same sample, so that profile shapes are meaningful. Moreover, the tests have been matched in difficulty so that all of them can be applied satisfactorily to the same subjects.

The intercorrelations and reliabilities of the tests are presented in Table 34. Reliabilities are split-half coefficients, except for the speeded Clerical

TABLE 34. Intercorrelations and Reliabilities of DAT Scores

	VR	NA	AR	SR	MR	Cler- ical	Spell- ing	Sen- tences
VR	.88							
NA	.50	.88						
AR	.51	.49	.86					
SR	.35	.35	.49	.92				
MR	.44	.25	.48	.43	.85			
Clerical	.10	.08	.10	.05	.04	.83		
Spelling	.48	.36	.25	.14	.16	.14	.92	
Sentences	.53	.43	.36	.23	.26	.11	.59	.86

SOURCE: Bennett *et al.*, 1947, pp. C-5, C-10.

test, where a between-forms coefficient was used. These data are for ninth-grade boys. It is evident that the tests measure with adequate precision. Second, we may note that the tests, except for Clerical, involve a general factor. Third, and of great importance, the correlations between tests are much lower than their reliabilities. This assures that each test is independent of the others to a substantial degree.

In order to emphasize the concept of multiple abilities, as distinct from the single composite ability commonly measured in previous tests, the DAT originally provided no total or general score. The authors later responded to the counselor's demand for an overall predictor by developing norms for the combination VR + NA. This composite serves the same purpose as the group tests of general ability or scholastic aptitude in common use.

1. The manual suggests that the DAT may be given in two, three, or six sessions, adjusting the length of session appropriately. Which arrangement would you consider wisest?
2. Prepare a composition diagram like Figure 37 to show the breakdown into common and independent elements of these pairs of tests.
   a. Verbal-Abstract
   b. Numerical-Clerical
3. If a person being counseled has been tested with the Wechsler, which of the Differential Aptitude Tests would add the most useful supplementary information?
4. In what high-school subjects would you expect the Space Relations score to predict success better than the Abstract Reasoning score?

THE GENERAL APTITUDE TEST BATTERY

In marked contrast to the DAT in form and function is the GATB. This battery was produced by the U.S. Employment Service and is used throughout the country for guiding persons seeking work. The construction of the battery was strongly influenced both by Thurstone's factor-analytic studies and by three decades of research on job performance. Several of the tests are descended from the pioneer Minnesota series of vocational aptitude tests, which date back to the 1920's.

The USES tests are given only through state employment services. The tests are often given to high-school juniors and seniors under a coöperative plan which makes the results available to both the high-school counselor and the employment service. Versions of the tests are now being prepared in at least 27 foreign countries.

The employment services are primarily concerned with guiding the person into suitable work. There are thousands of jobs in the modern industrial world, each having its own aptitude requirements. When an employer asks for referrals of potential employees, he wants applicants who are likely to succeed. The USES, working with state agencies, therefore conducts studies of the psychological characteristics of particular jobs and accumulates information on the meaning of test scores. Dvorak (1956) mentions the following occupations having been studied during a single year: assembler of dry-cell batteries, aircraft electrician, teacher, X-ray technician, nurse aid, sheet-metal worker, baker, cook, spot welder, comptometer operator, corn-husking-machine operator, knitting-machine fixer, and fruit packer. Prediction for such jobs takes us far beyond the academic and reasoning abilities which predominate in the tests studied so far in this book.

The diversity of occupations rules out the possibility of devising a separate aptitude test for each job. At one time, the USES had started to build different tests for each job family, but when the total number of tests passed 100, it became clear that such a collection could not be used for guidance, however suitable any of the separate tests might be for screening applicants for one job. For guidance we need a limited number of diversified tests which can be given to everyone and which can be linked together in various combinations to predict success in different situations. With this end in view, the current form of the GATB uses eight pencil-paper and four apparatus tests to measure nine distinct factors:

> G—General reasoning ability (a composite of tests titled Vocabulary, Three-Dimensional Space, and Arithmetic Reasoning)
> V—Verbal aptitude (Vocabulary)
> N—Numerical aptitude (Computation, Arithmetic Reasoning)
> S—Spatial aptitude (Three-Dimensional Space)
> P—Form perception (Tool Matching, Form Matching)

Q—Clerical perception (Name Comparison)
K—Motor coördination (Mark Making)
F—Finger dexterity (Assemble, Disassemble)
M—Manual dexterity (Place, Turn)

(An earlier form had an additional measure of Eye-Hand Coördination or Aiming [A], and factor K was referred to as T.)

We can skip over Vocabulary, Arithmetic Reasoning, and Computation without further description. The Space test is much like the DAT spatial test. Name Comparison, like DAT-Clerical, requires quick checking to detect discrepancies between two lists. The USES version gives two lists of names of business firms, identical except for errors of style and spelling. This technique of name comparison was invented for the Minnesota Clerical Aptitude Test, one of the earliest successful special aptitude tests.

Tool Matching calls for rapid visual comparison of pictures of tools, alike save for differences in shading. The only reason for showing tools rather than abstract forms is to increase the subject's interest. Form Matching is a pencil-paper adaptation of a formboard used in the Minnesota studies in which dozens of irregular shapes were cut out of a board. The subject was to fit each shape into the correct hole (see Figure 48). In the USES test, the shapes are printed in two different arrangements, and the subject must match identical forms. The test appears much like Figure 48, save

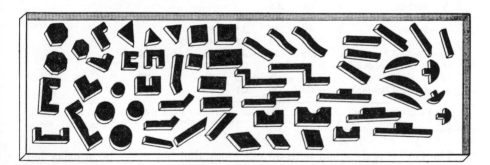

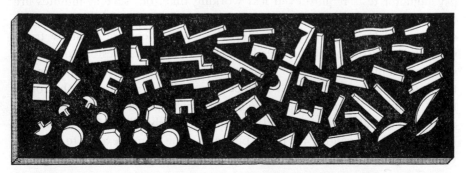

FIG. 48. Minnesota Spatial Relations Formboard. (Courtesy Educational Test Bureau.)

that the shapes are larger. Changing from a formboard to a printed test undoubtedly simplified the factor composition of the test by eliminating dexterity from the score, and so made it more interpretable as well as easier to administer.

Mark Making, a psychomotor test, is likewise designed to meet the needs of a program which tests a million people each year. The subject is asked only to make marks like these *ц* in each square, filling as many squares as he can in sixty seconds.

The Place and Turn tests are derived from the Minnesota Rate of Manipulation Test. Forty-eight pegs are placed in a pegboard. A second board with rows of holes is provided, and the subject transfers the pegs from one board to another as fast as possible. In the Turn test, he inverts each peg while transferring it.

The tests named Assemble and Disassemble call for finer coördination, using both hands. A board contains fifty holes. The person is to fit a rivet and washer into each hole. In Disassemble, he replaces the rivets in their original bin and puts the washers onto the rod where they are stored.

TABLE 35. Intercorrelations and Reliabilities of GATB Scores for High-School Seniors

	G	V	N	S	P	Q	K	F	M
G—General	.85								
V—Verbal	—	.86							
N—Numerical	—	.42	.82						
S—Spatial	—	.40	.34	.81					
P—Form Perception	.43	.34	.42	.48	.72				
Q—Clerical Perception	.35	.29	.42	.26	.66	.74			
K—Motor Coördination	−.04	.13	.06	−.03	.29	.29	.76		
F—Finger Dexterity	−.05	−.03	−.03	.01	.27	.20	.37	.65	
M—Manual Dexterity	−.06	.06	.01	−.03	.23	.16	.49	.46	.73

   All reliabilities are based on retests after three months for about 1000 boys. Intercorrelations are for a sample of 100 boys and girls. No correlation is given for G with V, N, or S, since these tests are included within G.
   SOURCE: *Guide to the Use of GATB*, 1958.

The GATB is designed with an efficiency that has never been exceeded. The working times for pencil-paper tests are close to six minutes each. The psychomotor tests require even less working time, but several minutes are used for demonstration and practice. The entire battery can be given in two and one-quarter hours. The procedures are simple enough to allow trustworthy administration of the tests by relatively untrained testers to subjects who have limited education or poor command of English. The psychomotor tests are so designed that each subject leaves all the materials as he found them, ready for the next subject. No doubt much has been sacrificed for efficient administration. The marked speeding of nearly all the GATB subtests may reduce their validity for many purposes. One cannot expect to measure with the precision of the DAT, using subtests only one-fifth as long.

With its access to workers in all areas of the country, all types of industry and agriculture, and most occupational levels, the USES was able to obtain a highly representative normative sample. Four thousand cases were drawn from the records on hand to form a group in which all occupational, sex, and age groups were properly represented in proportion to census data. Scores on the factors are expressed in standard-score form, with a mean of 100 and s.d. of 20.

Correlational data for the GATB are presented in Table 35. (These data are selected from several tables in the technical manual for the test and are not based on the same sample.) We note the usual common factor running through the pencil-paper tests, and another factor linking the psychomotor tests. In general, the test intercorrelations are low enough to give some promise of meaningful separation of aptitudes.

5. Compare the reliabilities of the DAT and GATB. How much was sacrificed by the use of short tests in GATB? What would the reliability of the S score be if the test were extended from six minutes to thirty minutes?

6. How do you account for the overlap of scores P and Q, which seem to involve neither reasoning nor dexterity, with the remainder of the battery?

7. Are local norms or national norms most relevant in occupational guidance?

8. The median coefficient of stability for GATB for high-school students is .81, but for adult applicants at employment service offices it is .89. Account for this difference. (Time between tests is short in both cases.)

9. Table 36 indicates stability of GATB scores over intervals of several years. Which aptitudes are stable enough to be used confidently for ninth-grade counseling? Which aptitudes appear to stabilize late in high school?

TABLE 36. Stability of GATB Scores

| | Correlation with 12th-Grade Scores of Tests Given in Grade | | | |
	8 N = 53	9 N = 61	10 N = 61	11 N = 53
G—General	.75	.82	.80	.84
V—Verbal	.70	.76	.73	.82
N—Numerical	.76	.77	.81	.85
S—Spatial	.76	.86	.86	.88
P—Form Perception	.61	.65	.71	.75
Q—Clerical Perception	.77	.80	.86	.89
A—Aiming	.55	.58	.69	.64
T—Motor Speed	.59	.61	.78	.75
F—Finger Dexterity	.59	.66	.68	.72
M—Manual Dexterity	.65	.65	.71	.73

SOURCE: Unpublished results supplied by Dr. Beatrice Dvorak.

Relation of DAT to GATB

One study has applied both DAT and GATB to the same high-school seniors, and the intercorrelations (Table 37) shed light on both tests. Each DAT score has its highest correlation with the corresponding GATB factor, except that DAT-VR and DAT-NA have higher correlations with GATB-General than with GATB-V and -N. The general factor has substantial influence in

TABLE 37.   Correlation of DAT and GATB Scores

	G	V	N	S	P	Q	T	F	M
					Form Perc.	Cler. Perc.	Motor Speed	Finger Dext.	Manual Dext.
	General	Verbal	Number	Spatial					
Verbal	.78	.72	.54	.54	.21	.41	.29	.20	−.03
Spelling	.66	.66	.57	.21	.03	.51	.32	.08	.10
Sentences	.74	.75	.56	.36	.05	.33	.33	.17	.12
Numerical	.66	.52	.62	.32	.01	.22	.27	.13	.05
Abstract	.68	.48	.45	.56	.14	.26	.21	.17	.00
Space	.59	.49	.24	.72	.21	.22	.19	.35	.11
Mechanical	.62	.56	.25	.68	.13	.09	.24	.39	.08
Clerical	.25	.18	.33	.07	.46	.53	.61	.27	.46

GATB Scores spans columns G through M. Left row labels are *DAT Scores*.

The values given are those for high-school boys; correlations for girls are similar, but generally lower. Correlations over .50 are in boldface type.
SOURCE: *Guide to the Use of GATB*, 1958, p. L-1.

every DAT score except Clerical, which correlates with all the GATB speed tests.

The GATB factors *P*, *F*, and *M* measure aptitudes not covered in the DAT battery. DAT-Mechanical Reasoning has no counterpart in the GATB, although it overlaps *G* and *S* to a considerable degree. DAT-Spelling and Sentences overlap considerably with Verbal Reasoning.

10. For what types of guidance does the content of GATB seem more useful than that of DAT? For what types is it less useful?
11. What do the correlations for DAT-Clerical tell about its meaning?
12. DAT and GATB spatial tests correlate .72, but each correlates only .50 with PMA-Spatial. How do you account for this?
13. Make composition diagrams to show the overlap and unique content of these pairs of tests:
    a. DAT-NA and GATB-N
    b. DAT-MR and GATB-S
14. Why does MR have a large spatial loading here, when a similar test showed no such factor in Table 30?

SPATIAL ABILITY

We cannot examine separately the psychological and practical significance of every factor so far isolated, or even of all the scores in the test batteries under discussion. We have selected spatial reasoning and mechanical comprehension as examples for close attention. After reviewing evidence on these two factors, we shall return to a general discussion of the test batteries. Psychomotor abilities will be further considered in the next chapter.

Spatial ability was present in some early nonverbal tests of general ability, but it was soon recognized that tests calling for comprehension of form relationships were not measuring the same thing as tests like Picture Arrangement which required comprehension of ideas. Early investigators of vocational aptitudes identified a number of jobs which seemed to require facile reasoning about forms, and spatial tests have since played a part in nearly all research on vocational aptitude. The DAT manual speaks of Space Relations in this way (Bennett *et al.*, 1959, p. 7):

> The *Space Relations* test is a measure of ability to deal with concrete materials through visualization. There are many vocations in which one is required to imagine how a specified object would appear if rotated in a given way. This ability to manipulate *things* mentally, to create a structure in one's mind from a plan, is what the test is designed to evaluate. It is an ability needed in such fields as drafting, dress designing, architecture, art, die-making, and decorating, or wherever there is need to visualize objects in three dimensions.

There appear to be several distinct spatial abilities. Comprehending static objects (as in Block Counting) seems to involve something quite different from visualizing how an object or machine will look after certain movements take place (Guilford, 1947, pp. 269–296; Michael *et al.*, 1951). A visualization factor (Vz) is found in tests such as Binet paper-folding and in some of Thurstone's tests where the subject must visualize how a figure will look when rotated.

Validity in Educational Prediction

One might expect spatial ability to be relevant to high-school courses such as geometry, shop, and engineering drawing. Validity coefficients for many schools are available in the DAT manual, some of which are reported in Table 38. For comparison, coefficients are also given for Numerical Ability and Abstract Reasoning. The coefficients reported are based on boys, but results for girls are similar.

Looking first at the correlations for geometry, we see that results from one sample to another vary, sometimes mysteriously. The two White Plains samples come from the same school in the same year, but coefficients in one class are strikingly higher than in the other. If differences such as this occur within one school in a well-defined course, it is obvious that generalizations about validity are hazardous.

In all schools, SR has positive relations with geometry, but NA is a better predictor. Insofar as we can judge from these coefficients, the contribution of SR to prediction of geometry is accounted for by its general-factor content. Other spatial tests show similar results. Though geometry undeniably requires reasoning about forms, tested spatial ability accounts for little of the variation in geometry marks. Here again we encounter evidence warning the test user against trusting his judgment as to what a test is likely to predict.

Note also, from this example, that the importance of a test cannot be judged solely from its correlation with the criterion. Considered alone, spatial ability has modest validity. Considered alongside other predictors, we find that the predictive value of the test is due to its general-factor content.

TABLE 38. Some Validity Coefficients for Differential Aptitude Tests Against Course Grades

Course	Grade	Location	Time Between Test and Marks	Number of Cases	Correlation of Marks with		
					Space	Numerical	Abstract
Plane Geometry	10	St. Paul, Minn.	1 year	48	.32	.47	.24
	10	White Plains, N.Y.	1 year	70	.20	.34	.19
	10	White Plains, N.Y.	1 year	77	.53	.57	.56
Solid Geometry	12	Baltimore, Md.	1 year	47	.13	.33	.41
	12	Hamilton, Ohio	1 semester	42	.18	.61	.25
Art	8	Yonkers, N.Y.	1 year	471	.20	.23	.16
	9	Worcester, Mass.	1 semester	44	.34	.41	.21
Mechanical Drawing	10	Gloucester, Mass.	1 year	46	.02	.17	.43
	10	Independence, Mo.	1 year	44	.57	.49	.28
Shop	9	Worcester, Mass.	1 semester	142	.26	.27	.22
	8	Yonkers, N.Y.	1 year	471	.18	.28	.14
	10	Independence, Mo.	3 months	42	.07	.06	.41
	8	Schenectady, N.Y.	1 semester	81	.33	.28	.50

SOURCE: Bennett *et al.*, 1959, pp. 42 ff.

The essential question about the practical value of a test is how much it adds to what other measures can tell.

The remaining coefficients in Table 38 tell the same story: variation from class to class, generally small positive correlations of SR with the criterion, equally good correlations for nonspatial tests. These data, and data on other tests, point to the conclusion that spatial ability does not, per se, predict success in high-school courses.

A study of college mathematics grades was made by Hills (1957), using Guilford's experimental tests of new reasoning factors. He included two separate spatial measures from the Guilford-Zimmerman Aptitude Survey. One, Spatial Orientation (a measure of S), shows pictures across a boat's prow, as seen from the cockpit. The pictures are paired, and the task of the subject is to locate in the second picture the "aiming point" toward which the prow was pointed in the first scene. The second, Spatial Visualization (Vz), requires the subject to identify how a clock will appear when tilted and rotated in a sequence of movements described verbally. Hills found consistent correlations of S with criteria in several mathematics courses for engineers, coefficients being as high as .55. In courses for physics and mathematics students at the same level of mathematics, however, S had negligible validities. Hills also found that the relevance of the factor to a specific course (e.g., calculus) depends on how the course is taught. Validities

FIG. 49.   Guilford-Zimmerman Spatial Orientation items. The subject is to mark whichever answer shows the position of the boat's prow (represented by the bar) in relation to the original aiming point (dot). The answers to the three items are C, B, and E respectively. (Copyright 1947, Sheridan Supply Co., and reproduced by permission.)

for Vz were much smaller than for S in the engineering sections but were consistently larger in sections for physics students. S gave a larger number of substantial validity coefficients than any other of the reasoning factors tested. Hills' results hint that special abilities may be more valuable as differential predictors in advanced courses than in high school. Special abilities contribute little to prediction of overall grade averages, since no ability save verbal or numerical affects many courses.

15. Give possible explanations for the differences between the two White Plains samples in Table 38.

16. How can one explain the negligible importance of spatial ability in predicting geometry?

Occupational Validity

The chief value of spatial tests is in vocational choice and employee selection. A study of watch repairing, for example, indicates a marked correspondence between spatial ability and performance, the validity coefficient being .69 (Bennett *et al.*, 1959, p. 63). Ghiselli's summary of published reports (1955) shows that spatial relations tests have predictive validities averaging greater than .30 for either training success or job proficiency in protective occupations, service occupations, mechanical repair-men, electrical workers, structural workers, processing workers, operators of complex machines, and gross manual workers.

A tremendous volume of information on vocational correlates of spatial ability is provided by the USES. Table 39 gives a sample of their results, along with data on General, Form Perception, and Manual Dexterity scores. These data were gathered on persons working in or training for the occupation who had already been selected to some extent, as is shown by the fact that the mean score departs from 100 and the s.d. is below 20. Evidently only persons very superior in space ability get into engineering and dentistry courses. Drill-press operators, at the other end of the scale, are drawn from the below-average workers who remain after those with better aptitude are siphoned into other jobs. The validity coefficients for occupations where the s.d. is low would be much larger if an unselected group had been hired.

Spatial ability is also important in several of these occupations. Both general and spatial ability contribute to success as draftsman or tabulating-machine operator; dentists, engineers, and machinists need form perception in addition. Careful distinction between aptitudes is important for job assignments. Although S and P are both, in a sense, "spatial," S is important in dentistry lecture courses while P is not. For bomb-fuse assemblers, the quick perception tested by P is much more important than the reasoning tested in S. The radio-tube mounter is likewise engaged in assembly of small parts, but his success depends on dexterity, not on S or P.

Few of the correlations in Table 39 are large. Spatial ability alone does not

TABLE 39. Validity of GATB-S Against Occupational Criteria

Occupation	Number of Cases	Criterion	Spatial Aptitude Mean	s.d.	r	Comparable Correlations for G	P	M
Dentist	96	Lecture grades	132	14	**.29**	**.24**	−.02	−.18
	89	Laboratory grades	—	—	**.33**	.13	**.33**	.14
Engineer	150	School grades	134	15	.11	**.42**	.11	unknown
Draftsman	40	Ratings	126	12	**.32**	**.42**	.06	.24
Machinist	71	Ratings	114	18	**.37**	**.29**	**.27**	.08
Tabulating-machine operator	203	Ratings	106	18	**.20**	**.34**	.10	.10
Bomb-fuse parts assembler	90	Ratings	102	15	.12	**.21**	**.33**	**.31**
Mounter (radio tubes)	100	Production records	101	14	−.02	.03	−.02	**.54**
Upholsterer	49	Ratings	97	17	**.43**	**.24**	**.25**	**.32**
Poultry laborer	72	Ratings	95	16	.03	**.24**	.09	**.56**
Drill-press operator	31	Production records	88	18	.05	**.32**	**.22**	**.47**

Values in boldface are significant ($P > .05$).
SOURCE: *Guide to the Use of GATB*, 1958, III J.

account for success in any of these jobs. Taking all the aptitudes into account simultaneously, however, can greatly improve employment decisions. In Chapter 12 we shall explain some of the procedures used to combine aptitudes into a selection formula.

17. Explain why the validities of the GATB tests are different for the two dentistry criteria.

MECHANICAL COMPREHENSION

We have previously discussed the Bennett TMC, which is the prototype for the Mechanical Reasoning Test of the DAT battery. No mechanical comprehension test was included in the USES battery, on the assumption that other tests in the battery cover much of what such a test would measure. As Table 37 showed, DAT-MR correlates about .60 with tests of G, V, and S. Factor analyses of an Air Force test patterned after the TMC, however, indicate that about 35 percent of its variance comes from Mechanical Experience, 25 percent from Visualization, and only 12 percent from G, V, and S combined (Guilford, 1947, pp. 336–339). These reports are less contradictory than they perhaps appear, since each analysis is based on different test batteries and statistical procedures. The Air Force analysis is the more satisfactory, being based on far more data and reporting correlations with factors rather than with single tests.

The validity coefficients for mechanical comprehension against high-school marks run a bit lower than coefficients for other abilities. In the DAT, the median correlation of MR with science grades for boys is .40, compared to VR, .54; NA, .52; AR, .42; and SR, .34. (See also Table 11.) Quite similar results are obtained for the Multiple Aptitude Tests, another high-school battery.

Adaptations of the Bennett test have frequently predicted success in civilian and military technical specialties (Bennett and Fear, 1943). The British Army found that a form of the Bennett test had a validity of .59 for selecting truck drivers; no other test was nearly so good (Vernon and Parry, 1949, p. 230). Among the average validity coefficients calculated by Ghiselli (1955) on the basis of the published literature, mechanical comprehension had the following notable validities for either training or job-performance criteria:

.50 to .59   machining workers, bench workers, and assemblers
.40 to .49   protective occupations, electrical workers, processing workers, complex-machine operators, inspectors
.30 to .39   mechanical repairmen, welders, vehicle operators, structural workers

Of particular interest is an Air Force study in which a factor analysis of pilot success was made. Out of 26 independent factors considered, the two most significant for pilot success were Spatial and Mechanical Experience (followed closely by Integration, Visualization, Psychomotor Coordination, and Pilot Interests; Guilford, 1947, p. 843). The Mechanical Principles test had a validity of about .35 as a predictor of pilot success.

A second type of mechanical test requires subjects to identify pictures of tools and is thus a measure of acquaintance rather than understanding. A recent test of this type is illustrated in Figure 50. The subject is to find the

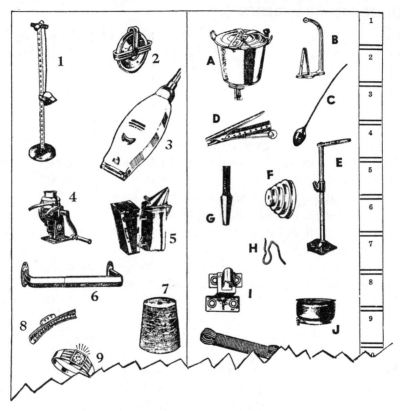

FIG. 50. Part of the Mellenbruch test. (Copyright 1957 by Psychometric Affiliates and reproduced by permission.)

lettered picture that goes with each numbered picture. Knowledge about a field may be regarded as an indication of interest in it, if people have more or less equal opportunities to get such information. Verbal tests of information about machinery, medicine, current events, sports, etc., may be useful in vocational prediction.

The U.S. Employment Service has done much to develop *trade tests* for use where an applicant claims to know a particular job. These questions about the job in effect constitute a short interview. Many men who claim experience in a trade fail on the questions. Such a screening test, used in an employment center, eliminates those who might otherwise be shipped across the country to a plant where skilled men are needed. Trade tests are also used in military classification to check whether men are qualified in the trades where they claim civilian experience. In the British Army such tests, because of their reliability, were sometimes more dependable bases for assigning men than records made in training courses (Vernon and Parry, 1949, p. 244).

Trade questions are selected to cover job processes and tools. Questions that would be unfair because of regional differences in methods of work or vocabulary are eliminated. To check item validity, three criterion groups are tested: expert workers, beginners in the trade, and workers in closely related trades. The items which discriminate these groups are retained. Items from several tests are (Stead *et al.*, 1940):

(Carpenter)   What do you mean by a "shore" in carpentry? *Ans.* Upright brace.
(Plumber)   What are the two most commonly used methods of testing plumbing systems? *Ans.* Water, smoke, peppermint, air (any two).
(Asbestos worker)   In stitching canvas covering over pipes, where is the seam run? *Ans.* Out of sight, back or top of pipe (either).

A good trade test discriminates between novices, apprentices, journeymen, and experts. In Figure 51 we see how a test of engine-lathe operators functions. Such a distribution of scores permits one to classify a job applicant with little error; a score of 22 almost certainly indicates a journeyman.

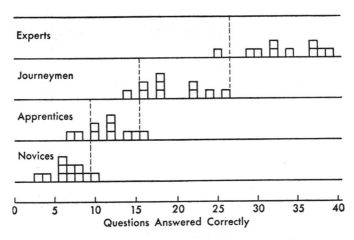

FIG. 51.   Scores on a trade test for engine-lathe operators (Burtt, 1942, p. 493).

18. a. The Purdue Assembly test is designed to include mechanisms using each important mechanical device: gears, levers, rack-and-pinion, etc. Does such a test assume that mechanical aptitude or comprehension is a single general ability, or that it is a group of specific abilities?

   b. If the latter theory is true, what implications does it have for selecting students for training in watch repairing?
19. Boys surpass girls on the Bennett test. How may this finding be explained?
20. Mellenbruch reports validity coefficients ranging from .50 to .60 for his mechanical aptitude test. The criteria used are teacher's ranking of engineering drawing trainees (women), experience in mechanical activities, and scores on the Air Force Mechanical Information Test. What other validity studies are needed to support his recommendation that those scoring low on the test should not be hired for mechanical work or should be placed only in routine mechanical jobs?

THE INTERPRETATION OF APTITUDE PROFILES

Differential ability tests are used in two ways: for institutional decisions and for individual decisions (Cronbach and Gleser, 1957). An institutional decision is one in which a factory, a school, a military organization, or the like selects and assigns individuals in order to obtain the best total result, i.e., the greatest possible attainment of institutional goals. This use of the tests rests primarily on efficient statistical combination of scores rather than on psychological interpretation. An individual decision is one which seeks to promote the welfare of one person, considered by himself. In career guidance, for example, the emphasis must be on psychological interpretation. We shall concern ourselves here with the use of profile information in individual decisions, and turn to institutional decisions in Chapter 12.

Perhaps there was once a hope among counselors that a test profile would permit a definite, final choice of vocation at the time the tests are given. If this were the case, the counselor and client together could reach a decision, and the client could rely on the counselor's interpretation of the tests. Today it is recognized that the client himself must fully understand the test results, for two reasons.

One reason is that vocational choice is not a single final throw of the dice. As a person goes through school and into his first jobs, he has many occasions to narrow his field of concentration or even to transfer to a new area. High-school courses and introductory college courses provide opportunities for him to explore and develop aptitudes and interests. In an expanding economy, workers change position or change responsibilities within the same establishment. The engineer in a technical firm, for example, may become a manager, a salesman, a creative designer, or an expert on detailed specifications. Wise choice requires self-understanding; no "prescription" filled out by a tenth-grade or freshman-year counselor can anticipate these subsequent decisions. Test interpretation is only one step in a long process of self-discovery.

Secondly, the client is more likely to accept recommendations which he understands. The counselor may be convinced that a freshman should get out of engineering and into advertising. Even though advertising is consistent with the boy's talents and interests, he may resist or ignore the recommendation. If he has been visualizing himself as an engineer for years, such a change of program requires him to alter his entire self-concept and may seem like an admission of defeat. To accept the new goal requires that he understand the facts the counselor considers significant. Acquiring a new self-image requires both factual and emotional learning.

The counselor must decide what meaning may justifiably be extracted from scores and must at the same time consider how this information is to be communicated so that it affects the client's conduct.

Limitations on Interpretation

A general ability test or a battery of aptitude measures has definite predictive value, as we have seen. At the same time, the scores have distinct limitations which must be remembered.

Profile Shape as a Function of the Norm Group. It is necessary to use test norms in order to plot a profile, and the choice of norms determines the profile shape. Profile shape changes when a different norm group is used. The most common example arises in interpreting mechanical comprehension scores for girls (see p. 92).

The USES profile is ordinarily plotted against norms for adult workers. The profile (Figure 52) of a (hypothetical) student engineer plotted in the

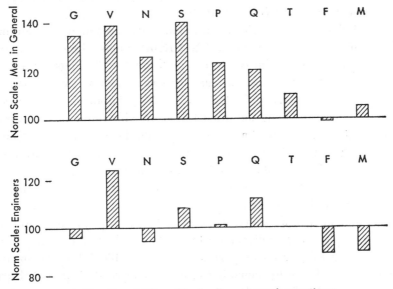

FIG. 52. Two GATB profiles for the same student engineer.

usual manner (upper profile, Figure 52) draws attention to his superior *G*, *V*, and *S* abilities, and shows him near the average in dexterity. If instead we use a standard-score conversion from data on engineering students, his profile (lower profile, Figure 52) takes on a strikingly different appearance. His greatest strength, relative to other engineers, is *V*. In *S*, he is just above average; he is average in *G*, and behind the group in dexterity.

It is important to compare the person with the group he will associate with and compete against rather than with "people-in-general."

Precision of Measurement. When we try to measure several aptitudes in a short period of time, reliability coefficients often drop to .75 or .80. Even with high reliability, a retest would show enough change to suggest different recommendations for a certain number of persons. These random errors, though present, do not cause much concern when tests are used for *institutional* decisions. Even if a test is seriously wrong in 10 percent of the cases, the decision maker reaches correct conclusions far more often than he could with other data. If an unintelligent man slips by an Army screening test, he can be detected later and discharged at no enormous cost. In an individual decision, however, we cannot be content with a small rate of error. One error may alter a person's entire life if the test leads him to decide, for example, not to continue his education.

Suppose it is known that 70 people out of 100 having IQ 110 fail in a certain profession. The counselor cannot make a clear prediction for Walter, IQ 110. Perhaps he would do better if tested again. Perhaps other qualities unknown to us make Walter one of the 30 who would succeed, rather than of the 70 who fail. *Almost never are psychological tests so valid that a prediction about a single case is certainly true.*

The counselor who is conscious of unreliability adopts many precautions to reduce its ill effects. He checks each test result against the case history for consistency. If in doubt, he confirms significant test findings by a second comparable test. He examines his case for special factors such as language difficulty which might make the test invalid. Most important, he thinks of a test performance as placing the subject in a probable range of scores, rather than as pegging him firmly at a particular percentile. Tests rarely miss fire in stating that a student is "somewhat, but not extremely, below average in scholastic aptitude." The statement "Walter is at the 32nd percentile of college freshmen" is almost certainly untrue, in the sense that further data would not precisely confirm it.

Clients and such professional workers as teachers, physicians, and social workers may place false reliance on test data which they regard as "scientific." Even when the tester's report is carefully qualified, the person receiving the report is likely to remember only portions of it. A parent, learning that his child's IQ is 87, may forget the tester's cautions about what the test does not measure, the possibility of growth or decline in IQ, and the approximate nature of predictions from it. Instead, the figure itself may stick vividly in mind and be used as a basis for significant decisions for years to come.

Profile Reliability. Special difficulties are encountered in interpreting multi-score tests where judgments rest on differences between scores. Such differences are usually much less reliable than the scores themselves. DAT-VR and DAT-NA are reliable, for example, but they overlap, and much of the reliability of each score is due to the overlapping part. When that is subtracted, the remaining test variance contains a high proportion of error (Thorndike and Hagen, 1955, p. 178).

The reliability of a difference between two standard scores A and B is calculated by this formula:

$$r_{(A-B)(A-B)} = \frac{r_{AA} + r_{BB} - 2r_{AB}}{2 - 2r_{AB}}$$

When tests have low reliabilities or a high degree of overlap, the difference is highly unreliable. Using the data of Table 34, we find that in the DAT the reliability of the VR-NA difference is .76. That of VR minus CSA is .82.

Small differences are generally chance effects. When a difference becomes twice as large as its standard error, there is only one chance in twenty that the person is equally good on both tests. We can have substantial confidence that a retest would confirm such a difference. Table 40 indicates

TABLE 40. Interpretability of Difference Scores

Average Reliability of Profile Scores	Difference in T-Score Units Required for Interpretation	Proportion of Subjects Showing Interpretable Difference if Test Intercorrelation Is			
		.00	.25	.50	.75
.95	6.3	66	61	53	38
.90	8.8	54	47	38	22
.80	12.5	37	31	21	8
.70	15.3	28	21	13	3

In this table, an interpretable difference is defined as one which would occur only one time in twenty, in testing persons whose two abilities are actually equal.

how large a difference must be to allow this degree of confidence. For DAT-VR and -NA, the average reliability is near .90. The table tells us that a difference between these scores must be at least 9 points to be significant. A difference smaller than that indicated by the table should be regarded only as a suggestion, to be confirmed by other data. If two tests are highly correlated, few difference scores will be large enough for interpretation. The test profile then is not very useful for differential measurement.

Test developers are giving increasing thought to ways of reporting scores so that their unreliability will be kept in mind. One device is the report form for an educational achievement test shown in Figure 53. Here the pupil's score is shown, not as a point on the scale, but as a range within which his ability almost certainly falls. The width of the band is twice the standard

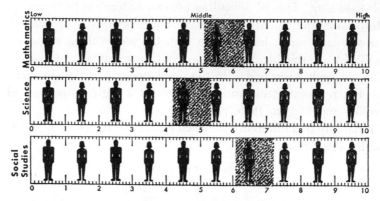

FIG. 53. Profile for the Sequential Tests of Educational Progress. The shaded areas for Mathematics and Social Studies overlap; there is no important difference in standings on these two tests. The same is true of Mathematics and Science. However, the shaded areas for Science and Social Studies do not overlap. The student is higher in Social Studies than in Science ability, as measured by these tests. (Copyright 1958, Cooperative Test Division, Educational Testing Service, and reproduced by permission.)

error of measurement. The student can see from the profile that about four persons in ten surpass his mathematics score, and that the difference between social studies and mathematics is not reliable.

21. Calculate the reliability of a difference between Spelling and Sentences in DAT.
22. Which pair of GATB tests appears to have the least reliable difference? Compute its reliability.
23. Examine the DAT profile in Figure 16. Which score differences are reliable enough to interpret?
24. In the PMA tests for ages 5 to 7, the correlation of V with S is .60. The reliabilities are .77 and .86, respectively. What can you say about the interpretability of the V-S difference?

Stability of Aptitudes. Vocational guidance involves an attempt to predict success far into the future. This prediction cannot be made unless the aptitude pattern is stable over a long period of time. Measures of general ability have substantial stability after about the age of 9, when the initial adjustment to schooling is completed. But how early does the pattern of specialized aptitudes emerge?

The DAT is designed for use as early as Grade 8. One study of its stability over time, based on tests in Grade 9 and retests in Grade 12, gives coefficients of stability for boys above .80 for Verbal and Spelling; near .70 for

Sentences, Numerical, and Mechanical; and near .60 for Space, Abstract, and Clerical (Bennett *et al.*, 1959, p. 68). Much of this stability is no doubt due to the general factor. Similar results were reported for GATB (Table 36).

The real question is the stability of differences within the profile. When ninth-grade *differences* were correlated with twelfth-grade differences, the correlations ranged from .20 (Numerical minus Abstract) to .74 (Mechanical minus Spelling) (Doppelt and Bennett, 1951). Differences among Clerical, Mechanical, and the overall level of the verbal-language-numerical tests are stable enough to be taken seriously. It is doubtful if long-range predictions can be based on Space scores in Grade 9, or on differences between Verbal, Numerical, and Abstract scores in that grade.

In view of the inadequacy of present data on the stability of factor scores, a firm conclusion cannot be reached. The following statement is a "best guess" as to what more complete research will show. Special ability tests may have some use for short-term prediction and classification in elementary school. This is suggested by Reed's finding (1958) that the PMA spatial score (visual discrimination) correlates .41 with achievement in primary reading whereas verbal ability correlates only .27. At higher grades, V correlates .52 and S only .18, a finding which reflects the shift in teaching emphasis, after basic skills are established, from perception to comprehension. Special ability tests are often relevant in studying children requiring remedial help. For most elementary pupils, guidance is best based on general measures of verbal and nonverbal ability rather than on more elaborate profiles whose implications for instruction are unknown.

There can be little long-range differential prediction before Grade 11. In Grades 7–10, aptitude tests suggest strong points so that the pupil will be encouraged to enroll in courses where these assets will be developed. In these grades low scores need not be considered seriously save where, as in Number and Spelling, remedial instruction can raise the score. By mid-adolescence, the individual's aptitude pattern is reasonably stable. Even at this age, irreversible decisions should be avoided. Later courses and job experience will add greatly to the student's knowledge of his aptitudes.

Meanings Attributed to Scores. For counseling, scores must be explained in common-sense terms. The client will continue to face choices between courses and between job openings, and the counselor cannot possibly give a recommendation that will anticipate all such questions. He must help the client to understand his own profile and to understand what tasks the various aptitudes are relevant to.

The DAT and GATB profiles are well designed for such interpretations. Labels like Numerical Reasoning and Spelling do not sound like mysterious inborn aptitudes; they are clearly measures of a certain type of performance.

The safest way to interpret scores is in terms of the items that constitute the test; i.e., "This score shows that you do well on problems like this." Any more elaborate interpretation leads quickly to misunderstanding. Mechanical reasoning is misinterpreted as "mechanical aptitude" though the test clearly does not cover dexterity. The clerical test is misinterpreted as a predictor of success in stenography and typing whereas it actually covers rapid checking of details, important only in very routine office jobs. The student may connect spatial ability to art, geometry, and shop courses even though the validity coefficients discourage such an interpretation.

Some degree of vagueness is absolutely essential. The student should be made to feel that he can improve many of his aptitudes. He should regard the test findings as hints to be checked in other experience. Nothing in our experience with testing justifies making firm individual decisions on the basis of differential abilities.

The case of Sarah Carrell provides an illustration of many of the comments we have made (Bennett *et al.*, 1951).

Early in her junior year, Sarah talked over her test scores with the counselor. Her school work had been satisfactory. She then appealed for help in persuading her mother that it was worth while to finish high school. The mother wished her to go to work since her father had been forced to retire on just a small pension. The mother felt Sarah was over-age (illness in childhood had retarded her one year), and that she would not do well in secretarial training because her school grades were not above average. Moreover, none of Sarah's older sisters had graduated from high school and the mother considered high school of little value for a girl.

Sarah's DAT profile showed that she fell in the middle range of high-school juniors. Her Spelling and Sentences scores were her lowest, at the 25th percentile. Her peaks were Numerical (75th percentile) and Abstract (70). All other scores were at the median. In Grade 9, a reading test had placed her at the 58th percentile, and the Otis group mental test in Grade 8 at the 47th percentile. All these agree with the DAT in indicating that Sarah had enough ability to finish school.

The test record was useful in showing Sarah's mother that the girl was superior in numerical and abstract performances. The counselor pointed out that Sarah could expect to do well in calculating and bookkeeping, which she could take if she stayed in school. (NA, AR, and Sentences are the best predictors of bookkeeping marks.) "The mother," says the counselor, "then admitted that her secret desire had been for Sarah to work in an insurance office where her brother-in-law could secure her a job. She conceded that if Sarah was that good, she ought to have a chance to finish school."

Sarah was deficient in language usage, and the counselor should point to its importance in office work. If this deficiency is repaired, as may well happen when study is motivated by a definite goal, Sarah could qualify for almost any office job at a modest level of responsibility. If this deficiency remains, the test analysis has shown that her best opportunity for success is in bookkeeping or the like.

The DAT scores of Robert Finchley (Figure 16) contradict his scores on other tests. His Otis score was at the 55th percentile, his reading speed at the 24th, and his comprehension at the 50th. But on the DAT, he had these percentile scores (Bennett *et al.*, 1951):

VR	NR	AR	SR	MR	CSA	Sentences	Spelling
95	95	97	92	95	10	14	9

His parents are college graduates, and his sister has a good school record. Robert's record had declined steadily during all his school years, and in high school he was doing little of his assigned work. The DAT had been given routinely in Grade 10, but no effort was made to discuss it with Robert, or even with his teachers, until a year later.

The story of the test scores is clear: outstanding overall ability, with a severe deficiency in clerical speed and in language usage. From the case history it appears that Robert's teachers had begun to regard him as a mediocre student who could not be expected to do well, and that he had come to share their opinion. Robert himself was openly delighted with the test report and put forth more effort as he regained confidence. He became interested in obtaining information on schools of engineering. The record suggests a need for remedial reading, but this could perhaps better be added to Robert's schedule after he gets his current work in hand.

25. Would the GATB have given valuable information to supplement Sarah's DAT scores?
26. Why did the Otis test fail to reveal Robert's superiority?
27. Is engineering the most suitable goal for Robert?
28. Interpret the profile of Ellsworth Newcomb. He has been preparing for engineering, but is making C's in mathematics. His tested interests are in verbal and personal-contact activities. He has done some selling, with success. On the OSU test, he scores at the 69th percentile of college freshmen. His DAT percentile scores in grade 12 are:

Verbal	Numerical	Abstract	Space	Mechanical	Clerical	Spelling	Sentences
86	48	44	40	36	13	73	93

IMPORTANT GUIDANCE BATTERIES

There is more to be said about interpreting tests so as to maximize the subject's insight, but before expanding on this point we provide a summary listing of some differential batteries now available to the tester. Comprehensive information on these batteries has been compiled and reviewed by Super (1958).

• Differential Aptitude Tests; George K. Bennett, Harold G. Seashore, Alexander G. Wesman; Psychological Corporation, 1947, 1952. Grade 8 to college. A well-constructed set of eight tests described on pp. 269 ff.

• Flanagan Aptitude Classification Tests; John C. Flanagan; Science Research Associates, 1953. High-school seniors. A seven-hour battery with 21 tests suggested by Air Force factor analyses. In addition to the customary aptitudes there are tests for ingenuity, tapping, speed of scale reading, carving skill, etc. The validity of the tests is still under investigation, and they should be restricted to research use at present. In particular, the "occupational scores" obtained by combining tests should not be used until satisfactory evidence of their validity is provided.

• Guilford-Zimmerman Aptitude Survey; J. P. Guilford and Wayne S. Zimmerman; Sheridan Supply Company, 1947. Measures V, R, N, P, S, Vz, Mechanical knowledge. Based on factors found useful in Air Force classification. Contains several unique tests which may have predictive value, but evidence on predictive validity in civilian tasks is not available. Primarily for research use at present.

• Holzinger-Crowder Uni-Factor Tests; Karl J. Holzinger and Norman A. Crowder; World Book, 1955. Grades 7–12. An excellently constructed test which in one hour gives measures of V, S, N, R, and a composite measure of scholastic aptitude. Reliabilities range from .80 to .90, with unusually low intercorrelations. Speed is of some importance in the short subtests. Predicts overall grade average very well, but the value of the factor scores for differential prediction appears to be quite limited.

• Multiple Aptitude Tests; David Segel and Evelyn Raskin; California Test Bureau, 1955. Grades 7–12. Nine tests in three hours cover vocabulary, reading, language usage, clerical, arithmetic, mechanical comprehension, and spatial abilities. Test scores may be combined into substantially intercorrelated scores for V, P, N, and S. The battery is technically satisfactory and uses tests of familiar types which can be interpreted by experienced counselors. Differential validity for course grades is not great, and occupational validities are not established.

• Tests of Primary Mental Abilities; L. L. and T. G. Thurstone; Science Research Associates, 1941, 1953. Ages 5–7, 7–11, 11–17. The battery measures several of Thurstone's factors, the list differing at each level. The tests at lower grades are best interpreted as measuring general ability by verbal and nonverbal tests. Evidence is inadequate to support diagnostic interpretation or differential prediction. The one-hour battery for ages 11–17 measures vocabulary, computation, fluency, space, and reasoning. Until evidence to indicate the meaning of profiles is available, the tests should be confined to research use. Incautious and incorrect claims have been made for the PMA tests (Anastasi, 1954, pp. 114, 365–368; Super, 1958, p. 87).

HELPING CLIENTS USE TEST INFORMATION

Client-Centered Counseling

In earlier days of psychological service, the counselor was often viewed as an expert passing judgment, in the same category as an engineer inspecting a bridge or a physician prescribing for a disease. The modern view is that the counselor does not decide or direct, but rather helps the client think for himself. In extremely directive or prescriptive counseling, the "expert" obtains facts, decides, and tells the client what to do. So-called "client-centered" counseling stresses the importance of the client's making his own decisions. This point of view, formulated by Rogers (1942), emphasizes that the important goal is the growth of the client toward maturity and adjustment. A person who has learned to rely on his own judgment has been helped more than one who must seek advice in each new crisis.

Expert advice often fails because factual questions are entangled in emotional attitudes. The true problem is often not the surface problem voiced to the counselor. Suppose Stan Howard, employed on a finishing machine, comes to inquire why he was not promoted to foreman. The directive personnel manager might give the facts, based on tests and ratings, which "prove" that he would make a poor foreman. He may even give Howard a pep talk on how well he produces, about the chance of raising his pay as a workman, and about the undesirability of seeking a job where he would fail. Howard is likely to nod his head and leave, but he may be far from convinced he should not be a foreman. He may quit and go to another company where he'll "have a chance." Howard may have failed to state or even to recognize that he is anxious to be a foreman because his brother-in-law is a foreman and he wishes equal status. Similar "irrelevant, nonobjective" factors may lurk within the case of the student who studies inadequately, the airman who longs to be a pilot, the mother who overrates her child's ability, or the unpopular girl. The client seeking counseling phrases his problem to protect the tender spots of his ego. The counselor who relieves a surface problem may be helping the client to avoid facing his real conflicts.

The nondirective methods suggested by Rogers help the client express his feelings. The counselor reflects the client's feelings by rephrasing what the client has said: "You think you'd rather be a foreman than a machine operator"; "It's discouraging when a man who came after you did is promoted over you"; "You feel that the management doesn't trust you." Acknowledging the feelings, instead of trying to prove them false, promotes ultimate adjustment. The client, freed from need to justify or apologize for his attitudes, gains insight into himself.

The client is made responsible. He asks the questions, limits the area discussed, makes the judgments, and decides when to terminate the counseling. If the counselor proposes a test, or suggests that poor arithmetic may be a source of difficulty, or lays down alternative solutions, he is taking responsibility. He thereby risks pushing the client faster than he is ready to move.

Tests designed to help the tester be wise become of secondary importance in client-centered counseling because they do not center on the feelings of the client. Says Rogers (1946):

> The counseling process is furthered if the counselor drops all effort to evaluate and diagnose and concentrates solely on creating the psychological setting in which the client feels he is deeply understood and free to be himself. It is unimportant that the counselor know about the client. It is highly important that the client be able to learn himself. (Not to learn *about* himself, but to learn and accept his own self.) In making use of these principles the counselor examines his own attitudes and techniques and endeavors to refine his procedures so as to eliminate all which are not in accord with the basic principles. Thus questions are eliminated from the interview because they invariably direct the conversation, advice is eliminated because it assumes the counselor to be the responsible person, diagnosis and evaluation are put aside because it has been learned that even when they are not voiced they tend to distort the counselor's responses in subtle ways and to break down his full acceptance of client attitudes.

Tests are not abandoned if one accepts this outlook. Instead of being ways of learning answers about the client so we can tell him, tests become ways of helping the client find out about himself. In strictly nondirective counseling, tests enter only when the client asks for them. The student who comes with the statement "I'm worried because it takes me so long to learn an assignment" is not immediately seated before a battery of tests. Instead, counseling may go through to completion with no use of tests. Perhaps, in the course of examining his difficulties, he says, "I've often worried about whether I'm as bright as the students I compete with. I thought you people had some tests that would tell about that." Then the counselor supplies him with the means of measuring himself, since he has apparently reached the maturity required to face his question honestly.

Most counselors compromise with the strictly nondirective approach, but its basic idea can be of great assistance. It is the repeated experience of counselors trying this technique that when tests are delayed, problems come to light which would otherwise never have been voiced. A student may request an intelligence test. Given the test, told that his score is normal, and dismissed, he has been reassured but not necessarily helped. Taking the test may have reduced his tension temporarily but left untouched the basic conflict that set him to wondering about his intelligence. Perhaps he is worrying about changing his major; perhaps he is concerned because his grades in college are lower than in high school. The problem may be as remote from that stated as a worry because his wife's family considers his pronounciation peculiar. The counselor who avoids bringing the conference to a head, giving an answer, and terminating the interview permits the client to dig into what really concerns him.

Bordin and Bixler (1946) suggests that counselors place on the client the responsibility of choosing the tests to be taken. In contrast to establishing a standard battery of tests to be taken, they invite questions about tests and discuss at length the sorts of tests available. They neither recommend a particular test nor limit their description to the tests the client asks about. After hearing what tests can be had, the client takes the initiative in deciding among them. This is particularly helpful in erasing the idea, common among those who seek counseling, that one or two tests will give definite answers to every problem.

Decisions made by the counselor apparently have less effect on most clients than those they make themselves. The counselor helps the client most when he helps him to reason out his own decision. Bixler and Bixler (1946) have made numerous suggestions to increase the client's involvement in test interpretation and his self-examination.

The counselor avoids giving opinions. The counselor is always tempted to comment on the goodness or badness of scores to build confidence or emphasize the seriousness of symptoms. Such evaluation comes between the client and the score and makes it harder for him to accept the score as a reality. Bixler suggests prediction in the form of an expectancy instead.

Bixler's second suggestion is that the counselor should be frank. Low scores must be faced honestly, if the client is to gain in self-knowledge. A test score inconsistent with the person's previous impression of himself forces him to take a new look at his plans. Students characteristically overestimate their ability and interest in the vocational field they have chosen. Test results which challenge these distortions can be beneficial, but they obviously generate emotional conflict which the tester must turn counselor to dispel.

What is less obvious is that favorable test results are equally likely to pose problems for the subject. Bordin (1951) tells of the college student who earned a high score on a "scientific aptitude" test because the test included achievement items and he had taken considerable science in high school. Although the student "had made a definite choice of business administration, he was thrown into a state of indecision by this test result, partly because his father was a successful engineer. Later counseling proved that his original choice was well founded and that his indecision would have been short lived if the tests had been properly interpreted to him by someone who could also have helped him to relate these results to his percept of himself as different from his father."

This does not argue against giving information to the subject. Testing is an opportunity for him to find out about himself, and it is better to create a correct self-image than to leave him with false impressions. But the counselor must decide what information the person is able to assimilate. One advantage of achievement tests such as the SCAT in college counseling, as distinguished from tests which appear to measure intelligence, is that the subject usually finds it easier to accept unfavorable evidence about his achievement than evidence of "low intelligence."

The client must always feel free to reject any interpretation. He must be able to say that, though his score is low, he expects to succeed. He must be able to reject his own interest test score by insisting that he really likes engineering despite a low interest in computation. It is only when he learns that he need not argue with the counselor that he becomes free to examine himself nondefensively. The counselor should help the client recognize his emotional reactions to the test scores. Emotional reactions block rational thinking; the client can use the scores wisely only after he has come to an understanding of his emotions.

These points are illustrated in the following dialog from a case record (Bixler and Bixler, 1946):

Counselor. Sixty out of one hundred students with scores like yours succeed in engineering. About eighty out of one hundred succeed in the social sciences. . . . The difference is due to the fact that study shows the college aptitude test to be important in social sciences, along with high school work, instead of mathematics.

Student. But I want to go into engineering. I think I'd be happier there. Isn't that important too?

C. You are disappointed with the way the test came out, but you wonder if your liking engineering better isn't pretty important?

S. Yes, but the tests say I would do better in sociology or something like that. (Disgusted)

C. That disappoints you, because it's the sort of thing you don't like.

S. Yes. I took an interest test, didn't I? What about it?

C. You wonder if it doesn't agree with the way you feel. The test shows that most people with your interests enjoy engineering and are not likely to enjoy social sciences—

S. (Interrupts) But the chances are against me in engineering, aren't they?

C. It seems pretty hopeless to be interested in engineering under these conditions, and yet you're not quite sure.

S. No, that's right. I wonder if I might not do better in the thing I like—Maybe my chances are best in engineering anyway. I've been told how tough college is, and I've been afraid of it. The tests are encouraging. There isn't much difference after all—Being scared makes me overdo the difference.

29. At what age is it appropriate for counselors or school psychologists to give a child or adolescent information about his abilities?

30. Reread the counselor's remarks carefully. Did he at any time suggest what he thought was right, or what he approved? Did he disapprove of any idea of the client?
31. In the dialog quoted, would it be helpful or harmful for the counselor to make these remarks?
    a. It's probably better for you to work in an area you like than to follow these tests strictly.
    b. Most people develop an interest in areas where they do well; you probably would learn to like social science if you tried it.
    c. If you stay in engineering, you should plan to take a course in remedial mathematics.
    d. It seems to you that it's wisest to work in the field where your chances are best.
32. Which is more likely to be threatening, a report on a general scholastic aptitude test or a report on a battery like the DAT?

Fact-Centered Counseling

Although emphasis has been placed on nondirective counseling above, it should not be assumed that prescriptive methods are obsolete. They are widely used under many circumstances. Some counselors prefer them. Administrative requirements often force a counselor to take responsibility for decisions, as when a veterans' counselor is required by law to approve the vocational plans of certain trainees. When a case is referred for counseling, rather than coming in voluntarily, the counselor cannot stick to client-centered methods. Cases in which the client is incapable of self-direction must also be prescribed for.

Those using tests prescriptively emphasize the importance of "objective facts" as a basis for rational decision, in contrast to Rogers' emphasis on the emotional meaning of the facts. The prescriptive counselor tends to think of the client as leaning on someone for direction, and considers tests an especially sound basis for giving the direction sought; in other cases, the problem of counseling is to convince the client that his plans should be changed, and tests are regarded as a forceful type of evidence (Staff, Advisement and Guidance Service, 1946). The counselor who wishes to bring his client to face the facts takes a stand similar to John Dewey's (paraphrased here from a passage dealing with children, 1938, pp. 84–85):

> The suggestion upon which clients act must in any case come from somewhere. It is impossible to understand why a suggestion from one who has a larger experience and wider horizon should not be at least as valid as a suggestion arising from some more or less accidental source. It is possible of course to abuse the office, and to force the activity of the young into channels which express the counselor's purpose rather than that of the client. But the way to avoid this is not for the counselor

to withdraw entirely. . . . The counselor's suggestion is not a mold for a cast-iron result but is a starting point to be developed into a plan through contributions from the experience of all engaged in the counseling process.

Prescriptive counselors generally obtain a variety of information, make an interpretation, and bring the client to act on this information. While they respect the right of the client to choose between alternatives of merit and do not force even a wise course of action upon him, their emphasis is on keeping the client from making errors. Williamson (1939, pp. 134–138) puts the position this way:

> The effective counselor is one who induces the student to want to utilize his assets in ways which will yield success and satisfaction. . . . Ordinarily the counselor states his point of view with definiteness, attempting through exposition to enlighten the student. . . . In respect to no student's problem does the counselor appear indecisive to the extent of permitting loss of confidence in the authority of his information. . . . If it is true that the counselor should not make the student's decision, it is equally true that someone must render this very service until some students are able, intellectually and emotionally, to think for themselves.

In helping the client make decisions, the counselor, whatever his technique, wishes the client to have a basis for optimism. The nondirective counselor would prefer that this come through insight, whereas the directive counselor tends to give direct encouragement. In either case, however, the client should leave the counseling with a positive plan for action, rather than merely with the knowledge that his former plan was inadequate. Similarly, he must have a feeling that he has some strong qualities, rather than a total feeling of failure because tests have brought to light only weaknesses. In every test performance, there are some praiseworthy aspects. The counselor who wishes to give support will call attention to such features as accuracy, originality, or persistence, in addition to giving the client facts about his score. Nearly all counselors working with normal late adolescents and adults agree in giving the client the facts on which recommendations (if any) are based. The counselor who refuses to give scores even in general form sets up a fear in the client that he was not told because his scores were too poor.

The most helpful single principle in all testing is that test scores are merely data on which to base further study. They must be coördinated with background facts, and they must be verified by constant comparison with other available data. This is the reason that continued counseling by an adviser over a year is more effective than "one shot" counseling where an answer is given to each new specific problem by a different adviser. The test score helps the counselor by warning him to look in the record for further symptoms of a particular problem. The score, and study of items within the tests, suggest topics to probe by interview methods. While sometimes it is necessary to act on a problem immediately, it is sound practice to defer a final decision as long as possible, meanwhile seeking confirmation of tentative diagnoses.

33. Discuss the advisability of delaying final decision in each of these situations. What supplementary information should be sought to confirm the tentative conclusions?
  a. A college student who is failing in engineering at midterm seeks a more suitable vocational goal. Aptitude and interest tests suggest journalism.
  b. An engaged couple, after a quarrel, seeks the help of a marital counselor. A personality test intended to predict marital adjustment (validity .50) shows that their score as a pair is low, in the range where there is an even chance of divorce.
  c. Students applying to enter a graduate school for social work are tested routinely. A girl shows severe neurotic signs on both a questionnaire and a subtle, moderately dependable personality test.

Suggested Readings

Bennett, George K., & others. *Counseling from profiles.* New York: Psychological Corporation, 1951.
  This booklet presents a general discussion of the DAT and a philosophy of counseling, then discusses thirty cases showing a variety of realistic problems where aptitude profiles are useful.
Bordin, Edward S. Test selection and interpretation and Illustrations and problems. *Psychological counseling.* New York: Appleton-Century-Crofts, 1955. Pp. 262–331.
  Bordin amplifies his view that tests imposed on the client without adequate preparation may delay improvement, and shows by extracts from interviews how skilled counselors deal with such problems as the client who expects tests to make decisions for him, and the client who has been forced into counseling.
Lamke, Tom A., & Nelson, M. J. Single-score tests vs. factor-score tests. *Examiner's manual, the Henmon-Nelson Tests of Mental Ability.* Boston: Houghton Mifflin, 1957. Pp. 19–22.
  The Henmon-Nelson test series yields a single measure of general ability. When it was revised, this section was added to the manual to explain why the authors had not shifted to the multiscore pattern. The authors' view that differential testing has little or no advantage over single-score testing should be compared to the views expressed in the Super reference, below.
Super, Donald B. (ed.). *The use of multifactor tests in guidance.* Washington:

American Personnel and Guidance Association, 1958. (Also published in *The Personnel and Guidance Journal*, 1957.)

In an unusual symposium each prominent differential battery is described by its authors. These articles combine factual information with a certain amount of "sales talk." Following each presentation, Super gives a short but pointed critique of the test and the validation research on it. Super's introductory paper (pp. 2–8) is a strong argument for differential testing and should be compared to the Lamke-Nelson reference above.

11

Other Special Abilities

THE tests discussed in the preceding chapter are the ones most often used in guidance. The present chapter describes other tests of special abilities including those for psychomotor and artistic aptitudes.

PSYCHOMOTOR ABILITIES

The only psychomotor performances considered to this point are the simple speed and dexterity measures of the GATB. Many tests using more elaborate apparatus and measuring more complex abilities have been tried, and many have shown predictive value. Since the tests are costly to construct, maintain, and administer, their use is largely confined to industrial and military classification.

The costliness of psychomotor testing, combined with the difficulties of obtaining adequate criteria of occupational success, has discouraged research on motor abilities. Our knowledge rests almost entirely on a few research programs, of which by far the most significant has been that of the Air Force, which has large samples of men, excellent equipment and control of testing conditions, and superior criterion data (Melton, 1947; Fleishman, 1956).

All psychomotor tasks involve intellectual abilities such as are found in pencil-paper tests. Many apparatus tests are correlated with factors P, S, and Mechanical Experience, as well as with strictly psychomotor factors. We shall concentrate here on the uniquely motor abilities and the tests which measure them. We shall describe a number of illustrative tests before turning to a factor-analytic classification of motor abilities.

Simple Performance Measures

Reaction Time. Measurement of reaction time goes back to the earliest days of experimental psychology. The techniques used today differ only in elegance of instrumentation from some of the procedures Wundt and Cattell introduced in the first psychological laboratory at Leipzig. The subject is told to react to a light or other signal as quickly as he can. When he presses the response button, an electrical timer records the interval that elapsed between signal and response.

Modern apparatus can present a whole series of stimuli, record times, and cumulate the score—all automatically. The signal apparatus is "programmed" by a tape or a cam so as to present signals at irregular intervals. Such automation is important for tests involving complicated stimulus patterns, as in measures of discriminative reaction time, because it speeds up testing and reduces the variation in testing procedure.

Although it has often been thought that simple reaction time is relevant to automobile driving and to many jobs, consistent evidence to support this view is lacking. Simple reaction is a different matter entirely from reaction with judgment. A test of discriminative reaction time, where a different button must be pushed for each pattern of light signals, correlates only about .30 with simple reaction time (Melton, 1947, p. 102). Most practical performances probably depend more on choice reaction than on simple reaction.

Steadiness and Simple Controlled Movement.   Steadiness is required where one must maintain a fixed posture or must trace a pattern accurately. Pos-

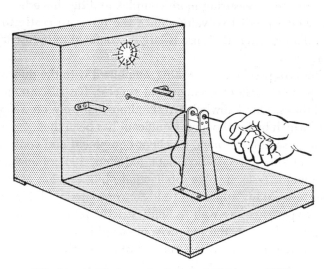

FIG. 54.   An Air Force steadiness test (Fleishman, 1954).

tural steadiness can be tested by recording movements of a platform on which the subject stands. Arm steadiness is tested by requiring the subject to hold a stylus outstretched in a small aperture without touching its sides. The stylus and base plate are connected electrically, and each contact is registered on a counter.

So-called "aiming" tests involve quick, precise eye-hand coördinations. Aiming may also be measured by a stylus-and-hole apparatus. The subject is required to thrust the stylus into successively smaller holes without touching the sides, or into holes momentarily uncovered by a rotating shutter. A pencil-paper version of this test requires the subject to place dots in small circles as fast as he can; this test involves motor speed as well as precision of movement.

Tests of aiming and steadiness had negligible validity for selection of pilots and bombardiers. Arm-hand steadiness is related to success of aircraft electricians, according to one study. Several studies have found very high correlations between aiming or steadiness tests and rifle marksmanship (Humphreys *et al.*, 1936).

1. Decide which type of steadiness test would be most promising for selecting persons for each of the tasks listed below. If none of the tests mentioned above seems fully suitable, attempt to describe one more comparable to the job.
   a. A jigsaw operator is to move a board, about eight inches square, so that a curved pattern is cut out.
   b. A rifleman must hold his sights steadily on a target while resting on an elbow in a prone position.
   c. A pistol marksman must hold his sights steadily on a target while standing.
   d. An engraver must follow a pattern with great precision, using a small power tool.

Speed and Dexterity.   We have already encountered speed of movement in the USES tests, where it enters into scores K, F, and M. The nearest to a pure measure of movement is the Mark Making test (p. 274). In Table 39 we noted that the manual factor M, involving speed and dexterity, correlated .30–.55 with success in many jobs, having a notably high correlation with success of persons mounting wires in radio tubes. Factor K has equally large correlations with such jobs as typing, telephone operating, packing, and outboard motor assembling. In general, motor speed is important in overlearned routine tasks.

The manual and finger dexterity tests of the USES require simple rapid movements. Some other tests require more complicated movements—for example, inserting pins into narrow holes with tweezers, or threading nuts onto bolts. Low-to-moderate positive correlations are reported for dexterity tests as predictors of office and factory jobs.

Complex Coördinations

Instead of the fairly simple tasks described above, one can ask the subject to do quite complicated acts. There is little rationale to guide in the design of these complex tasks, and a good deal of apparatus testing has been based merely on hunches.

One principle that has often worked well is that of the *job replica*. If we are selecting workers to perform a particular job, we might observe a *work-sample*, i.e., we might observe them briefly on the job itself and record their output. If the job requires training after selection or uses expensive apparatus, however, the true worksample may be impractical. In such a case, the tester tries to design an apparatus which reproduces much of the original task, without requiring skills that have to be developed during job training.

An excellent example of the job replica is the Complex Coördination test of the Air Force (Figure 2). One cannot observe a would-be pilot in an airplane, but the Complex Coördination test gives him a stick and rudder bar which he is to move much as the pilot does. Movements are dictated by signal lights. When a light appears at the top of the left center column, the man pulls the stick so that the right center light will move upward to match it. A sideways movement of the stick controls the light in the top row, and the rudder controls the light running across the bottom row.

This test had a validity of about .40 for predicting pilot success and was given the highest weight among all tests used in the selection battery. A factor analysis demonstrated the reason for this high validity: the Complex Coördination test duplicates better than any other test the common-factor composition of the student pilot's task. Table 41 (cf. Figure 44), gives the

TABLE 41. **Factor Loadings of the Complex Coördination Test and the Pilot Success Criterion**

Factor	Loadings of Complex Coordination Test	Graduation-Elimination Criterion	Product of Loadings
Spatial	.49	.34	.167
Psychomotor coördination	.34	.22	.075
Mechanical experience	.20	.26	.052
Interest in piloting	.17	.28	.048
Visualization	.17	.25	.042
Perceptual speed	.17	.15	.026
Numerical	.09	.01	.001
Verbal	−.01	−.02	.000
Reasoning	.02	−.02	−.000
Uninterpreted factor	.10	−.03	−.003
			.408

SOURCE: Melton, 1947, p. 995.

loadings of the test and of the criterion (graduation from pilot training vs. elimination). The products of the loadings, in the farthest right column, show how much each factor adds to the total validity. The total of these products agrees almost exactly with the observed validity of .39. The predictive validity is accounted for entirely by the common factors, which means that the specific content of the Complex Coördination test does not contribute to prediction of pilot success. Note that the spatial aspect of the test accounts for more of its predictive value than does the coördination factor.

Another type of complex task calls for "pursuit" or "tracking," i.e., following an irregular course or a moving target as in gunnery, radar operation, and high-speed maneuvering. The essence of a pursuit test is a moving target which must be followed with a pointer of some kind. Four pursuit devices are shown in Figure 55. The Rotary Pursuit Test is the simplest and the

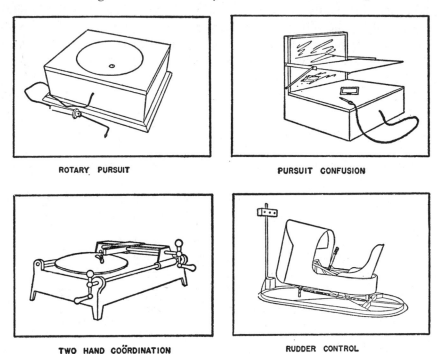

ROTARY PURSUIT   PURSUIT CONFUSION

TWO HAND COÖRDINATION   RUDDER CONTROL

FIG. 55. Four pursuit or coördination tasks (Fleishman, 1956). Except for Rudder Control, which is large enough for the subject to sit in, the tests are of desk-top size.

oldest. It has been used as a predictive device and as a laboratory instrument for the study of skill learning. A ¾-inch brass disk is set in a bakelite turntable. The subject uses a stylus with a hinged handle to follow the disk, his total contact time being recorded electrically. Many variations are possible. In the Pursuit Confusion Test, the speed of the target changes, and the subject has to guide his tracking by watching in a mirror rather than by viewing the target directly. The Two-Hand Coördination Test involves slower but more complex movement. One handle controls left-right motion of the follower arm, while the other controls front-to-back motion. Both must be moved at the same time, at different speeds, to stay on the target. The Rudder Control Test is another job replica, which has the honor of being the only psychomotor test invented during World War II which proved valuable enough to put into immediate use for pilot selection. The man sits in a cockpit and is to keep the cockpit pointed directly toward whichever of three target lights is lit. The direction of the cockpit is controlled both by the rudder and by the man's posture, so that this becomes a test of bodily balance as well as leg coördination.

Complex job replicas are of considerable value, provided they truly resemble the job to be predicted. An example is the so-called Metal Filing Worksample, intended to measure that skill as used in dentistry. This isolates one element of the job and measures it directly. It correlated .53 with grades in dentistry courses (Bellows, 1940). The I.E.R. Trimming Test, in which the subject cuts between a pair of narrowing lines with scissors, correlated .69 with ratings of power-sewing-machine trainees (Treat, 1929). The Hand-Tool Dexterity Test, requiring operations on nuts and bolts with wrench and screwdriver, correlated .46 with performance of machinists (Bennett and Fear, 1943).

TABLE 42.   Prediction of Quality and Quantity of Work of Sewing-Machine Operators

Test	Correlation with Quality Criterion (N = 52)	Correlation with Speed Criterion (N = 52)
Minnesota Clerical, Names	.36	.08
Minnesota Clerical, Number	.26	.22
Poppelreuter Tracing (time score)	−.31	.45
Poppelreuter Weaving	.27	.21
Paper folding	.30	−.10
Minnesota Spatial Relations (time)	.24	.28
Minesota Paper Form Board	.32	.17
O'Connor Tweezer Dexterity	.07	.46
O'Connor Finger Dexterity	.20	.27
Minnesota Rate of Manipulation	.08	.31
Otis Self-Administering (IQ)	.17	.11
Tests with correlations in boldface, combined	.57	.64

SOURCE: J. L. Otis, 1938.

In line with the suggestion that good predictors resemble the job, J. L. Otis (1938) found that tests which predict quality on a job may be poor predictors of speed. Correlations of predictive tests for sewing-machine operators with both speed and quality criteria are shown in Table 42. Otis points out that workers suitable for a shop stressing quality may lack aptitudes needed in a shop seeking high volume of production. The user of psychomotor tests must have clearly in mind the nature of the job he wishes to predict.

The difficulties of interpreting psychomotor tests which arise from their specificity and from the shortage of relevant psychological theory should not lead the personnel psychologist to underrate them. When the Air Force made a serious effort to use them on a large scale, they turned out to be not only practical but nearly indispensable. Their contribution to pilot selection was about equal to that of the much-better-understood printed tests.

2. The factor loadings for Complex Coördination, squared, give the percentage composition of the test variance. How do the values from Table 41 compare with those in Figure 44, p. 254? (The two results are based on different groups of student pilots, and a larger number of tests was used in arriving at the results in Figure 44.)

Factors in Psychomotor Performance

The extensive apparatus testing program of the Air Force continued from 1942 to 1955. During the program, Air Force psychologists collected data of an unprecedented type, giving batteries of reliable apparatus tests to large samples of men. The results promise to bring some order into the chaotic theory of psychomotor testing.

Hitherto, it was necessary to describe each test in turn. No basic list of abilities had been isolated, and factorial results had been incomplete and partly contradictory. Fleishman, on the basis of his recent work, now offers a list of factors which may account for much of the psychomotor domain. (This summary comes from Fleishman, 1956. Some of the original factor analyses are reported in Fleishman and Hempel, 1954b, 1956; Hempel and Fleishman, 1953; and Fleishman, 1954. See also Fleishman, 1953.) The list must be regarded as tentative, however, until it is cross-checked by work outside the Air Force. It seems fair to say that Fleishman has brought psychomotor testing to about the point that intellectual testing reached in 1940, following Thurstone's first report on the "primary abilities." Views in that field have changed extensively since 1940, and time will no doubt alter Fleishman's list.

Some of Fleishman's factors are old acquaintances like finger dexterity. Others represent distinctions never previously suggested. The list of major factors is as follows:

Reaction time. Quickness of a simple, overlearned movement in response to a signal.

Arm-hand steadiness. Precision and steadiness in positioning movements. Speed and strength irrelevant.

Rate of arm movement. Speed of gross arm movements. Precision irrelevant. The only test we have described which seems to measure this factor is the Place test of GATB.

Finger dexterity. Skillful, controlled finger movement. The GATB Assembly and Turn tests have loadings on this factor.

Manual dexterity. Skillful, controlled movements in manipulating larger objects with whole hand. The Turn test is one of the better measures of this factor.

Postural discrimination. Making precise bodily adjustments on the basis of postural cues. Walking a rail blindfolded would probably be a good test. The experimental measure of this factor is a test where the subject is seated blindfold in a tilted chair and must push buttons to bring the chair upright.

Fine psychomotor coördination. Also called "fine control sensitivity." Delicate, highly controlled adjustments involving large-muscle groups, as in Rotary Pursuit and Pursuit Confusion.

Multiple limb coördination. Using two arms, arms and legs, etc., in a simultaneous control movement such as clutching-and-shifting an automobile transmission. This is measured in Complex Coördination and Rudder Control.

Rate control. Involves continuous anticipations and adjustments of timing in tracking a target with variable speed and path.

Response orientation. Choosing the proper response among several alternatives. This has been tested by complex discrimination tasks where each signal pattern calls for movement in a different direction. Can be measured by pencil-paper tests as well as by apparatus.

Response integration. Combination of information into a single integrated motor response. Two-hand Coördination and Complex Coördination involve this ability.

In addition to this main list, a number of sheer physical factors such as "strength" are found, and a number of lesser psychomotor factors which are not yet well established.

Psychomotor tests which involve different factors often have very low correlations. (For example, Rate of Manipulation—Placing correlates only .02 with Rudder Control.) This definitely rules out the idea of a general psychomotor ability which makes some people good at any manual or athletic task.

3. Which factor involves complex movement of small-muscle groups, with little emphasis on speed?
4. Which factors do you think are involved in each of these tasks?
   a. Riding a bicycle.
   b. Typewriting.
   c. Cutting dress materials, following a pattern.
5. These items are included in the MacQuarrie Test of Mechanical Ability. All are given with short time limits. Which factors does each seem to measure?
   a. Dotting; $\frac{3}{16}$-inch circles, irregularly spaced. Place one dot in each circle.
   b. Tracing; a series of 1-inch vertical lines, each with a $\frac{1}{16}$-inch opening somewhere along its length. Trace a path through the openings.

   c. Tapping; ⅜-inch circles regularly spaced. Put three dots in each circle.
6. The Purdue Pegboard requires the subject to place small pegs into holes, first with his right hand, then with his left hand. Loadings for the right-hand and left-hand scores, respectively, on various factors were as follows: reaction time, .25, .02; arm-hand steadiness, .14, .06; rate of arm movement, .22, .13; finger dexterity, .46, .58. What explanation can you give for the differences observed between right- and left-hand scores?
7. The correlation of visual and auditory reaction time is only .56. How can the gap between this value and the reliability of .85 best be explained?

GENERAL PROBLEMS OF PSYCHOMOTOR TESTING

Apparatus Differences

Test apparatus is supposed to be standardized, especially when results at one time and place set standards to be used in future selection or guidance. The Air Force found that even when several pieces of apparatus were made in the same shop from the same blueprints they were rarely equivalent. Moreover, each apparatus changed over time as electrical contacts became dirty, rubber parts became less elastic, and so on. For example, in the relatively simple Arm-Hand Steadiness Test the mean scores earned on four different pieces of apparatus were 227, 230, 260, and 291 (Melton, 1947). These differences are of practical importance, since the standard deviation of scores is about 120 points. A score which was average on one machine would be near the 30th percentile on another.

Pencil-Paper Measures of Motor Performance

Apparatus tests are virtually out of the question in guidance testing, and it has rarely been practical to use them in industrial and military selection. Initial cost is not the critical factor; Melton estimates that $250,000 covered the total cost of apparatus for processing tens of thousands of Air Force men. The big cost is in time of the persons who must give the tests, for even with highly efficient arrangements a tester can handle only four to six subjects at once. So long as apparatus tests predict validly, they can save enough to more than repay their costs. In the Air Force, every man who failed pilot training represented a waste of $25,000. This easily justified using expensive tests to detect failure in advance. It is nevertheless obvious that testers would gladly substitute pencil-paper tests if these would measure the same aptitudes.

We have seen in the GATB Mark Making test an example of a pencil-paper psychomotor test. Some psychologists are convinced that with sufficient ingenuity other important motor abilities can be reduced to group pencil-paper tests. The evidence on the question is extremely fragmentary.

One Air Force study (Melton, 1947, pp. 1033 ff.) found that when apparatus tests and pencil-paper tests of motor speed were put in the same battery, the two groups defined quite separate abilities. Such small efforts as were made during the war to obtain validities for pencil-paper psychomotor tests were discouraging. More recently, Fleishman (1954) introduced several printed psychomotor tests into a battery and found that they were quite successful in measuring wrist-finger speed and fairly successful in measuring aiming and steadiness. The pencil-paper tests had little in common with the more complex coördination and dexterity tests.

Reliability

As in the case of performance tests of general ability, reliability has been a source of difficulty in psychomotor tests. It will be recalled that in the GATB, F and M are the least reliable scores. Reliabilities for apparatus tests as usually given are in the neighborhood of .70. This level may be satisfactory when the test is to be combined with several others in an overall prediction, but it makes the test untrustworthy by itself.

One might reasonably suppose that extending the test period would raise reliability, and if so, only cost of testing prevents us from boosting reliability just as we would for a pencil-paper test. The reliability of apparatus tests does not increase with length in the normal manner, however, because two successive sections are not "equivalent." This is best shown with the Rotary Pursuit Test, where the internal consistency of a ten-trial score is .97, but the correlation of the first ten with the second ten trials is only .84. For all the Air Force tests the same thing was found: reliability increases with length, but more slowly than the Spearman-Brown formula predicts.

The reason is that the test measures different things at different stages of practice. The first and second ten trials are outwardly similar, but psychologically they pose different tasks for the subject. To that topic we now turn.

Changes in Meaning with Stage of Practice

In an aptitude test it is important to obtain a stable measure, characteristic of the person over a period of time. Scores are unstable if we apply a psychomotor test without giving the subject a chance to learn the task in preliminary trials. This is again an example of the principle that abilities, while emerging, cannot be accurately measured.

On complicated testing devices, a subject cannot show his full ability until he has become familiar with the reaction required. Fleishman and Hempel (1954a; Fleishman, 1957) gave 64 two-minute trials on the Complex Coördination Test. (Eight minutes is the usual testing time.) The scores, together with reference tests, were factored. Figure 56 shows that the factor content of the test depends on the amount of practice. That is, different men score high at different stages of practice. In the early stages, cognitive factors such as S and Vz are most important, along with Psychomotor Coördination. These interpretative factors account for little variance after subjects become familiar with the task. Psychomotor Coördination, a factor common to this test and to other motor tests administered, increases in importance during the first 40 minutes of practice but then drops back. Two

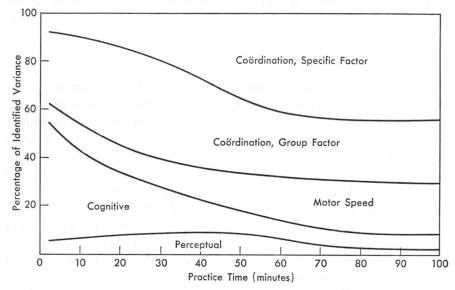

FIG. 56. Composition of Complex Coördination Test as a function of practice. (Data from Fleishman and Hempel, 1954a.) Curves show proportion of variance accounted for by each factor after removing error variance and unidentified minor factors from consideration. Curves have been smoothed, and factors have been combined as follows: Cognitive includes Spatial, Visualization, and Mechanical Experience; Motor Speed includes Rate of Movement and Psychomotor Speed.

factors grow steadily in prominence: rate of movement and a specific factor which we shall discuss further in a moment. Evidently the early trials measure the person's adaptation to a new task, and intellectual factors play a large part in the variance. At the end, sheer speed has become one of the leading sources of individual differences.

The substantial specific factor found in the Complex Coördination scores and not in other apparatus tests, such as Rotary Pursuit, becomes the largest source of individual differences after the first hour of practice. This factor involves some difference among individuals generated during the test and presumably corresponds to particular coördinations or work methods which the individual develops as he practices (Stevens, 1951, pp. 1341–1362). If a man with good general aptitude happens to fall into a bad habit, his final score may be far below his potential. Specific bad habits are highly persistent from trial to trial, as any athlete knows. They are not just a matter of low aptitude; the professional coach makes a career of recognizing and eliminating such faults from the performance of talented athletes. Not all specific responses are harmful; sometimes one stumbles into a fortunate pattern or rhythm which gives him a higher score than his aptitude would have predicted. The specific factor built up only in the Complex Coördination Test is unlikely to be of much predictive value. There is no reason to think that a man who acquires a certain bad sequence of actions on this test will form a similar habit when learning to fly a plane. In learning that task, other specific habits will develop.

Stability

When enough research has been done to provide a basis for practical interpretations of the factors, measures of these factors may be able to play a major role in vocational guidance. Before tests can be used to make long-range predictions, however, research on the stability of psychomotor aptitudes will be necessary. There is considerable evidence of stability of scores over periods of a few months, but little is known about stability over several years. For guidance of adolescents, it is necessary to know at what age psychomotor abilities begin to stabilize. The only substantial follow-up data so far available come from a study made in a Texas high school, where the same 114 pupils were tested with the GATB each year (Table 36). These data, though limited, suggest strongly that simple psychomotor abilities stabilize at about the same age as intellectual abilities.

Validity

Any verbal or intellectual test is likely to predict many criterion tasks. A numerical reasoning test may predict English, mathematics, science, and shop grades, all equally well, simply because all the measures depend on general ability. Despite popular legends about boys who are "good with their hands," there is no such general psychomotor ability. Any psychomotor test is much more valid for some jobs than for others. Psychomotor tests must be chosen for each particular job. They can be trusted as predictors only after an empirical tryout. There have been many disappointing studies in which tests which "ought to have" predicted occupational criteria failed to do so (Stevens, 1951, pp. 1341–1362).

In trying out tests with the hope of finding a good predictor, past experience suggests the job replica as the best bet. The common-sense rule that the test which resembles the job ought to predict the job has generally paid off

with encouraging validity coefficients. If intelligently designed, the job replica can demand the same coördinations, speed, and precision as are called
for in the criterion task. Furthermore, it looks like a reasonable test and
therefore appeals to the subject and to the employer in whose behalf the tests
are used. There is little doubt that job replicas will continue to be used in industrial and military selection for some time.

Some of the results for the Complex Coördination Test raise a serious question as to whether the job replica deserves its good reputation. Much of the
validity of that test in pilot selection was due to intellectual abilities which
could be measured in pencil-paper tests. The psychomotor aspect of the test
which predicted the criterion was the coördination factor common to several
apparatus tests which were *not* replicas of the pilot's job. Rotary Pursuit,
which does not "look like" anything the pilot does, was a better measure of
the coördination factor than Complex Coördination. If there is anything special about the Complex Coördination Test as a replica of the pilot's job, it
must be in the specific factor, and that contributed nothing to validity. So the
magic of the Complex Coördination Test appears to be that it involves about
the right mixture of common factors. If so, such a mixture could be put together by adding scores from other tests measuring the same factors.

One of the reasons for wishing to avoid the job-replica principle in test design is that it leads to an endless process of inventing and revising tests to
cover additional jobs or to take changes in job requirements into account.
Vocational guidance could not possibly be based on such tests, since hundreds of tests would have to be given to cover the occupational spectrum.

Fleishman believes that it will be possible to prepare a short battery to
measure the chief psychomotor factors, and to combine scores from this battery so as to predict the psychomotor component of any job. At present, no
one can say how well the factor scores will predict jobs, and one cannot guarantee that the list of psychomotor abilities will remain short. The factors do
account for about half of the variance in current tests; therefore combinations of the factor scores may be able to do much of what the original tests can
do. While psychomotor abilities are often of value in predicting occupational
performance, they are generally of less importance than intellectual abilities.
In the USES studies, there were relatively few occupations where motor factors were substantially better predictors than the nonmotor factors. These exceptional occupations fall into two broad categories: bench work or assembling (cheese wrapper, telephone diaphragm assembler, paper-pattern
folder) and manipulative machine operating (machine clothes presser, bag
sealer). Motor tests have excellent validity for these routine jobs, but as soon
as a job becomes less repetitive, perceptual and intellectual factors make
large contributions. Ghiselli's study (1955) of other published coefficients
supports this conclusion, but adds that motor tests make a substantial con-

tribution in predicting success of structural workers. Tiffin (1952, p. 126) comments as follows on the failure of motor tests to predict skilled work (see also Patterson, 1956):

> A consideration of the skills demanded of the industrial tradesman or skilled machine operator indicates that this employee usually succeeds or fails in proportion to his training and general mechanical comprehension, not in proportion to his basic dexterity. This fact does not mean that successful tradesmen do not need skilled movements, but it does mean that such muscular coordination as may be needed can be developed by the majority of tradesmen in training and that it is lack of mechanical comprehension rather than inability to develop the muscular aspects of the job, that may prevent them from becoming really proficient in this line of work. This implies that only in the most repetitive performance can psychomotor tests alone provide an adequate basis for selection. In complex jobs where psychomotor tests do not predict ultimate proficiency, they nonetheless may make a valuable contribution by identifying which persons can master the motor components most rapidly.

8. What function might psychomotor tests play in making school physical education programs more profitable?
9. Experimenters wish to study the effect of vitamin lack on motor performance. They plan to test a group, then alter the diet, and test again after some time. Would it be desirable to offer training on the tests before the first measurement?
10. Under what circumstances would extending a psychomotor test so that it measures fatigue or endurance lower its validity?
11. Bennett and Cruikshank (1942) say, "Vocational guidance (not selection) on the basis of motor skill alone is quite deplorable, except in the case of individuals who have gross incapacitating motor disabilities." Do you agree?

ARTISTIC ABILITIES

General mental tests measure ability to succeed in courses, but a high score does not guarantee creativeness even in strictly intellectual work. In painting, architecture, and other graphic arts, special talents must certainly play a large part in success. To identify such talents has proved exceedingly difficult, but several tests of artistic ability have been tried. (In addition to these approaches, some effort has been made to predict from personality tests.)

Worksamples

One way of identifying those who will do well in art training is to obtain a sample of the person's creative drawing. This may measure training just as much as talent, but it is a fair basis for comparing persons with similar training. Merely asking the subject to draw or paint a picture, or to submit a piece of completed work, however, does not make for a standardized comparison. To standardize the task by requiring everyone to draw from the same model, on the other hand, leaves no room for creativeness.

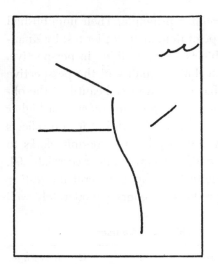

FIG. 57. Specimen item from Horn Art Aptitude Inventory, showing stimulus lines and two drawings based on them (C. A. Horn and L. F. Smith, 1945).

The Horn Art Aptitude test attempts to solve this problem by a job replica calling for high-level creativeness under very slight constraints. In the "imagery" section of the test the subject is given several cards, each bearing a pattern of lines. Around these lines he is to sketch a picture. The pictures are judged by art instructors as to imagination and technical drawing quality. Using careful scoring directions, competent judges can attain a correlation of .86 between independent scorings. The other chief section of the test calls for arrangement of rectangles and other simple figures into balanced compositions.

The test is intended for use with applicants to art school, most of whom have had previous training. The scores at the beginning of the year correlated .66 with grades in a special art course for high-school seniors (C. A. Horn and L. F. Smith, 1945).

Gilbert and Ewing also favor the job-replica principle. Their unpublished Illinois Art Ability Test (based on one type of item in an earlier test by Knauber) asks the subject to draw certain objects (e.g., a table) in perspective. The drawing is scored not only for the technical quality of the perspective but for the extent to which the subject has elaborated or beautified the object. A table which shows attractive lines and proportions receives a higher score than a graceless one. The test requires artistic skill, but it also reflects creative effort. Scoring rules have been developed which permit clerks to score the papers objectively; two scorings of the same papers correlate .94.

A validation study on students of architecture shows several interesting facts. In Table 43 we see that the test predicts art courses moderately well

TABLE 43.   Prediction of Success in Freshman Architecture Courses

Test	General Engineering Drawing	Freehand Drawing	Grade Average, Other Courses Combined
Illinois Art Ability Test	.26	.42	.27
Object Aperture Test (spatial)	.57	.30	.27
Coöperative Mathematics Test	.40	.27	.45
ACE (general ability)	.40	.25	.45
Bennett TMC	.60	.10	.09
Rank in high-school class			.49

NOTE: The criterion for the drawing courses is a composite of grades and ratings by instructors. The number of cases varies from 27 to 69.
SOURCE: These are unpublished data from a study by W. M. Gilbert, T. N. Ewing, D. R. Krathwohl, and L. J. Cronbach.

but gives a poor prediction in engineering drawing. The latter is predicted very well by the TMC and a spatial test. The average in other courses, including English and mathematics, is best predicted by high-school marks, the ACE tests, and a mathematics achievement test. This points to a fact of great importance in vocational counseling. Even though a student possesses special aptitudes in high degree, he cannot use them in a profession unless his general ability is good enough to carry him through general college courses. Specialized abilities, in fact, play little part in determining the architect's overall freshman grades, where the drawing courses are outweighed by nonspecialized courses. The TMC and the Art Ability Test correlate only .12 with the overall grade average.

Analytic Tests

The job replica gives valuable information about students who have had some art training, but it neither clarifies the nature of artistic talent nor gives a basis for comparing untrained persons. For these purposes, it is necessary to test components of artistic ability prior to training. These components have not been adequately identified, and the tests now available are based only on some investigator's hunch as to what makes an artist. One such test is the Lewerenz Test of Fundamental Abilities in Visual Art (California Test Bureau). Among the aspects of artistic ability measured are preference for designs, drawing a sketch to fit a pattern, locating proper positions of

FIG. 58. Item from the Meier Test of Art Judgment. The arrangement of the woman's burden has been changed. Which arrangement is better? (Item copyright 1940, Bureau of Educational Research, State University of Iowa. Reproduced by permission.)

shadows, art vocabulary, reproducing a form (vase) from memory, correction of perspective, and color matching. Practically no information on the validity of the test has been published.

The most adequate analysis of art ability to date is that of Meier (1939), who took into account biographies of artists and experimental test results. He concluded that six traits distinguish the artist: fine eye and hand coördination, energy and concentration, intelligence, keenness of observation, creative imagination, and aesthetic judgment. While Meier planned tests for "creative imagination" and "aesthetic perception," only a test of artistic judgment was actually completed.

The Meier Art Judgment Test (and an earlier form by Meier and C. E. Seashore) has been more widely used than any other art test. The test measures taste rather than ability to use art media. A "good" work of art is altered in composition, shading, or some other quality so as to damage its aesthetic appeal. The original and altered pictures are presented to the subject, who selects the more pleasing one (Figure 58). If he agrees with "experts" who have taken the test, he gets a high score. The needed validity studies on this test have not been performed; a few studies give favorable but very fragmentary evidence.

One difficulty with tests of judgment is that the subject may give, not his own opinion, but his guess as to what experts will accept as best. An experiment on the Graves Test of Design Judgment showed that by giving such guesses the subject could gain several points over the score his own preferences would earn (Buros, 1953, p. 336).

Artistic judgment is distinct from ability to perform artistically. Rose Anderson (1951) warns against reliance on the test of judgment as a predictor in the fine arts. Persons with poor Meier scores often are judged highly promising by art instructors. Her counseling experience, she says,

> has led to considerable caution in encouraging clients toward fine-art specialization. On the other hand, the combined results of several tests provide a more adequate basis for appraising potentialities for such applied fields as advertising art, format, interior decoration, costume design, and crafts. The appropriate combination of supporting aptitudes includes superior artistic judgment reflected in a high McAdory score, superior facility for spatial visualization and fine eye-hand coordination, manual dexterity, evidence of drawing ability reflected in the Lewerenz Originality of Line Drawing Test [subtest], in the Horn Art Aptitude Test, or in work samples.

The McAdory test is a test of taste in furniture, clothing, and automobiles as well as in fine art (Rose Anderson, 1948).

Research on artistic abilities is still in a most primitive stage. No systematic research has been done using modern tests and adequate criteria. Most of the tests have been left as they were when first designed as much as thirty years ago, without follow-up research or revision. The nature of artistic aptitude remains an unsolved—and neglected—problem.

12. What criterion would the Meier test be expected to predict better than the Horn test, and vice versa?

13. What aspects of art aptitude do not appear to be measured by any of the tests described?

14. Are the six traits listed by Meier most likely to reflect talent, training, or temperament?

15. Assuming that the validities reported in Table 43 are confirmed by further studies, what advice would a counselor give an applicant to the school of architecture who scores at the 80th percentile in the Art Ability Test, TMC, and

Object Aperture Test but at the 30th percentile in mathematics and general ability?

SOCIAL INTELLIGENCE

A recurrent interest of aptitude testers has been to identify qualities which help one to get along with other people. It was once suggested that there might be three categories of intelligence: abstract, practical, and social. We have found some evidence permitting us to distinguish the first two, though both of them must be further subdivided. After fifty years of intermittent investigation, however, social intelligence remains undefined and unmeasured.

There are wide individual differences in performance of such roles as salesman, Army officer, teacher, and psychotherapist. General intelligence has something to do with success in most of these assignments, but it surely is not the whole story. Perhaps the difference between the successful and the unsuccessful performer depends chiefly on personality and interests. Many testers have tried to identify an intellectual component in ability to respond successfully to others, and these tests merit brief attention.

In 1926, a Test of Social Intelligence was developed by F. A. Moss and others (published by George Washington University). There are four subtests in the revised (1944) version: judgment in common-sense social problems (e.g., "What is the best way to ask a favor of someone you know only slightly?"), matching statements with the emotions expressed, everyday psychological generalizations in true-false form ("In social relations, demands are usually more effective than requests"), and completion of a joke (multiple-choice). This test measures general or verbal ability to some degree, but there is no evidence that it measures any distinct ability which has practical predictive value. Enough attempts were made to establish the validity of the test for selection of salesmen, etc., to indicate that this line of approach is fruitless (R. L. Thorndike and Stein, 1937).

The last few years have seen a large number of tests of "social sensitivity," "insight into others," or "empathy." Personality theorists have argued that good personal relations depend upon good communication, and that a good leader or therapist is he who is sensitive to the ideas and feelings of others, even the unvoiced ones. We measure A's understanding of B by asking A to describe some aspect of B and comparing this judgment with an independent criterion. The most common method, because it is the simplest to apply, is to have B fill out a personality questionnaire describing himself, and to have A fill out the questionnaire *as he thinks B would*. The method is capable of endless variations, depending on whether A is asked to judge friends, work associates, or strangers, on what opportunities he is given to observe the strangers, and on what questions he has to answer.

This is a job replica which encounters all the pitfalls of an approach resting on surface similarity rather than psychological understanding of the variable measured. It is a reasonable assumption that a teacher or therapist or leader ought to understand what those he works with are thinking. The test design seems like a simple translation into scorable form of an act which he performs every day. Careful analysis of these tests, however, shows that the responses do not depend on insight into the individual (Cronbach, 1955b; Gage and Cronbach, 1955). No evidence of validity is yet available which warrants confidence in any present technique for measuring a person's ability to judge others as individuals.

SPECIAL APTITUDE TESTS FOR COURSES AND PROFESSIONS

About thirty years ago, numerous attempts were made to develop specialized aptitude tests for particular school subjects or curricula such as algebra, foreign language, engineering, or law. The test was usually prepared on the basis of a superficial analysis of the course of study. Test problems were based on the type of content to be encountered in the course (e.g., a foreign language test might involve substituting nonsense symbols for words in a sentence; a legal aptitude test would ordinarily present hypothetical problems in legal reasoning).

The tests of this first period have virtually disappeared. The primary reason is that the introduction of content specially relevant to the course of study did not raise validity appreciably above that which could be obtained with a good measure of general ability. When group tests began to provide separate scores for verbal, quantitative, and later spatial and mechanical comprehension, these broader-purpose tests appeared to offer all the advantages of a special test for particular subjects. Prediction ordinarily can rest on either a general mental test, a verbal test, or a general proficiency test, although there may occasionally be an advantage in considering special abilities also.

When thorough psychological study is made of a type of training which is of widespread importance, it may be possible to discover component abilities not covered in general ability tests. The best example is the *Modern Language Aptitude Test* of Carroll and Sapon (Psychological Corporation). This test, originally designed to select overseas employees to take special intensive language courses, showed validities in the range .60–.75. When used with high school students, predictive validities vary from school to school and from course to course. For four languages in one high school, validities ranged from .53 to .60; these validities are about .20 higher than corresponding correlations for general mental ability. The test correlates .61 with general ability, implying that not all very bright pupils are superior at language learning. The test is administered by means of a tape recording so as to test the pupil's ear for strange sounds, his ability to learn new material, and his sensitivity to grammatical forms (Carroll, 1959; Harding, 1958).

Many aptitude tests have been developed in recent years for use in graduate and professional schools. The tests are for the most part measures of general ability or academic achievement, such as might be used for general college counseling. They are adjusted in difficulty to the level of students tested, and place extra emphasis on the abilities of obvious interest to the profession in question. This special emphasis may make the test a slightly better predictor than a general-purpose test.

TABLE 44. Validation Research on the University of California Engineering Examination

Section		Part	Time Limit	Relia-bility	Correlation with Freshman Grade Average	Decision Regarding Test
I General scholastic ability	1	Word meaning	15	.93	.11	Study further
	2	Verbal fluency	10	.63	—	Drop
	3	Figure classification	30	.73	.12	Revise
	4	Technical vocabulary	20	.95	.27	Use
II Mathematical reasoning	5	Quantitative inference	70	.91	.39	Use
	6	Numerical progression	20	.89	.11	Drop
III Scientific	7	Understanding scientific relationships	90	.93	.23	Use
IV Spatial visualization	8	Figures	10	.92	.06	Study further
	9	Cubes	10	.90	.06	Study further
	10	Length of time	10	.64	.04	Drop
	11	Hidden forms	10	.61	.07	Drop
	12	Line location	15	.95	.09	Study further
	13	Matching parts	10	.79	.03	Drop
High-school grade average					.39	

SOURCE: M. H. Jones and H. W. Case, 1955.

The development of a professional aptitude test is illustrated by a report from the University of California regarding a test for the selection and guidance of applicants to the Engineering School (M. H. Jones and H. W. Case, 1955). Four sections were developed: a general ability test, a mathematics test, a test requiring interpretation of scientific data, and a spatial test. Each section had several parts, adjusted in length according to their presumed importance. Table 44 shows reliability estimates on limited samples, and validities based on 533 engineering freshmen. Test 2 was dropped without complete trial, because of low reliability.

The previous (high-school) grade average is the best predictor; this is a common finding in academic prediction. Such a predictor is to some degree unsatisfactory because grading standards vary in different schools, and test scores are a valuable supplement. The best tests are 5 (quantitative inference), 4 (technical vocabulary), and 7 (scientific interpretation). These tests, combined with high-school average, correlate .51 with freshman marks. Note that these tests are all measures of achievement. The prediction from this three hours of testing would not be bettered by adding the tests with lower validities, so tests 6, 10, 11, and 13 were dropped. Tests 1, 8, 9, and 12 and a revised form of 3 were retained because it was thought that this information might be useful in predicting advanced courses.

The California data do not tell clearly whether the special battery does better than a general predictor test would. For evidence on this point, we turn to a report from the University of Utah (Pierson and Jex, 1951). The Utah College of Engineering had used the Pre-Engineering Inventory, a six-hour battery (which has subsequently been shortened to an eighty-minute test) covering mathematics and scientific comprehension. It was found that high-school marks predicted college engineering marks with an r of .57. Adding subtests of the Pre-Engineering Inventory raised the correlation to about .68. The nonspecialized Coöperative Achievement Tests, combined with high-school average, correlated about .65 with engineering grades. (Just why the correlation at Utah is so much higher than at California is uncertain. One possibility is that the California engineering students are more severely preselected.)

This result is consistent with studies of other tests. A specialized professional aptitude test is not appreciably more effective as a predictor than a suitably weighted combination of ordinary measures of achievement and general mental abilities. The only professions which constitute exceptions to this rule are dentistry, where spatial and dexterity tests have predictive value, and architecture, discussed above. The main reason for having separate professional tests is administrative. Such tests are ordinarily distributed through the national professional association or some comparable group and are not available to individual counselors. This protects the secrecy of questions so that tests can be used fairly as a basis for admission to professional schools.

16. Why do measures of past achievement predict college marks better than measures of general mental ability? In view of this fact, what function can group mental tests perform in college admission and counseling?
17. How could a high school coach students desiring to enter Engineering School

at the University of California so as to raise their aptitude test scores? Is it desirable to use tests which allow such coaching?

Suggested Readings

Fleishman, Edwin A. Psychomotor selection tests: research and application in the United States Air Force. *Personnel Psychol.*, 1956, 9, 449–468.

    This is a description of the Air Force psychomotor tests and a summary of research on factors underlying them.

Schultz, Harold A. Review of the Meier Art Tests: I. Art Judgment. In O. K. Buros (ed.), *The fourth mental measurements yearbook.* Highland Park, N.J.: Gryphon Press, 1953. Pp. 338–340.

    In a critique of the Meier test, largely from the point of view of content validity of the items, Schultz indicates how complex, and how little understood, is even this one aspect of artistic ability.

Traxler, Arthur E., & others. Validation of professional aptitude batteries. *Proceedings, 1950 Invitational Conference on Testing Problems.* Princeton: Educational Testing Service, 1951. Pp. 13–54.

    A symposium describes efforts to develop special tests for accounting, law, dentistry, and medicine.

12

Personnel Selection and Classification

WHEN we wish to predict success in task X, it would be convenient if we could look in a test catalog, find a test labeled "Test of Aptitude for Task X," and begin using that test for selection. Unfortunately, the procedure required to establish a selection program is much more complicated. One difficulty is that tests with similar names measure different things, and that a test intended to predict a particular performance may be a poorer predictor than a test made for quite another purpose. More than one test may be required to cover all the aptitudes a particular job demands. Another problem is that jobs are difficult to classify. Some mechanical jobs seem to make psychomotor demands which almost anyone can satisfy, whereas success in other jobs with similar titles depends almost entirely upon the psychomotor factors. No matter how well a test has been developed and how thoroughly its author has validated it, no one knows how well it will predict in a particular practical situation until it is tried out there.

The employment manager or educational admissions officer can accept no test on face value, nor can he accept a test solely on the basis of research conducted elsewhere. Sooner or later, nearly every test worker must carry out his own validation studies to determine whether his prediction methods are working. While the practicing tester may limit his studies to relatively simple follow-up, it is important to know the full procedure for validation research, since this establishes the basic logic of any study of prediction.

In Chapter 2 we distinguished among various types of decisions for which tests are used: selection, classification, evaluation of treatments, and verification of scientific hypotheses. While in one sense prediction is involved in using tests for any of these purposes, the empirical, criterion-oriented validation procedures to be examined in this chapter are most directly relevant to selection and classification. We shall devote the greater part of our discussion to selection, centering on employee selection for the sake of clarity. The statements are equally relevant, however, to institutional selection (or rejection) decisions in military, educational, and clinical settings.

PROCEDURES IN PREDICTION RESEARCH

To predict success in a job one chooses a number of tests for tryout, determines their effectiveness experimentally, and devises a plan for using test scores in making decisions. One procedure relies on crude trial and error: the experimenter assembles a "shotgun" battery of all kinds of tests in the hope that one or more of them will prove effective. This method is declining as we understand better why some tests are valid and others are not. Psychologists developing test batteries today devote considerable thought to the characteristics of the job and the establishment of adequate criteria, as well as to the search for promising tests.

The stages in prediction research are as follows:

Job analysis, to determine what characteristics appear to make for success or failure.

Choice of possibly useful tests to measure these characteristics.

Administration of tests to an experimental group of workers.

Collection of criterion data showing how the experimental group of workers succeeded on the job.

Analysis of the relation between test score and success on the job, and installation of most effective selection plan.

Job Analysis

The first step is to analyze the job to be predicted. This analysis sets up hypotheses stating which abilities and habits contribute to or limit success in the job. No machine-like procedure of checking off one by one all possible factors has ever been found successful. Instead, the psychologist studies the task with whatever insight and psychological knowledge he can muster. Job analysis is in large measure an art.

In order to make a successful analysis, one must first of all have wide background in psychology. Understanding of motivation, motor habits and the organization of abilities, and knowledge of the multitude of tests now available are required. Detailed motion analysis will suggest what dexterities or coördinations are important. Analysis of the stimuli to which the worker responds may suggest need for certain perceptual or sensory abilities. One frequent approach is to compare good and poor employees. Simple studies often reveal essential differences between good and bad performers. Study of workers in training is helpful, since their difficulties in learning may show what aptitude is needed to avoid failure. Research on prediction for other jobs draws attention to tests worth trying and sometimes suggests that certain tests can be eliminated without further trial. No routine or stereotyped approach is likely to be successful, however. The analyst must take off from the experience of others, but unless he brings in new hypotheses he is unlikely to find a better method of predicting.

A job analysis should be highly specific. One should not state that successful workers have "mechanical ability"; one should instead define the ability as "knowledge of and ability to apply principles of gears," or "speed in routine two-handed manipulation, not involving much finger dexterity or thinking." Such clear definitions permit one to obtain or construct the most appropriate test. The analysis should not be confined to "aptitudes." It should range over the entire field of abilities, habits, personality characteristics and interests, previous experiences, knowledge, physique, and so on.

Impressionistic job analysis places heavy reliance on the opinions of a few observers. A more systematic procedure for collecting opinions from a larger body of informants and reducing the effect of folklore on the job analysis is the "critical-incident" technique developed by Flanagan (1954). The analyst asks a foreman or some other person well acquainted with the job to think of an individual who has done excellently on the job, and then to recall one particular incident which showed this person's superiority. Likewise, the informant recalls a poor performer, perhaps one who had to be discharged, and the incident which led to the final verdict of unsuitability. These incidents are concrete, and only one stage removed from field observation of good and poor performance, as can be seen in these two examples (Preston, 1948):

This officer was instructed to land his P-80 on runway 15. He pedaled on the right runway but lined up to land on runway 9. He was told to go around and line up and land on runway 15 again. This time he overshot and had to go around. He was getting dangerously low on fuel so I personally talked him around the pattern, putting him on his down-wind leg, and instructed him when to turn on base. I asked him if he had runway 15 spotted and he said "Roger." After acknowledging, he flew right by runway 15 and almost "spun-in" trying to turn in on runway 9. Being low on fuel, I told him to go ahead and land. He came in hot and ran off the end of the runway.

In meeting and acting as a pilot for general officers this lieutenant has brought favorable comment upon himself through the accomplishment of the mission. One specific case was when, through no fault of his own, an aircraft was allowed to depart without a retired Major General on board. Immediately upon being confronted by the general—a rather crusty old bird—he, without calling on me or any other superior, arranged for his departure to the original destination in time to overtake his original aircraft.

The incidents are classified into logical categories in order to identify variables that may be measured for the purposes of prediction.

The critical-incident method collects richly suggestive data, avoiding vague generalities such as "This job requires good judgment." It is not, however, a truly objective method. If the folklore of the business says that truck drivers must have stamina but not necessarily much intelligence, the informant is likely to bring to mind incidents which support the stamina theory, and to forget the cases in which drivers made themselves valuable by recognizing mixups in their orders. The person who classifies incidents likewise can introduce stereotypes into the final result, but this disadvantage is present in any judgment of job requirements.

1. Prepare a list of the factors composing aptitude for one of the following jobs: making pie dough, operating a calculator of a particular type, driving a taxi, or schoolteaching of some one type.
2. For many jobs requiring long training, e.g., physiotherapy, it is undesirable to take girls into training who will probably marry and drop out. What characteristics might distinguish between probable marriers and nonmarriers?

Choice of Tests for Tryout

Having a list of characteristics presumed to be important in a job, the investigator must then find tests to measure each. He must make a choice between seeking one test which is a composite of the job requirements and seeking a group of tests, each of which is a pure and independent measure of one of the characteristics. The former method, which usually leads to tests of the job-replica type, requires the investigator to design a new test for the job. As we have seen in considering mechanical, psychomotor, artistic, and academic aptitudes, the relatively complex test which comes close to the requirements of the job generally gives higher validity coefficients than simple tests, although simple tests may be equally useful when a number of them can be combined. The specially designed job replica has distinct disadvantages:

● In employee placement and in guidance it is more economical to use a few tests which give information about many jobs than to use a separate test for each job.

● Work samples must be revised, restandardized, and revalidated when any change in the nature of the job is made. A battery of simple tests can be revised to fit minor changes in the job by altering weights assigned to the tests or by adding perhaps one more test.

Assuming that the investigator decides to use many tests, each for a particular function, he must then choose among available tests or construct new ones. If the abilities the job seems to demand are already measured in published tests, such tests should be tried. Naturally, not every test with a relevant name will be suitable; the investigator must consider the difficulty of the test, its appropriateness to the intelligence and education of his subjects, and the like. If the job calls for an ability only approximately represented in available aptitude tests, it is more desirable to make a new test to measure this ability than to obtain a pale distorted image of it from an indirect measure. Without condemning the useful TMC, we can use it to illustrate this point. The items measure some general factor, but there are also group and unique factors among its items, which are drawn from all portions of physics and mechanics. To select men for advanced electrical training, background and comprehension are significant; but it is probable that Bennett's items dealing with electricity will give better correlations than his items on forces, motion, and buoyancy. Inclusion of the latter items might, in fact, dilute the test so that it will fail to select good workers, whereas a test covering only electrical comprehension might be a good predictor. Unless there is a close psychological correspondence between an available test and the job, a new test of the ability must be constructed.

There is no simple answer to the question of published versus homemade tests. Tests validated on many jobs are of distinct advantage in educational guidance, and to a lesser extent in employment work. Counselors would prefer to predict all jobs with a few tests. But the test designed for a specific job often has significantly higher validity than the test for general use.

In addition to tests designed to yield predetermined scores, many selection studies employ tests which are no more than collections of heterogeneous items. The most common of these is the biographical inventory, used to identify background factors capable of predicting success. There is no published biographical inventory of this type, but it is a simple matter to prepare a suitable collection of items covering work and educational experience, hobbies, athletic background, social activities, and family. In this miscellaneous collection, each item is treated as a separate test, and its relation to success on the job is examined empirically. Each job will correlate with some of the items, and a score based on just those items can be used to predict success in that job. The same technique of trying out a mixed assemblage of items and keying only those which predict the criterion can be applied to interest and personality tests. Inventories scored in this manner have often predicted job success as well as ability tests. The wartime Air Force Biographical Data Blank correlated .30 with pilot success (the items scored being those which distinguished successes from failures in the first group studied). Among eighty different types of tests studied, the only ones yielding coefficients higher than .30 were a pencil-paper test of knowledge about automobile driving (.32), instrument comprehension (.32), and mechanical principles (ca. .35) (Guilford, 1947). Two of these three tests clearly depend on background experience.

3. What practical conditions would a department store consider in deciding whether to make a special test for each type of clerk or to use a published test for salespeople in general?

Experimental Trial

The crucial step in prediction research is experimental trial of the instruments. One gives the tests to typical *applicants* and observes the correspondence of test scores to success. In practical work there is much pressure to omit the experimental study; this pressure must be resisted. When the psychologist reports to his boss that he believes test X will eliminate poorer employees, the boss is far more anxious to install the test and benefit from it at once than to withhold judgment during weeks or even years of investigation. Full experimental trial is indispensable. No hypothesis can be trusted, because there have been many instances in which "likely" tests proved to be of no value in selection.

The nonpsychologist may propose to use the test to eliminate poor men, and to study the survivors to determine the relation between test and performance. This is not a satisfactory plan. A test might not predict which of the acceptable men would do well on the job even though it could weed out failures. (Example: A hearing test would rule out some people as music students; but within a selected group, all of whom could hear, it would not predict success.) Trial on an unselected group is necessary, moreover, to establish critical scores and weightings of tests. So important is experimental trial on an unselected population that the Air Force went to the trouble to validate its selection methods by sending through training 1300 men, a random sample of all eligible recruits, even though it knew in advance that the majority of these men would be failures (DuBois, 1947).

Subjects should take the tests with the same motivation that would exist in their ultimate use (see p. 53). The investigator will try more tests than he can use in his final prediction battery, since some will probably not be helpful. This makes the trial battery long, and special attention must be paid to maintaining coöperation from the subjects. Sometimes one test can be tried at a time, but sooner or later the entire selection battery must be validated on a single group.

4. Suppose an employer puts a test in use without tryout. What harm can result from this, assuming that the validity of the test is zero or low positive?

The Criterion

After giving his tests, the experimenter waits for evidence of good and poor job performance. The experimental group is treated in the same way as other workers, being given normal training and duties. After a suitable interval, data on success are obtained. Among the criteria often used are quantity of production, quality of production, turnover, and opinions of foremen or supervisors. As was explained on p. 108, it is important that the criterion possess a high degree of validity. A test which can predict quality of work will seem to be a poor test if it is judged by a criterion which does not fairly indicate quality of work. The criterion (or set of criteria) should cover all important aspects of the job.

Criteria may be based on measured output, field observations, or ratings.

The criterion must have high reliability. An adequate number of observations representative of normal performance is required. If a proficiency test is the criterion, it must meet the usual requirements of objectivity, stability, and validity. Ratings are particularly common criteria and are subject to many errors. Methods of making ratings more dependable are discussed in a later chapter (pp. 506 ff.).

Frequently no single measure of success is suitable. One reason is that different workers seem best at different times. The fast learner who does well at the end of a short training course may not give as good ultimate results as a learner who continues to gain in ability after he starts work. The worker who makes good grades in training sometimes lacks temperamental qualities for success on the job.

In every study, there is some hypothetical "ultimate criterion" which best represents what the selector desires to obtain. The medical school would, if it could, judge the success of its students by their lifetime contribution to the community where they practice. This probably depends more on personality attributes than on abilities; it certainly is not very closely related to grades in biochemistry. The student's grades, however, are likely to be the criterion in any selection research done by the medical school; they are available, and it is certainly true that the student who never graduates will make no medical contribution. The most extensive effort to study an ultimate criterion is the work on combat effectiveness in Korea. Teams of observers and interviewers went to the theater of combat to obtain information on performance; these data were supplemented by ratings from field commanders. The validity of an Army test battery developed to predict performance in training and in maneuvers was .27 against these peacetime criteria, but only .17 against a combat criterion. A battery developed using the combat criterion correlated .36 with both training and combat criteria. The important difference between the two batteries was the inclusion of a personality questionnaire in the combat-valid battery (Willemin et al., 1958).

More and more attention is being given to establishing plural criteria for success in the same job. This is particularly important for high-level jobs; there are a great many patterns of success among officers, executives, consulting engineers, or artists. Teachers, for example, may be successful in different ways: one may develop into a friend and counselor for youth; one may stimulate independent and courageous thinking in the few brightest pupils; another may overcome the blockings that cause failure among poor students. No one of these teachers is best, but all are necessary types. It is impossible to find a single criterion that is adequate for comparing these different types of teaching success.

A striking study by Lennon and Baxter (1945) inverts the normal procedure and determines what aspects of the criterion can be predicted by available tests. Each item on a ninety-item checklist applied to clerical workers was correlated against a revision of Army Alpha and an aptitude test requiring alphabetizing, number checking, coding, digit counting, computation, and reading of tables. For some aspects of job performance, correlations with the predictors were high, but other qualities were not predicted. Checklist items were well predicted which dealt with understanding of the work, quantity and speed of work, performance of multiple tasks, and avoidance of duplication of effort. Faults in quality of work, typing, shorthand, grammar, orderliness, and "personality" were not predicted successfully. Some of the results are shown in Table 45. This study shows why it is difficult to predict such a composite criterion as "supervisor's rating of all-round performance."

TABLE 45. Percentage of Office Workers Having High and Low Aptitude Scores Rated as Having Particular Characteristics

Characteristic	Learning Ability Test		Clerical Aptitude Test	
	High 27% (N = 58)	Low 27% (N = 58)	High 27% (N = 58)	Low 27% (N = 58)
His working instructions have to be repeated frequently	7	12	5	5
Has made helpful suggestions about work handled	31	29	**38**	**22**
Often does necessary but unrequested work on his own initiative	**37**	**26**	39	25
Checks his work for errors before releasing it	51	45	52	48
Sometimes forgets matters which should receive prompt attention	5	7	7	7
Is inclined to sacrifice accuracy for speed	4	3	6	5

Boldface type indicates that the difference between low and high group is probably a true difference, rather than the result of chance in sampling.
SOURCE: Lennon and Baxter, 1945.

When records have been collected to show which workers are most successful, the final procedure in a selection study is to process the data and identify the best predictors. Before discussing the analysis of prediction data, it will be desirable to see the entire research process by examining an actual study.

5. What procedure might be suggested for selecting clerical workers, in view of the findings of Lennon and Baxter?
6. List several independent (nonduplicating) criteria which might be used to evaluate teacher success.
7. List several independent criteria to consider in judging branch managers of an equipment firm. Branches are responsible for both sales and service.
8. McNemar (1952) makes the following comment about a study of performance in clinical psychology: "It is sheer nonsense to have proceeded with an extensive testing and assessment prediction program without first having devised satisfac-

tory measures of that which was to be predicted." Yet this study was conducted by well-qualified and experienced persons and supported by a large appropriation from equally responsible psychologists in the Veterans Administration. What arguments can be given on each side of this controversy?

Development of a Stenographic Aptitude Test

Among girls who undertake the study of shorthand, quite a few fail. A test which could be given before training would save time and money spent in stenography courses and permit girls to select a more appropriate vocation. Moreover, tests of general intelligence and the commonly measured abilities have had only moderate success in predicting failures in shorthand. Deemer therefore decided to develop a test geared specifically to the problem of predicting success in learning stenography. The abilities to be built into the test would be those important in stenography, even if they were of no significance anywhere else in business or education.

A job analysis was made. It was based upon a study of the shorthand systems and the nature of the job, rather than upon observation of stenographers. The resulting list of abilities was as follows (Deemer, 1944):

During dictation: The more efficient stenographer will probably be superior to the less efficient in:
1. Ability to listen to what is being said during dictation, i.e., facility with which she attaches meaning to each word dictated.
2. Ability to write correct outlines fluently and rapidly.
3. Ability to hold a number of words in mind while writing others.
4. Ability to be "behind the dictator" without becoming flurried.
5. Knowledge of symbols for complete words. The less efficient stenographer will have to compose more outlines sound by sound during dictation.
6. Thoroughness in checking, during pauses in dictation, the outlines just written.

During transcription: The more efficient stenographer will probably be superior to the less efficient in:
1. Ability to judge from the length of her notes where to begin the letter on the page.
2. Ability to produce letters which are neat and clean.
3. Ability to read the outlines she has written.
   a. To call up the word or words for which an outline stands, either by recognizing the outline as a whole or by deciphering the outline sound by sound.
   b. To choose, when necessary, the word that fits the context.
4. Ability to spell the words.
5. Ability to type the words accurately and rapidly.
6. Ability to judge how far ahead to read before beginning to type.

This list of abilities was shortened by eliminating aptitudes which all girls might be expected to possess to an adequate degree, by eliminating those abilities which would be developed in training, and by combining some abilities. Preliminary forms of the test were then designed, using the following exercises:[1]

Speed of writing. Girls were required to copy the Gettysburg Address in longhand as rapidly as possible. This may be considered a coördination or rate of movement test, duplicating many motor elements of shorthand writing.

Word discrimination. In this test, girls choose which of two words best fits a particular context, as in "We are satisfied that our (**personal personnel**) is completely loyal to the firm." This simulates the problem in shorthand of choosing the correct word when an outline fits more than one word. This is a complex intellectual action involving verbal intelligence, vocabulary, and spelling.

Phonetic spelling. Girls are to write, correctly spelled, the words represented phonetically by *oshen, akshn, vejtabl, bleef,* etc. This simulates the problem in shorthand of recalling the entire word from a phonetic symbol, and at the same time tests spelling.

Vocabulary.

Sentence dictation. The tester reads aloud sentences of varying length which the subjects take down. The sentences increase in length, so that the subject must eventually carry many words in mind.

The next stage in the study was to try the preliminary forms of the test. Some items proved ambiguous, too easy, or too hard and were removed. The final form of the test for validation was then prepared. Validity was determined by administering the test to 500 students entering shorthand classes. During the next two years, various measures of achievement were collected. For the total test score, the validity coefficients were as follows, for different criteria:

Accuracy of transcription after one year of study: dictation at 60 w.p.m. or less	.54
Accuracy of transcription after two years of study: dictation at 80 w.p.m. or less	.65
Accuracy of transcription after two years of study: dictation at more than 80 w.p.m.	.70
Accuracy of transcription after two years of study: dictation of material, the shorthand outlines for which had not been studied (80 w.p.m.)	.58
Accuracy of transcription after two years of study, shorthand notes being transcribed two weeks after dictation (90 w.p.m. or less)	.65
Rate of transcription at end of two years of study	.35

These validity coefficients are high enough to justify using the test to identify girls likely to have difficulty in the course. Since a coefficient of .65 means that many false predictions will be made in individual cases, a school will usually prefer to use the test to point out those who should have special attention from the teacher rather than arbitrarily to bar girls with low scores from trying shorthand.

9. What abilities listed in the job analysis are not represented in the final test?

10. Deemer's manual says, "No reliability coefficients are reported for this test because it is felt that they add nothing to the reported validity coefficients. If the validity coefficient is satisfactory, the reliability coefficient must be satisfactory."

[1] Items copyright 1944 by Walter L. Deemer and reproduced by permission of Science Research Associates.

Although the latter sentence is defensible, one sometimes wishes reliability data also. What important questions about Deemer's test would be answered by reliability coefficients for subtests and total score?

11. What explanations can be offered for the failure of the validity coefficient to reach 1.00? What does this imply regarding ways to improve the prediction in further studies?

12. The DAT battery, developed later than Deemer's test, includes measures of spelling and verbal ability. In a sample of 43 girls, the validity coefficients for predicting shorthand grades are: VR, .45, Spelling, .68, Sentences, .58. Does Deemer's test appear worth using when DAT results are available? If neither test has been given, which should a school adopt to reduce the number of failures in shorthand?

DRAWING CONCLUSIONS FROM SELECTION TESTS

Strategy of Decision Making

The test scores, once obtained, are translated into decisions according to some plan. The plan or *strategy* describes how scores from various tests are to be combined, how they are to be combined with nontest information, and what decision will be made for any given combination of facts.

For the moment, we shall consider only decisions based on a single test score. Where there is a definite number of vacancies to be filled, the obvious strategy is to rank individuals and fill vacancies from the top of the list. If there is no limit on the number of persons to be selected, the strategy takes the form of a "cutting score." All persons below this score are rejected.

The cutting score is determined from the scatter diagram or expectancy table. The validation data indicate what degree of success is to be expected from persons in each score level. The decision maker decides what level of risk he is willing to accept and fixes the critical score accordingly. The expectancy table in Figure 59 shows how engineering marks at the University of Idaho in a certain year correspond to ACE scores. A grade average below 2.0 is regarded as unsatisfactory. The investigator, after examining the successive columns of the table, set 85 as his critical score. Any person below that score was discouraged from entering the School of Engineering.

A standard terminology borrowed from medical diagnosis is applied to decisions involving two definite categories, such as "succeed" and "fail" or "brain damaged" and "not brain damaged." A person who shows the "bad" sign on a test is said to be a "positive." This terminology is in some ways confusing, but the medical slang is, of course, a short cut for "cases where the test gives a positive indication of the disease." A follow-up study divides positives into two groups: "hits" or true positives, who do turn out to have the weaknesses indicated, and "false positives," who turn out not to belong in the "bad" category where the test placed them. Among those who are cleared

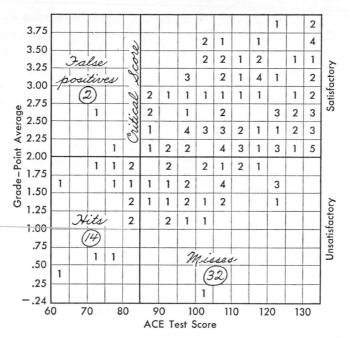

FIG. 59. Scatter diagram for the ACE test as a predictor of engineering grades (Sessions, 1955).

by the test (the "negatives"), the persons who should have been identified as positive are called "misses." No special name is given to the true negatives, who are ordinarily much the largest fraction of the sample. In the engineering study, there were 16 positives out of 147. Of the 16 positives, 14 were hits and 2 were false positives. The test let 32 misses slip into the engineering school.

It is generally unwise to set a cutting score directly from the raw data in the scatter diagram. In the engineering data, it looks as if there is a marked difference between persons scoring 85–89 and those scoring 80–84. Three-fourths of one group pass, whereas none of the others pass. This abrupt decline is almost certainly due to the fact that only a limited sample was studied. With more cases, there would be more misses in the 85–89 column and some false positives in the 80–84 column. Figure 60 permits us to estimate what will happen in a large population. The dots in that figure are the proportions of failure in each five-point interval. The line fitted to the points gives an estimate of the trend of failure in the population of which these 131 cases are a sample, i.e., of the trend to be expected in other samples. Estimating from this line, the failure rate at 85 (the cutting score originally proposed) is about 62 percent.

Setting a cutting score requires a value judgment. If we accept a cutting score of 85, it means we wish to reject persons who have less than an even chance of passing. One college administration might decide that it could not afford to admit boys unless they have a 70 percent chance for survival; if so, the cutting score should be 105. Another administration might leave the choice to the student except where there is a very high probability of failure. For this purpose a cutting score of 75 might be set to rule out those boys who have a 4-to-1 chance of failing. The administrator who lowers the cutting score reduces his false positive rate; that is, he runs less risk of cutting out a satisfactory student. At the same time, however, he increases his number of

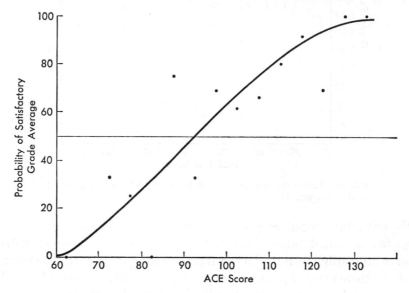

FIG. 60.   Probability of success in engineering as a function of test score.

misses. The choice of cutting score cannot be made scientifically. It is a decision based on personal, social, and economic values, combined with practical considerations.

Some of the arguments which lead one to shift the cutting score downward (accepting more students who will fail) are these:

● A "failure" is not a total loss. The student will gain a good deal from a year of college, even if he then drops out. If admitted he will become of greater value to society because of whatever he learns.

● If the boy is refused admission, he may be a total loss to higher education. If he is enrolled, further investigation can perhaps identify deficiencies to be removed or help him work out a plan in which he has a greater chance of success.

● When the country needs engineers very badly, it is important to process even low-grade ore to get a few students who will graduate.

● Tests are fallible. A decision to admit the boy is really a decision to continue testing him by means of his class performance. There is no way to continue testing a boy who is rejected. Erroneous decisions to reject cannot be corrected.

On the other side, the arguments for a high critical score include these:

• Accepting a boy who is unlikely to succeed wastes educational resources. He takes staff time which might better be spent on more promising students. His presence in the group lowers the level of discussion and thus robs the better students.

• The boy who is going to fail is better off facing the fact at once, rather than after he has wasted a year. He can use the year to get started in a more suitable trade or course of study.

In general, the problem is to weigh the loss from accepting a failure against the loss from rejecting a person who will make good. The proper cutting score is one at which these two risks are in balance.

The examples discussed above assume that performance increases as test score increases. When turnover is used as a criterion, a different type of relation is at times encountered. Turnover sometimes is found to be relatively great for men with very high and very low aptitude, whereas men in the middle range tend to stay on the job. In a study of taxi drivers, seven out of ten tests of discrimination, motor speed, and reasoning showed such a relation to the criterion. Data for two of the tests are plotted in Figure 61. It is rea-

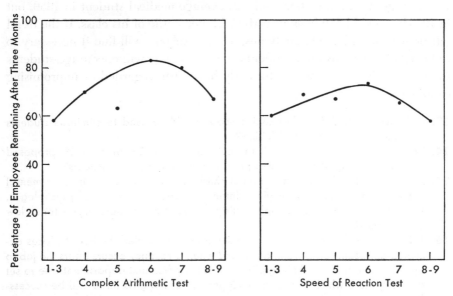

FIG. 61. Curvilinear relations between predictors and turnover of taxi drivers (C. W. Brown and E. E. Ghiselli, 1953).

sonable to suppose that the poorest men drop out because of difficulty on the job, while the best men are able to move to some more satisfying or better-paid job. For a situation like this, a double cutoff plan might be necessary to eliminate men at either extreme of the ability scale.

Expectancies and critical scores may change rapidly in a period when institutions are changing. One striking example of such change is the report of grades of students entering medical school summarized in Table 46. The 1955

TABLE 46.   Caliber of First-Year Medical Students in Successive Years

| | Percentage Having an Undergraduate Grade Average of | | |
	A	B	C
1950–1951	40	43	17
1951–1952	30	55	15
1952–1953	18	68	14
1953–1954	21	69	10
1954–1955	17	69	14
1955–1956	16	71	14

SOURCE: Anon., 1956.

admissions are strikingly poorer than those in 1950. The schools evidently were able to hold the same critical score for admission, but they attracted far fewer "A" applicants. For the college counselor and his client considering medical school, the change is of great importance. An undergraduate with a B+ average would have been only an average medical student in 1950, but in 1955 he would have been near the 75th percentile of his class. If the trend (at present unexplained) continues, medical schools will find it necessary to reduce their demands upon students, and counselors will encourage students to enter medicine who would formerly have been regarded as unpromising candidates.

13. In Figures 59 and 60, what cutting score would be used to eliminate students with one chance in three of failing?

14. What assumptions are made if the cutting score of 85 on the ACE, proposed for the University of Idaho, is applied in other engineering schools?

15. A screening test is applied to school children to identify those in poor mental health so that they can be given intensive study by the school psychologist. What factors argue for a high cutting score? What factors argue for a low cutting score?

16. A large office has about ten vacancies a month for clerk-typists. It places accepted applicants on a waiting list, and when a vacancy occurs offers the job to applicants in order of their application. Is the personnel department free to set a cutting score which insures that 95 percent of the girls hired will be successful?

17. Which is to be preferred, false positives or misses, in each of these situations?
    a. Patients entering a hospital are given a reasoning test which gives a rough indication of organic brain damage. Positives are given a thorough neurological examination.

b. Candidates for admission to teacher training are screened for ability.

c. It is important to hire skilled sheet-metal workers to fill vacancies, during a time of tight labor supply. Men cannot be trained on the job.

d. In inducting soldiers, a mental test is used to determine which men are too dull to be useful to the service.

e. A company wishes to hire mechanics and put them through an expensive training program; success cannot be observed until the end of the course.

18. The following is taken from a letter to the *New York Times:*

"I submit that 'slaughter on the highway' will continue until state licensing authorities recognize some simple facts: To drive a car on today's highways demands a rather complex set of sensori-motor skills. These skills are 'normally' distributed; i.e., some folks have them, some do not. Instruments are available to measure these skills. Authorities have some remote responsibility here to see that such instruments are used before licensing."

a. What degree of validity should be required before tests are used as proposed?

b. If scores are normally distributed, how should the cutoff score be fixed?

Combining Data from Several Tests

When several tests are tried out, the results must be evaluated in order to decide which test is best, and to determine the most useful combination of tests for predicting. If only one test is to be used in selection, we will ordinarily select that which has the highest validity. An exception to this rule occurs when the best test is quite expensive to apply and some simpler test yields nearly as good a correlation. A second exception occurs when the tests tried out have quite unequal reliabilities. If a reliable test has the best validity, and the runner-up is notably unreliable, the best procedure may be to lengthen the latter test to increase its validity (cf. p. 130). Prediction is ordinarily improved by combining several tests which cover different relevant aptitudes.

Multiple Correlation and Statistical Weighting. It is customary to employ *multiple-correlation* techniques to select the most effective combination of tests, to determine how they should be weighted in arriving at a final prediction, and to assess the effectiveness of the composite predictor. Formulas for computing multiple correlation are given in most statistics texts.

To obtain a high multiple correlation, tests are sought which have a positive correlation with the criterion and low correlations with each other. There is little value in combining tests of the same ability; this is equivalent to making the original test more reliable, and usually raises the validity only slightly. But if a new test measures a component of the job not estimated by the first test, it will improve the multiple correlation appreciably. The example in Table 47 shows how prediction improves when we combine several tests with low validity. It also shows that the multiple correlation reaches a ceiling very rapidly, so that adding tests beyond the first three or four rarely

TABLE 47. Effect on Multiple Correlation of Adding Tests to Battery

Tests	Correlation with Criterion (Shop Performance of Junior-High-School Boys)	Multiple Correlation of Criterion with First Test, First Two Tests, First Three Tests, Etc.
Paper Form Board	.43	.43
Stenquist Assembly	.26	.44
Steadiness	.29	.53
Card sorting	.27	.563
Tapping	.18	.580
Spatial Relations Formboard	.36	.594
Packing blocks	.28	.5953

SOURCE: Paterson *et al.*, 1930, p. 83.

is valuable. More elaborate prediction batteries are worth while only when each added test measures a new factor.

One can afford to discard tests from a trial selection battery even though they have positive correlations with the criterion. There is little value in extending a battery by adding even reliable tests, if they duplicate abilities already measured. The following correlations between tests and elimination from flight training were found by the Air Force (DuBois, 1947, p. 194):

Pilot stanine (i.e., composite score on selection battery)   .653
Stanine plus Qualifying examination   .655
Stanine plus Qualifying plus General Classification Test   .655

The multiple-correlation procedure starts with the test validities and test intercorrelations. Customarily, one selects the test having the highest validity as the first member of the composite predictor. Then the intercorrelations are examined systematically to determine which test predicts the criterion and at the same time least duplicates the test already chosen. The third test, in turn, must be one which overlaps little with the first two. Out of the same computations come a set of weights, which place heavy emphasis on the tests first selected for the battery and smaller emphasis on the tests added later. A cutting score for the weighted composite is established in the same manner as for a single test.

Such a set of weights is illustrated in Table 48, which shows how tests were combined by the Air Force to predict graduation from pilot, bombardier, and navigator training. The same tests were used for all entering cadets, but a different combining formula was required for each job. In selecting bombardiers, for example, discrimination reaction time and finger dexterity counted heavily, whereas reading and arithmetic had very little weight. The

TABLE 48. Validity Data and Combining Weights Used in an Air Force Classification Program

Test	Correlation with Criterion			Relative Weight		
	Bomb.	Nav.	Pilot	Bomb.	Nav.	Pilot
Printed tests:						
Reading Comprehension	.12	.32	.19	8	2	—
Spatial Orientation II	.09	.33	.25	—	10	5
Spatial Orientation I	.12	.38	.20	—	9	6
Dial and Table Reading	.19	.53	.19	14	18	4
Biographical Data—pilot	—	—	.32	—	—	15
Biographical Data—navigator	—	.23	−.03	—	9	—
Mechanical Principles	.08	.13	.32	—	—	8
Technical Vocabulary—pilot	.04	.10	.30	—	—	13
Technical Vocabulary—nav.	.04	.22	.09	—	—	—
Mathematics	.10	.50	.08	—	18	—
Arithmetic Reasoning	.12	.45	.09	8	12	—
Instrument Comprehension I	—	—	.15⎫	—	—	9
Instrument Comprehension II	—	—	.35⎭			
Numerical Operations, front	.13	.26	.01	—	—	—
Numerical Operations, back	.11	.28	.02	—	—	—
Speed of Identification	.09	.19	.18	—	—	—
Apparatus tests:						
Rotary Pursuit	.14	.10	.21	12	—	4
Complex Coördination	.18	.24	.38	12	—	17
Finger Dexterity	.16	.20	.11	19	6	—
Discrimination Reaction Time	.22	.36	.22	27	6	4
Two-Hand Coördination	.12	.26	.30	—	11	4
Rudder Control	—	—	.42	—	—	12

NOTE: The criterion for the various validity coefficients is graduation or nongraduation from training.
SOURCE: DuBois, 1947, pp. 99, 101.

navigator score, on the other hand, depended primarily on these intellectual abilities.

A combination of tests makes the greatest contribution when the original battery contains independent tests measuring quite different factors. If the tests overlap to a large degree, the procedure will eliminate most of the tests and it is almost certain that some aspects of the criterion will not be measured. One of the major claims of factor analysis is that it will ultimately permit the preparation of "pure" tests, each measuring one factor and very little else. These various factors can then be put together in whatever proportion a given criterion demands, whereas an impure test puts both wanted and unwanted factors into the composite. This argument is logical enough, and is increasingly being attained in such batteries as the GATB. Pure tests have not been easy to devise, however.

19. The Holzinger-Crowder manual offers weights for estimating relative scores on certain general mental tests. Interpret this equation:
Estimated CTMM standing = $7.5V + .3S + .9N + 1.3R$
20. How do you account for the different weights assigned the first two tests in

Table 48 for navigator prediction, in view of their similar validity coefficients?
21. Which of the three aircrew jobs has the smallest psychomotor component, according to the prediction weights?

Multiple Critical Scores. Instead of pooling all scores into a composite, some personnel workers select their tests either by multiple correlation or by other methods and then use a strategy known as the *multiple cutoff* or multiple critical score. For each test a separate critical score is determined. The critical scores are adjusted so that persons who pass all the hurdles have a satisfactory probability of acceptable performance.

The most extensive use of this plan is in the application of the GATB battery. Occupational standards are established by considering the average score of successful workers in the job, and also the correlation of the tests with the criterion and with each other. An example is the standard for the job of "mounter." A mounter assembles radio-tube mounts and connects very small parts and wires, welding them in place. The passing standard for this occupation on the older form of the GATB is Form Perception (P) 85, Aiming 85, Finger Dexterity 90, Manual Dexterity 85. The cutting score eliminates the lower third of the workers, thereby weeding out the most probable failures.

The validity data in Table 49, used to establish the standards, were based on 65 cases. The validity coefficients suggest selecting on scores F, M, A, and T, but the high correlation of A with T indicates that only one of the two

TABLE 49.   Data Used in Establishing GATB Occupational Standards for Mounters

Aptitude Score	M	s.d.	Correlation with Production Records
G—General	106.9	15.3	−.075
V—Verbal	102.2	14.7	−.061
N—Numerical	105.8	13.3	.064
S—Spatial	109.3	16.6	−.009
P—Form Perception	111.8	15.6	.015
Q—Clerical Perception	106.2	15.9	.097
A—Aiming	107.1	13.9	.229
T—Motor Speed	103.6	15.5	.191
F—Finger Dexterity	109.5	18.4	.437
M—Manual Dexterity	98.7	20.7	.353

SOURCE: *Guide to the Use of GATB*, 1958, p. I-1.15.

need be used. (In the more recent form, which does not measure Aiming, a cutoff of 85 on K [motor speed] has been substituted.) The USES noted the additional fact that these workers were distinctly above average in P. The implication is that perceptual ability may be a selective influence leading some people to enter or remain in the job of mounter even though it does not correlate with performance within the selected group. For this reason, P was added as a hurdle.

The validity of the composite pattern (F, P, A, M) was tested by a tetrachoric correlation calculated from a table of hits, misses, and false positives. The correlations for three samples, using production records as a criterion, were .46, .49, and .52. The composite is thus a trifle better than prediction from F alone would be.

22. In a fourth sample of mounters, supervisors' ratings were used as a criterion. How do you account for the fact that the correlation was only .24?

Comparison of Composite and Cutoff Procedures. The weighted composite ranks individuals according to their expected criterion scores, and a single cutoff is established. All persons whose composite is above that level are accepted. A graphic illustration is given in the left panel of Figure 62; all per-

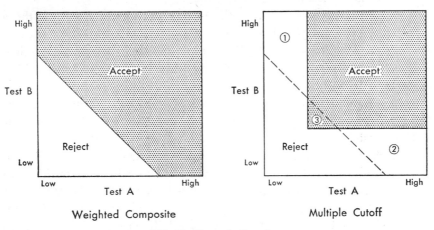

FIG. 62. Two selection plans.

sons above the line are accepted. The multiple cutoff eliminates persons who are low on either test, with the result diagramed in the right-hand panel of Figure 62. For most individuals both procedures lead to the same decision. Persons in areas 1 and 2, in the lower-right and upper-left corners of the scatter diagram, are low on one test and high on the other. They are rejected by the critical-score procedure but are accepted when a weighted composite is used. The persons in area 3 are just above the minimum on both tests; they are accepted by a multiple-cutoff plan but are rejected when the composite score is used.

The advantages of the weighted composite are as follows:

● It gives additional information, indicating how each accepted man ranks within the group. This is useful for identifying men requiring special assistance during training, or for singling out superior men for special responsibility.

• By estimating the man's probable success in the assignment it permits comparison with his probable success in other lines instead of merely ruling out the assignments where he would fail.

• If there is a linear relation between tests and the criterion—a matter to be discussed further below—it gives a higher proportion of correct decisions than the multiple cutoff.

The multiple cutoff has these advantages:

• It is easier to compute, administer, and explain to laymen than is the composite score.

• Retaining the scores of separate tests provides a valuable basis for counseling.

• When the relation between tests and criterion is configural rather than linear, the multiple cutoff can yield a higher proportion of correct decisions than the customary weighted composite.

The essential difference is that the weighted composite acts on the assumption of compensation among abilities. A person weak in dexterity may be accepted if he has exceptional perceptual ability; strength in the one is presumed to make up for weakness in the other. In most predictions this assumption is justified, but not in all.

At one time during World War II the Navy desired to train men to operate antisubmarine listening gear. By the usual correlation procedure, psychologists established a prediction formula: men were screened on general intelligence, and within the surviving group, predictions were based on the average of the Bennett TMC and several Seashore tonal tests. Following standard Navy procedure, acceptable men were sent to training school, and those who failed in school were assigned to general sea duty. It was therefore a serious matter when a man of good intelligence was sent to a school for which he was unqualified, since his ability would not be properly used. Many men who failed in sonar school did so because of very poor tonal judgment, which made them unfitted for listening duty. How had they happened to be sent to sound training? Their high mechanical comprehension (many had studied college physics) raised their composite enough to conceal their weakness. Such men, despite an adequate "average" ability, were doomed to fail in sound training whereas they would have been excellent in engineering, radar maintenance, or navigation. In fact, a few were salvaged by school officers and sent to other training, where they did well. Ultimately, a multiple-cutoff procedure was adopted.

Configural Prediction.   The estimation equation derived by the usual multiple-correlation method is a linear, additive equation. That is to say, estimated scores are obtained by adding predictors. The criterion score is assumed to increase regularly as a function of the predictor score. This linear assumption is not always justified. A certain amount of manual dexterity may be required on an assembly line, but increased dexterity above the minimum makes little or no difference in the value of an employee if the assembly line moves at a fixed speed. A worker who keeps ahead of the line produces no more than one who can just comfortably keep up. His greater dexterity does not compensate for weakness in some other ability.

Many writers have condemned conventional additive prediction methods, claiming that "patterns" or "configurations" of scores will yield better prediction. We cannot consider this issue fully here, and confine ourselves to a few summary statements:

• The writers who propose to interpret "patterns" are often vague in their proposals, and writers mean different things by that term. Some of the writers advocate examination of simple differences between abilities which the multiple-correlation procedure automatically takes into account. Others are arguing for nothing more complicated than a multiple-cutoff procedure.

• The multiple-correlation method can be extended to take into account configural relationships of any degree of complexity. It need not be limited by the linear assumption.

• In practical prediction problems, a linear assumption has almost always proved adequate to account for the data, and nothing is gained by introducing configural formulas unless data are uncommonly reliable.

• In a limited number of investigations, configural treatment of scores has permitted much better prediction than a linear composite. Most of these investigations have involved personality variables as predictors.

One pioneer, highly tentative study suggests what may be done with configural prediction. Frederiksen and Melville (1954) thought it possible that for compulsive students, who work hard on tasks even when they are not interested, achievement in engineering would be predicted by ability tests and not by interest tests. Among noncompulsive students, however, who work hard only on what interests them, they thought an interest test might be an important additional predictor. The investigators used two indications of compulsiveness or unusual concern with accuracy: having interests like those of professional accountants; and having low speed on a reading test relative to the vocabulary score. Some of the validity coefficients of predictors against average grades were as follows:

	Compulsives	Noncompulsives
High-school grades	.47	.50
Mathematics test	.31	.61
Interest in engineering	−.18	.36
Interest in selling real estate	−.04	−.55

The evidence thus supports the hunch that for noncompulsive students interest in the subject matter is an important factor in success, but that for compulsive students interests make no difference. If this relation were verified in further work, the correct selection procedure would be to divide men into two groups. For the compulsive group, a composite ability score would be used; for the noncompulsives, a different combining formula considering interests would be needed.

Sequential Strategies

In the multiple-cutoff or composite-score plan, all the tests are given at once and the decision is then made. For many personnel decisions a more economical procedure is the sequential plan, in which testing is divided into several stages. After each stage, a decision is made to reject some men, to accept others, and to continue testing those close to the borderline.

The decisions in the first stage of a sequential plan are based on a short and incomplete test, and the method therefore makes somewhat more wrong decisions than a plan in which every man takes all tests. The plan reduces costs, however, because relatively few men take the second and later sets of tests. Especially when the later stages include expensive apparatus tests or interviews, the saving can be considerable. Sequential methods are generally superior to single-stage testing, since great savings in testing cost can be accomplished with a very small reduction in the correctness of final decisions (Arbous and Sichel, 1952; Cronbach and Gleser, 1957, pp. 48–63, 82–87).

23. What practical considerations determine whether a sequential plan should be used in hiring workers for training?

Nonstatistical Combination of Scores

All the procedures discussed so far involve an experimental determination of the best possible rule for selection, and rigorous application of that rule. The assumption underlying these approaches is that a statistical formula will more often point to the correct decision than will a procedure which depends on the judgment of a psychologist. The psychologist with a clinical orientation often complains that such a mechanical method is insensitive to the unique characteristics of the particular case and cannot possibly be as wise as a psychologist.

It seems that a competent professional interpreter, bringing reason to bear on the data, should do no harm and might well improve decisions, but this expectation is contradicted by experience. In the Navy, for example, trained classification specialists interviewed each man, having at hand his test scores, a life history, and other data. The interviewers gave a final rating as to the man's probable success in the training to which he was assigned. A mechanical prediction formula combining two tests (Electrical Knowledge and Arithmetic Reasoning) correlated .50 with success in training of electrician's

mates. The interviewer's rating, based on these tests plus judgment, correlated only .41 with success. In other words, judgments departing from the
statistical formula reduced the correctness of prediction (Conrad and Satter, 1945). P. E. Meehl (1955) made a major comparison of "clinical vs. statistical prediction" in which he examined every study where predictions
made by judges could be compared with predictions made from the same
data by statistical formula. In some twenty studies where such a comparison
could be made, he found that the actuarial, cookbook prediction was equal
or superior to the judgmental prediction in every case save one. The statistical method, which is obviously cheaper to apply, beats the judge time after
time, whether the judge be a counselor, a clinical psychologist, or an industrial personnel manager.

Why does the judge do so poorly? The foremost reason is that he combines
the data by means of an intuitive weighting which he has not checked. The
statistical formula, on the other hand, has been carefully checked on a sample of cases like the one for whom the new prediction is made. It uses the
best possible set of weights. The judge can beat the formula only by bringing in additional data and combining those data in the proper manner with
the facts used by the formula.

It is very difficult for a judge to function efficiently. In the first place, he
does not know what weights he uses to arrive at a decision. He looks at the
man from various angles and finally comes to an intuitive decision. Almost
certainly, he gives greater weight to some factors than they deserve, and
changes his weights from one case to the next. Moreover, his judgment is unreliable, in the sense that he might judge the same case differently on different days. The formula never varies. There is some reason to think that judges
give too much weight to the additional facts they add to the test data.

Judges make many constant errors. They have stereotypes and prejudices;
for example, they make different predictions for women from what they
would for men with similar scores even when there is no evidence that men
and women perform differently on the job. In one of the most interesting
studies, counselors judged badly because they applied a completely sound
principle in a situation where for some strange reason the principle was inappropriate. Sarbin (1943; see also Cronbach, 1955b) asked counselors to
predict grade averages of students at Minnesota from their high-school records, ACE test scores, and a whole dossier of information on interests, experiences, and motivations. The statistical formula combining ACE and high-
school rank had a validity of .45 for men, .70 for women. The counselors did
a little worse: .35 for men, .69 for women. When we examine the weights
used, we find that the formula placed almost its entire weight on high-school
rank and paid no attention to ACE scores because in the three preceding
classes at Minnesota the ACE had made no independent contribution to pre-

diction. The counselors, however, gave about equal weight to high-school marks and to ACE scores. Such a weighting had been found best in most of the reported investigations of college success, and is quite consistent with experience of colleges generally. For some reason, the Minnesota situation during the period of this study was unique; quite reasonable weights used by the counselors were the wrong ones for this situation. The statistical formula was custom-made for the Minnesota situation and of course it did better than the counselors working from general psychological lore.

What does this imply? It implies that counselors, personnel managers, and clinical psychologists should use formal statistical procedures wherever possible to find the best combining formula and the true expectancies for their own situation. They should then be extremely cautious in departing from the recommendations arrived at on the basis of the statistics, unless they are strongly convinced that the additional information they bring in is a valid basis for decision. When they do use their own judgment, they should make careful follow-up studies, comparing their number of hits with the number of hits the formula would have yielded. Moreover, those who make judgments must try to formulate the bases they use, stating just what they take into account and how heavily they weight each bit of information.

The proper province of the statistical formula is the institutional decision, where a definite and irreversible decision is required to carry out the purposes of the institution. The admissions officer having to choose the most promising applicants for a limited number of openings should certainly make decisions in whatever way will be most accurate. In counseling, on the other hand, decisions are personal decisions of the client and cannot be dictated by the experience table. The counselor's responsibility is to help the client understand himself; if, having the facts before him, he wishes to embark on a course in which failure is likely, it is his right to use his life that way.

INTERPRETING SELECTION STUDIES

What Is an Acceptable Validity Coefficient?

As validity coefficients for various tests have been presented in past chapters, the reader probably has been classifying them mentally as "good" or "poor." Many tests, particularly those of special abilities, do not seem very satisfactory at first glance. But, in one sense, a test has a satisfying validity coefficient if it is better than other tests for the same purpose. The only sound standard for judging a validity coefficient is the question: Does the test permit us to make a better judgment than we could make without it—sufficiently better to justify its cost? The older literature on testing placed little value on tests with moderate validity coefficients. A so-called "coefficient of forecasting efficiency" was computed which purported to tell how much better a prediction from the test was than a random guess. According to this coefficient, validity had to reach .86 before a test was "50 percent better than chance." Tests with validity below .50 were thought to have negligible practical value. This line of reasoning, we now know, is based on inappropriate assumptions (Cronbach and Gleser, 1957). The reader is advised to disregard the coefficient of forecasting efficiency and its implications, if he encounters them in his reading.

Psychologists have abandoned their insistence on validity coefficients of .70 or .80 for all tests. While we would be pleased to reach these or better levels, the experience of thirty years of practical testing shows that we cannot often attain such standards. Coefficients as low as .30 are of definite practical value (cf. Table 48). Occasionally, a test with much lower validity is promising for further development, if it measures what no other test does. In discussing this point, Strong comments that the test critic who is contemptuous of low positive correlations is quite willing to accept information of no greater dependability "when he plays golf or employs a physician." The correlation of golf scores between the first and second eighteen holes in championship play is, he says, about .30, and the reliability of medical diagnosis near .40 (Strong, 1943, p. 55).

In his discussions with executives, the personnel psychologist would like to state just how much benefit a selection program offers to a business, a school, or a military force. He can give a partial answer by comparing selected and unselected men with respect to number of failures in training, average length of training required, rate of turnover, average production, and so on. All these sources of evidence have been used, and all of them show that tests with validities in the range from .30 to .50 make a considerable contribution to the efficiency of the institution even though they make faulty judgments in many individual cases.

The best single rule of thumb for interpreting validity coefficients is the one developed by Brogden (1949). Making certain reasonable assumptions, he showed that the benefit from a selection program increases *in proportion to the validity coefficient*. Suppose the 40 applicants out of 100 who score highest on a test are hired. We can consider the average production of randomly selected men as a baseline. An ideal test would pick the forty men who later earn the highest criterion score; the average production of these men is the maximum that any selection plan could yield. A test with validity .50, then, will yield an average production halfway between the base level and the ideal. To be concrete, suppose the average, randomly selected worker assembles 400 gadgets per day, and the perfectly selected group of workers turns out 600. Then a test with validity .50 will choose a group whose average production is 500 gadgets, and a test of validity .20 will select workers with an average production of 440 gadgets. The assumptions under-lying Brogden's rule are these:

> The job to be performed remains the same, whether men of high or low ability are selected.
>
> Production (or other measure of benefit) has a linear relation to test score.

The benefit derived from a selection plan depends on the *selection ratio*, as well as on the validity of the test. The selection ratio is the proportion of persons tested who are accepted. If there is a large labor supply, the selection ratio can be very low, but when applicants are scarce the selection ratio may be forced up toward 1.00. Even an ideal selection plan has no effect on the quality of workers when every applicant must be hired. If one can pick and choose, average output can be much improved. Figure 63 shows the relation of production to selection ratio and test validity for the hypothetical gadget assemblers used in the illustration above. In this figure we have assumed that among unselected workers the average production is 400 gadgets, and the standard deviation is 100. Tests of low validity have considerable value when the selection ratio can be very low, when individual differences in job performance are large, and when small increases in production have a large dollar value.

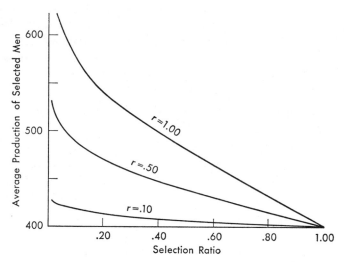

FIG. 63.   Benefit from a selection program as a function of validity and selection ratio, under Brogden's assumptions.

In evaluating a validity coefficient to decide whether a test is worth using for selection, one must ask the following questions:[2]

---

[2] The questions are so worded that an answer of "no" indicates that tests of relatively low validity are likely to be helpful.

Are individual differences in job performance or other outcomes fairly small?

Can we afford to discharge or transfer to other duties men who prove to be unsuccessful? I.e., can we tolerate "misses"?

Is it important to hire every applicant who will be satisfactory, even though this also involves hiring many men who will fail? I.e., must we avoid "false positives"?

Does this test measure an ability which is already fairly well measured by other tests or procedures already in use?

Is it possible to modify the job so that it makes less demand on the aptitude tested?

Is the validity coefficient much lower than the reliability coefficient of the test? (If not, lengthening the test should raise validity.)

Is administration of the test difficult and costly?

24. In the light of the foregoing questions, how satisfactory is Deemer's validity coefficient of about .65 for selecting shorthand students?

25. In one pilot-selection study, the predictive validity of pencil-and-paper tests was .64 (elimination-graduation criterion). The coefficient was raised to .69 when apparatus tests were added. Is such a small increase worth while, in view of the questions listed above?

26. State employment offices use tests to guide workers into appropriate positions. A very low selection ratio may be used, since a particular unemployed worker may be directed into any one of hundreds of job families. In a particular insurance agency, on the other hand, it is necessary to employ about 60 percent of those who apply for clerical jobs. Are the same tests equally suitable in both situations?

27. In which of these situations is there likely to be a fixed number of vacancies, and in which can the decision maker set the critical score as high or low as he likes?

a. A parole board decides which prisoners may be released.

b. An engineering school admits well-qualified applicants.

c. A school psychologist identifies mentally handicapped children to be placed under a special teacher.

d. A college counseling bureau identifies clients likely to profit from psychotherapy.

Restriction of Range.   Tests predict less accurately when they are applied to a homogeneous group. Validity coefficients rise when a test is applied to a group with a wide range of ability, and drop when the test is used on a restricted, preselected group. Many studies are based on selected groups. Deemer, for example, did not test how well his instrument predicted shorthand learning of all girls. Instead, it was tried on girls already planning to take the course. Many girls of low aptitude were not included, since normally those entering a shorthand course have successfully completed some work in typing. If Deemer's test were applied to an entirely unscreened group, a higher coefficient would result.

The effect of screening upon validity coefficients is illustrated by the Air Force study referred to earlier. The validity coefficient of the battery for pilot selection was in the neighborhood of .37 for men who met standards for flight training. When, for experimental purposes, a completely unscreened group was sent into pilot training, the failure rate rose enormously. In this unrestricted group, the validity coefficient rose to .66 (DuBois, 1947, pp. 103, 193).

Investigators are frequently perplexed when a variable listed in the job analysis fails to predict the criterion of success. The job analysis may have been correct in listing the ability as essential to the job, yet selection may have reduced its significance as a predictor. If future applicants will be drawn from a similarly selected group, this variable will not help in prediction. But if the tests are applied to an unselected group, the variable which had no predictive value in the restricted group may turn out to be a good predictor. For example, intelligence tests have consistently been poor predictors of success in teaching. The explanation is obvious: Nearly every teacher has survived years of schooling with at least adequate grades, which assures a fair to superior degree of intelligence (Figure 64). Among those so selected, differences in tested intelligence play little part in determining success as teachers. Granted that an intelligence test will not help a school system hire teachers, an intelligence test is still a major factor in advising a girl in high school whether she is likely to be able to complete a teacher-training course. Failure to recognize the effects of restricting range sometimes leads to discarding useful tests. In 1930, Moss developed a test for selecting medical students which in tryout studies had good correlations with grades. When schools selected students on the basis of scores on the Moss test, they began to discover that the predictive coefficients were quite low. Ultimately, in 1946, the Moss committee was discharged and the test was abandoned. Then, when the test was no longer used to select students so that scores again covered the full range, research studies began to report higher coefficients again.

28. If one were considering the probable success in industrial jobs of graduates from an engineering school, what characteristics would have a restricted range owing to preselection? What characteristics would probably not have been restricted?

Contamination of Criteria. It is important to guard against contamination of criteria, which spuriously raises correlations. Wherever ratings are used as criteria, there is a possibility that teachers, foremen, or other judges are influenced by knowledge of the prediction data. Teachers may be influenced in their grading by knowledge of a pupil's IQ. A foreman may rate a man higher than his performance warrants because he knows the man has considerable experience. These influences raise the correlation between grade

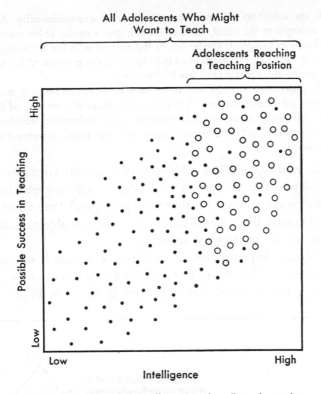

All Adolescents Who Might
Want to Teach

Adolescents Reaching
a Teaching Position

FIG. 64. Hypothetical data illustrating the effect of preselection upon correlation. Dots show scores to be expected if every
ninth-grader interested in teaching later enters the profession.
Circles show scores of persons likely to survive gradual elimination as a consequence of low school marks.

and intelligence, or rating and experience. The only way to eliminate contamination is to keep predictor data secret until all criterion scores have been
collected.

29. In each of the following situations, trace how contamination might occur, and
suggest an improved procedure to avoid it.

    a. A psychologist administers aptitude tests to entering college freshmen and
from the results predicts each student's success. Success is determined after
two years by noting which students have been dropped from school by the
school guidance committee for unsatisfactory work. The predictions are kept
in a locked file and not made available until the two years have passed.
The psychologist is a member of the committee but does not disclose the
predictions.

    b. Test data on pupils' intelligence, mathematical ability, and other facts are
made available to science teachers so that they can do better teaching.
Learning in science is judged not by ratings but by an objective test of
ability in science given at the end of the course. The pretests are correlated
with this final score.

c. Tests for selecting salesmen are being tried experimentally. Because they are thought to be valid, the results are given to the sales manager for his guidance in assigning territories to the salesmen in the experimental group. After a year of trial, each man is judged by the amount of his sales in relation to the normal amount for his territory.

d. Flight instructor's ratings are used as a basis for promoting men from primary to advanced training. It is desired to check the validity of these ratings as predictors of success in advanced training. Advanced training is taken at the same field, with a different instructor. This man's judgment supplies the criterion.

Criterion Unreliability and Bias. The size of a validity coefficient is limited by the reliability of the criterion. A low validity coefficient may be the result of poor criterion measurement rather than poor prediction. Grades and ratings are particularly likely to be unreliable, whereas objective measures of achievement can be made very accurate.

In many studies improvement in validity coefficients is obtained by refining the criterion rather than by continued development of the predictors. An example of the effects of better criteria is shown in Figure 65. When

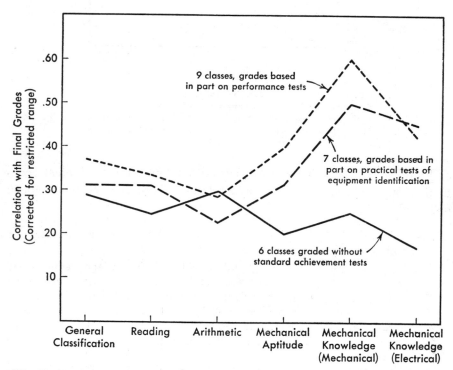

FIG. 65. Correlations of Navy classification tests with grades in Basic Engineering School, before and after introduction of standard achievement tests (Stuit, 1947, p. 307).

grades for Navy classes in ship's engine operation were based only on instructor's judgments, school grades had rather small correlations with predictor tests. But when two highly valid achievement tests were used in allotting school grades, the classification tests were much better predictors. It is to be noted that the subjective grades were influenced most by academic and intellectual abilities. When a valid measure of job knowledge and skill was applied as a criterion, the prediction rested most heavily on Mechanical Knowledge and Mechanical Aptitude. The tests that predict a valid criterion may be different from those that predict a biased, incomplete criterion.

Necessity for Confirmation of Findings

When an investigator has once obtained a satisfactory validity coefficient, he tends to install his program and stop research. Other workers, reading his report of the study, may accept his test as valid and put it to work in their own situations. This practice is unsound. In the first place, any validation result is influenced by chance, and correlations will fluctuate from sample to sample. Consequently the test which proves best in one sample may prove not to be the best predictor in another similar sample. Even when the results are based on a large sample, the particular critical score or the particular weights most effective in a multiple correlation are certain to change when a new group is tested. If the same formula is applied in other groups, the correlation is sure to drop. Moreover, the supply of men and the conditions of training change from time to time. It follows that the investigator must redetermine the validity of his prediction technique periodically.

The weights for a composite score, or the critical scores in a multiple-cutoff procedure, are determined so as to get the best possible prediction in the sample studied. In the next sample, the same formula will have lower validity. We speak of this as the "shrinkage" of validity. Shrinkage is likely to be great when many possible predictors are tried and when weights are determined from small samples. Shrinkage is relatively small when the predictors are chosen initially on the basis of substantial past experience and theory, and relatively large in a "shotgun" study where miscellaneous predictors are tried with no particular rationale.

To estimate properly the validity of any scoring formula one must cross-validate by trying the formula on a sample not used in selecting tests and establishing scoring weights. Sometimes the validity remains nearly the same in the second sample, but sometimes there is considerable shrinkage.

The term *cross-validation* usually indicates a second study in the same factory or school where the prediction formula was developed. The general psychological reader wants to know how well the formula holds up in other situations. This is the question of *validity generalization*. We have seen several examples of the fact that formulas cannot be transferred automatically to new situations. DAT scores had different validities in different schools.

The value of a formula for selecting sewing-machine operators shifted when the job emphasis shifted from speed to quality. Minnesota counselors went wrong when they gave the same weight to ACE scores as had been used at other colleges. No matter how well a selection procedure is validated and cross-validated in the original situation, it must be validated anew when it is carried into a new situation. Published results help only by suggesting what tests should be included in the tryout battery.

30. In a configural scoring formula, weights may be assigned to every variable and to every pair of variables. How many scores are weighted (or considered for possible weighting) when a configural method is applied to a set of ten subtests? What does this imply about the shrinkage of configural validities?

CLASSIFICATION DECISIONS

The employment manager and the college admissions officer make genuine selection decisions. They hire or admit some applicants and have nothing further to do with those they reject. Classification decisions are far more numerous than selection decisions, and many so-called selection programs really lead to classification decisions. A classification decision is one in which persons are assigned to different jobs, courses, therapeutic treatments, etc. The task in classification is to assign each person to the job where he can do best, subject to limitations imposed by the number of vacancies in each job category. The decision maker is concerned about the subsequent performance of everyone, rather than just the persons assigned to one treatment. The Air Force program for "pilot selection" is really a classification program, because men who do not pass the tests are retained in the service and assigned to other duty.

The theory of classification testing must probe into the same questions as the theory of selection. There are methods of combining scores for classification purposes, strategies for assigning persons to fill quotas, and so on. The methods differ quite a bit from those appropriate in simple selection. We shall not attempt to summarize these methods and the related theoretical principles, except to comment on the relation between test validity and classification efficiency.[3]

A test which predicts success within many jobs is a poor instrument for classification because it does not tell which job the person can do best. The ideal classification test is one which has a positive correlation with performance in one job and a zero—or better yet, negative—correlation with performance in other jobs. A general mental test is of little value for deciding which curriculum a college student should enter, even though it correctly indicates that he will do well in academic work.

[3] For a summary of much of the theory, and further references, see Cronbach and Gleser, 1957, esp. chaps. 6, 9.

When we apply Brogden's assumptions to classification, we find that the value of a test used to assign persons to one of two treatments is proportional to its *differential validity*. Differential validity is expressed by the formula

$$s_1 r_{1t} - s_2 r_{2t}$$

Here s_1 and s_2 are the standard deviations of criterion scores for the two treatments for randomly selected men, the two criteria being expressed in comparable units such as dollar value of the worker's production. r_{1t} and r_{2t} are the usual predictive validity coefficients for test t (Brogden, 1951).

Looking back at Table 48 (p. 341) let us assume that the criterion standard deviations for pilots and navigators are about equal—that is, that the difference in value to the Air Force between an ace pilot and a borderline pilot is equal to that between an outstanding and a mediocre navigator. We see that the Two-Hand Coördination Test has a validity of .26 for navigator and .30 for pilot. It therefore has no differential validity. Numerical Operations has a validity of .26 for navigator and .01 for pilot. It is therefore a good classification test. The Mathematics test, with validities .50 and .08, is even better.

One of the remarkable values of differential predictors is that they make much better use of a pool of manpower than can a general predictor. Suppose we have three tests, A, B, and C. Test A is a general test which has

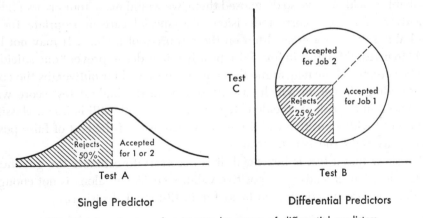

Single Predictor   Differential Predictors

FIG. 66. Superior use of manpower by means of differential predictors.

validity .40 for job 1 and job 2. If we want to rule out below-average performers, we accept the best 50 percent of the men. We must divide them randomly between the two jobs because test A has no differential validity. Test B has validity .40 for job 1, .00 for job 2, and zero correlation with test C. Test C has validity .00 for job 1, and .40 for job 2. Now we can accept all men above average on *either* B or C and assign each one according to which test he does better on. With these differential tests, 75 percent of the men can be used, yet each one is average or better in aptitude for the job in which he is placed.

All decisions in clinical diagnosis are essentially classification decisions, i.e., choices between treatments. Even discharging a patient is a decision that return to the community is the most beneficial treatment for him. There are usually no quotas to be filled in clinical diagnosis; every person can be called "normal" or every one called "schizophrenic" if such uniform classification appears correct. Meehl and Rosen (1955) have drawn attention to the fact that such uniform classification is often the best strategy even when we are using a test which has significant positive validity. This occurs when the clinician is trying to identify a rare condition; Meehl and Rosen take the problem of predicting suicide as an example. If a test identifies a person with a high probability of suicide, the clinician will probably recommend that he be given closer attention and more intensive treatment than a probable nonsuicide. Suicide is rare; perhaps 5 percent of those tested in a certain clinic will later attempt suicide. A person with a low test score (on a hypothetical test) may have expectancy of only 0.1 percent of a suicide attempt, and one can confidently place him in the nonsuicide category. With higher test scores, probability of suicide increases, so that the test has undoubted validity. The highest score in the clinic sample, however, may indicate only a 20 percent expectancy of suicide. These people cannot be called probable suicides. If we so diagnosed them, we would make four errors (false positives) for every correct decision. The special care appropriate for a probable suicide is a great drain on the resources of a clinic. It may not be able to invest this effort in four false positives in order to prevent one suicide. To be sure, the clinic may argue that one person saved far outweighs the cost of guarding all five, in which case persons with the highest test score will be placed in the risk-of-suicide category. The principle still holds: a classification test with a positive validity is not worth using if the cost of false positives outweighs the benefit from hits.

To show that a test is beneficial, it is necessary to estimate the goodness of the decisions it leads to. A positive validity coefficient alone is not enough to demonstrate practical usefulness for institutional decisions.

31. Suppose that pilot performance is judged to be three times as important as navigator performance ($s_1 = 3s_2$). Then what tests have greatest differential validity for these jobs?

32. What tests have greatest differential validity for distinguishing pilots from bombardiers?

33. A twenty-point test for parole prediction gives these expectancies of violating parole: for a score of 20, 40 percent; score 10, 20 percent; score 0, 5 percent. Can this test be used practically by a parole board, or should all prisoners be classified as likely to obey probation rules?

Suggested Readings

Flanagan, John C. The critical incident technique. *Psychol. Bull.*, 1954, 51, 327–358.
> Procedures used to obtain and interpret critical incidents are described, together with suggestions for using the information in measurement and training.

Ghiselli, Edwin E., & Brown, Clarence W. Analysis of jobs. *Personnel and industrial psychology.* (2nd ed.) New York: McGraw-Hill, 1955. Pp. 17–58.
> The authors survey and critically compare methods of job analysis which may be used in deciding what tests deserve tryout.

Kirchner, Wayne K., & Dunnette, Marvin D. Applying the weighted application blank procedure to a variety of office jobs. *J. appl. Psychol.*, 1957, 41, 206–208.
> A simple experiment shows how a score derived from personal history can predict job tenure.

Perrine, Marvyn W. The selection of drafting trainees. *J. appl. Psychol.*, 1955, 39, 57–61.
> A compact report of a selection study on a small scale illustrates nearly all the principles and problems of selection research. This technically excellent investigation was done as an undergraduate honors project.

Tiffin, Joseph, & McCormick, Ernest T. General principles of personnel testing. *Industrial psychology.* (4th ed.) Englewood Cliffs, N.J.: Prentice-Hall, 1958. Pp. 75–109.
> Procedures used in validating tests for industrial selection are described. Particular emphasis is placed on the difference between studies on present employees and studies conducted on new applicants, tested at the time of hiring but not screened on the basis of test performance. The importance of the selection ratio as a factor determining the usefulness of a test is fully explained.

13 |

13 |

Proficiency Tests

PROFICIENCY tests measure present performance in some important task. A test of typing proficiency evaluates job applicants, a test of driving proficiency indicates whether a person meets standards for a license, a test of proficiency in calculus determines the student's course mark. The proficiency test can be thought of as a sample of the criterion. In this it differs from the usual test of general or special ability, which presents novel problems quite different in form from the criterion.

Functions of Proficiency Tests

Proficiency tests may be used for forward-looking decisions such as selection and classification and also for evaluation decisions which look back at some completed experience. Tests which look forward are often called "aptitude" tests, and those used to measure educational gains are called "achievement" tests. Items measuring proficiency (in, for example, reading and arithmetic) are used in both.

Measures of proficiency, being evidence of past attainment, are among the best predictors of future academic attainment. In the California study of engineering (p. 321), the best predictors were high-school record, a mathematics test, and a test of proficiency in interpreting scientific data. In the DAT guidance battery, the two Language Usage tests and the Numerical Reasoning test are predictors which measure school-learned abilities.

Proficiency tests for hiring employees are quite varied, since each test must deal with the skills or knowledges of a particular job. Tests for specific jobs can be standardized whenever the requirements of jobs in several places are similar. A few such tests for clerical skills and shop knowledge have been published. The wide range of tests usable in hiring and promotion is illustrated by the list of tests used by Macy's department store (Table 50). The variety of tests and the adaptation of the tests to the specific demands of jobs are noteworthy. We have also pointed earlier to the use of information tests in selection of college students (as in the College Qualification Tests) and in screening of skilled workers (trade tests, p. 283). An "automotive information" test is a valuable supplement to aptitude tests for classifying soldiers into artillery and armor duties (Birnbaum *et al.*, 1957).

While the proficiency test has an obvious place in selection and guidance,

TABLE 50. Tests Used in Employee Selection by R. H. Macy & Company, Inc.

Category	Test	Remarks
General ability	Wonderlic adaptation of Otis Self-Administering	For nonexecutives
	Mental ability	Difficult one-hour test for prospective executives
Arithmetic	Mental arithmetic	For cashiers, adjusters, and various clericals
	Sales arithmetic	For Telephone Order Board operators
Office skills	Thurstone typing	Rough draft typing and tabulation
	Junior typing	Simple copying
	Comptometry: 1. addition 2. addition and subtraction 3. all operations	Various degrees of skill on the comptometer
	Stenography	Three letters are dictated and transcribed
Language ability	Spelling	For typists, correspondents, and secretaries
	Correspondent's test	Worksample; subject composes three letters answering sample inquiries from customers. Graded by prospective supervisors on composition and grammar
Clerical ability	Speed and accuracy	Measures ability to count or locate numbers and letters
	Same-different	Comparisons of written and printed names
Manual Ability	Minnesota Rate of Manipulation	For kitchen employees, packers, stockmen
Color vision	Pseudo-Isochromatic Plates for testing color perception	For guards and stockmen handling colored merchandise (e.g., men's ties)

SOURCE: Information supplied by Mrs. Iseli Krauss of Macy's Personnel Division. All tests except the Wonderlic, Thurstone, Minnesota, and color vision test were specially constructed by Macy's.

its unique function is in evaluation of treatments. It is our best means of measuring the effectiveness of instruction. The teacher and student may think of the test primarily as a basis for assigning fair marks but its more important function is to indicate what the student is ready to do next, and to tell the teacher how well his instructional methods have succeeded.

Tests are such a common fixture in the schools that it is difficult to appreciate their influence, which can be more clearly seen in a situation where standardized testing was suddenly introduced. The Navy has long operated a vast and successful program of vocational education. Navy recruits receive training in the various skills needed to maintain a complex fighting force. When educators and psychologists were given responsibility for some Navy schools during World War II, one major change they proposed was the development of standard proficiency tests. The advantages the Navy found may be summarized as follows (Stuit, 1947, pp. 287–354):

• Tests aided in holding instruction constant in all schools preparing men for a given duty (e.g., torpedomen). Although objectives of instruction and curricula were standardized, individual schools tended to neglect or overemphasize particular topics. Since any neglect would lower test scores, the tests forced teachers to do as the course planners intended.

• The tests provided a basis for revising the curriculum and improving instruction. If results showed that certain skills were not mastered in the time allotted, it was necessary to reconsider the length of the course or the emphasis placed on these skills. Without such tests, instructors often assumed that, having "covered" a topic, they had taught it. Test results were of great interest to instructors and often caused them to ask supervisors or specialists to suggest ways to improve their teaching.

• Proficiency scores identified classes which were not making adequate progress, so that supervisors could investigate the cause.

• Some tests required the student to demonstrate job skills rather than merely to give verbal answers. Such tests directed the attention of instructors to the behaviors the course was intended to produce. Reliance on the lecture-discussion method of teaching declined, and training improved.

• Tests which placed emphasis on all significant aspects of the course made sure that all-round proficiency would be considered and deficiencies noted. In the Basic Engineering school, before the introduction of standard testing, grades were strongly influenced by performance in mathematical aspects of the course, probably because this ability was easy to test. The new examinations stressed mechanical understanding. As a result, attention was drawn to men who, despite skill in arithmetic, were poor in other essentials.

• In the absence of tests, grades had been assigned to students on the basis of subjective impressions, with, at best, the aid of teacher-made tests. Such marks were unreliable and subject to bias. Even objective tests, made by teachers without special training, measured poorly. Careful preparation of tests led to fairer and more accurate grading.

• Standard tests permitted analysis of grading standards and reduced variation between graders. When marks were based solely on standard tests, grades given at different places represented the same degree of proficiency.

• More accurate final marks were a better criterion against which to validate selection tests.

• Motivation of students and instructors was improved by developing rivalry based on a fair standard. Showing a man his particular deficiencies was useful for motivating and directing study.

In effect, the program of proficiency testing introduced into personnel management "quality control" like that imposed on manufacturing processes. Substandard individuals were thrown back for further polishing, or for discard. Substandard teaching methods were detected and changed. These advantages have their counterparts in industrial training and in schools and colleges. Marks are unreliable, and may emphasize some aspects of the course to the exclusion of others. Different instructors in the same department grade differently and teach with different effectiveness. Teachers depart from planned curricula. But stringent control by testing can be undesirable in general education, for reasons to be discussed later in this chapter.

One significant contribution of standardized tests has been to break down the "time-serving" concept of education. A person's standing in school is frequently judged by the number of years he has put in, or the number of courses he has passed through. Time spent is no index of education received. In one study, where thousands of college students took standardized tests of knowledge in various fields, many college seniors knew less than the average high-school senior. Since number of units accumulated tells little about proficiency, tests are being given increasing weight as evidence of educational development. In most communities, an adult who did not complete high school may receive a diploma by passing an examination and use this diploma to enter college if he wishes. Colleges exempt from certain required courses those who perform well enough on proficiency tests. Control by proficiency examination is widespread in professional education. Lawyers, for example, must take a state examination before being admitted to practice. Psychologists wishing a diploma certifying their competence as clinical, industrial, or counseling psychologists take an examination given by the American Board of Examiners in Professional Psychology (ABEPP).

In this chapter we can introduce only the major problems of proficiency testing and illustrate a few techniques that have been used. The psychologist and the teacher frequently have to construct proficiency tests. This is an art which requires both experience and technical training. For advice on construction of tests for various purposes, the reader should consult such specialized books as these:

Dorothy C. Adkins and others, *Construction and Analysis of Achievement Tests*, Washington, Government Printing Office, 1947. This discusses test construction from the point of view of the Civil Service Commission.

E. F. Lindquist (ed.), *Educational Measurement*, Washington, American Council on Education, 1951. This major handbook on test construction covers both procedures and theory.

J. R. Gerberich, *Specimen Objective Test Items,* New York, Longmans, Green, 1956. This book discusses the use of objective tests in various fields and gives over 200 examples of test items developed for special purposes. It also has excellent bibliographies.

1. In the United States, a high-school diploma is awarded to almost any pupil who has stayed in the school system for twelve years. In Great Britain, where fewer persons complete secondary education, the evidence of "completion" is the General Certificate of Education, granted not by the school but by a regional examining body controlled by the universities. Only pupils who meet the passing standard on a test are given the certificate. What assumptions about society underlie each plan? What are the social consequences of each plan?
2. What consequences would follow if ABEPP published the proportion of applicants trained by each university who pass the examination for their diploma in clinical psychology?

VALIDITY OF PROFICIENCY TESTS

Content Validity

Among the four types of validity introduced in Chapter 5, little has yet been said about content validity. Content validation is primarily relevant to proficiency testing. General and special ability tests, for the most part, employ one type of content to assess ability to learn to deal with some other content. The typical proficiency test, on the other hand, assesses ability to deal with content of which the test is supposed to be a sample, and its content validity must be established.

Whereas predictive and concurrent validation judge a test by statistical study of results, content validity is established by logical examination of the test and the methods used in its preparation. The question is, How well does performance on the test serve as an index of performance on some defined "universe of situations?" The test questions are only a sample of all the possible questions that might be asked, and they may or may not be representative of the total domain of appropriate questions.

Ideally the author of a test would define a universe to be measured and then sample his items so as to represent that content. To specify the universe, he has to define both the stimuli and the responses that concern him. Consider first the stimuli. Each of the following describes a universe of content in which some tester might be interested:

● All the flags used in the U.S. Navy signal system.

● All the words likely to be read in everyday German, i.e., in newspapers, correspondence, etc.

● All possible addition problems involving two numbers, each of three digits or less.

● All facts regarding schizophrenia given in a certain textbook.

To specify the response he intends to observe, the test developer would indicate what he desires the subject to do. Is the subject to name the flag, taking as long as he needs? Or is he to recognize it rapidly? Is he to tell what a German word means when he hears it? Or to recall the German word when given the English equivalent?

When an author has defined a universe of content, he then can prepare a sample to represent that universe. For instance, he might tabulate all the words used in German newspapers and use this as his basic list. A random sample could be taken, perhaps every 200th word on the list. The sample could be chosen on a representative basis rather than randomly. The words might be grouped according to frequency of use: the thousand most frequent, the next thousand, and so on. Then twenty words might be taken at random from each level. The resulting sample would have an average frequency of use similar to that of the universe. The representative sample generally gives a somewhat more accurate measure than the random sample of equal size.

Formal sampling plans are most used to select items for educational tests. Spelling words, arithmetic combinations, shorthand symbols, and other collections of factual associations can be catalogued and sampled. In subjects like history and science the content cannot be reduced to a list of specific items, but it is still possible to sample so as to represent each section of the course in proper proportion.

Sampling is sometimes very poor in tests developed by an inexperienced or untrained tester. A spelling test may consist of the words someone believes workers should know, rather than words actually used on a job or actually covered in a course of study. A test in physics may overemphasize items on the parallelogram of forces if the tester finds such items easy to invent, and may neglect topics where he lacks good ideas for items. Competent test developers take great care to match their proficiency tests to a careful job description or to the course of study.

If a test is prepared according to a clearly described sampling plan, a prospective user can judge content validity very simply. He needs only to decide whether he is satisfied with the author's choice of universe and his sampling method. If a German teacher is interested in preparing his students to read everyday German, he should be content with a test based on newspaper vocabulary. If the course is intended to teach literary German or scientific German, the same test would be less appropriate. The teacher can adopt it only with some risk of drawing false conclusions. The student who has the largest scientific vocabulary may not earn an especially high score on the test of newspaper vocabulary.

Although sampling items from a definite universe is a pleasing and logical ideal, very few of the situations that concern testers reduce to such simple terms. Most often the test constructor has some general idea of the stimulus he wishes to place before the subject, but he cannot give a neat definition. Can an investigator who wants to measure sociability of preschool children catalog the situations where sociable behavior arises? Can we list all the human relations problems a foreman should be able to deal with? Can one define the universe of situations in which scientific reasoning is to be shown by a science student? Obviously not.

Examining content validity therefore requires judging whether each item, and the distribution of items as a whole, covers what the tester wants to measure. This judgment rests on the test user rather than on the test author. The test author can state the sources of his items, but they will rarely correspond perfectly to what the tester intended to measure. How close a correspondence should be demanded is a highly subjective judgment, unless there happens to have been a correlational study showing whether one performance can substitute for something a bit different.

3. A tester wants to measure attitude toward the Negro, so as to compare schools having different programs of student activities. What is the universe from which he will draw test items?
4. Skill in the use of library reference materials is to be measured at the end of a college freshman course. Define a possible universe of situations from which the test might be drawn.
5. The Morse code consists of a short alphabet of characters. The receiver must respond to units made up of several characters in rapid succession; the most difficult part of the task may be to separate one letter from the next.
   a. Describe an appropriate test for a person learning to receive ordinary non-secret communication in English.
   b. Describe an appropriate test for a person learning to receive secret (encoded) messages of the form GFVG JHBI YGTA FBSJ. . . .
6. In a written test for drivers, how could the tester decide how many questions to devote to speed laws, how many to safety rules, how many to interpretation of signals, etc.? Would the decision reached have any effect on a learner's chance of success? Would it have any effect on the way he studies for the test?

Statistical Selection of Items

Often the test constructor supplements logical procedures with a statistical item analysis. He gives a trial form of the test, separates groups of students who do well and poorly on the test as a whole, and compares these two groups item by item. An item on which the good students surpass the poor ones is judged satisfactory. One which shows no difference or on which the poor group is more successful is regarded as questionable. A discrimination index or a correlation between item score and test score may be calculated to formalize this comparison.

An item shows a low item-test correlation (i.e., fails to discriminate good from poor students) for one of three reasons:

It is so easy that nearly everyone passes, or so hard that nearly everyone fails.

It is ambiguous or confusing.

It measures something different from what the bulk of the test measures.

Some test constructors, routinely discard any item which discriminates poorly. In a test purporting to sample a defined body of content, it is highly undesirable to drop items just because their correlations are low.

Easy and hard items are needed if the test score is to give a fair picture of the proportion of the content a person knows. If the easy items were eliminated, the average percentage score on the test would be much lower than that on a random sample of the content. If items on a certain topic prove to be very hard, this may be important information for the instructor, and the items should perhaps be left in the test just to bring this fact home to him.

The chief value of the discrimination index is to point out ambiguities. A badly written item which confuses good students has no place in the test. The test constructor who examines an item with an unsatisfactory index may see a flaw in the item which explains the errors of good students: a double negative, a supposedly true statement which the critical reader can find an exception to, a too-plausible alternative answer, etc. If such a flaw can be found, the item should be rewritten. Dropping a particular item probably will not spoil the content validity of the test. The danger is that many of the poorly constructed items will fall in the same content area. When they are dropped the test loses its representativeness.

The third cause of a low discrimination index is that the item differs psychologically from the bulk of the test. The content that a proficiency test is intended to sample is ordinarily mixed. Dropping unusual items "purifies" the test in one sense, but it no longer represents the original universe of content. A person might master the verbal portions of chemistry and still be badly confused on the quantitative parts of the course (such as balancing equations). To drop the quantitative sections just because they correlate less with the total than do verbal items makes the test a false sample of the content. On the other hand, if a question correlates poorly with the total because it requires knowledge of a certain compound that few pupils have read about, the item ought to be replaced. The special element it brings in is irrelevant to the purpose of the test.

Matching Achievement Tests to the Curriculum

If a test is used to evaluate instruction, it is necessary to compare the content of the test with the objectives of the instruction. A test might have excellent content validity as a measure of skill in arithmetic computations and yet be a most unfair evaluation of instruction if the course was primarily designed to develop reasoning abilities. Brownell and Moser (1949) wanted to know which of four ways of teaching subtraction was best. Some pupils were taught by the equal additions method and others by the decomposition or borrowing method. Each method was presented meaningfully in some classes and as a mechanical or rote procedure in other classes. Subtraction of two-digit numbers (e.g., 27 from 41) was the content used in the instruction. On a test of accuracy in two-digit problems there was a small advantage for the borrowing method, meaningfully taught, but the differences between groups was so small that one might advise a teacher to use whichever method he happened to prefer. Arguing that an important purpose of beginning instruction in subtraction is to pave the way for later complicated problems, the investigators also tested the children on subtracting three-digit numbers (e.g., 358 from 644) even though this had not been taught. On this test the borrowing-meaningful group did 50 percent better than the other groups; this was unquestionably the best teaching procedure.

To take into account the variables that ought to be measured, one has to find out just what the objectives of instruction are. Objectives do not end with factual knowledge and a limited group of skills. When you ask a teacher why he is teaching his course, he lists a large number of objectives. The geometry teacher, for example, denies that the purpose of his course is to transmit a certain number of theorems, a few practical principles, and some skills with ruler and compass. Instead, he speaks of developing habits of reasoning, skill in identifying assumptions, skepticism about unverified conclusions, and so on. Yet achievement tests have traditionally stressed specific facts and skills to the exclusion of other important outcomes of the course.

In a series of studies of college and high-school teaching (Smith and Tyler, 1942), R. W. Tyler and his coworkers identified a large number of purposes schools claimed to hold. These aims may be grouped as follows (Raths, 1936):

> Functional information. Not mere rote knowledge, but knowledge that
> can be applied to new situations where it is relevant.
> Thinking skills and habits.
> Attitudes and social sensitivity. (Tolerance, spirit of scientific inquiry,
> appreciation of music, etc.)
> Interests, aims, purposes. (Vocational goals, secretarial interests, etc.)
> Study skills and work habits.
> Social and personal adjustment.
> Creativeness.
> Physical health.
> A functional philosophy of life.

Before one can determine how well the student has developed these qualities, it is necessary to define them in terms of behavior. How does a person act who has "ability to draw sound conclusions from scientific data"? Skill in interpretation of data is shown by certain definite actions. If we give a skilled person a table or graph carrying unfamiliar information, he does certain things. He identifies major trends. He disregards fluctuations that are due to variations in sampling. He concludes that factor A and factor B change together, not that factor A causes factor B. Having defined precisely what actions give evidence that the subject possesses the desired skill, it is a fairly simple matter to observe those actions and translate the observations into a measurement.

Facts and skills loom so large in the usual classroom that teachers and test designers have emphasized them out of proportion to other types of outcome. Although it is important to measure knowledge and skill, a pupil may earn a high score on memorized material and yet have made little progress

TABLE 51.   Improvement in Abilities in Zoölogy, Measured at the End of the Course and One Year Later

Type of Examination Exercise	Mean Score			Percent of Gain During Course Which Was Later Lost
	Beginning of Course	End of Course	One Year Later	
Naming animal structures pictured in diagrams	22	62	31	77
Identifying technical terms	20	83	67	26
Recalling information				
a. Structures performing functions in type forms	13	39	34	21
b. Other facts	21	63	54	21
Applying principles to new situations	35	65	65	0
Interpreting new experiments	30	57	64	−25

SOURCE: R. W. Tyler, 1934, p. 76.

toward understanding the course. A course in cooking presumably is supposed to improve ability to cook. But one teacher tested a college class on knowledge of scientific principles underlying cookery, and also had them cook food. The quality of cooking correlated only .25 with the verbal knowledge (Arny, 1953, p. 25).

Studies of forgetting give weight to the argument that thinking and attitudes should be measured. Facts poorly understood are quickly dropped from the mind, whereas attitudes and changes of thinking habits are usually much more lasting. Tyler gave a series of tests to one college class before they studied zoölogy, at the end of the course, and again after a second year in which they studied no zoölogy. The most lasting changes were in ability to apply principles to new problems and to draw conclusions from data (Table 51).

In stating objectives and in designing tests it is especially important to distinguish ability (maximum level of performance) from typical performance. Knowing the right answer is no guarantee that a person will behave in the right way. It is easy, for example, to prepare a true-false test for a course in "how to study." After a few lectures on principles of study, most students know how they should study and can pass the test. But the gap is wide between what students know about study and what they do about it. Tests of typical behavior are needed to evaluate the effectiveness of courses teaching handwriting, leadership or personnel, management, resistance to propaganda, accuracy in arithmetic, and many other objectives. Proficiency tests measure abilities produced on demand. To evaluate instruction fully, it is necessary to supplement proficiency tests with observations and other measures of typical behavior (see Part Three).

7. For one of the following courses, try to list all the important objectives:
   a. Study of literature in the junior high school.
   b. A course to train union officials for collective bargaining.
   c. A course to train junior executives in human relations.
8. Define each of the following objectives in terms of specific behaviors:
   a. "To train young people for wise parenthood."
   b. "To increase appreciation of good literature."
   c. "To prepare young people for the duties of citizenship."
9. The Brownell-Moser test of ability to do a performance that had not been taught is a "transfer" test.
   a. Is it fair to judge the student's learning by asking what he has not studied?
   b. A man is trained to repair certain models of a radar set. What would be a suitable transfer test and what would be learned from it?
   c. It is claimed that study of French improves English. Would it be useful to include an English test in a research study on a new method of teaching French?

Construct Validity

The listing of various objectives implies a list of distinct kinds of behavior. Are "thinking skills" really distinct from "functional information"? This is a problem of construct validation.

Tyler's evidence that applying principles and interpreting experiments are much less subject to forgetting than factual information indicates that these abilities are distinct. In a more extensive study of fourteen college courses he found that the correlations between different types of proficiency were quite small. Even after correction for errors of measurement, the correlations were (Judd *et al.*, 1936):

Knowledge of facts vs. application of principles, about .45
Knowledge of facts vs. inference from experiment, .35
Application vs. inference, .40

10. In a certain course, the correlation between a factual test and a test of ability to apply knowledge to new situations is .40. Assume that grades are assigned as follows: 10 percent A, 20 percent B, 40 percent C, 20 percent D, and 10 percent F. What grades will A students on the first test receive if the second test is used as a basis for grading? (Use the scatter diagram on p. 114.)

Effects of Item Form on What Is Measured.   Tests having the same "content" may measuure different abilities because of variables associated with item form. Reading ability, for example, affects scores on almost all achievement tests. A valid measure of knowledge is not obtained if a person who knows a fact misses an item about it because of verbal difficulties. The Navy Mechanical Knowledge Test contained four types of item: mechanical facts, tested verbally; mechanical facts, tested pictorially; electrical facts, tested verbally; and electrical facts, tested pictorially. Similarity of content produced lower correlations than similarity in form (Table 52). In other words,

TABLE 52.   Correlations of Tests Having Similar Form and Tests Having Similar Content

	Correlation	Correlation Corrected for Unreliability
Tests similar in form, different in content:		
Verbal tests: mechanical vs. electrical	.63	.79
Pictorial tests: mechanical vs. electrical	.64	.86
Tests similar in content, different in form:		
Mechanical: verbal vs. pictorial	.61	.71
Electrical: verbal vs. pictorial	.51	.74
Tests different in both form and content:		
Mechanical verbal vs. electrical pictorial	.49	.63
Electrical verbal vs. mechanical pictorial	.45	.59
Kuder-Richardson reliability coefficients:		
Mechanical verbal	.89	
Mechanical pictorial	.82	
Electrical verbal	.71	
Electrical pictorial	.67	

SOURCE: Conrad, 1944.

the form of the items largely determined the score received. Another study provides even stronger evidence that the verbal element in tests may be undesirable. Training of Navy gunners had been validly evaluated by scores made in operating the guns. As an economical substitute, verbal and pictorial tests were developed. Identical information was tested in the two forms, the same question being asked in words alone or by means of pictures supplemented by words. Questions dealt with parts of the gun, duties of the crew, appearance of tracers when the gun was properly aimed, etc. The pictorial test had a correlation of .90 with instructors' marks based on gun operation whereas the validity of the verbal test was only .62. The verbal test was in large measure a reading test; it correlated .59 with a Navy reading test, while the picture test correlated only .26 with reading (Training Aids Section, 1945).

Speed is relevant and important in tests of typing attainment or reading facility, or in tests of arithmetic for cashiers. Speed is irrelevant when we wish to know how large a pupil's vocabulary is, how much science he knows, or how accurately he can reason. Speeding can usually be justified in proficiency tests only if the test is intended to predict success in a task where speed is helpful.

Many popular testing techniques are strongly affected by response styles. A *response style* is a habit or momentary set which causes the subject to earn a different score from the one he would earn if the same items were presented in a different form. In true-false tests particularly, some people have the habit of saying "true" when in doubt, while others are characteristically suspicious and respond "false" when in doubt. If the tester has included a large proportion of true statements in his test, the acquiescent student will earn a high score even if his knowledge is limited. Other response styles include tendency to gamble, working for speed rather than accuracy, and use of a particular style in essay tests.

Aptitude tests are also affected by response styles, though to a lesser degree than proficiency tests (Cronbach, 1950). In one of Thurstone's spatial tests, the student is to mark all the figures in a row of six which are just like a given figure save for being rotated. Some students consistently mark many figures in the row, while some mark only one figure even when several are correct. This caution, or lack of thoroughness, lowers scores. The Seashore pitch test requires subjects to judge whether the second of two tones is higher or lower than the first. Some students are strongly biased toward one of the two answers; in one class of ten students, the most biased student marked 75 items H and only 25 L. After the class was given a short talk on the nature of bias, their scores improved. This particular student gained 14 points (on a 50-point scale from pure chance to perfect).

For measuring ability, multiple-choice or best-answer tests are distinctly preferable to tests having fixed response categories such as true vs. false or agree vs. disagree. The best-answer test is not only virtually immune to response biases other than tendency to gamble but is especially well adapted to testing of comprehension.

11. A mental test uses items like the following:

      sweet-sour .... SAME-OPPOSITE
      obscure-lucid .... SAME-OPPOSITE
      occult-mystical .... SAME-OPPOSITE

What response styles is such a test affected by when given with a time limit? Design a test for the same ability which would be less influenced by response style.

Recognition vs. Recall.   A major issue in educational testing is whether recognition tests and recall tests on the same content measure the same ability. Multiple-choice and other recognition items are necessarily given great emphasis in standardized testing because they are easy to score. This has been a source of concern to teachers who feel that only tests requiring free responses can measure adequately what they teach. Especially where the purpose of teaching is to produce ability to recall or invent new solutions, teachers tend to prefer free-response tests. The English teacher prefers to judge a student from a sample of his free writing, rather than on tests where he merely identifies errors. The mathematics teacher feels that his students should be required to solve problems, rather than merely to select alternatives in what one writer calls "place-your-bet" questions.

To evaluate this argument requires an experiment to determine whether the recognition and recall tests rank subjects in the same way. The result of this experiment depends on the ability measured. In arithmetic, the two rankings correspond closely; at the other extreme, penmanship performance has negligible correlation with ability to recognize good writing. In college mathematics, multiple-choice questions had reliability coefficients and correlations with grades in later mathematics essentially the same as those for free-answer questions (College Entrance Examination Board, 1946).

One might think that ability to generalize from data could be tested only by requiring that the student form his own generalizations. But a test requiring undergraduates to identify the best and poorest generalizations from a set of data correlated .85 with ability to draw generalizations directly from the data. Planning an experiment is a creative function, yet a recognition test calling for choice among alternative plans correlated .79 with a free-response test of ability to make plans (R. W. Tyler, 1934, pp. 27–30).

It seems likely that free-response tests can be superior to recognition tests where one is required to measure very accurately. Among graduate students who have overlearned the verbally stated principles of scientific method, probably all would do well on any reasonable objective test of experimental design. But even among such students there is marked variation in inventiveness in attacking new problems, and a long, carefully scored free-response test may be the best measure. Similarly, an objective recognition test sorted students accurately on French pronunciation (Tharp, 1935). But in an advanced group it is doubtful that fine discrimination between those with authentic and those with false accents could be obtained by anything but a performance test.

The most serious charge against recognition tests is that they have often been confined to measurement of simple, even trivial knowledge of facts. It is possible, as many examining bodies in universities have demonstrated, to devise objective questions which call for deep comprehension and subtle reasoning. Recognition tests are by no means limited to simple mental processes. The difficulty is that ingenuity and effort are needed to prepare a penetrating objective test, whereas a taxing (if not necessarily valid) essay question can be scribbled off in minutes.

12. A course in psychological testing is intended to prepare students to perform the skills listed below. For which would a recognition test be acceptable?
   a. Selecting a test battery for a college counseling bureau.
   b. Administering and scoring the WAIS.
   c. Drawing proper conclusions from a validation study.
   d. Making proper interpretations of technical terms used in test manuals.
13. What is the relative importance of free recall and recognition of correct responses in
   a. learning to interpret children's problem behavior in terms of probable causes.
   b. learning to play bridge.
14. Discuss the following comment by a newspaper columnist:

   "I view with some misgivings the purely utilitarian course in 'Communications' which has been substituted for the traditional freshman composition course at S_____. Students' needs in this course, we are told, are ascertained by the administration of 'batteries of tests.' I venture to assert that nothing will be learned from these tests which a skilled teacher would not find out from a single theme and a half-hour interview; and that these would be better for the student psychologically, as motivation for the course, than the 'batteries of tests.' "

Taxonomy of Educational Outcomes. In contrast to the vast effort to map out aptitudes by factor analysis, there has been almost no systematic research on proficiency variables. Tyler's correlational studies barely illustrate the questions to be asked: How many distinct types of outcome are there in a particular content area? Is scientific inference a general ability, or specific to one science? Are the correlations between outcomes the same at all ages? How do the relations between outcomes depend on the method of instruction? And so on. Research on such questions remains utterly fragmentary.

Proficiency testing is usually an *ad hoc* effort to satisfy a practical need: a test for torpedomen in this Navy school, a test for clerks in this particular civil service agency, a test of French for freshmen in this college. The test developer moves from one such assignment to the next, never pausing to ask fundamental psychological questions. Tests marketed nationally undergo extended developmental research, but that research is more concerned with removing ambiguous items and developing accurate norms than with clarifying the nature of proficiency.

The structure of proficiencies has been less appealing as a research problem than "the structure of mental abilities." It is obvious that the correlation between proficiencies depends upon what one has studied. Factual knowledge of college physics correlates with skill in mathematics, if only because most physics students also take mathematics. When he investigates whether an "aptitude" such as mechanical comprehension is correlated with mathematical reasoning, the psychologist often has the illusion that he is dealing directly with the natural organization of the mind. That this is an illusion is shown on the one hand by the substantial correlation between the TMC and the biographical inventory, and on the other hand by theoretical research such as Piaget's. The aptitudes treated by the factor analyst are no less dependent on experience than are the proficiencies. How mathematical understanding of science, after training, is related to understanding of the concrete aspects of science is fully as challenging and urgent a problem as any question about predictive abilities.

The only major advance in conceptualizing proficiency variables has come from a logical rather than an empirical investigation. A group of specialists in educational testing, most of them university examiners, has developed a "taxonomy" of educational objectives. This is a grand index of all the variables which instructors and educational testers have suggested measuring for the purpose of evaluating instruction. The variables are classified logically; these groupings provide hypotheses that certain types of behavior are psychologically similar (for example, that they might be developed by similar teaching methods).

As outlined in Table 53, the taxonomy has six major sections: Knowledge, Comprehension, Application, Analysis, Synthesis, and Evaluation.[1] The abilities are listed in an approximate order of complexity; sections are also subdivided to separate more and less complex processes. One must comprehend something before he can apply it, generally speaking, and he must be able to analyze elements before he can analyze organization. The taxonomy gives a complete definition of each category and illustrates the category with several educational objectives and several pages of test items.

The taxonomy has considerable value in improving communication between testers and instructors. It offers a standard vocabulary for discussing testing problems and provides a sort of checklist so that evaluators can recognize whether they have listed all the objectives that ought to be measured. At present, the taxonomy is limited to "cognitive" performance, i.e., to knowledge, comprehension, and reasoning.

The illustrative test items for measuring higher mental processes are of unusual interest. We can select only a few illustrations here, beginning with a simple factual item falling in category 1.12 (knowledge of specific facts):

[1] Table 53, Figure 67, and the test items in this section are taken with minor modifications from Bloom (1956). Copyright 1956 by Longmans, Green and Company and reproduced by permission.

TABLE 53.   Synopsis of the Taxonomy of Educational Objectives

---

1.00 *Knowledge*   Remembering something previously encountered.
    1.10 *Knowledge of specifics.* Recall of bits of concrete information.
        1.11 Knowledge of terminology.
        1.12 Knowledge of specific facts.
    1.20 *Knowledge of ways and means of dealing with specifics.* Includes methods of inquiry, chronological sequences, standards of judgment, patterns of organization within a field.
        1.21 Knowledge of conventions: accepted usage, correct style, etc.
        1.22 Knowledge of trends and sequences.
        1.23 Knowledge of classifications and categories.
        1.24 Knowledge of criteria.
        1.25 Knowledge of methodology for investigating particular problems.
    1.30 *Knowledge of the universals and abstractions in a field.* Includes organization of ideas by means of theories.
        1.31 Knowledge of principles and generalizations.
        1.32 Knowledge of theories and structures (as a connected body of principles).
2.00 *Comprehension*   Understanding of material being communicated, without necessarily relating it to other material.
    2.10 *Translation* from one set of symbols to another.
    2.20 *Interpretation.* Summarization or explanation of a communication.
    2.30 *Extrapolation.* Extension of trends beyond the given data.
3.00 *Application*   The use of abstractions in particular, concrete situations.
4.00 *Analysis*   Breaking a communication into its parts so that organization of ideas is clear.
    4.10 *Analysis of elements.* E.g., recognizing assumptions.
    4.20 *Analysis of relationships.*
    4.30 *Analysis of organizational principles.* E.g., recognizing techniques of propaganda.
5.00 *Synthesis*   Putting elements into a whole.
    5.10 *Production of a unique communication.*
    5.20 *Production of a plan for operations.*
    5.30 *Derivation of a set of abstract relations.*
6.00 *Evaluation*   Judging the value of material for a given purpose.
    6.10 *Judgments in terms of internal evidence.* E.g., logical consistency.
    6.20 *Judgments in terms of external evidence.* E.g, consistency with facts developed elsewhere.

Number of annual rings at *the base of the trunk* of an old tree is
        greater than
        less than   the number of rings *half-way up the trunk*
        the same as

Knowledge of methodology (1.25) is also at the level of sheer recall, but the content is more general. For example:

Fossils on rocks constitute valuable clues to the past. Some of these fossils are identical with animals existing today. How does this affect the investigation of geological history? (Choose one)
    a. Such fossils make the work much simpler since they can be easily traced.
    b. These fossils are rare and therefore do not weaken the overall results very much.
    c. These fossils are extremely valuable since observation of their living counterparts yields much information as to climates and physical conditions of the geologic past.
    d. The existence of living counterparts of fossils is immaterial since only the fossil itself is important.

An item is not classified entirely by its content, since the processes the student uses will depend on his experience. In a biology course which has been studying about fossils, this is likely to be a recall item, but in a general science course which has not touched on fossils, this item requires application of scientific method to a new problem. In the taxonomy, the item would have to be classified as a measure of application (3.00) for the general science student.

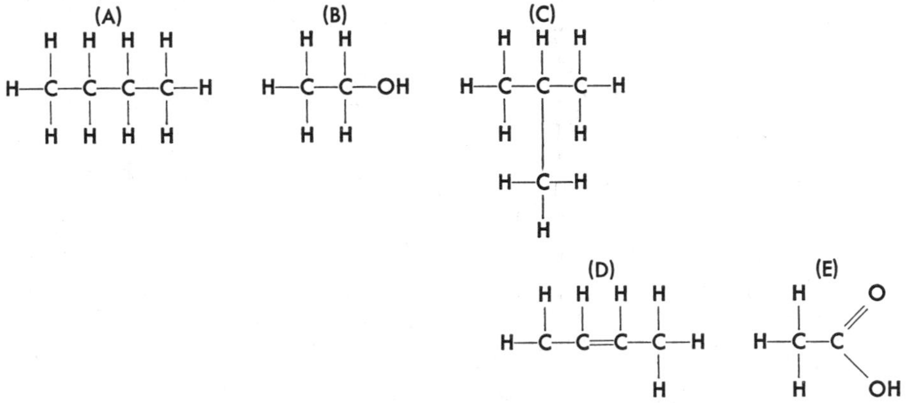

.... 1. The compound which can neutralize bases and form salts.
.... 2. The hydrocarbon which has the least tendency to "knock" among those listed above.
.... 3. The compound which decolorizes bromine and potassium permanganate.

FIG. 67. Item testing comprehension of organic chemical formulas rather than memory alone.

Comprehension items go beyond recall and ask the student to restate material. The item in Figure 67 requires matching organic chemical compounds with their properties. The compounds are representative of familiar types (e.g., B is an alcohol), but the student is not expected to know the specific chemical formulas given. This item is classified as translation (category 2.10) since the formula must be recognized as equivalent to the verbal definition of an acid, etc.

The following application item (category 3.00) calls for free response:

John prepared an aquarium as follows: He carefully cleaned a ten-gallon glass tank with salt solution and put in a few inches of fine washed sand. He rooted several stalks of weak elodea taken from a pool and then filled the aquarium with tap water. After waiting a week he stocked the aquarium with ten one-inch goldfish and three snails. The aquarium was then left in a corner of the room. After a month the water had not become foul and the plants and animals were in good condition. Without moving the aquarium he sealed a glass top on it.

What prediction, if any, can be made concerning the condition of the aquarium after a period of several months? If you believe a definite prediction can be made, make it and then give your reasons. If you are unable to make a prediction for *any* reason, indicate why you are unable to make a prediction (give your reasons).

The items in categories 4.00 to 6.00 tend to run considerably longer. The student may read an argumentative passage and be asked to tell the function of a certain sentence (4.20, analysis of relationships) or he may listen to a recorded musical selection and answer questions on the development of the themes (4.30, analysis of organizational principles). "Synthesis" ordinarily requires free response; e.g., one item asks the student to develop a chemical process to satisfy given specifications. As a final example, we cite part of an "evaluation" item (6.00). The student is to suppose he reads some surprising statements about language by an Otto Jespersen, and is to tell whether each of the following facts would lead him to trust Jespersen's statement, or to distrust it, or would have no significance:

   a. Mr. Jespersen was Professor of English at Copenhagen University.
   b. The statement in question was taken from the very first article that Mr. Jespersen published.
   c. Mr. Jespersen's books are frequently referred to in other works that you consult.

The taxonomy is an impressive analysis of constructs which perhaps describes the way intellectual processes are organized. Many decades ago, however, the collapse of faculty psychology taught psychologists to be suspicious of purely logical categorizations. Though the faculty psychologists had defined innumerable independent powers of the mind such as memory, judgment, and reasoning, they could find no way to measure these powers separately or to distinguish them from general adaptive ability. The categories of the taxonomy refer, not to hidden mental powers, but to observable abilities to solve specific types of problems. These abilities are obviously measurable. Nevertheless, one must ask whether the categories describe separate types of behavior. If the tests given different names correlate highly, the distinctions are of little value; and if tests within the same category correlate little, the grouping is artificial.

The one recent study of the organization of intellectual skills appeared prior to taxonomy. Furst (1950) administered 27 tests covering several subject fields to two groups of students at the start of the eleventh grade, and again late in the twelfth grade. Within each subject there were tests of factual knowledge, judgment of relations, application of principles, etc. One group in a private experimental school was taught by a method emphasizing integration of courses and development of higher mental processes. The other group, from public high schools, was taught by more formal methods, the content areas being sharply separated from each other. Furst determined whether the tests of different intellectual processes had different correlations at the start and end of the experimental period, whether the training program affected the pattern of correlations, and how highly tests measuring similar intellectual processes were correlated. The total study involved 1600 correlations, and only a superficial résumé of results can be given here.

Despite the differences in the two educational programs, the correlational patterns for the two groups were nearly alike. The most important finding is that tests dealing with the same subject area had higher intercorrelations than tests dealing with the same mental process. In Table 54, based on

TABLE 54. Correlation Among Proficiency Tests Categorized by Subject Matter and by Mental Processes

	Average Correlation Within Group of Tests	Average Correlation with Tests Not in Group
Subject-matter groupings:		
English	.48	.32
Humanities	.28	.23
Social studies	.45	.35
Physical sciences	.45	.31
Mathematics	.55	.34
All categories	.44	.31
Mental-process groupings:		
Critical thinking	.38	.32
Recall of information	.25	.31
Reading	.52	.39
Language expression	.44	.29
Application of principles	.24	.29
Interpretation of data	.33	.28
All categories	.36	.34

SOURCE: Furst, 1950.

the public school, the average correlation among a group of tests is compared with the average correlation of those tests with all other tests. The former value must be higher before one can argue confidently that tests within the group measure some common ability. Subject-matter groupings clearly meet this requirement; mathematics tests or science tests do have more in common with other tests of the same subject than they do with tests outside the subject. This is to be expected. Knowledge of scientific facts, application of scientific principles, and interpretation of scientific data are developed in the same class, and the same pupils who do well in that class tend to do well on all tests in that subject. The evidence on mental-process groupings is essentially negative. There is no general "ability to apply principles"; the tests of application in various subjects actually have less in common with each other than they do with tests of other processes. Likewise, Furst found little evidence for a general ability to think critically or to interpret data.

This study leaves considerable need for further information. The correlation between tests in the same field is not high; evidently the various tests within the science field, for example, do measure somewhat distinct abilities. But we have little knowledge as to why some students develop one scientific ability more than another, and little understanding as to how interpretation of data in science differs psychologically from interpretation of social data.

15. **a.** List several outcomes which might be considered in evaluating proficiency in algebra.
    b. Classify these outcomes according to the taxonomy.
    c. What empirical questions might be asked about the relation between these several proficiencies? What value might this information have in designing subsequent tests, in altering instruction, and in guiding students?
16. In question 15, substitute clinical psychology for algebra, and answer the same subquestions.
17. Would a logical taxonomy of psychomotor abilities have led to the same results as factor analysis?
18. The following quotations from want ads specify proficiencies that an employer might want to test by interview, written test, or other methods. Locate the proficiencies in the taxonomy as well as you can.
    a. "Wanted: Young man for advertising agency with 'a flair for writing.' "
    b. "Wanted: Senior marketing research analyst, thoroughly familiar with customer testing procedures."
19. What might a person studying psychological testing learn that would fall in each of the following categories of the taxonomy: 1.11, 1.21, 1.23, 1.24, 1.31, 2.30, 4.10, 5.20, 6.20?

PUBLISHED TESTS OF EDUCATIONAL OUTCOMES

Among the myriad tests which have been published for measuring pupil accomplishment, some are concerned with single subjects like history or science. Batteries of achievement tests have subtests measuring several important areas of school attainment. The subtests are standardized together, so that one can compare the pupil's relative standing in one subject with his standing in other subjects. The areas most commonly measured in elementary-school batteries include reading, spelling, language usage, arithmetic, and social studies. On the whole, because of the way schools are organized, single-subject tests have been more widely used at the high-school and college level than comprehensive batteries, but tests of general educational development are now widely used for selection of students and for guidance.

Tests of General Educational Development

If one's purpose is to determine how much science a student contemplating a premedical course knows, his general scientific competence is of more interest than his mastery of a particular subject. A few recent test batteries for high school and college attempt to measure general educational development without regard to narrow subject-matter divisions. One important use of such tests is to evaluate a man's readiness for college (Dressel and Schmid, 1951). GED tests were first designed to assist men returning from military service to reënter the educational system at the appropriate level, regardless of the amount of formal credit they had received. Lindquist, a designer of the original tests, indicates their philosophy (1944, p. 366):

> The real ends of instruction are the lasting concepts, attitudes, skills, abilities, and habits of thought, and the improved judgment or sense of values acquired; the detailed materials of instruction—the specific factual content—are to a large extent only a means toward these ends. Since the detailed materials out of which a self-educated serviceman might have developed his . . . thinking might differ considerably . . . from those used in formal classroom instruction, we felt that . . . we must try to measure as directly as possible the ultimate outcomes of a general education, and to minimize as much as possible the formal pedagogical procedure that may be used to attain them in classroom instruction.

GED batteries measure mathematical ability and English expression by rather conventional items, but in science, social studies, and literature, instead of testing what scientific facts or works of literature student is familiar with, the battery uses "tests of interpretation." He is asked to read a passage resembling those in college science texts, and then is tested for comprehension. Similarly, he is required to interpret social science materials and passages from literature. The test draws on knowledge but requires few specific facts. It should be noted that these tests are measures of *general* education, i.e., of proficiencies that may apply to a wide range of future experiences. Readiness for a specific course (e.g., college zoölogy) depends both on general intellectual development and also on specific attainments from prerequisite courses. The latter are measured by proficiency tests in particular subjects.

For teaching purposes, measures of overall proficiency are not sufficient. The teacher needs to know specific strengths and weaknesses of each pupil, and diagnostic tests provide this information. Diagnostic tests focus on the process by which the student responds, rather than the product. Diagnostic procedures in reading will be described below. Since they stress analysis of the individual's errors rather than comparison between students, diagnostic procedures are rarely standardized.

Early proficiency tests have measured knowledge and routine skills, neglecting higher intellectual processes. Recent tests have paid more attention to complex intellectual skills such as interpretation of experiments. Many of these are "transfer" tests requiring application of skills and ideas to situations not studied. Tests of ability to apply principles ask the pupil to solve unfamiliar problems using the principles he has learned. If a pupil can solve a problem he has not studied and defend his solution with a sound scientific principle, it is certain that he understands the principle. The TMC is in effect a test of application of principles of mechanics. Another example is the "aquarium" item above.

20. If admission to college depends in part on a test which stresses knowledge of historical facts, what instruction given high-school seniors would improve their chances of passing? What instruction would help them most if admission is based on a test of interpretation of social studies materials?

21. Discuss the argument: "The GED tests of interpretation are measures of intelligence and reading ability rather than of educational development in subject fields."

Important Educational Achievement Batteries

The following list of educational tests is by no means exhaustive, but it covers many prominent types including those a psychologist or counselor is most likely to encounter. Most of the batteries are divided into parts which can be given separately where measurement in only one area is required.

● California Achievement Tests; Ernest W. Tiegs and Willis W. Clark; California Test Bureau, 1933, 1950, 1957. Grades 1–2, 3–4, 4–6, 7–9, 9–14. Earlier edition known as Progressive Achievement Tests. A comprehensive three-hour battery yielding separate scores in vocabulary, reading comprehension, arithmetic reasoning, arithmetic fundamentals, English mechanics, spelling; these scores have reliabilities .79–.95 (Grade 6). Large differences between a pupil's subtest scores are significant. The proposed "diagnostic analysis" based on small subgroups of items is not a dependable basis for studying learning difficulties. Norms are derived from a representative national sample also used for norming the CTMM, thereby permitting accurate comparison of achievement for each pupil with that of pupils having similar general ability (see below).

● California Tests in Social and Related Sciences; Georgia Sachs Adams and others; California Test Bureau, 1946, 1953. Grades 4–8, 9–12. A test of three parts, yielding six scores with reliability .85–.95 (6th grade). Four sections cover history, geography, and other social studies; two sections cover science content. Items at the elementary level test knowledge of the important facts and central concepts of the typical program in general social studies and science. The advanced level deals specifically with American history (four sections), and with a mixture of factual and reasoning questions selected from various science courses.

● Essential High School Content Battery; David P. Harry and Walter N.

Durost; World Book, 1951. Grades 10–13. A three-and-one-half-hour battery measuring knowledge in mathematics, science, social studies, and English. Each section covers specific course content rather than general comprehension. For example, the mathematics test includes algebraic factoring, recognizing graphs of conics, and recalling theorems about perpendicular chords. Other problems cover everyday arithmetic reasoning, use of tables, etc. The science section surveys factual and vocabulary knowledge and also measures ability to reason from principles to conclusions. The single score for each area is less analytic than the finer subdivision given in ITED or STEP.

• Evaluation and Adjustment Series; Walter N. Durost (ed.); World Book, 1950. A series of tests for high-school use, each test with a different author and for a different subject. (Examples: Anderson Chemistry Test, Davis Test of Functional Competence in Mathematics, Engle Psychology Test.) The several tests vary in quality, but each of the better tests represents a comprehensive survey of outcomes regarded as important by specialists in the field. The chemistry test covers principles such as valence and photosynthesis, practical applications, interpretation of experiments, chemical formulas, and quantitative problems. Norms are for students who have had one year of chemistry. In general, tests in this series are well designed for end-of-year evaluation of attainment in basic courses.

• Iowa Tests of Basic Skills; E. F. Lindquist and A. N. Hieronymus; Houghton Mifflin, 1940, 1956. Grades 3–9. A battery requiring about five hours, yielding scores on vocabulary, reading, arithmetic, language, and work-study skills, each having a reliability .90 or over (Grade 6). Norms are based on carefully selected national samples for each grade early in year, at midyear, and at end of year. Each test contains sections of increasing difficulty; pupils in any grade take only those sections appropriate in difficulty for them, but questions for adjacent grades overlap. All sections require use of skills in meaningful contexts. The section on work-study skills measures ability to read maps, graphs, and charts, and ability to use reference material, indices, etc.

• Iowa Tests of Educational Development (ITED); E. F. Lindquist and others; Science Research Associates, 1942, 1952. Grades 9–13. An eight-hour battery of nine tests designed to measure general educational development in skills and thinking abilities, regardless of particular courses or content studied. Scores include understanding of basic social concepts, interpretation of reading materials in social studies, use of sources of information, quantitative thinking, correctness and appropriateness of expression, etc. The tests are carefully normed; reliabilities range from .81 to .94. The battery predicts college grades with validity near .60, this high validity being attributable in part to the length of the battery. "Secure" versions of ITED, of various lengths, are used in scholarship competitions, and in the American

College Testing Program, which obtains information on high school seniors for use by college admissions officers.

• Metropolitan Achievement Tests; Gertrude H. Hildreth and others; World Book, 1931, 1946, 1959. Grades 1, 2, 3–4, 5–6, 7–9. The elementary level provides nine scores in three hours of testing, measuring vocabulary, reading, arithmetic, and language usage. At higher levels, tests of study skills and information in science and social studies are added.

• SRA Achievement Series; Louis P. Thorpe, D. Welty Lefever, Robert A. Naslund; Science Research Associates, 1954, 1957. Grades 2–4, 4–6, 6–9. A seven-hour battery measuring work-study skills, reading, language usage, and arithmetic. (Other tests in preparation.) An attractive test using story materials to measure fundamental skills in meaningful contexts. Designed to give accurate end-of-year measures for average and able students. Retarded pupils earn such low scores on the test for their grades that for accurate measurement they should be retested on the next lower level of the series.

• Sequential Tests of Educational Progress (STEP); various authors; Cooperative Test Service, 1958. Grades 4–6, 7–9, 10–12, college. A battery of seven tests, each requiring ninety minutes to obtain a score with reliability .83 to .91. Norms can be compared to scores on the School and College Ability Tests. In reading, quantitative ability, science, and social studies, the student is required to comprehend and draw conclusions about complex selections, realistic problems, unfamiliar experiments, etc.; the tests thus require a deeper mastery than many skill or content tests do. One novel subtest is a measure of listening comprehension for passages read by the teacher. Another is an ingenious objective test of ability to judge and improve writing style. This battery is particularly likely to encourage teaching for understanding.

• Stanford Achievement Test; Truman L. Kelley and others; World Book, 1923, 1943, 1953. Grades 1–3, 3–4, 5–6, 7–9. The several revisions of the Stanford test have been more widely used than any other achievement battery. Revisions have greatly improved the norms and score conversions without radically altering the test content. There are five scores at the primary level (80 minutes) and eight at the advanced level (215 minutes); two-thirds of the reliability coefficients are .88 or better. The skill tests (paragraph meaning, arithmetic computation, language, etc.) contain carefully written items. The problems are very similar to those used for practice in traditional lessons. The social studies and science sections ask miscellaneous, unrelated factual questions; modern educational theory regards understanding of central concepts in these fields as more important than such recall of isolated facts.

22. Some achievement test manuals report no information on score intercorrelations. What value is there in knowing not only the reliabilities of the California

Mathematics Reasoning and Mathematics Fundamentals scores (.91 and .93, respectively) but also the intercorrelation (.77)?

23. The GED tests require up to two hours to obtain a single score, whereas the California battery obtains about twenty scores in two hours. What differences in viewpoint underlie these different practices?

24. Some test manuals encourage teachers to study answer sheets to determine what items each individual student missed. The Iowa Tests of Educational Development, however, discourage this practice, saying that such analysis does not provide a dependable basis for individual diagnosis. Why not?

25. Some achievement tests have end-of-school-year norms, whereas others report norms for the beginning of the school year. For what purpose is each type better suited?

Norms for Educational Tests

Grade Norms. When standardized tests were first introduced, the manuals began to translate raw scores into "grade equivalents." These equivalents are somewhat analogous to the mental age. A "grade equivalent" of 6.0 is assigned to the score the average beginning sixth-grader makes. Just as mental ages have proved to be an unsatisfactory and misleading system for general mental tests, so grade equivalents have proved unsatisfactory for reporting educational development.

Grade norms are based on samples of pupils throughout the nation. Some sections of the country are far superior to others, because of differences in pupil ability, differences in the quality of teachers, and differences in expenditures for education. No teacher or superintendent from a superior school can take pride if his group merely reaches the national norms; no one from a handicapped school district should be condemned if his group cannot attain the national average. The only fair basis for comparing schools is to judge each school against schools with similar organization, similar curricula, and similar promotion policies. Rarely are published norms based on such meaningful segments as "New England public elementary schools, in cities with population 2000 to 10,000" or "Southern rural elementary schools."

Norms are not "standards." It is a common mistake to assume that all pupils in the ninth grade should reach the ninth-grade norm. This is of course a fallacy; 50 percent of the pupils in the standardizing sample fall below the norm. Furthermore, the test shows only what schools are doing at present. It is highly unlikely that the schools are doing so well that the national average represents what pupils could attain with the best teaching methods. The teacher whose class reaches the average has no cause for complacency. There is much room for the development of better educational methods.

Grade norms are based on grossly unequal and artificial units of measurement. It looks as if a pupil is greatly superior if he reaches the "ninth-grade level" in science when he is only in Grade 6. But in many standard

tests such a difference in score represents very little difference in ability, because the average rises only slightly from Grade 6 to Grade 9. In Figure 68
we see curves for two tests of the Stanford Achievement series in which
grade norms are compared to statistically derived "K scores." We cannot here
consider the assumptions made in deriving the K scores, but the general
implication of Figure 68 would hold for almost any scoring method. In
Language, grade increments above Grade 7 imply only very small improve-

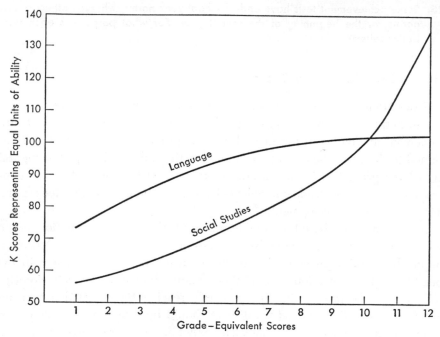

FIG. 68. "True" increases in ability corresponding to equal changes in grade scores for two
subtests of the Stanford Achievement Test.

ments in performance. In Social Studies, on the other hand, a three-grade
gain represents a large increase in knowledge.

"Ninth-grade levels" in different subjects are not equally hard for sixth-
graders to reach. The pupil who is "two years beyond his grade" in a subject
may sometimes be markedly superior; at other times this standing is equaled
by a large proportion of his class.

One further serious limitation of grade equivalents arises when conversions
for very high and low scores are derived statistically rather than by direct
observation. In a test battery intended for Grades 4 to 6 the author measures
pupils in those grades and then may determine by extrapolation what score
"ought to correspond" to the Grade 2 or Grade 8 average. This is sometimes
done just to save effort in standardization, and sometimes because it is impossible for second-graders to take a sixth-grade test.

Grade norms imply that two pupils with a grade equivalent of 7.0 are similar, even if one is in Grade 4 and one in Grade 9. This is just as unsound as assuming that an MA of 12 means the same thing for a 9-year-old and for a 14-year-old. The advanced pupil and the retarded pupil with the same score make different errors, and they are by no means ready for the same type of instruction. Grade norms can lead teachers and parents only to unsound conclusions and should be replaced by percentile scores based on single-grade groups in a defined type of school, or by some similar system. We may expect the grade norm to remain in use long after all test specialists agree on its inappropriateness, just as it took a long time to displace the ratio IQ. Teachers and school administrators are used to it and look for it; the pub-

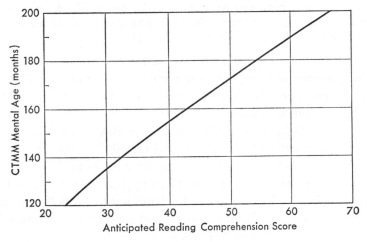

FIG. 69. Expectancy chart for California Achievement Test in Grade 7. (Redesigned from the chart presented in the CAT manual, 1957.)

lisher of a new test feels that he must satisfy this demand; and the vicious circle rolls on.

Expectancy Norms. The employer who uses a proficiency test to screen out poor performers is concerned only with raw scores. The educator, however, wants to know if the student is making as much progress as he should. He therefore wants to evaluate performance relative to ability, and gain over performance at the beginning of training. The proper procedure compares the pupil to the normal expectancy for his ability. The technique is illustrated by the expectancy charts developed for the California Achievement Tests. The expectancy chart shows what proficiency score can be expected for pupils with each score on a mental test. Figure 69 shows a simplified version of the chart for reading comprehension in Grade 7. The tester enters at the left with the pupil's MA from CTMM. The line indicates the normal achievement for pupils with his general ability. For example, a pupil with

MA 180 (15 years) is expected to earn a reading score of about 54. Any lower score indicates that he is performing below his ability.

One great advantage of the expectancy chart is that it enables the teacher to evaluate the attainment of his group even if it is not typical in mental ability. A teacher who finds that end-of-year performance is below average usually dismisses the finding if he knows that the group was weak to start with. The chart can show whether this class is performing as well as did comparable weak pupils in the norm group.

26. What reading score is expected, according to Figure 69, for a seventh-grader whose CTMM MA is 14 years?
27. Might there be an advantage in preparing separate expectancy charts for pupils from lower-class homes?
28. Tests of the Evaluation and Adjustment Series are provided with expectancy charts in which expectancies are shown as a function of IQ. Is this more or less satisfactory than the use of mental age as in Figure 69?

Conversion Scales for Recording Progress.   There are obvious advantages for the school program in using the same tests from year to year, though it is necessary to use more difficult tests as the pupil advances through school. It is also advantageous to standardize tests for the several subject areas on the same or comparable groups. Publishers of educational tests have invented single conversion scales which can be used for all the tests they publish.

The usual method for articulating consecutive tests at different levels is the equipercentile technique (see p. 93). Suppose a reading test has two levels, one for Grades 7 to 9 and one for Grades 9 to 12. Both tests may be given to a large sample of ninth-graders, and percentile scores may be determined. The results will look like this:

	Lower-Level Raw Score	Upper-Level Raw Score
80th percentile	62	49
50th percentile	48	33
20th percentile	32	18

Then a raw score of 49 on the upper-level test is regarded as equivalent to a raw score of 62 at the lower level. This permits measurement of growth for a pupil who is given the lower form in Grades 8 and 9 and the upper form in Grade 10.

29. On the test discussed above, interpret the growth shown by a pupil whose eighth-grade score (lower level) is 32, ninth-grade (lower level) is 48, and tenth-grade (upper level) is 35.

Reading Tests

Reading deserves special attention in this book for two reasons. First, reading tests have been developed in greater number and variety than any other type of achievement test and demonstrate numerous problems in test construction. Second, they are used more widely in guidance and clinical examinations than other achievement tests.

Definition of Abilities. At a glance, reading seems to be a clearly defined skill which could readily be measured, but tests having the same name measure quite different behaviors. Authors disagree on what reading tests should include and on the most useful definition of rate, comprehension, word knowledge, etc., for testing purposes. One author examined 24 reading tests and found that between them they measured 48 differently labeled skills (Traxler, 1941). This does not mean that reading involves 48 specific abilities, however. One test claimed to measure several "entirely different" reading skills, but correlations showed that these scores actually measured the same function over and over under different names. In factor analysis of 25 tests of reading and study skills, the following common factors were found: tendency to read carefully (an attitude or habit), inductive reasoning, rate of reading, verbal ability, vocabulary, rate for disconnected facts, and chart reading (W. E. Hall and F. P. Robinson, 1945). In view of such variety of test content, the person who needs a reading test must be careful to define what reading ability he wishes to measure.

Survey Tests. Survey tests are ordinarily intended to assess general level of reading development. They are used to screen pupils for remedial teaching, to predict success in courses, and to check whether poor reading explains a poor score on a group mental test.

Reading development includes both speed of reading and comprehension, and a useful test must consider both these elements. Most testers have tried to measure the two aspects of performance independently, but they have been largely unsuccessful. This problem occurs in most testing, but rarely is it so obvious as in reading: when an act has several integral aspects, one cannot divide the act into fragments for testing purposes.

In theory, the way to separate speed and comprehension is to hold one constant while the other is measured. Speed can be minimized by giving a test without a time limit; the subject's understanding of what he reads then should be a measure of comprehension alone. Rate is much harder to isolate because every person has many reading rates, which he changes with his purpose and with the material read (Blommers and Lindquist, 1944). The usual device for controlling comprehension is to require the subject to answer questions about what he has read, or to cross out absurdities as he reads.

The most prominent reading tests for the lower grades are those contained in standard batteries (also capable of being administered separately). For college guidance and screening to detect remedial needs, there are several carefully developed tests including the Survey Section of the Diagnostic Reading Tests (see below), the Davis Reading Test (Psychological Corporation), the Coöperative Reading Test (Educational Testing Service), and the Kelley-Greene Reading Comprehension Test (World Book).

The following limitations should be borne in mind in evaluating reading survey tests:

● The scores on rate and comprehension are often interdependent, so that the subject can raise one at the expense of the other. When only a single "rate of comprehension" score is obtained, thoroughness may lower the subject's rate score.

● Time-limit tests supposed to measure comprehension often are strongly influenced by rate of reading. Such tests have little diagnostic value, although they may be good predictors of school success.

● The reading test covers only a selected range of content, yet reading ability varies somewhat with different materials. Some people can read history well but not science; some do well on stories, poorly on textbooks. Different content is appropriate for different testing purposes.

● Many tests measure only a limited type of comprehension. The skilled reader must be able not only to follow sentences but also to take the main idea from a long passage, put together ideas from separate sentences, follow a logical argument, and so on. Some reading tests measure only the simplest comprehension, whereas others demand deep and thorough interpretation.

Diagnostic Methods.   A diagnostic proficiency test at its best is an impressive tool. With or without such tests all teachers and school psychologists must at times determine why students are having difficulty. An ideal diagnostic reading test calls attention to every aspect of the reading process wherein the pupil might have stumbled. Checking off one at a time the many sorts of possible error, the tester is left with a picture of the specific weaknesses that must be remedied before the pupil can make normal progress.

Such a diagnostic procedure must be based on extensive research to determine the common types of errors. Once the errors are listed, it is necessary to devise test procedures to reveal which errors the pupil makes. Systematic diagnostic methods have been worked out for arithmetic and a few other school subjects, but they have reached their highest development in reading. Reading specialists have available a great variety of diagnostic techniques, and a few of these have been organized into batteries sufficiently simple for nonspecialists to use. Among the widely known methods is the Durrell Analysis of Reading Difficulty (Durrell, 1940).

Durrell based his tests on study of the reading errors made by 4000 school children. The tests provide an opportunity to observe the child at work in oral and silent reading, and in special tests. The first tests deal with oral reading. The tester records the time required to read the standardized paragraphs, and notes errors as they occur. Silent reading is then checked on a set of paragraphs of difficulty equal to the oral series. Questions are used to check recall, and the teacher observes such reading habits as lip movement. A flash-exposure device is used to show words briefly; this detects perceptual habits and errors. Finally, there is a phonetic inventory for children who have difficulty in word perception. The analysis is not a mechanical device —it calls for keen observation by the tester. In the oral tests, the tester must record phrase reading, hesitation on words, mispronunciation, omission of words or syllables, neglect of punctuation, and enunciation. The virtues of the test are that it presents materials of standardized difficulty and that the checklist of errors calls the tester's attention to all the significant facts.

The type of information that comes from a careful diagnosis is illustrated by Durrell's report on Anthony, age 9–8, in the fourth grade. His Binet MA was 9–4, but his general reading achievement was at the low second-grade level.

On the Durrell *Analysis of Reading Difficulty*, Anthony made a low second-grade score on oral-reading tests, but seemed quite unable to keep his attention on silent reading. He did poorly on quick perception of words, and had no method of word analysis. He read a word at a time in a strained voice and a monotone. He was markedly insecure in his reading and repeated words continually. He was unaware of the errors in his reading, indicating a lack of concern about meaning. When his errors were corrected in his oral reading, his comprehension was excellent.

The silent reading was marked by a high rate at the expense of mastery. He skipped all the hard words; as a result his recall was scanty and inaccurate, although he did the best he could with it. Strictly speaking, he did not read silently at all, since his reading was accompanied by constant whispering of the words, vague sounds being given for the difficult words. His eye movements in silent reading were irregular and unrhythmic, with seven to ten per line and many regressive movements.

Much simpler diagnostic tests are designed for group administration. These contain subtests presumed to measure various types of reading ability. Performance is represented as a profile showing the relative strengths and weaknesses of the pupil. The Diagnostic Reading Tests contain a survey section and a diagnostic battery to be applied to pupils who do poorly on the survey. The diagnostic battery designed for Grades 7 and above offers the following scores:

Vocabulary in special areas
   English grammar and literature
   Mathematics
   Science
   Social studies
Comprehension
   Silent reading of textbook material
   Comprehension of similar material read to the student

Rate of reading
General
Social studies
Science
Word attack
Oral. An individual test for observing speed and errors in attacking new material
Silent. A group test of skills such as syllabication

TESTS OF SKILLS IN PERFORMANCE

Development of skilled performance in a repetitive task is the goal of instruction in typewriting, comptometer operation, shopwork, blueprint reading, dressmaking, and industrial training. Measurement of maximum ability to perform is based on the principle of the worksample. One rates a sample of the work produced, or observes and judges the performance itself. Many of the methods described can also be applied to the study of typical behavior on the job. Methods discussed in Chapters 17 and 18 are especially designed to assess typical performance.

Product Rating

For product rating, we must compare specimens of the best work of each person. To compare people, it is desirable to have them work on similar material. One standard test in stenography accomplishes this with a recorded dictation which the subject must take down and transcribe. This method holds constant not only the difficulty of material but also the speed of dictation and clarity of speech. McPherson (1945) standardized a test in simple woodworking by requiring each boy to construct a wood block like a model. The block was designed to demand use of saw, drill, and chisel. Scoring was done objectively by imposing a plastic pattern on the block to check dimensions.

Objectivity in scoring is aided by a checklist or rating scale. This forces

	1	2	3	Score
Appearance	1. Shriveled		Plump and slightly moist	1.
Color	2. Pale or burned		Well browned	2.
Moisture content	3. Dry		Juicy	3.
Tenderness	4. Tough		Easily cut or pierced with fork	4.
Taste and flavor	5. Flat or too highly seasoned 6. Raw, tasteless, or burned	Well seasoned Flavor developed		5. 6.

FIG. 70. Score card for rating sample of cooking (Clara M. Brown et al., 1946).

judges to notice the same features of each sample and to use a comparable numerical scale. Two product rating forms are illustrated in Figures 5 and 70.

Observations

Observations or measures of active performance are needed when the product is not an adequate index of a skill. The civil service typing test is such a measure, indicating both speed and quality of performance. Some tests use regular factory or shop equipment, while others use special apparatus. Use of regular equipment is illustrated by a test of ability of packers in a cannery. Production on the job could not be used as a test, because of factors varying from day to day and because the job is normally affected by teamwork. For test purposes, one conveyor belt was set aside and one worker at a time assigned to it. A count was made of the number of cans he packed per hour (Stead *et al.*, 1940, p. 86).

Special equipment is used to obtain a worksample where regular equipment cannot be used, because of either cost or danger. It is essential for every submarine crewman to learn to use the escape hatch of his ship in case it should sink in shallow water. The only sure test of ability is to have him try to use it, but it is obviously impossible to make the test at sea. To test (and to train) crewmen on shore, a replica of the escape hatch was built in a deep tank. Since this test reproduces all essential features of sea conditions, a valid worksample is obtained.

Motion pictures have occasionally been used to assess ability to observe. Ability of aerial navigators was tested by showing them a motion picture, taken from a plane, giving a view of the ground and of the essential instruments. Aided by a map, students were to make a plot just as they would in flight. This, like many worksamples, proved to have little reliability (Carter, 1947). Low reliability is characteristic of worksamples where one error may disturb the entire sequence of performance, and several samples of performance must therefore be obtained. The more successful motion-picture tests usually include a large number of short, similar items, rather than a few complex sequences of performance (Gibson, 1947).

Observations are far from trustworthy. Men with experience in administering worksample tests were asked to record facts about the performance of a man sharpening a drill point, as shown in a film, on two occasions one month apart (Siegel, 1954). Even though the questions dealt with readily observable facts (e.g., Did the man wear goggles while grinding?), the raters' answers on the second occasion agreed with their first answers only 82 percent of the time (50 percent being chance expectancy).

Evaluation of performance is improved by recording systematically what the subject does. Mechanical recording devices are especially valuable where a performance is rapid or where subtle details are important. An example from industrial training is provided in Lindahl's study of disk-cutter

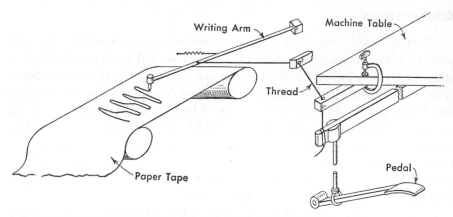

FIG. 71. Schematic diagram of Lindahl's recorder (Lindahl, 1945).

operation (1945). The difference between good and poor performers was found to lie in the speed with which they went through each phase of the cycle of operation. The operation called for pressing a pedal to drive the cutting wheel, and releasing it for a new cut. Lindahl devised the recording device shown in Figure 71, which yielded records such as that in Figure 72. These objective records showed which workers were the best producers and, more important, what errors each was making. The records also provided a means of teaching the worker what errors he was making and helping him recognize the "feel" of the pedal when he was doing the act correctly.

30. Outline a plan for obtaining product ratings and performance observations for each of the following situations. In each case, discuss the relative merit of the two procedures.
   a. Testing a boy's knowledge of how to wire batteries in series.
   b. Testing the improvement in technique of a concert violinist.
   c. Testing ability to operate a calculating machine for all types of operation.

STANDARDIZED PROFICIENCY TESTING IN SCHOOLS

Standardized tests are a comparatively modern innovation. Fifty years ago teachers around the country taught in their own ways, set their own expectations of their pupils, and assigned grades independently. If the average fourth-grader in Mill Corners could outread sixth-graders down the road at Pinetown, that fact was never brought to light. Parents and employers looked at the performance of school graduates and, according to their dispositions, were pleased or displeased with the results. There was no sound

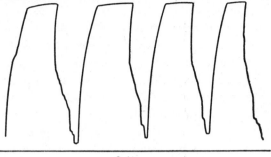

9 Hours

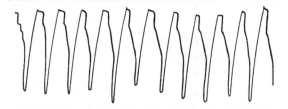

45 Hours

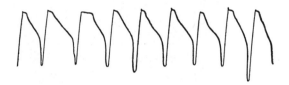

141 Hours

239 Hours

FIG. 72. Improvement in the foot-action pattern of a trainee. The record at the top shows long pauses between strokes, uneven speed during the cutting (downstroke), and jerky foot action at the end of the stroke. All these faults were eliminated in the final record (Lindahl, 1945).

basis for judging whether the school had taught as well as might reasonably be expected.

The first systematic comparison of school attainment was made by an educational crusader, J. M. Rice (1897). He was convinced that the pressure for perfection in certain accomplishments was leading to faulty emphasis in education, and he prepared a spelling test to collect evidence for an article on the subject. His test, given in 21 scattered cities, showed that the test scores of eighth-graders were about the same in all cities regardless of the time devoted to spelling. Although children in some cities were superior spellers during early grades, presumably because of stress on that subject, such differences vanished by the end of schooling. Rice hoped to convince teachers that they could reduce the time spent on formal skills, saving more time for an enriched curriculum. Ironically, the testing movement which he fathered tended instead to chain the schools to limited curricula and to increase the emphasis on a few skills.

Educators were quickly impressed with the advantages of determining whether schools were "up to standard," and tests of reading and arithmetic were prepared and widely used. Tests in other subjects followed. In some cities, at the height of the enthusiasm for standard tests, every pupil was given a nationally distributed examination each June in nearly every course he studied. Despite the marked benefits conferred by tests, the testing craze eventually produced serious dislocations in the school program.

The Navy program described at the start of the chapter demonstrated that tests are a powerful instrument for administrative control of the classroom. The tests show which teachers are bringing their groups "up to standard," so that administrators can take prompt remedial action. The fact that tests can be used in this manner constitutes an obvious threat. Even if a teacher knows that no one in his school system has ever been discharged or reprimanded after his class made a poor showing, the desire to make a good impression on his superiors will cause him to take the tests seriously. The teacher relieves his anxiety by making a greater effort to teach effectively, and by putting pressure on his pupils to work harder. This increase in effort on both sides might increase the amount pupils learn, but it has frequently raised tension in the classroom to an unhealthy level. It is one thing for a teacher to demand thorough preparation and work of good quality; it is quite another for the teacher to whip his charges on so they will "make the best record in the school."

Administratively imposed tests not only intensify the effort in the classroom; they channel that effort until teaching can become entirely a matter of preparing for the examination. The situation in New York State has been described as follows (Brickman, 1946):

The New York State Education Department, better known as the Regents, administers uniform examinations, also better known as the Regents, semiannually to all high-school students pursuing key subjects. To prepare their students for this ordeal, many teachers abandon the regular textbook in favor of a special booklet containing a review of the subject and a reprint of recent Regents' examinations. The general practice is to begin the review about four to six weeks in advance of the big test, although some teachers start Regents preparation as early as the first day of the term.

Such concentration may be reasonable if the test measures what the pupils ought to be learning, but it severely restricts education when the test covers the wrong outcomes or covers only a few of the desired outcomes. The writer recalls visiting a rural school which was alarmed because all the boys, upon finishing the compulsory eighth grade, left school to work on the farm. The principal believed they should stay in high school, but the boys considered school a waste of time. A look at the "literature book" for Grade 8 supplied one clue to the difficulty. Pupils were being held to selections about a Hindu boy and his village, mountain climbing in Tibet, and other topics of remote interest. When the teacher was asked why she did not encourage the boys to develop their language skills on bulletins from the agriculture extension service that the boys would consider valuable, her answer was: "I know this book isn't good, and the boys don't like it, but I have to teach it because it prepares pupils on topics covered in the standard test given at the end of the year by the County Office."

A test (or set of tests) is said to have "curricular validity" if it represents the objectives of the curriculum the pupils have studied. Instruction should not be identical in all classrooms of a given grade. Even within the same class, it may be proper for different pupils to work on different skills at a given time. A standardized test necessarily fits one particular set of objectives and one particular body of content. Uniform instructional aims may be assumed in Navy training; every torpedoman must learn the same things no matter what school trains him. In public schools there is much less justification for uniform content. Everyone would agree that elementary-school pupils should learn certain basic concepts about society and the community (for example, interdependence of communities and nations). One school might approach this by a survey of local industries. Another might develop the same concept with a unit on Great Britain. Perhaps a school in Texas would find pupils more responsive to a unit on South America. All of these programs would aim toward the same goal, and yet their content is so different that no one test fits all three approaches.

The same problem arises even in fundamental skills such as spelling and arithmetic, where objectives are more definite. Some teachers develop spelling incidentally to instruction in other subjects. Drill on long lists of words, as Rice first pointed out, produces very small permanent gains. It is reasonable to suppose that pupils will learn spelling just as well if they master words they have occasion to use. But when the teacher knows that the test will be a random sample of words from a "standard word list," he cannot hope to make a good showing by concentrating on words that pupils misspell in writing about South America. One published spelling test, for example, uses words such as *anxious, foreign, vitamins, biscuit, admission,* etc. The only way to insure a high score on a test like this is to have a daily spelling drill with a miscellaneous list of words. In arithmetic, all teachers cover the same content, but there are wide differences in opinion regarding the appropriate timing of a particular topic. Should fractions be introduced in the third grade? If the test will include such items, the teacher is likely to try to squeeze it in even though it would be wiser to put extra time on short division. Conversely, if the test omits fractions, a teacher hesitates to spend time on them even when a class is interested in fractions and ready for such work.

Tests have effects on the pupils also. The pupil learns that "what really matters" in any course is what shows up on the tests. Anything the teacher introduces which will not be tested is likely to be regarded as a side show. A mathematics teacher may try to show the similarity between geometric postulates and the premises hidden in advertising appeals or political debates. Students who know that their tests will cover mathematics alone may be entertained by the digression, but they will not study the material. By the time of college, the student is keenly alert to the fact that tests cover only part of the course, and is sure to focus his study on what he thinks he will be examined on.

Because of increased recognition of these problems, there was a swing away from wholesale, administratively imposed testing in the years following 1930. Many school testing programs became inadequate with respect to both the amount of information collected and the use made of it. The national concern with educational quality, brought to a peak by the successful launching of a Russian satellite in 1957, revived public and professional concern with tests as a means of quality control. President Eisenhower, speaking shortly after the Russian success, suggested that a national examination might be the best way of raising educational standards. The educational legislation adopted by Congress in 1958 made special provision for state testing programs, and a report prepared to guide such programs (*Identification and Guidance of Able Students,* 1958) said that achievement tests are "the most valuable single testing investment for the statewide program."

The chief risk in using standard tests as a means of quality control is that they will discourage teachers from introducing untraditional material or trying new methods. The test is likely to focus attention on those outcomes easiest to test, to the neglect of attitudes, originality, and complex ideas. Choosing and using tests wisely can overcome these difficulties without sacrificing the benefits that standardized testing can offer. There are four questions to answer in planning such a program: When should the tests be used? What should be tested? Which tests should be selected? How should the results be used? Of these questions the last is paramount.

The proper function of a school test is to improve the educational program. It may do so by helping plan learning experiences for a pupil, by indicating ways to improve teaching, or by building attitudes in pupils and teachers which will promote better teaching. Once this point of view is accepted, it follows that tests are initial, not terminal, parts of the educative process. There is little merit in testing after it is too late to profit from the results. For this reason, more and more schools are using achievement survey tests at the beginning of the school year. When the results of suitable tests are placed in the hands of the teacher in September, they provide a sound basis for planning the year's work. There is no argument against testing again in June to measure improvement, but in fall testing the emphasis is on diagnosis and curriculum planning rather than on marking and recrimination.

In guidance, tests are used *for* the pupil rather than *on* him. They show him his weaknesses, and are a more effective argument for his taking certain courses or changing certain habits than is pressure from the teacher. In guidance testing, it is important to minimize competition and concern over the effect of tests on marks. In the most successful programs, the pupil takes the tests because *he* wants to know the results.

It follows that the tests have to measure something of importance. Some schools will seek to measure acquisition of subject matter. Others will be more concerned with educational development defined less in terms of specific knowledge and more in terms of skills such as interpretation of data. In general, it appears that the most useful standardized tests are those which cover highly general objectives rather than those covering specific content. A test of ability to reason from a scientific principle to a conclusion about a strange situation is a fair test for almost anyone. It is not necessary for the student to have studied either the specific situation or the principle; if he can think scientifically, he can draw the correct conclusion. The GED tests calling for ability to interpret new reading selections likewise measure proficiency regardless of what the person has studied.

Tests should not be the sole determiner of the pupil's mark. Equal attention should be given to locally constructed tests of objectives not covered in the standard instruments, and to evidence the teacher has collected from the pupil's continued class performance.

It is important to interpret scores in the light of the background of the pupils and of the school program. The fact that a school is "behind" the national norms is no cause for alarm. The reasons for the lag need to be found, but they may not justify any change in the school program. For example, a school which takes in many pupils from Spanish-speaking families may quite properly decide to spend most of its effort during the first two years on developing English vocabulary, even if this delays instruction in arithmetic. A fifth-grade class which has been enthusiastically composing original stories and poems need not be criticized if grammar has been neglected in the process. Such evidence would suggest extra effort on grammatical usage at some other time, but would suggest changing the fifth-grade work only if the teacher thought it possible to improve formal usage while at the same time developing creative abilities.

Achievement testing has been detrimental when it forced schools into training rather than educating pupils. So long as tests are considered in the light of the pupil's past development and as a guide to future instruction, they need have no harmful results. They will have to be improved to meet these new demands adequately. Tests of limited validity may serve tolerably as impartial marking instruments. But when a test bears the responsibility of describing what a pupil knows and can do, and what he needs to attain, it will have to meet a high standard of validity. It is in this direction that improvement is to be anticipated.

31. If a teacher knows that a test containing items such as the following will be given at the end of the fifth grade, how will it influence her social studies instruction? (Items from Stanford Achievement Test; copyright 1952, World Book Co., and used by permission.)

1. A chief food of Eskimos is
   fish   vegetables   fruits   cereals
2. A man who works with wood is a
   plasterer   carpenter   plumber   painter
3. Each star in the United States flag stands for a
   state   city   president   battleship
4. A large ranch in a mountainous area is most likely to sell
   wool   milk   vegetables   chickens
5. The great pioneer leader in Kentucky was
   Boone   Clark   Marion   Carson
6. The invention of the steam engine made possible the invention of the
   reaper   locomotive   sewing machine   Bessemer converter
7. A popular amusement in ancient Rome was
   soccer   chariot racing   cricket   golf

32. What effect on the high-school social studies curriculum would be expected to follow if tests of ability to interpret data (charts, graphs, government reports, etc.) were given annually to all pupils? Would this effect be beneficial or harmful?

33. Most states require high-school students to study American history as a way of developing their proficiency as citizens. Would it be beneficial or harmful to give every pupil a test of historical information based on a random sample of persons and dates in American history?
34. A writer says, "As a general rule, no achievement test printed or revised more than five years ago, or any other test more than ten years old, should be used." Do you agree?
35. Are there school subjects in which the content in a certain grade ought to be uniform for all schools?

Suggested Readings

Katz, Martin R. *Selecting an achievement test: principles and procedures*. Princeton: Educational Testing Service, 1958.

This thirty-page brochure (available without charge from the publisher) covers the major considerations in selecting tests for school purposes. In addition to a review of reliability and validity as they apply to achievement tests, the author considers school characteristics which affect the choice of tests and gives advice on how scores should be interpreted.

Noll, Victor H. Objectives as the basis of all good measurement. *Introduction to educational measurement*. Boston: Houghton Mifflin, 1957. Pp. 90–107.

This chapter, from a representative textbook dealing with problems of testing in schools, describes and illustrates the process of stating educational objectives and using them to direct test construction and test selection.

Travers, Robert M. W. The trend toward the measurement of skills. *Educational measurement*. New York: Macmillan, 1955. Pp. 94–115.

Travers explains the reason for growing interest in intellectual skills as distinct from mastery of facts, and describes tests used to measure thinking skills and study skills.

PART THREE

TESTING OF TYPICAL PERFORMANCE

14

Interest Inventories

WE NOW turn from the study of ability tests (tests of maximum performance) to the assessment of typical behavior. We shall begin with interest inventories, paying particular attention to selected inventories which illustrate different techniques of measurement. With these concrete examples before us, we shall discuss in Chapter 15 some general problems of obtaining information on typical behavior.

Functionally, interest inventories are closely related to the aptitude tests we have been considering in preceding chapters, since their main use is in vocational and educational guidance. An interest "test" is a lengthy questionnaire. It applies the "self-report" technique referred to in Chapter 2, obtaining information by having the individual describe his own characteristics. The questionnaire or inventory may be regarded as a written interview which, since it uses numerous rather indirect questions, is in some ways more satisfactory than the direct oral interview. A single direct question, "Would you like to be a teacher?" does not give adequate information for guidance because answers may be based on ignorance or superficial understanding of the vocation. A girl may reject teaching for no better reason than that she thinks correcting papers would be tedious, little realizing the numerous other activities in a teacher's day. Likewise, some boys choose law because it calls for public speaking, ignoring its long hours of isolated research and thinking. To get around such difficulties, the blunt question is replaced by the indirect, comprehensive, objectively scored inventory.

An important advantage of the standardized inventory over the interview is the possibility of comparing responses to those of reference groups. A student may indicate that he likes 25 computational activities out of 80 such activities listed in a particular questionnaire. This, on its face, appears not to indicate much liking for computational work. But since our culture views computation more often as work than as fun, this raw score of 25 places the student near the 80th percentile for high-school boys. Though he may not be strongly attracted to computation, he evidently finds it much less distasteful than most boys do. He is a much-better-than-average prospect for a vocation which combines computational duties with duties in which he would have a positive interest.

THREE APPROACHES TO INVENTORY CONSTRUCTION

Empirical Keying: The Strong Blank

One of the two most widely used tests of interests is the Strong Vocational Interest Blank (SVIB), first published in 1927 (Strong, 1943). This inventory has been developed by means of a strictly empirical procedure; that is to say, it makes very few psychological assumptions and develops scoring formulas entirely on the basis of observed correlations of responses with criteria. The Kuder Preference Record, its chief competitor, describes the individual in terms of psychological traits (e.g., mechanical interests). The Strong inventory is comparable to the aptitude test designed for a particular occupation, where trial-and-error selection of items maximizes predictive power and theory of abilities plays little part in the test construction. The Kuder inventory is more comparable to multiscore aptitude tests intended to describe distinct aspects of ability; the practical implications of such abilities remain to be established after the test is developed.

The SVIB consists of questions on hundreds of activities both vocational and avocational. Most of the 400 items require a "like-indifferent-dislike" response to activities or topics: biology, fishing, being an aviator, planning a sales campaign, etc. Strong tried to select activities that adolescents would know or be able to imagine, rather than activities that become meaningful only as a result of work experience.

Assignment of Item Weights. Since the majority of men in a particular occupation have roughly similar interests, Strong assumes that a person having the pattern typical of an occupational group will find satisfaction in that field. Strong identifies, for example, the interests characteristic of practicing engineers. College students who have the same interests are advised to consider engineering as a vocation, and students with some other interest pattern are warned that they may not enjoy the work of an engineer.

The questionnaire was given to successful members of a particular profession, and the interest pattern for that profession was determined by comparing the responses of the group with those of men of similar age selected randomly from the whole range of occupations ordinarily entered by college men. A weighted scoring key was prepared to assess how closely the subject's interests correspond to those of the professional group. Table 55 illustrates the plan by which the key was constructed. On each item, the percentage of men-in-general giving each answer was compared with the percentage of men-in-the-occupation giving the answer. Engineers dislike "Actor" more commonly than other men; therefore, response D is assigned a positive weight in the Engineer scale. The weighting is proportional to the

TABLE 55.   Determination of Weights for Strong's Engineer Key

First 10 Items on Vocational Interest Blank	Percentage of "Men-in-General" Tested			Percentage of Engineers Tested			Differences in Percentage Between Engineers and Men-in-General			Scoring Weights for Engineering Interest		
	L	I	D	L	I	D	L	I	D	L	I	D
Actor (not movie)	21	32	47	9	31	60	−12	−1	+13	−1	0	1
Advertiser	33	38	29	14	37	49	−19	−1	+20	−2	0	2
Architect	37	40	23	58	32	10	+21	−8	−13	2	−1	−1
Army officer	22	29	39	31	33	36	+9	+4	−13	1	0	−1
Artist	24	40	36	28	39	33	+4	−1	−3	0	0	0
Astronomer	26	44	30	38	44	18	+12	0	−12	1	0	−1
Athletic director	26	41	33	15	51	34	−11	+10	+1	−1	1	0
Auctioneer	8	27	65	1	16	83	−7	−11	+18	−1	−1	2
Author of novel	32	38	30	22	44	34	−10	+6	+4	−1	1	0
Author of technical book	31	41	28	59	32	9	+28	−9	−19	3	−1	−2

SOURCE: Strong, 1943, p. 75.

difference. Liking to be the author of a technical book is especially common among engineers; since it is a significant indicator of engineering interests it is given a weight of +3. In contrast to engineers, who tend to dislike acting, 40 percent of artists respond "Like" to "Actor." The weights of "Actor" in the Artist scale are +2 for L, 0 for I, and −1 for D.

Occupational scores are converted into letter grades ranging from A to C. Seventy percent of successful men in the occupation fall into the A group on that scale. The interests of a person who falls below B+ are quite different from those of the bulk of the occupational group. Only 2 percent of the men in the occupation fall as low as C.

Strong's key is based on no psychological theory about engineers; he relies entirely on test data to define what engineers are like. Some of the weights, such as +2 for liking to be an architect, fit our expectations. Other weights may seem quite "unreasonable." Liking to write a novel lowers the Engineer score and disliking such work counts zero, but being indifferent counts +1. A few weights are illogical because they come entirely out of the numerical findings (some of which are chance effects) and are not influenced by the author's judgments.

The empirical key is a more or less heterogeneous mixture. In Table 55, the ten responses weighted for the Engineer key encompass interest in mathematical-scientific subjects (Architect, Astronomer, Author of technical book), dislike for verbal activities (Actor, Advertiser, Author of novel, Auctioneer), indifference to Athletic director, and liking for Army officer. The remainder of the key—to give only a few examples—puts substantial weight on the following likes: calculus, chemistry, *National Geographic,* repairing a clock, writing reports, and improving the design of a machine. These items all reflect scientific-technical interests. Small weights are given to numerous miscellaneous likes not obviously related to engineering: taking long walks, symphony concerts, military drill, talkative people, courteous treatment from superiors. Since these scattered items have much less influence on the score than the many highly correlated technical items, they can be neglected in psychological interpretation of the Engineer score.

Keys for as many as 47 male occupations (Printer, Musician, etc.) are available. There is also a women's blank which can be scored for Nurse, Stenographer, Dentist, and 24 other occupations. The items of Strong inventories, like those of the biographical inventories mentioned in Chapter 12, are so varied that they can be used to predict almost anything. A new key can be made for any vocation or specialized group. For example, Strong originally provided separate keys for accountants, office workers including bookkeepers, and certified public accountants. A later study of nearly 3000 practicing accountants, however, found that only about 40 percent of certain CPA subgroups make a score of A on CPA whereas 70 percent of men in an occupation are expected to make A. Strong therefore prepared a new key for "Senior CPA." The original scale seems to apply well to partners managing accounting firms and was renamed the "CPA Partner" scale. The "Accountant" scale seems to apply to junior accountants, and probably also to men who move from accounting into business management. The "Partner" scale stresses verbal interests; the new "Senior" scale involves mathematical interests and has a negative relation to such verbal interests as Lawyer and Advertiser. Senior CPA and Partner CPA scores correlate only .07 (Strong, 1949).

Strong keys are not confined to vocational interests. By scoring answers which men give more frequently than women, for example, a "masculinity-femininity key" was prepared. In principle, the test could also be keyed to give an indirect measure of scholastic aptitude, of neurotic tendency, or even of soundness of financial credit.

When the SVIB was first produced, calculating weighted scores on the many keys was extremely laborious. Fortunately, several methods of efficient scoring have now been developed, and most guidance services arrange to send the tests to centers where they can be processed electronically.

1. Estimate the approximate weights for the Chemist scale, of the item "Actor," if responses of chemists are as follows: 16 percent L, 34 I, 50 D.

2. Estimate the weights for the Musician scale, of "Actor," if responses of musicians are 34 percent L, 48 I, 18 D.

3. Suppose you wished to make a key for the Strong blank for women to measure interest in being a mother, i.e., to predict whether a girl will enjoy raising a family. Outline the steps you would follow to prepare the scale, with special attention to the persons you would use as a basis for the key.

4. Each of the following assumptions is implied in the construction or in some uses of the SVIB. For each one, state a contradictory hypothesis that might be reasonable.
   a. One is not likely to succeed in an occupation unless the work is interesting to him.
   b. One is not likely to succeed in an occupation unless his interests are similar to those of most other men in the profession.
   c. Interest in the school subjects required for preparation for a profession is not an adequate basis for predicting satisfaction in the profession.
   d. The interests leading to satisfaction in a vocation in 1930 will also be associated with satisfaction in 1970.

5. Research psychologists generally find considerable mathematical work necessary, yet liking for mathematics is assigned a weight of zero in the Strong scale for psychologists. How can this seeming inconsistency be explained?

6. "An A rating in psychologist with B+ in physician and dentist should suggest a different preparation and career than an A rating in psychologist with B+ rating in engineer, production manager, and carpenter" (Strong, 1943, p. 54). What differences in advice are justified in these cases?

7. How might an interest test be used to distinguish, among prospective teachers, those likely to be traditional subject-matter teachers from those likely to emphasize the development of the pupil as a person? Outline a plan for research to develop such a procedure.

8. Kuder's Occupational inventory (not to be confused with his Vocational inventory) is scored empirically by weighting items in a manner similar to Strong's. Kuder mentions the following principles used in developing his scale. Comment on the reasonableness of each principle.
   a. The vocabulary should be kept simple.
   b. To keep obvious vocational significance of the item to a minimum, items should not consist of occupational titles to be checked as liked or disliked.
   c. It is generally more important to sample a large number of relevant areas than to obtain large samples of only a few areas.
   d. When the purpose of a test is to differentiate between groups, reliability within groups (e.g., within the group of engineers) is relatively unimportant.

9. Would Strong improve his Engineer key by discarding weights which do not seem logical even though the item in question shows a difference between Engineers and men in general?

Interest Clusters. Although Strong's original purpose was to make predictions about suitability for specific occupations, his test is used equally often to obtain a general description of the person being counseled. Such a description must organize the responses in terms of psychologically meaningful traits. Factor analysis of the vocational keys has produced a set of descriptive traits for the SVIB.

The analysis indicates the following clusters of occupational interest for men:

> Group I, Creative-scientific: Artist, psychologist, architect, physician, dentist.
> Group II, Technical: Mathematician, physicist, engineer, chemist.
> Group III: Production manager.
> Group IV, Sub-professional technical: Farmer, carpenter, printer, mathematics-science teacher, policeman, forest service.
> Group V, Uplift: YMCA physical director, personnel manager, YMCA secretary, social science teacher, school superintendent, minister.
> Group VI: Musician.
> Group VII: Certified public accountant.
> Group VIII, Business detail: Accountant, office man, purchasing agent, banker.
> Group IX, Business contact: Sales manager, real-estate salesman, life insurance salesman.
> Group X, Verbal: Advertising man, lawyer, author-journalist.
> Group XI: President of manufacturing corporation.

Special keys for those groups involving several occupations have been prepared, so that the counselor can score the blank on these eleven factors and thus arrive at a meaningful overall description. The counselor using hand scoring may find it efficient to score the blank for the occupational groups as a first stage in counseling, and then to apply specific occupational keys only for occupations which seem important after discussion of the group-key profile with the subject. Such two-stage scoring is inefficient, however, when the blanks are processed electronically.

Darley and Haganah (1955, p. 34) advise against the use of group keys, warning that a student may not have a high score on a group key within which some of his high occupational scores lie. Physicists, to be sure, will definitely be identified by the Group II key (Technical), where 97 percent of them earn A's. Among engineers, only 62 percent earn A's in Group II. Since only 70 percent of engineers earn A's in the Engineer key, this does not appear to be a damaging criticism of the use of group keys. The writer recommends that counselors use group keys in hand scoring, but that they give attention to groups where the client scores B+, as well as those where he scores A.

Strong has designed a "map" for plotting the families of occupations. The chart represents the surface of a globe. The record shown in Figure 73 has high scores running from Group V over the "North Pole" to Group X. This pattern of interests was shown by a psychology major tested in his senior

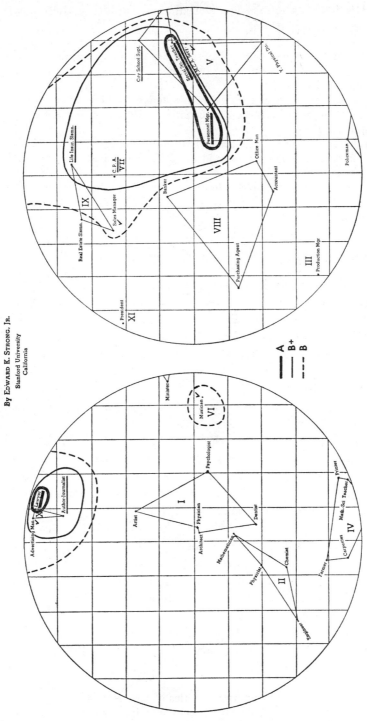

FIG. 73. Interest chart for the Strong blank. (Chart copyright 1945, Stanford University Press, and reproduced by permission.)

year. His interests emphasize "verbal" and "uplift" activities, with lower scores on accounting and selling.

10. If the student represented in Figure 73 has done good academic work and has been satisfied in his courses in psychology, what possible vocational aims are suggested by the test?
11. There are many groups in which this student has low scores. Which of these lacks of interest would be significant in deciding against certain positions in psychology?
12. The three dimensions (up-down, left-right, front-back) of the chart represent the three chief interest factors in the SVIB scores. How might these factors be named?
13. How would one use the SVIB in counseling a boy who is considering becoming a librarian or an English teacher, since there are no keys for those occupations?

Homogeneous Keying: The Kuder Preference Record

The evolution of Kuder's inventory was almost exactly opposite to that of Strong's. Kuder began with a factor analysis of single items in order to identify clusters of interests, and then organized these items into descriptive scales. The scales were used in educational and vocational guidance even though predictions rested on inference rather than evidence of predictive validity. With the passage of time, information on the predictive validity of Kuder profiles has been collected. Today scores for specific occupations can be constructed from the Kuder profile just as for the Strong, although the instrument is still used most often as a trait description.

We shall discuss primarily Form C of the Kuder Preference Record. Form A, also in current use, is a personality test (see p. 496). Form B is an early version of the vocational inventory, now replaced by Form C, and Form D is a recently developed set of questions designed to yield specific occupational scores like those of the SVIB and not intended for description. Thus Form C best illustrates the development of descriptive keys.

Kuder identified ten clusters of occupational interests, a cluster being a group of items which have substantial correlations with each other. Such a group is said to be homogeneous, i.e., there is a common factor running through the items. The ten scores constituting the Kuder profile are: Outdoor, Mechanical, Computational, Scientific, Persuasive, Artistic, Literary, Musical, Social Service, and Clerical.

Each item is in the "forced-choice" form. Three activities are listed, for example:

a. Develop new varieties of flowers.
b. Conduct advertising campaign for florists.
c. Take telephone orders in a florist shop.

The subject is to select the one he likes most and the one he likes least, leaving the third unmarked. A person who chooses "a" as most liked receives credit under Scientific and Artistic; choice of "b" scores as Persuasive; and choice of "c" is counted as Clerical. These scorings are not arbitrary; the items are counted in that key whose other items they correlate with. Judgment entered the test construction only when Kuder decided what items to use in his original tryout.

The occupational interpretation is usually made by identifying the two highest scores in the profile and referring to a list of occupations for which those scores are believed or known to be relevant. According to the test manual, a "3–6" profile (i.e., one with highest scores in categories 3, Scientific, and 6, Literary) suggests the occupations author, editor, reporter, physician, surgeon, psychologist, and etymologist.

Kuder scores are most often interpreted on the basis of their "common-sense" meanings. A person like Mary Thomas whose profile (Figure 74)

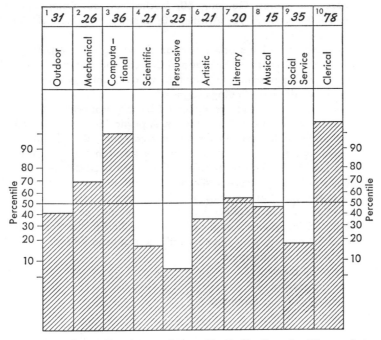

FIG. 74. Kuder profile of Mary Thomas. The Profile Sheet for Women of the Kuder Preference Record. (Adapted by permission of Science Research Associates, publisher.)

shows high Clerical and Computational scores presumably will enjoy positions demanding such activities. The low-interest areas are also important, since the person might dislike work demanding such activity. In Mary Thomas' case, the interest test was highly informative. She was majoring in child development in college at the time she took the test. Her grades were mediocre, and her work with children was not especially successful. When questioned regarding her choice of major, she explained that she had set her heart on work in an orphanage. This desire had arisen in childhood when she read a book about a woman who helped orphan children, and this had seemed to her a "wonderful" thing to do as a lifework. The low Kuder scores in Persuasive and Social Service activities suggested a somewhat withdrawn personality, while the high Mechanical, Computational, and Clerical scores suggested a liking for routine, uncreative activities. When questioned about office work, she enthusiastically described her previous summer's work as a file clerk; her duties apparently consisted solely of alphabetizing folders, yet she had "just loved it." Moreover, she had done well in secretarial training courses. Evidently both ability and interest fell in an area she had not considered as a vocational goal.

14. What tentative conclusions can be drawn about a college man with the following percentile scores: Outdoor, 60; Mechanical, 50; Computational, 30; Scientific, 70; Persuasive, 98; Artistic, 70; Literary, 90; Musical, 50; Social Service, 40; Clerical, 15?
15. A boy majoring in business administration shows high interests in Persuasive and Social Service. He is near average in Clerical and Computational. He has a high score (78th percentile) in Scientific, which is not usual among business managers. What do these findings suggest?
16. A person's absolute interests are indicated by the proportion of the possible preferences he marks in a given category. A particular man earns 40 percent of the highest possible score in the Literary category; this places him at the 80th percentile. He earns 50 percent of the possible points in Mechanical; this places him at the 59th percentile in that score because the average man has a higher percentage score in Mechanical than in Literary. In what sense is it correct to say that this man has a higher interest in mechanical than in literary activities? Should guidance be based on relative or absolute scores?
17. What high and low points would you expect to find in the Kuder profiles of these groups? Compare your answers with the results in Kuder's manual.
    a. Female personnel managers.
    b. Female retail buyers.
    c. Female secretaries.
    d. Male manufacturing foremen.
    e. Male photograpers.

Occupational Keys. When Kuder published the first form of his instrument in 1940, he suggested interpretation solely on logical bases. This required assumptions about the interests relevant to various occupations, and studies of occupational groups were needed to validate those assumptions. Kuder's data, gathered more or less as opportunity has permitted, do not necessarily represent adequate samples for the various professions. Information on psychologists, for example, was obtained by asking 260 Fellows in four Divisions of the American Psychological Association to fill out the scale; 111

persons (46 percent) provided data (Baas, 1950). Separate tabulations are made for the 27 clinical psychologists, 26 counseling psychologists, 29 theoretical psychologists, and 29 industrial psychologists. For all psychologists combined, the median fell at the 84th percentile (of men in general) in Scientific and Literary, between 60 and 70 in Computational and Social Service, and at or below 30 in Clerical, Mechanical, and Persuasive. The only noticeable differences between subgroups were in Artistic (Theoretical and Clinical above 60, others below 40) and Social Service (Clinical and Consulting above 70, others below 50).

The results found by Kuder generally support the logical expectations. The median profile for accountants shows peaks in Computational and Clerical. Authors, editors, and reporters have a peak in Literary, chemists in Scientific, musicians in Music. At the same time, there are enough departures from expectation to demonstrate that logical presuppositions must be tested (D. N. Wiener, 1951). The median for Engineers, for example, is 64 in Mechanical; 68, Computational; 73, Scientific. These depart from 50 in the expected direction, but not very far; and many engineers are below average in one or all of these scores. Camp counselors of the YMCA might be expected to have distinctly high Social Service scores, but they average only at the 69th percentile, being equally high in Persuasive, Musical, Artistic, and Literary.

Regression equations may be used to combine interest scores into a composite which distinguishes men in an occupation from men in general. The best simple formula for identifying carpenter interests counts Mechanical positively and gives equal *negative* weights to Scientific, Literary, and Clerical. A formula of this type was highly effective in separating carpenters from men in general and from men in other trades (Mugaas and Hester, 1952). Kuder profiles can therefore be transformed into occupational scores like those for the SVIB. In practice, such translation is uncommon, because counselors are more interested in helping students toward a general self-understanding than in selecting particular occupations for them.

Logical Keying: The Lee-Thorpe Inventory

There is still a third approach to questionnaire construction. The Occupational Interest Inventory by Lee and Thorpe is a set of questions selected and organized on the basis of judgment rather than on statistical grounds. This, which we may refer to as a "logical" approach, contrasts with the Strong and Kuder procedures, which depend primarily on statistical findings. The logical approach is similar to the technique of constructing proficiency tests by defining a universe of situations and selecting items randomly from that universe.

Lee and Thorpe took as their starting point the description of occupations given in the *Dictionary of Occupational Titles*. This handbook prepared by the USES defines and classifies virtually all American occupations. Within each of six areas, tasks were selected to represent high, medium, and low levels of responsibility. Brief job descriptions are presented in pairs; the subject indicates which of the pair he prefers. Scores indicate the relative frequency of choices in the Personal-Social, Natural, Mechanical, Business, Arts, and Sciences categories.

This inventory differs from the SVIB in that the original selection and classification of items is based entirely on job descriptions rather than on empirical evidence that persons in the job like the activity. It differs from the Kuder in that the first grouping of items came from a logical analysis rather than statistical isolation of factors. The Mechanical category, for instance, includes a great variety of tasks: labeling bottles, operating a lathe, making drawings with ruler and compass, repairing shoes, operating an elevator, testing the strength of steel structures, designing airplanes, etc. Such a heterogeneous category is difficult to interpret either descriptively or predictively. Knowing that a person likes half of the activities in such a mixed group tells us little about what jobs he will find satisfying. Although the original classification of items was based completely on logical criteria, a subsequent correlational analysis was made to improve homogeneity. Items which had nothing in common with the rest of the category were eliminated in revising the test.

Relations Between the Inventories

Initially, the three inventories were designed by quite different techniques. Strong starts with almost no theory and searches out those interests which go with membership in an occupation. Relations need be neither logical nor psychologically interpretable. Lee and Thorpe begin with the occupational category, basing items on duties which fall within the occupational field. If Strong finds that engineers like mountain climbing, he uses that item; Lee and Thorpe, however, would find such an item irrelevant to the occupational description. If engineers have to check blueprints, on the other hand, Lee and Thorpe would presumably include that in the Mechanical score even if engineers dislike the task. Kuder ignores the occupational structure at the outset; instead, he searches for a set of traits which summarize the main differences between persons. Only after interest factors are identified does he turn to logical analysis of occupations and then to vocational interpretations based on statistical evidence.

Despite the differences in initial conception, we find that the three inventories have converged on much the same sort of measurement. Through factor analysis of Strong keys and through case studies, it has become possible to translate SVIB occupational scores into a trait description. Through use of regression equations and profiles of occupational groups, Kuder scores can identify occupational categories into which people fit. Lee and Thorpe have begun to purify their scales to increase interpretability and if they desired could collect occupational norms for the test. In principle, therefore, all tests can fulfill all functions. Each has its own characteristics, but research gives no definitive answer as to which approach is best.

The inventories measure approximately the same interests and the corresponding keys have substantial overlap, as can be seen in Table 56. This

TABLE 56.   Selected Correlations Between Strong and Kuder Scores

SVIB Group keys	Kuder Scales							
	Artis-tic	Scien-tific	Me-chanical	Compu-tational	Social Service	Cleri-cal	Persua-sive	Liter-ary
Creative-scientific	.45	.34				*	*	
Scientific-technical		.67	.58	.14		*	*	
Uplift		*	*		.39			.30
Business detail	*			.50		.60	.36	
Business contact	*	*	*	*		.29	.70	
Verbal		*	*	*				.48

Asterisks indicate substantial negative relationships. The remaining correlations are between +.30 and —.30.
SOURCE: Cottle, 1950b; see also Triggs, 1943.

table gives correlations for selected scales of the Strong and Kuder instruments. Most of the correlations are in the neighborhood of .50–.70 for closely corresponding scales. The corresponding scores for any two inventories, however, involve a substantial amount of independent content.

18. A college student states that he is interested in a career in the diplomatic service. This may be a response to the glamor of the field rather than a genuine interest. Which inventory would give the most relevant information for guiding him?

VALIDITY OF INTEREST MEASURES

Stability of Interests

The first assumption in using interest tests for counseling is that they measure a stable characteristic. Evidence of stability is not enough to establish validity, but it is a necessary first consideration.

Strong, in his extensive follow-up studies, finds that interest scores are indeed stable after age 17. When Stanford students were retested after an eighteen-year interval, the two measures of interest were substantially correlated: .76 on the Physician scale, .54 on Personnel Manager, .68 on Sales Manager, .73 on Lawyer, etc. (Strong, 1955, p. 63; Darley and Haganah, 1955, pp. 37, 53). Scores in high school are less stable. Between tenth and twelfth grades, the average correlation was .57 (Canning *et al.*, 1941).

Another way of examining stability is to compare the test and retest profiles of each individual to see whether the same scores remain high. In Strong's eighteen-year follow-up, only about 6 percent of all A ratings changed to C, 3 percent of C's to A. For 17 percent of the cases, the correlation between the test and retest profiles was .90 or higher. Fifty percent of the cases had profile correlations of at least .80, which means that the two tests—eighteen years apart—would lead to essentially the same occupational advice. There are a few exceptional cases whose profiles on the two occasions were markedly dissimilar. In eight cases, there were negative correlations (ranging as low as −.47) between the two profiles, indicating that the peaks and valleys of the profile had actually been reversed in the interval (Strong, 1955, p. 64; see also, Darley and Haganah, 1955, p. 43).

Since the Kuder inventory was developed more recently than the SVIB there have been fewer studies of its stability. One study (Herzberg and Bouton, 1954) covering changes from age 17 to 21 in a group who went to college finds correlations ranging from .50 to .75 for the various scales. Mechanical was especially stable for boys, but otherwise no important differences between scales were found. Mallinson and Crumbine (1952) warn against making long-range decisions from Kuder scores in Grade 9. On retests in Grade 12, they found considerable stability, but many patterns showed important changes. For only 74 percent of the pupils did the two highest interests in Grade 9 remain among the *three* highest in Grade 12. And for only 76 percent did the lowest Grade 9 interest remain among the lowest *three* in Grade 12.

Interests gradually crystallize as the individual begins to discover himself and to pile up rewarding experiences in a few fields. Individual differences in interests are evident even in the preschool years. Little has been done to investigate childhood interests save for tabulations of typical interests at various ages. Leona Tyler (1951, 1955), however, measures individual interests during the elementary grades.

In junior high school the pupil begins to form a mature picture of adult occupations and of the branches of knowledge. He also begins to form a conscious picture of how he differs from other persons. His experiences in science, shop, and other courses give him opportunity to learn what he likes, but his acquaintance with these areas remains superficial. As he pursues more specialized high-school courses, reads more adult magazines, and indulges in hobbies, his interests become more definite. The boy who likes sports spends more time in them, increases his athletic proficiency, makes friends having the same interests, and so builds a little world in which he receives social reinforcement for this interest. Since high-school activities are intended to develop interests, vocational guidance prior to the senior year should be aimed chiefly to point out areas for exploration. A student who enters high school with greater-than-average liking for persuasive activities should enroll in courses and activities which will test and clarify that interest, but he should certainly not commit himself to become a lawyer or salesman.

Vocational choice is a continuous process. Certain doors are closed to a person who does not get the right training at the right time, but whatever training he does get leaves him with many options. Opportunities to specialize, to turn to administration, or to learn new skills are constantly before the professional man and white-collar worker. Long after the skilled worker leaves school, he likewise continues to make vocational decisions—to change jobs, to acquire a new skill, or to go into business for himself. The worker in a routine factory job has less chance for vocational choice; change, when it comes, is forced on him by a layoff, and his interests have little to do with the choice among openings available to him. During the years from 40 to 60 there may be little change in vocational responsibilities—research on this period is virtually nonexistent—but the approach of retirement brings further demands for self-knowledge and choice of activities.

Interests never become permanently fixed. Broad lines of interest remain unchanged for many years, but there is a constant reshaping of the detailed pattern. The beginning psychologist may enjoy everything about the job: testing, directing an experimental laboratory, analysis of data, vocational advising, giving talks on occupations. After a while he finds his greatest satisfaction in advising and begins to leave the other tasks to someone else whenever he can. His specialization may become even narrower, if he finds that his greatest rewards come from dealing with students whose vocational questions are part of a broader emotional conflict between a student and his parents. No label really tells what a person entering a professional field will do. Interests are quite stable enough to help a student choose between broad lines of training, but in that training and subsequent experience he will modify his interests and make further career decisions. If jobs were highly stereotyped, so that every 25-year-old worker in the occupation did the same thing and kept on doing the same thing until retirement, interests would need to be far more stable than they are to insure continued satisfaction with one's work.

Prediction of Vocational Criteria

Overlap with Claimed Interests.   Does the interest inventory give more information than could be obtained merely by asking the person what fields of work he thinks he would like? The evidence on this point shows that inventories fulfill an important function. Students were asked to estimate their own Kuder profiles, i.e., to report the strength of their various interests. The average correlation between estimated interest and measured interest was .52 (Crosby and Winsor, 1941). Another investigation compared claimed vocational interests with interests measured by the SVIB (Haganah, 1953; cited in Darley and Haganah, 1955, p. 67). Roughly two-thirds of those with claimed interests in business detail, business contact, and technical fields had similar measured interests, but the test supported the statements of only about one-third of those who claimed a primary interest in scientific, social service, and verbal-linguistic fields. At least two factors account for such disagreements between scores and claimed interests. The use of a large number of items, many of them indirectly related to the job in question, provides a thorough sampling of interests which is more reliable and more penetrating than the self-estimate. Secondly, even the student who knows his own interests is unable to judge how his interests compare with those of other persons.

The counselor must not, however, assume that interest tests are more valid than expressed interests. For the older subject whose expressed and measured interests differ, there is some evidence that his expressed interests better predict what field he will enter (Wightwick, 1945). Where the two disagree, the counselor will want to make sure that the expressed interest is based on mature consideration, but he would be unwise to dismiss it as "wrong."

Prediction of Occupational Choice and Satisfaction. Interest scores discriminate between men in various occupations; this in itself is partial evidence that the scores are a sound basis for guidance. Both the Strong and the Kuder tests have been studied sufficiently to verify that the majority of persons successful in an occupation have corresponding interest scores. It will be recalled that the SVIB is keyed so that 70 percent of successful adult engineers earn A's on the Engineer scale. Among students, 30 percent of those who later make a career in engineering score A in college. Data for the Kuder test are not so fully reported, though there is evidence that scientific and computational interests are characteristic of those who persist in engineering (Barnette, 1951).

While either test can point out occupations for which the person seems to have appropriate interests, it is obvious that the usual scores do not pin down the vocational choice narrowly. Indeed, subclasses within the same profession differ a great deal in their interests, as Strong's accountant study illustrated. Dunnette (1957) tested four types of engineers employed in the same company. High interests in each group are plotted in Figure 75. The "pure research" group show interest in both scientific and technical fields,

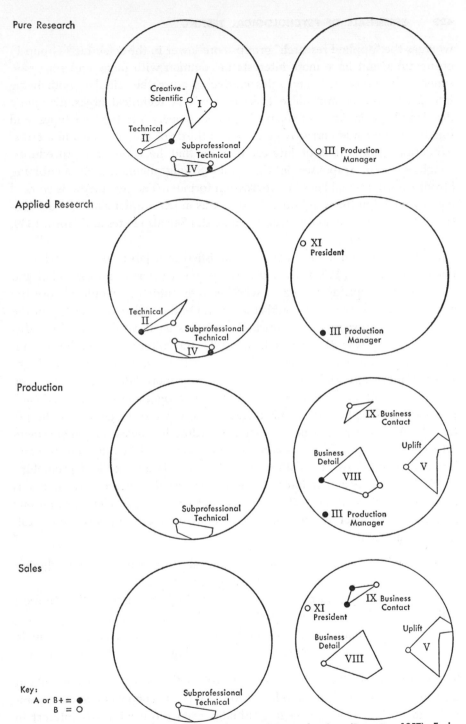

FIG. 75. Interests shown by engineers performing different functions (Dunnette, 1957). Each dot shows a Strong score in which the average score of these engineers was A or B+; a circle shows an average of B. For names of specific occupations, refer to Figure 73.

whereas the "applied research" group score lower in the scientific (Group I) occupations and have more interests in common with office and sales personnel. The production and sales engineers are rather similar, both being interested in sales and office tasks and not in technical areas. Dunnette developed special keys for separating the engineers into the four types, and found that he could correctly classify two-thirds of the engineers in a cross-validation group. It is of interest to note that he tried two procedures: weighting item responses in the usual Strong manner, and combining Strong's occupational keys in a regression formula. The two methods worked equally well, but the weighting of scores was much simpler since the occupational scores had previously been calculated. (See also Estes and Horn, 1939; Strong and Tucker, 1952.)

Interest tests can discriminate men satisfied in a job from those who are dissatisfied. Perry (1955) divided Navy yeomen (clerks) into satisfied and dissatisfied groups, according to whether they said they would choose the same service career if they could start over. On the Office Worker key of the SVIB, the mean score of the satisfied yeomen was 48 while that of the dissatisfied group was 21. (The s.d. being 33, the difference is highly significant.) A guidance service which had given the Kuder inventory to high-school seniors and adults asked them, a year or more later, what work they were doing and how well they liked it. The investigators then classified each person according to whether his tested interests were "suitable" for the job he held. A similar judgment was made regarding his measured general mental ability. As Figure 76 shows, interests do forecast satisfaction, and the combination of interests and ability taken together is an excellent predictor.

Further evidence that interest differences predict future satisfaction is found in Strong's studies (1943, pp. 114 ff.) of men who change from one field to another after leaving school. His follow-up study supports all the following statements:

> Men who remain in an occupation for ten years or more average higher scores for that occupation than for any other.
> Men continuing in an occupation have higher scores in that interest than men who try the occupation and change.
> Men who change from one occupation to another change to one in which their interest scores were about as high as for the first choice.

The correlation of interest scores with professed satisfaction is low (about .20) in Strong's study and in other studies he cites. The principal reason appears to be that among college graduates even those with low interest in their work usually report satisfaction, presumably because prestige, working conditions, and role in the community play a large part in job satisfaction.

Strong's most impressive data (1955) are those showing that college interest scores predict what occupation the man will actually be engaged in eighteen years later. Among men later employed in an occupation, five times as many had A+ ratings in that occupation in college, three times as many had A— ratings, and one-fifth as many had C ratings as among men em-

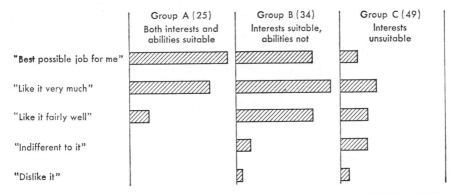

FIG. 76. Dependence of job satisfaction on suitability of interests (Lipsett and Wilson, 1954).

ployed in other fields. In the Stanford sample an A in Engineer indicates one chance in three of becoming an engineer, one in three of entering a related occupation, and one in three of entering an occupation having little resemblance to engineering. This indicates good validity, since a man may have several A's yet can enter only one field of work.

McArthur (1954; McArthur and Stevens, 1955) challenges too simple an assumption that interest scores ought to predict what a person will become. He argues that many forces other than interests determine what field a person will enter. Particularly, the family of the well-to-do boy may dictate what field he will enter, and provide the economic support to assure success. When the presumably wealthier Harvard students who had come from private schools were considered separately from those who were public-school graduates, a marked difference appeared. The private-school group, in general, entered an occupation corresponding to their claimed interests and not to their measured interests. The public-school group (generally upward-mobile middle-class boys) entered fields corresponding to measured interests.

This evidence does not deny that the SVIB accurately measures interests of upper-class boys. "It is not," Darley says (Gee and Cowles, 1957, p. 26), "that the Strong doesn't 'work,' it is that you don't need it when students' occupational choices are so completely determined by the subculture from which they come. All you need to do is to ask a boy in this particular private prep school what he is going to be and you get the right answer since this is totally predetermined by his entire environment. The Strong may truly reflect another pattern of motivation which his subculture does not allow him to use, and this is the tragedy of that subculture."

For those entering professions or skilled jobs, interest measures are highly meaningful. In the occupational world, however, a large number of jobs are essentially routine and offer little possibility of self-fulfillment. As Darley and Haganah (1955, pp. 8–9) point out,

> Only at [professional, managerial, and skilled] levels do students tend to say "*that* would be an interesting job." We as adults also tend to feel that the really "interesting" jobs are to be found only in the upper categories and that many workers are doomed to tasks requiring little training, repetitive and routine activities, and rather undemanding or unchallenging work assignments. . . . In the various job satisfaction and morale studies, a crude division of responses appears to be related to the hierarchy of occupations. Respondents at lower occupational levels stress as sources of satisfaction economic factors, security, a chance to get ahead, a need for recognition as persons. Respondents at upper economic levels define satisfaction in terms of "interesting work.". . . For the former group, satisfaction derives from sources *external* to the work.

There probably are no special patterns of interest characteristic of the unskilled occupations. Strong developed keys only for responsible positions —even his Group IV covers only skilled trades. When Clark (1950) tried to develop interest keys for various jobs by Strong's method, he found no distinction among men in various unskilled trades. He did, however, succeed in differentiating skilled trades from each other. The few Kuder data available on lower-level groups support this view. Average profiles for such groups as filling-station attendants, department store help, and painters are similar, being much flatter than the profiles for professional and skilled groups.

This result makes sense when we think about job duties. The mounter, whose aptitudes we discussed earlier, spends hour upon hour fastening wires together; wherein lies his vocational satisfaction? If he is to be satisfied, his pleasure must come not from the work itself but from companionship, good working conditions, and freedom from responsibility. The very essence of interest is a changing environment, presenting new situations to be interpreted and dealt with. Thus, while some people can be content in a routine job, it probably cannot command active interest.

19. Darley and Haganah estimate that the Strong vocational keys cover only 20 percent of the male working population. Does this constitute a serious criticism of the Strong scale?

20. Production engineers average only B— and sales engineers average C on the Strong Engineer scale. What does this imply regarding the use of Strong scores in guidance?

21. Assuming a normal distribution of Office Worker scores, and the same s.d. in both groups, sketch distributions for satisfied and dissatisfied yeomen in Perry's study. How well does the Strong distinguish these groups?

22. Expressed interests of private-school graduates predict what they will be doing more accurately than their inventoried interests. Does this mean that the SVIB is an invalid indicator of their interests?

23. How is the interpretation of Strong's follow-up studies influenced by the fact that interest scores were discussed with the subjects during college?

24. In addition to the original Physician key, Strong and Tucker developed two sets of keys for medical specialties such as surgery. One key is based on items which differentiate surgeons from men in general, the other on items which differentiate surgeons from a mixed group of physicians. Which of the three keys could best be used
   a. for guidance of a college freshman?
   b. for advising medical-school seniors about their careers?
   c. for assigning Army medical officers to duty and advanced training?

25. Among veterans who planned to enter engineering, a success and failure group were distinguished by Barnette, according to whether they continued in engineering training. How do you explain the fact that the Kuder Mechanical score, though high in both groups, had no relation to continuance whereas Computational had a very marked relation?

26. Do you agree with the following statement?

   "Insofar as stated choice of occupation by groups of individuals (high school girls) may be considered a true criterion of interest, the lack of relationship between statement of occupational choice and interest scores . . . may be considered evidence of the lack of validity of the interest inventories."

Prediction of Occupational Success.   Only a few studies have examined whether the usual interest scores predict job performance. The most adequate studies are Strong's investigations of insurance agents (1943, pp. 486–500). The Strong scores predict either ratings or records of business produced, with correlations of about .40. Men with A scores in sales interest wrote, on the average, $169,000 per year of new policies, whereas C men averaged only $62,000. A few C men, however, were unmistakably successful.

E. L. Kelly and D. W. Fiske (1951) tested students entering training for clinical psychology with predictors of all types: ability measures, personality questionnaires, performance tests of personality, and interview ratings. Four years later they collected such criteria as grades, scores on performance tests, and ratings by training supervisors. Particular interest attaches to the ratings on Overall Clinical Competence and Research Competence. In a study with hundreds of predictive scores and a dozen criteria, no single coefficient is dependable, but several findings regarding interest tests emerged. The Kuder proved to have rather little predictive value: out of 117 correlations, only 16 (13 percent) reached .20. For the SVIB, which has more scales, a total of 677 coefficients were determined, and 140 of these (21 percent) reached .20. Except for the Miller Analogies Test, a measure of verbal ability, no test yielded better predictions than the Strong. Most of the larger correlations for the overall clinical and research criteria are summarized in Table 57. The correlations may well have been reduced by restricted range in the group and by unreliability of the ratings. Verbal interests and creative-scientific interests appear to be associated with success in clinical psychology, while interest in business activities is associated with low ratings. There are some differences between those high in research and those high as clinicians, the former being stronger in scientific interests and distinctly lower in business interests. Strong's original Psychologist key, prepared in the 1920's, emphasized the interests of research psychologists and here correlates quite high with rated research competence. The Kriedt (1949) keys for various types of psychologists show that among interests characteristic of psychologists there are numerous patterns and each pattern is relevant to a different type of success.

TABLE 57. Correlations of SVIB Scales with Ratings of Trainees in Clinical Psychology

| | Correlations with Ratings on | |
	Overall Clinical Competence	Research Competence
Group I: Artist, Architect, Physician	.10 to .22	.22 to .34
Group II: Mathematician, Physicist, Chemist	−.04 to +.09	.27 to .36
Group III: Production Manager	−.25	−.10
Group V: Personnel Director, Social Science Teacher	−.03 to +.06	−.15 to −.01
Group VIII: Office Man, Purchasing Agent, Banker	−.24 to −.08	−.30 to −.25
Group IX: Sales Manager, Life Insurance Salesman	.02 to .07	−.24 to −.21
Group X: Advertising Man, Lawyer, Author-Journalist	.24 to .35	.15 to .27
Psychologist keys:		
Original Strong Psychologist	.18	.43
Kriedt Psychologist	.20	.38
Kriedt Clinical	.26	.01
Kriedt Experimental	−.08	.16
Kriedt Guidance	.00	−.22
Kriedt Industrial	−.21	−.22

SOURCE: E. L. Kelly and D. W. Fiske, 1951, pp. 150–155.

Interest inventories have shown negligible value for predicting success in vocational training. The Air Force correlated scores on various interest categories with grades in thirteen training schools. Almost all correlations were below .20 (Brokaw, 1956).

Many students confuse interests with aptitudes and misinterpret the interest test as a measure of what they can do best. Interests obviously tell nothing about abilities; in general, the correlations between interests and corresponding abilities (e.g., between Kuder Clerical and DAT Clerical) are close to zero. A high interest score should be interpreted as indicating that *if* a person survives training and enters the occupation, he is likely to enjoy his work. Though interests imply motivation, their influence on success is rather small. The Frederiksen-Melville study (p. 345) explains this in part. They found that grades of "compulsive" students depend only on abilities; such students make an effort whether interested or not, and their interests have no predictive value. Among noncompulsive students, however, interests predict achievement with validity .36–.55. While it is dangerous to generalize from this one study, it seems reasonable to conclude that a person with interests and abilities suitable for an occupation can and will do well in it, a person with suitable abilities but unsuitable interests can do well but may not, and a person with suitable interests and low aptitude will do badly (cf. Fig. 76).

Efficient prediction of success cannot generally be expected for interest scores based on differences between men-in-the-occupation and men-in-general. It is necessary to establish differences between good-men-in-the-occupation and poor-men-in-the-occupation. The characteristics differentiating good from poor veterinarians might have no resemblance to the pattern distinguishing successful veterinarians from the average man. Only a few studies have developed keys distinguishing good from poor men. One study of salesmen and servicemen for office equipment has demonstrated that this method of treating interest inventories may have substantial predictive power (Ryan and Johnson, 1955).

27. Assume that certain interest scores of veterinarians are distributed in the manner described below. What advice would a discriminant key of the Strong type lead to? What advice would be given if expectation of success within the field were considered?
    a. In Outdoor interests, veterinarians are higher than the average man, and their success is positively correlated with the interest score.
    b. In Persuasive interests, veterinarians have the same average as men in general. Persuasive interests are positively correlated with success in the field.
    c. In Social Service interests, veterinarians tend to be below the average for all men, and the correlation between interests and success is positive.
28. Do you agree with this opinion?

   "Various criteria have been suggested in connection with vocational counseling. . . . Success is often employed as a criterion. It is more appropriate in connection with aptitude tests than with interest tests. But it is doubtful if it is as good as it seems. Fifty per cent of people must always be less successful than the average. Counseling evaluated on such a basis must always appear rather ineffective" (Strong, 1955, p. 11).

Prediction of Academic Criteria

There is no overall interest pattern significant of superior academic performance. Among several groups studied at Yale, overachievers were consistently a bit higher in scientific, uplift, and verbal scores on the Strong, and lower on business scores, but the overlap of the overachievers and underachievers was very great (R. M. Rust and F. J. Ryan, 1954). Other studies such as that of Kelly and Fiske confirm this result. Correlations of interests with grades in specific fields or courses are generally below .30, which implies that interest tests add only a small amount to formulas for predicting grades. Interest scores may predict persistence even if they do not predict grades. In one study of dental students 92 percent of those with A and B+ scores on the Strong Dentist key graduated, compared with 67 percent of B's and 25 percent of C's (Strong, 1943, p. 524).

Segel (1934) found definite correspondence between interests and *differences* in achievement between courses. The correlation of Strong Engineer interests and mathematics-marks-minus-history-marks was .61. This is a finding of great potential importance in classification and guidance, but unfortunately other investigators have not attempted to confirm and extend it.

Specially constructed keys have had some success in predicting grades. Various "studiousness" keys have been made for the Strong blank by scoring on items which distinguish good and poor achievers. Mosier (1937) found that studiousness scores and grades correlated .47 for students in liberal arts, .24 for engineering students, and only .05 for business administration majors. Though such a score can improve prediction by some amount, its validity must be established in each new situation. Hundreds of studies have tried to use interest scores to predict average marks, but no technique has been satisfactory enough for practical use. The only approach that can be viewed as promising is the prediction of specific marks by means of specific interest scores chosen on theoretical grounds, as in the studies of Segel and Frederiksen and Melville.

INTERESTS AND PERSONALITY

In adjustment inventories the subject frequently conceals his attitudes and feelings. The person is usually pleased with and proud of his interests, however. Especially where it is understood that the tests will be used to provide the person with activities which will interest him, there is likelihood of honest self-report. Interests give clues regarding adjustment and personality.

Highly intellectual interests or concentration in some field where one has developed unusual competence may be an attempt to withdraw from fields where one cannot be sure of superiority.

Some persons with conflicts arising from self-criticism find satisfaction in activities which others find monotonous. Mathematical and clerical work, for example, appeals to some workers who need to be sure that what they do is right. Having added a column of figures and checked themselves, they can feel an assurance they could never have after writing a story or planning a party, or in some other activity where "rightness" is less objective. There are others who can be satisfied only when imposing their own individuality upon their work. Such people frequently dislike routine or stereotyped activities but respond eagerly to artistic tasks where originality is essential.

This suggests going behind the interest test score in an attempt to infer the type of personality consistent with the interests. Because it relies on the insight of the interpreter, any such attempt is open to error. A good many empirical studies (Darley and Haganah, 1955, pp. 103–133) have found modest relations of interests to personality tests, but clinicians and counselors have not found these studies very illuminating because they reveal little about the nature of the stresses within each personality. Clinicians therefore fall back on cumulated experience with individual cases. Rarely is such experience collected and systematized; the most complete research of this character is Anne Roe's work on eminent scientists (1952, 1957). Her findings, based on interviews and projective tests, deserve close study by anyone concerned with vocational counseling.

The implications of personality interpretations are well illustrated by these comments on medical students (E. L. Kelly in Gee and Cowles, 1957, pp. 185–196):

> As a group, the medical students reveal remarkably little interest in the welfare of human beings. For example, one of the sharpest distinctions I can find between a group of physicians at Michigan and a group of clinical psychologists whom we have been studying is [the physicians' higher] Farmer score on the Strong. . . . The Farmer key . . . is based on the modal interest pattern of highly successful graduates of scientific agricultural schools. . . . Such persons are not scientific in the sense that they want to discover new truths; their concern is rather the application of science toward the goal of increasing production. . . .
>
> Another characteristic of medical students is reflected by their relatively high scores on the Aviator scale. . . . The one thing they [various kinds of pilots] have in common is maleness and a lack of interest in anything cultural.
>
> Our data suggest that if you want to select the kind of lad who is go-

ing to be interested in public health, general practice, and so on, you should pick the person with a high Strong score on the Carpenter key. This is a person who has a relatively low upward mobile ambition in our society.

Kelly's data, from incomplete research in one medical school, illustrate that interest scores shed some light on the role the person is likely to perform within his profession. Among other criteria, sociometric ratings were obtained from the student's peers, indicating (1) his social relationships, likelihood of becoming a hospital administrator, and personal acceptability as a colleague, and (2) his likelihood of entering some public service role such as medical-school teaching, and willingness to sacrifice high income. A miscellaneous group of Strong scores were used as predictors of these criteria. For Kelly's 112 cases, the Strong Mortician key predicted the social relationship rating ($r = .30$), and Mathematician and Chemist had negative correlations of $-.29$ with the rating. The highest correlations with the rating on service orientation were Carpenter, .44, and Sales Manager, $-.42$. Other scales showing positive correlations between .30 and .39 were Industrial Arts Teacher, Math-Science Teacher, Physicist, and Dentist; negative correlations were shown by Advertising Man, CPA, and the Strong keys for sales occupations. There are many pathways to success in medicine or any other profession; vocational self-understanding is not complete when the person is fitted into a broad occupational category.

The most comprehensive information now available on personality correlates of interest scores comes from a study at the University of California (Block and Petersen, 1955; see Darley and Haganah, 1955, pp. 128–129). One hundred Air Force officers were assessed by a great variety of techniques, including tests and interviews. Clinical psychologists recorded their impressions by rating each man on an adjective checklist. For each Strong scale, a tabulation was made of the personality characteristics on which men high on that category differed from the remaining men. It was found, for example, that the following descriptions tended to fit those with high Mathematician scores: concerned with philosophical problems, introspective, lacking in social poise, lacking confidence in own ability, self-abasing, reacts poorly to stress, sympathetic; and not ostentatious, aggressive, or socially ascendant.

It is important to warn against interpreting particular interest patterns as indicating "good" or "bad" personalities. Perhaps the reader has already been inclined to judge the mathematically oriented officers described above as being maladjusted. Any such value judgment can be made only on the basis of some personality theory which is open to challenge. Most contemporary psychological writing appears to assume that the ideal personality is confident, interested in social contacts, and effective as a leader. Roe (1952), however, points out that many distinguished, highly effective, and apparently contented physical and biological scientists are not at all socially oriented. They care little for making friendships or for earning the good opinions of others. Eminent and effective psychologists (including laboratory experimenters), on the other hand, typically are concerned with having good relationships with others. Roe finds that both groups had had difficulties with social relationships at some time in their preadult development, and believes that each group chose a different method of adjusting successfully to these difficulties. The physical scientists became absorbed in tasks not involving other persons, while the psychologists made other persons their professional concern. This leads Roe to question whether psychologists, merely because their personalities have now crystallized about an active relationship with others, build such a relationship into the definition of "good adjustment" they apply to others. Quite possibly, says Roe (1953), the psychologists are critical of effective and healthy patterns of adjustment which do not coincide with their own. Conversely, if physical scientists were to define the healthy personality after studying all the data available to psychologists, their ideal might place little emphasis on warm friendships and ability to lead, and a great deal of emphasis on responsibility, freedom from suggestibility, and independence of group opinion. This argument is supported by another study of ratings of graduate students at the University of California. To the clinical psychologists, "soundness" of personality depends strongly upon warmth in interpersonal relations, and eccentricity or deviation from the norm is regarded with suspicion. When faculty members rate the same students, however, "soundness" is judged almost entirely by the student's effectiveness in getting his work done (Barron, 1954).

USE OF INTEREST TESTS IN COUNSELING

Interest inventories are rarely used for selection or for administrative decisions about classification, even where suitable scoring formulas permit valid prediction. Historically, interest tests have always been a method for helping the individual attain satisfaction for himself rather than a method for satisfying institutions. As a result, the interest inventory is used almost entirely in academic and vocational counseling.

One may conceive such counseling as intended to arrive at a decision— i.e., of selecting a definite goal and working out a training and career plan— or one may conceive the counseling as intended to promote the client's understanding of himself. More and more, counselors are shifting to the second point of view. As we have pointed out earlier, vocational development necessarily involves new choices as new facts become available, as the individual matures, or as his social circumstances and opportunities change. The student and counselor in high school may set down a definite plan to study certain subjects, to enroll in a certain college curriculum, to complete training in a certain professional school, and to find an opportunity to enter a certain type of practice. This plan has an almost negligible probability of being carried out. Somewhere along the line instructors will open new vistas to the student or arouse new interests. Somewhere along the line concrete experience will show him that he does not enjoy some aspect of the work and will reveal an unsuspected talent in another direction. Counseling should realistically assume that any plan is a road with many branches. In a good plan most of the branches are conceivably appropriate for the client to follow, and he is able to reach any of the goals which at present seem most appropriate. If the goal in counseling is not to be definite planning, save with regard to immediate decisions, the goal must be to equip the student to make future decisions as choice-points are reached. The aim in counseling should be to give the student a more sophisticated view of the world of work, of the choices open to him, and of his own range of potentialities for achievement and satisfaction.

Interest inventories are peculiarly well adapted to vocational counseling. The student expects his interests to be considered, and he is not threatened by the questionnaire as he might be by personality or ability tests. The interpretation, when given, carries considerable force, because the student can see that he is looking at himself in a mirror, that he is only receiving an analysis of what he himself has said. No psychological mysteries becloud the interest test as they do tests involving more esoteric constructs of personality and aptitude. From the counselor's point of view also, the interest inventory is less fraught with emotional significance. The counselor hesitates to tell a student his aptitude and personality tests scores unless there is ample evidence that he can accept and comprehend the findings. Scores on interest tests can be discussed freely, however; while they may require the student to examine discrepancies within his self-concept, they rarely threaten his esteem.

For the counselor or high-school instructor who wishes to encourage thinking about future plans, the interest inventory is a helpful device. It can be given to entire classes or entire student bodies. Students are quite willing to reveal their interests and are eager to have a report of scores. Although there is some risk of misunderstanding, interpretation of profiles can be carried out in group discussions rather than in individual counseling (Layton, 1958, pp. 32 ff.). Such a process, leading each student to list vocational possibilities suggested for him by the test, is an excellent preliminary either to further group study of careers or to individual counseling.

The interest inventory also assists counselors in dealing with many other student problems. A promise to interpret interest scores is an excellent, non-threatening gambit to entice the student into the counselor's office. In the course of the discussion of vocations he will necessarily talk about his family, his social relations, and his academic difficulties, and so may touch upon problems for which the counselor can provide help ranging from a diagnostic reading test to psychotherapy. The conference opens a natural opportunity for the student to express his desire for such help, a desire which he might otherwise never have acknowledged even to himself.

In view of the aims described above, it is most unwise to concentrate the interview upon an analysis of scores for specific occupations. This tactic gives the student far too narrow a description of himself and leaves too many things out of consideration. It is absolutely essential that the student should go beneath occupational labels and stereotypes, that he should understand the variety of roles different members of the same occupation play, that he should understand the differences between demands of the training program and demands of the occupation, and that he should recognize the shifting nature of occupations. He must consider his abilities and academic prospects, the pressures from his family, his motivations and values, his financial resources, and the probability that his present interests may shift.

Darley and Haganah (1955, p. 195), speaking from this point of view, sharply criticize some common practices in vocational counseling. They take as an example the student with peak interests in the social service group.

> At some point in the counseling interview series, the counselor can make this bald statement: "You have the same kind of interests as successful personnel managers or Y.M.C.A. secretaries or school superintendents." With minor modifications, this is probably the standard approach to interpretation. It is also the least effective approach and the one most likely to lead the student and counselor into ever deeper morasses of interpretive difficulties.

They give eight reasons for condemning this approach, most of which we have touched on already. Most specifically, such an approach immediately causes the student to think in terms of occupational stereotypes, instead of trying to see what interests of his match activities common in the jobs mentioned. Moreover, since he may attach a negative connotation to—let us say —"school superintendent" if he sees himself as a business executive in an all-male world, the student may find it necessary to resist the test interpretation.

Instead of a narrowly occupational interpretation, counselors should help the student identify the groups of activities in which he has expressed interests. The Kuder scores lead directly to this type of interpretation, and the occupational groups of the Strong are similarly a good starting point for discussion. A high score in literary interests, for example, can be amplified by questioning which will clarify whether this is an interest in reading, in writing, or in speaking; whether it is an interest in face-to-face verbal activities or in isolative verbal activity; and whether it is accompanied by any evidence of talent in expression. The discussion will ultimately come around to specific vocations used as examples of ways in which the expressed interests might be satisfied. Such illustrative vocations can be selected by the counselor in the light of the student's claimed interests, his probable ultimate level of education, and his abilities. They may or may not correspond to the limited number of occupations for which keys exist.

It is particularly necessary to reconcile differences between claimed interests and measured interests in a way that is emotionally acceptable to the student. To have told Mary Thomas, "You don't really want to work in child development; you want to be a secretary," would have precipitated an emotional conflict. No one can abandon a long-standing self-concept easily. An authority who bluntly contradicts firm beliefs invites the counselee to reject him as an authority. In Mary's case, it might have been better to inquire as to the reasons for her choice of child development, to ask her to envision the activities she might be engaged in ten years hence, and to compare those with the activities rated high in the interest blank. The fact that the inventory contains only her own ratings brings her face to face with her self-contradictions. The psychologist is no longer the "authority"; he is merely holding the mirror for her.

We may compare the three types of interest inventories in terms of their suitability for counseling purposes. The Strong blank is undoubtedly the most highly developed and best understood of the inventories; indeed, it ranks very near the top among psychological tests of all types.[1] The specific occupational keys with complex weights are rather inconvenient to score by hand and, indeed, may be no more valid than keys with unit weights. Those who prefer the Strong over its competitors will not find the cost and delay of electronic scoring a severe handicap. The scoring charge is currently about $1 per person. The great number of keys make interpretation both rich and complex. Speaking generally, this militates against its use by high-school teachers and relatively untrained counselors, and against its use in mass counseling programs. But its length and complexity, together with its research foundation, make the Strong the preferred instrument of most highly trained counselors and psychologists dealing with college students. The blank is relatively unsatisfactory for clients entering occupations below the professional-managerial level.

[1] The amount of effort involved in painstaking test construction is indicated by Strong's report that over $45,000 was spent, and blanks from over 23,000 people were obtained, in the course of his research.

The Kuder blank has a much simpler format. Even ninth-graders can take the test in groups, score their own tests, and plot their own profiles. There is evident danger if this invites teachers to leave interpretation to the students, but this is not a necessary fault of the inventory. The scores lend themselves directly to interpretation in terms of patterns of activity, with vocational interpretation secondary. For this reason scores of the Kuder type seem slightly preferable to those of the Strong type, especially in the hands of counselors with limited training. It is of interest that Darley, a leading advocate of the Strong test, urges that it be interpreted in terms of interest categories such as technical, social service, business detail, and verbal-linguistic, rather than in terms of the occupational scores *per se*. While the Strong can be so treated the Kuder is designed for just this use. It appears more suitable than the Strong for girls, and for students headed for lower-level occupations. Both the Strong and the Kuder inventories are long and tedious, which makes them somewhat unsuited for application to large groups. Canfield (1953) has shown that Kuder profiles are not greatly altered if only the odd pages are administered, thus cutting testing time in half. He has prepared norm tables for this short form. (See also Clark and Gee, 1954).

Inventories such as the Lee-Thorpe, developed on a logical or content-sampling basis, are much harder to evaluate. The items are more directly descriptive of vocations than are those of the Strong and Kuder, and are therefore more likely to invite responses on the basis of stereotypes. A more serious difficulty is that one cannot say whether the category scores represent suitable constructs for describing individuals. The heterogeneous mixture of activities called "mechanical" by Lee-Thorpe define a less clear interest pattern than the mechanical items of Kuder, whose intercorrelations have been established empirically. The Lee-Thorpe inventory would be a more useful instrument if considerable empirical work were done to revise the groupings and to provide a background of facts with which to interpret scores. In the absence of such facts, scores on Lee-Thorpe categories appear to deserve little emphasis. The items, covering a wide range of occupations, may be regarded by counselors as a checklist or pencil-paper interview. Innumerable leads for interviewing will come out of consideration of the separate items.

A final consideration in choosing between inventories is a statistical comparison of reliabilities, intercorrelations, and relations with criteria. Unfortunately, the available information is spotty at best, since only a few isolated studies have administered two or more inventories to the same sample. The Strong and the Kuder are about equally reliable, with the Strong having a slight advantage. The "corresponding" keys sometimes agree very closely but at other times seem to have different psychological meanings. Differences of this kind indicate how important it is for the counselor to become thoroughly familiar with the particular test he is using and with the research indicating the meanings of scores.

29. The Thurstone Interest Schedule consists of a set of paired comparisons of occupational titles such as Engineer-vs.-Accountant. Titles are assigned to areas on a logical basis. The choices made in a given area are counted, yielding scores in ten areas such as Physical Science, Business, Linguistic, and Humanitarian. The scale requires about ten minutes. Discuss the advantages and disadvantages of such an inventory for counseling.
30. The Thurstone profile is expressed in terms of percentage of choices in each area. No norms are used, interpretation being based on the shape of the raw-score profile. Is this advantageous or disadvantageous?
31. Compare the extent to which the Strong and the Kuder are influenced by response style (p. 372).
32. An interest test is to be used in helping junior-college freshmen make vocational plans. Among the training programs offered are those for photoengraver, dietitian, and others not directly represented in the Strong and Kuder keys. How could each test be extended to assist students in judging whether they would like these fields? Which test seems to be more adaptable?
33. What errors are likely to occur when ninth-grade students score and interpret their own Kuder profiles, in the course of several days of class discussion? How can the teacher reduce such risks?

PROSPECTIVE DEVELOPMENTS

Interest testing and test interpretation have changed markedly since Strong's test was first published, and there is much reason to expect continued rapid development. The initial investigations were blunt empirical comparisons of occupational groups on items selected almost at random. There was no theory as to the nature of interests or as to the types of interests most deserving consideration; there was no theory about the structure of occupations and careers; and the interpretations placed on test scores were entirely pragmatic and unpsychological. Kuder's approach and Strong's factor analyses led to the beginning of a theory of interests. Guilford and his associates, in a tentative but comprehensive study (1954), found over twenty interest factors, most of which seem to reflect general personality styles rather than vocational orientations. Guilford recognized several familiar factors such as mechanical, scientific, and social-welfare, but he adds adventure vs. security, aesthetic appreciation, cultural conformity or orderliness, need for diversion, aggression, and many other interest dimensions. Longitudinal studies and case histories have also begun to present a clearer picture of the significance of interests. The original crude empiricism has declined in importance.

The next development that may be forecast is the systematic interpretation of interests in terms of more fundamental personality constructs. The work of Roe, Tyler, Kelly, Guilford, and the California investigators all represent preliminary steps in this direction. Whereas interests were once viewed almost as a product of chance conditionings, today it is thought that interests are an expression of deeply rooted needs and adjustment patterns. Interest tests are perhaps superior to many other techniques for assessing personality because of their diverse content and their acceptability to the subject. But considerable research must be done to place such interpretations on a sound footing.

Every current writer on interests and on vocational counseling stresses the great need for a theory of interest development and for a theory of occupational adjustment to replace the present piecemeal collections of facts. Much current research is intended to produce at least the beginnings of such a theory, and as it emerges this theory will no doubt have radical effects upon test interpretation. It will also reopen questions as to the appropriate age to begin the measurement of interests, and the appropriate items to be used.

LISTING OF INTEREST INVENTORIES

Among the interest inventories currently in use are the following:

• Kuder Preference Record, Occupational, Form D; G. Frederic Kuder; Science Research Associates, 1956. A collection of 100 forced-choice items drawn from the Kuder Vocational and Personal inventories. Intended for institutions which wish to develop keys to place the most suitable persons in particular jobs. For use in guidance, Kuder is developing and releasing keys for various occupations. The 1957 manuals discuss keys for 22 occupations, including those of electrical engineer, farmer, minister, etc. The information available to date on discrimination between occupations is encouraging, but until longitudinal studies and correlations with job satisfaction are available, it is not possible to judge whether this inventory can become as serviceable as the much longer Strong inventory.

• Kuder Preference Record, Vocational, Form C; G. Frederic Kuder; Science Research Associates, 1939, 1951. For high-school students and adults. A descriptive blank yielding ten scores showing the person's percentile standing in various interest categories. (See pp. 412 ff.)

• Guilford-Shneidman-Zimmerman Interest Survey; J. P. Guilford and others; Sheridan Supply Company, 1948. For high-school students and adults. An inventory based on factor analysis which identifies nine categories, each of which has two subscores (e.g., aesthetic appreciation vs. expression). Guilford's later work suggests revision and extension of the categories. The instrument is primarily suitable for research on interest development rather than guidance in its present stage of development.

● Minnesota Vocational Interest Inventory; Kenneth E. Clark; unpublished. For high-school students and adults. Can be expected, when published, to fill an important place in counseling and classification. Forced-choice triads are scored empirically to indicate how closely an individual's interests resemble those of men in various trades such as bakers, plasterers, retail sales clerks, and truck drivers. The inventory thus covers a portion of the occupational range for which the SVIB is inadequate.

● Occupational Interest Inventory; Edwin B. Lee and Louis P. Thorpe; California Test Bureau, 1943, 1956. For Grades 7 upward. Yields scores for six fields (personal-social, arts, business, etc.) and another set of scores for verbal, manipulative, and computational interests. (See pp. 415, 435.)

● Strong Vocational Interest Blank for Men; E. K. Strong, Jr.; Consulting Psychologists Press, 1927, 1951, with supplementary research reports. For high-school students and adults. The outstanding example of an empirically scored interest inventory. Keys for 47 occupations, plus group factors. (See pp. 406 ff.)

● Strong Vocational Interest Blank for Women; E. K. Strong, Jr.; Consulting Psychologists Press, 1947, 1951. For high-school students and adults. Scores for 27 occupations. This instrument has not shown satisfactory validities and is rarely used. In counseling women who plan to enter occupations for which the men's blank is scored, it is preferable to use the men's blank.

● Vocational Interest Analyses; Edward C. Roeber and Gerald G. Prideaux; California Test Bureau, 1951. Grades 9 and up. To be used as a second step, following rough mapping of interests by the Lee-Thorpe inventory. This instrument has six sections of 120 items each, corresponding to the sections of the Lee-Thorpe. The counselor administers those sections corresponding to high scores on the first test to obtain a more detailed analysis of interests within the area. As no evidence of validity is available, the inventory should be regarded as a written interview rather than as a scored test.

Suggested Readings

Callis, Robert, Polmantier, Paul C., & Roeber, Edward C. The case of Bill Davis. *A casebook of counseling.* New York: Appleton-Century-Crofts, 1955. Pp. 77–103.

In transcribed interview notes a senior engineering student who expresses his lack of interest in engineering goes over his Strong and Kuder profiles with a counselor.

Darley, John G., & Haganah, Theda. The Strong Vocational Interest Blank in individual cases. *Vocational interest measurement: theory and practice.* Minneapolis: University of Minnesota Press, 1955. Pp. 194–263.

The authors explain how to proceed from the profile showing primary interest areas to a discussion of specific occupational choices. Ten cases are described, showing how the use of SVIB information varies according to the client's aptitudes, maturity of self-concept, and background influences. Of particular interest is a history (Karl Brooks) showing development from age 14 to 25.

Kuder, G. Frederic. Research methods for development of an occupational key. *Research handbook for the Kuder Occupational Preference Record Occupational.* Chicago: Science Research Associates, 1957. Pp. 27–38.

This is a brief account of the procedures used in developing and testing the efficiency of a key to distinguish persons of one type from men in general.

Strong, Edward K., Jr. Interpretation of interest profiles. *Vocational interests of men and women.* Stanford: Stanford University Press, 1943. Pp. 412–456.

Strong presents data on typical patterns among college students and suggests how the relevant information can best be conveyed to the student seeking guidance.

15

General Problems in Personality
Measurement

PERSONALITY, attitude, and interest measures were introduced in Chapter 2 as measures of "typical behavior," and thus distinguished from the ability tests, which measure maximum performance. In assessing typical behavior, the investigator wants to know what the person normally does rather than what he can do under exceptional motivation. In this chapter, we shall examine the notion of "typical behavior" and compare various ways of gathering and interpreting information about it. Before proceeding to this discussion, it would be wise to reread the introduction to procedures used to investigate typical behavior given on pages 31 to 34.

TYPES OF DATA

Observations in Representative Situations

The logical way to determine typical behavior would be to observe the individual repeatedly in situations likely to reveal the aspect of personality in which we are interested. To study interests, one would observe what the person does during his leisure. To evaluate a businessman's generosity one would observe his responses to charitable appeals, his tipping, and his dealings with employees.

The first requirement is a sufficient number of suitable observations. No one act can be taken as typical, since it is influenced by mood, immediately preceding experience, details of the surroundings, and other factors. There are cycles and trends in behavior. If a subject appears quarrelsome on several occasions, quarrelsomeness seems typical for him. Perhaps, however, he is in a continuing state of irritability due to some worry, and some months earlier or later he would appear well adjusted. It could be argued that we took too small a sample and as a result had observed a mere temporary deviation. Yet the deviation was real, and the behavior reported was typical for the subject during that time.

Careful attention must be paid to definition in attempting to observe typical behaviors. One can be sure what a report of typical behavior means only when the observer specifies the range of time represented in the data, the range of situations, and the range of motivations. When these are not specified formally, they are often implied in the description of the observation method.

The second procedural requirement is that the act of observing must not alter the behavior observed. Just as the presence of a traffic cop at an intersection raises drivers from their habitual level to their best ability, so the presence of the observer may cause the subject to try harder. This seems to occur even when no reward or punishment will result. Roethlisberger and Dickson attempted to compare work output under various conditions at a Western Electric manufacturing plant. Relay assemblers were placed in a small experimental room where they could be observed and their output recorded in great detail. Various experimental rest pauses and privileges were introduced; as each change was introduced, no matter what it was, production climbed. Finally, in the twelfth and thirteenth periods, the rest pauses and privileges were removed, and production per hour still remained as high as under the "best" working conditions. Another striking change was that absenteeism dropped from 15.2 days per year per worker before entering the study to 3.5 days per year in the test room. The heightened morale of the workers—as a result of being singled out for study, of being better acquainted with their supervisors, and of feeling personal responsibility for their rate of output—changed their performance so that it was no longer comparable to that in the regular workroom.

Distortion is less when the judging is a regular part of the work procedure. Ratings by foremen can reasonably be regarded as reports of typical behavior in the plant, for the foreman is usually present; how the man would act if no foreman were provided is not of interest. Wherever the rater or observer is a regular member of the group, his presence will have little distorting effect.

An ideally random sample of the subject's total behavior can never be observed. Those moments of his life which are open to the psychologist's inspection are by no means typical. It is a fantasy to think of assessing generosity by tabulating the businessman's responses to appeals; these private moments are not open to observation. Observation in representative situations can be used only to learn about the individual's typical *public* behavior: in classrooms, on playgrounds, and in certain work situations. Indeed, direct observation of samples of "natural" behavior is restricted almost entirely to research, particularly research on children who are young enough to ignore the presence of the observer.

1. Define the range, in time and situations, of the behavior which should be studied to answer these questions:
   a. How well does this supervisor handle grievances?
   b. Does study of philosophy make an adult more rational in his daily life?
   c. Does viewing a film on nutrition improve housewives' practices in menu planning?
   d. Do graduates of the modern elementary school write legibly?
   e. How anxious is this patient at this point in therapy?

Reports from Others and from the Subject

If we are willing to sacrifice the precision and detachment of the scientific observer, we can obtain useful information from the subject's acquaintances and coworkers. The rating by a foreman is more nearly a general impression than a dependable record of typical behavior, but it is nonetheless useful Similarly, mothers give information about children, nurses about patients, and so on.

It is common to regard such ratings and descriptions as information given by a competent authority who is in a sense the professional ally of the psychologist. Any one such report, however, must be regarded as one individual's perception of another, subject to as much distortion as any perception of a fluctuating, ambiguous stimulus. Indeed, investigators are now beginning to use such reports as information about the personality of the rater rather than solely as information about the person observed.

Sociometric or peer-rating techniques obtain reports on the individual from his fellows. Children rate other members of their school groups, college girls rate other members of their sororities, and officer candidates rate classmates. The interpreter may assume that such a report is a valid summary of typical behavior or, refusing to make this assumption, may still be interested in the report as evidence of the impression the subject makes on others.

Similar comments may be made about the self-report. The subject is indeed an authority on his own behavior, but there are distortions in his perception of himself and in his report. We shall discuss the interpretation of self-reports at some length below.

Performance Tests

Obtaining reports from others, or self-reports, avoids some of the difficulties of field observation. Such reports can (in principle) shed light on corners of the subject's life where the observer may never go, can cover past behavior which is no longer observable, and can take into account far more incidents than any observer could record. These benefits are offset, however, by the distortions which result when subjective impressions are substituted for precise quantitative records. Performance tests seek to obtain precise and dependable information—but they do so by giving up the attempt to take a representative sample. Just as in a measure of aptitude or achievement, the tester places the individual in a standardized situation to which he must respond. His performance is evaluated either by an objective performance score or by observation of the way he responds.

A great variety of techniques fall into this category. One might measure interests, for example, by a current events test covering developments in science, engineering, music, public affairs, and so on. Knowledge in the various fields is to some degree a reflection of relative interest. One might allow the subject a supposed "rest period" during a battery of other tests and let him browse in a library; the books which attract his attention might be presumed to represent his interests. A third approach is to require him to make up stories about pictures showing people at work in settings such as a hospital operating room. The ideas and feelings he attributes to the characters in the pictures may indicate his attitudes about various types of work.

There is no accepted classification system for performance tests. Cattell has proposed that the term *objective test* be applied to devices like the current events test of interests which yield a direct measure of performance unmodified by any observation or interpretation. This name, however, is not accepted by other workers. The name *situation test* has also been applied to tests of performance in complex, lifelike situations. It was first used for work-samples of leadership. The candidate for a leadership position was placed in a standardized situation, given a crew of men, and observed as he directed them. Another subcategory is the *projective technique*. A projective technique gives the subject material with which to work creatively; e.g., the tester presents an ambiguous stimulus (inkblot, picture, unfinished story, etc.) and asks the subject what he sees in it or what he thinks will happen next. These interpretations are regarded as projections of the subject's unconscious wishes, attitudes, and conceptions of the world.

The great advantage of the performance test is that it permits fair comparison of individuals. A rating of leadership may reflect differences in opportunity rather than differences in readiness to lead, but a performance test gives each individual in turn the same opportunity to lead. Individual differences in use of that opportunity reflect personality. Behavior in this standardized situation may be far from "typical." At best, we obtain a sample of response to a very special stimulus, namely, a-leadership-opportunity-when-being-tested-by-a-psychologist-whose-good-opinion-will-have-certain-consequences. The performance test gives neat data, but interpretation is far more difficult than interpretation of observations in representative situations or reports from others.

2. How well can the four procedures—observation in representative situations, report from others, self-report, and performance tests—satisfy the following requirements? Rank them from best to poorest in each respect.
   a. The data reflect differences in personality rather than differences in environment and opportunity.
   b. The data reflect the individual's behavior, undistorted by perception of those who provide data.
   c. The data provide a summary or estimate of the individual's behavior during all moments of his life.
   d. The results are the same, whether or not the subject wishes to make a good impression on the psychologist.

THE SELF-DESCRIPTION AS A REPORT OF TYPICAL BEHAVIOR

The simplest view of the self-report is to treat it as a record of typical behavior, which the subject is in a uniquely excellent position to observe. There is some justification for so interpreting the interest inventory, since the person seeking guidance wants his interests to be satisfied in the work he selects. Even the interest inventory, however, is not proof against distortion as a result of status aspirations. In other questionnaires, there are many sources of distortion which prevent accepting the score as a true summary of behavior.

The first difficulty in questionnaire interpretation is that items are somewhat ambiguous. "Do you make friends easily?" seems a straightforward question, but it is hard to say just what behavior the question refers to, and what the tester means by *easily*. The subject, reflecting upon his past behavior, is unable to count up particular incidents. If he could, his report would be a simple factual statement. But he will recall some cases where he formed a friendship quickly and other cases where an acquaintance remained somewhat distant over many months. If he tries to push for a more literal interpretation of the question, he soon bogs down. What does *friend* mean—close and intimate companionship, pleasant interaction without emotional involvement, or something in between? The subject taking a questionnaire does not ask such fussy questions (though a scientific observer tabulating typical behavior would have to). The subject answers the question in terms of a general feeling or self-concept. If he regards himself as being the type who makes friends easily—hang niceties of definition!—he says "yes" to the question. Another equally popular boy may have a different self-concept and respond "no."

Similar difficulty arises because most questionnaires ask about responses to the hypothetical "typical" situation, instead of asking about response in well-defined situations. "Do you seek suggestions from others?" is a fairly clear question, but most people would have to answer, "Sometimes I do, but not always." This might be further qualified: "I do on difficult problems"; "I do if someone is around whose ideas are especially good"; "I don't if I'm supposed to make the decision myself." These qualifications would have to be stated if the subject tried seriously to report typical behavior. Since he cannot average his memories to determine what percentage of the time he has sought suggestions, the question will be answered offhand. When one person defines "yes" to mean "with very few exceptions" and another defines it as "fairly often; at least in difficult situations," they are answering different questions and their responses are not comparable. Another example is the apparently clear item: "Do you like to operate an adding machine?" Many students say that they enjoy this but would be dissatisfied with a job where they had nothing to do but operate an adding machine. It is impossible to qualify items to eliminate such problems of interpretation.

Many self-report tests provide a response scale using such words as "always," "frequently," "seldom," and "never." Simpson (1944) examined how

TABLE 58. Range of Meanings Assigned to Words Commonly Used in Personality Inventories

	What Percentage of All Occasions Is Indicated by the Word at Left?	
	Median Answer	Range of Answers of Middle 50 Per-cent of Subjects
Usually	85	70–90
Often	78	65–85
Frequently	73	40–80
Sometimes	20	13–35
Occasionally	20	10–33
Seldom	10	6–18
Rarely	5	3–10

SOURCE: Simpson, 1944.

such ratings might compare with quantitative observations. He asked students what percentage frequency of a particular response would correspond to a report that this was what they "usually" did. Twenty-five percent of them applied "usually" only to events occurring at least 90 percent of the time; another 25 percent said that "usually" meant a frequency below 70 percent. The quantitative interpretation of other words is shown in Table 58. It is evident that two subjects with identical behavior may choose entirely different adverbs to describe what they do.

Response Styles

The use of fixed response categories such as "Yes," "Agree," and "Like" makes questionnaires particularly subject to individual response biases. This was first noted by Lorge (1937; see Cronbach, 1946, 1950), who counted how often people responded "Like" to SVIB items. One subject uses the word for every activity he would not positively dislike; another applies the word only to activities to which he is strongly attached. Such differences can lead to quite different Strong profiles.

Where response style has considerable effect it becomes difficult or impossible to interpret self-reports as if their face content were true (Jackson and Messick, 1958). The California *F* scale is a questionnaire developed for research on authoritarian personalities (Adorno, *et al.*, 1950). The items consist of strongly worded opinions most of which express a critical attitude about human nature. People who endorse these items tend to show other symptoms of readiness to follow strong, repressive political leadership, and hence the scale is labeled *F*, for "fascist." It was supposed, for a number of years following the publication of this scale, that it gave a dependable report of the subject's attitudes. Later, it was noted that virtually all the items in the scale were worded in hostile language, so that the response "Yes" was consistently scored as undesirable. Several investigators questioned whether the score reflected the content of attitudes or an acquiescent response style. To investigate this, a "reflected" scale was constructed. For each item an alternate version was written which had the opposite ostensible meaning. We may label this scale *F'*. Then a pair of items might be:

(F) Obedience and respect for authority are the most important virtues children should learn.
(F') Self-reliance and lack of need to submit to authority are the most important virtues children should learn.

In one study the number of statements marked in the authoritarian manner on the two scales ("Yes on *F*, "No" on *F'*) correlated only .20. The correlation would be .50 or beyond if responses were determined primarily by the content of attitudes (Bass, 1955; Messick and Jackson, 1957; Ancona, 1954; Chapman and Campbell, 1957).

Faking

The tester would like to view his inquiry as a scientific project to which the subject is willing to contribute valid information. The subject comes to the test with a quite different purpose. In a clinical test, he may want to avoid certain threatening diagnoses. In employment testing, his first concern is to land the job. In vocational guidance, he may be more concerned with convincing the tester that he should enter a certain occupation than with learning the truth about his suitability for it. When industrial workers filled out identical health questionnaires under two conditions, the results were strikingly different. One questionnaire was turned in to the company medical department, as a preliminary to a medical examination designed to improve the worker's health. The other questionnaire was mailed directly to a research team at a university. The workers listed far more symptoms on the research questionnaire (which would not help them) than on the other, even though an honest report to the company physician might bring them medical help (Streib, unpublished).

As might be expected, the subject most often presents himself in a favorable light (Edwards, 1957). On an item (e.g., Do you make friends easily?) where one response is socially desirable, the great majority of subjects will give that desirable answer. The subject's tendency to make favorable statements about himself, i.e., to put up a good front, is often referred to as a "façade" effect. Striving to make a favorable impression can be identified by counting how often favorable self-descriptions are checked. A high façade score may occur, of course, because the person is truly superior in behavior and adjustment; but persons whose behavior approaches the ideal on many dimensions are so unusual that faking is suspected.

Not all the subjects "fake good." Some deliberately give an unfavorable picture of themselves. A draftee who believes that a poor score on a personality questionnaire will get him a discharge may report an astonishing array of emotional symptoms. In an ordinary clinical test, exaggerating symptoms may be a gambit to enlist sympathy and attention. The subject may prefer to have the tester believe that troubles as a student are due to emotional disturbance than to be thought stupid or lazy.

A type of distortion which confounds evaluation of psychotherapy is the so-called "hello-goodby" effect. Upon entering the clinic, the client tends to present the worst conceivable picture of himself. He may not lie outright, but on borderline responses he selects unfavorable alternatives. This may be a calculated strategy to get the clinic to take his problems seriously and make therapy available to him or a sign of high awareness of symptoms.

Just the opposite effect is often noted when the client is discharged after treatment. Now the self-description glows with the psychological counterpart of "Thanks, Doc. I feel fine." This may involve self-deception, to prove that the sacrifice of time, money, and privacy was not foolish. One important motivation of faking good, Hathaway suggests, is the client's desire to repay the therapist by letting him see how much help he has given. It would be ungrateful indeed for the client to dwell on the symptoms the therapy had left untouched. On his exit questionnaire the client may be disposed to give himself (and his therapist) the benefit of all the borderline decisions. The number of symptoms is thus below the number reported at intake. The therapy may have produced genuine improvement, but true improvement is hard to distinguish from change in test-taking attitude.

Investigations of faking compare scores made under instructions to describe oneself honestly, with scores made when directed to try for a good score or a bad score. All these studies demonstrate that faking is possible; we need cite only two representative findings. Longstaff gave the Strong and Kuder tests to students with the usual instructions, and then asked them to try simultaneously to fake a particular pattern: high on certain keys and low on others. The results, some of which are given in Table 59, indicate that

TABLE 59. Percentage of Male Students Able to Fake Strong and Kuder Scores Successfully

Scores "Faked Upward"								
Percentage reaching A on Strong keys	Carpenter	9	Chemist	91	Artist	86	Author	83
Percentage reaching 75th percentile on Kuder keys	Mechanical	32	Scientific	5	Artistic	83	Literary	51
Difference		−23		86		3		32
Scores "Faked Downward"								
Percentage reaching C on Strong keys	Accountant	26	Life insurance sales	20	Personnel manager	37	Office man	54
Percentage reaching 25th percentile on Kuder keys	Computational	30	Persuasive	70	Social service	70	Clerical	41
Difference		−4		−50		−33		13

Source: Longstaff, 1948.

both tests are fakable. On the whole, it is easier to fake high interests on the Strong and easier to fake aversion on the Kuder. The several keys are not equally fakable. Wesman (1952) gave the Bernreuter Personality Inventory with the following instructions: "I want you to pretend that you are applying for the position of salesman in a large industrial organization. You have been unemployed for some time, have a family to support, and want very much to land this position. You are being given this test by the employment manager. Please mark the answers you would give." The next week, the same inventory was filled out "as if you were applying for the position of librarian in a small town." The scores on the two occasions differed spectacularly, as Figure 77 shows. Studies such as these prove beyond dispute that personality tests can be falsified, no matter how constructed. Probably most applicants give more honest answers than did the students in these experiments, but the fact remains that the dishonest applicant can probably beat the test.

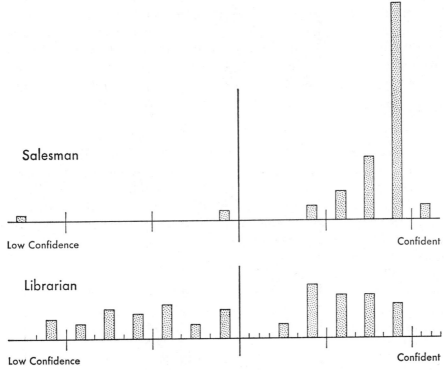

FIG. 77. "Self-confidence" scores of the same students when playing the role of applicant for sales and library positions (Wesman, 1952).

3. Some Strong items are obviously related to certain occupations, and these items are usually given higher weights than the subtler items which have a less direct relationship. Garry (1953) finds that when subjects attempt to fake interest in a particular field they answer the "obvious" items correctly. Most of them are unable to fake successfully on the items whose correlation with the criterion is lower and less obvious. Would it be a good idea to base Strong scores entirely on the latter items in order to thwart fakers?

OVERCOMING DISTORTION IN SELF-REPORT

Establishment of a Coöperative Relationship

In any interview or personality test, the psychologist appeals for coöperation and employs his skill as best he can to produce rapport. But rapport is a complex interpersonal relationship, depending on many factors other than the tester's technique. Never may the tester safely assume that he has established the ideal relationship which will cause the subject to want to tell "the whole truth." The tester's choice of questions and his subtle modification of the testing situation may cause the subject to shift back and forth from concealing to confessing, but there is little chance that he will come to rest at "objectivity." Moreover, as psychoanalytic interviews make clear, the subject's memory of his own life is so distorted by his emotional conflicts that long therapeutic sessions are required before he can bring to consciousness some of the important facts about himself.

Constraint upon Responses

Variation in response style is reduced or eliminated by forcing all persons to respond to the same issue. The most common technique is the "forced-choice" item seen in the Kuder inventory. Instead of using the somewhat ambiguous categories L, I, and D, Kuder asks which of three activities the subject likes best. Now the subject cannot say he likes everything, or withhold information by checking "Indifferent." The forced choice demands information regarding specific attitudes, traits, and interests.

Forced choice is especially useful as a means of reducing façade effects. The popularity ("social desirability") of each statement can be determined in a preliminary study. The test constructor then forms sets of statements having equal desirability. This increases the amount of information obtained, as can be seen from the following example. Three interest items might be:

	Percent of Subjects Saying "Like"
Watching Western movies	90
Driving in the country	90
Bird-watching	10

Administered separately, these would be inefficient for detecting individual differences, since 90 percent of the subjects give the same answer. If movies were paired with bird-watching in a preference item, results would be little better; at least 80 percent of the subjects would prefer movies. If the movie item is paired with the equally popular driving item, the forced choice will divide the subjects into nearly equal groups, thus obtaining a maximum amount of information about differences in interest.

The subject who wants to "fake good" is outwitted by the forced choice between equally desirable traits. He is required to describe *which* good statements are most characteristic of him, and *which* faults he suffers to the greatest degree. Navran and Stauffacher (1954) asked student nurses to rank fifteen needs (e.g., deference) in order of their social desirability. Each nurse also ranked the needs from most to least characteristic of herself. The correlation between these two rankings for any nurse would indicate her tendency to give a favorable picture of her own needs; this correlation was higher than .44 for the majority of nurses. A quite different result was found on the Edwards forced-choice inventory. In not one case did the rank order of Edwards scores correlate as high as .44 with the desirability ranking. Another study employed a direct measure of façade or self-favorableness. This score correlates .50 to .90 with Taylor's anxiety, Guilford's coöperation, and similar scales which score Yes-No answers. The highest correlation among the fifteen scales of the Edwards forced-choice instrument is .32 for the Endurance score (Edwards, 1957; R. E. Silverman, 1957). Although the Edwards scale forces the subject to give a profile with some low points, it is by no means proof against faking. A subject who can guess that certain good qualities are more important than others in decisions the tester will make can distort his responses to earn high scores in those qualities and low scores in qualities which seem unimportant on this occasion.

The forced-choice method has its defects. It requires more time to obtain an equal number of responses. It is sometimes resisted by subjects who object to its "Have you stopped beating your wife?" character. And it may reduce the validity with which the test predicts external criteria, for reasons discussed below.

4. What sort of personality would you try to show if "faking good"
   a. in a test to select Boy Scout leaders?
   b. in a test to select scientists for advanced training?
   c. in a test for psychiatric ward attendants?

Empirical Validity of Forced-Choice Instruments.   In some inventories, eliminating response sets eliminates the significant, criterion-related information from the scores. As mentioned earlier, the F scale measuring fascist tendencies seems to be largely influenced by acquiescence. This seemingly irrelevant influence may be desirable. Tendency to accept extreme statements may in itself be a symptom of an authoritarian outlook; if so, a forced-choice scale which ruled out differences in acquiescence would eliminate important evidence (Christie et al., 1958; Gage et al., 1957).

Our present knowledge about acquiescence, façade, and other response styles may be summarized as follows (Cronbach, 1950):

● General response styles obscure descriptive information. A person who says that he likes nearly everything tells us little about his particular interest patterns.

● Response sets can be modified by changing the directions. They are therefore to some extent transient, and irrelevant to the intended measurement.

● Response styles often correlate with practical criteria, but the correlations are not high.

• The response style involves three types of variation: transient and un-reliable attitudes, stable patterns which reflect criterion-relevant aspects of the personality, and stable but psychologically unimportant verbal habits. The forced-choice technique eliminates all three types of variation so that scores depend only on reactions to the content of items.

• Reliability is decreased by shifting to the forced-choice form, because choice is made difficult. The forced-choice instrument is ordinarily a purer measure of the criterion-relevant qualities in the test, because irrelevant verbal response habits are eliminated. Changing to the forced-choice form may or may not raise predictive validity because the loss in reliability may offset the gain in relevance.

The foregoing statements seem to vacillate between regarding response styles as beneficial and regarding them as an interference. The statements are reconciled when we recognize that the effect of response styles depends on test length. According to the argument developed on page 130, the effect of length depends on the purity of a test. A short impure test capitalizes upon the limited predictive validity of response styles and ordinarily gives a higher correlation with a criterion than does a short forced-choice test. When the number of items is very large, the purer forced-choice test is more valid (Osburn, Lubin, Loeffler, and Tye, 1954).

When the subject is motivated to give a favorable report on himself, even a short forced-choice questionnaire is likely to be advantageous. On an opinion or interest questionnaire, faking is not generally a serious problem. Since "every man has a right to his own opinion," no one set of answers is usually considered especially desirable. Unless the subject has a special reason for concealing his views, he will answer frankly. "The respondent's understanding of the purpose of the test and the psychologist's understanding are in agreement. Were the respondent to read the psychologist's report of the test results, none of the topics would surprise him" (Campbell, 1957).

Concealing the Purpose of the Test

Some tests of personality openly refer to themselves as measures of adjust-ment. More commonly, the title is less informative: for example, "The California Personality Inventory." The subject does not know what scores will be recorded and what interpretations will be made. He may guess something from the content of the items, but he is unlikely to suspect that interpretations will be made about his tendency to delinquency, among other things. It is harder for the subject to fake when he does not know what the tester is looking for, though in that situation he may become even more suspicious and defensive in his responses.

An effective method of concealment is to state a plausible purpose which is not the tester's real center of interest in giving the test. The F scale, for instance, is on the surface an inventory of opinions, but it is used to draw conclusions about the underlying personality. If the content of a test is such that subjects regard it as a measure of some ability, faking can be reduced or even eliminated. Campbell (1957) discusses use of measures of knowledge or reasoning ability as disguised measures of attitude. Another type of disguise uses questions having one ostensible content but employs a scoring method which has little or nothing to do with that content. One investigator asked boys to check which books they had read, seemingly to measure reading interests. Actually, he had inserted fictitious titles in the list, and the number of such titles checked was taken as one indicator of deceit or boasting.

While disguising one's purpose may be effective, it skirts the edge of unethical practice. And, as one writer has commented, to try to prevent deceptive subject behavior by becoming deceptive oneself merely encourages the view that psychologists are tricky, and in the long run may drive subjects to even greater degrees of evasiveness.

Verification and Correction Keys

The Kuder interest inventory has a special verification score, obtained by counting the subject's responses to certain items which are rarely chosen. A subject who made a large number of these rare responses probably answered the items without proper concentration. This by no means detects all types of distortion, but it is of value in group testing. Some subjects are too little motivated to make the many preference judgments seriously, and there are even some who lose interest and simply mark at random from that point to the end of the test.

The Edwards inventory uses 210 forced-choice pairs of statements. Fifteen pairs are presented a second time at random intervals within the test. A verification score indicates whether the student gave the same answer on the two occasions when he made the same choice. Some inconsistencies are to be expected, but numerous reversals suggest either careless response, resistance, or a seriously confused self-picture. Other inventories use a variety of check scores, including façade or social desirability keys and keys to detect response styles (e.g., a count of evasive "Cannot say" responses in the Minnesota Multiphasic).

The check score may be used most simply to eliminate suspect records. It is also possible to apply statistical corrections which estimate the score that would have been obtained with a normal response style.

5. If a high-school senior earns a suspiciously high verification score on the Kuder, what should the counselor do?

ALTERNATIVE INTERPRETATIONS OF RESPONSE CONTENT

No matter what special procedures are used to reduce distortion, the test re-sponses depend upon how much of the truth the subject is willing and able to report. Interpretation must take this fact into account.

Interpretation as True Self-Description

Simplest but most hazardous is to interpret the responses as a frank report of the subject's typical behavior. If the relationship between tester and sub-ject is such that this is a reasonable expectation, then no subtleties of test de-sign are required.

Complete frankness cannot be anticipated in any situation where the sub-ject will be rewarded or punished for his response. Some degree of reward and punishment is implicit in any institutional use of tests, such as clinical di-agnosis or employee selection. Honest self-examination can be hoped for only when the tester is helping the subject to solve his own problems, and even then the subject may have a goal for which he wishes the support of the counselor's authority, which biases his response.

Interpretation as "Published" Self-Concept

It is more reasonable to interpret the report as a statement of the subject's public self-concept than as a statement of his typical behavior or of his pri-vate self-concept. To be sure, his public self-concept should correspond in some measure to his behavior, but the ambiguity of test items and the inevi-table distortion in self-observation reduce this correspondence.

A historian, examining a diary written by a long-dead statesman, refuses to assume that the statements made therein are true reports of the man's be-liefs and feelings. Unless there is considerable evidence that the document was a private one never intended for the light of day, the safest assumption is that the statements represent the image the man wished to leave in his-tory. The psychologist likewise can regard the responses of his subject as a "published" self-concept, a statement of the reputation the subject would like to have.

Sometimes this information may be of considerable value. The fact that an individual is unable to admit certain kinds of tabooed impulses may be highly diagnostic. A person who presents too perfect a picture of himself may be expressing his fear that others are critical and punitive, and that he can maintain their respect only by keeping his halo bright. Unless there is some obvious motive for deceitful response, the psychologist should suspect that the person who presents so perfect a façade on the test maintains a similar façade in all his social relations. The façade of perfect control and freedom from impulse is a brittle one and can be maintained only at considerable emotional cost. Hence the façade itself has diagnostic and prognostic significance.

The person who admits to certain emotional problems may also be building up a public image. These may not be the most important problems of which he is conscious. It is commonly observed in psychotherapy that people do not bring out their main problems until several interviews have passed. When a person admits to problems which call for counseling, his report is an invitation to open counseling with an examination of the area mentioned. He is saying, first of all, that he is willing to be counseled; second, that this area is one which concerns him but is not too sensitive to be discussed. His most serious conflicts may be completely concealed by his questionnaire responses, but if he is unwilling to admit these conflicts he is probably also unwilling to deal with them immediately in psychotherapy.

6. A questionnaire is filled out by all parents belonging to a study group, as a means of identifying problems to be taken up in group discussion. Mr. Smith checks many problems having to do with developing the child's honesty, respect for the property of others, and care for his own property. The school counselor knows, however, that his son has been in difficulty several times because of aggressive fighting on the playground, window breaking, and other aggressive offenses which have been called to Mr. Smith's attention. Can the counselor draw any useful conclusion from Mr. Smith's self-report?

7. An attitude test for foremen presents hypothetical problems that might arise on the job and asks the subject to indicate what action he would take if he were foreman. Scores are based on response patterns (e.g., "takes quick action," "seeks facts," "emphasizes morale," "emphasizes cost-cutting"). What use can be made of the responses, in view of the obvious temptation to give a desirable picture?

Dynamic Interpretation

The clinical psychologist is unwilling to reduce personality to a statistical report of overt behavior. The clinician is concerned not with the number of times a person becomes emotionally upset but with the conditions under which this happens and the forces, internal and external, that lead to it. An individual who now becomes upset once per month might become chronically disturbed if conditions changed in a certain manner. In this event, a statistical average of his past behavior would have almost no predictive value. A "dynamic" picture of an individual is a picture of the forces changing his response as situations change. Important in such a picture are his perceptions of the people he deals with, his feelings about himself, and the needs which he is trying to satisfy. If the clinician has insight into these hidden characteristics, he then has some hope of predicting reaction to particular opportunities or stresses.

Drawing conclusions about personality dynamics even from an extended series of interviews is difficult, and a brief test or series of tests can only offer hypotheses of questionable validity. Tests are commonly used as a basis for dynamic interpretation, however, and highly experienced and insightful interpreters can use them profitably. The basic assumption of any dynamic interpretation is that every act of behavior is meaningful, even when it is inconsistent with other observations. The task of the interpreter is to seek some underlying unity which resolves the contradiction.

Dynamic interpretation requires extensive data about the individual's environment and difficulties as well as his test score, and considerable knowledge of personality theory. It can be demonstrated in a brief example, using an analysis by a University of California counselor. Barbara Kirk (1952) describes the pattern often found among academic failures or near-failures who do well on aptitude tests given at the Counseling Center. (Our summary is drastically condensed.)

The explanation and the excuses for the academic deficiency are unrealistic, superficial, and largely implausible. The counselee demonstrates no real recognition or admission of the reasons for this deficiency, but, on the other hand, he evidences no surprise at the results of the tests. He may be surprised that he was not tense or bothered on tests administered to him during counseling because he frequently has been tense or bothered during academic examinations. The impressions regarding the Minnesota Multiphasic Personality Inventory records in these cases are:

Most frequent is "psychoneurosis with compulsive and depressive features." Such [persons] tend to be pervasively resistant on an unconscious level to any externally imposed task. Since childhood, however, they have concealed such resistances from themselves and others by a façade of hard-workingness, meticulousness, and earnest dutifulness. In the unstructured environment of a university, the loss of the continued external pushing of teachers and parents permits the overthrow of the process of grudging achievement, and the resistances then manifest themselves in nonperformance.

The academic failure probably has meaning in terms of unconscious satisfaction of the hostility usually directed towards some member of the family who demands success, while the excellent scores on tests taken in a counseling situation may be interpreted also as hostile gestures. Because no importance is attached to these tests, the counselee is free to do with them as he wishes. It is a declaration, perhaps, of the lack of significance of his academic failure.

It can be seen that such interpretations involve considerable speculation, but they alert the counselor to conflicts that may emerge during counseling.

INTERPRETATION OF RESPONSES AS DIAGNOSTIC SIGNS

The risky assumption that the subject is telling the truth can be avoided if we interpret his response, not as self-description, but as an act of verbal behavior that is correlated with his inner nature. These two approaches have been characterized by Florence Goodenough as the "sample" and "sign" approaches. In regarding responses as samples of behavior, we use transparent items and pay primary attention to the content of the responses. We are at the mercy of the subject who wants to mislead us. If we plan to regard responses as signs, we can use items whose surface content is irrelevant to what we wish to measure, and even distorted responses may have diagnostic value.

The Strong blank, as originally employed, is based on the "sign" principle. Strong did not include activities in his Engineer key because they are part of the engineer's work; he asked only whether the response was characteristic of engineers. By counting dozens of such "signs," he distinguishes men who resemble the typical engineer from those who have little in common with engineers. The interpretation that a person belongs in a category is made on a strictly actuarial basis. Strong can say, "Persons with this combination of responses tend to become engineers" in the same way that an insurance examiner might say, "People with this combination of weight, blood pressure, and heart condition rarely live beyond 70." In strict actuarial interpretation, the tester makes no pretense of a rational connection between a particular response and the criterion. Engineers have greater than average liking for *The National Geographic Magazine;* prediction can be based on this fact whether or not any psychological significance can be attached to it.

The actuarial approach eliminates the assumption of honest self-report. The question "Is your health better or poorer than average for your age?" does not obtain valid facts about health. One person overrates his health in reporting; another who has only minor ills exaggerates them. If clinically diagnosed neurotics reply "poorer" more often than do normals, this answer may be diagnostic even when it is "untrue"—in fact, it may be diagnostic just because it is untrue. Empirical scales take the "attitude that the verbal type of personality inventory is *not* most fruitfully seen as a 'self-rating' or self description whose value requires the assumption of accuracy on the part of the testee in his observations of self. Rather is the response to a test item taken as an intrinsically interesting segment of verbal behavior, knowledge regarding which may be of more value than any knowledge of the 'factual' material about which the item superficially purports to inquire. Thus if a hypochondriac says that he has 'many headaches' the fact of interest is that he *says* this" (Meehl, 1945, p. 9).

The empirically scored test can be used for purposes the subject never suspects. The Strong ostensibly assesses vocational interests, but one scoring key combines those items which men answer differently from women into a "masculinity-femininity" score. It is presumably possible to distinguish communists from noncommunists, or girls who are likely to marry and stop working from those who are likely to remain in an occupation. The inventory could likewise be keyed to distinguish juvenile delinquents from nondelinquents, or potential suicides from nonsuicides. The basic principle is that any group which differs on one psychological quality differs on other qualities. Reports on some of these qualities are likely to be falsified to gain social approval. The remaining qualities, which carry no connotation of approval or disapproval, permit valid indirect measurement. Actuarial scoring is by no means certain to eliminate distortions, as the faking studies on the Strong blank show. Basing the scoring weights on empirical connections makes it more difficult for the subject to guess what significance will be attached to his statement that, for example, he likes to read the *Geographic*.

Within an empirically scored test, one can distinguish between items that are "obviously" related to a key and those whose connection is indirect. For example, in taking the Strong blank a boy trying to fake a high score as Engineer could be expected to indicate a marked liking for mathematics and technical subjects; these are "obvious items." He would be less likely to realize that interest in *The National Geographic* is characteristic of engineers; this item may be classified as "subtle." If we were to make up two scoring keys, one for obvious and one for subtle items, we would perhaps be able to make much more valid distinctions. A person who has a high score on both keys is more surely like an engineer than one who is high only on the obvious ones.

This suggestion was introduced in connection with the MMPI by D. N. Wiener (1948; see also Seeman, 1952) and regrettably has received little attention. Wiener developed separate keys for five of the MMPI clinical scales. No direct validity studies on these keys were carried out. There is evidence, however, that the subtle and obvious keys differ in their susceptibility both to façade effects and to response sets (Table 60).

TABLE 60.   Correlations of MMPI Scores with Measures of Façade Effect

Scale	Correlations with Façade Score for	
	Obvious Items	Subtle Items
Depression	−.78	.33
Psychopathic deviate	−.85	.27
Paranoia	−.72	.06
Manic	−.53	.40
Hysteria	−.71	.54

SOURCE: Fordyce and Rozynko, see Edwards, 1957, p. 47; see also Fricke, 1957; Hanley, 1957.

The usefulness of empirical tests depends primarily on the adequacy of the validation experiments. Sometimes absurd weights are assigned to items, suggesting that the original validation was based on inadequate sample. Allport (1937, p. 329) protests against a scale in which the word association "green" to the stimulus "grass" is scored +6 as a sign of "loyalty to the gang."

Loyal boys might have given this response more often in the sample tested than disloyal boys, but it is implausible that the same result would be found in further studies. Large and representative samples are crucial for establishing empirical keys. At best the validity of empirical keys is only moderate, since they rely on indirect information. Because they use subtle items they are less readily explained to clients than are tests using content interpretation.

8. Distinguish in each of these cases whether the investigator is assuming that self-reports are truthful:
   a. The clinical symptoms of condition x are determined by observation. A list of symptoms (swollen feet, rash, etc.) is prepared. This list is used to determine how frequent condition x is in several localities. Each subject is asked to check whatever symptoms he has.
   b. There are three general stages in social development in which a child names as favorites (1) other children without regard to sex, (2) persons of his own sex exclusively, (3) persons of the opposite sex. The investigators ask a child to name his favorite playmates as a means of determining his level of development.
   c. A psychologist administers to a group of applicants a checklist in which each marks the adjectives that describe him. The success of these men is observed, and a record is made of the characteristics checked by the successful applicants but not by the others. This checklist is then given to further applicants, and those who check the same characteristics as the previously successful men are hired.
9. What use could be made of a scale predicting what girls are likely to marry?

ETHICAL ISSUES IN PERSONALITY TESTING

Personality testing has flourished in two contexts, one institutional, the other individual. Valid information about personality would presumably be of great value to employers, college admissions officers, and others who make decisions to carry out institutional policies. In fact, personality tests were first applied to screen potentially neurotic soldiers. Such institutional testing tries to determine the truth about the individual, whether he wants that truth known or not. In noninstitutional testing, tests are applied for the benefit of the person tested. Here also the tester believes that learning the truth will be valuable but does not feel free to violate the person's wishes. The client who comes with an emotional difficulty wants the psychologist's assistance, but he may be quite unprepared to pay the price of unveiling his soul.

Any test is an invasion of privacy for the subject who does not wish to reveal himself to the psychologist. While this problem may be encountered in testing knowledge and intelligence of persons who have left school, the personality test is much more often regarded as a violation of the subject's rights. Every man has two personalities: the role he plays in his social interactions. and his "true self." In a culture where open expression of emotion is discouraged and a taboo is placed on aggressive feelings, for example, there is certain to be some discrepancy between these two personalities. The personality test obtains its most significant information by probing deeply into feelings and attitudes which the individual normally conceals. One test purports to assess whether an adolescent boy resents authority. Another tries to determine whether a mother really loves her child. A third has a score indicating the strength of sexual needs. These, and virtually all measures of personality, seek information on areas which the subject has every reason to regard as private, in normal social intercourse. He is willing to admit the psychologist into these private areas only if he sees the relevance of the questions to the attainment of his goals in working with the psychologist. The psychologist is not "invading privacy" where he is freely admitted and where he has a genuine need for the information obtained.

Some testers are regarded as "espionage agents" in industry (Otis, 1957). The newspapers have reported one case of a psychologist who developed for an industrial client an inventory intended to detect applicants with strong prounion attitudes, so that the client, by rejecting such men, could keep the union weak in his plant. As the tester finds increasingly valid ways of detecting what men feel and think, and as tests are increasingly imposed by schools, employers, and military services, there will be serious danger of conflict between the demands of the psychologist's employers and the rights of the person tested.

Responses have to be evaluated in terms of conformity to some ideal. The employer who used tests to detect union supporters dictated the attitude he wanted employees to have. If it is repugnant to find a powerful figure dictating what a citizen may say, it is unthinkable that he should have the power to punish unuttered thoughts. Yet that is what a subtle measure of attitudes threatens when used for institutional purposes. Defining certain score patterns as good necessarily makes the test a force toward conformity and standardization.

The use of personality tests for selection arouses resistance, as the prevalence of faking indicates. Calls for open rebellion flare up from time to time in the public press, a notable example being *The Organization Man*, the challenging book of essays by William H. Whyte, Jr. (1956), one of the editors of *Fortune*. He warns men seeking executive positions that they can count on favorable recommendations from the psychologist who examines them only if they display a particular pattern: extrovert, uninterested in the arts, and acceptant of the *status quo*. He advises them to fake "normality":

> . . . Give the most conventional, run-of-the-mill, pedestrian answer possible. When in doubt about the most beneficial answer to any question, repeat to yourself

I loved my father and my mother, but my father a little bit more.
I like things pretty much the way they are.
I never worry much about anything.
I don't care for books or music much.
I love my wife and children.
I don't let them get in the way of company work.

Whyte is certainly incorrect in describing this one interpretation as representing the practice of all industrial psychologists concerned with executive selection, but regardless of what the psychologist concludes, the firm to which he reports is likely to prefer the man who has "safe" attitudes.

The *Standards of Ethical Behavior for Psychologists* (1958) include the following principles:

● The psychologist in industry, education, and other situations in which conflicts of interest may arise among varied parties as between management and labor, defines for himself the nature and direction of his loyalties and responsibilities and keeps these parties informed of these commitments.

● [When serving the individual] the psychologist informs his prospective client of the important aspects of the potential relationship that might affect the client's decision to enter the relationship.

● The psychologist who asks that an individual reveal personal information in the course of interviewing, testing, or evaluation, or who allows such information to be divulged to him, does so only after making certain that the person is aware of the purpose of the interview, testing, or evaluation and of the ways in which the information may be used.

No ethical objection can be raised to the use of subtle techniques and even of misleading instructions when the information so obtained will be used entirely for research purposes, the subject's identity being concealed in any report. Even when the tests are intended solely for research, the tester should not be a person who has other responsibilities toward the subject (e.g., his teacher or therapist) except under the conditions described below.

Whether serving an institution or serving an individual client, the tester should not use indirect and misleading techniques unless the subject clearly understands that "anything he says may be used against him." To be sure, an employer may regard his refusal to submit to tests as grounds for denying him employment, but this is ethically preferable to obtaining deceitfully information he does not wish to give.

In a clinical setting, the psychologist can likewise offer a choice, with an introduction of approximately this character (see also pp. 293–296): "It might help to solve your problem more rapidly if we collect as much information as we can. Some of our tests use straightforward questions whose purpose you will readily understand. Some of our other tests dig more deeply into the personality. Sometimes they bring to light emotional conflicts that the person is not even conscious of. Few of us admit, even to ourselves, the whole truth about our feelings and ideas. I think I can help you better with the aid of these tests."

The client may refuse to take disguised tests if he is not ready to trust the psychologist with full knowledge of his personality. If this is the case, the information probably could not be used constructively in counseling him. In counseling it is both advantage and disadvantage that direct, unsubtle tests are no more than tabulations of statements made by the person about himself. While they uncover no secrets, they frequently accelerate the counseling process because they represent things he is ready to discuss with the counselor.

There remains the question of using personality tests when the tester has authority over the person tested. The psychologist diagnosing mental patients, the military psychologist, or the schoolteacher can enforce tests on his charges. The standards with regard to such practice probably should vary from institution to institution. In general, it seems that subtle tests may properly be used if they are valid and relevant in making decisions which would otherwise rest on less valid information. The tester should avoid misrepresentation in giving the tests. For example, it is quite improper to study an individual's beliefs under the guise of an opinion poll. Test records made for employee counseling should never be made available to the employee's superiors.

10. Would it be proper for a psychologist working in a government intelligence agency to develop a key for scoring the Strong or MMPI so as to detect communists among college students?
11. Should a test used in premarital counseling, given separately to both engaged persons to determine their suitability and probable success as marriage partners, use direct or subtle questions?
12. Is it ever "an invasion of privacy" to administer an ability test to a prospective employee?
13. The Minnesota Teacher Attitude Inventory attempts to identify teachers who have the attitudes that lead to high ratings from principals. Which would be best in a school staff: uniform attitudes or variety?

Suggested Readings

Krugman, Morris. Changing methods of appraising personality. *Proceedings, 1956 Invitational Testing Conference.* Princeton: Educational Testing Service, 1957. Pp. 48–57.

In an evaluation which stresses the inadequacy of questionnaires and projective techniques, Krugman's composite of extracts from test reviews and his statement of emerging trends are of particular interest.

Longstaff, H. P., & Jurgensen, C. E. Fakability of the Jurgensen Classification Inventory. *J. appl. Psychol.*, 1953, **37**, 86–89.

This describes an illustrative experiment on faking of a forced-choice inventory under different sets of directions.

McClelland, David C. Roles and role models. *Personality.* New York: Dryden, 1957. Pp. 289–332.

Describing personality in terms of typical behavior is not completely satisfactory because behavior varies with the situation. McClelland illustrates and accounts for such inconsistency in terms of changing social roles.

Meehl, P. E. The dynamics of "structured" personality tests. *J. clin. Psychol.*, 1945, **1**, 296–303. (Reprinted in G. S. Welsh & W. G. Dahlstrom (eds.), *Basic readings on the MMPI in psychology and medicine.* Minneapolis: University of Minnesota Press, 1956. Pp. 5–111.)

Meehl argues that self-report is undependable and uninterpretable if taken at face value, and defends actuarial keying as the only suitable method of obtaining useful insight from questionnaires.

Whyte, William H., Jr. The tests of conformity. *The organization man.* New York: Doubleday Anchor, 1956. Pp. 201–222.

This is a scathing critique of personality tests as used in executive selection. Examine also the Appendix, How to cheat on personality tests.

16

Personality Measurement Through Self-Report

HISTORY OF PERSONALITY INVENTORIES

IN INTRODUCING personality measurement we have spoken of it as an attempt to assess "typical behavior." This phrase, which has served our purposes to this point, echoes the viewpoint of behavioristic psychology, which is concerned primarily with overt, observable responses. The behavioristic outlook is somewhat limiting, however, and we can understand personality assessment better if we recognize that its development has been strongly influenced by the attitudes of *phenomenological psychology*. Phenomenological psychology is concerned with the way the world appears to the individual, with his so-called private world. Such expressions as *self-concept, feelings of hostility,* and *attitude toward authority* refer to perceptions and reactions occurring within the individual. Many important psychological events such as hallucinations and dreams exist only in the person's consciousness. It can be argued that almost all crises of adjustment are shaped more by the individual's perception of events than by the events themselves. As a consequence, many psychologists are more concerned with the subjective reactions of the person than with his outward responses.

The first personality questionnaires were developed in an attempt to study the inner world of perception and feeling. Sir Francis Galton in the 1880's devised the technique when he needed a standard procedure which could be applied to numerous subjects for his studies of mental imagery. Use of questionnaires, again for research purposes, was extended later in the nineteenth century by G. Stanley Hall in his vast studies of adolescent development. He used information given by large samples of adults to delineate normal trends in development, being little concerned with single individuals.

The questionnaire served rather different functions for the two men. In

Galton's work, self-report was used as the only possible way to obtain information on events within the respondent's head. Hall's self-report was used to avoid the labor and delay involved in direct observation of behavior.

1. Which of these problems or topics of research falls within behavioristic psychology, and which within phenomenal psychology?
   a. How frequently does mood change in the typical woman?
   b. How much does speed of reading decline in the presence of loud, continuous noise?
   c. Do managers and workers describe the company policy on selecting workers for promotion in the same way?
   d. What is this child afraid of?

Adjustment Inventories

The first inventory primarily concerned with assessing the individual was the Woodworth Personal Data Sheet. The U.S. Army, at the beginning of World War I, wanted to detect soldiers likely to break down in combat, but individual psychiatric interviews were not practicable when recruits were processed by the thousand. Woodworth made a list of symptoms such as psychiatrists would touch upon in a screening interview and presented the list as a questionnaire. This pencil-and-paper version of the interview presented questions such as a psychiatrist would ask: "Do you daydream frequently?" "Do you wet your bed?" etc. It differed from the interview only in that the sensitivity of individual questioning was sacrificed for speed. Men who reported numerous symptoms were singled out for further examination. The test was valued because it had appreciable power to detect maladjusted soldiers in a situation where individual interviewing of every man was totally out of the question.

The Woodworth scale was a forerunner of a number of "adjustment inventories," which consist primarily of lists of problems, symptoms, or grievances to be checked. These instruments make little claim to subtle description of personality, often yielding only a single score representing level of adjustment. Sometimes only one type of symptom is emphasized, as in the Cornell Medical Index covering psychosomatic complaints. Sometimes the items are grouped by logical categories, as in the Bell Adjustment Inventory, which has scores for home, health, social, and emotional adjustment based (respectively) on items such as[1]

[1] Items quoted in this chapter come from various tests and are used by permission of the copyright holders: Bell Adjustment Inventory, copyright 1934, 1938, 1959, Consulting Psychological Press; Minnesota Multiphasic Personality Inventory (MMPI), copyright 1943, University of Minnesota, published by The Psychological Corporation; Thurstone Temperament Schedule, copyright 1949, Science Research Associates; Minnesota Personality Scale, copyright 1941, The Psychological Corporation; Minnesota Counseling Inventory, copyright 1953, University of Minnesota, published by The Psychological Corporation.

Has either of your parents frequently criticized you unjustly?

Are you subject to eye strain?

Would you feel very self-conscious if you had to volunteer an idea to start a discussion among a group of people?

Do you get discouraged easily?

An adjustment inventory consists of items that differentiate subjects known to be maladjusted from subjects judged normal.

One principal use of such inventories is to identify those who should be offered counseling. While "problem cases" who cause trouble are easily recognized, children and adults who are withdrawn and insecure may not attract the attention of observers. An adjustment inventory brings to light many of these cases. Simple though the inventory may be, it can play a valuable role in large guidance programs. Some indication of the demand for such aids is the fact that one modest inventory reported, after ten years of distribution with no special advertising, that half a million copies had been sold.

Adjustment inventories are best regarded as screening instruments which single out persons who freely check symptoms and self-criticisms. They are not definitive measures of any clearly defined trait; such information as they provide is superficial at best.

Trait Descriptions

During the period from 1920 to 1945, psychologists were largely behavioristic in outlook and unwilling to base conclusions on the individual's introspections. The inventory was thought of as primarily a substitute for observation of behavior, and the questions placed more emphasis on what the individual did than upon how he felt or what he thought. The questionnaire was broadened to describe as many aspects of behavior as possible, and responses were summarized by giving scores on a number of "traits" or response patterns. Personality was conceived during this period as a bundle of habits. The individual was described by the strength of such traits as friendliness, confidence, persistence, etc. A "strong" trait was one describing a response which he usually or frequently made.

In early inventories this list of traits or behavior categories to be scored was arbitrarily chosen. Some traits such as self-confidence came from common experience, and some such as introversion from personality theories. Dozens of instruments were produced, each taking items from its predecessors, adding a few new ones, and scoring them in new combinations. The best-known instrument of this period was the Bernreuter Personality Inventory, like the Bell Inventory in form but using more varied questions. It was scored for Neurotic Tendency (i.e., adjustment), Self-Sufficiency, Introversion, and Dominance.

A study of this scale by Flanagan marked the introduction of trait scores defined according to statistical rules. Flanagan adopted the principle that to deserve separate names, traits must have low correlations. He intercorrelated the Bernreuter scores of 305 adolescent boys (Table 61) and found

TABLE 61. Intercorrelations of Bernreuter Scores for Adolescent Boys

	Neurotic Tendency	Self-Sufficiency	Introversion	Dominance
Neurotic Tendency		−.39	.87	−.69
Self-Sufficiency			−.33	.51
Introversion				−.62
Dominance				

SOURCE: Flanagan, 1935.

the traits by no means independent. "Introversion," as there measured, is little different from "Neurotic Tendency," since items on social isolation and daydreaming carry large weight in both scales. Applying factor analysis, Flanagan found that Confidence and Sociability scores could account for the information carried by the four original keys, and he developed scoring keys for these traits. The scores correlate negligibly and thus do represent independent aspects of the self-report.

There followed a period when personality theory was wholly subordinated to a statistical search for "dimensions" which could summarize personality. Item intercorrelations led Guilford, for example, to suggest that introversion could be separated into social introversion (S), thinking introversion (T), depression (D), cycloid tendencies (frequent shifts of mood) (C), and restraint (R). Accordingly, he developed the Inventory of Factors S-T-D-C-R. Later he added eight more aspects of personality. The Guilford scales were not uncorrelated (resembling verbal and numerical reasoning scores in this respect). Other investigators therefore rearranged them into scoring patterns which they regarded as more efficient. Thurstone, for instance, accounted for much of the information in Guilford's thirteen scores by seven factors which he renamed reflective, sociable, emotionally stable, vigorous or masculine, ascendant or dominant, active, and impulsive. This game is interminable. One psychologist classifies the items finely, the second puts some of the small bundles together, the third redivides the large bundles in a new way—and each gives his own names to the factors. Until trait lists can be tied down to a definite theory or to external criteria, choice can be made only on aesthetic grounds. There is at present no consensus among factor analysts as to the number of factors that have been reliably identified, the best organization of them, or their most appropriate names.

Trait names, we may note in passing, are a source of serious confusion in the personality field. The meaning of "introvert" is twisted and turned so that it represents for one author a brooding neurotic, for another anyone who would rather be a clerk than a carnival barker. "Ascendance" ranges from spontaneous social responsiveness, in one theory, to inconsiderate and overbearing behavior in another. The verbal coinage has been so debased by popular usage and by questionnaire makers that some investigators try to free themselves by coining completely new terms. R. B. Cattell (1957) has succeeded in popularizing his word *surgency* to describe a certain pattern of energetic behavior, but he will surely encounter considerable resistance to such new-minted trait names as *parmia, premsia,* and *abcultion* (akin respectively to social extroversion, emotional sensitivity, resistance to intellectual culture). In the present Babel of trait names, the only useful way to discuss personality test data is to speak of "Guilford's Ascendance score," "CPI Dominance score," or "Thurstone Ascendant score," according to the measure used.

2. Does the Woodworth inventory employ the "sign" or the "sample" approach?
3. Some testers have treated Flanagan's two scoring keys as supplements to the four supplied by Bernreuter, reporting all six scores to describe an individual. Discuss the advisability of this practice.
4. Do you think that most introverts are emotionally maladjusted? Does the correlation of the *N* and *I* scales indicate good or poor construct validity?
5. What is a desirable score on a test such as the Bernreuter?
6. What does it mean to say that Henry falls at the 50th percentile in Sociability? Can his behavior be described in terms of a "habit"?

Criterion-Oriented Tests

Construction of personality questionnaires according to the "sign" principle used by Strong has been rare, chiefly because criteria in the personality field are disputable at best. One obvious point of departure is psychiatric classification. D. G. Humm developed the Humm-Wadsworth Temperament Scale with empirical keys to distinguish such groups as manic and paranoid. The use of this test was restricted to industrial psychologists given special training in Humm's method, and little of the research done with the test was reported.

Essentially the same approach to test construction and many of the same items were used in the Minnesota Multiphasic Personality Inventory. This scale, published in 1942, was very rapidly accepted and remains today the most widely used and most widely investigated of questionnaires. Although strictly empirical in its original conception, it proved to be relatively ineffective in allocating patients to diagnostic groups. The test has, however, grown in prominence because accumulated research and clinical experience permit the tester to interpret scores. It will be discussed at length below.

7. In developing an empirical scale for college students one might develop a key consisting of items that distinguish campus leaders from nonleaders. Suggest other criteria that might mark important personality dimensions.

8. An investigator believes that teachers can be characterized by the trait "content-centered" vs. "child-centered." Outline the procedure needed to make a self-report test by means of criterion keying.

Tests Derived from Personality Theory

Whereas both the factor analysts and the empiricists developed tests by blind groping to find what-correlates-with-what, the more recent trend in personality measurement is to define constructs on the basis of personality theory and to prepare items specifically to elicit information about those constructs. This is not wholly new; indeed, the earliest work on introversion was stimulated by Jung's personality theory. But that theory had little influence on the actual tests, beyond suggesting items for trial. Today, considerable research is going into the Myers-Briggs Inventory, whose items and scoring keys are explicitly dictated by Jungian theory. Other instruments which illustrate this trend are the Edwards Schedule (which derives from the Murray theory of needs), the Taylor Manifest Anxiety Scale (designed in connection with research on Hull-Spence behavior theory), and the California F scale for identifying "authoritarian" personalities. The theoretically oriented instrument often is confined to one single trait. To validate a test as a measure of even one construct requires extensive and painstaking research, and it is a brave investigator who tries to advance on more than one theoretical front at a time.

9. How many scores would you consider necessary to give a complete picture of personality?
10. The following items are taken from various personality inventories. Is any apparent purpose served by the alterations in form and wording?

    Did you ever have a strong desire to run away from home?
        Yes   No   (Bell Adjustment Inventory)
    At times I have very much wanted to leave home.
        True   False   Cannot Say   (MMPI)
11. Is any apparent purpose served by these changes of form and wording?

    Are you at ease in a large group of people?
        Yes   No   (Thurstone Temperament Schedule)
    I am a good mixer.
        True   False   (Calif. Personality Inventory)
    Do you like to mix with people socially?
        Almost always   Frequently   Occasionally   Rarely   Almost never   (Minn. Pers. Inventory)

DESCRIPTION OF THE MMPI

The Minnesota Multiphasic Personality Inventory (MMPI) holds a place among personality questionnaires comparable to that of the Strong among interest measures. It was constructed in a similar empirical manner and was subjected to exceptionally thorough research by its authors. It appeared at an opportune time, and great reliance was placed upon it during the rapid wartime and postwar expansion of clinical psychology. It contributed to and benefited from the postwar interest in clinical research, and as a result has been studied more adequately than any other personality test. There are 689 titles included in a bibliography covering MMPI research through 1954; at that time, the number of MMPI studies was 100 per year and the rate was still increasing (Welsh and Dahlstrom, 1956).

The MMPI was originally constructed by a psychologist, Starke Hathaway, and a psychiatrist, J. C. McKinley, to aid in diagnosis of clinical patients. A collection of 550 items was prepared by borrowing from older inventories and rephrasing diagnostic cues used by psychiatrists. Among the items to be answered "T," "F," or "?" (cannot say) are these:

> I believe I am being plotted against.
> It takes a lot of argument to convince some people of the truth.
> I wish I could be as happy as others seem to be.
> I drink an unusually large amount of water every day.

The content of these items is quite diverse. Some report observable behavior, some report feelings that could not be observed from the outside, and some express general social attitudes. Some items frankly report symptoms of abnormal behavior, whereas others appear to have no favorable or unfavorable connotation.

Scoring Procedures

Psychiatric Discriminant Keys. The scoring keys were developed with the intention of identifying patients with respect to such recognized psychiatric states as hysteria. Patients of each type were compared, item by item, with a so-called normal group drawn from visitors coming to a large city hospital. Items which distinguished paranoids from normals were counted in the *Pa* (paranoid) key. Paranoid patients tend to say "True" to the first of our specimen items ("plotted against") and it is included in the *Pa* key. The second item ("argument to convince some people") seems to imply a paranoid insistence on one's own ideas, but it does not differentiate paranoid patients from normals and is not in the *Pa* key. Instead, the evidence shows that responding *F* to this item is indicative of hysteria.

The contrast between the MMPI "sign" approach and the content-oriented approach of its predecessors is illustrated by the fact that certain items of the MMPI are also found in the Guilford homogeneous scales but are scored in the opposite direction.

For example, to say that most people inwardly dislike putting themselves out to help others, that most people would tell a lie to get ahead,
. . . are responses scored as paranoid on the Guilford-Martin; whereas
it is found empirically that these verbal reactions are actually significantly *less* common among clinically paranoid persons than they are
among people generally. This kind of finding suggests that paranoid
deviates are characterized by a tendency to give two sorts of responses,
one of which is obviously paranoid, the other "obviously" not. [Meehl
and Hathaway, 1946.]

The original scales developed by the test authors are as follows:

1. *Hs*—hypochondriasis ⎫
2. *D*—depression   ⎬ the so-called "neurotic triad"
3. *Hy*—hysteria   ⎭
4. *Pd*—psychopathic deviate
5. *Mf*—masculinity-femininity
6. *Pa*—paranoia
7. *Pt*—psychasthenia
8. *Sc*—schizophrenia
9. *Ma*—hypomania

Data for the reference group of normals provide a standard-score conversion
so that results can be plotted on a profile sheet as shown in Figure 78. Primary significance is attached to scores greater than 70 (50 being the average
for the reference group). This cutoff is somewhat arbitrary, and interpreters
examine all peaks whether or not they cross this line.

Control Keys.   The MMPI is provided with several correction or control
keys intended to identify or make allowance for exceptional response
styles. The simplest group of control keys are known as *?*, *L*, and *F*.

The *?* score is the number of times the person replies "Cannot say." Exces-
sive evasion of questions of course makes it meaningless to compare the subject's responses with the standardization group. Profiles showing high *?*
scores are recognized as invalid.

There are some test items so worded that a person who denies having
these symptoms is almost certainly not evaluating himself frankly. One example is the "I sometimes put off until tomorrow what I ought to do today."
The *L* (lie) score is based on a count of such improbable answers. A high
L score indicates that answers are untrustworthy but need not indicate deliberate lying. The *L* key detects some cases of "faking good," but it cannot
be depended upon to detect faking by sophisticated subjects.

The *F* (false) score consists, like the Kuder verification score, of responses
given extremely rarely. A high *F* count reveals carelessness, misunderstanding, or otherwise invalid answers. The *F* score tends to be high for subjects

who attempt to fake bad records, because rare responses are usually un-favorable self-descriptions.

K, the fourth and most important control key, was designed on an empirical basis. It was found, early in the test development, that some quite nor-

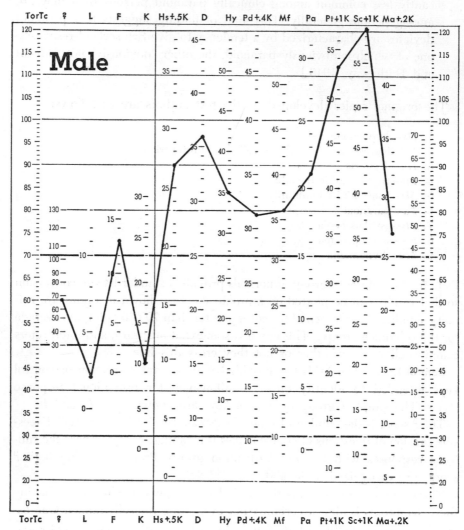

FIG. 78. MMPI record of a male mental patient. (Data from Shneidman, 1951, p. 221. Profile form copyright 1948, The Psychological Corporation. Reproduced by permission.)

mal individuals earn scores above 70 in *Hs*, for example, because of what have been called "plus-getting" attitudes. That is to say, these persons reply with such complete frankness or self-depreciation that their response patterns appear abnormal. Among patients, on the other hand, there are a large number whose scores remain below 70 because of defensive denial of symptoms. In order to reduce the number of such misses and false positives in MMPI diagnosis, a key was made to measure defensiveness. The investigators identified items commonly marked by the clinical cases whose profiles were less deviant than they should have been. The K key composed of those items expresses a bland "all is well" façade, e.g.:

I have very few quarrels with members of my family. (T)
Criticism or scolding hurts me terribly. (F)

Whereas most control scores are used simply to signal untrustworthy profiles, the K scale is employed in a regression formula to correct the regular scales for test-taking attitude. Thus the original Hs scale was replaced by Hs + .5K. These corrected scales became the main keys for the test about 1946. Although our discussion of validity is to come later, we can give here one example of the effect of the correction. When 200 normals were compared with 101 hypochondriacal patients 5 percent of the normals and 62 percent of the patients exceeded an Hs score of 69.8. After correction, a cutting score which picked off 5 percent of the normals could detect 72 percent of the patients (McKinley et al., 1948). The "misses" were thus reduced from 38 to 28 percent. In subsequent studies by other authors, the K correction has not been found consistently valuable.

Still a further method of identifying faking is to score separately the obvious and the subtle items in any key (see pp. 458 ff.).

12. A client coming to a social agency has these MMPI scores:

Hs	D	Hy	Pd	Mf	Pa	Pt	Sc	Ma
43	45	50	50	50	68	42	67	69

How would the interpretation be affected if the "control scores" were as follows:
a. ?, 72; L, 50; K, 50; F, 50.
b. ?, 50; L, 73; K, 50; F, 50.
c. ?, 50; L, 50; K, 72; F, 50.
d. ?, 50; L, 50; K, 35; F, 50.

Descriptive Interpretation of Coded Profiles. Although MMPI scores derived from psychiatric diagnosis, the diagnostic categories *per se* play little part in its interpretation. At some point in the late 1940's, as Dr. McKinley reached the point of retirement and Paul E. Meehl became more actively identified with research on the scale, a new viewpoint began to replace the original diagnostic emphasis. By 1951 Meehl was ready to say (Meehl, 1951):

These days we are tending to start with the test, sort people on the basis of it, and then take a good look at the people to see what kind of people they are. This, of course, is different from the way in which the test was built, and different from the usual psychiatrist's notion of a test

> where you start with groups of people sorted out on some basis—for in-
> stance, by formal psychiatric diagnosis—and you try to build a test
> which will guess or predict or agree with that . . . criterion. . . . The
> idea that the primary function of psychometrics is to permit me . . . to
> prophesy what the psychiatrist is going to say about somebody is . . .
> not a very powerful way of looking at . . . the Multiphasic.

For Meehl's purpose, any set of reasonably uncorrelated scales would presumably have been at least as appropriate as the psychiatrically oriented
keys of MMPI. By the time this new viewpoint emerged, so much experience had been accumulated on the psychiatric scales that they could be replaced only with great loss. The subsequent work on the test has been an
attempt to work out meaningful interpretations for obsolete scales.

In arriving at a description of personality, it is customary to consider the
salient features of the MMPI profile simultaneously. The high and low
points are listed in terms of the code numbers given above. For example, a
32–6 profile is one in which scales 2 and 3 are exceptionally high with 3 being
highest, and 6 is exceptionally low. (This individual, that is, has high counts
in depressive and hysteric response categories, and is very much unlike the
paranoid.) Some clinicians use extremely elaborate codes, but two- or three-
digit codes are sufficient; if more detail is required, the original profile is
more satisfactory than the code.

When they introduce a numerical code, the MMPI developers attempt to
sidestep some of the consequences of having started originally from psychiatric diagnoses. The counselor should never tell a client that he has "a
high schizophrenic score." Such labels confuse even trained psychologists
when the test is applied outside the mental hospital. Thus, although the test
record forms still carry the labels *Pd, Sc,* etc., Meehl (1951) advises,

> If you can, get into the habit of using the code to talk about curves,
> instead of talking about the psychiatric category names. . . . It's worst
> to talk about the schizophrenia key; it's better to talk about the Sc key;
> it's best to talk about code 8. That is, of course, entirely in line with
> . . . starting with the test and looking at the people, instead of trying
> to guess the diagnosis. When you are working chiefly with relatively
> normal individuals, . . . it is still more desirable to avoid the psychiat-
> ric implication. . . . If you talk about the 87's and the 23's, then you
> can set up relatively fresh associations with the significance of those
> numbers.

Psychological significance is given to coded patterns by cumulating experience with each type. The principal depository of this information is an *Atlas*
which gives descriptions and case histories for nearly 1000 psychiatric patients, classified by profile type. To take one example, a 50-year-old man

tested upon admission showed score 2 (D) over 70 with 3 (Hy) next high-est, and with 9 and 6 (Ma and Pa) as low points. The staff diagnosis was "psychosis, manic-depressive, depressed state." After a month of treatment in a hospital, his profile had changed so that 8 and 9 (Sc and Ma) were above 70 and 2 (D) was lowest; but high L and F made this record suspect. At this time the staff changed the diagnosis to "paranoid," because the symptoms had changed. The third test for this patient came two years later, upon a readmission. At this time, he had returned to the 23 pattern, with no very low scores. His diagnosis was again manic-depressive, depressed. The case history from the *Atlas* follows (Hathaway and Meehl, 1951, p. 120):

The admission of this patient with severe depression of about two months' dura-tion was the latest of several such episodes, with seclusiveness, poor memory, in-ability to work, and somatic complaints the outstanding characteristics of the de-pression. When he was working, he misplaced tools; and he was convinced that people watching him noticed the poor quality of his work. He complained of fail-ing memory; he slowed down physically and mentally; he suffered from insomnia; there was loss of appetite; and in general he lost contact with his surroundings. Lacking energy, he found it very difficult even to dress himself or go to meals. His speech was retarded and incoherent at times.

A year before admission there had been a similar attack from which he had re-covered after six electroshock treatments. Until this first attack, his behavior had always been normal. His intelligence was average. A shy person, not socially ag-gressive, withdrawn, and moderately religious, he had always been kind and had never lost his temper. A premarital dependency on his mother was later transferred to his wife. His general adjustment to society was adequate although he was known as a "drifter," and at best he held only semiskilled jobs. Throughout his life there had been a history of cyclic mood swings in which he moved from periods of elation to periods of depression.

On admission he showed rather severe psychomotor retardation. He did not appear to be delusional. He had no paranoid ideas, nor was he suicidal. His sen-sorium and intellect were intact, and he had some insight into the depression. There was marked apathy, but he was cooperative and expressed the hope that he might be "well again." After shock therapy, which brought about rather marked change, he became more disoriented, careless, and talkative. He showed some regression, answered questions foolishly, and was occasionally euphoric, unco-operative, loud, and demanding. With the continuation of the shock treatments his behavior became more acceptable and five days after the last of the eleven treatments he was discharged with almost complete remission of his symptoms. At that time it was felt that he would probably have another depression. Twenty months later the patient returned to the hospital. Following his first discharge, he had been euphoric and unstable for about three months, then had begun to slip into another depression which persisted until the second admission. He was dis-charged after seven shock treatments and was to return to the outpatient clinic for supportive care. The prognosis about a further relapse was very guarded.

In this record we may note several points, the first being the essential con-sistency of the two records taken upon admission, two years and eleven shock treatments apart. The intermediate record, taken while behavior was disorganized, showed a markedly different pattern, but its truthfulness was challenged by the control scores. The high D scores in the admission profiles are consistent with the clinical picture, and the high Hy scores are consistent with his "withdrawn, kind, dependent" exterior. The inadequacy of his defenses, however, led the psychiatric staff to classify him as psychotic rather than neurotic. This illustrates the important point that even though MMPI scales use psychiatric language, they are descriptions of personality patterns rather than direct diagnoses.

There is no simple translation from MMPI information into descriptive terms. The user of the test must build up a repertoire of information from the *Atlas,* from other studies scattered through the literature, and from his clinical experience. For our purposes, the meanings of the scales can be introduced by Black's study with an adjective checklist. Each of 200 women students at Stanford rated other girls residing in her dormitory by checking adjectives which best described her. The girl also described herself on the checklist and took the MMPI. The statistical tabulation then showed which adjectives were applied to girls with high scores on any MMPI scale. Table 62, based on a portion of the results, shows what reputation (i.e., typical overt behavior) and what "published" self-concept goes with each MMPI score. The tabulations are based on small groups and are therefore indicative of general trends rather than of well-established associations.

Studies such as this extend MMPI interpretation to normal personalities. The various MMPI scales do seem to depict different types of personality. A high score on 9 (Ma) may not indicate pathological lack of control, but it does indicate a colorful, dynamic, self-assertive person. Many other scales pick out recognizable types of overt behavior.

The difference between the self-ratings and ratings by others is striking. The girls frequently use favorable adjectives to describe characteristics which others describe in less flattering terms. The high 9's say, for example, that they are enterprising and courageous, while others call them boastful and selfish. The self-description in some cases, indeed, is diametrically opposed to the reputation. The high 9's see themselves as popular and peaceable, but acquaintances apply these adjectives to them rarely. This strongly reinforces the view that the self-description is a statement of what the person believes about himself or what he wants others to believe, and not an adequate report of typical behavior. On the other hand, the MMPI's indirect "sign" interpretation of the self-description may come close to typical behavior by stating what a claim of popularity "really" means.

Supplementary Keys. Numerous investigators have tried to develop supplementary keys to identify subgroups of various types. Welsh and Dahlstrom (1956) mention 100 supplementary keys, including scales for socio-economic status, dominance, prejudice, and social introversion. These scales have not gained wide usage.

Among the many scales derived from the MMPI, one has attained special prominence in clinical diagnosis and research, and it, oddly, was not intended

TABLE 62. Typical Behavior and Self-Descriptions Associated with MMPI Scores of College Women

Scale or Pattern with High Score	N	Description by Dormitory Mates	Self-Description
2. Depression	16	Shy, not energetic, not relaxed, not kind	Shy, moody, not energetic, not relaxed, not decisive
3. Hysteria	25	Many physical complaints, flattering, not partial, not clever	Trustful, friendly, not emotional, not boastful
13 or 31. Hypochondriasis with hysteria	9	Many physical complaints, indecisive, high-strung, seclusive, eccentric, apathetic	Affectionate, partial, not orderly, not conventional
4. Psychopathic deviate	26	Incoherent, moody, partial, sociable, frivolous, not self-controlled	Dishonest, lively, clever, not adaptable, not friendly, not practical
5. Masculinity	15	Unrealistic, natural, not dreamy, not polished	Shiftless, not popular, unemotional, not having wide interests
5 low. Femininity	68	Worldly, not energetic, not rough, not shy	Self-distrusting, self-dissatisfied, sensitive, shy, unrealistic
6. Paranoia	24	Shrewd, hard-hearted	Arrogant, shy, naïve, sociable
7. Psychasthenia	20	Dependent, kind, quiet, not self-centered	Indecisive, soft-hearted, depressed, irritable
9. Hypomania	52	Shows off, boastful, selfish, energetic, not loyal, not peaceable, not popular	Enterprising, jealous, courageous, energetic, popular, peaceable, self-confident

SOURCE: After Black; see Welsh and Dahlstrom, 1956, pp. 151–172.

for practical use. Spence and Taylor wished to test the effect of anxiety upon learning, in an extension of Hull's theory of drive (Spence, 1958). They presumed, from previous theory, that persons with marked, admitted anxiety symptoms had higher levels of drive and thus would more quickly acquire a conditioned defense reaction. In order to identify extreme groups by a simple, unsubtle measure of anxiety, Taylor requested experienced counselors to choose MMPI statements which constituted overt admissions of anxiety. The items so selected were combined into a short questionnaire and used for the laboratory studies of learning. When a puff of air onto the eye was associated with a bright light, eyeblink responses to the light stimulus were far more numerous among the "nonanxious" subjects (J. Taylor, 1951). The questionnaire was subsequently adopted by many investigators and clinical counselors, under the name of the Taylor Manifest Anxiety Scale. The scale has not been standardized, validated, or published in the usual sense, and it appears to have no special virtues to recommend it for clinical purposes over other adjustment indicators.

VALIDITY OF INVENTORIES FOR SPECIFIC DECISIONS

Screening of Deviant Personalities

Separating Patients from Normals. Although the MMPI was designed with psychiatric diagnosis as a criterion, the authors early abandoned claims that the test had great power as a discriminant. Some of the scales had reasonably satisfactory relations to the criterion, but others were regarded as questionable even at the time of publication. In papers by the test authors one finds many remarks like these: "The evidence for the validity of *Ma* is certainly not conclusive." The published version of the *Sc* scale "was only slightly better than the ones that were rejected." "The *Pt* scale has never been considered very satisfactory." And for *Pa,* "Cross-validation was always disappointing." This frankness is in welcome contrast to the glowing accounts of other test developers who have made less effort to validate their instruments.

Under favorable conditions, the various scales (except 5, 7, and 8, which are especially weak) have more or less the same discriminating power. A cutting score which yields 5 percent false positives among normals will identify from 62 to 74 percent of the patients in the category to which the scale corresponds. The precise character of the data is indicated in Figure 79, which shows the distribution on scale 2 (*D*) of 690 normals and 35 patients who had previously been identified as clinically depressed. The data show a distinctly higher mean for the patient group, 63 percent of them falling at or above 73, which is the 95th percentile for normals. It is hard to say without further analysis whether the screening validity is high enough to be useful. In order to face this question, we must take into account the number of true depressive cases in the population likely to be tested (Meehl and Rosen, 1955).

As an illustration, let us assume that among the persons coming to a clinic 50 percent are depressed. Then let us change this figure to other base rates: 20 percent, 5 percent, and 2 percent. Figure 80 plots the probability that a person with each score will be depressed, using the distributions of Figure 79 with each base rate in turn. Again, we see the clear relation between score and probability of being properly called a depressed patient. The value of the test in diagnosis depends heavily on the base rate. One will be right 80 percent of the time if classifying a person with a score of 70 on scale 2 as depressive—*if* depressives constitute half of a clinic's intake. If, as is more probable, the proportion of depressives is 20 percent, one must shift the cut-

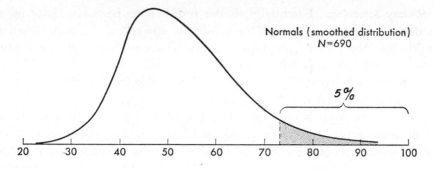

Normals (smoothed distribution)
N=690

5%

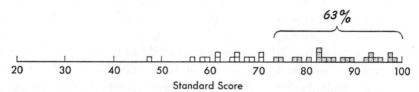

Depressed Patients N=35

63%

Standard Score

FIG. 79. Distributions of normal and patient groups on MMPI scale 2 (D) (Starke R. Hathaway and J. C. McKinley, 1942).

ting score to 83 to have the same confidence in a borderline diagnosis. Such a shift, however, leaves over half the depressive group undetected. A poor *D* score is therefore far from dependable as an indicator of maladjustment. A good score does permit confident judgments; with any reasonable base rate, the tester can be sure that a person scoring 50 or below is very unlikely to be depressive. If these low scores are passed over while the remaining cases are submitted to further interviewing or testing, virtually no depressives will be overlooked.

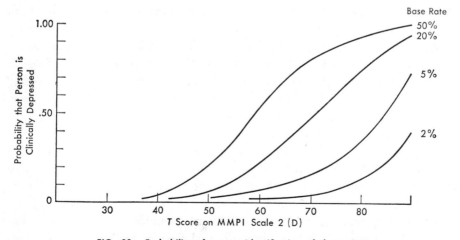

FIG. 80. Probability of correct identification of depressives.

Military Screening.   Essentially similar results have been found for other modern questionnaires, though the validity of any test varies from situation to situation. Short, undisguised questionnaires have been of distinct value for screening military populations (W. A. Hunt and I. Stevenson, 1946). An inventory of only twenty items was profitably used by the Navy to determine which men should be seen by psychiatrists for examination and possible discharge as unfit. With a cutting score set to allow 5 percent false positives, 53 percent of the discharges could be identified. A questionnaire given 2081 Seabees successfully identified 281 cases later adjudged by psychiatrists to present neuropsychiatric conditions, missed 16 who came to the psychiatrists' attention through difficulty on duty, and falsely picked up 244 men judged normal upon further study (D. H. Harris, 1945). This means that the tests permitted psychiatrists to omit individual interviews with 1540 men—not a trifling saving.

Screening of Students.   Attempts to screen students to find those requiring counseling have been more disappointing. Over 800 college students were interviewed repeatedly during the year by counselors who then made a diagnosis of the kind and extent of maladjustment (Darley, 1937). The Bell Adjustment Inventory given at the start of the year identified 40 students truly having problems relating to home adjustment, but missed 41, and produced 73 false positives. On emotional adjustment, there were 32 hits, 75 misses, and 42 false positives. In a study of the Bernreuter, an exceptionally good criterion was used—observation records gathered continually during the year. Of sixteen girls at the maladjusted extreme on the Neurotic Tendency scale (out of 81 subjects), only six were considered actually maladjusted, whereas two of those least maladjusted according to the test were rated maladjusted on the criterion. The Self-Confidence scale was more successful. Ratings agreed with test scores for all ten girls showing extremely low confidence on the test, and for six of eight whose test scores showed high confidence (Feder and Baer, 1941).

Although errors are too frequent to warrant trust in questionnaires as indicators of maladjustment, scores have validity better than chance. Stogdill and Thomas (1938) found that the *mean* score among students reporting voluntarily for counseling was significantly deviant on the Flanagan keys. The correlation of Self-Confidence with rated maladjustment was .59 for men. Overlap in scores between normal and counseling groups was too great for screening validity. Correlations with ratings were of negligible size in a group of probationary students referred for assistance; any such test is more likely to be valid in groups seeking assistance than in groups who are uncooperative.

Identifying problem cases by self-report methods at earlier ages has proved to be very difficult. Investigators who compare known delinquents with normals find some differences in scores, but the scores of the groups overlap so much as to discourage reliance on the tests for screening. On the Heston Personal Adjustment Inventory, 30 to 48 percent of delinquents (compared to 8 to 16 percent of a matched control group) fell below the 20th percentile on Emotional Stability, Confidence, and two other scales (Hathaway and Monachesi, 1953). This relation is far poorer than the level of discrimination achieved by psychiatric interviewing.

An exceptional study tested all ninth-graders in Minneapolis and followed the 4000 cases for two years. Predictive validity was examined by comparing those who later became delinquents with the remainder. Several significant differences were found, the main results being indicated in Table 63. Scales F and 4 were prognostic of delinquency, and codes 2, 5, and 7 were relatively rare among delinquents. The F scale proved to be the most indicative of potential delinquency. Scale 4 indicates an acting-out, impulsive personality, insensitive to social controls.

TABLE 63.   Rate of Juvenile Delinquency for Various MMPI Profile Types

High Score	Percent of All Boys Falling in Code Class	Percent of Boys in Code Class Who Became De-linquent	Percent of All Girls Falling in Code Class	Percent of Girls in Code Class Who Became De-linquent
F	5	48	3	22
4 (Pd)	21	28	19	12
9 (Ma)	21	22	17	8
2 (D)	4	12	1	3
5 (Mf)	5	9	17	5
7 (Pt)	6	19	7	4
Total, all classes	100	22	100	7

SOURCE: Hathaway and Monachesi, 1953, p. 131.

13. What does Table 63 indicate about the practical value of MMPI for screening potential delinquents?

14. Is concurrent or predictive validity the primary concern in screening studies?

15. What importance can be attached to the finding that *Pd* scores decrease markedly with age?

Limitations of Validation Studies.   The studies above are based on a consideration of one score at a time. Writers on the MMPI have stressed judgments based on all scores together. It is well established that a deviant group has high averages on several scales, not just the one "appropriate" to its diagnosis, and this is a reasonable finding since a disorder often involves many types of symptoms. The argument is made, therefore, that screening should take into account many scores at once by means of a linear combination, a nonlinear combination, or a multiple cutoff pattern. (See Chapter 12 for the distinctions between these methods.) While one can find dozens of papers arguing for such screening methods, it is difficult to locate evidence about the accuracy of multiscale analysis or evidence comparing it to single-scale screening. Statistical studies of this question are few and inadequately reported. One reason, of course, is the shift in emphasis from actuarial interpretation to descriptive interpretation shortly after the MMPI scales were put into their final form; another, the fact that too few cases of any one pattern are found for adequate statistical summary. Some evidence on the use of MMPI patterns to distinguish between types of patients is presented below.

Before trying to explain the generally poor performance of inventories as screening devices, let us emphasize certain aspects of the design of validation studies. These points are important because some articles report striking success in predicting various criteria, and in many instances the apparent success merely results from improper analysis. The first error to be noted is validation of a key or scoring formula on the same cases used to select items and establish weights. As was pointed out in Chapter 12, cross-validation is essential to avoid giving credit for chance discriminations peculiar to the sample studied.

A second common fault is to demonstrate significant differences (e.g., between delinquents and normals) without examining the base rate. The usefulness of a screening or categorizing instrument depends upon the number (not the percentage) of misses and false positives at any cutting score. Given enough cases, highly significant differences can be established for instruments which have no practical value.

A similar remark is to be made about comparisons of extreme groups. Gough (1957) shows a very significant difference on the *Sa* scale of the California Psychological Inventory between boys nominated by principals as most and least self-accepting. This comparison is based on 52 boys in each group, selected from among six high schools. Gough computes a biserial correlation of .46 for these data. But as can be seen in Figure 20, there can be a great difference between extreme groups even when the correlation based on the entire population is very low. A correlation coefficient must be computed on (or estimated for) the entire population to whom the test will be applied. If, as Gough's report seems to indicate, the principals nominated the extreme 1 percent of their student bodies, a recomputation indicates that the true validity of *Sa* is approximately .15, not .46.

Explanation of Results. The discouraging results for even the best available inventories can be explained in two rather different ways. The defender of the inventory will argue that the evidence is, on the whole, favorable; the critic will argue that the inventory is inefficient either in principle or because of poor design. The defender can argue that the criteria used in validation and in scale construction are themselves invalid, and, indeed, that a test which predicts diagnosis perfectly would be far from a true picture of personality. The diagnosis of maladjustment is controversial at best. Psychiatrists disagree as to what categories should be used and disagree in their classification of individuals. Clinical staffs have such marked biases toward the use of certain diagnoses that it has been said, only half jokingly, that whether a patient is called psychotic or neurotic depends as much on the hospital he enters as on his symptoms.

Meehl insists that the diagnosis is at best only a starting point. Just as Binet started with bright pupils selected by teachers, the Minnesota testers started with diagnosed hypochrondriacs; but the intention in both cases was to develop an instrument which would be superior to the starting criterion—i.e., which would in the end disagree with it. The Binet scale, they point out, has value precisely because it detects bright children that teachers overlook, and corrects the teacher's overfavorable evaluation of other cases. While the attack upon diagnoses is legitimate, one must be wary of any implication that when test and psychiatrist disagree the test is the more dependable. Evidence to support this type of claim has not been developed for the MMPI as it has for the Binet scales.

A second pertinent defense is that in many studies the criterion is crudely determined, even if in principle it could be made dependable. Thus the data on depressives presented above are probably unfair to the MMPI. The patient group included some cases who might have recovered from their depressive phase before testing, and the normal group, including as it did unhospitalized relatives of patients, may well have included numerous undetected depressives. More generally, nonpatient status is no guarantee of sound personality; many persons in the community have serious maladjustment which remains undetected only so long as they are exposed to no exceptional stress. The fact that the pressures of life are not the same for all persons greatly reduces the prospect of predicting behavior from personality measures.

It remains a question whether some other investigator could produce a better screening instrument than the MMPI. There are many reasons for thinking that it is far from the most efficient actuarial instrument that could be developed. In the original derivation of scales, the number of cases of each patient group was generally below fifty, and often below thirty; as a consequence, chance may have played a large part in assigning items to scales. Moreover, the patients and normals were quite differently motivated in taking the test, and neither had the motivation likely to be encountered when the test is used for screening. The scales have lower stability than desirable, the median for normals over one week being .80 (Cottle, 1950a). Items were combined with little regard for their intercorrelations, yet in actuarial prediction it is profitable to maximize item heterogeneity so as to raise the correlation of the scale with the criterion. Separate scoring of subtle and obvious items would probably be of value; despite the empirical origin of MMPI keys, there is evidence (McCall, 1958) that the obvious face-valid items carry almost all of the discriminating power. Finally, although it is evident that combining several scales can improve differentiation, no formula for combining the scales to separate normals from patients has been systematically validated. Even with improved test construction, the variation from one population to another (e.g., between a community clinic in a small town and a city hospital) may be so great that even the most powerful actuarial test will have very limited general validity.

We may summarize the findings on personality tests as screening instruments as follows: In dealing with large populations (military recruits, college students, etc.) where individual attention cannot be given to everyone, questionnaires validated on that type of population are of great value as a preliminary screen. Persons with better scores can be passed over while more systematic diagnostic procedures are applied to the remainder. The number of deviant cases missed is reduced if suitable methods to control faking are applied. It is never proper to assume that those earning poor scores on a questionnaire are seriously maladjusted; the number of false positives makes it imperative to regard the test as only a first stage of investigation.

Differential Diagnosis of Patients

The second original aim of the MMPI was to distinguish one type of psychopathology from another. Clinical psychologists are commonly required, especially in mental hospitals and outpatient clinics, to make a rapid decision as to the probable nature of the patient's disorder.

MMPI profiles for various diagnostic groups differ significantly, and experienced MMPI users can classify profiles with some success. Guthrie (1950) asked them to classify 89 records into six piles (paranoid, anxiety state, depressed, etc.), and found that accuracy ranged from 36 to 54 correct placements for various judges. Though substantially better than chance, this represents rather low accuracy for diagnostic purposes. Sullivan and Welsh (1952) found a set of eight "pattern" characteristics (e.g., score 1 higher than 3) which, considered simultaneously, differentiated ulcer patients from unselected neuropsychiatric patients with some success (70 percent of ulcers correctly identified at a cost of 37 percent false positives). One is forced to conclude that analysis of MMPI scores, whether impressionistic or actuarial, is at best a source of hypotheses about diagnosis to be checked by other methods. In this role, it can be of definite assistance in the clinic.

Results on differential diagnosis with questionnaires other than MMPI have in general been unencouraging, and in recent years the MMPI has displaced all competing questionnaires for this purpose.

16. SVIB keys for differentiating medical specialist groups from each other had little correlation with the key for separating physicians from men in general. What does this imply regarding the design of keys for distinguishing one type of patient from another?

Prediction of Vocational Criteria

Inventories have had rather little success in predicting employee perform-ance. Ghiselli and Barthol (1953) found 113 correlations between job pro-ficiency and presumably relevant inventory scores. Nearly all correlations were positive. The average correlation was as high as .36 for sales personnel but only .14–.18 for supervisors and foremen. There was a wide range among coefficients for the same occupation. The Ghiselli-Barthol averages are prob-ably unrealistically high. Since investigators file and forget hundreds of studies with small samples which showed unpromising relations, only a biased selection reaches publication.

The experience of Household Finance Corporation is consistent with these statistics. Wonderlic and Hovland (Moore, 1941, p. 60) report: "Our early in-vestigations were carried on with published tests which have been standard-ized by others. . . . We were unable to find any test in which the total score was significantly prognostic of success in our organization to warrant its inclusion as part of a selection program. In the cases of many of the purchas-able personality tests, results were obtained which ran counter to expecta-tions. Clerical workers seemed to be more aggressive than salesmen, sales-clerks were higher than managers."

Inventories must inquire about typical behavior rather than behavior un-der specific conditions. Regardless of what a person is prone to do when given free choice, he adapts himself to the demands of different situations. He can be assertive as a parent, submissive in reporting to his commanding officer, boisterous at a party, decorous in church. People vary in their ability to assume roles, but there is no evidence that one can assume convincingly only the roles which match his typical behavior. In this sense, personality is like posture; the young man who slouches habitually can be placed in uniform and trained to hold as rigid a military bearing as anyone else. Per-sonality, as commonly measured, probably has much to do with the sort of work and personal relations a person *seeks,* but has little to do with his abil-ity to perform a role when thrust into it. The adjusted person is able to adapt his style to role demands.

Dependable use of personality inventories for guidance requires empirical study of men who succeed and remain in particular occupations. The most adequate work of this kind has been done with the Kuder Preference Record—Personal. Figure 81 shows some of Kuder's evidence that occupational

		A Being active in groups	B Being in fa- miliar, stable situations	C Working with ideas	D Avoiding con- flict	E Directing others
High Scores	85–			Clergymen		
	75–84					Lawyers
	65–74	Insurance salesmen Clergymen	Farmers	Lawyers Physicians	Clergymen Accountants	Insurance salesmen
	60–64		Clergymen		Physicians	Accountants
Low Scores	35–44	Farmers	Insurance salesmen			Physicians
	25–34	Physicians	Lawyers	Farmers		

FIG. 81. Occupational differences in preference profiles. Mean scores for men satisfied in each occupation are shown. In the columns where an occupation is not mentioned, the average score was not significantly away from the general average of 50. (Data from the manual for the Kuder Preference Record—Personal.)

profiles are often quite distinctive; when more evidence is accumulated, occupational interpretations of profiles may be of distinct value in counseling.

Inventories may have some place in employee selection. The average correlation of .36 for salesmen found by Ghiselli and Barthol, and the several high correlations for small samples of clerical workers, should not be dismissed. Combining personality and aptitude data might give excellent prediction. In view of the variation from situation to situation, however, one can predict success or failure only in a definite job in a specific firm. Each agency must develop its own prediction formula. Where a large number of employees in an organization are doing similar work, best prediction can be obtained by developing a new key for the inventory using responses characteristic of successful employees.

The most successful device of this nature is the Aptitude Index designed for use in life insurance agencies. It is a combined personal history and personality questionnaire, scored by an empirical formula developed after tryout on a nation-wide sample of agents. The correlation with sales volume is .40. Although individual prediction is inaccurate, selection by means of the Index leads to considerable improvement of average sales per man in the long run. Ignoring those men who quit in their first year, it was found that agents rated A on the Index produced 206 percent as much business as the average agent, while those rated E produced only 41 percent of the average (Kurtz, 1941). In general, for prediction of success biographical inventories seem to be more satisfactory than questions about personality.

17. Should inventories be used to advise students about their probable vocational success?
18. What advantages does a biographical inventory have over a personality questionnaire in employee selection?
19. What differences among clerical jobs might account for variation in the validity of personality tests?
20. How might lack of self-confidence help one student to attain high marks, yet be a drawback to another?

VALIDITY OF INVENTORIES FOR TRAIT DESCRIPTION

The Test as a Mirror for the Counselee

In counseling, the personality inventory is used like the interest inventory to help the individual examine his own characteristics as in a mirror. He knows what he has said, but the test permits him to compare himself with others. His percentile standing in various traits is an appropriate initial topic in counseling. For this purpose, it is probably not wise to use subtle scales or scales whose meaning is difficult to communicate, since the instrument serves primarily to reflect the counselee's own professed attitudes. To show a counselee his MMPI profile could lead only to difficulties in explaining the meaning of the categories, and possibly to his rejection of interpretations based on subtle items.

What inventory is preferred will depend upon the nature of the counseling. General adjustment inventories or other single-score instruments are of little use in counseling since they pose few questions for discussion. A descriptive scale reporting introversion, impulsiveness, and so on is of potential value in vocational guidance and may open discussion of traits which the client regards as faults. Descriptions in terms of preferred activities (e.g., Kuder Preference Record—Personal) and values (Allport-Vernon) are somewhat better suited to vocational guidance than scales which describe emotional reactions. The Mooney Problem Checklist is of considerable value because it draws attention to specific concerns the client is ready to talk about and wants help with. It is, in effect, a preliminary interview rather than a measuring device.

A descriptive inventory useful in initiating counseling of college students is that of Edwards. The profile describes fifteen "needs" which presumably direct the subject's actions. Some of the needs, and items related to them are:

      Abasement—to accept blame when things do not go right
      Achievement—to be a recognized authority
      Affiliation—to be loyal to friends
      Aggression—to attack contrary points of view
      Autonomy—to be independent of others in making decisions

The items are paired and the subject chooses the goal or behavior he prefers in each pair. The interpretation of the scales clings very close to the explicit content of the items, which aids communication, and yet the summary in terms of needs may add to the subject's insight into himself. The counselor can help him examine how his major needs are currently being frustrated, how well his future plans will satisfy these needs, or how factors in his earlier development caused certain needs to develop.

Where a test is used as a reflection of the client's remarks, several questions related to validity are of interest. Only partial answers can be given here, but further information on particular tests being considered as counseling aids should be obtained from the test manuals.

• Are the scores adequate measures of the published self-concept? Would another set of items give the same profile? This is to be answered by parallel-form or internal-consistency reliabilities, or by correlations between inventories having similar scales. The better inventories show reliabilities of .80 and above, which is sufficient to pick out salient characteristics. Scores with the same name in different inventories may have low correlations, which emphasizes the need for cautious interpretation.

• Do scores reflect lasting characteristics? E. L. Kelly administered several questionnaires to 300 engaged couples during the years 1935–1938 and retested nearly all the subjects again in 1954. Among the instruments used were the SVIB, the Bernreuter, the Allport-Vernon, and the Remmers generalized attitude scales. The stability coefficients in Figure 82 show a striking degree of similarity between self-descriptions given twenty years apart. The interest scores are most stable, but when we allow for the initial unreliability of the Allport scale it appears that values are equally stable. Personality scores are only slightly poorer. Attitudes, on the other hand, are quite temporary. While the self-concept seems to remain relatively stable, the meanings attached to the rest of the world change greatly with experience.

We may also present evidence on stability arising from a study of children's personalities. These data are not from questionnaires or self-ratings. Trained interviewers asked mothers to tell the extent to which their children showed such problems as insufficient appetite, nailbiting, and quarrelsomeness. The reports were coded on a five-point rating scale for each problem, and a total score indicating severity of problem behavior was derived. The procedure was repeated each year from infancy to age 14. The correlations in Table 64 should be compared with the correlations for repeated men-

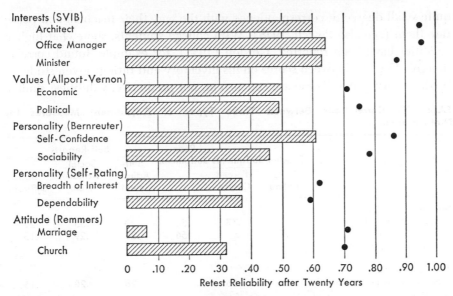

FIG. 82. Stability of various aspects of personality (Kelly, 1955). The dot indicates the reported reliability of the scale over a short time interval (usually one week).

tal tests in Table 21 (p. 176), which come from the same longitudinal study. In both tables, we find that correlations from year to year are much higher at later ages, after development is more stabilized. The stability coefficients for personality scores are lower than those for mental tests, but the drop is surprisingly small. While we do not have information on the stability of

TABLE 64.   Correlation of Problem Behavior Score of Boys with Score at a Later Age

Approximate Age at First Rating	Years Elapsed Between First and Second Score			
	1	3	6	12
$1\frac{3}{4}$	.38	.40	.27	−.01
3	.50	.31	.35	.47
4	.56	.57	.54	—
6	.67	.70	.81	—
7	.73	.55	.51	—
9	.70	.75	—	—
11	.86	.80		

SOURCE: Macfarlane *et al.*, 1954.

personality questionnaire scores for children, these data show beyond a doubt that problem behavior itself has a great deal of stability over at least a three-year span.

● Do the descriptions agree with external evidence of typical behavior? Research comparing self-descriptions with objective records of behavior is lacking. There have been numerous comparisons of scores with judgments. The study reported in Table 65 shows that children's self-reports have a quite small degree of correspondence with the way their teachers and peers rate them (see also Powell, 1948). With college students, somewhat higher validities have been reported. Gordon (1953), for example, found correlations of .47 to .73 between scores on his inventory and ratings given students by dormitory mates. These are concurrent, not predictive, validities; similar

TABLE 65. Correlations Between Three Types of Adjustment Measures for Ninth-Graders

| | Teacher Judgments | | Peer Judgments | Self-Reports | | |
	Rating	Forced Choice		Self-Adjustment	Social Adjustment	Basic Difficulty
Teacher judgments:						
Rating of adjustment		.77	.56	.30	.33	.22
Score on forced-choice descriptive questionnaire	.77		.56	.28	.29	.15
Peer judgments:						
Nominations on desirable traits	.56	.56		.28	.28	.16
Self-reports:						
California Test of Personality Self-Adjustment	.30	.28	.28		.73	.61
California Test of Personality Social Adjustment	.33	.29	.28	.73		.47
SRA Youth Inventory, Basic Difficulty score	.22	.15	.16	.61	.47	

Source: Ullmann, 1952.

correlations for the EPPS were obtained in an unpublished study by Tamkin and Klett. (Cf. also Table 62.)

● Do the descriptions agree with the true self-concept? A criterion could be obtained by asking a therapist who is well acquainted with the person's inner attitudes to describe him. Evidence of this sort, however, is rare. Rogers cites correlations ranging from .38 to .48 between scores on his adjustment inventory and ratings by clinicians, but this is an isolated investigation, not adequately reported (1931).

21. Applying the method of p. 138 to Figure 82, about what proportion of the variance in self-confidence is due to random error of measurement, what proportion to genuine but unstable characteristics, and what proportion to stable characteristics?
22. In counseling with the Edwards inventory, should raw scores (ranging 0 to 15 on each scale) or percentiles be used to plot the profile?

Descriptions to Aid Institutional Decisions

The second major descriptive use of inventories is to provide others with insight regarding the individual. This may be important in clinical diagnosis or other institutional decisions, and in prescriptive counseling. The therapist may wish to know as much as he can about the person's conflicts long before they emerge in interviews. The college counselor (see p. 456) may wish to know what hidden attitudes are preventing a student from doing his best work. For these purposes, subtle tests may have distinct advantages in the hands of highly experienced testers.

The MMPI is the generally preferred instrument for clinical patients and for many counseling uses. The interpreter must bring to bear information from the *Atlas* and other sources in order to translate scores into psychological constructs. An illustrative description is that given by Grayson (Shneidman, 1951, pp. 268–269) for a 25-year-old veteran (see Figure 78):

This profile may, with a good deal of confidence, be considered as a valid representation (F within limits) of a seriously disturbed patient (unusually elevated profile), who has a tremendous amount of anxiety and depression (D), with sad, worrisome feelings of inadequacy (high D, Pt). The patient is self-depreciative (low L, low K) and lacking in self-assurance to the point of being a "compulsive doubter" (high ?). He has attempted to resolve his anxiety through hysterical displacement (high Hs) and obsessive-compulsive mechanisms (high Pt) but these have been unsuccessful, with the result that the overwhelming anxiety has cracked his weak ego structure (high Sc). In addition, the patient has a considerable degree of hostility directed both against self (high Pd) and others (high Pa). The strong feelings of anxiety and depression (D) combined with introverted and extraverted aggression (Pd, Pa), in an individual who possesses insufficient ego control (Sc) to inhibit his tendency to act out impulses (Ma) add up to an explosive picture which presents strong possibilities of suicidal and homicidal behavior. Diagnostically, the patient may be classified as incipient paranoid schizophrenia.

The validity of the description is attested by the full case history and therapy protocol. The following statements are made in a summary by the man's psychotherapist: "He seemed suspicious, indecisive and unable to relax. . . . There seems to be considerable guilt in relation to his own hostility. He has established some defenses against this through obsessions but these defenses are cracking and he fears that his hostile impulses might become so great that he would be unable to control them. . . . The patient seemed obsessed with thoughts about death, homicide, and suicide."

The MMPI is not entirely suitable for normal groups, particularly younger ones. Some of the items ("My sex life is satisfactory") arouse criticism from teachers and parents, and the scales of clinical origin produce information principally on undesirable traits. The California Psychological Inventory (CPI) and Minnesota Counseling Inventory (MCI) are descendants of the MMPI specifically designed for relatively normal high-school and college students. The MCI keys are labeled Family Relationships, Emotional Stability, Conformity, Adjustment to Reality, Mood, and Leadership. Some of these keys correspond rather closely to the MMPI clinical scales in general purpose (e.g., Conformity is a substitute for *Pd*), but the MCI labels carry less damaging connotations.

The validity of descriptive interpretations is difficult to assess, especially when the construct employed cannot be equated with any one observable behavior. MMPI scales have been given meaning by integrating evidence from all manner of studies, gradually formulating a psychological hypothesis about the meaning of each score. Meehl's remarks on the *Pd* scale illustrate the process (Cronbach and Meehl, 1955):[2]

> The Pd scale of MMPI was originally designed and cross-validated upon hospitalized patients diagnosed "Psychopathic personality, asocial and amoral type." Further research shows the scale to have a limited degree of predictive and concurrent validity for "delinquency" more broadly defined. Several studies show associations between Pd and very special "criterion" groups which it would be ludicrous to identify as "*the* criterion" in the traditional sense. If one lists these heterogeneous groups and tries to characterize them intensionally, he faces enormous conceptual difficulties. For example, a recent survey of hunting accidents in Minnesota showed that hunters who had "carelessly" shot someone were significantly elevated on Pd when compared with other hunters. . . . The finding seems to lend some slight support to the construct validity of the Pd scale. But of course it would be nonsense to *define* the Pd component "operationally" in terms of, say, accident proneness. We might try to subsume the original phenotype and the hunting-accident proneness under some broader category, such as "Disposition to violate society's rules, whether legal, moral, or just *sensible*." But now we . . . are using a rather vague and wide-range class. . . .
>
> We want the class specification to cover a group trend that (nondelinquent) high school students judged by their peer group as least "responsible" score over a full sigma higher on Pd than those judged most "responsible.". . . Again, any clinician familiar with MMPI lore would predict an elevated Pd on a sample of (nondelinquent) professional actors. Chyatte's confirmation of this prediction tends to support *both:* (a) the theory sketch of "what the Pd factor is, psychologically"; and (b) the claim of the Pd scale to construct validity for this hypothetical factor. Let the reader try his hand at writing a brief phenotypic criterion specification that will cover both trigger-happy hunters and Broadway actors! And if he should be ingenious enough to achieve this, does his definition also encompass Hovey's report that high Pd predicts the judgments "not shy" and "unafraid of mental patients" made upon nurses by their supervisors? And then we have Gough's report that *low* Pd is as-

---

[2] References for the studies described are given in the original.

sociated with ratings as "good-natured," and Roessell's data showing that high Pd is predictive of "dropping out of high school." The point is that all seven of these "criterion" dispositions would be readily guessed by any clinician having even superficial familiarity with MMPI interpretation; but to mediate these inferences explicitly requires quite a few hypotheses about dynamics, constituting an admittedly sketchy (but far from vacuous) network defining the genotype *psychopathic deviate*.

This body of evidence leaves little doubt that *Pd* has some relation to internal personality structure. The correlations cited do not represent strong relations; if they did, we would find the same person dropping out of school, rated ill-natured, becoming a Broadway actor, and shooting a fellow hunter. Circumstances dictate much of behavior. Personality structure, even if perfectly measured, represents only a predisposition rather than an absolutely determining force.

Granting that *Pd* and other scores have some validity, we are still uncertain as to the closeness of correspondence between the scores and the true, hidden personality structure. Before interpretations can be used with confidence, we require evidence as to how often we go wrong in assuming that a person with high *Pd* has this vaguely defined pattern of arrogant, unruly, irresponsible attitudes.

The facts required to assess the adequacy of descriptions are seriously incomplete, and many of the findings strike a pessimistic note. Gough (1957) correlated a number of CPI scores with ratings of students made by a staff of psychological assessors. These ratings are based on comprehensive psychological study and provide a reasonable criterion to test the statement that persons with certain scores tend to be seen in certain ways. The correlations between CPI scores and the ratings to which they supposedly relate range from .21 to .48. Such modest correlations warn against depending on any single aspect of the description from the CPI.

We may not, however, judge a description of a whole personality by the validities of the scales taken separately. The personality description covers many dimensions, and a little information about each feature may add up to a revealing portrait. Moreover, considering the whole pattern of scores at once possibly permits much more accurate description than the single-scale interpretations for which Gough gives validity coefficients. Gough argues that the interpretation of one score depends upon the level of another in the manner shown in Figure 83. The interpretation might be further modified if other scales were taken into account.

Clearly needed, at this point, is evidence not now available. Using single scales, pairs of scales, or whole profiles, the interpreter should divide cases into three piles according to whether he regards them as strikingly high, strikingly low, or in the middle range on some trait (e.g., compliant). This classification could be correlated with ratings by others who know the person well.

From the evidence now available (see also p. 592) we must continue to regard descriptive interpretations as hazardous. Those familiar with a par-

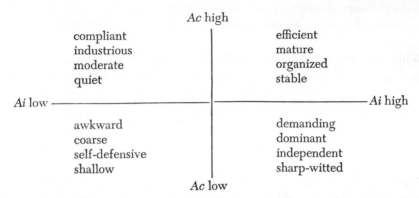

FIG. 83. Proposed pattern interpretation of CPI scores labeled Achievement through conformity (Ac) and Achievement through independence (Ai) (Gough, 1957).

ticular test often believe that it gives them clear pictures of personality. This may be a self-delusion nurtured by recall of successful cases, but one cannot deny that many inventories measure individual differences reliably and that those differences have some relation to personality as observed in other ways. When the description from the test is a point of departure for further study of the individual, errors of interpretation can be corrected. Under no circumstances should such a description be passed on to a school principal, an employer, or any other decision maker not trained to check the interpretation critically against other evidence.

23. Grayson diagnosed his case as "incipient paranoid schizophrenia." What diagnosis would be suggested from the peak MMPI scores if no effort had been made to interpret the dynamics of the personality as a whole?

Establishment of Scientific Laws

A recent development is the employment of personality measures in the establishment of psychological theory. Test scores are interpreted in terms of theoretical concepts and related to behavior under various experimental conditions. The outcome of such experiments is, first, interpretation of the test in terms of a refined concept rather than an ambiguous or arbitrary trait name and, second, development of theory as to the significance of the trait. In addition to the study of Taylor scores and eyelid conditioning summarized earlier, we may mention the more elaborate study by Cervin (1957) testing the hypothesis that in a two-person discussion the more emotionally responsive subject will take more initiative, participate more, and change opinion less. In order to bring out this effect, he found it necessary to use a specially purified measure of emotional responsiveness (akin to anxiety or neuroticism) rather than a published questionnaire. In experimental groups formed by pairing high scorers with low scorers, the predicted differences were found in about 80 percent of the cases.

Relations of this type can be considered well established only when confirmed by other investigators. As more such relations are verified and woven into psychological theory, tests will come to have an important role in the science of psychology as well as in practical decisions. Theoretical clarification should also have practical consequences, though these may be far in the future.

REPRESENTATIVE PERSONALITY INVENTORIES

The following inventories illustrate the variety among currently published inventories, but by no means exhaust the field:

● Billett-Starr Youth Problems Inventory; Roy O. Billett and Irving S. Starr; World Book, 1958. Grades 7–9, 10–12. A problem checklist covering such areas as health, boy-girl relationships, personal finance, and planning for the future. Designed for general screening of pupils for individual study, and for identification of common problems to be taken up in group guidance.

● California Personality Inventory; Harrison G. Gough; Consulting Psychologists Press, 1957. High school. A lengthy inventory covering fifteen traits such as sociability, tolerance, and intellectual efficiency, plus three control keys. The scoring keys were developed empirically but have rather low correlations with their criteria. Interpretation is based primarily on an impressionistic psychological integration of the entire profile. The profile covers personality more broadly than most other inventories, but scores often intercorrelate too highly for efficient measurement. Interpretation has not yet been adequately standardized and validated.

● California Test of Personality; Louis P. Thorpe, Willis W. Clark, Ernest W. Tiegs; California Test Bureau, 1942, 1953. Primary, elementary, secondary, and adult forms. A questionnaire yielding percentile scores on personal adjustment and social adjustment. Such subscores as "sense of personal worth," "nervous symptoms," and "family relations" have skewed distributions and are capable of giving meaningful information about patterns of adjustment only in rare cases. The evidence on validity presented in the manual is incomplete, and misleading in places. The manual attempts to summarize theory and practices of mental hygiene for teachers, and the necessarily brief presentation runs considerable risk of being misinterpreted and misapplied.

● Edwards Personal Preference Schedule; Allen L. Edwards; Psychological Corporation, 1954, 1959. High school, adult. The 225 paired comparisons lead to scores on 15 "needs." Designed so as to eliminate "façade" effects, but patterns can be faked. The scale is recent and research is limited. Gives a description likely to be helpful in counseling.

● Gordon Personal Profile and Gordon Personal Inventory; Leonard V. Gordon; World Book, 1953, 1956. High school to adult. Uses eighteen to twenty forced-choice items in each form. The profile measures ascendancy, responsibility, emotional stability, sociability; the Inventory measures cautiousness, original thinking, personal relations, vigor. Either can be given in fifteen minutes, yet reliability of scores is about .83. An efficient instrument for obtaining a self-description profile. Evidence regarding significance of scores is extremely limited but encouraging.

● Guilford-Zimmerman Temperament Survey; J. P. Guilford and Wayne Zimmerman; Sheridan Supply Company, 1949. Adolescent and adult. Measures ten relatively independent traits defined through factor analysis, including ascendance, sociability, thoughtfulness, objectivity, and restraint. A more efficient version of the earlier Guilford scales. A typical descriptive instrument. Little evidence on significance of scores is available.

● Kuder Preference Record, Form A—Personal; G. Frederic Kuder; Science Research Associates, 1948, 1953. Adolescent and adult. A companion to the vocational interest inventory, this set of forced-choice items measures preference among sociable, intellectual, etc., activities. (See Figure 81.) Occupational patterns have been collected which enhance the usefulness of the scale in vocational guidance, but little is known about the scale as a descriptive or diagnostic instrument. It is free from façade effect, but patterns can be faked. Since scores have no obvious "good-bad" implications, the Kuder is likely to be suitable for introducing counseling, especially in high school.

● Minnesota Counseling Inventory; Ralph F. Berdie and Wilbur L. Layton; Psychological Corporation, 1957. High school. Many of the 413 true-false self-description statements are rewritten MMPI items. Seven scales measure adjustment to family and social relations, emotional stability, mood, conformity, etc. Two control keys are provided. The scales have positive but very modest validity for separating (for example) pupils known to have poor family adjustment from those rated as having good adjustment. Retests after three months show reliabilities in the .70–.80 range. Interpretation of this instrument will remain uncertain until considerably greater experience and validating evidence have been accumulated.

● Minnesota Multiphasic Personality Inventory; S. R. Hathaway and J. C.

McKinley; Psychological Corporation, 1943, 1951. Late adolescents and adults. (See pp. 469 ff.)

• Mooney Problem Check Lists; Ross L. Mooney and Leonard V. Gordon; Psychological Corporation, 1948, 1950. Forms for junior high through college, and adult. Subject checks his problems in eleven fields: morals and religion, finances and living conditions, adjustment to school work, social relations, etc. High scores identify those who should receive counseling, and items checked provide a basis for individual or class discussion.

• SRA Youth Inventory; H. H. Remmers and Benjamin Shimberg; Science Research Associates, 1949. High school; also, SRA Junior Inventory for Grades 4–8, 1955. A checklist of unusually efficient format covering typical adolescent problems of educational and vocational planning, and social and emotional adjustment. Chiefly useful as a starting point for individual and group guidance; may also be used as a screening inventory to detect individuals requiring intensive study.

• The 16 P. F. Test; R. B. Cattell, D. R. Saunders, and Glen Stice; Institute for Personality and Ability Testing, 1950. Age 16 and over. Sixteen scores measure dimensions such as dominance, general intelligence, emotional stability, radicalism, and will control. The dimensions are relatively independent and have some advantages for research purposes. The short scales have extremely low reliability (.45–.55) and the information on norms is unsatisfactory. Not recommended for assessment of individuals. (Versions of the test for various school ages are either available or in preparation.)

• Study of Values; Gordon S. Allport, Philip E. Vernon, Gardner Lindzey; Houghton Mifflin, 1931, 1951. Later adolescence and college. Forced choice between preferred activities and beliefs. Scored according to Spranger's system to indicate relative emphasis on Theoretical, Economic, Political, Aesthetic, Social, and Religious values. Of some value as a supplement to interest inventories in vocational guidance; much used for research in social psychology.

• Survey of Study Habits and Attitudes; Wm. F. Brown and Wayne H. Holtzman; Psychological Corporation, 1953. College students. Covers study behavior and attitudes (e.g., "Whether I like a course or not, I still work hard to make a good grade"). Out of 75 items on this questionnaire about half are keyed; these distinguish students with good marks from those who do poorly. This score correlates about .45 with grades and, combined with an ability test, yields a predictive validity of about .60. The test is fakable and is not recommended as an admission test. Both the total score and the item responses are useful in counseling and in how-to-study courses.

Three levels of test were mentioned in Chapter 1: Level A, appropriate for use by teachers and others without special training in testing; Level B, for use by counselors and others with a good general understanding of testing; and Level C, for use by persons with considerable psychological knowledge and relevant supervised experience. Most personality tests belong to the higher levels, because their interpretation requires considerable judgment. There is some risk that the interpretation will create difficulties which only a professional counselor or clinical psychologist is likely to recognize. For example, to tell a subject that he is low in emotional stability may aggravate his difficulties. Giving the same facts to his employer—no matter how cautiously presented—may blight his chances of promotion and ultimately increase his maladjustment. Allowing a test to damage the person's opportunities and self-satisfaction would be dubious even if the test were highly valid. Since it is not, the results of personality tests should generally be reported only to professional workers who know their limitations. In the light of these dangers, the author suggests the following categorization of the tests listed above:

A. Can safely be interpreted by teachers:

● Mooney, SRA, and Billett-Starr inventories. Teachers should not attempt to analyze individual test scores, and unless a counselor is to interpret individual records pupil's answer sheets should probably be unsigned. A tabulation of the frequency of particular problems is an excellent basis for group guidance, curriculum planning, and modification of school conditions which create problems.

B. Can safely be used by the counselor with basic training in vocational and educational counseling.

● Allport-Vernon-Lindzey, Kuder Personal. These inventories reflect the person's preferred choices and in that respect resemble interest inventories. Interpreting the scores is unlikely to threaten self-esteem.

● Billett-Starr, Mooney, SRA inventories. These may be used to identify pupils for interviewing, and as a starting point for interviewing. Little attention should be paid to the scores themselves. The counselor should not attempt to resolve deep emotional conflicts that call for experience he does not have.

B′. Can safely be used by counselors with considerable training in personality theory and handling of emotional conflict.

● Bell, California (CTP), Edwards, and Gordon inventories. These should ordinarily be interpreted as a part of an individual case study; except in research studies it is rarely advisable to apply them routinely to groups. Since some scores in the Bell, CTP, and Gordon may threaten the individual, the counselor should consider carefully before deciding whether to interpret the test to the subject.

C. Require comprehensive training in counseling psychology or clinical psychology, including understanding of test theory, personality theory, and handling of emotional conflict.

● CPI, Guilford-Zimmerman, Minnesota Counseling Inventory, MMPI. Further reports of research on the meanings of profiles on some of these inventories may ultimately make them trustworthy in the hands of counselors at Level B or B'. Most promising in this respect is the relatively simple MCI. This instrument is not difficult to interpret, but its use in schools carries some risk. The Leadership score, for example, is not very valid; it may be that if such a score is made available to teachers they will give leadership opportunities to pupils with high scores and deprive pupils with low scores of this valuable learning experience.

24. A Leadership score identifies pupils whose responses resemble those of other pupils who have become leaders. What characteristics other than leadership ability and interest are likely to distinguish student leaders in high school from the students who take little part in student affairs?
25. If school officials make use of leadership scores in encouraging certain pupils to take leadership responsibilities, will this tend to increase or decrease the correlation between the original scores and leadership record by the end of high school?
26. Scores on certain instruments purport to identify students likely to be trouble-makers and potential delinquents. Assuming that such a score has very high stability and validity, what use might be made of such a test by high schools? If, as is the case, the validity coefficients are quite low, what undesirable effects may follow if such scores are collected by principals?
27. The restrictions on use of personality inventories in counseling suggested above are admittedly conservative. Some psychologists argue that it is unwise for counselors to "imitate the secrecy of the medical profession" in withholding scores from teachers and other laymen. These psychologists argue that laymen continually make judgments about personality, and that if discouraged from using test scores they will base their judgments on casual observations of even less validity than the tests. What do you think?

IDIOGRAPHIC ANALYSIS OF THE SINGLE PERSONALITY

Criticisms of the Concept of "Trait"

If a test is to assign a rank or score to the individual, there must be a characteristic or dimension along which this score is located. The desire for scales analogous to those for size, temperature, and reaction time led psychologists to postulate that personality has dimensions or traits. A *trait* is a tendency to react in a defined way in response to a defined class of stimuli. Traits are deeply embedded in Western languages; nearly all the adjectives which apply to people are descriptive of traits: happy, conventional, stubborn, and so on. Traits are elusive in scientific analysis, however, and are defined and measured only at the risk of some ambiguity.

The postulate that traits exist is supported by three facts:

● Personalities possess considerable consistency; a person shows the same habitual reactions over a wide range of similar situations.

● For any habit, we can find among people a variation of degrees or amounts of this behavior.

● Personalities have some stability, since the person earning a certain score this year usually has a somewhat similar score next year.

These facts lead one to consider personality traits as habits, capable of being evoked by a wide range of situations. It would be tedious to catalog a series of traits such as "habit of bowing politely when meeting a pretty woman of one's own age on the street on Sunday," "habit of bowing politely when meeting a not-pretty woman . . . ," etc. Therefore traits are sought which describe consistent behavior in a wide range of situations. The trait approach to personality hopes to describe economically the significant variations of behavior, neglecting unduly specific habits. Since the English dictionary offers no less than 17,953 adjectives describing traits, the problem of economy is a serious one.

A trait is a composite of many specific behaviors. To say that a boy is *perfectly* honest predicts his behavior in any situation involving honesty. Ordinarily, however, one possesses an intermediate degree of a trait; he is honest in some situations but not others. Two people with the same score need not be alike in personality. Saying that a boy is "50 percent honest" implies an even probability of honest or dishonest behavior. The description conceals the fact that he is perfectly honest with money and perfectly dishonest when grades are the reward. A trait scale permits faultless inference only when all the behaviors collected under the trait definition are present in the same person, i.e., when all scores are 100 percent or zero.

"The normal personality" presents troublesome problems of measurement. The deviate at either end of a trait distribution is well characterized by his score; he exhibits the trait in unusual degree and in a large number of situations. Intermediate scores tell the investigator little. Yet every normal personality has its unique characteristics. Even a person who is "normal" in all the traits we measure has individuality. Reducing his performance to a standard list of traits on which he proves not to be exceptional, we lose patterns which make him different from his also-normal neighbors.

Allport (1937, pp. 248–257) criticized the entire trait approach on this ground. One man may act from need; he will take money to feed his family, but will not cheat or lie. Another may be prudent rather than honest; he will be as honest as he must to avoid being caught. Another may define honesty in a limited way; he would never steal, but he thinks it right to operate a business on the principle of "buyer beware." These men are all honest to an intermediate degree; statistically, their honesty is near the average.

Since mapping a personality in terms of a few common traits does not represent the way the individual's behavior is organized, many investigators have tried to develop what Allport calls an "idiographic" description. An idiographic analysis would define new traits as needed to fit each individual (e.g., "shy with women of his own age in non-business relationships"). The difficulties that face such efforts are enormous, but some initial steps have been taken successfully.

The trait approach describes responses as if they were general over a very large class of situations. "Dominant," "paranoid-like," and "honest" describe responses independent of particular situations. The idiographic approach looks for equivalences among situations. Sometimes student X shows dominance, sometimes not. If we can find out what situations bring out dominant reactions—i.e., are equivalent for him—we can then hope to predict his behavior with some exactness.

As a first step in studying situational equivalences, C. E. Osgood and G. A. Kelly have developed techniques for studying perception of the significant persons in a subject's life. These others are an important part of the person's world, and many reactions are determined by his perception of them.

28. Show how "stubbornness" might be present in some situations and absent in others for the same person, even though both actions are typical for him.

The Semantic Differential

Osgood's method was developed for research on perception, meaning, and attitudes, rather than as a personality test (Osgood *et al.*, 1957). Known as the Semantic Differential, it measures indirectly the connotations of words or objects. The stimulus is rated on a seven-point scale, various scales and stimuli being mixed in random order. Successive items might appear as follows:

My Father	soft	___	: ___	: ___	: ___	: ___	: ___	: ___	hard
Fraud	rich	___	: ___	: ___	: ___	: ___	: ___	: ___	poor
Confusion	fair	___	: ___	: ___	: ___	: ___	: ___	: ___	unfair
My Father	deep	___	: ___	: ___	: ___	: ___	: ___	: ___	shallow

In most studies Osgood and his students have been interested in specific stimuli (e.g., "physicians," "Presidential candidate A") as perceived by a large group. For examining an individual, Osgood employs stimuli of personal significance, e.g., "my father."

The subject is to check the scale rapidly, recording his first impressions. Naturally it is difficult to defend any single response as "right" when judging *communism* on the scale *thin-thick,* but subjects have little difficulty in checking associations. The scoring can be accomplished in two ways. Using factor analysis, the scales can be grouped into *good-bad, strong-weak,* and *active-passive* keys. Average scores can be assigned for each stimulus. Thus we could say that a subject has indirectly described his father at +1 on good (on a scale from +3 to −3), 2.4 on strong, −0.4 on active. The other scoring method compares stimuli two at a time, converting the differences between their ratings into a "distance score" measuring the degree to which the subject perceives the stimuli as similar.

The best illustration of the technique is its application to a case of triple personality. A dissociated personality is one in which the person possesses two or more different "selves" and shifts back and forth between them (a bit like Dr. Jekyll and Mr. Hyde). Eve White had three such identities who "took possession" at various times, and her therapists were able to administer the Semantic Differential to each self in turn (Thigpen and Cleckley, 1953, 1957). In Figure 84 we present the configurations from two of the tests. The

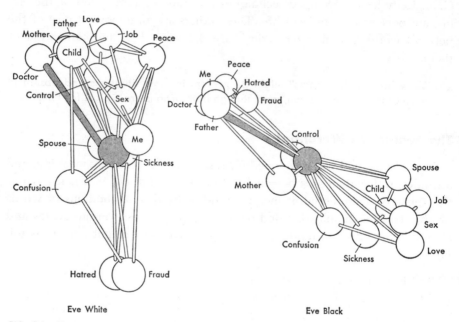

FIG. 84. Meaning systems of Eve White and Eve Black on the Semantic Differential (Osgood and Luria, 1954).

black ball represents the midpoint on all scales. "Good" is at the top, "active" at the left, and "weak" toward the viewer. The solid line connecting the black ball with "doctor" (who is always good, strong, very active) helps to orient the figure.

Two psychologists interpreted the patterns "blindly," i.e., with no further knowledge of the cases. Looking first at a few salient indicators, they pointed out in Eve White's record the separation of love and sex, the meaningless-ness of the spouse, the weakness of "me." Eve Black seems to place hatred and fraud in a favorable cluster with "me" and rejects spouse, love, job, and child. (The pattern of the third self, Jane, which will not be discussed here, is normal; love and sex are closely linked and favorable.) An impressionistic "guess" by the interpreter led to this summary of the first two personalities (Osgood and Luria, 1954):

Eve White is the woman who is simultaneously most in contact with social real-ity and under the greatest emotional stress. She is aware of both the demands of society and her own inadequacies in meeting them. She sees herself as a passive weakling and is also consciously aware of the discord in her sexual life, drawing increasingly sharp distinctions between love as an idealized notion and sex as a crude reality. She maintains the greatest diversity among the meanings of various concepts. She is concerned and ambivalent about her child, but apparently is *not* aware of her own ambivalent attitudes toward her mother. . . . Those psycho-analytically inclined may wish to identify Eve White with dominance of the *superego:* certainly, the superego seems to view the world through the eyes of Eve White, accepting the mores or values of others (particularly her mother) but con-tinuously criticizing and punishing herself. . . .

Eve Black is clearly the most out of contact with social reality and simultane-ously the most self-assured. To rhapsodize, Eve Black finds Peace of mind through close identification with a God-like therapist (My Doctor, probably a father symbol for her), accepting her Hatred and Fraud as perfectly legitimate aspects of the God-like role. Naturally, she sees herself as a dominant, active wonder-woman and is in no way self-critical. She is probably unaware of her family situation. . . . Like a completely selfish infant, this personality is entirely oriented around the assumption of its own perfection.

The pattern corresponds well with the therapists' picture of Eve. The therapists described the same personalities in these phrases, among others:

Eve White: demure, almost saintly, seldom lively; tries not to blame her husband for marital troubles; every act demonstrates sacrifice for her little girl; meek, fragile, doomed to be overcome.
Eve Black: a party girl, shrewd, egocentric; rowdy wit; all attitudes whimlike; ready for any little irresponsible adventure; provocative; strangely secure from inner aspect of grief and tragedy.

The correspondence of the portraits is remarkable. A single brilliant hit, however, is not to be regarded as adequate evidence of validity.

Mapping stimulus equivalences gives a different type of information from that of the trait-oriented questionnaire, but the semantic map does give in-formation about traits. Eve White is unquestionably dissatisfied with her-self, perfectionist, unwilling to express emotion—any questionnaire would show a high score on introversion and hysteric tendencies. The Semantic Differential adds information about specific sources of conflict: lack of acceptance of spouse and sex, and her child's weakness and need for protection. (Indeed, Mrs. White's feeling that she could not give her child adequate protection was a precipitating cause of her illness.) Eve Black is shallow, uncontrolled, self-centered—extrovert on any questionnaire and on MMPI surely extreme on *Ma* and *Pd*. This is apparent in the Semantic Differential association of me, hatred, and fraud as "good and strong." But the map gives the additional picture of strong identification with men and rejection of child and spouse. One can judge what persons and treatments are likely to win her respect and coöperation, and what rewards she is likely to work for. Such information goes far beyond what one can get from even the most valid description of her general personality style. The rewards that a therapist might ordinarily offer—opportunity to hold a job, restoration of marriage—were spurned by Eve Black. The coöperation that eventually permitted some success in therapy was won only when the therapist appealed to Eve Black's fear of sickness.

The Role Concept Repertory (Rep) Test of G. A. Kelly (1955) is much like Osgood's procedure, save that the subject himself now picks the scales on which he will respond. This device reflects Kelly's theory of social behavior and psychotherapy, which places great stress on the way the person's conceptualizations shape his behavior. The principal aim of the Rep test is to obtain information useful to a therapist.

The subject is given a list of about twenty roles, of which the following are representative:

Your wife or present girl friend
Your mother
A person with whom you have worked who was easy to get along with
A girl you did not like when you were in high school
The person whom you would most like to be of help to (or whom you feel most sorry for)

The subject names the people who fill these roles for him. The examiner then selects three of the persons and asks, "In what *important way* are two of them alike but different from the third?" If the response is superficial ("These two are tall") the examiner asks for some further similarity. A useful response might be, "These two are self-confident and this one is shy." The subject has then stated a bipolar scale along which he perceives people to differ. The procedure is continued until many scales have been elicited and applied to the significant others.

29. Is the Semantic Differential fakable? Can one argue that it assesses unconscious attitudes?
30. How might the Semantic Differential be used to study transference relations during psychotherapy?
31. Osgood finds only three predominant factors among his scales. Do three dimensions appear adequate to describe one's perception of others?
32. Is Osgood's test primarily behavioristic or phenomenological in outlook?

Suggested Readings

Diamond, Solomon. The factorial approach. *Personality and temperament.* New York: Harper, 1957. Pp. 151–183.

This review attempts to classify dimensions of personality by factor analysis, considers lists of possibly important traits and also gives an introductory explanation of factor-analytic procedures.

Hathaway, Starke R., & Monachesi, Elio D. Personality characteristics of adolescents as related to their later careers. II. Two-year follow-up on delinquency. *Analyzing and predicting juvenile delinquency on the MMPI.* Minneapolis: University of Minnesota Press, 1953. Pp. 109–135.

This massive study of score patterns indicative of delinquency shows both the advantages and the disadvantages of analyzing combinations of scores. The first and last chapters of the book deal with the practical meaning of the research.

Meehl, Paul E., & Hathaway, Starke R. The K factor as a suppressor variable in the MMPI. *J. appl. Psychol.,* 1946, **30,** 525–564. (Reprinted in G. S. Welsh and W. G. Dahlstrom (eds.), *Basic readings on the MMPI in psychology and medicine.* Minneapolis: University of Minnesota Press, 1956. Pp. 12–40).

Several theoretical aspects of the development of MMPI are discussed, including the authors' reasons for not forming homogeneous clusters of items and the need for corrections for bias in self-reports.

Schiele, B. C., & Brozek, Jozef. "Experimental neurosis" resulting from semi-starvation in man. *Psychosom. Med.,* 1948, **10,** 31–50. (Reprinted in Welsh and Dahlstrom, *op. cit.* Pp. 461–483.)

In a study of MMPI changes during an experimental stress of six months' duration, nine cases are described in detail, showing the relationship between MMPI profiles and behavior patterns.

Ullmann, Charles A. Teachers, peers, and tests as predictors of adjustment. *J. educ. Psychol.,* 1957, **48,** 257–267.

Evidence is given on the difference between information contained in teacher ratings and in self-report questionnaires. Attention focuses on pupils who drop out of school or who perform poorly in school. Items capable of identifying such students are listed.

17

Judgments and Systematic Observations

WHETHER an individual's reputation corresponds to his behavior or not, it is unquestionably significant. A person who has impressed his former teachers as imaginative is favored by a college admissions committee. Business and military organizations file supervisors' opinions and use them in deciding whom to promote. Teachers find out what children think of each other in order to understand relationships in the classroom and to identify social misfits. Furthermore, as we have seen, ratings are an important criterion for studying job performance and adjustment. In this chapter we shall consider problems and techniques of obtaining ratings by superiors and by peers (companions at the same level in the organization). We shall then turn to systematic observations of behavior.

RATINGS AND SOCIOMETRIC REPORTS

Ratings by Supervisors

Descriptions by supervisors (foremen, teachers, superior officers, etc.,) are hard to compare because styles of writing vary. Rating scales are therefore used to reduce impressions to manageable form. A rating scale consists of a list of traits to be rated. The form of the scale may vary from a simple list of adjectives to be checked to a continuous scale with several descriptive labels, as illustrated in Figure 85. Before evaluating specific forms of rating scale, let us consider the chief difficulties to be overcome.

Sources of Error. The first problem is *generosity error*, i.e., the tendency of raters to give favorable reports. The teacher, asked to indicate on a report card whether the pupil is coöperative, will usually rate all except the most troublesome pupils at the highest point on the scale. Company commanders rate 98 percent of their junior officers in the top two categories (out of five)

Name of student...

A—How are you and others affected by his appearance and manner?	☐ Sought by others ☐ Well liked by others ☐ Liked by others ☐ Tolerated by others ☐ Avoided by others ☐ No opportunity to observe	Please record here instances on which you base your judgment.
B—Does he need frequent prodding or does he go ahead without being told?	☐ Seeks and sets for himself additional tasks ☐ Completes suggested supplementary work ☐ Does ordinary assignments of his own accord ☐ Needs occasional prodding ☐ Needs much prodding in doing ordinary assignments ☐ No opportunity to observe	Please record here instances on which you base your judgment.
C—Does he get others to do what he wishes?	☐ Displays marked ability to lead his fellows; makes things go ☐ Sometimes leads in important affairs ☐ Sometimes leads in minor affairs ☐ Lets others take lead ☐ Probably unable to lead his fellows ☐ No opportunity to observe	Please record here instances on which you base your judgment.
D — How does he control his emotions?	☐ Unusual balance of responsiveness and control ☐ Well balanced ☐ Usually well balanced ☐ Tends to be unresponsive ☐ Tends to be over emotional ☐ Unresponsive, apathetic ☐ Too easily depressed, irritated or elated ☐ No opportunity to observe	Please record here instances on which you base your judgment.
E—Has he a program with definite purposes in terms of which he distributes his time and energy?	☐ Engrossed in realizing well formulated objectives ☐ Directs energies effectively with fairly definite program ☐ Has vaguely formed objectives ☐ Aims just to "get by" ☐ Aimless trifler ☐ No opportunity to observe	Please record here instances on which you base your judgment.

FIG. 85. The ACE Personality Report, Form B. (Reproduced by permission of American Council on Education.)

on efficiency reports. Such ratings have little value because they do not discriminate between individuals. There are several reasons for generosity errors: the rater may feel that he is admitting poor leadership if he says that his subordinates are not performing well; he tends to feel kindly toward his associates; he thinks he may have to justify any implied criticism; and he often finds it easier to say good about everyone than to pause to make careful discriminations.

Ambiguity is a second difficulty. Just as a self-report question on leadership can be variously interpreted, so a rater may define leadership in many ways. To one judge "leadership" suggests conscious wielding of authority, crisp decisions, and general dominance. A person rated high by this judge would receive a lower rating from a judge who looks for a leader to encourage subordinates, bring out coöperative decisions, and subordinate his own views to the decision of the group.

The rater is usually instructed to mark one of several alternative scale positions, and these response positions may also be ambiguous. In some of the early rating scales the respondent was asked to rate "Friendliness," for example, on a scale from 0 to 100. No particular definition can be given for a number such as 85 on that scale, and the same score may indicate quite different behavior to different raters. Such words as *average* and *excellent* are equally indefinite. They should be replaced by specific descriptions of behavior.

Judges have *constant errors* or biases. A constant error can be identified when two judges rate the same individuals. If the judges' averages differ, they are observing different aspects of behavior or are defining the scale differently. Generosity is one such constant error. The response styles mentioned in connection with achievement tests and personality questionnaires are also observed in ratings; e.g., one judge rarely uses the extremes of the scale in describing subjects, whereas another describes most persons in black-and-white terms.

A further source of differences between judges is that each has *limited information* about the individual. Since a physical education teacher and an English teacher see entirely different sides of the student, their ratings on initiative, imagination, or reaction to frustration will disagree. Even when an observer sees an individual in a great variety of situations, his sample of behavior is still limited. The supervisor can base his ratings only on what the man does under his supervision, and this may not be at all representative of his work elsewhere.

The so-called *halo effect* is an error which obscures the pattern of traits within the individual. The observer forms a general opinion about the person's merit, and his ratings on specific traits are strongly influenced by this overall impression. Even productivity may be rated erroneously because of the influence of a pleasing or displeasing personality. Halo is responsible for the substantial correlations shown in Table 66 among ratings given to 1100 industrial employees. The ratings on quite dissimilar traits show a marked

TABLE 66.   Intercorrelations of Ratings Given 1100 Industrial Workers

Traits	Safety	Knowledge of job	Versatility	Accuracy	Productivity	Overall job performance	Industriousness	Initiative	Judgment	Coöperation	Personality	Health
Safety	.35c	.61	.52	.63	.55	.60	.49	.54	.62	.61	.55	.25
Knowledge of job	.61	.46	.81	.85	.79	.82	.78	.78	.80	.67	.67	.52
Versatility	.52	.81	.47	.80	.72	.80	.71	.78	.82	.68	.63	.50
Accuracy	.63	.85	.80	.45	.81	.67	.80	.78	.84	.74	.70	.84
Productivity	.55	.79	.72	.81	.46	.86	.86	.80	.81	.81	.73	.45
Overall job performance	.60	.82	.80	.67	.86	.46	.85	.83	.88	.80	.74	.60
Industriousness	.49	.78	.71	.80	.86	.85	.47	.82	.84	.80	.67	.53
Initiative	.54	.78	.78	.78	.80	.83	.82	.48	.86	.72	.72	.77
Judgment	.62	.80	.82	.84	.81	.88	.84	.86	.45	.76	.75	.43
Coöperation	.61	.67	.68	.74	.81	.80	.80	.72	.76	.37	.80	.52
Personality	.55	.67	.63	.70	.73	.74	.67	.72	.75	.80	.39	.71
Health	.25	.52	.50	.84	.45	.60	.53	.77	.43	.52	.71	.36

a Boldface figures show correlations of two raters' judgments on each worker, i.e., reliability of judging.
SOURCE: Ewart et al., 1941.

general factor, apparently corresponding to the foreman's opinion of the man's industriousness and productivity.

These sources of error have four undesirable consequences:

• Ratings may not reveal important individual differences because they pile up at the favorable end of the scale.

• Ratings may be seriously invalid, representing chance effects or traits other than the one supposedly rated. Psychologists rating intelligence on the basis of observation, for example, overrated the ability of men with more introspective, less outgoing personalities (Barron, 1954).

• Halo effect obscures the descriptive picture.

• Ratings by different judges disagree. Evidence of unreliability is seen in Table 66. Reliability of rating is greatest for behaviors which can be clearly specified and for traits which are descriptive rather than interpretative. Traits reliably rated include talkative, assertive, bashful, and cultured. Reliability is lowest for general, vaguely stated attributes such as adaptable, sensitive, and kindly (Hollingworth, 1922; Mays, 1954).

Improvement of Ratings. The problems in improving ratings are similar to the problems in improving self-reports. Again, the tester must assume that the respondent will give false information if he thereby gains psychological rewards. To be sure, the information affects the subject's future rather than the rater's, but this does not mean that the rater is uninvolved. We have mentioned the rater's inclination to interpret reports on the subject as a reflection of the adequacy of his own teaching or supervision. Bias is even more certain when the therapist's ratings are used as a criterion of personality change during psychotherapy. Sometimes a rater gives a low rating because he wishes to retain an employee who might be promoted if he got a high rating. A teacher who rates a scholarship applicant may enlarge upon his merits nearly to the point of perjury in order to help the student.

Selection of raters is the first point at which to improve ratings. Raters cannot give valid information unless they know the subject well. Other things being equal, those in immediate contact with the subject can give better information than those who rely on hearsay. A high-school teacher usually can give more dependable information on a pupil's work habits and social behavior than can the principal.

One elementary precaution, often overlooked in practice, is to include in the rating blank a question regarding the extent of the rater's acquaintance with the subject and the kinds of situation in which observations were made, and a space where the rater can indicate "insufficient opportunity to observe" each trait instead of making an estimate from inadequate information. The American Council scale (Figure 85) not only provides a space to indicate lack of information but requests specific evidence for each rating so that the reader can judge for himself whether a favorable rating is justified by the rater's knowledge. If a judge is directed to mark every trait, some ratings are little better than guesses. Conrad (1932) directed raters to star traits which they regarded as especially important in the child's personality. Interjudge correlations on all traits ranged from .67 to .82. But for the traits which three judges agreed in starring, the ratings correlated as high as .96.

When the same judge is used repeatedly, it may be possible to keep a record of his ratings and ultimately to estimate his constant error. For example, a college learns to allow for the fact that one high school has a "tough" grading or rating policy, whereas another school is lenient. It is rarely practical to make exact statistical corrections for such differences between raters.

One can raise the reliability of ratings by combining impressions of several judges. If, as in Table 66, the reliability of a rating is about .45, the average of two independent judges is expected to have a reliability of .60 and the average of five judges a reliability of .80. (These results are given by the Spearman-Brown formula, p. 131.) In the average the bias of one judge tends to cancel the bias of another, and each adds information the other had no opportunity to observe. Reliability may be lowered rather than raised, however, when the additional judges are only remotely acquainted with the subject.

Careful preparation of the rating scale is of great value. There is some advantage in using several questions dealing with a particular aspect of personality, just as there is advantage in basing self-report scores on many related items. On the other hand, anything which enlarges the rater's task invites perfunctory answers.

The rater may be asked to make a simple checkmark beside satisfactory qualities, respond on a numerical scale, or make choices among carefully described alternatives. Where ratings on each trait are to be considered separately the last of these forms, known as the *descriptive graphic rating scale,* is generally best (cf. Figure 86). The scale is descriptive, since each point

Is he abstracted or wide awake?

Continually absorbed in himself (5)	Frequently becomes abstracted (4)	Usually present-minded (2)	Wide-awake (1)	Keenly alive and alert (3)

Is he shy or bold in social relationships?

Painfully self-conscious (4)	Timid, Frequently embarrassed (2)	Self-conscious on occasions (1)	Confident in himself (3)	Bold, Insensitive to social feelings (5)

How does he accept authority?

Defiant (5)	Critical of authority (4)	Ordinarily obedient (3)	Respectful, Complies by habit (1)	Entirely resigned, Accepts all authority (2)

FIG. 86.   Items for the Haggerty-Olson-Wickman Behavior Rating Schedule. (Copyright 1930 by World Book Company and reproduced by permission.)

corresponds to a recognizable behavior pattern. It is graphic, in that the rater is allowed to mark at intermediate points if he does not find any one of the descriptions entirely suitable. In general, 5- to 7-point scales seem to serve adequately. With informed and serious professional judges, much finer subdivisions of the scale prove profitable (Champney and Marshall, 1939).

The 5-point scale obtains more discrimination than the "yes-no" checklist. A judge will ordinarily say "yes" when asked "Does the subject have good judgment?" but if given several alternate choices he may check "Sometimes overlooks relevant facts in making decisions." The 5-point scale also has the advantage of drawing attention to various kinds of deviation. A simple "yes-no" question, "Does he accept authority?" would not distinguish, as does the

Haggerty-Olson-Wickman scale, between the respectful, obedient child and the slavish, spiritless conformer.

To predict an external criterion, traits for rating can be selected empirically. The Haggerty-Olson-Wickman scale is intended to screen maladjusted pupils for psychological study. A direct interpretation might be made simply by scoring socially desirable behavior. The investigators found, however, that behavior which on its face seems desirable may actually be a sign of maladjustment, appearing more often among problem children than among pupils in general. Weights were therefore assigned to each response, as indicated by the numbers in Figure 86. A score of 1 was given for descriptions rarely applied to problem children, and a score of 5 for responses characteristic of the problem group. We see, for example, that "Wide-awake" is a favorable description, but that "Keenly alive and alert" describes children who get into trouble about as often as it does the well adjusted.

This weighting technique suggests the possibility of concealing the scoring plan to outwit the rater who is unwilling to give an unfavorable report. One might count only those ratings which correlate with the criterion. For example, in selecting salesmen one might give credit for high ratings such as energetic, ambitious, and friendly (if these traits correlate with success in the job) and no credit for equally high ratings such as hard-working, well-adjusted, and coöperative (if these traits have no predictive value). Indeed, we may go farther, and assign a *negative* weight to these irrelevant favorable ratings to compensate for rater generosity.

Forced-Choice Methods.   This idea underlies the forced-choice method of merit rating pioneered by the military services. Periodic ratings of each officer by his superior are required for use in promotion and reassignment. The tradition of giving favorable ratings, however, means that conventional rating forms bring in almost no information. Psychologists therefore invented a forced-choice scale. As a first step in making such a scale, superiors are asked to describe men by checking a list of phrases. A follow-up is then made to determine which men perform best in subsequent assignments, and for each adjective or phrase two figures are obtained: a favorability index and a validity index. A favorable-valid item is one which raters apply frequently and which predicts success: an unfavorable-valid item is rarely applied and when applied forecasts failure. Invalid items are those not associated with success or failure.

The forced-choice item is then developed. One technique used by Army psychologists employs two pairs of statements. A favorable-valid item was matched with a favorable-invalid item, and an unfavorable-valid item with an unfavorable-invalid item. These four were presented together, the rater being instructed to indicate the one statement which best describes the man and the one which least describes him. Thus the rater is forced to make at least one unfavorable statement, and to choose only one favorable statement. An item might consist of the following alternatives:

Wins confidence of his men	(Favorable-valid)
Inclined to gripe about conditions	(Unfavorable-invalid)
Punctual in completing reports	(Favorable-invalid)
Has weak tactical judgment	(Unfavorable-valid)

The response is scored by assigning a plus credit for each favorable-valid choice and a minus credit for each unfavorable-valid choice.

The aim in the forced choice is to separate the rater's task of describing what the individual does from the task of evaluating what he does (Richardson, 1949). The responsibility for description must rest on the rater, but evaluation is left to the decision maker.

The score indicates the man's probable merit. For a combat command, it appears likely that winning confidence is more important than punctuality in reports, and tactical judgment more important than contentment. The scoring weights, however, are assigned on the basis of statistical evidence, not on the basis of judgment. The weights are kept secret from the raters, but since raters can guess to some extent how the scale will be scored, the choice is only relatively free from distortion.

Highland and Berkshire (1951) compared several types of forced-choice instrument for rating instructors. Whereas a graphic rating scale correlated only .40 with rankings, validities for forced-choice scales ranged from .53 to .62. The most valid form presented four favorable traits, two relevant to the criterion and two irrelevant, with the rater instructed to mark the two most descriptive of the instructor. Such a form can be distorted by a desire to give "good" ratings, but only to a limited degree. When supervisors filled out the scale a second time with instructions to give as favorable an impression as possible, the median of the "faked" scores fell near the 67th percentile of the "honest" distribution. As Figure 87 shows, the bias raised many scores from the "bad" end of the scale to the average but did not lead to a piling up of very high scores. It is evidently possible for the rater to avoid giving a bad impression on this type of scale, but not to fake a very good one. Raters preferred the form using all favorable traits to the one using two favorable and two unfavorable traits. The latter was also more subject to distortion, since "faked" scores did pile up at the high end of that scale.

Raters are generally antagonistic to forced-choice techniques. They want to know how their reports will be interpreted and want to be free to give an entirely favorable impression. Whether a forced-choice scale can be used in a given situation depends upon the coöperation the data gatherer can anticipate or upon the authority he can bring to bear. The Army, after developing the technique and establishing its validity, concluded that resistance from officers was too great to justify continued use of forced-choice scales in effi-ciency reports. It has continued to use forced choice, however, in self-report forms. In industry, forced-choice merit ratings have had considerable appli-cation.

A method of restricting raters which encounters less opposition is to re-quire rankings. Where large groups of men are to be judged, the instructions

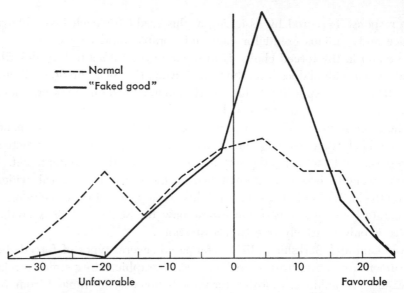

FIG. 87. Distribution of ratings on a forced-choice scale under normal and faking conditions (Highland and Berkshire, 1951).

may call, not for complete ranking, but for dividing men into groups such as top 5 percent, next 20 percent, middle 50 percent, next 20 percent, and bot-tom 5 percent. This forced distribution obtains more differentiation under some circumstances than does the graphic scale. Ranking presupposes that the judge is giving consideration to the proper trait; a ranking on overall merit will be misleading if the rater stresses obedience and dependability when the institution wishes to select men with initiative and imagination. The chief limitation of the ranking method is that groups are rarely compara-ble, so that a top man in one group might rank tenth in another.

The "Q-sort" technique developed by Stephenson (1953) is valuable for certain purposes. In comprehensive personality assessment, for example, in-terviewers and observers may collect a great deal of information and arrive at a comprehensive picture of the man's strengths and weaknesses. Much of this information is lost if it is reduced to a few simple numerical ratings. In a descriptive report, the psychologist sometimes makes general remarks which might apply to any subject and omits some important findings.

Stephenson's method calls for the preparation of a set of phrases covering the aspects of personality or performance that concern those who will use the report. There is no single list of statements for Q-sorting, since the traits to consider in selecting executives may differ a good deal from the descriptions useful in appraising patients during psychotherapy. The following statements are representative of a list used by assessors for evaluating superior men (Block, 1957):

Communicates ideas clearly and effectively
Is rigid; inflexible in thought and action
Takes an ascendant role in his relations with others
Is masculine in his style and manner of behavior
Lacks insight into his own motives and behavior
Overcontrols his impulses; is inhibited; needlessly delays or denies gratification
Allows personal bias, spite, or dogmatism to enter into his judgment of issues

The statements or phrases are written on separate cards. The rater is told to sort the cards into eleven piles, with those most descriptive of the subject in the first pile and those least descriptive in the eleventh. The rater must place a specified number of items in each pile; if there are 100 statements to be sorted, he might be told to put them into this distribution:

	Most descriptive						Least descriptive				
Pile	1	2	3	4	5	6	7	8	9	10	11
Number of cards	2	4	8	11	16	18	16	11	8	4	2

The number of piles and the number of cards differ in different studies.

The sorting procedure has some advantage over the usual rating form, since the rater can shift items back and forth. In the usual inventory or checklist his definition of a category such as "Definitely true" may shift while he is making his ratings, but in a Q sort we may expect the items placed in the same pile to be truly comparable. The fixed distribution eliminates rater differences in response style. It cannot, however, eliminate rater bias. The rater can easily arrange the items so as to describe the subject favorably (Edwards, 1957). The Q-sort method may also be used in obtaining self-descriptions.

Q-sort data can be handled in several ways. One may compute the median position of statements representing a single dimension of personality, just as a personality test is scored for anxiety or dominance. One may develop an actuarial key for items predictive of a criterion, as in forced-choice rating scales. One may compute a correlation showing how similar one subject is to another. Some of the elaborate techniques used with Q sorts are open to serious criticism (Cronbach and Gleser, 1954). Properly designed Q statements, however, have unquestionable value for obtaining complex descriptions which can be systematically compared.

The choice among rating techniques depends upon the purpose of rating, the qualifications of raters, the information they have about the subjects, and the likelihood of distortion, deliberate or unconscious. The short, unsubtle, but carefully prepared descriptive graphic rating scale is probably best when each subject is rated by different individuals and one may assume a reasonable degree of honesty in rating. Ranking is advantageous when a single judge gives information on the complete group or a representative sample of the group. The forced choice is often superior when ratings are used for institutional decisions regarding selection or classification but is less suitable for guidance or description of the individual. The Q sort is of greatest value where a comprehensive description of a single individual is desired and the rater can be expected to give patient consideration to a long list of questions. Asking the rater to fill out a standard personality questionnaire so that the responses describe the subject has similar advantages.

1. Which rating technique would be most suitable for each of these purposes?
    a. Obtaining ratings from principals to be used in deciding which teachers should receive salary increases for special merit.
    b. Obtaining information for school records regarding parents' impressions of their children's personalities.
    c. Maintaining weekly records of ward behavior of patients as seen by attendants.
    d. Recording teacher characteristics as judged by an observer in research evaluating teacher-training methods.
    e. Obtaining reports from supervisors of student teachers, to be used by campus instructors in helping the student to improve.
    f. Obtaining reports on pupils to be used in awarding college scholarships to the most deserving graduates in a state.
2. Why might keenly alive children have more behavior problems than those rated as wide-awake (Figure 86)? Would "keenly alive and alert" ordinarily be considered a sign of poor mental hygiene?
3. In the American Council rating scale, the trait scale for leadership (C) is defined by five specific phrases. What advantage does this scale have over the set of adjectives "excellent," "good," "average," "poor," "unsatisfactory"?
4. Why might integrity and kindness be especially hard to rate reliably?
5. Which of the following traits would probably be hardest to rate reliably after observations: skill in self-expression, freedom from tension, freedom from anxiety, leadership (Hollingworth, 1922, p. 32)?
6. Ratings on leadership made at Officer Candidate School correlated only .15 with ratings on efficiency of combat leadership by superior officers who observed the men in combat (Jenkins, 1947). Why is the correlation so low?
7. Could a complex description be obtained by having the rater mark the MMPI responses that fit the subject? Would such a method be less satisfactory than a Q sort?
8. The rating form shown in Figure 88 is used by high schools to send reports to colleges. Compare this form with the ACE scale (Figure 85) with respect to
    a. format.
    b. traits covered.
    c. adequacy of phrasing of scale positions.

Personality Record (Confidential)
(REVISED)

Room.............
Grade.............

PERSONAL CHARACTERISTICS OF.............. ....
                                     Last Name   First Name   Middle Name

School.............. ....
             Town or City   State

The following characterizations are descriptions of behavior. It is recommended that where possible the judgments of a number of the pupil's present teachers be indicated by the use of the following method or by checks:

Example: MOTIVATION

M (5) indicates the most common or modal behavior of the pupil as shown by the agreement of five of the eight teachers reporting. The location of the numerals to the left and right indicates that one teacher considers the pupil *vacillating* and that two teachers consider him *highly motivated*. If preferred, the subject fields or other areas of relationship with the pupil may be used to replace the numerals.

Example: MOTIVATION	Purposeless	Vacillating 1 √	Usually purposeful M (5) √ √ √ √ √	Effectively motivated	Highly motivated 2 √ √
1. MOTIVATION	Purposeless	Vacillating	Usually purposeful	Effectively motivated	Highly motivated
2. INDUSTRY	Seldom works even under pressure	Needs constant pressure	Needs occasional prodding	Prepares assigned work regularly	Seeks additional work
3. INITIATIVE	Merely conforms	Seldom initiates	Frequently initiates	Consistently self-reliant	Actively creative
4. INFLUENCE AND LEADERSHIP	Negative	Co-operative but retiring	Sometimes in minor affairs	Contributing in important affairs	Judgment respected—makes things go
5. CONCERN FOR OTHERS	Indifferent	Self-centered	Somewhat socially concerned	Generally concerned	Deeply and actively concerned
6. RESPONSIBILITY	Unreliable	Somewhat dependable	Usually dependable	Conscientious	Assumes much responsibility
7. INTEGRITY	Not dependable	Questionable at times	Generally honest	Reliable, dependable	Consistently trustworthy
8. EMOTIONAL STABILITY	Hyperemotional / Apathetic	Excitable / Unresponsive	Usually well-balanced	Well-balanced	Exceptionally stable

FIG. 88. The Personality Record. Prepared by a joint committee representing high schools and colleges. (Copyright 1958, National Association of Secondary School Principals of the NEA, and reproduced by permission.)

Validity of Ratings by Superiors. It is extremely difficult to state whether, in a given situation, ratings by superiors will be valid measures of behavior. One might expect supervisors to rate job knowledge accurately. The trait is well defined, the behavior is observable, and the supervisor has ample opportunity to observe. Nonetheless, supervisors' ratings of job knowledge usually correlate only about .35 with the knowledge measured by a formal test, though ratings in one department reached a validity of .55 (Peters and Campbell, 1955; Morsh and Schmid, 1956).

Another study investigated ratings given by department heads to foremen. These ratings correlated only .22 with objective records of the work performance of the crews. The rating supposedly reflected productivity but it actually correlated .59 with how long the rater had known the foreman, and .65 with his liking for the foreman (Stockford and Bissell, 1949). Such findings are particularly distressing in view of the widespread use of ratings as criteria for validating tests.

Although the evidence demands that one be suspicious of the validity of ratings, they are sometimes excellent sources of data. Jack (1934) found that ratings of "ascendance" by nursery-school teachers correlated .81 with a score derived from objectively recorded observations of the child's acts on the playground. For ratings to be depended upon, the validity of the rating procedure should be established in the particular situation where it is used.

Peer Ratings

In many situations ratings by peers give more useful information than ratings by superiors. Even where ratings by superiors are available and dependable, the peer ratings cover a different aspect of personality. A "peer" is an individual who has the same status within the organization as the person rated. Black's study in which girls rated others living in the same college dormitory is one example. Another is the rating of each other by officer candidates. In military studies, such reports are often referred to as "buddy ratings."

Whereas only one or two superiors know a subject well, ten to thirty raters may give information when ratings in a class or a dormitory are collected. As a consequence, the average rating on any trait is highly reliable. Indeed, for well-defined traits in a group which has had reasonable opportunity to become acquainted, composite peer ratings generally have reliabilities in the neighborhood of .90.

A child who impresses his peers as being a leader may not be the one whom the teacher regards as a leader; the peers, for example, may place great weight on popularity whereas the teacher notices originality and initiative. It is of value for the teacher or counselor, however, to know which persons are regarded as leaders by their own group. Indeed, the information may be most significant in just those cases where the superiors and the peers have different impressions. The peer rating is an objective statement about the individual's reputation. Reputation is based to some extent on behavior, but the social pattern and role relations in the group introduce biases of various sorts. Among adolescents, correlations between reputations and careful observations of corresponding behaviors range from .45 to .70 (Newman and Jones, 1946).

To obtain peer ratings it is usually necessary to simplify the task. Raters are untrained, and we desire each rater to describe many individuals. The adjective checklist (see p. 477) can be marked much more quickly than the descriptive graphic scale and can cover many aspects of behavior. In using the checklist to obtain information about particular individuals, related adjectives are classified into groups and a count is made of the frequency with which adjectives in each category are checked. Such a checklist leads to a descriptive profile.

Nomination Techniques. If thirty persons in a group rate each other on twenty traits, each person is being asked to give 600 responses. This means that considerable carelessness and halo effect may be expected, and various alternative devices are employed to reduce the labor without reducing the amount of significant information. The most important of these devices is the nomination technique. Each member of the group is asked to name a fixed number of persons who are outstanding in a particular respect, such as leadership. A similar nomination of persons who are most lacking in leadership may also be solicited, but this arouses anxiety because subjects know that they are being considered for such unfavorable nominations and because, as raters, they are reluctant to speak unfavorably of associates. The data gatherer can usually infer that the person who is never mentioned for a certain favorable trait belongs somewhere toward the other end of the scale.

For young children, Hartshorne and May disguised the nomination technique as a guessing game. The "Guess Who" test describes various roles children may play, and each member of the group names the children he thinks each description fits. Typical descriptions are (Hartshorne and May, 1929, p. 88):

Here is the class athlete. He (or she) can play baseball, basketball, tennis, can swim as well as any, and is a good sport.
This one is always picking on others and annoying them.

A profile for each child is made by counting the frequency with which he is mentioned for each description.

Sociometric Ratings. The sociogram is a method of studying the social structure of groups. Characteristics of an individual, including his popularity, may be studied by the Guess Who method, but the sociogram gives further insight by identifying cliques, hierarchies of leadership, and other social groupings. The sociogram was developed by Moreno (1934). Although the technique has been amended in various ways which sacrifice effectiveness for convenience, the best procedure is to request members of a group to indicate their choices for companions in a particular activity. Gronlund (1959) suggests the following directions for use with pupils in the upper elementary grades.

During the next few weeks we will be changing our seats around, working in small groups, and playing some group games. Now that we all know each other by name, you can help me arrange groups that work and play best together. You can do this by writing the names of the children you would like *to have sit near you,* *to have work with you,* and *to have play with you.* You may choose anyone in this room you wish, including those pupils who are absent. Your choices will not be seen by anyone else. Give first name and initial of last name.

Make your choices carefully so the groups will be the way you really want them. I will try to arrange the groups so that each pupil gets at least two of his choices. Sometimes it is hard to give everyone his first few choices so be sure to make all five choices for each question.

Directions should be concerned with real group activities, and the choices should be real choices. The data are not obtained in a test setting; instead, they are obtained as a means of dealing with the group. If data are obtained from a less real question, such as "Who are your friends?" there is more likelihood of answers given to make a good impression. Subjects must know that their reports will be treated confidentially. The sociometric data should be used as promised to set up work groups, committees, homeroom seating, or whatever; this permits one to obtain coöperation when the technique is used again at a later date.

Though sociometric ratings are easy to obtain in most situations, the tester must be wary of arousing anxieties. In a group of adolescent girls where popularity is a matter of great concern, a girl may resist the injunction to indicate the one person she most prefers, or may worry about how she will be rated.

After the choices are obtained, they are plotted in a sociogram. Figure 89 is the sociogram of a class of fourth-grade girls early in the school year. Pupils indicated one to three choices and were permitted to list also any classmates they would not choose. This sociogram shows several typical configurations. There are two groups or cliques. In one Emily is the most-sought-after person, with Jane, Lenora, Caroline, Rhoda, and Louise as accepted members. In the other group, Agnes is the key figure, with Lurline, Patricia, and Ann as members. Patricia is not thoroughly integrated with the clique; while accepted by Agnes, she is also reaching toward Emily in the other group, rather than Lurline or Ann. Agnes, who might be a popular leader of all the girls, instead shows considerable hostility, rejecting three popular girls. Ella is not chosen by any of the others, and Tess is even more isolated.

The sociogram obtained depends upon the question asked. For example, if sorority girls are asked to indicate their choices for roommates, and their choices of persons with whom to study, the sociometric patterns will differ.

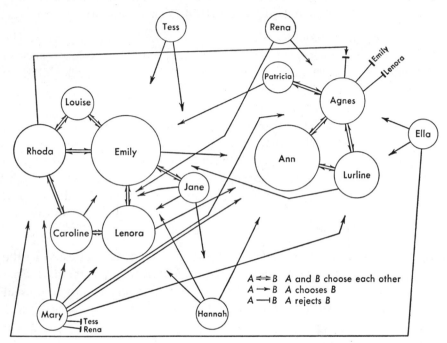

FIG. 89.   Sociogram for a class of fourth-grade girls. (Adapted from Staff, Division on Child Development, 1945, p. 297.)

A best friend may be thought of as too noisy or untidy for a good roommate, and an unpopular girl may be regarded as an excellent helper on school assignments. Basic social configurations are fairly stable when different questions are used, but one cannot assume that the interpersonal structure of a group is the same under all conditions.

The structure changes with time. By December, Agnes was a "star" in her class, along with Rhoda and Emily. The cliques had disappeared, thanks to the skill of the teacher. Ann and Lurline still chose each other, but Agnes now turned her back on them, ignoring Ann and rejecting Lurline. Even though social relationships change, an individual's level of popularity is remarkably constant. Gronlund (1959) points out that among elementary pupils the stability over a one-year interval is about as high as for intelligence and achievement.

The term *sociometric rating* applies generally to all methods of identifying social relationships among group members. No sharp distinction is to be made between the descriptive peer rating and the sociometric rating, but in general the latter is restricted to questions about whom the rater likes best or would prefer to work with, and thus is as much concerned with the rater's reaction as with the rater's personality. When given willingly, however, the ratings may be much more dependable than other sorts of ratings, as Lindzey and Borgatta point out (Lindzey, 1954, Vol. I, p. 406):

> There is no need to train raters to engage in sociometric ratings. The difficult and time-consuming task of attempting to produce common frames of reference and homogeneous criteria in terms of which ratings shall be assigned is avoided. The rater is asked to apply exactly those particular, unique, and sometimes irrational criteria he has spent a lifetime developing. Everyone is an experienced or expert rater when it comes to sociometric judgments. Each of us has a vast body of experience in deciding with whom we wish to interact and whom we wish to avoid. Liking and disliking, accepting and rejecting are part of the process of daily living. . . . One might say that the individual who uses these techniques is taking advantage of the largest pool of sensitive and experienced raters that is anywhere avilable.

The validity of responses to the sociometric questionnaire is attested by the finding that choices given by pupils as to preferred fellow actors in a class play correlated about .80 with actual choices when an opportunity to present impromptu plays was given (Byrd, 1951).

9. What children besides Tess and Ella are fringers?
10. What interpretations of Agnes' hostility can be suggested?
11. Prior to this study, the teacher had characterized Tess as hard working, interested in accomplishing tasks, "fits in nicely with the group." Tess helps others with their sewing, at which she is superior. How would the teacher's outlook and treatment of Tess be affected by the information from the sociogram?
12. The following choices were made in a group of tenth-graders. Plot a sociogram and discuss the interactions shown.

> Shirley chooses Charles, Jim, and Sam.
> Charles chooses Shirley, Sam and Jim; rejects Tom.
> Phil chooses Jim, Charles, and Shirley; rejects Wallace and Tom.
> Wallace chooses Phil and Jack; rejects Tom.
> Jim chooses Jack, Sam, Charles, and Shirley; rejects Tom.
> Jack chooses Jim and Tom; rejects Phil.
> Shirley is chosen by several girls whom she does not mention. Sam and Tom were absent.

13. When sociograms were made of squadrons of Navy fliers on combat duty, it was found that the "administratively designated leaders" were often not the ones chosen as preferred work leaders by the men (G. A. Kelly, 1947, p. 133). What practical suggestions follow from this finding?

14. In a group of sorority girls, the sociometric question "Whom would you choose as a roommate?" is asked; will results be the same if the question is changed to "With whom would you choose to go on a double date?"

15. What would be the best way of studying the reliability of sociometric data?

Uses of Peer Ratings.   Information about the individual's reputation or status in the group can be used in many ways. The group leader uses it to identify individuals who require special attention and individuals who can be developed into leaders. Sociometric information has frequently been of use in reorganizing a group so that it will function better. For example, Roethlisberger and Dickson used sociometric data to organize factory workers into congenial teams. Moreno, in an institution for delinquent girls, assigned the girls to small living groups on the basis of sociometric choices.

Peer ratings can be used as a basis for selection and classification. Among officer candidates, for example, the impression a man makes on his companions during the early phases of training is likely to forecast his ability to win confidence and acceptance as an officer. One study (Wherry and Fryer, 1949) refers to the peer rating as the "purest measure of leadership . . . better than any other variable." Kelly and Fiske (1951, p. 169) found that peer ratings of clinical psychology trainees after only a few days' close association were significant predictors of ratings of clinical competence made by university departments three years later. The median correlation of .25 is only a little below the coefficient of .34 for ratings by a team of trained psychological assessors using full test and interview data. Neither validity coefficient is high, partly because of the inadequacy of the criteria. Similarly, composite peer ratings of officer candidates correlate about .50 with later ratings by superiors in duty assignments. This correlation is extremely impressive, in view of the criterion reliability of about .50. The rated traits which predict the criterion include coöperative, emotionally stable, assertive, intellectual, and determined (Tupes, 1957).

For the counselor, the peer descriptions point out characteristics of the individual which impede his acceptance. Especially when the student seems to lack insight regarding his reputation, the peer rating points to behavior which should be examined during counseling.

16. Cattell and Stice (1953) find that surgency (i.e., energetic, talkative, enthusiastic behavior) correlates very little with leadership behavior as rated by observers, but correlates substantially with frequency of election. Explain this finding. What does it imply regarding the use of peer ratings as criteria?

Noteworthy Rating Scales

Few rating scales are distributed commercially, since the common practice is to develop a new instrument for each institution or each investigation.

Some scales have been carefully designed and standardized for common research and administrative purposes. Figures 85 and 88 show scales for use by high schools in making recommendations about college applicants. Several scales for industrial merit rating have also been published or distributed through management consulting firms. Here we shall examine selected scales for two other uses.

The rating of personality has particularly widespread application. Both for practical personnel decisions and for research, we wish to record the impressions of peers and supervisors. A suitable set of scales will include traits which can be rated reliably and which are relatively definite and free from halo effect.

Scales for ward observations and clinical diagnosis emphasize symptoms. In large hospitals, for example, it is useful for ward attendants to fill out such forms periodically on each patient, since shifts in observed behavior may imply that the patient's treatment should be altered. Several scales for rating patient behavior have been developed, one being the Wittenborn Psychiatric Rating Scales published by the Psychological Corporation (1955). (See also Lorr *et al.*, 1955.) The Wittenborn form presents 52 scales, organized into nine scores representing different types of symptoms. Figure 90 shows the ratings of a patient on the first five items. The clusters I to IX were defined through factor analysis, and the unshaded block in the rating form indicates that a particular response is relevant to one of the dimensions. The rater need only circle the number (0, 1, 2, or 3) which indicates his impression of the patient. The scorer then copies that number into the corresponding block. For example, the rating given on scale 1, indicating difficulty in sleeping, adds one point to the score in cluster I and cluster V. Two unshaded blocks in a given column indicate that double weight is given to an item.

The dimensions, established by examining symptoms in a large number of patients, are named in psychiatric terminology: I. Acute anxiety; II. Conversion hysteria; III. Manic state; IV. Depressed state; V. Schizophrenic excitement; VI. Paranoid condition; VII. Paranoid schizophrenic; VIII. Hebephrenic schizophrenic; IX. Phobic compulsive. With few exceptions (e.g., Acute anxiety and Phobic compulsive) the correlations between scales are low. The scores are moderately reliable, the median split-half correlation being .82. Combining two or more independent ratings would be necessary to get a dependable picture of the individual's condition. This is not a serious limitation, since clinical decisions are likely to be based on trends over several weeks. It should be noted that the rating scale indicates the patient's condition rather than his diagnostic category. A patient may shift through different patterns of behavior as he progresses toward recovery or is tem-

Scale	Rating	I	II	III	IV	V	VI	VII	VIII	IX
1. Gives no evidence of difficulty in sleeping.	0									
Without sedation may have difficulty in falling asleep, or sleep is readily or spontaneously interrupted.	(1)	1								
Without sedation long periods of wakefulness at night.	2									
Acute insomnia; without sedatives gets less than 4 hours sleep in 24.	3									
2. Rate of change of ideas (e.g., topics of conversation) does not appear to be accelerated, nor are changes conspicuously abrupt.	0									
Ideas may change *abruptly*.	1					1				
Ideas are in the process of *rapid* and *constant change*.	(2)			2		2				
Ideas change with spontaneous and unpredictable rapidity as to make sustained conversation *impossible*.	3									
3. No evidence that he imagines people (who probably are wholly indifferent to him) have an amorous interest in him.	(0)									
Believes (without justification) that certain persons have an amorous interest in him.	1									
Believes (without justification) that a sexual union has occurred or has been formally arranged for him.	2					2				
4. No evidence for obsessional (repetitive, stereotyped) thinking.	(0)									
Obsessive thoughts recur but can be banished without difficulty.	1									
Patient is able to banish obsessive thoughts but only with difficulty.	2									
Cannot banish or control obsessive thoughts.	3									
5. No evidence that patient considers himself to be particularly unworthy or blameworthy.	0									
Patient tends to blame himself or refer to his unworthiness.	1									
Patient blames and criticizes self to an unrealistic and inappropriate degree.	2									
Patient appears to have a *delusional* belief that he is an extraordinarily evil, unworthy or guilty person.	(3)	3								
		3								
Subtotals (p. 1)		7		2		5				

FIG. 90. Ratings of a 26-year-old male patient on the Wittenborn Psychiatric Rating Scales. (Form copyright ©, 1955, The Psychological Corporation. Reproduced by permission.)

porarily upset, and the function of the scale is to record such changes rather than to give him a label.

As a further example of rating scale development, we may mention the Fels Parent Behavior Rating Scales. These scales were developed to study the preschool child's family. Trained observers visited each home periodically and wrote a descriptive report; to provide systematic data which could be treated statistically, the observer also gave ratings on thirty scales. These scales were designed to cover emotional relations, disciplinary methods, and values of the home.

The directions and definitions for one scale, for example, are as follows:

Quantity of Suggestion (*Suggesting—Non-suggesting*)

Rate the parent's tendency to make suggestions to the child. Is the parent constantly offering requests, commands, hints, or other attempts to direct the child's immediate behavior? Or does the parent withhold suggestions, giving the child's initiative full sway?

This does not apply to routine regulations and their enforcement. Rate only where there is opportunity for suggestion. Note that "suggestion" is defined broadly, including direct and indirect, positive and negative, verbal and nonverbal, mandatory and optional.

—Parent continually attempting to direct the minute details of the child's routine functioning, and "free" play as well.

—Occasionally withholds suggestions, but more often indicates what to do next or how to do it.

—Parent's tendency to allow child's initiative full scope is about equal to tendency to interfere by making suggestions.

—Makes general suggestions now and then, but allows child large measure of freedom to do things own way.

—Parent not only consistently avoids volunteering suggestions, but tends to withhold them when they are requested, or when they are the obvious reaction to the immediate situation.

Such lengthy scales, requiring patient and thoughtful discrimination, contrast markedly with the simple rating scales used in obtaining recommendations on prospective employees or routine judgments from teachers. The elaborate definitions and fine subdivision of traits permit a much more reliable and comprehensive picture of the home than a simple form would. Interrater reliability on single traits ranges from about .50 to .90. The technique is designed to be used by a qualified professional observer who has a substantial amount of information to record, information which could not be communicated fully in a coarse scale. Such an elaborate scale is unnecessary when the rater has only casual impressions to convey.

The scale is organized around these factors: Warmth (first five variables in Figure 91), Adjustment, Restrictiveness, Clarity of Policy, and Interference. The detailed picture of five areas which are themselves further differentiated forestalls any tendency to characterize homes as simply "good" or "bad." The scale results show that democratic homes can be cold and conflictful, orderly yet affectionate, or warm and still maladjusted. The profile in Figure 91 illustrates the volume of information recorded in quantitative form about a single home. The Stones are warm, protective, rather coercive,

Left pole	20	30	40	50	60	70	80	Right pole
Child-subordinate						√		Child-centered
Disapproval					√			Approval
Rejection					√			Acceptance
Hostile				√				Affectionate
Isolation			√					Close rapport
Inert contacts				√				Vigorous contacts
Withholds help					√			Over-helps
Exposing					√			Sheltering
Nonchalant					√			Anxious
Nonsuggesting					√			Suggesting
Uncritical				√				Critical
Inactive				√				Active
Chaotic				√				Coordinated
Arbitrary policy				√				Rational policy
Dictatorial			√					Democratic
Retardatory					√			Acceleratory
Thwarts curiosity				√				Satisfies curiosity
Obtuse		√						Keen
Freedom					√			Restriction
Suggestions optional				√				Suggestions mandatory
Lax enforcement		√						Vigilant
Vague policy			√					Clear policy
Maladjusted		√						Well-adjusted
Harmony				√				Conflict
Unsuccessful policy			√					Successful policy
Concordant			√					Contentious
Seclusive family			√					Expansive family
Brief contact			√					Extensive contact
Mild penalties		√						Severe penalties
Objective					√			Emotional
	20	30	40	50	60	70	80	

FIG. 91. Rating of the home treatment of Ted Stone (Baldwin et al., 1949, p. 28).

giving, as the authors say, a picture of "restrictive indulgence." But more can be learned from the profile (Baldwin et al., 1949, p. 29; see also Baldwin et al., 1945):

The rating of readiness of enforcement contributes a definite flavor to the interpretation. The mother is restrictive, but lax in enforcement and also, we see, mild in her punishments. The home begins to appear verbal and nagging, but without any core of enforced disciplinary policy. When ratings of low adjustment, high discord, low effectiveness of policy, and high disciplinary friction are added, the suspicion arises that Ted does not conform to his mother's standards. She talks and nags, but achieves little. The fact that approval is still high in spite of all this conflict and discord might be interpreted as a determined effort by the mother to see the boy in the best possible light. . . . A low rating on understanding makes it clear that the mother has little insight into what Ted wants and needs but instead is projecting on him her own motivation.

This rating pattern fits the full clinical description given by the visitor. This evidence of validity raises the question whether careful and elaborate ratings cannot accomplish all that a clinical description might hope to do. An attempt to reduce individuality to a limited list of dimensions always loses some idiosyncratic features, however. The ratings characterize the Stone family in terms of those qualities on which all homes can be judged, but not in terms of its own recurrent themes and conditions. From the clinical notes we learn facts such as these: Mrs. Stone has had lifelong trouble in forming emotional ties, with the significant exceptions of her mother and her son. She is contemptuous of her husband. She thinks that no one, not even her husband, understands that she has "sacrificed her life for Ted." "Having identified herself completely with her product, it was necessary that the child himself be immaculate, perfect in behavior, precocious intellectually." Ted is prone to respiratory infections and subject to allergies; these intensify his mother's anxiety. Discipline is pulled in opposite directions by Mrs. Stone's desire for perfection and her identification with Ted. "On one occasion when he was sent to bed an hour early as a punishment, Mrs. Stone decided she had been overly severe and went to the bedroom to read to him for the extra period." Such descriptive color and texture, while of no use for statistical research, is informative both to the clinical worker and to the research psychologist. There is no reason to think that even elaborate rating systems can replace descriptive accounts in exploratory research or casework.

17. Would an elaborate rating instrument such as the Fels scales be advantageous when obtaining ratings of a child by his teacher?
18. How much of the "individual" information quoted from the caseworker's notes on the Stones could have been covered by adding additional traits to the rating scale?
19. No evidence on agreement between raters is given in the manual for the Wittenborn scales. Why is this information needed? Plan a study to obtain it.

OBSERVATION OF BEHAVIOR SAMPLES

Self-reports and judgments by peers and supervisors are based on a more or less haphazard composite of observations. The rater has not seen the individual in all situations, and selective recall operates in both rating and self-report. Systematic observations can give a more accurate description of typical behavior. A distinction must be made between observations intended to cover a representative sample of behavior and observations in a standardized test situation. The former attempts to estimate typical behavior from a statistically representative sample of situations actually occurring in life; the situations may and usually will differ for different persons. The latter observes reaction to the same situation for everyone. The situation used may be quite uncommon in the subject's life.

Field observations—i.e., observation of the subject under his normal circumstances—are relatively easy to carry out and for some studies they are more suitable than standardized observations. Many investigators feel that it is impossible to know personality unless we watch the subject react to the conditions that are most significant for him. Different stimuli are significant for different people. Standard situations are perhaps not as likely to elicit the important behavior patterns as are the normal (dissimilar) conditions under which the subjects live. The difficulty lies in seeing enough of the person's normal behavior and in obtaining dependable records.

Sampling Problems

Whenever one wishes to know the typical behavior of an employee, a student, or a patient, the most direct way to find out is to observe him in normal situations. If he does not know that we are watching him, we obtain a truthful picture limited only by our skill as observers and our persistence. This is our usual basis for judging associates and friends. Judgments based upon observation, however, are likely to be untrustworthy on account of sampling errors and observer errors.

To know the "typical" behavior of an individual, it is necessary to know how he characteristically acts in a particular situation. But situations change from day to day and from moment to moment. If we observe the attentiveness of an employee before lunch, we get a different impression from the one we would get in midafternoon. If we observe cheerfulness or politeness when he is worried, our impression may be unfair. The only way to be even moderately certain of typical behavior is to study the subject on many occasions, which is expensive. In practice, one must compromise between perfect sampling and economy.

Inference about individual differences is difficult because one can never observe two individuals in the same situation. Even when the situation is externally constant, previous conditions cause people to behave differently. When Jimmy fidgets more than John in the classroom, one is likely to infer that Jimmy is "restless," "nervous," or "jumpy." If the impression is confirmed by repeated observations, this difference seems to be fundamental. But if

Jimmy usually comes to school without breakfast, if he expects to be criticized by the teacher for poor work, or if he is large for the chairs provided, the difference in activity may tell nothing about the boys' basic restlessness. In fact, if conditions were reversed, Johnny might be more restless than Jimmy is now. At best, comparative observations show how different people act under their present conditions, but do not guarantee that the differences would persist if background conditions changed.

One of the best approaches to precise comparison is *time sampling*. In time sampling, a set schedule of observations is planned in advance. The schedule is randomized so that each subject is seen under comparable conditions. In one study of social contacts of preschool children, for example, a schedule of one-minute observations was drawn up. After the observer

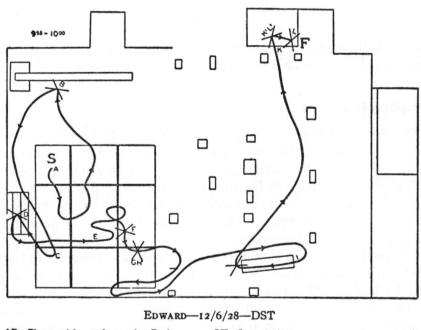

EDWARD—12/6/28—DST

AB—Plays with and mauls Paul.		GH—Somersaults	3″
Teacher intervenes	60″	IJ—Slide	30″
CD—Goes up to Alma. Throws cover		KL—In closet	50″
at her	11″	K¹L¹—Knocks Paul down; teacher	
EF—Jungle gym	100′	intervenes	2″

FIG. 92. Record obtained in a five-minute observation of a preschool child (Thomas *et al.,* 1929, p. 43). The diagram shows the nursery school play yard and traces Edward's movements. Letters mark the start and finish of each activity.

watched a child for one minute, noting all social interaction, he wrote down a full record. Children were watched in a predetermined order which was altered from day to day. During the study each child was observed an equal number of times during the first five minutes of the free-play hour, during the second five minutes, and so on (Barker *et al.*, 1943, pp. 509–525).

The advantages of short well-distributed time samples is that the cumulative picture is likely to be far more typical than an equal amount of evidence obtained in a few longer observations. Moreover, errors of memory are reduced, since the observer can make full notes during or just after observing. Time samples are especially suitable for recording specific facts that can be expressed numerically, such as the number of social contacts with other children. A slightly more elaborate record shows the complete activity pattern during the observation period. Figure 92 reports the behavior of Edward during a five-minute period: what he did, for how long, and where.

A much more extensive sample is obtained in the "day record" technique of Barker and his associates. Their general aim is to study the pattern of a child's life, with particular attention to the various settings in which he moves. For example, they wish to see what behaviors are evoked from small-town children in the course of a day, as compared to those evoked from children in larger communities. For this purpose, an observer goes with the child throughout his whole day's program, from the moment of awakening until the end of the day. The form of the record is illustrated by this description of three boys playing with a crate in a vacant lot (Barker and Wright, 1951, pp. 349–350):

5:39. Raymond tilted the crate from side to side in a calm, rhythmical way.
   Clifford's feet were endangered again. Stewart came over and very protectively led Clifford out of the way. [Observer's opinion.]
   Raymond slowly descended to the ground inside the crate.
   When Stewart came back around the crate, Raymond reached out at him, and growled very gutturally, and said, "I'm a big gorilla." Growling very ferociously, he stamped around the "cage" with his arms hanging loosely. He reached out with slow, gross movements.
   Raymond reached toward Clifford but didn't really try to catch him.
   Then he grabbed Stewart by the shirt.
   Imitating a very fierce gorilla, he pulled Stewart toward the crate.
   Stewart was passive and allowed himself to be pulled in. He said "Why don't you let go of me?" He spoke disgustedly and yet not disparagingly.
   Raymond released his grasp and ceased imitating a gorilla.
   He tilted the crate so that he could crawl out of the open end. As he crawled out, he lost control of the crate and it fell over on its side with the open end perpendicular to the ground.
   Stewart said, "Well, how did you get out?"
   Raymond said self-consciously, "I fell out," and forced a laugh.
   He looked briefly at me as if wondering what I thought.
5:40. He slowly and carefully crawled inside and went directly through the crate and out the open end.
   Stewart and Clifford got in front of Raymond and tried to get him to chase them and continue imitating a gorilla.
   Raymond stood immobile and didn't cooperate.

> Finally Stewart said to Clifford, "Maybe if he'll follow us through, then we can crawl out this end. Then we can tip it up and have him caught again."

The day record has some advantage in showing the total sequence of activities, but it also has disadvantages. The unconcealed observer may have some effect upon behavior, an effect which cannot be assessed. And the use of a single full day does not obtain completely typical information for the child in question, since each day has its own unique characteristics. Neither of these is a serious drawback for the Barker studies, where the goal is an overall report of the normal experience of a group of children. Observing many children, each on a different day, irons out sampling error so far as group data are concerned. The observer is present in all the data and therefore does not prevent comparisons among groups.

A series of time samples gives at best a statistical composite of different responses. Responses which the observer counts as the same may actually have quite different meanings, and situations which appear similar to him may evoke quite different responses. Newcomb (1929) observed boys in a summer camp, making daily records of many particular responses such as coöperation in after-meal work, fighting with other boys, and persistence. When these day-to-day records were studied, most boys were found to be inconsistent. As Newcomb points out, situations are only superficially alike. "Whether or not Johnny engages in a fight may depend on whether or not he thinks he can 'lick' his opponent." The apparent inconsistency of Johnny's action from an observer's frame of reference may be highly consistent from Johnny's point of view. Correlations were computed between observed behaviors which were supposed to represent single traits, such as showing off or dominance over peers. Behaviors grouped within one of these supposed traits correlated little higher than obviously dissimilar behaviors. Another study found only trivial correlations (median .20) between punctuality observed in different situations (Dudycha, 1936).

Conclusions formed in one situation—even on the basis of many cumulated observations—are valid only for that situation. Inference as to how a person would act in another situation is warranted only when responses under the two conditions have been shown to be correlated, or when observation yields so much understanding of his underlying personality structure (his stimulus equivalences) that we can see what a new situation means to him.

Symonds (1931, p. 5) has commented emphatically on the need for adequate sampling:

> A single observation is unreliable, a single rating is unreliable, a single test is unreliable, a single measurement is unreliable, a single answer to a question is unreliable. Reliability is achieved by keeping up observa-

tions, ratings, tests, questions, measures. . . . If you ask one teacher for her judgment of a boy's trustworthiness, you obtain what she has been able to observe in those few narrow classroom situations that appeared when her attention was particularly directed to some act involving honesty. An adequate rating, on the other hand, requires the judgment of several raters in several situations at several different times. Reliable evidence is multiplied evidence.

The extreme variation in performance is illustrated by a study of navigators. Students were taken on missions where their task was to continually compute their own position, air speed, etc., by dead reckoning. On each mission, four separate legs were run, and the accuracy of the man's air speed report for the leg was recorded. The score for each mission had a split-half reliability of .77; this is an indication of the man's consistency from one leg to the next, under the same wind conditions, with the same plane, etc. A correlation was also computed between scores on different days. While this correlation varied from class to class, the mean reliability coefficient was .00 (Carter and Dudek, 1947). Differences in score are determined almost entirely by transient conditions rather than by the individual's ability. Under these circumstances, even combining information from several missions would not give a useful report on the individual.

How many observations are required to obtain reliable data depends on the problem. The experimenter can estimate reliability of sampling by correlating ratings of "odd" with "even" observations. By this means, it was determined that 24 or more five-minute time samples permitted "reasonably stable" estimates of individual differences in preschool children (Arrington, 1939). In general, many short observations are superior to a few longer samples of behavior.

20. Why might an unfair picture of a child's behavior be obtained if he were always observed during the first five minutes of the play period and never during the second five minutes?
21. What sorts of information about Edward's personality could be obtained from a cumulation of records such as Figure 92?
22. What sorts of information about Edward's behavior are discarded in making an objective record such as Figure 92?
23. As a criterion in selection research, would it be better to test every flier with repeated landings on the same day or with a similar number of landings spread over several days?
24. May one say, paraphrasing Symonds, "Valid evidence is multiplied evidence"?

Observer Error

Whenever a person observes an event, he notices some happenings and ignores others. This is a necessary difficulty, since any activity has too many aspects for the mind to attend to all at once. Especially in social situations, the complexity of interaction prevents exhaustive reporting. If errors in observing were merely random omissions, they would be unimportant. But observers make systematic errors, overemphasizing some types of happenings and failing to report others.

Viewing the identical scene, observers give widely different reports. The following reports were written by four observers, each of whom saw the same motion-picture scene of about ten minutes' duration (from the film *This Is Robert*). The film was shown twice without sound. The film sequence, taken in the classroom and on the playground, showed several activities which revealed much of Robert's personality. The observers were directed to note everything they could about one boy, Robert, and were told to use parentheses to set apart inferences or interpretations. Numbers in these accounts, referring to scenes in the film, have been inserted to aid comparison.

Observer A: (2) Robert reads word by word, using finger to follow place. (4) Observes girl in box with much preoccupation. (5) During singing, he in general doesn't participate too actively. Interest is part of time centered elsewhere. Appears to respond most actively to sections of song involving action. Has tendency for seemingly meaningless movement. Twitching of fingers, aimless thrusts with arms.

Observer B: (2) Looked at camera upon entering (seemed perplexed and interested). Smiled at camera. (2) Reads (with apparent interest and with a fair degree of facility). (3) Active in roughhouse play with girls. (4) Upon being kicked (unintentionally) by one girl he responded (angrily). (5) Talked with girl sitting next to him between singing periods. Participated in singing. (At times appeared enthusiastic.) Didn't always sing with others. (6) Participated in a dispute in a game with others (appeared to stand up for his own rights). Aggressive behavior toward another boy. Turned pockets inside out while talking to teacher and other students. (7) Put on overshoes without assistance. Climbed to top of ladder rungs. Tried to get rung which was occupied by a girl but since she didn't give in, contented himself with another place.

Observer C: (1) Smiles into camera (curious). When group breaks up, he makes nervous gestures, throws arm out into air. (2) Attention to reading lesson. Reads with serious look on his face, has to use line marker. (3) Chases girls, teases. (4) Girl kicks when he puts hand on her leg. Robert makes face at her. (5) Singing. Sits with mouth open, knocks knees together, scratches leg, puts fingers in mouth (seems to have several nervous habits, though not emotionally overwrought or self-conscious). (6) In a dispute over parchesi, he stands up for his rights. (7) Short dispute because he wants rung on jungle gym.

Observer D: (2) Uses guide to follow words, reads slowly, fairly forced and with careful formation of sounds (perhaps unsure of self and fearful of mistakes). (3) Perhaps slightly aggressive as evidenced by pushing younger child to side when moving from a position to another. Plays with other children with obvious enjoyment, smiles, runs, seems especially associated with girls. This is noticeable in games and in seating in singing. (5) Takes little interest in singing, fidgets, moves hands and legs (perhaps shy and nervous). Seems in song to be unfamiliar with words of main part, and shows disinterest by fidgeting and twisting around. Not until chorus is reached does he pick up interest. His especial friend seems to be a particular girl, as he is always seated by her.

Every observer is more sensitive to some types of behavior than others. How does he regard nailbiting, failure to look one in the eye, or profanity? If he considers these significant, he will note them and base his impression on them. In the same situation, another observer might give greatest attention to voice modulation, careful use of grammar, or friendliness of conversation. Ideally, an observer would base his impression on every revealing act, but when he is looking for one thing, he necessarily overlooks something else.

Observers interpret what they see. If observers recorded only objective facts, others studying the data might reach quite different interpretations, but people always try to give meanings to what they see. When they make an interpretation, they tend to overlook facts which do not fit the interpretation, and may even invent facts needed to complete the event as interpreted.

25. What do you think really happened in scene (4)? Which observer came closest to adequate reporting of it?
26. Which of the numbered scenes appears to give the most significant information about Robert? How many of the observers reported that information?
27. Did the observers of the film about Robert succeed in identifying and marking all their judgments and hypotheses?
28. Do the observers of the film about Robert ever disagree, or are the differences entirely due to omissions and oversights?
29. A clinical psychologist asks a parent how well his 6-year-old child gets along with other children. Illustrate how each of the following errors might operate:
   a. The observer has not observed an adequate sample for judging typical behavior.
   b. The observer notices events which fit his preconceived notions.
   c. The observer is likely to note the behaviors he considers significant and to ignore others of equal importance.
   d. The observer may give a faulty interpretation to an event.

Systematic Recording.   Where possible, it is desirable to record countable units of behavior. For example, the extent to which factory workers attend to their work may be described by a time record which notes the exact moments when they are at work, and the time spent in looking around, obtaining tools, and visiting. The causes of distractions can also be noted. Such records for different workers and departments can be analyzed both for judging the workers and for planning rest periods or improved tool distribution.

Child development has been studied through records of social contacts, play activities, speech, and other objectively defined behaviors (Barker *et al.*, pp. 509 ff.; Thomas, 1929). Such precise reports are especially useful for measuring changes, since the observer's memory cannot compare performance now with performance several months ago.

Even if the behavior observed is too varied for direct tabulation, it may be possible to define categories of actions so that the observer needs only to check each incident as it occurs. One of the best examples is Bales' method (1951) of categorizing social interaction for the purposes of research on small groups. Twelve categories describing various types of response are defined, including:

> *Shows solidarity,* raises other's status, gives help, reward.
> *Shows tension release,* jokes, laughs, shows satisfaction.
> *Asks for orientation,* information, repetition, confirmation.
> *Disagrees,* shows passive rejection, formality, withholds help.

The observer tallies responses moment by moment. By noting who makes each remark and its approximate time, he can keep a full record of the interplay of thought and emotion. An "interaction recorder" using a motor-driven tape has been designed to facilitate such recording. Later analysis can examine individual differences such as the emergence of conflict and other group processes.

30. What advantages and disadvantages would a checklist or schedule have for each of the following purposes, compared to a one-paragraph descriptive report?
  a. A social agency wishes its visitor to report the condition of homes of its clients, including furnishings, conveniences, and neatness.
  b. A department store sends shoppers to be served by its clerks and to observe their procedure and manner.
  c. A state requires an observation of the applicant's driving before issuing a license to drive.

31. An investigator wishes to measure punctuality, for research purposes. He stations himself where he can observe the arrival of each student attending a particular class. Number of minutes early or late is recorded for each person. Records are made on several days. What assumptions are involved in using the average of these records as an index of punctuality?

32. Tape recordings of group discussions are used to study individual differences in dominance, leadership, and other traits. What types of observable information about personality could not be obtained from the tape?

Anecdotal Records.   Although objective counts and tabulations are well suited to research, their information is of limited value for individual guidance. Anecdotal records escape the bleakness of quantitative methods, offering a more lifelike sketch of the subject. The observer is free to note any behavior that appears significant, rather than having to concentrate on the same traits for all subjects. Often the anecdotes are reports of incidents noted by a teacher or supervisor in daily contacts.

In an anecdotal record, the observer describes exactly what he observed, keeping interpretation and fact separate. The record is made as soon after the action as possible, to eliminate errors of recall. Cumulated over a period of time, the incidents provide a richer picture of behavior than any other equally simple technique. The following are typical anecdotal reports:

Paul, after projecting the film for the class, took it back to the office (where I happened to be) to rewind. He is not very skilled, and missed his timing, so that much of the film cascaded onto the floor instead of going onto the takeup reel. John came up just then and said something sarcastic about Paul's clumsiness. Paul gave no answer, but kept on at work with no change of manner and a stolid face. Richard, who had been watching Paul, turned on John, told him to "shut up and give Paul a chance," and muttered something about "some of these kids make me sick." (Paul seems to suppress emotion; he certainly heard John's very unpleasant tone.)

Joan spent the entire science period wandering from group to group instead of helping Rose as she was expected to. She interrupted many of the others, telling them they were doing the work wrong. She asked a lot of (foolish) questions ("Does filter paper make certain things go through or just keep certain things out?") and was teased a good deal by the boys. By the time Rose was finished she returned; Rose was quite angry, but they made up and Joan helped put things away. But on her first trip to the storeroom she stayed to plate a gold ring with mercury, while Rose made repeated trips with the equipment.

The reporter has two responsibilities: he must select incidents worth reporting, and he must be objective. Both incidents characteristic of the person and striking exceptions to his normal conduct are helpful. The typical incidents provide a more individualized picture than the hackneyed trait names that would otherwise be used—friendly, showing initiative, rude, and so on. Exceptional actions are rarely reported in ratings and general impressions, but they too are significant. A single incident showing interest in the company's welfare from a man known as a troublemaker or a sign of enthusiasm for learning on the part of a boy who rebels against school may be the key to a new and successful treatment. The observer must weed out value judgments and interpretations, attempting to report the exact occurrences, including significant preceding events and environmental conditions. One can never report "everything" about the incident. The reporter selects for his record the facts he considers relevant.

Single anecdotes tell little. As anecdotes accumulate, however, they begin to fill in a picture of the person's habits. If a particular response is typical, it will recur. An effective method of determining personality characteristics of an individual is to search through the anecdotes about him to detect repetitions. A summary based on these recurring patterns usually requires confirmation by further directed observation.

Suggested Readings

Biber, Barbara E., & others. Recording spontaneous behaviors. *Life and ways of the seven-year-old.* New York: Basic Books, 1952. Pp. 33–53.

An account of procedures used in ten-minute schoolroom observations, together with illustrative anecdotal records and evidence of observer reliability.

Gronlund, Norman E. Validity of sociometric results. *Sociometry in the classroom.* New York: Harper, 1959. Pp. 158–188.

A review of studies shows how sociometric choices of school children relate to observed behavior, teacher opinions, and adjustment.

Lindzey, Gardner, & Borgatta, Edgar F. Sociometric measurement. In Lindzey (ed.), *Handbook of social psychology,* Vol. I. Cambridge: Addison-Wesley, 1954. Pp. 405–448.

A comprehensive summary of the major sociometric techniques includes correlations between sociometric evidence and other measures of personality. The authors draw particular attention to limitations of research or practical decisions based on sociometric findings alone.

Newman, Frances B. The development of methods in the adolescent growth study. In Frances B. Newman and Harold E. Jones, The adolescent in social groups. *Appl. Psychol. Monogr.,* 1946, No. 9, 16–29.

This describes different techniques, ranging from quantitative ratings to narrative accounts, used in the same program for observing adolescent personality. Special advantages of each approach are indicated. Subsequent chapters give information on reliability and validity, and the use of the data in case analysis.

Prescott, Daniel A. Interpreting behavior. *The child in the educative process.* New York: McGraw-Hill, 1957. Pp. 99–150.

Anecdotal records collected on one boy throughout a school year are compared to show consistencies and deviations from his normal pattern. The discussion shows how teachers form and test hypotheses when using such records as a case-study technique. Several other chapters in the book also give useful information on the collection of anecdotal information.

Tuddenham, Read D. Studies in reputation: II. The diagnosis of social adjustment. *Psychol. Monogr.,* 1952, **66**, No. 1.

Reports on school children obtained by the nomination technique can be used for personality analysis. Five illustrative records are interpreted.

18

Performance Tests of Personality

THE preceding chapters have considered the well-established and unquestionably useful techniques for studying personality: interest measures for use in counseling, adjustment inventories for screening purposes, sociometric and peer ratings, empirically keyed predictive questionnaires, and systematic sampling of behavior. Some of these are of value to the practicing personnel psychologist and others are better suited to gathering research data, but each of them is capable of giving reliable data, the major sources of error in interpretation have been identified, and score interpretations are adequately supported by combined evidence and theory.

We now turn to procedures whose value is unsettled—indeed, is vehemently disputed. Although performance tests and projective techniques have been in use for about thirty years, they have reached a much less mature stage of development than methods discussed to this point. The complexity of personality and the instability of personality theory are one source of difficulty. When there is no consensus as to the most important traits to measure, or even, as Allport says (Lindzey, 1958), on whether it is fruitful to conceive of personality in terms of traits, test developers have no target on which to concentrate. Conversely, when there are no outstanding tests in an area, research is scattered so widely that no coherent body of evidence becomes available as a base on which to build theory. When the theory of intelligence was confused and primitive in the first quarter of this century, the focus Binet's scale gave to research effort made it possible to move toward a much clearer theory regarding the nature and growth of ability.

Since there are no performance tests of salient importance and few clear principles, we must confine ourselves in this chapter to describing enough illustrative tests to show the range of approaches. In addition to a variety of performance tests, this chapter describes projective tests, there being no sharp distinction between the two classes. We shall present some evidence on the validity of scores as psychometric predictors, that is, on the use of performance and projective tests as quantitative measuring instruments. Many of these instruments, however, are used primarily for impressionistic assessment in which the scores become raw material to be integrated with other data into a portrait of the whole person. The complex and controversial issues regarding such assessment we reserve for Chapter 19.

The aim of the performance test may be clarified by contrasting it with the time-sampling method of determining typical behavior by observation. The limitations of time sampling are its high cost and the fact that scores, when obtained, depend upon both the subject and the situations in which he happens to have been observed. It has been the great dream of personality measurement to invent procedures which would give quantitative results, would directly represent behavior rather than biased impressions, and would permit direct comparison of individuals in the same situation.

A performance test is an observation in a standard situation designed to elicit a particular type of response. One trait of great interest, for example, is how the person controls and expresses aggression. It is difficult to judge this by observing the daily life of most subjects, because the person is only occasionally in an aggression-provoking situation. Testers have therefore developed standardized procedures for annoying the subject, such as condemning the opinions he voices in a standard interview. This almost certainly does arouse hostile feelings, and the subject's behavior in this short test may be more revealing than several hours of field observation.

Galton once compared psychological testing to the geologist's "sinking shafts at critical points" to obtain samples of significant material. Whereas ratings return, for the most part, strictly surface impressions, and the time sample sinks its shafts entirely at random, the performance test is designed to provoke exhibitions of truly critical behavior. The usual features of such a test are as follows:

● The stimulus situation is made as nearly uniform as possible for all subjects.

● The situation is designed to permit variation in those types of behavior which the tester wishes to observe.

● The subject is led to believe that one characteristic is being tested while the observer is actually observing some other aspect of performance.

● The observer makes careful records of the subject's method of performance, rather than noting only the amount performed.

An example is the Operational Stress technique developed to assess whether men entering pilot training can resist pressure. During administration of an apparatus test, the candidate is subjected to stress-producing stimuli. The apparatus has seven controls (pedal, throttle, stick, and various levers), which the examinee resets continually as signal lights change and buzzers sound. The time required to react to each signal is recorded electrically. The examinee is told that he will be observed by a concealed observer "just as a checkpilot will rate you in flying." Administration is stand-ardized: one minute of rest and anticipation, one minute of directions regarding signals and controls, and three short test periods. In each period, the examinee is given increasingly reproving "stress directions" while he is busily moving levers. The signals are made more complex. In test period C, the pattern of lights changes six times, after intervals of about fifteen sec-onds, while the examiner is delivering the following speech in an urgent manner: "Don't make lights flicker on and off. Be steady. . . . Quit making errors. You aren't moving fast enough. . . . More speed. . . . Hurry and stop the clock. . . . Last chance. . . . Set controls quickly. . . . You are still making errors." The concealed observer, meanwhile, makes extensive ratings of manner and reaction to criticism, and objective clock scores are recorded (Guilford, 1947, pp. 660–664; Melton, 1947, pp. 811–814).

The greatest advantage of a test observation is that it reveals characteris-tics which appear only infrequently in normal activities—characteristics such as bravery, reaction to frustration, and dishonesty. Second, desire to make a good impression does not invalidate the test. In fact, just because he is anxious to make a good impression, the subject reveals more than he nor-mally would. It is necessary, however, to take this motivation into account in interpreting results. The third advantage of the performance test is that it comes closer than other techniques to comparing subjects under identical conditions.

Performance tests vary greatly in purpose and in design. They may be strictly psychometric instruments measuring single narrowly defined con-structs such as persistence in routine work, or they may be a basis for impres-sionistic evaluation of the person's total life-style. They may be worksamples for predicting success in a specific assignment, or cross sections of behavior without reference to any single future situation.

Situations used to elicit performance range from highly structured to almost totally unstructured. A situation is structured if it has for all subjects a definite meaning. An unstructured situation presents so few cues or has so little pattern that he can give it almost any meaning he wishes. A common-place unstructured stimulus is the strange sound in the night. Is it the wind? a burglar? the cat? water dripping? The interpretation we make is strongly influenced by our interests, by fears conscious and unconscious, and, of course, by knowledge. In a structured situation, the subject knows exactly what he is expected to do and how he is expected to do it. In the un-structured situation, he guides himself. The more ambiguous the situation, the more opportunity there is for individual method of interpretation and performance. An extremely unstructured situation is established in Waeh-ner's (1946) procedure for studying personality. She observed her subject's behavior and products after turning him loose in a studio equipped with all types of art media and materials, with little more instruction than "You may do anything you like with these."

Highly structured tasks are excellent for measuring ability just because they force everyone to try the same thing. Projective situations, at the opposite extreme, use almost totally unstructured stimuli. The projective test is so named because it permits the subject to project into the situation his unconscious thoughts, wishes, and fears (L. K. Frank, 1939). Thus the householder who interprets the creak in the dark as a burglar may be revealing that he is more anxious than another man, who interprets the same stimulus as a natural phenomenon and goes back to sleep.

1. In each of the following situations, discuss whether it would be preferable to employ observations in natural conditions, or standardized observations where conditions are fixed in advance and identical for all subjects.
   a. The telephone company wishes to rate its operators on courtesy and clarity of speech. It is able to tap conversations and make recordings.
   b. It is desired to screen Navy personnel for tendency to panic under conditions of extreme noise, as in amphibious landings.
   c. An investigator wishes to study the habitual recklessness of 7-year-old boys in climbing and jumping.
2. To what extent may each of the following be considered an unstructured stimulus?
   a. A teacher, during a test, glances up from her desk and barely observes a hasty movement of one boy who is pulling his hand into his lap from the aisle.
   b. A group of people play duplicate bridge, the same set of hands being played at each table.
   c. A questionnaire is designed to obtain information about age, income, education, etc. All possible answers are anticipated and presented on the blank in multiple-choice form.
3. To what extent is each of the following unstructured? If the test is at all unstructured, discuss whether that is an advantage or a disadvantage.
   a. Stanford-Binet test, Memory for Sentences.
   b. Wechsler Comprehension test.
   c. A test of addition which presents in random order the combinations up to $9 + 9$, the pupil being directed to do as many items as he can in the time allowed.
   d. In the Porteus test (Figure 1), the subject is to solve a maze. The time it takes him to trace the correct path with his pencil is scored.

STRUCTURED TESTS MEASURING SINGLE TRAITS

Character and Persistence

The Character Education Inquiry of Hartshorne and May (1928, 1929, 1930) was the only extended effort to evaluate personality by strictly quantitative and objective methods. Character traits can be validly assessed only by subjecting people to temptation in a situation where they believe they can violate standards without detection. Traits studied by Hartshorne and May include truthfulness, honesty with money, persistence, coöperativeness, and generosity.

Honesty with money was tested by presenting arithmetic problems in which each pupil had to use a boxful of coins. The box provided for each pupil was secretly identified. At the end of the work each pupil carried his own box to a pile in front of the room. Since pupils were unaware that boxes could be identified, many took advantage of the opportunity to keep some of the money. Honesty in a situation involving prestige was tested by asking the child to do an impossible task, such as placing marks in small circles while keeping his eyes closed (Figure 93). Many children turned in "suc-

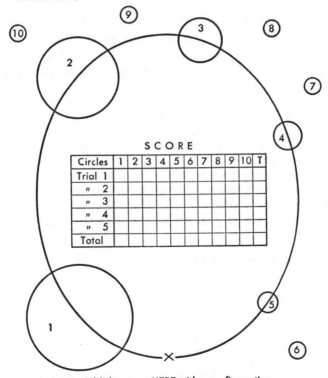

CIRCLES PUZZLE
First Trial

Wait for the signal for each trial. Put the point of your pencil on the cross at the foot of the oval. Then when the signal is given shut your eyes and put a small cross or X in each circle, taking them in order.

Circles	1	2	3	4	5	6	7	8	9	10	T
Trial 1											
" 2											
" 3											
" 4											
" 5											
Total											

SCORE

Hold the page HERE with your finger tips

FIG. 93. An "improbable achievement" test of honesty (Hartshorne and May, 1928, p. 62).

cessful performances" which could have been obtained only by cheating.

Motivation to work has been of particular interest because it is thought of as the link between aptitude and achievement. The employer, the teacher, the clinician, and all other users of tests wish they could predict whether a person's behavior will bear out the promise shown in tests of ability. Many investigators have explored possible performance tests. Hartshorne and May tested how long children persist as a task becomes difficult. Pupils read a story which builds to a climax: "Again the terrible piercing shriek of the whistle screamed at them. Charles could see the frightened face of the engineer. . . ." Here the examiner tells them that if they wish to learn the ending they must read the difficult printed material that follows:

CHARLESLIFTEDLUCILLETOHISBACK"PUTYOURARMSTIGHT
AROUNDMYNECKANDHOLDON
. . . .

NoWhoWTogETBaCkoNthETREStle.HoWTOBRingTHaTTErrIFIED
BURDeNOFACHiLDuPtO
. . . .

fiN ALly tAp-taPC AME ARHYTH Month e BriD GeruNNing fee Tfee
TcomING

The pupil separates each word with a vertical mark as he deciphers it; the amount deciphered is an index of persistent effort (Hartshorne and May, 1928, p. 292). Some other tests have determined how long the subject will continue to work on an exceedingly difficult or impossible problem, presented in a series with solvable problems.

4. If Bill does better than Fred on the circle-dotting test of honesty, what conclusions can be drawn about Bill's character?
5. Joe is a known delinquent, having gotten into trouble together with a gang of boys for several minor thefts and disturbances. How can you explain the fact that he does well on all the tests of honesty, coöperation, and generosity?
6. The test illustrated in Figure 94 is a test of self-control, requiring the pupil to work in the presence of attractive distractions. Does this measure the same motivational factors as the story-completion test of persistence?

Perceptual and Cognitive Styles

The psychologist observing any problem-solving behavior is quickly impressed by individual differences in the way subjects attack problems and surmount difficulties. Individual tests such as the Wechsler are commonly used as opportunities to observe such styles or habits (see p. 191). Information of this type might predict what problems a person could best deal with and what errors he would make, and might open the way to remedial training to improve his thinking.

Tests of cognitive processes are concerned primarily with how a person

Copyright, 1927, Institute of Educational Research
Teachers College, Columbia University, New York
Devised by Allen M. Ruggles

FORM C-2

Begin here:

7 2 3 4 5 3 7 8 6 1 3 5 =

9 1 7 6 8 4 3 1 2 8 4 3 =

A CLOUD The man in When the SWALLOWS M J

Peter Piper picked a

MARY

NO How do

6 3 2 1 5 4 2 5 7 2 3 7 =

3 7 4 3 7 5 3 6 8 3 1 5 =

VACATION Kodac Loova

CANDY 2+1=? appetite you manage

One more and away we

Oh DEAR!

PICKFORD

9 1 5 4 3 2 7 5 4 8 9 4 =

7 3 6 5 7 8 3 2 8 4 3 6 =

A C ICE CREAM
B L The earth is flat. It
M can be proved.

HANG ON

when

Sigaret

HONG GONG

2 6 3 5 3 2 4 5 7 1 2 4 =

3 6 4 1 3 6 2 3 4 2 7 1 =

S
V LL BEGIN OVER
L
D

Why DON'T YOU —
see next line

you

CANDY TI NOP

A APPLE

8 2 7 5 2 3 4 5 9 6 4 2 =

5 2 3 4 1 3 5 4 7 2 1 7 =

THIS
SPACE
RE
SERVED

SHAKE
S
P
A
R
E

STAN I AM SICK

A few dance

5 4 6 4 2 5 6 1 3 4 5 3 =

2 5 3 2 4 8 6 5 1 2 5 4 =

COOTIES
NEW YORK

N. A.

CON FIRE

Circus
ITS PINK

6 4 5 3 2 1 4 6 7 8 3 2 =

7 2 4 5 6 1 3 7 6 4 3 2 =

A
F CAT
T
E SPAROWS THIS
R ALSO

3+1-4=0

4 5 1 2 9 4 3 6 5 6 3 2 =

3 4 2 4 8 7 6 5 1 4 5 4 =

BANG Jonny's First Drawing WARNING
WHO ?
Hot Dogs

four seven

5 4 6 1 2 5 3 4 1 3 5 4 =

3 4 5 8 9 4 3 2 1 6 3 2 =

Cows
Horses
SHEEP
CHILDREN
GOATS
SKUNKS

SKANA-

Gwenkiskwischckw
Iowa, U.S.A.

A YANKEE SETTLEMENT

BREAD LARD

NUT & JEFF

4 6 5 3 4 2 5 8 6 1 2 5 =

9 1 7 6 5 4 3 1 4 6 5 7 =

FIG. 94. A test of self-control or resistance to distraction. (Hartshorne and May, 1929, p. 308. Reproduced by permission.)

organizes information. This patterning has been the chief interest of Gestalt psychology, and many of the tests in this area come from Wertheimer and other Gestaltist investigators. Gestalt psychology has always been concerned with the brain as an information-processing organ. If the organism is an information-processing system, simple perceptual tests may identify its constant characteristics. These tests are analogous to the test performed by an electronic technician when he puts a perfect sine-wave signal into an amplifier and examines the distorted signal put out by the speaker. This gives the unique "signature" of that particular system.

Simple stimuli have been used to test the functioning of the total perceptual system. Flicker fusion and apparent movement may be described as examples. When a person views a light through spaces in a rotating shutter, "flicker" is perceived at low rates of rotation. At high rates, however, no interruption or flicker is noticed. As we increase the rate gradually, the subject can report the point where the flicker just disappears. The "fusion threshold" is fairly stable, and there are great individual differences. It has been suggested that this fusion point provides an index of the ability of the nervous system to register details of incoming stimulation, and measures of flicker fusion have been found useful in diagnosis of brain damage. Halstead (1951) comments that fusion "represents a dramatic change in consciousness for the subject. For once he reaches the rate at which separate flashes . . . fuse for him, he cannot tell the unsteady light from a steady one. He has broken with physical reality. The rate is much higher in our normal individuals than in our frontal brain-injured patients. It is as if the mental engine were running in the brain-injured, but running on inadequate power. It fails at the first little hill. . . . It seems clear that the test reflects an important aspect of cerebral metabolism."

When two lights, side by side, are flashed on and off in quick succession, the light appears to jump back and forth. This "phi phenomenon," as Wertheimer called it, is the basis for traveling light patterns in theater marquees and neon signs. In apparent movement the nervous system integrates stimulation into a pattern. Klein and Schlesinger (1951) arranged to vary the interval between flashes. As the interval is reduced there is a definite threshold where apparent movement first appears and a second threshold where it disappears, beyond which point the subject sees two steady lights. The separation of these thresholds, i.e., the range of intervals which permit an impression of movement, is much wider for some subjects than others.

Other tests deal with mental flexibility and rigidity. It is frequently observed that unsuccessful problem solvers cling to incorrect ideas—for example, repeatedly entering the same blind alley in a maze. Successful adaptation requires reorganizing perceptual fields on the basis of new information or new requirements. Investigators associated with Wertheimer in Berlin in the 1920's invented the "Water Jar" or Einstellung test (Luchins, 1942). *Einstellung* may be translated approximately as "mental set" or "orientation." The test makes use of water-jar problems like those of the Stanford-Binet: "If you have a 7-quart jar and a 4-quart jar, how can you get exactly 10 quarts of water?" To follow the logic of the test, call the jars A(7) and B(4). The solution is: Fill A, fill B from A (leaving three quarts in A), empty B, fill B from A, fill A. Thus three quarts are obtained by the rule (A − B), and the additional seven quarts from A; i.e., (A − B) + A = 10. The series of problems in a test might be as follows:

	Jars A	B	C	To Be Obtained	Rule	
Example:	7	4	—	10	2A − B	
a.	21	127	3	100	B − A − 2C	
b.	14	163	25	99	B − A − 2C	
c.	18	43	10	5	B − A − 2C	
d.	9	42	6	21	B − A − 2C	
e.	20	59	4	31	B − A − 2C	
f.	23	49	3	20	B − A − 2C or A − C	Critical
g.	15	39	3	18	B − A − 2C or A + C	Critical
h.	28	76	3	25	A − C	Extinction
i.	18	48	4	22	B − A − 2C or A + C	Critical
j.	14	36	8	6	B − A − 2C or A − C	Critical

The subject may be given help in solving the first few problems. The long series of problems *a* to *e* solved by applying a particular rule builds up a mental set to use that formula. "Critical" and "extinction" problems are then introduced. In a critical problem such as *f*, the "set" solution works but there is a much easier way to achieve the answer. In the extinction problem *h* the set solution does not work, but another simple rule can be found by the flexible subject.

To get a good score in the Einstellung test the subject must attend to the immediate problem, discarding memories of the previous solutions. Inflexible behavior perhaps indicates inability to separate conflicting sources of information. Three other tests relevant to this specific aspect of mental functioning may be described briefly.

The Embedded Figures test (EFT) based on work of Gottschaldt (1926) presents a strange geometric pattern and requires the subject to find it in a larger complex field. In some versions, the background is colored irregularly to increase confusion. The score is the time required to solve the problems (Witkin, 1950).

The Stroop Color Word test uses three test sheets. The first sheet consists of color names to be read as fast as possible. The second sheet consists of rows of dots whose colors are to be named rapidly. The third and most important sheet again presents color names but this time the words are printed in color. The colors used conflict with the names, the word *yellow* being printed in red, for example. The subject is required to call off the colors as rapidly as possible. Finally, he is asked to read the words on this sheet. The decline in speed from second to third trial (color naming) and from first to fourth (reading) indicates the degree to which conflicting cues block his thinking.

The Rod and Frame test of Witkin (1949) is similar in psychological con-

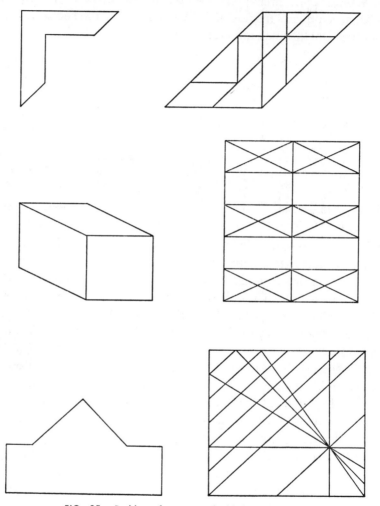

FIG. 95.   Problems from an Embedded Figures test.

ception, though radically different in stimulus material. A person ordinarily judges "which way is up?" by combining visual and kinesthetic cues. A "crazy house" in which walls and objects are built at a slant requires the subject to disregard visual cues and rely wholly on bodily cues. In the Witkin experiment in a dark room, the subject is strapped into a fixed position in a chair which can be tilted. He is then asked to judge when an adjustable luminous rod several feet in front of him is in the upright position. The person's success on the rod alone is a measure of kinesthetic acuity. When the rod is placed within a luminous tilted square frame, however, visual cues tempt the subject to call the rod vertical when it is parallel to the sides of the frame. Most subjects judging the rod-in-frame select as vertical a compromise position between the gravitational vertical and the tilt of the frame. The greater the tilt of the chosen position, the less the subject has cast aside the irrelevant cue. A second test of the same nature is Witkin's Tilting Room, where the entire chamber, in which the chair is mounted, can be tilted.

Validity of Structured Tests

The performance tests have several common characteristics. Each is employed to measure a stable personality trait. The investigator usually hopes to obtain, from a measurement at one moment in time, information on the individual's general level of persistence, rigidity, prejudice, etc. Performance tests have also been used to study how persistence, for example, varies over time or with changing experimental conditions. In discussing field observations we noted that numerous samples are required to estimate typical behavior, because any particular observation catches the subject only in one of many possible situations. By standardizing the situation, eliminating the random variation from subject to subject, the performance test hopes to make extensive sampling unnecessary.

Motivation can be more nearly standardized for the performance test than for any other personality measure. In the field observation the subject is given no directions, simply exhibiting whatever motivation he brings to his own affairs. In EFT, the Circle test of honesty, and in nearly every other performance test, the subject is told that an ability is being measured. This provides him with a culturally defined ideal of behavior; he understands, in each case, how he can earn a high score and understands that a high score is desirable. The "good performance" referred to in the directions is not the performance the investigator is observing; for example, the child who "raises his score" on the Circle test by peeking lowers his honesty score. A performance test of personality tries to standardize motivation to the same degree that motivation for a test of mental ability is standardized. Motivation is not uniform for every subject, but neither is it uniform in a school achievement test or a test for selecting policemen.

Nearly all performance tests contain an ability component which is irrelevant to the personality trait supposedly examined. Some control for level of ability is therefore required. In the Color Word test the reading rate without interference is a necessary baseline for the interference measurement. General reasoning or spatial ability accounts for as much of Embedded Figures performance as does difficulty in handling perceptual interference. Separation of ability from personality factors in problem-solving tests is not easy, and may not be reasonable to attempt. Embedded Figures correlates .35 to .60 with ability tests such as Block Design, Number Series, and Thurstone's tests of the spatial factor. Yet these are problem-solving tests just because the answer is "hidden." If there were no interfering stimuli there would be no problem.

Do perceptual and cognitive tests measure nothing but general ability? This suspicion is readily dismissed. Although they overlap with ability tests, particularly in samples of college students, they also carry information not predictable from ability tests. An entire battery of intellectual, spatial, and psychomotor tests accounted for only half of the reliable variance in Embedded Figures in one study (Guilford, 1947, pp. 895, 897).

Performance tests are closely linked to specific theories about personality and brain functioning; in this they contrast with most questionnaires and field observations. Hartshorne and May assumed that character consisted of collections of responses or habits and sought to measure those habits by sampling. The perceptual and cognitive tests assume that mental functioning has a definite overall structure and seek to measure specific subprocesses. Since each performance test relates to one narrow element in behavior, it gives little basis for describing the overt personality as a whole. Structured tests of broad traits like cheerfulness and friendliness do not exist and indeed are difficult to imagine.

The most important question about structured tests is their degree of generality. If honesty is a generalized habit, the Circle test will correlate with honesty in many more significant situations. If inability to separate two streams of information is a general pattern of behavior, such superficially dissimilar tests as Color Word and Rod and Frame will correlate. And if so, we can expect the same trait to be important in many types of problem solving.

The questionnaire obtains information by means of general questions dealing with average situations, for example: "Do you feel unhappy much of the time?" The hope is that these superficial summary questions will permit inferences to specific situations. The structured performance test, on the other hand, starts with a single artificial situation and hopes that behavior in that situation is largely determined by some fundamental quality of habit, temperament, or brain structure which will influence response in situations having a very different surface appearance. The test is meaningless unless it measures something accurately. It is equally pointless to develop the test if it measures behavior only in this specific task. If it correlates repeatedly with tasks which are on the surface quite dissimilar, it takes on considerable psychological interest. It can then be regarded as measuring a difference between individuals which is in some sense fundamental. Once this is established, a program of validation should be undertaken to determine just how much of socially significant behavior such a score can account for.

The developers of performance tests must study the potential usefulness of their methods in three stages: establishing that the test measures some characteristic dependably (reliability studies), establishing that the characteristic is found in distinctly different tasks or situations (generality), and establishing that the characteristic is related to socially significant aspects of behavior (criterion-oriented validity).

We cannot point to any one "official" version of a performance test, and we have no manual systematically reporting its technical qualities. Each investigator modifies a test for his own purposes and reports such findings about reliability and validity as emerge from studies of his own theories. For this reason, we can give only illustrative rather than definitive evaluations of the tests we have described.

7. What "ability" is involved in the Rod and Frame test and how may it be corrected for?
8. Are the tasks used in performance tests of personality any more "artificial" than those used in aptitude tests?
9. Discuss this statement: "A test presented to the subject as a test of ability should be regarded as a measure of ability if the subject knows what aspect of his performance will actually be scored, and as a measure of personality if he does not know."
10. The Water Jar test tends to produce U-shaped distributions rather than normal distributions. Is this an advantage or a disadvantage?

Reliability.   A coefficient of equivalence for a performance test calls for correlating different trials or stimulus arrangements on the same occasion. Some performance tests are quite reliable and others are quite unreliable. A low coefficient of equivalence may indicate that the proposed test is too brief to be a good measure, or that there is no common characteristic running through performance on different items. A high coefficient of course implies that we are getting an accurate score for the individual's standing at this time. Table 67 illustrates some reported coefficients of equivalence. Evidently one can measure many traits with very satisfactory precision, but reliability cannot be taken for granted. Users of performance tests often neglect to check reliabilities, and it is very likely that unreliability accounts for the failure of many experimenters to discover significant correlations and differences with such tests.

Lengthening a performance test to improve reliability measurement is sometimes impossible. In the Water Jar test, for example, once the subject discovers that the solution rule changes for different problems, subsequent

TABLE 67. Coefficients of Equivalence for Selected Performance Tests

Test	Scores Compared	Coefficient	Remarks and Source
Rod and Frame	Rod and Frame with Tilting Room	.64, .52	(Witkin, 1949)
Rod and Frame	Eight odd vs. eight even trials, corrected	.99, .98	(Gardner *et al.*, unpublished)
Deception tests		.62 to .87	Scores corrected for differences in relevant abilities (Hartshorne and May, 1928)
Critical flicker frequency of paretics and schizophrenics	Thresholds on six trials	.98 in each group	(Irvine, 1954)
Embedded Figures	Odd vs. even items, corrected	.68 to .88	Subtests composed of more-embedded figures correlate only .35 with easy figures (Gardner *et al.*, unpublished)

trials are likely to show much less "rigidity." There is no way to reinstate the subject's initial naïveté to obtain an equivalent trial. The only way to extend the sample of behavior is to find a second task which measures the same quality.

If the coefficient of equivalence is large enough to guarantee accurate measurement, the coefficient of stability tells whether the quality being measured is a stable one. Stability is desirable when we intend to interpret the trait as a long-standing, generally significant aspect of personality. An unstable score reflecting mood, temporary inefficiency of thinking, or the like may also be useful, particularly for testing transient effects of experimental conditions such as stress or drugs. The illustrative results in Table 68

TABLE 68. Coefficients of Stability for Selected Performance Tests

Test	Interval	Coefficient	Remarks
Cheating	Six months	.75–.79	(Hartshorne and May, 1928, II, 88–89)
Cheating	Early adolescence to adulthood	.37	(V. Jones, 1946)
Rod and Frame	More than one year	.86	(Witkin, 1949)

leave no doubt that some performance tests measure characteristics of considerable permanence.

Correlations with Nonperformance Measures. Positive relations between performance tests and other types of personality measures are considered evidence that the tests are getting at personality variables. Pemberton (1952a) administered several questionnaires to subjects who also took the Embedded Figures test. There were 29 significant correlations between self-reports and EFT, indicating that good performers on EFT describe themselves as follows:

I stay in the background
I am not sensitive to social undercurrents
I am not interested in humanitarian occupations
I do not feel need to apologize for wrong-doing
I am not conventional
I have high theoretical interests and values
I am interested in physical sciences

It appears that in this sample, at least, good EFT performance is associated with self-centeredness or nonconformity. We cannot judge the strength of this relationship from Pemberton's report.

L. Ainsworth (1958) correlated rigidity on the Water Jar test with a questionnaire on insecurity or general life adjustment. For 120 students in a British university, the correlation was .24. An important subsidiary finding was that the performance of insecure students changed as the test was administered with various degrees of emotional pressure. As stress increased, the most insecure students actually showed greater adaptation on critical trials than they had shown under minimum stress.

Generality.   In one sense, every performance test appears to be highly specific. Very slight modifications in conditions of administration, scoring procedure, task, or sample produce significant differences in the meaning of results. In the Tilting Room, errors have different correlations and different psychological implications depending on whether the trial begins with both chair and room tilted to the left or with the two tilted in opposite directions (Witkin, 1949). This has a theoretical explanation, since the degree of conflict between cue systems is far greater in the second case. In the Water Jar test, behavior on critical trials (where the "set" solution works but is unnecessary roundabout) has different psychological properties and correlates from behavior on extinction trials (where the "set" solution does not work) (L. Ainsworth, 1958; Back, 1956).

Most of the performance tests of personality are used in many different versions. One EFT presents key figures one at a time; another places several key figures before the subject at once; in a third, the subject is to look for the same key figure in every item. One may keep the key before the subject during his search, or may require him to remember the key figure while examining the complex figure. We need engineering studies of the promising tests to determine what version is potentially most valuable. Even where modification is desired, it appears necessary that the new form and a standard form be used side by side to evaluate the importance of the change. No one would think of adopting a modified Wechsler or Binet procedure without comparing it systematically with the original; yet the tradition of standardization is almost entirely neglected in performance testing of personality.

To summarize the research on generality is next to impossible. For some traits such as "rigidity" there have been a dozen papers summarizing correlations, and even the summaries are in disagreement. Some conclude that there is a general trait of rigidity, some find three or four rigidity factors (never the same from study to study), and some argue that the very concept of rigidity is invalidated by the data. Levitt (1956) summarized more than thirty correlations of the Water Jar test with other alleged measures of rigidity and found that negative results outnumbered significant correlations three to one. Such a finding must be regarded as evidence that investigators have been too quick to label a test as a measure of rigidity. Among the tests which have been claimed to measure rigidity were an anxiety questionnaire, a questionnaire measure of rigidity, the California F scale, Wechsler Similarities, and mirror writing of words. To expect all these measures to agree reflects an unreasonable simple view of mental organization.

Luchins (1951), though he popularized the Water Jar test, is critical of those who are content to measure a trait of "rigidity." He regards the test as an observation of mental process, and would expect its meaning to shift (as Ainsworth found) under different conditions. Those who seek to measure an abstract trait underlying the test performance

err in assuming that every Einstellung solution to a test problem is brought about by the same psychological process—namely, rigidity of behavior. . . . Moreover, the alleged rigidity in solving the criticals is taken as an indication of rigidity in the respondent's personality or of rigidity in his ego-defense system. His behavior is rigid because he possesses rigidity. One is reminded of the outmoded belief that a thing burns because it has fire in it. . . . Rigidity of behavior is sought for in the respondent; it is considered as relatively independent of the field conditions under which the individual is operating.

. . . I do not think that there is anything inherently wrong with attempting to determine within a short period of time, a few hours of testing, the probability that an individual will shift his behavior in real life situations in order to meet changing circumstances. . . . At the present time the most fruitful approach seems to me to involve intensive observation of and experimentation with rigidity of behavior under various conditions, if possible suspending biases as to the nature of the behavior involved. . . . The aim should be to vary conditions systematically and to observe what happens. As a final step—and not as a first, step as is so common today—one may be able to propose an explanation for such behavior.

Devoted, painstaking exploration of a single type of test does not appeal to investigators who want to isolate important individual differences. They prefer to seek some general dimension among several diverse tests. They are seriously attempting to identify a quality which is "in the person" yet accounts for behavior over a wide range of situations or conditions. This line of attack meets many setbacks; one attempt to establish generality after another has failed. Yet the approach is not entirely without success, and sufficiently patient revision of tests and theories has a reasonable chance of identifying significant traits. Any consistent positive correlation between two superficially dissimilar tests encourages continued effort to define and clarify the underlying variable.

Positive correlations do commonly occur, but there are puzzling inconsistencies. Witkin (1949) finds that EFT correlates with Rod and Frame .64 for men but only .21 for women. Gardner (unpublished data) finds a correlation of .65 for women but a near-zero correlation for men. Small samples, differences in technique, and subtle differences in subject motivation all contribute to these inconsistencies. One can conclude that performance tests generally have correlations consistent with the theories offered to explain them, but the correlations are often low. We are far from having the reproducible high correlations which would permit us to argue that any two performance scores measure the same factor of personality.

Each task has its specific elements, and a satisfactory general measure will have to be built up by combining short trials on various tests each containing the same common element along with different specifics. The original Hartshorne-May studies of generality in character support this conclusion. They were the first to cast doubt upon the assumption that general traits of behavior can readily be measured by one or two specific samples. Although the specific tests were reliable, different measures of deception correlated little with each other. The correlation between cheating on a classroom test and on the Circle test of coördination was only .50 even after correction for unreliability. These data contradicted the notion that honesty is a unified trait which can be measured in any tempting situation. Furthermore, correlations between different character tests were so low as to prove untenable the view that a generalized "good character" accounted for desirable traits. Intercorrelations of honesty, coöperation, and so on were only about .25. The "general factor" in character has small influence on any specific behavior (Hartshorne and May, 1930).

Similar results are found for persistence (Thornton, 1939; MacArthur, 1955). MacArthur obtained 21 measures on English schoolboys, all the tests being presumed to have something to do with persistence. A very large proportion of the intercorrelations were insignificant, though some correlations were in the .50–.60 range. The general factor accounted for only 14 percent of the performance on the collection of tests. Among the scores which seemed to be good measures of "general persistence" were time spent in completing a magic number square, time spent on a difficult three-dimensional wooden puzzle (Japanese Cross), and ratings of persistence by teachers and peers. Combining eight scores could provide a measure of general persistence with reliability .79. MacArthur also found four group factors. One factor linked tests where pupils had a chance to see if their classmates were still working (in contrast to those where each had to set his own standards). This factor MacArthur named "social suggestibility in situations demanding persistence." Reputation measures formed a group factor. Two more factors were required to account for persistence on intellectual tasks and persistence in physical tasks. It is evident that persistence is to a large degree situational.

It should not be concluded that tests of specific traits have no place. They are invaluable for many research purposes, and the findings of such research may have practical significance. Maller (J. McV. Hunt, 1944) tells us that the Hartshorne-May findings on character led one national agency working with youth to revise its program completely, because the study showed that those who had received most recognition in the agency's character-building activities were on the average *most* likely to cheat. This is not hard to explain when we consider that striving for recognition in competition, and working for high scores even in a puzzle test, may stem from the same basic feeling of inadequacy.

There are three ways to interpret structured performance tests:

● They can be regarded as specific measures of one type of performance, defined only by the operations used in measuring. When they are used as dependent variables in psychological experiments, any positive findings are likely to be of ultimate theoretical importance even though the test cannot at present be interpreted in terms of general attributes.

● They can be used to measure general traits of personality. But because of the low correlations among tests of the same supposed trait, any such measurement requires a composite of diverse tasks. Performance testing of any personality construct seems to require a "hodgepodge" such as Binet invented to measure intelligence when no single type of problem proved adequate.

● They can be used singly or in combination to predict practically important variables. Any significant findings (see below) would be important whether or not the tests could be interpreted in terms of constructs.

11. Analyze the story-completion test of persistence, identifying all the factors which might cause one fifth-grader to earn a higher score than another.
12. According to *Studies in Deceit* (Hartshorne and May, 1928), children from homes with low socioeconomic status cheat more on achievement tests than other children ($r = .49$). What factors must be taken into account before concluding that these children are more likely to violate standards of good conduct?

Practical Correlates.   Comparisons with socially important criteria have been few and unsystematic. As comprehensive as any evaluation program has been the work of the Air Force, whose conclusions are summarized by Melton (1947, pp. 848–849):

> A continuing effort was made during the Aviation Psychology Program to obtain a test of the reaction of the candidate to emotion-producing stimuli, either directly through the application of such stimuli as distractions during the course of performance on some psychomotor task or indirectly through the measurement of muscular tension or other psychophysiological variables. . . . The available data do not support the hypothesis that additional validity for the prediction of success in elementary pilot training accrues to a test situation when verbal threats and other distractions, including presumably fear-producing stimuli, are administered.

Though the Operational Stress Test had validities of .20–.30, it overlapped so much with ability tests that it made no useful contribution to prediction.

Structured tests have been widely applied in clinical research, and many studies demonstrate differences between patients and normals or among patients of different types. Such results are difficult to interpret; diagnostic categories have uncertain psychological significance, and results can often be attributed to differences in coöperation and attention rather than to more fundamental psychological processes. Burdock, Sutton, and Zubin (1958) summarize much tentative evidence for various positive relations; for example, discharge of schizophrenics from hospital is predicted by low flicker-fusion thresholds and good performance on the Color Word test. Confirmation of these results would have obvious practical importance. It might also lay a basis for theories about qualities which predispose to recovery. According to Burdock and his colleagues, previous applications of performance tests to patients have picked variables too unsystematically, have not distinguished conceptual from perceptual performances, and have failed to compare complex performances against "baseline" measures of physiological and neurological functioning.

Performance measures of personality are related to social-psychological variables. Linton (1955), for example, measured attitudes before and after reading a biased but allegedly authoritative article. An index based on the Rod and Frame and Embedded Figures tests together correlated .66 with change scores. Subjects who could not disentangle relevant from irrelevant stimuli were most easily persuaded.

Significant predictions of resistance to propaganda or of recovery from schizophrenia are illustrative of the many studies which encourage hope for practical application of performance tests. None of the relationships, however, is well confirmed. Few correlations are checked by repeat studies, and not infrequently a repeat study fails to confirm the initial finding. One can find no correlation between a performance test and a practical criterion that is at present well enough established to warrant basing individual or administrative decisions on the test.

OBSERVATION OF COMPLEX PERFORMANCE

We turn from the highly structured measures of single traits to tests which assess style of performance in relatively complex tasks.

Problem Solving

During an ability test such as Block Design one can observe method of attack and response to frustration. Better information is obtained by modifying the test and by specifying precisely what is to be observed. Goldner (1957) defined "method of attack" in terms of two more definite variables, "whole-part approach" and rigidity. He used six tests: a modified Block Design test; the Arthur Stencil Design test, in which cutouts of various colors must be superimposed to form a specified pattern; Anagrams I, in which the subject builds numerous words from a set of letters; Anagrams II, requiring identification of a scrambled ten-letter word; the Rorschach inkblots; and a "Function test." In the last named, the subject is asked "What are the possible different uses of ——— (box, broom, pliers, paper)?" Goldner developed scoring rules for each test. For the Function test, the whole-part score was assigned according to whether the answer used the whole object ("Put things in the box") or broke it into parts ("Use it for firewood"). In the Block Design test, a "whole" attack is shown by the person who turns each block to the correct face before beginning assembly, and then assembles the pattern as a unit, paying attention to symmetry, etc. The "part" approach is shown by the person who starts at one corner and adds one block at a time, building up the pattern piecemeal. To bring out differences in approach, Goldner made three changes from the original Kohs test. He used irregular, nonsquare designs so as to make analysis of the pattern more difficult. He presented every design, whether it used nine or sixteen blocks, in the same size, so that the subject had to decide how many blocks to use.

Goldner also judged rigidity. In Block Design, for example, rigidity was scored if the subject had difficulty in judging the correct number of blocks, retained the same attack after a failure, or gave up without finishing a problem. In the Function test, rigidity was identified with a tendency to give many logically similar uses ("as a tool box," "for mailing," "to pack things") whereas flexibility was identified with variety.

This technique contrasts with the Water Jar test used as a measure of rigidity. In that simpler task the score reports a particular countable symptom. In Goldner's battery each score is a rating of an assumed mental process which can appear in the performance in several different ways. The more complex task "spreads out" performance so that mental process can be inferred.

Goldner found substantial support for the hypothesis of generality of the two traits observed. The results above the diagonal in Table 69 show that

TABLE 69.   Generality Among Tests of Problem-Solving Style

	Inkblot	Func-tion	Ana-grams I	Ana-grams II	Stencil Design	Block Design	Total "Whole-Part" Score Minus Particular Test
Inkblot		25	40	40	**58**	40	**67**
Function	42		00	−02	−02	10	08
Anagrams I	51	19		25	**53**	36	**48**
Anagrams II	10	25	−30		29	−03	27
Stencil Design	17	32	−19	**50**		62	**66**
Block Design	26	16	00	34	**83**		**48**
Total Rigidity score minus particular test	**54**	**43**	06	30	**58**	**54**	

Note: Correlations above diagonal are for whole-part scores, those below diagonal for rigidity scores. Correlations in boldface are significant.
Source: Goldner, 1957, p. 14.

five of his six "whole-part" scores are correlated. Each test agrees substantially with the total of the other measures. Particularly striking is the correlation between tasks as dissimilar as Anagrams I and Stencil Design. The Function test is an exception; whole approach on this test either is unreliable or is a different trait from whole approach on the other tasks. Goldner's findings on rigidity are quite similar: five tasks have marked correlations with each other. This time, however, Anagrams I is independent.

Concept-formation tests have been specially designed for study of abnormalities of thought processes. The Hanfmann-Kasanin test may be taken as an example. Twenty-two wooden blocks of several colors, shapes, heights, and sizes are placed on the table. On the hidden underside of each block is printed a nonsense syllable. The syllable defines a type of block (all *mur* blocks are small and tall). The examiner tells the subject that the blocks are of four different kinds, one of which is named *mur*, and that he is to discover the basis for classification and sort the blocks. The subject proceeds as he likes to discover the classification, except that he may not invert the blocks to look at the name. After each trial sorting, the examiner points out one mistake and asks for another trial. This goes on until the problem is solved and the principle of classification is stated. Observation shows whether the subject uses a logical hypothesis ("perhaps all *mur* are triangles"), an arbitrary hypothesis, or pure guessing. One observes ability to profit from a correction, ability to discard a false set and form a new concept, bizarre procedures and verbalizations, and so on. More significant than the numerical score is the insight and conceptual thinking displayed. The theory behind the test is that schizophrenics are unable to think abstractly and must respond to each object in the environment as a separate thing.

Though clinical groups differ on conceptual tests, they are by no means infallible diagnostic indicators. Some brain-injured patients show normal concept formation; and tests of either schizophrenics or of disturbed patients with low ability may easily be misinterpreted as indicative of brain damage (Zangwill, in Buros, 1949, p. 79). The designers of such tests argue for impressionistic analysis as the only dependable method of interpretation, but reviewers conclude that the advantages of the tests could be retained in a strictly objective scoring of processes observed (A. J. Yates, 1954).

13. Which of Goldner's tests are most structured? Do they correlate more highly with each other than with unstructured tests?

Perception

The Bender Test. Perceptual tests examine how the subject takes in, rearranges, and reports information. One such test is the Bender Visual Motor Gestalt Test (or Bender-Gestalt). The Bender, like many other tests we have mentioned, grows out of Gestaltist research on perception (Bender, 1938). Figures with different patterns of organization, including those in Figure 96, are shown. The tester asks the subject to copy the set, and observes his mode of attack and his success.

Each structured personality test was pointed specifically toward measuring some single trait. Goldner, using more complex tests, was able to score each one for two qualities, approach and rigidity. The Bender cannot be characterized as a measure of any one trait or set of traits. Responses of individuals may differ in a hundred different ways, which the tester attempts to observe, collate, and interpret. Scoring rules have been developed (Pascal and Suttell, 1951), but the clinician generally attempts a qualitative integration (see Chapter 19).

Performance may be treated statistically by observing "signs" which char-

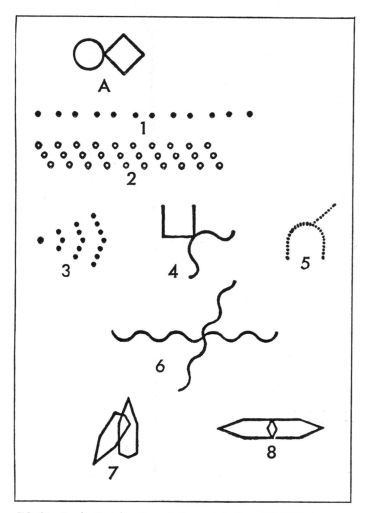

FIG. 96. Bender-Gestalt patterns to be copied. (Copyright 1946, American Orthopsychiatric Association. Reproduced by permission of Dr. Lauretta Bender and the American Orthopsychiatric Association.)

acterize some criterion group. Gobetz (1953) listed behaviors which distinguished neurotics from normals, for example:

Upward slope in reproducing rows of dots
Incorrect number of wave crests
Counting aloud during reproduction
Figures crowded into half of page

When Gobetz counted the number of such signs he found a significant difference: 19 percent of a cross-validation group of neurotics showed nine or more signs, compared to 4 percent of normals. Many of the signs reported by other authors as characteristic of neurotics did not differentiate in his study. Gobetz concluded that the test could be helpful in locating emotionally disturbed persons, provided that other data were used to confirm any diagnosis of maladjustment.

14. Judging from Gobetz' signs, what traits does the Bender measure?
15. Compare the screening effectiveness of Gobetz' scoring system with that for the MMPI (p. 479).

The Rorschach Test.   The Bender is a test of mental efficiency. The subject is set a simple, objective, and literal task; any emotional perturbation of mental processes can impair the performance. In the Rorschach test, "reality" plays a much smaller role in guiding responses. The subject is asked to tell what he sees in ten inkblots, blots whose form is so irregular as to permit innumerable interpretations. The blots are calculated to arouse emotional response with their bloody reds, ominous blacks, and luminous grays, and with their forms suggestive of nursery animals, overbearing giants, and sex organs. While the task as stated is purely intellectual, it also reveals emotional patterns. Patients often become extremely agitated while responding to the cards, and emotion is sufficient to damage some responses of seemingly normal individuals.

The technique was invented by Hermann Rorschach, a Swiss psychiatrist. He used the blots for "an experimental study of form perception" and found that patients of different types had different ways of responding to the blots. His diagnostic method, published in 1921, has been elaborated by subsequent investigators, with a shift of emphasis from attempted psychiatric classification to a description of psychodynamics. In the United States S. J. Beck (1945, 1952) has made minor changes in Rorschach's scoring system and developed crude norms; a more radical revision of the scoring system has been offered by Bruno Klopfer (Klopfer et al., 1954).

The Rorschach is used very extensively in clinical testing, even though its dependability is seriously questioned by nonclinical psychologists and by some expert clinicians. The Rorschach became prominent because psychiatrists have great interest in the descriptions of personality it yields. In the 1940's, when psychologists were first used in large numbers in mental hospitals and treatment centers, the chief duty assigned them by the medical staff was the administration of intelligence tests and Rorschachs. As a result, training in Rorschach interpretation became a requirement for clinical psychologists.

The interpretation begins with a systematic scoring according to fairly objective rules. There are about a dozen major scores, which fall into three major categories: location, determinants, and content. Location scores indicate whether the response uses the whole blot (W), commonly perceived subdivisions (D), or unusual details (Dd). The "determinants" are the shape, color, and shading of the blot which the subject takes into account. "Movement (M)," for example, is scored when the subject describes humans in motion, and CF when the response depends on both form and color, with color the more significant in determining the response. The scorer also notes how well the response fits the form of the blot, scoring form quality $+$ or $-$. Finally, the content score notes whether the response refers to persons (H), parts of persons (Hd), clothing (Cg), etc.

The scoring of four responses will illustrate the procedure. Card X is a mixture of brightly colored forms. Suppose that these four responses are given:

1. A big splashy print design for a summer dress.
2. Enlarged photograph of a snowflake [refers to a large irregularly shaped area].
3. Two little boys blowing bubbles. You just see them from the waist up.
4. Head of a rabbit.

The scoring of these responses (based on supplementary explanation obtained by inquiry) is:

Response	Location	Determinant and Form Level	Content
1	W	CF+	Art, Cg
2	D	F−	Nature
3	D	M+	Hd
4	D	F+	Ad

Norms can be collected for Rorschach scores, but to be meaningful the norms must be based on subgroups of the population rather than people in general. The procedure for testing can also be standardized. Interpretation, however, has never been reduced to a systematic procedure.

The quality of responses indicates something both about the subject's intellectual level and about the effort and carefulness he puts into an intellectual task. Much is made of the subject's control over his impulses and his emotional reactions. In Rorschach interpretation, movement responses are thought to represent imagination and creative impulses arising from within, and color responses are thought to represent emotional reactions to external stimuli. "Form" is equated with ability to take reality into account. A person who harmonizes form and movement is said to accept and use constructively his inner impulses; a person who rarely reports a movement response is regarded as lacking in imagination or as repressing it. Hertz (1942) expresses a view shared by most specialists in Rorschach method:

In the final analysis the procedure of the interpretation in terms of other clinical and test data defies standardization, as Rorschach originally contended. The information gleaned from the Rorschach material is projected against family background, education, training, health history, past life, qualitative judgments of the examiner and of other people, and other clinical and test data. This is then interpreted in terms of the examiner's experimental knowledge of the dynamics of human behavior. Final conclusions are made by inference and analogy depending upon the experience, ingenuity, the fertility of insight, and, not to be forgotten, the common sense of the examiner. Prolonged and extensive experience is necessary, not only with human personality but with all kinds of clinical problems. This last step by definition, therefore, is personal to the examiner and subjective in view. It permits no norms, and it eludes all standardization.

The impressionistic interpretation is constructed through the use of a great number of interrelated hypotheses about the internal forces and controls which lead to each type of response. Each of these hypotheses must ultimately be verified to make interpretation trustworthy. Successful experience with individual cases is the chief basis on which users defend the Rorschach method. There has been considerable formal research on the hypotheses, but the complexity of the problems posed by the tests has made comprehensive research exceedingly difficult (Cronbach, 1949; Mary D. Ainsworth, in Klopfer *et al.*, 1954, pp. 405–500). Sometimes the evidence is strikingly favorable.

Rorschach (1921; see 1942, p. 7) said that movement responses are indicative of personalities that "function more in the intellectual sphere, whose interests gravitate more towards their intrapsychic living rather than towards the world outside themselves." This introversion interpretation was checked by Barron (1955), who employed a psychophysical technique to obtain an M score, like Rorschach's but much more reliable. This score was compared with ratings made by clinical assessors using other data. The persons with strong M tendencies were described as inventive, having wide interests, introspective, concerned with self as object, valuing cognitive pursuits. The low M subjects were described as practical, stubborn, preferring action to contemplation, inflexible in thought and action. Although this supports Rorschach's interpretation, Klopfer's use of M as a prime indicator of intelligence is questioned; there was no correlation between Barron's M score and objective tests of intelligence and originality. To be sure, the psychologist assessors rated the high M's as more intelligent, but in view of the objective test results this implies that assessors are biased toward judging persons intelligent if they appear "thoughtful." In another study, similar mixed confirmation of Rorschach theory is found. S responses, which interpret the white space between the blots, are presumed to indicate oppositional tendencies, and Bandura (1954) found a correlation of .35 between the S score and ratings of negativism. No support was found, however, for the configural hypothesis that the meaning of this oppositional tendency depends on the M:C balance, S in high M subjects implying self-criticism, and in high C subjects implying opposition to others. (See also D. C. Murray, 1957.)[1]

Hundreds of additional studies could be cited, each dealing with one bit of Rorschach theory. The trend of the results (Benton, 1950; Holtzman et al., 1954; Sarason, 1954) is this:

● About half of the experimental tests of Rorschach hypotheses give results consistent with clinical theory. The interpretation certainly has "validity greater than chance."

● These confirmations indicate rather small degrees of relationship between Rorschach indicators and postulated traits. (Bandura's correlation of .35 is typical). Many different personality factors and abilities influence any one score, and no direct trait interpretation can be made with confidence.

● Some aspects of the theory are definitely incorrect and should be revised.

Just how adequate the test, with these limitations, is for global impressionistic assessment will be considered in Chapter 19.

There have been attempts to use single quantitative scores from the Rorschach either as trait measures or as empirical predictors. Sets of "signs" have been developed, for example, to identify persons with organic brain damage (A. J. Yates, 1954; Fisher, Gonda, and Little, 1954). Generally, these proposed special formulas prove valueless on cross-validation, either showing no validity or having too high a false positive rate to be useful. Trait scores such as Goldner's measures of approach and rigidity sometimes correlate with external criteria, but the correlations are generally too small to warrant use of the Rorschach as a quantitative measure. Some investigators feel that these deficiencies could be removed by redesigning the test in order to obtain a better sample of behavior. Holtzman (1958) has prepared two parallel sets of 45 blots and developed a scoring system for them. The subject gives one response to each blot. Score reliability is expected to surpass that of the conventional ten-blot test, but validity remains to be determined.

---

[1] An amusing and possibly profound analysis of the disagreements among validation studies in contained in a study by Levy and Orr (1959) on "the social psychology of Rorschach validation." When university psychologists set up experiments to test construct interpretations of the Rorschach, their predictions are confirmed 70 percent of the time. Comparable studies by psychologists working in clinical settings succeed only 50 percent of the time. When working clinicians try to establish criterion validity, however, they succeed in 60 percent of their studies whereas academic psychologists are successful in only one-third of their attempts to validate the test against clinical criteria.

16. Why might a "perfect" accuracy score, 100 percent $F+$, indicate a personality pattern undesirable for many situations?

17. Do the Rorschach scores related to quality of output reveal maximum ability or typical behavior? How does the Rorschach compare with the Binet test in that respect?

18. "Responses to ten inkblots, presented by one tester on one occasion, constitute too small a sample of behavior to measure any intellectual or emotional trait reliably." Do you agree? To what extent does Holtzman's test overcome this objection?

19. It was pointed out (p. 131) that lengthening a test improves validity most if the score is a pure measure of the quality measured by the criterion. In view of this principle, would increasing the sample of inkblot responses in Holtzman's manner be expected to have much or little effect on validity?

Group Behavior

Group Discussion.   The Leaderless Group Discussion (LGD) is a systematic observation procedure used to study social behavior (Bion, 1946). A group of persons, perhaps applying for the same job, are told to discuss a certain problem (e.g., how to increase movie attendance). Observers rate predetermined aspects of each member's performance. The LGD is unstructured: no rules of procedure are established, the topic is left largely undefined, and the group, being strangers to each other, have no initial friendship or dominance relations. During the discussion, however, social patterns are quickly built up, and the role the person plays is presumably similar to the role he is prone to adopt in natural groups.

The variables most commonly rated have to do with three traits: prominence, goal facilitation (efficiency, suggesting useful ideas), and sociability. Bass (1954) measures prominence by rating the following behaviors (on a scale from "a great deal" to "not at all"):

> showed initiative
> was effective in saying what he wanted to say
> clearly defined or outlined the problems
> motivated others to participate
> influenced the other participants
> offered good solutions to the problem
> led the discussion

What the test chiefly measures, Bass says, is "tendency to initiate structure in an initially unstructured situation."

The effectiveness of the LGD can be evaluated in several ways. Stability over trials is fairly high; with a week between tests, the correlations range from .75 to .90. Over longer time intervals or with radical changes in the type of problem, correlations drop to about .50. The test is measuring some consistent and general aspect of personality. Behavior in practical situations is no doubt determined by many forces other than personality (seniority, relative prestige, specifically relevant knowledge, etc.) but LGD scores nonetheless have striking predictive value. Bass and Coates (1952) compared LGD scores with ratings by superiors given as much as nine months later and found correlations of .40 to .45. Arbous (1955) reports a validity of .60 for LGD against rated promise of executives in training. Suitability for the British foreign service as rated after two years on duty was predicted (validity .33) by LGD scores at the time of selection (Vernon, 1950).

The LGD procedure illustrates the advantage that can be obtained from systematic observations. Social relations are important in personnel assignment, yet it is very difficult to judge validity from questionnaires, letters of recommendations, or interviews. The LGD is an economical "worksample" of group behavior. By scoring observed behavior it avoids much of the bias inherent in summary impressions. Army colonels' ratings of cadet potential were much poorer predictors of later merit ratings than were total scores recorded by these same colonels acting as observers for an LGD session (Bass, 1954).

20. Give reasons for each of the following recommendations by Bass regarding LGD technique:
   a. Counts of actual behavior (e.g., new approaches suggested) should be substituted for ratings of the subject's tendency to suggest new approaches.
   b. Problems should be equally ambiguous to all participants.
   c. Examinees tested in a group should all have the same rank.
21. Compare LGD and peer ratings as methods of assessing leadership potential.

Task Leadership. The Leaderless Group Discussion is one of a number of "worksample" techniques for measuring personality which originated in German and British military psychology. Psychologists selecting officers thought it necessary to observe complex behavior combining intellect, emotion, and habit. One simple team-performance task devised by the Germans uses two pairs of shears linked by rods so that they must move in unison. While one shear is opening, the other is closing. Each subject operates one pair of shears, cutting a series of increasingly complex patterns from a sheet of paper. The shears are so arranged that if one man goes directly and forcefully at his task, the shears of the other man move in a rhythm which makes accurate cutting almost impossible. By means of observation, automatic recording, and inspection of the product, the tester looks for evidence of initiative, dominance, and coöperation (Kunze, 1931). In a group leadership test used by OSS, the American wartime intelligence service, candidates were directed to move a heavy eight-foot log, and themselves, over two walls ten feet high, eight feet apart, and separated by an imaginary bottomless chasm. Observers noted which men took initiative and leadership, how they directed others, how they accepted orders, and so on.

Perhaps the high point of fiendish ingenuity was the OSS construction test. The subject is assigned to build a five-foot cube with a set of super-Tinkertoys. Poles and spools must be fitted together, and since the parts are too large to be managed by one man, two helpers are assigned. After giving directions, the tester ostentatiously clicks his stop watch and retreats. What the subject does not know is that his helpers are highly trained stumble-bums. Kippy is negative, indolent, a drawback. Buster is an eager beaver, ready to do all manner of things, mostly wrong, and also primed to needle the candidate with personal criticism. This is reported as a typical dialog (Anon., 1946):

Candidate: Well, let's get going.
Buster: What is it you want done, exactly? What do I do first?
Candidate: Well, first put some corners together—let's see, make eight of these corners and be sure you pin them like this one.
Buster: You mean we both make eight corners or just one of us?
Candidate: You each make four of these, and hurry.
Kippy: Whacha in, the Navy? You look like one of them curly-headed Navy boys all the girls are after.
Candidate: Er, no, I'm not in anything.
Kippy: Just a draft dodger, eh?
Candidate: Let's have less talk and more work. You build a square over here and you build one over there.
Kippy: Who are you talking to—him or me? Why don't you give us a number or something—call one of us number one and the other number two?
Candidate: I'm sorry. What's your name?
Buster: Mine's Buster and his is Kippy. What's yours?
Candidate: You can call me Slim.
Buster: Not with that shining head of yours. What do they call you, Baldy or Curly? Did you ever think of wearing a toupee?
Slim: Come on, get to work.
Kippy: He's sensitive about being bald.
Slim: Just let's get this thing finished. We haven't much more time. Hey, there, you, be careful. You knocked that pole out deliberately.
Kippy: Who me? Now listen to me, you———, if this———thing had been built right from the beginning, the poles wouldn't come out. For———, they send a boy out here to do a man's job. . . .

Kippy and Buster are psychologists and are in a position to make an excellent report on the man's reaction. (The fact that they had served as Army privates, and that some of the candidates they were privileged to torment were generals being considered for special assignment, probably also set an untouchable record for job satisfaction among psychologists.)

22. A field performance test of an NCO's ability to lead his squad was developed by the Army as a criterion measure of proficiency. Why are some performance tests regarded as measures of personality and some as measures of proficiency?

THEMATIC PROJECTIVE TECHNIQUES

The Bender-Gestalt and the Rorschach illustrate one type of projective technique, in which the subject's style of handling a problem is the focus of attention. These primarily *stylistic* tests may be contrasted with *thematic* tests, in which the interpreter is especially concerned with the content of the subject's thoughts and fantasies. This distinction resembles that between trait questionnaires such as Guilford's, which focus on response patterns, and techniques for studying stimulus meanings such as the Semantic Differential and the Rep test. The stylistic and thematic categories are not mu-

tually exclusive. One can identify specific fears or obsessions in the Rorschach protocol, and can even interpret "content" of Bender reproductions through Freudian symbolism. Conversely, mental style is observed in the Thematic Apperception Test. But the stylistic tests generally yield richer stylistic information than the thematic tests and are rather poor sources of thematic information. The thematic test comes nearer to examining "the whole person" at once than any other testing technique,

FIG. 97. Cartoon stimulus for a thematic test. The picture is presented with the statement "Here is Blacky with Mama's collar." (From the Blacky Pictures by G. S. Blum. Copyright 1950, The Psychological Corporation. Reproduced by permission.)

seeking information on emotions, attitudes, and cognitive processes, so that it does give a comprehensive, if tentative, portrait of the whole personality.

The Thematic Apperception Test

The Thematic Apperception Test of H. A. Murray and his coworkers (1938) requires the subject to interpret a picture by telling a story—what is happening, what led up to the scene, and what will be the outcome. The responses are dictated by the constructs, experiences, conflicts, and wishes of the subject. Essentially the person projects himself into the scene, identifying with a character just as he vicariously takes the place of the actor when he sees a movie. The TAT consists of twenty pictures, different pictures being used for men and women. Since two one-hour sessions are required for the full test, investigators often use shortened versions. The subject is led to believe that his imagination is being tested. The interpreter gives particular attention to the themes behind the plots. The stories may indicate a defeatist attitude, concern about overbearing authority figures, or preoccupation with sex. In addition to these aspects of response content, the interpreter considers the style: use of the whole picture rather than piecemeal attack, fluency, concern with accuracy in fitting the story to the picture, etc.

The interpreter looks at each story in turn, deriving hypotheses from the plot, the symbolism, and the style. The hypothesis from one story (e.g., "This man represses all hostile feelings") is checked against subsequent stories. The interpreter must decide how much weight to give to each of many conflicting indications and must integrate the information on intellectual powers, emotional conflicts, and defense mechanisms indicated by the test protocol.

Only a few illustrations of the analysis can be given here. Card I of the TAT shows a boy, perhaps 10 years old, looking at a violin lying on a flat surface. A girl, age 14, with a Binet IQ of 143, gives this story (Henry, 1956, p. 111):

> Right now the boy is looking at the violin. It looks like he might be kind of sad or mad because he has to play. Before he might have played ball with the other boys and his mother wouldn't let him. He had to go in and play. Looks like he might practice for a little while and then sneak out.

Henry, working from this and other stories, estimated her IQ at 140, commenting on how clearly the story "takes into account the basic stimulus demands of the picture" and goes on to "entirely relevant elaborations of good quality . . . [which] attribute motive and action to the characters." Whereas this story led more to a study of process than of plot, the story of a 42-year-old clerk is interpreted thematically (Henry, p. 145):

> The story behind this is that this is the son of a very well-known, a very good musician and the father has probably died. The only thing the son has left is this violin which is undoubtedly a very good one and to the son, the violin is the father and the son sits there daydreaming of the time that he will understand the music and interpret it on the violin that his father had played.

Henry comments that the first sentence shows preoccupation with excellence and a conviction that to match the example is impossible. The man dreams only of things within himself, and takes no action to carry out his ambition.

Contrasting with this rather direct interpretation of a plot as reflecting the teller's drives and style of behavior, another story shows the possibility of identifying deeper symbolism behind the fantasy. A recent immigrant, a man age 29, tells this story (Henry, p. 178):

> A young boy sitting in front of a violin spread out on white table, or white linen. It is not clear in the expression of the face if he thinks in glorification and admiration of that what the violin and music could hold for him or if he is bored and in disgust with the lesson he has to take and doesn't want.

Note, says Henry, the emphasis on conflicting alternatives: glorification or disgust, has to take and doesn't want. This personality "may well be marked by its attraction to opposites." The core of conflict appears to be sexual, the basic issue being whether woman can be "both the Madonna and the sexual object. . . . This is an instance of the use of the violin as a sexual symbol. The man is basically preoccupied with some strong emotional issue; hence he utilizes form details in a distorting manner [e.g., "violin spread out"]. . . . He feels impelled to make a formal heterosexual adjustment as well as a conventional social adjustment, even though both are somewhat forced and against his will."

These excerpts by no means represent the intricacy of a full interpretation in which stories are compared with each other and with background information about the subject. For examples of such full interpretations the reader is referred to Henry (1956) and Shneidman (1951). We should also emphasize that such interpretations as Henry makes are—if the psychologist is properly trained—extremely tentative, and are discarded unless there is supporting evidence elsewhere in the test and the subject's history. These illustrations do indicate the individuality of style which TAT responses exhibit, and the variation in the interpreter's attack. At one moment he views the performance entirely as an intellectual effort; at another he treats the response as a symbolization of unconscious conflict. How he interprets each response depends upon the story and perhaps upon his own artistic impulses of the moment.

Though interpretation has been primarily qualitative and impressionistic, it is possible to develop objective scoring systems for the TAT. There are dozens of common variables whose strength can be observed in almost every TAT performance: perception of authority, reaction to extremely difficult tasks, originality, reliance on luck and magical intervention. The themes themselves are often highly individualistic, but common elements can be tabulated. Shneidman (1951) presents fifteen TAT scoring systems used by various clinicians. Such scoring reports the percentage of stories whose outcome is unhappy, the number of female characters seen as predatory or demanding, etc. These scores play a larger part in research than in clinical analysis of individuals. Use of TAT scores for diagnosis appears worthy of further exploration. Dana (1955, 1956) developed four scores for expressive aspects of the performance which separated neurotics, psychotics, and normals. Mussen and Naylor (1954) validated an aggression score for TAT stories, showing that it correlated with frequency of overt aggressive behavior in problem boys. More than that, when the frequency of mention of punishment in the TAT was used as a measure of fear of punishment, it was shown that behavior depended on both aggressive drive and fear. Every one of the seven boys with high TAT aggression and low fear of punishment showed high behavioral aggression; only two out of nine with high TAT aggression and high fear of punishment were overtly aggressive. This is an example of the oft-reiterated principle that no one personality score is fully interpretable by itself.

Stability coefficients over two months are in the range .60–.90 for such scores as need for abasement, giving stories with positive outcomes, and use of tension-relief words. Though the evidence is scanty, this is a very favorable indication of the possibility of accurate measurement, since the strength of needs measured by TAT changes somewhat from occasion to occasion and consistency cannot be perfect (Crandall, 1951; Lindzey and Herman, 1955). From these and other studies, it appears that the TAT collects sufficient information to permit fairly accurate scoring of traits, if scoring keys are carefully developed toward this end.

23. How many traits are mentioned in Henry's three interpretations?
24. Can one regard the frequency of punishment by authority in TAT stories as a sample of behavior indicating how often the subject is punished in life?

Measurement of Need for Achievement

The TAT is designed to cover the whole range of ideas and behavior and therefore cannot cover any one topic thoroughly. While a person obsessed with independence conflicts may bring them into every story, most people reveal their relationships with authority only on one or two cards specifically designed to elicit such stories. As the examples above show, any single picture is indefinite enough to bring out different types of information from different subjects. This flexibility, which permits the subject to reveal almost any trait or theme that is prominent in his personality structure, is an advantage in a free-ranging exploration of personality. But it is a serious disadvantage when one wishes to answer a specific question.

Focused tests are designed to elicit thematic responses all of which bear on the same question. For example, Murphy and Likert (1938) carried out research on labor-management conflict by presenting pictures of strikers in conflict with police, etc. Shapiro, Biber, and Minuchin (1957) tested teachers' attitudes by presenting cartoon pictures of classroom scenes and pupil groups. A focused test for Air Force personnel was based on the hypothesis that outwardly directed aggression would be associated with tolerance for high centrifugal forces. The criterion was a measure of the force (number of "G") required to produce blackout in a human centrifuge. In the best-designed of several validation studies, the score from the thematic test classified 18 of 25 subjects correctly as having high or low tolerance (A. J. Silverman et al., 1957).

The possibilities of the focused thematic test have been most thoroughly exploited by McClelland and his associates (1953). He selected four pictures (two from the TAT) intended to bring out attitudes toward achievement. The four cards are a work situation (men at a machine), a study situation (boy at desk with book), a father-son picture, and a boy apparently daydreaming. Achievement motivation was scored in every story suggesting competition with a standard. For example,

A worker is putting a hot plate of metal back in the oven with a pair of tongs in order to heat it up again. The gentleman beside him is a helper.

is scored as showing need for achievement (n Ach) because the reheating implies "desire to move ahead to the ultimate goal" (Atkinson, 1958, p. 722). Detailed scoring manuals have been developed (McClelland et al., 1953; Atkinson, 1958, pp. 685–735).

A second projective measure for the same purpose is the French Test of Insight (Atkinson, 1958, pp. 242–248). A brief description of behavior is given, e.g., "Bill always lets the 'other fellow' win"; the subject is to provide an explanation. The test consists of twenty such items, ten in each form. The score is the number of times desire for achievement is mentioned as a motive.

There is evidence that such projective measures are getting at a different aspect of personality than that shown in other measures. De Charms et al. (McClelland, 1955, pp. 414 ff.) made up a questionnaire on desire for achievement (called v Ach). This correlated only .23 with n Ach. The subject with high v Ach is concerned with conformity, is deferential to expert authority, and disapproves unsuccessful people. High n Ach, on the other hand, is more associated with striving and effectiveness. Scores on the French test correlated near zero with peer judgments of motivation to achieve (Atkinson, 1958, p. 247). French was able to show that the peer judgments of motivation depended heavily on observed success and thus are probably reflections of ability rather than motivation.

Even though it is unrelated to observations and self-report, the projective test is related to behavior. High n Ach is generally associated with striving and effectiveness (de Charms et al., in McClelland, 1955, p. 421). French and Thomas (1958) divided a selected group of highly intelligent subjects into those with high and low n Ach on the Insight test and required them to solve a difficult intellectual problem of the type described in Chapter 1 (p. 7). The problem had several acceptable solutions. The high n Ach group worked, on the average, twice as long as the others before giving up, and were much more successful in arriving at at least one solution. In the highly motivated group, performance correlated .36 with ability, but the correlation was zero in the low n Ach group. Ability predicts only when men are motivated to use that ability.

It is hypothesized by McClelland that thematic tests reflect strength of motives at a given moment, as well as the average need level of the individual. This is supported by the finding that *n Ach* scores are higher when tension is raised by ego-involving directions (French, 1955), as well as by studies with focused tests of sexual, affiliative, and hunger drives.

Prominent Projective Techniques

During the decade 1945–1955 there was a wave of indiscriminate enthusiasm for developing new projective techniques. Dozens of approaches were tried, but in most cases the research was so superficial that the unique merit of each procedure, if any, was not established. Only a few of the techniques have survived, and some of them retain popularity only because a cult of specialists keeps the test prominent. The following projective tests, in addition to those previously described, are encountered with greatest frequency in the current research literature or in clinical practice.

● The Blacky Pictures; Gerald S. Blum; Psychological Corporation, 1950. A set of cartoons involving a small dog; situations are designed to elicit stories revealing sexual attitudes (Figure 97). The pictures suggest various types of conflict derived from psychoanalytic theory (e.g., castration anxiety). Validation is seriously inadequate.

● Children's Apperception Test (CAT); Leopold Bellak, 1948, 1951. (See Bellak, 1954.) A TAT-type instrument for ages 3–10. Pictures of animals such as might be used in nursery stories are aimed to elicit information on feeding conflicts, sibling rivalry, and other childhood problems. Validity is presumably very similar to that of TAT.

● Four-Picture Test; D. J. van Lennep; M. Nijhoff, The Hague, 1930, 1948, 1958. The subject is given four pictures showing two solitary figures and two social scenes; one story is to be woven around all four pictures. In the hands of an experienced user, the test should have values similar to those of the TAT. (See H. H. Anderson and Gladys L. Anderson, 1951, pp. 149–180; van Lennep, 1958.)

● House-Tree-Person (HTP) Test; J. N. Buck; Western Psychological Services, 1946, 1950. This is one of several tests in which the subject merely executes a drawing. Different interpreters emphasize different aspects of the production. Although claims are made for successful interpretation in clinical cases, careful validation studies cast doubt upon the specific interpretative principles offered (Anastasi and Foley, 1952; Fisher and Fisher, 1950.) There is no doubt that drawings reflect personality, but there is great uncertainty as to how to make sound inferences from them.

● Make-a-Picture-Story Test (MAPS); Edwin S. Shneidman; Psychological Corporation, 1947. A variant of TAT in which the subject assembles paper cutout figures against backgrounds to make his own pictures. Presumably similar to TAT in value though even less structured (Shneidman, 1951).

● Rosenzweig Picture Frustration (PF) Test; Saul Rosenzweig, 1944, 1948. A set of cartoons in which one figure thwarts another; the subject, taking the part of the second person, is to tell how he would reply. The PF is therefore a self-report test using focused fantasies. The test is objectively scored. Though it is of definite research value, there is no clear theory for interpreting individual scores.

● Sentence Completion Technique; J. B. Rotter; Psychological Corporation, 1950. Another version, Amanda R. Rohde and Gertrude Hildreth; Psychological Corporation, 1947. The sentence-completion method is one of the simplest methods of obtaining information on conflicts either for screening of disturbed persons or as a preliminary to interview. Unfinished sentences such as "My mother . . ." or "When I make a mistake . . ." are to be completed by the subject. Several versions of the test have been crudely standardized. Although responses can be consciously controlled, the coöperative subject generally gives a useful picture of some of his salient attitudes (Rotter *et al.*, 1949).

● The Szondi Test; L. Szondi, 1937, 1951. (See Deri, 1949.) Photographs of patients having various diagnoses are presented to the subject, who indicates which ones he prefers. It is assumed that even though the patient does not know the diagnoses, his unconscious tendencies to approach one type or another reflect his personal needs. Available evidence indicates that the Szondi-Deri hypotheses are invalid (Lubin in Buros, 1953, pp. 255–256).

Some summary may be attempted regarding the value of performance tests and projective tests when used as psychometric instruments, even though their variety requires that generalization be cautious. We have seen that tests vary greatly in their degree of focus. Some, such as the flicker-fusion measure and the box-of-coins test, sample behavior of an exceedingly specific type. Composite scores such as MacArthur's general persistence score or Goldner's whole-part score derived from several techniques cover a broader range of behavior. Likewise, the focused measures of *n Ach* and the Leaderless Group Discussion procedure give reliable scores which have appreciable correlations with nontest variables. When focus is almost completely removed, as in the TAT and Rorschach, it becomes much harder to measure any one variable accurately. In the present state of performance testing, therefore, these conclusions seem justified:

● Highly structured tests of narrowly defined variables have little usefulness today save in development of psychological theory. Such tests are unlikely to have ultimate practical value except in a composite or battery, or in some rare situation comparable to the use of a color-vision test as a measure of occupational aptitude, where a specific test factor duplicates a specific task requirement.

● Less narrowly focused tests have potential value as measures of general personality attributes. The one procedure now known to have practical value is the LGD, which is a worksample. With composite performance scores like MacArthur's or focused tests like McClelland's, significant traits can be measured. These trait measures are of potential value as measures of dependent and independent variables in research. Because numerous traits interact to determine behavior in any situation, any one such measure will rarely have a large correlation with any practical criterion.

● Unfocused projective techniques are poorly adapted for quantitative measurement, although scores can be derived from them. Their chief function is in impressionistic assessment of individuals, as part of a thorough case study employing numerous other sources of information. The next chapter will discuss this.

Suggested Readings

Bass, Bernard M. The leaderless group discussion. *Psychol. Bull.*, 1954, **51**, 465–492.
    This is a comprehensive account of evidence on the practical validity of LGD scores, together with an analysis of the personality and ability factors which lead to good LGD performance.
Biber, Barbara, & others. Problem-solving situations. *Life and ways of the seven-year-old.* New York: Basic Books, 1952. Pp. 298–344.
    The authors applied four tests of problem-solving behavior to ten 7-year-olds, primarily to observe their approach, insight, and reaction to blocking. The chapter describes the tests and method of scoring and summarizes results for the group. It also describes problem tests used by other investigators. Elsewhere in the book, case descriptions of the separate children are given, so that the information from the performance observations can be compared with other data.
Burdock, Eugene I., Sutton, Samuel, & Zubin, Joseph. Personality and psychopathology. *J. abnorm. soc. Psychol.*, 1958, **56**, 18–30.
    Research is described involving nineteen structured tests of traits ranging from the physiological to the conceptual. Preliminary results are given on the possible diagnostic and theoretical significance of each test, together with critical comments on performance measures previously used in clinical work.
Levitt, Eugene E. The water-jar Einstellung test as a measure of rigidity. *Psychol. Bull.*, 1956, **53**, 347–370.
    Levitt summarizes numerous investigations of the generality of this test. He shows that the same test takes on different psychological properties with only slight changes in design. Levitt's critique of the psychometric properties

of the Water Jar test raises questions applicable to nearly all performance tests.

McClelland, David C. Performance traits. *Personality*. New York: William Sloane, 1951. Pp. 162–199.

A penetrating discussion of the use of performance tests and ratings to isolate useful dimensions for describing typical behavior includes an excellent survey of factor-analytic studies of personality.

19

Assessment of Personality Dynamics

THE psychometric tradition isolates separate dimensions of ability and personality and represents the individual by assigning scores on those dimensions. Other testers follow a more artistic tradition in which tests are seen as just one procedure for gaining insight into a complexly organized system of needs, concepts, and perceptual attitudes. The impressionistic interpreter is not primarily concerned to arrive at quantitative scores on abstracted dimensions. He is concerned with the organization of processes within the individual which give unity to his behavior. The impressionistic interpreter asks what "personality structure" (intrapersonal organization) could account for the observed facts—for the ways he perceives significant others in his life, for the discrepancies between his abilities on various tests, for the seeming differences between his fantasy needs and his overt behavior, etc. Such a coherent picture is of great potential value in making decisions about a case, though its usefulness depends entirely upon its quality and completeness, and these in turn depend on the range of information available and the astuteness of the clinician's synthesis of it. The clinician's judgment makes full use of his psychological theory and his experience with other cases, but his final portrait of the case is an artistic reconciliation of diverse impressions.

Almost any psychological test, observation, or interview can be used as a basis for such a portrait. We have illustrated this with many examples: Jones' description of John Sanders from the Stanford-Binet (p. 187); Kirk's description of a type of underachiever (p. 456); Grayson's description of a patient from the MMPI (p. 491); Osgood's and Luria's description of Eve from the Semantic Differential (p. 503); Henry's three partial TAT interpretations (p. 570). These examples vary considerably in the extent to which the interpreter speculates beyond the observed facts. Henry's three sketches range from an almost literal description of the young girl's reasoning methods to a symbolic translation of the story given by the immigrant man. As one further example which shows how freely a clinician employs creative imagination, psychoanalytic theory, and even frank speculation, we may quote a Bender interpretation given by Max Hutt (Shneidman, 1951, pp. 227–233) for the same patient whose MMPI Grayson interpreted.

Hutt first notes that the reproduced figures are arranged in the same sequence as in the original, the first six being aligned with the left margin, but that the last two drawings are fitted into the right half of the page.

Our first hunches then are: this individual has strong orderly, i.e., compulsive needs, tending towards a sort of compulsive ritual, but tries to deny them [the first drawing being displaced away from the margin and the examiner having noted that the man draws fast and unhesitatingly] . . . , and he is oppressed with some (probably) generalized feelings of anxiety and (more specifically) personal inadequacy (clings to the left margin and is "constrained" to use all of the space available to him on this one sheet). We raise the question for consideration, at once, "How strong and from what source is this anxiety and what is his defense?" We can speculate, from his use of space, that he attempts in some way to "bind" his anxiety, i.e., he cannot tolerate it for long or in large amounts, and that one of the features of this young adult's functioning is the need of control. . . . The super-ego is very strict.

Here Hutt has looked at the style of the man's performance, and then has tried to infer what inner tensions and defenses could generate such a style. As he says, these are hunches and speculations to be checked against other evidence in the protocol and against all other information about the patient. As in most "dynamic" interpretations, Hutt uses Freudian concepts of drives, conflict, and defenses.

As an example of more detailed analysis, consider Hutt's remarks on the subject's reproduction of the rows of circles (see Figure 98).

. . . the ten diagonal columns of circles [offer] further evidence of the marked variability which begins to appear to be characteristic of this "S." The examiner notes, "Checks number of rows (i.e., columns) about two-thirds through." We note that the angles of the columns of dots differ, becoming more obtuse (from the vertical) with a correction towards the end. The whole figure is exaggerated in the lateral plane. Together, these findings suggest a strong need to relate to people, but difficulty in establishing such relationships. The orientation of the first column is correct, so the variation in "angulation" is not a simple perceptual difficulty. "S" gets the number of columns correct, but varies *both* angulation and spacing. We have evidence, then, for the presence of considerable internal tension with an attempt at denial of its existence. How can we explain the apparent contradiction of the need for order and control with the speed and variability of performance?

Without giving further details of Hutt's reasoning about perceptual style, we quote a few of his conclusions for comparison with the MMPI report and the opinions of the therapist (p. 491). All the following descriptions are used, in a context which explains how they were derived and with what degree of confidence: compulsive defenses not effective . . . acting out . . .

regressive impulsivity breaks through . . . possibility of psychotic episodes
. . . depressive reaction.

The clinician's interpretation of scraps and shreds of evidence is daring.
Can one really know a person from the minor irregularities of his rows of
dots? But if Hutt's interpretations of style seem bold, there are more startling
things to come. From statements about defenses and controls, Hutt turns to

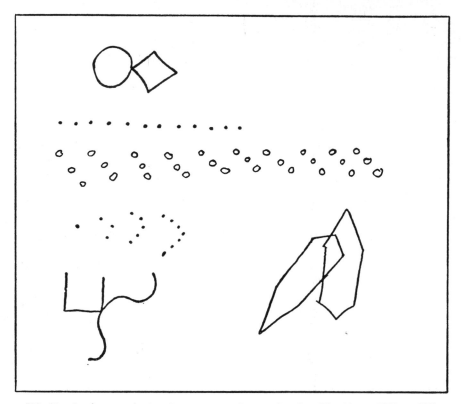

FIG. 98.   Bender reproductions by a young male mental patient (Shneidman, 1951, p. 228).

the symbolism of the figures, following certain Freudian ideas about "masculine" and "feminine" designs:

[In the figure composed of an open square with a wave form at one corner]
"S" has increased the vertical sides of the open square. . . . S's reaction to authority figures can now be inferred more completely: he is hostile to such figures,
unable to express this hostility directly, and reacts either symbolically or impul-
sively. In line with the "acting out" hypothesis, the former is more likely. The
curved portion of this figure is enlarged, flattened out in the middle and reveals an
impulsive flourish at the upper end. Now we may speculate that S's major identification is with a female figure, but she is perceived as more masculine (i.e., dominant, aggressive) than feminine and is reacted to openly with antagonism. It is

interesting that the upper portion of the curved figure extends well above its position on the stimulus card, and is at least as high up as the vertical lines. Here we may conjecture that S's mother (or surrogate) was stronger psychologically than his father, or at least seemed so to S, and that S would like to use his mother (or women) to defy his father (or men).

Such test interpretation is often severely criticized as unscientific. In defense of the method, we may note that Hutt is able to give a detailed rationale for each of his inferences; he is by no means allowing his fantasy free rein. A much stronger defense is that his description of the patient agrees well with the clinical picture given both from the MMPI self-report and in the therapist's notes. Word for word, we find confirmation there of ineffectual defense through obsession, hostile impulses the subject fears to express, and so on. Other remarks of the therapist support some of Hutt's most hazardous-seeming guesses: "The father seems to be a hazy person in the patient's life." "He talked of wishing to strangle his mother." "Had difficulty with authority figures." While the Bender analysis was not a perfect description, it yielded much better information about the depths of personality than one might expect from seemingly wild interpretations of a little task suitable for a child's drawing exercise.

The fact that clinicians continually have such striking successes with individuals gives them considerable right to feel confident in their methods and theory. At the same time, the clinical tests rarely satisfy the demand for systematic validation. If it was difficult to nail down the validity of the Pd score on MMPI, it is impossible to put into statistical form the evidence for such innumerable hypotheses as that enlargement of the Bender wave-form indicates a particular attitude toward one's mother.

The dynamic interpretation of the person by means of a single complex test or a whole assortment of techniques is frequently called "assessment," to distinguish it from psychometric measurement. Assessment most commonly takes one of two forms. The first is clinical analysis, well illustrated in the Grayson and Hutt interpretations. The second is prediction of performance of normal or superior persons assigned to responsible jobs.

Personality assessment of normals grew out of the German military testing of the 1930's, whose team-performance tests were mentioned earlier. In the hands of German testers, tests were regarded primarily as samples of character traits such as will power and rigidity. The techniques were adapted in Great Britain for War Office Selection Boards. When wartime conditions made it necessary to select officers from the ranks instead of relying on professionals from the upper classes, these boards took responsibility for judging ability and character of applicants for commissions. In the United States, Professor Henry Murray and his associates described the application of a large number of asessment techniques to Harvard students in the ground-breaking *Explorations in Personality* (1938). During World War II, Murray was asked to select staff for the Office of Strategic Services, the forerunner of today's Central Intelligence Agency (OSS Assessment Staff, 1948). In that program, use was made of group discussions, team-performance tests, stress interviews, observation at meals and social events, peer ratings, projective techniques, and structured tests of many types. The range of the testing program, its claim to penetrate hidden depths, and its cloak-and-dagger mystery have provided vivid material for unsympathetic writers; see A. P. Herbert's *Number Nine* (1952), an attack on British civil servant selection, and Morgan's *The OSS and I* (1957). In recent years, assessment methods have been used for selecting officers and executives, and in numerous research programs.

The principal features of assessment procedures are: use of a variety of techniques, primary reliance on observations in unstructured situations, and integration of information by experienced psychologists. No assessment program refuses to employ intelligence test scores or other relevant facts, but the emphasis remains upon synthesizing these data quasiartistically rather than upon combining separate scores in a statistical formula.

Our chief concern in this chapter is to evaluate impressionistic assessment. There have been many validity studies, some penetrating and some superficial. We shall review the best of these.

VALIDATION STUDIES

Attempts to Predict Job Performance

The original assessment programs in the military and intelligence services were never adequately validated, largely because candidates were scattered to far places and to diverse duties, so that criterion data were lacking. Perhaps the most meaningful figure is the report from the British Army that ratings of 500 officers in combat by their noncommissioned subordinates correlated .35 with Selection Board ratings. (This validity is corrected to apply to the entire range of candidates processed rather than the restricted group recommended for commissions—Vernon and Parry, 1949, p. 125.) These British studies also found that assessment may be seriously unreliable. One group of candidates was assessed separately by two boards, and the correlation between ratings was only .67. Reliabilities of .80 were achieved, however, by teams trained to use similar standards and procedures.

Assessment of British Civil Servants.   Three-day "house-party" assessments of candidates for the British civil service were validated by Vernon (1950a), who collected follow-up data on the men accepted. Though measurement of individual differences among such superior university graduates is extremely difficult, the validity coefficients were encouraging. Grades in a training course were predicted by final assessment rating with a validity of .82. For job-performance criteria the validities were .50–.65.

Two hundred administrators were rated by superiors after a two-year probationary period. Vernon gives fifty correlations of predictors with this criterion, and the predictors fall into two distinct groups. There are 27 validities for written ability tests; every coefficient is below .30, and the median is about .12. There are 19 correlations for ratings made by observers after performance tests or interviews; these correlations range from .26 to .49, the median being .41. Peer ratings had validities near .25 for this group. Evidently the impressionistic procedure identified aptitudes the pencil-and-paper tests did not.

It is important to note that in this successful assessment study selectors had "a clear and agreed conception of what they were selecting for, based on a thorough job analysis." The performance tests were for the most part job replicas of civil service paper work, committee tasks, and group discussions. Little use was made of personality theory. Projective tests, field observations, and stress interviews were absent or were given minimal attention by the raters.

The VA Study of Clinical Psychologists.   When the Veterans Administration began to support training of clinical psychologists in 1947, it sponsored a program of selection research directed by E. Lowell Kelly. Kelly's team, which included prominent clinical psychologists and experienced OSS assessors, applied "every promising technique and procedure: objective, projective, subjective, clinical and quantitative" to a group of 137 graduate students in a nine-day assessment program. Supplementary groups were also tested. Criterion data collected from universities in 1950 included information on the trainee's ability as a therapist, as a diagnostician, and as a student of research methods.

During assessment, ratings had been made of general surface habits (e.g., readiness to coöperate), underlying personality (e.g., characteristic intensity of inner emotional tension), and potential performance as a psychologist in various roles (e.g., group psychotherapy). Ratings were made by some persons who knew only the situational data, by some who knew only the interview, and by some who had access to various combinations of data; this procedure permitted comparison of techniques. Only a partial account of the hundreds of correlations can be given here.

Table 70 indicates how well single test scores or ratings based on them predicted certain important criterion ratings. The correlations, though frequently better than chance, are much too small for the predictors taken singly to be of substantial value in selection or guidance. The general ability

test was much better than other methods for predicting academic performance, and also best for predicting rated clinical competence. The next best
measure is peer ratings; these had some validity even for the criterion ratings
of diagnosis and therapy. The Bender-Gestalt did remarkably well on two

TABLE 70. Selected Validity Coefficients for Single Predictors of Competence in Clinical Psychology

	Criterion Ratings			
	Academic	Therapy	Diagnostic	Clinical Competence
Miller Analogies (verbal ability)	**.47**	.02	**.24**	**.35**
Guilford self-report questionnaires				
S (social extraversion)	.06	**.22**	**.23**	.11
T (thinking extraversion)	.05	.09	.17	.19
Highest of 13 r's	(.14)	(.22)	(.23)	(.19)
MMPI				
Highest of 9 r's, regular scales	(.26)	(−.16)	(−.12)	(−.16)
Gough Psychologist key	.16	.15	**.22**	**.25**
Strong VIB				
Group I (creative-scientific)	**.26**	.06	.04	**.21**
Kriedt Clinical Psychologist key	.10	**.23**	**.23**	**.26**
Ratings from Bender-Gestalt	.15	.02	**.33**	**.32**
Ratings from TAT	.08	.16	.24	.15
Ratings from performance tests (pooled)	.19	.19	.02	**.24**
Self rating	**.25**	−.20	.05	.00
Peer ratings	.13	**.28**	**.23**	**.25**

Boldface correlations are statistically significant.
SOURCE: Kelly and Fiske, 1951, pp. 146 ff.

of the criteria. Validities are lowered by the unreliability of criteria and the
fact that the trainees had already been screened to eliminate obviously unsuitable candidates.

Table 71 shows the overall validity for impressionistic assessments combining all sources of data. The correlations of .46 for academic prediction
and .38 for clinical competence compare very favorably with the best that

TABLE 71. Validity of Ratings of Clinical Psychologists Based on Comprehensive Assessment

	Criterion Rating			
Assessment Rating	Academic	Therapy	Diagnosis	Clinical Competence
Academic	.46	.09	.21	.45
Therapy	.24	.24	.29	.36
Diagnosis	.36	.14	.16	.32
Overall suitability for clinical psychology	.27	.18	.22	.38

SOURCE: Kelly and Fiske, 1951, p. 161.

could be expected from a statistical combination of scores and ratings. The coefficients for diagnosis and therapy are lower, as in Table 70. This is partly to be explained simply by the inadequacy of those criteria. Probably an even more pertinent explanation is that the assessors, some of whom had no experience in analyzing personalities of graduate students and none of whom had studied the personality required in such roles as psychotherapist, were unable to make competent ratings on these two scales.

The third table indicates how much each part of the assessment program added to the final judgment. (Since this final judgment is based on only

TABLE 72.   Evidence on Change of Validity with Added Information

	Criterion Rating	
	Academic	Clinical Competence
Credentials file plus objective tests (one rater)	.36	.37
Above plus autobiography, projectives (one rater)	.38	.40
Above plus interview (one rater)	.32	.37
All above information (conference of three raters)	.32	.42
Above plus performance tests (one rater)	.31	.39
Final pooled judgment of three raters	.33	.37

SOURCE: Kelly and Fiske, 1951, pp. 168–169.

three assessors rather than the whole staff, the figures cannot be matched with those in Table 71.) Apparently, assessors did just as well when they had only the credentials file and objective test scores as they did with the addition of interviews and performance tests. This information, considered along with the modest validity coefficients for the performance tests taken alone (Table 70), does not encourage faith in the performance observations, at least in the absence of psychological job analysis.

Menninger School of Psychiatry Study.   A similar problem was investigated by Holt and Luborsky (1958) at the Menninger School of Psychiatry. Several classes of applicants were interviewed and evaluated by projective tests. One principal criterion was the competence of the accepted man as judged by his supervisor during the residency which completed his training.

The original assessment employed the usual practice of estimating success on the basis of the assessor's judgment. This judgment is based on psychological or psychiatric theory, which is presumably able to evaluate how well a person functions in challenging situations. The results were in general unsatisfactory. The average validity for the combined information from tests was .27, and that for interview assessments was .24. Even allowing for the fact that the correlations are based only on the restricted group who were accepted and finished training, these validities indicate a high rate of error.

Holt and Luborsky (1958, II, p. 139) examined whether some interviewers or test interpreters were markedly better than others, and although they did find differences, they conclude that the evidence "throws cold water on a frequently encountered suggestion for improving selection methods: 'Find the interviewer who does the best job and have him teach the others how he does it.' Even if one entertained the dubious assumption that an interviewer knows 'how he does it,' and is able to teach the helpful rather than the erroneous parts of his technique, there is still too little difference between the predictive performance of the best interviewer and those of the others to make such an endeavor worth while."

One comment by a test interpreter is particularly significant in pointing to a central difficulty in assessment: "Reviewing some predictions on which we erred, we were impressed with our correct assessment of many specific qualities and our inability to cast these up into proper balance so as to judge ability to develop skill as a psychiatrist" (Luborsky, 1954).

Predicting Emotional Difficulty in Flying Training. Just as the Menninger data indicate that highly competent psychiatrists may make poor evaluations, predictions made by the best of projective testers are sometimes no better than guesses. Holtzman and Sells (1954) asked nineteen clinicians including some of the most prominent authorities on projective methods to separate aviation cadets into two groups, those who succeeded in flight training and those eliminated because they had developed overt personality disturbances. Each judge classified twenty cases, of whom from eight to twelve were successes. The judge was given the subject's responses to group forms of the inkblot, draw-a-person, and sentence-completion tests, a biographical inventory, and an inventory of psychosomatic complaints. The mean number of correct classifications per judge was 10.2, compared to 10 expected by chance alone. Even where judges were unanimous in their rating, accuracy was 56 percent, compared to a chance expectancy of 50. The results were not improved by treating single tests as a basis for judgment or by considering only those judgments which the clinician said he felt sure of.

Assessment of OCS Candidates. In contrast to the three preceding studies, where ratings were made by highly qualified psychological assessors, an Army study showed that recent graduates of Officer Candidate School were successful in assessing candidates (Holmen et al., 1956). Squads of ten selected applicants were observed for two weeks in an assessment center. There were four assessors, each a recent OCS graduate. Leadership exercises designed by psychologists as performance tests were administered by these officers. Data collected included ratings by the officers and by the other squad members, and self-report scores. Pass-fail records in OCS were the criterion.

For all men combined, average ratings by the assessors had a validity of .55, and peer ratings of .58. Ratings based on specific performance tests generally had validities between .25 and .50. Self-report tests had essentially zero correlations with success. It was recommended that a five-day version of the procedure be used for selection whenever a reasonably large supply of qualified applicants is available. Although the assessment is time consuming, there is evidence that the procedure provides sufficient training and orientation to increase the man's chance of success in OCS, and therefore is economical.

IPAR Study of Air Force Officers. The most extensive research on assessment methods is the program of the Institute for Personality Assessment and Research at the University of California. The Institute was organized by D. W. MacKinnon, one of the original OSS staff, for the purpose of testing and improving assessment procedures, particularly as applied to superior men. Studies have been conducted on student, military, and professional groups, but the only major report is of an assessment of Air Force captains (MacKinnon et al., 1958; Gough and Krauss, 1958; Barron et al., 1958; Gough, 1958; MacKinnon, 1958; Woodworth and MacKinnon, 1958).

This is an exceptionally good test of what assessment can and cannot do. An expert staff was assembled, and an enormous range of procedures was applied to a large sample of men for whom several appropriate criteria were later available. The staff had a reasonable understanding of the criterion task, having previously carried out several studies of military personnel. Pencil-and-paper tests (ability measures, personality and interest questionnaires, biographical data) were taken by 343 captains eligible for promotion. Of these, 100 officers were brought together in groups of 10 for "living-in" assessment. For three days, they lived with the psychologists, being interviewed, having a medical examination, taking projective tests, objective tests of perceptual performance, and group performance tests, and being evaluated by the staff in informal contacts. In all, there were 233 "field test" (pencil-and-paper) scores and 398 scores or ratings from "living-in" assessment. These scores were compared with nine major criteria. In all, including analyses of various subgroups of subjects, more than 15,000 validity coefficients were calculated.

Such a dragnet search for correlates of officer effectiveness is difficult to interpret. Just by chance, 5 percent of the variables will show "significant" correlations with any criterion, and it is always possible to invent a plausible explanation for such relations. The investigators, however, guarded against serious misinterpretation by dividing the sample and confining interpretation to results which appeared in several subsamples.

A second serious difficulty is the dubious validity of the criteria. Independent criteria of officer effectiveness correlated in the neighborhood of .30

(Barron *et al.*, 1958, p. 5). Consequently, test validities cannot be expected to rise much beyond this level. Even the most valid assessment techniques cannot predict unstable criteria. The probable reasons for low agreement among various criteria are the restricted range of ability in the group studied, and the difference in standards of judgment employed by various superiors.

The staff ratings in which a global assessment was attempted ("overall military effectiveness") did not correlate beyond the chance level with any of the criteria of effectiveness. All correlations were below .20 (MacKinnon, 1958, p. 36). From the psychometric field testing, a composite "good-officer index" was computed on the basis of a formula developed in previous research on officers. This composite correlated no higher than .18 with the Air Force criteria (MacKinnon, p. 28). Three "clusters" summarizing the assessment ratings had "disappointing" correlations with criteria of effectiveness (median .13). But although impressionistic ratings were unsuccessful as predictors of effectiveness, a reanalysis provided some encouragement. When flying officers were separated from ground officers, the medians were .21 and −.02 respectively. That is, the assessors did reasonably well in sizing up flying officers—considering the instability of the criteria—and had no success at all in evaluating ground officers (Woodworth and MacKinnon, 1958, pp. 11–13).

Whereas effectiveness was hard to predict, a criterion rating on interpersonal relations (uncorrelated with the criterion of effectiveness as an officer) was successfully predicted. Several assessment ratings had validities in the range .20–.30, which is about as good as the criterion permits. No test score had appreciable validity for this criterion; the valid information came from staff appraisals. In general, the person seen by the staff as tolerant, conforming, and relaxed was rated by his superior as having good relations with others (Barron *et al.*, 1958, p. 24).

The validity of psychometric measures was evaluated for the total officer group, but not for flying and ground officers separately. The results varied slightly from one criterion to the next, but no measure gave consistent evidence of validity. In fact, out of 194 test variables not a single one correlated significantly with the officer effectiveness rating in three successive subsamples (Barron *et al.*, 1958, p. 15). A few scattered correlations in the neighborhood of .30 indicate that there is promise of predictive value in empirical keys based on successful performance (e.g., a CPI key based on responses of high achievers) and in self-ratings on adjustment (Gough, 1958, p. 6). Rorschach and TAT were not useful in assessing officers (MacKinnon, 1958).

Summary. The foregoing studies include the major validations of global predictions to date. The most favorable results were obtained in OCS assessment, followed by British civil service selection. The VA psychologist study showed about equal validities for psychometric prediction and for assessment based on those tests plus a credentials file, with interviews and performance tests evidently adding little. The initial Menninger study of psychiatrists (their later study remains to be discussed) was less successful, and the classification of emotional failures among pilots by projective tests showed zero validity. Common elements in the more successful procedures may be noted:

• There is no evidence that psychological training gives the assessor an advantage. The best results occurred when officer candidates were rated by recent OCS graduates. The worst, as it happens, were obtained where the assessors were expert clinicians who, however, lacked specific experience with the types of candidates and criteria under study. The clinician's experience and theoretical background gives him confidence in the judgments he makes but seems not to make his judgments actually superior to those of the intelligent untrained observer who knows the job requirements. This conclusion is supported by the frequent finding that peer ratings have validities as good as those of ratings by observers.

• Structured tests, or performance tests which are very near to work-samples of the criterion task, have considerable validity. These tests are directly interpreted without use of intervening personality theory and can be used by nonprofessional judges. Tests requiring the judge to infer the subject's personality structure and then to predict behavior were rarely beneficial in these studies. Group performance tasks including LGD make an important contribution in predicting criteria where acceptance by one's group is necessary for success. They contribute much less to prediction when the criterion task calls for individual performance.

• The most important requirement for valid assessment is that the assessors have a clear understanding of the psychological requirements of the criterion task. The civil service and OCS assessors understood the ability requirements of the criterion task and made little effort at subtle psychological evaluation. The VA assessors and the Menninger assessors tried to match the candidates against their mental pictures of the successful psychologist or psychiatrist. The IPAR assessors assumed that the requirements for effectiveness were the same for ground officers as for flying officers. These stereotypes had never been checked by controlled observation of successful performers. If such an "obvious" relation as that between spatial aptitude and success in geometry is contrary to the facts, it is not surprising that stereotypes concerning therapists prove false.

It seems fair to conclude that impressionistic interpretations are often used where they have no validity. The assessor must learn to distrust even the most compelling hunch until it has been independently verified. In Kelly's apt phrase, too many psychological techniques are used on the basis of nothing more than "faith validity."

The generally black picture painted above of psychologists' most ambitious efforts at assessment is not, however, the final answer. There is the difficult problem of reconciling the statistical evidence with the claimed "clinical validity" of assessment techniques. We need to identify the sources of error in assessment and to arrive if possible at a statement of the conditions under which they are or can be made profitable.

1. When a group has been preselected before collection of validity data, correlations are reduced. In which of the assessment studies cited are the correlations based on groups more restricted than those which would usually be assessed?
2. In the OCS study, peer ratings were collected from nine men and assessment ratings from four judges. How is this fact relevant to the interpretation of the validity coefficients of .58 and .55, respectively?
3. In which studies did the criterion depend substantially upon ability to make a good impression upon and win the coöperation of peers?

Sources of Error in Assessment

In order to understand the difficulties of assessment, we need to recognize the steps involved in information gathering and inference. Figure 99 compares three types of personnel evaluation: inference based on dynamic interpretation, direct impressionistic evaluation from behavior samples, and psychometric prediction.

Let us begin with the right-hand column, which outlines the stages leading to the criterion. Each box distinguishes one stage. Between boxes, the small type lists some of the sources of error which preclude a perfect correspondence among the findings at successive stages. Time intervenes between assessment and criterion performance; changes in personality during this period reduce the possibility of perfect assessment. Job performance (2b) depends not only on personality but on the specific conditions of the individual's job. Given a different superior or different assignments, the man's performance might change. The criterion 6d reflects performance (2b) indirectly, being affected by the bias and incomplete observation of the supervisor. The sources of error in the right-hand column imply that even with perfect information about personality one could not predict job criteria perfectly.

The simplest assessment method is psychometric scoring of behavior and application of a "cookbook" formula to arrive at a prediction (center column of Figure 99). Reduction of behavior to scores discards some amount of information. The combining formula may introduce error if it was developed under conditions that do not apply perfectly to this new sample. Every stage

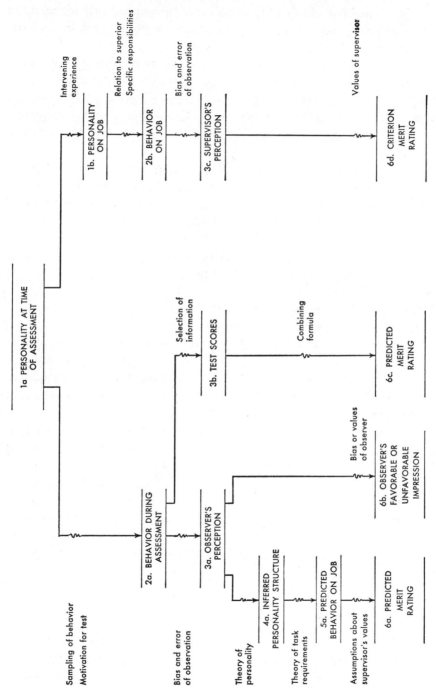

FIG. 99. Stages in assessment and in criterion development.

from 1a to 6c and from 1a to 6d involves an additional opportunity for error. By this analysis, there are seven places where error can lower the correlation between prediction 6c and criterion 6d.

Impressionistic rating from observed behavior is illustrated in the OCS study, where value judgments were made directly, without intervening dynamic analysis of personality. Here again there are seven possible sources of error between 6b and 6d. These may not be damaging to the correlation if, as in the OCS study, the bias of the raters resembles the bias of work supervisors.

Dynamic assessment, in the left-hand column, involves two added stages of inference. The step from 3a to 4a is hazardous because personality constructs are poorly developed and poorly matched to test behavior. The step from 4a to 5a involves equally undependable constructs about the nature of the criterion task and about how personality differences affect job behavior (Cronbach, 1956). The added links of hazardous inference make dynamic prediction far more prone to error than the more conservative predictions 6b and 6c.

This diagram leads to several suggestions for validation research and for the improvement of assessment. If criterion 6d is affected by errors, perhaps a better criterion could be obtained. A worksample of job behavior should correlate higher than the rating criterion with 5a and 3b. The psychologist may quite accurately predict a high degree of initiative, for example, and yet not be able to predict whether the man's (unknown) supervisor will evaluate that initiative favorably or unfavorably.

Even more important is the possibility of comparing the inferred personality structure (4a) with personality on the job (1b). It will be recalled that Luborsky was able, he said, to judge personalities accurately and yet was not able to judge whether the men would make good in psychiatry. If this type of claim is valid, then the weak links of the assessment chain are in translating knowledge of personality into expected behavior. The generally low validity coefficients in studies attempting dynamic assessment indicate that something is wrong along the chain of inferences, but it may be that 4a corresponds excellently to 1b.

Validity of Clinical Descriptions

The validity of inferences about personality structure cannot be deduced from the assessment studies discussed above, where descriptive inferences were not recorded in a form suitable for verification, and where the criterion was an overall evaluation rather than a description. This evidence must come from studies in which inferences are compared with other descriptions of personality structure.

The literature contains a great many impressive case reports in which clinical analyses agree strikingly with other data on the individual. The Hutt and Grayson case descriptions are examples; it will be recalled that these clinical impressions corresponded very well with the therapist's case notes. Nearly every clinician can point to cases where projective techniques gave him insight into unique features of individuals, features so rare that they could not possibly be attributed to chance. George DeVos once made a blind analysis of the Rorschach record of a research worker and, in reporting on the inferred personality structure, commented, "This man ought to be an historian. He'd be completely happy down in Washington digging minute details out of the Lincoln archives" (these being a set of century-old documents which had just been opened to scholars). The man was a specialist in a field where historical research is most uncommon—but he actually was in Washington at the time the analysis was made, extracting detailed information from fifty-year-old files of a Congressional committee! Such "hits" cannot be explained away, and constitute the most persuasive evidence of the value of projective methods.

The critical thinker must ask, however, just how often the descriptions are correct; perhaps we hear about only the successful predictions. Formal testing of the validity of descriptions is difficult, and few adequate studies have yet been reported. One method, asking an informed judge to state whether a description fits the individual, is unsatisfactory. Judges tend to say that the description fits even when it was actually written about someone else. This is due partly to noncriticalness and partly to the tendency to write vague descriptions that might fit anyone, e.g., "prefers a certain amount of change and variety" (Sundberg, 1955; Davenport, 1952).

A second procedure uses matching. Descriptions may be prepared for, say, six persons. Judges who know all the individuals, or who have folders of case material on them, may be asked to match each clinical description with the correct person. Judges have had success far beyond a chance level in studies of this character (e.g., Vernon, 1935; Henry, 1947; Palmer, 1951), but this alone is not an adequate validation method. A successful match may be made on one aspect of the description even if other parts of the description are incorrect, and sometimes there will be a mismatch because of one minor error in the portrait. A more specific technique which indicates the validity of particular predictions is required (Cronbach, 1948).

One method of considerable value when properly applied is Q sorting. Statements may be prepared covering dozens of aspects of behavior. These statements may be judged as fitting or not fitting the individual both by the assessor and by others well acquainted with his behavior. Various statistical methods may then be applied to investigate whether the two descriptions correspond. The most satisfactory procedure is to correlate all descriptions by the assessor with descriptions of each case by the criterion judges. If the clinical descriptions are discriminating rather than universally applicable, the correlation between the two descriptions for the same person will be much higher than that for descriptions of different persons.

No ideal study of this type is available. Samuels (1952) examined trait-by-trait interpretations from the projective tests taken by the VA psychologists. He found that ratings on such traits as depressed-vs.-cheerful, social adjustment, and quality of intellectual accomplishments by interpreters of different tests (Rorschach, TAT, Bender, Sentence Completion) had a median correlation of only .05–.08. This in itself indicates that there is no agreement among projective interpreters. A comparable analysis of TAT data alone was made by Hartmann (1949), with records of 35 delinquent and dependent boys. Two raters given a complete case record judged each boy on 42 variables. These "criterion" judges had a median correlation of .44, which indicates how difficult it is to make trait judgments. When the TAT interpreter, W. E. Henry, rated each boy, his correlation with the criterion judges averaged .16. Hartmann also obtained a correlation indicating how well the description for each boy separately, over all 42 scales, agreed with Henry's evaluation. While the median correlation between the criterion raters was .39, Henry's median correlation with these judges was .25. The TAT description fell short particularly in judging aggressiveness, stability, attachment to father, school adjustment, activity in recreation, and moral standards. It did best on taciturnity, self-reliance, and maturity. In another study Henry (1947) compared TAT descriptions with other sources of data; there was essential agreement between TAT and at least one other source in 83 percent of the specific statements. Regarding only 2 percent was there definite disagreement. These are much better results than in the Hartmann study but the comparison is less well controlled.

The foregoing series of findings implies that projective techniques as currently interpreted are not dependable sources of complex descriptions, although some reports are appreciably better than random guesses. Their value can be improved with further development of scoring reliability and interpretative theory. No evidence is available on the adequacy of personality descriptions from observations in complex performance tests or interviews.

IMPROVING THE USEFULNESS OF ASSESSMENT METHODS

Some critics of projective methods and of impressionistic assessment have concluded that these methods are indefensible, and that psychologists who depend on them are deluding themselves and those to whom they report. Confirmed believers in assessment methods, on the other hand, reject their critics as "methodological bluenoses" (Bellak, 1954) and even deny the relevance of such formal evidence as is available. This denial goes much too far; as R. R. Holt (1958), a proponent of clinical techniques, says, "If the issue were whether some clinicians have made themselves look foolish by claiming too much, then I should agree: these studies show that they have, and unhappily, brought discredit on clinical methods generally." Since the claims made in the past have frequently been discredited, *any would-be assessor is responsible for presenting indisputable public evidence of the dependability of his judgment;* vague claims regarding successful experience will not suffice.

On the other hand, the evidence does not demand abandonment of assessment methods. Personality testing has had a shorter history than ability testing. With personality as difficult to analyze as it is and with the available techniques all open to one serious objection or another, it is important to turn attention to how assessment techniques can be improved. It is equally necessary to understand just what function each procedure is best for. Many of the attacks on projective techniques and many of the defensive arguments have been based on a misconception of their proper role in the study of personality.

Improving Test Interpretation

Projective tests and situational observations have been interpreted by means of whatever theory a particular interpreter adopts. Some TAT interpreters view the stories as samples of stable traits likely to be shown in overt behavior, some consider the test a measure of strength of motives which shift from occasion to occasion, and some consider the test as a measure of unconscious and unexpressed drives. If the interpretation of a test has not yet been stabilized and verified, no one knows what that instrument might do at its best. Recent years have shown many defects in the theories used to interpret complex tests, and personality theory itself is undergoing substantial change.

We cannot examine detailed questions about particular weaknesses in interpretation, but we can note studies having very general implications. The first is the finding of serious bias in certain techniques. Soskin (1954, 1959; see also Samuels, 1952) asked judges to indicate the probable behavior of a subject, using a multiple-choice test based on incidents from his life. One group of judges responded knowing only the subject's age, sex, and social background. Other judges had Rorschach and TAT records. Answers were scaled from 4.0 (implying excellent adjustment) to 1.0 (implying severe maladjustment). The median of the responses representing what the subject actually had done was 2.5. Judges relying on general background data gave a generally favorable assessment (median prediction of his response scaled at 3.1), but judges relying on projective data were unfavorable (median response 2.0). On the whole, the projective interpreters misjudged the subject whenever his actual behavior showed good adaptation. In uncertain situations, they expected the worst of him.

This apparent bias toward psychopathology in Rorschach interpretations is implied also in Roe's work on eminent scientists, the Menninger psychiatrist study, and other investigations. Within any group of normal persons one encounters records which, considered by themselves, would seem to be indicative of gross emotional disturbance or psychopathology (Gallagher, 1955). As one Menninger assessor commented, "The TAT usually exposed a man's weakest points, without giving compensatory signs of his strong ones. . . . To some extent the same thing is true of the Rorschach. . . . Latent conflicts show up in these tests much more plainly than the compensating strengths; . . . [it is necessary] to be very cautious in assuming that such *potential* liabilities are *actual* if they are not seen operating in much more direct fashion" (Holt and Luborsky, 1958, p. 246).

One reason for the bias is that projective theory was developed through the study of mental patients without appropriate control studies of normals. Only fairly recently have extensive data on normals and superior individuals been collected. A projective technique reveals drives and impulses, but it does not indicate clearly how they are controlled. Strong hostility is likely to be an unfavorable sign in a person tested by a clinic; in an executive, author, or school superintendent, the same force may be harnessed to creative and socially constructive activity. Until further research enables the tester to distinguish unchanneled from controlled forces, one must interpret damaging indications with caution. Ultimately, we may learn to identify control mechanisms as well as disruptive forces through projective protocols.

Projective and performance tests are not comprehensive cross sections of personality. On the contrary, they are observations in a specific situation, and one generalizes to future situations only with considerable risk. Edith Lord (1950) showed that a cold, forbidding female Rorschach examiner elicited a high frequency of unhealthy, uncontrolled emotional response and strongly compulsive behavior from the same subjects who gave moderate, passive, unimaginative responses when tested by a soft "mother-figure." Moreover, deliberate efforts on the part of the examiner to be more permissive altered the test performance. No test is a measure of personality in isolation; it is always a sample of social interaction with a specific other person (Schafer, 1954; Sarason, 1954). There is considerable risk when one generalizes to other social interactions.

"Blind analysis" is the custom in validation studies aimed to determine what can be done with a single test, but practical interpretation should be based on considerable background knowledge. Indeed, Holt and Luborsky wisely recommend study of projective tests *only* along with intellectual tests and a case history. "If one could give only the Rorschach and TAT, it would be better to give no tests at all rather than spend time with so dubious a prospect of satisfactory results. Projective tests give valuable insights into personality, but the level of material from which they draw varies so much from one case to another and its significance is so dependent on a framework of realistic knowledge about the person that projective techniques can make their proper contribution only when used in conjunction with other methods" (p. 303).

The statement about "levels from which they draw" makes reference to one of the most confusing problems in interpretation of projective tests. Sometimes a story or free association appears genuinely to reflect deep-lying repressed conflicts, but one cannot be sure which records or parts of records have such hidden meanings. The interpreter will do well to heed Schafer's warning (1954, p. 150) against "arbitrary, presumptuous efforts to deepen interpretation in spite of the patient."

Still another difficulty which can be remedied only by improving personality theory is semantic confusion. If the test interpreter uses words which mean different things to different people, he cannot hope that his interpretations will be confirmed or that they will be practically beneficial. Many of the key words in dynamic interpretations are highly ambiguous. Grayson and Tolman (1950) asked psychologists and psychiatrists to define such words as *bizarre* and *aggression*. Twenty-three of these clinicians defined the aggressive person as hostile and destructive; but 21 of them used the word to describe positive, assertive, dominant behavior. As the authors said, "The most striking finding of the study is the looseness and ambiguity of many of these terms. . . . For the most part, the lack of verbal precision seems to stem from theoretical confusion in the face of the complexity and logical inconsistency of psychological phenomena. Verbal discrepancies can only be reconciled by a deeper understanding of these underlying phenomena which will require many years of careful, penetrating, and analytical psychological experience."

Psychological Study of Treatment Situations

No psychometric tester would willingly introduce a selection plan without first validating his tests against criterion information, but the assessor has generally made blind predictions. The assessor has picked Army officers, civil servants, espionage agents, and fliers with no better standard than his hunches about the demands of the situations involved. While one might excuse such presumptuousness on the grounds of wartime necessity, when men must be selected according to someone's best guess, prudence demands realistic job analysis and test tryout when circumstances permit. Nearly all the validations of assessment methods have examined the merit of "naïve clinical assessment," which Holt (1958) describes as follows:

> The data used are primarily qualitative with no attempt at objectification; their processing is entirely a clinical and intuitive matter, and there is no prior study of the criterion or of the possible relation of the predictive data to it. Clinical judgment is at every step relied on not only as a way of integrating data to produce predictions, but also as an alternative to acquaintance with the facts.

The choice of sound psychometric methods and interpretations has, from the days of Wissler and Binet, depended upon thorough empirical follow-up; similar follow-up is even more essential in personality appraisal, where problems are more complex. Holt suggests the following as a "sophisticated" clinical method:

> Qualitative data from such sources as interviews, life histories, and projective techniques are used as well as objective test facts and scores, but as much as possible of objectivity, organization, and scientific method are introduced into the planning, the gathering of data, and their analysis. All the refinements of design that the actuarial tradition has furnished are employed, including job analysis, pilot studies, item analysis, and successive cross-validations. Quantification and statistics are used wherever helpful, but the clinician himself is retained as one of the prime instruments, with an effort to make him as reliable and valid a data-processor as possible; and he makes the final organization of the data to yield a set of predictions tailored to each individual case.

This procedure was applied as well as possible in the second phase of the Menninger psychiatrist study. Naïve assessment, as described above, had been applied with mediocre success, validity being .24. In the "sophisticated study" the investigators examined enough successful and unsuccessful men to formulate a concept of the good psychiatrist. Specific cues in the TAT and other data were identified, to provide an objective framework for judging the remaining cases. Despite this effort, the resulting scores or judgments developed in this manner had no validity when based on a single projective test. Predictive ratings based on all data had validities of .57 for one judge, .22 for the second (average, .40). Holt and Luborsky conclude that the validities from the final study are "impressive" and recommend application of refined assessment methods to the selection of psychiatrists. The issue appears still to be in doubt, however. The one coefficient of .57 is high, but it gives no assurance that the validity of judges would be consistently superior to the naïve predictions. Moreover, when Verbal IQ correlates .39 with the criterion, it is hard to believe that clinical judgments represent an improvement sufficient to justify the labor involved. Even with careful analysis of the personalities of men whose criterion scores are known, assessment must overcome serious difficulties.

Every test represents performance in a highly specific situation, as we noted earlier; there is a counterpart problem with respect to the criterion. A criterion rating is generated by the specific interaction of a man and one set of duties. The psychiatrist who might do well with children can be rated a failure if he proves unable to cope with hospitalized adults early in his practical training. An unfortunate first assignment or an incompatible first supervisor may develop feelings of incompetence and a bad reputation which prevent the man from reaching his potential. Likewise, the success of the psychoanalysis the student of psychiatry often undergoes is a significant but rather unpredictable feature of the situation. Assessment is rarely used to select men for uniform, well-defined jobs. The usual problem in executive appraisal or clinical evaluation is to judge how the individual will get along in an ill-defined or unspecified situation. Where many variable conditions intervene between prediction and follow-up, high validity cannot be hoped for.

One might hope for test data to predict the average success of a man in many independent situations. A statistical composite such as a college grade average is a "convergent phenomenon" (Langmuir, 1943; L. K. Frank, 1948). Despite lucky or unlucky experience in single courses, the average becomes more and more stable and hence easier to predict as more courses are added. All-round popularity is a similar convergent phenomenon. A person's standing may vary greatly from church to office to bowling team, but as more groups are added his average "seeks its level." A phenomenon is said to be *divergent* if the successive events that cause it to develop are highly interrelated. A landslide is an example. One stone jars another, the two moving together dislodge others, and soon an irresistible stream of debris is pouring downhill. This force is a sum of many separate movements, but not an average of independent events. Rather, every added stone is an amplification of the original movement; if the first stone had not moved, there would have been no landslide.

Prediction of divergent phenomena is not possible. Possibilities can be identified ("that hill looks loose enough to slide"), but what will occur can be predicted only on the average over independent situations ("Landslides will cost the state road department x thousands of dollars"). The social scientist can predict accurately how many women in a college class will marry. He can predict much less well whether a particular woman will marry. Whether she will marry the man she met last night is extremely uncertain. Successes and failures do not average out; one quarrel at the wrong time may end all chance for compensating pleasant experience. Even with full day-to-day information, the fate of this possible marriage will be unpredictable for many months.

The assessor can reasonably hope to figure out how many men of a certain type will succeed in psychiatry. He can perhaps judge what any one man would do on the average if he could have ten independent careers in psychiatry. But any one career is like a horse race; a delay in the starting gate, a jam on the track, one mistake by his rider—and the favorite loses. The psychiatrist has just one career, in one group, under one set of demands. If he establishes a good relation with the significant figures in this environment, the beneficial consequences will rebound through his whole life. Yet that relation depends on chance events as much as on his stable personal qualities. As William James warned, psychology can establish general expectations but cannot hope to give biographies in advance.

4. Show that each of these is the result of a divergent phenomenon:
   a. The ceremony was a moving emotional experience.
   b. Terry is coöperative, but his brother Mike no one can manage.
   c. Charles' interest in science is becoming focused on genetics.
5. How reasonable is it to try to predict each of the following?
   a. Will men of this type respond better to close supervision or to freedom?
   b. How will this man respond to close supervision?
   c. Will Mark like selling?
   d. Will Mark like this job as salesman?
6. Defend the statement: "After a certain point in its development, the divergent phenomenon becomes predictable." What sort of information is needed for this prediction? What does this imply for the psychologist?

The Unique Functions of Assessment Procedures

In the writer's opinion, assessment techniques have been asked to do a job for which they are ill suited. It has been necessary to emphasize the extensive and discouraging negative results on the use of clinical techniques as predictors, but there is another, more positive evaluation to be made.

Assessment techniques have three related features which set them apart from conventional psychometric methods. Stated simply, these are as follows:

They provide information both on typical response patterns and on stimulus meanings.

They cover a very large number of questions about the individual.

They provide information about different questions for different individuals.

Coverage of Stimulus Meanings. The psychometric approach is to confront the individual with a carefully selected task or set of tasks which represent a criterion situation in some way. This description applies to proficiency tests, to aptitude tests, to questionnaires on typical performance, and to worksample performance tests such as the LGD. We saw that even impressionistic interpretation of such samples of behavior gave valid predictions for civil service and OCS selection. The essential assumption in this type of testing is that we can generalize from a sample of behavior to performance in *one class* of situations.

A person's behavior changes from situation to situation, however, and whenever one must understand the person as a whole, or must select situations to fit him, a simple prediction by sampling within one class is impossible. One must begin to learn what situations mean for him. Much of the content of an interview deals with situational meanings: attitudes toward parents, former employers, school subjects, etc. The thematic projective tests elicit similar information, though in a more disguised and perhaps less censored form.

The Semantic Differential is the only psychometric technique designed to study meanings the person gives to significant others. Even this procedure, though structured and quantifiable, is interpreted impressionistically when a single individual is under study. Hence there is no psychometric technique for obtaining information about the subject's reactions to various persons and situations—unless one wishes to prepare dozens of questionnaires or Q sorts, each dealing with one person or situation. While research along the lines recently opened by Osgood and G. A. Kelly may lead to well-controlled psychometric techniques, at this time there is no alternative to some type of clinical assessment if we want attitudinal information covering a wide range of objects. It is unfortunate that there have been no controlled validation studies to show just how well such procedures as TAT and Semantic Differential identify significant attitudes. Virtually all systematic validation of impressionistic methods has examined their adequacy as measures of traits (i.e., of response information).

7. What value does information about situational attitudes have for a decision maker or counselor in each of these situations?
   a. Counseling a couple having marital difficulty.
   b. Appraising junior executives in a corporation.
   c. Evaluating a student on probation because of poor grades.
8. Why is information about attitudes to diverse situations more important in dealing with divergent phenomena than with convergent phenomena?
9. Evaluate the suggestion that situational attitudes might be assessed by administering a large number of scorable questionnaires, each dealing with a different attitude-object. To what extent would this overcome the limitations of impressionistic assessment?

10. Is the assessment of stimulus meanings really distinguishable from assessment of traits? (Example: Is "hunger drive" distinct from "attitude toward food"?)
11. List the persons or situations about which attitudinal information would be useful in clinical study of a bright 9-year-old child who is unable to read.

Bandwidth. Shannon's "information theory" (1949), developed for the study of electronic communication systems, provides a model for considering the second important feature of assessment methods. He distinguishes two attributes of any communication system: bandwidth and fidelity.

Home record players have made "high fidelity" familiar to everyone. The complementary concept of bandwidth refers to the amount or complexity of information one tries to obtain in a given space or time. The fidelity of recording depends upon the width of the groove; if grooves are crowded together to put more music on a record, fidelity suffers. Fidelity could be improved over present standards by designing record and playback systems which would carry less information (e.g., a 33-rpm record lasting only ten minutes instead of thirty). With other things held constant, any shift in the direction of greater fidelity reduces bandwidth; and increase in bandwidth may be purchased at the price of bandwidth. In any particular communication system there is an ideal compromise between bandwidth and fidelity. The record industry settled on the 33-rpm "long-play" record; the FCC allows the FM station a bandwidth of 22 kilocycles.

The classical psychometric ideal is the instrument with high fidelity and low bandwidth (Cronbach and Gleser, 1957; Hewer, 1955, pp. 3–19). A college aptitude test tries to answer just one question with great accuracy. It concentrates its content in a very narrow range, using correlated items to increase reliability. Because its parts are highly correlated, part scores give little information for choosing majors or diagnosing weaknesses. Most other excellent predictors such as the LGD participation score and the peer rating have similar limitation to one central variable.

At the opposite extreme, the interview and the projective technique have almost unlimited bandwidth. Whereas the aptitude test may devote three hours to obtaining just one score, the interviewer may cover twenty topics in a half-hour, and note an even larger number of traits. In some TAT studies ratings were made on more than forty variables, all on the basis of about an hour's testing. The individual description adds a dozen or more statements about individual traits or attitudes not commonly encountered.

There are tests with intermediate bandwidths, and a particular technique like the Binet or MMPI may be used as a narrowband method by some testers and as a wideband method by others. All the validity studies we have reviewed substantiate Shannon's principle: increases in complexity of information are obtained only by sacrificing fidelity. The Wechsler Verbal IQ is highly valid. Patterns of subtest scores are of some but quite limited value.

And interpretations of responses to single items, or judgments about observed processes are distinctly untrustworthy. The most successful combinations of large bandwidth with relatively high fidelity are the GATB and the SVIB, both of which are designed for counseling where many alternatives must be considered and useful prediction can be made from about a dozen scores.

Extremely large bandwidth is disadvantageous because the information becomes too unreliable for use. Extremely small bandwidth, on the other hand, is appropriate only where there is one specific, all-important question to be answered, to which all testing effort should be devoted. While no rule can be given specifying the ideal bandwidth for testing, we can point to conditions favoring wider or narrower bandwidth:

● The first is the number and relative importance of decisions to be made. If an institution is concerned with a simple decision and only one outcome, it should concentrate on the information most relevant to that decision. (Example: a college wishing to admit students who will make good academic records, without regard to values, social or emotional adjustment, or probable post-college career.) If many outcomes or alternatives are to be considered, more types of information are needed and bandwidth must increase. Counseling, diagnosis, remedial teaching, and supervision of professional workers generally involve multifaceted decisions. The testing effort should be balanced to obtain relatively dependable information on the most important questions or those which are most likely to arise. It is better to ignore minor questions than to spread one's inquiry too thin (Cronbach and Gleser, 1957, p. 96).

● Bandwidth can be greatly increased when it is possible to confirm or reverse judgments at a later time. Lack of fidelity does no harm unless it leads to costly errors. Narrowband instruments are desired for making final, irreversible decisions about important matters (e.g., scholarship awards). The wideband technique, on the other hand, serves well as the first stage in a sequential measuring operation. As a first stage, the wideband test scans superficially a range of important variables, pointing out significant possibilities for further study. In this use the wideband procedure is used for *hypothesis formation*, not for final decisions.

This is the proper function of the Strong blank, for example. It is not a highly valid basis for career choice. It is an inexpensive pencil-and-paper interview which gives an excellent preliminary mapping of the vocational field. Its ease of administration, objective scoring, and norms make it superior to the unconstrained interview (which has even greater bandwidth). Following the test, the counselor uses a more focused interview to confirm high scores and to determine their implications. Even this discussion should not lead to a final decision. It is better to narrow the choice to two or three areas; these hypotheses can be tested by enrolling in suitable courses and by trying relevant summer jobs.

Comparable opportunities for follow-up and confirmation of assessments or score interpretations exist in virtually every decision except selection. Fallible tests can suggest assignments for an employee, treatments for a patient, teaching techniques for a student. Even if the test is little better than a guess, it has some value when there is no sounder basis for choice. Since trying out the hypothesis permits verification, and change when the hypothesis was wrong, little has been lost. We may say, in sum, that the fallibility of wideband procedures does no harm unless the hypotheses and suggestions they offer are regarded as verified conclusions about the individual. And of course some degree of skepticism is required in interpreting the score from any psychological test, however precise and narrowly focused it may be.

Impressionistic procedures, and psychometric procedures in clinical settings, are chiefly used for hypothesis formation. Clinicians bring a Rorschach interpretation or a Wechsler IQ to a case conference, where it is considered along with other data, and this conference concludes that it is better to try one therapy than another. Only where the decision is irreversible, as when surgery is prescribed or where the patient once classified is forever left in the same pigeonhole, is this use of impressions and imperfectly valid scores dangerous. Likewise in executive appraisal or school psychology, the recommendations of the tester are recommendations about experiments to be tried. Unfortunately, assessors (and psychometric testers) have far too often claimed that their methods give valid final conclusions. This has two bad consequences: nonpsychologists expect more than the assessor can deliver, and the psychologist tries to live up to his claim by giving one description or recommendation instead of outlining the reasonable alternatives.

12. Defend the analogy of a psychological examination to a communication system.
13. Would you characterize the DAT as wideband or narrowband? the MMPI? the test of flicker-fusion frequency?
14. Did the Hartshorne-May tests of honesty serve better as a wideband or narrowband procedure?
15. Why is sequential testing of hypotheses more important for wideband than for narrowband procedures?

Adaptation to the Individual.   Closely related to the foregoing comments are the advantages of assessment procedures for shaping the testing to the individual. The psychometric tester standardizes his test to answer a question presumed to be important for everyone. The impressionistic tester may vary the problems and topics covered by the testing to fit the individual. The psychometric tester tries to standardize every aspect of his measuring procedure, so that precisely the same information is obtained about each subject. The impressionistic tester wishes to obtain whatever information is most significant regarding a particular individual, even if this means asking different questions of each person. The flexibly administered interview, the individualized Rep test, and the unstructured projective technique elicit idiosyncratic, personally significant responses for which there is no counterpart in psychometric methodology. These responses can only be interpreted impressionistically.

Meehl (1954) gives several examples of such interpretations, which he properly regards as the essence of the clinical art. One is from the psychoanalyst Reik (1948, p. 263):

Our session at this time took the following course. After a few sentences about the uneventful day, the patient fell into a long silence. She assured me that nothing was in her thoughts. Silence from me. After many minutes she complained about a toothache. She told me that she had been to the dentist yesterday. He had given her an injection and then had pulled a wisdom tooth. The spot was hurting again. New and longer silence. She pointed to my bookcase in the corner and said, "There's a book standing on its head." Without the slightest hesitation and in a reproachful voice I said, "But why did you not tell me that you had had an abortion?"

How Reik made this correct inference from the patient's chain of associations and silences is not our concern here. The skill is compounded of theory, imagination, experience, and willingness to make (and verify or discard) rash guesses. The important point is that this interpretation, which might accelerate appreciably the therapy, could not possibly have been reached by a formal testing procedure. In the first place, such a procedure would be unlikely to touch upon the particular topic of abortion. Even if it did, there is no "trait" on which the response could be scored, unless one envisions keying the MMPI to distinguish ex-abortion patients from other women—and similarly for every other group having conceivable clinical interest. Secondly, the response cannot possibly be interpreted by any multiple-regression or other formal procedure. How could one establish frequency tables to give the meaning of associations-about-a-dental-extraction-plus-silence-plus-observation-about-an-inverted-book? This is a unique datum to be interpreted only by a creative act of applying such a theory as the psychoanalytic hypothesis that tooth extraction is a disguised symbol for birth. This extreme example of symbolic communication shows clinical idiographic interpretation in its purest form, but unique content is interpreted by every assessor.

The interpreter must likewise deal with the unprecedented when he predicts response to a specific situation. "Should this child be sent back to his mother or placed in a foster home?" is a decision in which statistics cannot aid. No experience table can predict from IQ, anxiety level, or anything else whether he will adjust well to his mother. This can be estimated only from her particular character, the child's character, and the precise home situation. Any decision about this problem is likely to be wrong, but that is beside the point. The decision must be made, and insofar as psychological study of the child can improve the decision, the risk of error is reduced. In this case, impressionistic appraisal is the best available basis for decision. All the "little" decisions that take place from minute to minute in therapy and teaching are similarly resistant to measurement and statistics. In these judgments, where the psychometric tester would have nothing to say, the hints from the TAT or a case history may provide valuable guidance (Meehl, 1954, p. 120).

The difference between psychometric and impressionistic assessment, we find, is not that one uses multiple-choice questions and one uses inkblots, or that one is compulsively cautious, the other erratically overambitious. The two approaches to observation and interpretation are suited to different purposes. When clinical testers answer questions for which their methods and theory are badly suited, their answers are next to worthless or at best are costly beyond their value. When psychometric testers are faced with a clinical problem calling for understanding rather than simple evaluation (e.g., what lies behind a given child's anxious withdrawal?) they are unable to give any answer at all. Each in his own proper province will surpass the other and each outside his province is nearly impotent. Assessment methods have earned a bad name for themselves by trying to compete with measurement techniques on their own ground. In the absence of excellent research to guide the combination of information, the wideband technique should not be advanced as a means of predicting specific, recurring criteria. The precisely focused instrument, on the other hand, should not be exalted into the sole approved technique for gathering information. It is efficient only when the decision maker asks the particular question for which it has been designed and validated. Even the TMC must be interpreted impressionistically when one wants to explain a low score, or to predict performance in a new training program.

We expect an evolution from naturalistic to highly structured techniques. Alfred Binet began to explore and define intelligence by means of impressionistic interpretations of imaginative performance. It was only after this study had disclosed the important variables that he began to design the structured tests from which all later ability tests sprang. The personality questionnaire developed out of psychiatric observations of symptoms, and the interest questionnaire out of counseling interviews. Pure naturalistic observation is always the first step in science, followed by gradual structuring of the observations, and ultimately by definition of specific variables and quantitative measurement. Whenever the importance of some treatment and criterion becomes great enough to warrant quantitative measurement, formal psychometric procedures can be developed to measure them. The psychometric method can give increasingly more refined and trustworthy answers to any recurrent question than can an exclusively natural-history observational approach, because successive stages of research eliminate sources of error.

This does not mean that impressionistic methods will or should ultimately disappear. There will always be unique problems to deal with and unique facts to interpret. Indeed, since every person is unique in certain ways, each case will present some problems which are beyond the reach of standard interpretative formulas. Moreover, treatments will continually change, and judgments about assignment to the new treatments will have to be made without waiting for years of follow-up research. Even the growth of psychometric testing creates a demand for greater and more skillful use of wideband techniques. As more and more specialized scales are developed for measuring aptitudes, traits, and situational meanings, it will become even more important to have suitable wideband procedures for use as a first stage to determine which of these psychometric scales are relevant to each person. Psychometric and impressionistic testing procedures will always be needed to supplement each other.

Here again we find illustration of the principle introduced very early in this book: one cannot identify one group of tests as good and recommend it for use. For every type of decision and for every type of psychological information, there are many techniques and many specific instruments. The instruments differ in practicality, in the degree of training required to use them, in the variety of information they obtain, and in fidelity. The instrument that works best for one tester will not be best for another tester making the same decision. Tests must be chosen by a highly qualified professional worker who has a thorough understanding of the institution and persons he serves.

All in all, psychological testing is an accomplishment its developers may well boast of. Errors of measurement have been reduced year by year, and the significance of tests has been increased, until today all facets of American society feel the impact of the testing movement. The school, industry, marriage, governmental policy, and character-building agencies have all been aided by tests. Interpretations of test data are daily creating better lives by guiding a man into a suitable lifework, by placing an adolescent under therapy which will avert mental disorder, or by detecting causes of a failure in school which could turn a child into a beaten individual. Methods are now available which, if used carefully by responsible interpreters, can unearth the talents in the population and identify personality aberrations which would cause those talents to be wasted. Building on these techniques, we are in a position to capitalize as never before on the richness of human resources.

Suggested Readings

Holt, Robert R., & Luborsky, Lester. Theoretical issues in selection research. *Personality patterns of psychiatrists.* New York: Basic Books, 1958. Pp. 79–107.
 A reconsideration of past studies of clinical and statistical prediction criticizes Meehl (see below) for giving undue recognition to the contribution of impressionistic prediction, properly used. Elsewhere in the book (esp. p. 213) the success of the authors' attempt at a sophisticated method can be examined.
Hooker, Evelyn. The adjustment of the male overt homosexual. *J. proj. Tech.,* 1957, **21,** 18–31; and Hooker, Evelyn. Male homosexuality in the Rorschach. *J. proj. Tech.,* 1958, **22,** 33–55.
 The former paper describes, with case examples, an unsuccessful attempt by highly qualified judges to distinguish homosexual from heterosexual Rorschach records. The second paper studies differences that might be used to make an actuarial key, compares this method with the judging method, and discusses why Rorschach data cannot disclose homosexual behavior.
Macfarlane, Jean W., & Tuddenham, Read D. Problems in the validation of projective techniques. In H. H. Anderson and G. L. Anderson (eds.), *An introduction to projective techniques.* New York: Prentice-Hall, 1951. Pp. 26–54.
 The authors classify and review methods of validation, concluding that there has been too little adequate research to disclose whether projective tests have value in analyzing personality dynamics. Requirements of sound validation are set forth.
Meehl, Paul E. Empirical comparisons of clinical and actuarial prediction. *Clinical vs. statistical prediction.* Minneapolis: University of Minnesota Press, 1954. Pp. 83–128.
 This is a review of twenty studies in which controlled comparison of impressionistic and psychometric prediction was attempted, and in which the psychometric method was overwhelmingly superior. The reader should consider carefully in each study whether the impressionistic prediction was "naïve" or "sophisticated," and whether judgment was one where the impressionistic method could show at its best.
Meehl, Paul E. Wanted—a good cookbook. *Amer. Psychologist,* 1956, **11,** 263–272.
 In an experiment psychometric methods were devised for obtaining from the MMPI profile a clinical "description" which proved to be more highly related to the therapist's impression than the judgments of qualified clinicians.
Merrill, Maud A. Oscillation and progress in clinical psychology. *J. consult. Psychol.,* 1951, **15,** 281–289.
 The conflict between the practical demands for clinical service and the inadequacy of clinical diagnostic techniques is considered in the light of the similar history of intelligence tests, which were attacked in the 1920's for promising too much. The present uncertainties are seen as a step toward clarification.

Leading Test Publishers, Distributors, and Service Agencies

Bureau of Publications, Teachers College, Columbia University, New York 27, New York.

California Test Bureau, 5916 Hollywood Boulevard, Los Angeles 28, California.

Centre de Psychologie Appliquée, 15 rue Henri Heine, Paris XVI, France.

Consulting Psychologists Press, 270 Town and Country Village, Palo Alto, California.

Educational Test Bureau, 720 Washington Avenue, S.E., Minneapolis 14, Minnesota.

Educational Testing Service, 20 Nassau Street, Princeton, New Jersey.

Grune & Stratton, Inc., 381 Fourth Avenue, New York 16, New York.

Houghton Mifflin Company, 2 Park Street, Boston 7, Massachusetts.

Institute for Personality and Ability Testing, 1602 Coronado Drive, Champaign, Illinois.

Measurement Research Center, Inc., Iowa City, Iowa.

National Foundation for Educational Research, 79 Wimpole Street, London W1, England.

Personnel Press, Inc., 188 Nassau Street, Princeton, New Jersey.

Psychological Corporation, 304 East 45th Street, New York 17, New York.

Psychological Test Specialists, Box 1441, Missoula, Montana.

Psychometric Affiliates, Box 1625, Chicago 90, Illinois.

Science Research Associates, Inc., 57 West Grand Avenue, Chicago 10, Illinois.

Sheridan Supply Company, P.O. Box 837, Beverly Hills, California.

C. H. Stoelting Company, 424 North Homan Avenue, Chicago 24, Illinois.

Western Psychological Services, 10655 Santa Monica Boulevard, Los Angeles 25, California.

World Book Company, 313 Park Hill Avenue, Yonkers 5, New York.

Bibliography

Adorno, T. W., *et al. The authoritarian personality.* New York: Harper, 1950.

Ahmavaara, Yrho. On the unified factor theory of mind. *Ann. Finnish Acad. Sci.,* 1957, Ser. B, No. 106.

Ainsworth, Leonard H. Rigidity, insecurity, and stress. *J. abnorm. soc. Psychol.,* 1958, **56,** 67–74.

Allen, Mildred M. The relation between Kuhlmann-Anderson tests and achievement in Grade IV. *J. educ. Psychol.,* 1944a, **35,** 229–239.

Allen, Mildred M. The relationship between Kuhlmann-Anderson tests in Grade 1 and academic achievement in Grades 3 and 4. *Educ. psychol. Measmt,* 1944b, **4,** 161–168.

Allport, Gordon W. *Personality: a psychological interpretation.* New York: Holt, 1937.

Anastasi, Anne. *Psychological testing.* New York: Macmillan, 1954.

Anastasi, Anne. Age changes in adult test performance. *Psychol. Rep.,* 1956, **2,** 509.

Anastasi, Anne. *Differential psychology.* (3rd ed.) New York: Macmillan, 1958.

Anastasi, Anne, & Drake, John D. An empirical comparison of certain techniques for estimating the reliability of speeded tests. *Educ. psychol. Measmt,* 1954, **14,** 529–540.

Anastasi, Anne, & Foley, J. P., Jr. Psychiatric screening of flying personnel. V: The Human-Figure Drawing Test as an objective psychiatric screening aid for student pilots. *USAF School of Aviation Medicine, Res. Rep.,* Proj. 21–37–002, 1952.

Ancona, Leonardo. Indagine sulla natura psichica del "response set." La "motivazione al successo." *Archivio psicologica, neurologica, e psychiatria,* 1954, **15,** 23–74.

Anderson, Harold H., & Anderson, Gladys L. (eds.). *An introduction to projective techniques.* New York: Prentice-Hall, 1951.

Anderson, John E. The limitations of infant and preschool tests in the measurement of intelligence. *J. Psychol.,* 1939, **8,** 351–379.

Anderson, John E. Freedom and constraint or potentiality and environment. *Psychol. Bull.,* 1944, **41,** 1–29.

Anderson, John E. (ed.). *Psychological aspect of aging.* Washington: American Psychological Association, 1956.

Anderson, Rose G. Modification of the McAdory Art Test. *J. consult. Psychol.*, 1948, **12**, 280–281.

Anderson, Rose G. A note on the McAdory and Meier Art tests in counseling. *Educ. psychol. Measmt*, 1951, **11**, 81–86.

Anon. A good man is hard to find. *Fortune*, 1946, **33**, 92–95 *et seq.*

Anon. Medical education in the United States and Canada. *J. Amer. med. Ass.*, 1956, **161**, 1659.

Arbous, A. G. Selection for industrial leadership. London: Oxford University Press, 1955.

Arbous, A. G., & Sichel, H. S. On the economies of a pre-screening technique for aptitude test batteries. *Psychometrika*, 1952, **17**, 331–346.

Arny, Clara B. *Evaluation and investigation in home economics.* New York: Appleton-Century-Crofts, 1953.

Arrington, Ruth E. Time-sampling studies of child behavior. *Psychol. Monogr.*, 1939, **51**, No. 2.

Atkinson, John W. (ed.). *Motives in fantasy, action and society.* New York: Van Nostrand, 1958.

Ayres, Leonard P. *A scale for measuring the quality of handwriting of school children.* New York: Russell Sage Foundation, 1912. (Now published by Educational Testing Service, Princeton.)

Baas, Malcolm L. Kuder interest patterns of psychologists. *J. appl. Psychol.*, 1950, **34**, 115–117.

Back, Kurt W. The Einstellung test and performance in factual interviewing. *J. abnorm. soc. Psychol.*, 1956, **52**, 28–32.

Baldwin, Alfred L., Kalhorn, Joan, & Breese, Fay Huffman. Patterns of parent behavior. *Psychol. Monogr.*, 1945, **58**, No. 3.

Baldwin, Alfred L., Kalhorn, Joan, & Breese, Fay Huffman. The appraisal of parent behavior. *Psychol. Monogr.*, 1949, **63**, No. 4.

Bales, R. Freed. *Interaction process analysis.* Cambridge: Addison-Wesley, 1951.

Bandura, Albert. The Rorschach white space response and "oppositional" behavior. *J. consult. Psychol.*, 1954, **18**, 17–21.

Barker, Roger, Dembo, Tamara, & Lewin, Kurt. Frustration and regression: an experiment with young children. *Univer. Ia. Stud. Child Welf.*, 1941, **18**, No. 1.

Barker, Roger G., Kounin, Jacob, & Wright, Herbert F. (eds.). *Child behavior and development.* New York: McGraw-Hill, 1943.

Barker, Roger G., & Wright, Herbert F. *One boy's day.* New York: Harper, 1951.

Barnette, W. Leslie. An occupational aptitude pattern for engineers. *Educ. psychol. Measmt*, 1951, **11**, 52–66.

Barron, Frank. *Personal soundness in university graduate students.* Berkeley: University of California Press, 1954.

Barron, Frank. Threshold for the perception of human movement in inkblots. *J. consult. Psychol.*, 1955, **19**, 33–38.

Barron, Frank. Dignity for unquantified children. *Contemp. Psychol.*, 1957, **2**, 69–70.

Barron, Frank, and others. An assessment study of Air Force officers. Part III: Assessment correlated of criteria of officer effectiveness. *WADC Technical Report* 58–91 (III), Wright Air Development Center, 1958.

Bass, Bernard M. The leaderless group discussion. *Psychol. Bull.*, 1954, **51**, 465–492.

Bass, Bernard M. Authoritarianism or acquiescence? *J. abnorm. soc. Psychol.*, 1955, **51**, 616–623.

Bass, Bernard M., & Coates, C. H. Forecasting officer potential using the leaderless group discussion. *J. abnorm. soc. Psychol.*, 1952, **47**, 321–325.

Bayley, Nancy. Mental growth during the first three years. *Genet. Psychol. Monogr.*, 1933, **14**, 1–93.

Bayley, Nancy. Consistency and variability in the growth of intelligence from birth to eighteen. *J. genet. Psychol.*, 1949, **75**, 165–196.

Bayley, Nancy. On the growth of intelligence. *Amer. Psychologist*, 1955, **10**, 805–818.

Bayley, Nancy. Data on the growth of intelligence between 16 and 21 years as measured by the Wechsler-Bellevue Scale. *J. genet. Psychol.*, 1957, **90**, 3–15.

Beck, Samuel J. *Rorschach's test. I: Basic processes.* New York: Grune & Stratton, 1944.

Beck, Samuel J. *Rorschach's test. III. Advances in interpretation.* New York: Grune & Stratton, 1952.

Beckham, A. A. Minimal intelligence levels for several occupations. *Personnel J.*, 1930, **9**, 309–313.

Bellak, Leopold. *The Thematic Apperception Test and the Children's Apperception Test in clinical use.* New York: Grune & Stratton, 1954.

Bellows, Roger M. The status of selection and counseling techniques for dental students. *J. consult. Psychol.*, 1940, **4**, 10–16.

Bender, Lauretta. A visual motor gestalt test and its clinical use. *Res. Monogr. Amer. Orthopsychiat. Ass.*, 1938, No. 3.

Bennett, George K. *Test of Mechanical Comprehension, Form AA, manual.* New York: Psychological Corporation, 1947.

Bennett, George K., & Cruikshank, Ruth M. *A summary of manual and mechanical ability tests.* New York: Psychological Corporation, 1942.

Bennett, George K., & Fear, Richard K. Mechanical comprehension and dexterity. *Personnel J.*, 1943, **22**, 12–17.

Bennett, George K., Seashore, Harold G., & Wesman, Alexander G. *Differential Aptitude Tests, manual.* New York: Psychological Corporation, 1947. (Loose leaf pages added in later years.)

Bennett, George K., Seashore, Harold G., & Wesman, Alexander G. *Counseling from profiles.* New York: Psychological Corporation, 1951.

Bennett, George K., Seashore, Harold G., & Wesman, Alexander G. *Manual for the Differential Aptitude Tests.* (3rd ed.) New York: Psychological Corporation, 1959.

Benton, Arthur L. Influence of incentives upon intelligence test scores of school children. *J. genet. Psychol.*, 1936, **49**, 494–496.

Benton, Arthur L. The experimental validation of the Rorschach test. *Brit. J. med. Psychol.*, 1950, **23**, 45–58.

Berdie, Ralph, Dressel, Paul, & Kelso, Paul. Relative validity of the Q and L scores of the ACE Psychological Examination. *Educ. psychol. Measmt*, 1951, **11**, 803–812.

Bernreuter, Robert G., & Carr, E. J. The interpretation of IQ's and the L-M Stanford-Binet. *J. educ. Psychol.*, 1938, **29**, 312–314.

Berry, Richard, & Porteus, S. D. *Intelligence and social valuation.* Vineland, N.J.: The Training School, 1920.

Biber, Barbara, & others. *Life and ways of the seven to eight year old.* New York: Basic Books, 1952.

Bingham, W. V. Great expectations. *Personnel Psychol.*, 1949, **2**, 397–404.

Bingham, W. V. Expectancies. *Année psychol.*, 1951, **50**, 549–555. (Reprinted in *Educ. psychol. Measmt*, 1953, **13**, 47–53.)

Bion, W. R. The leaderless group project. *Bull. Menninger Clin.*, 1946, **10**, 77–81.

Birnbaum, A. H., White, R. K., Rosenberg, N., & Willemin, L. P. Selection and standardization of tests for improved combat aptitude areas. *Personnel Res. Branch tech. Res. Note*, 1957, No. 87.

Bixler, Ray H., & Bixler, Virginia H. Test interpretation in vocational counseling. *Educ. psychol. Measmt*, 1946, **6**, 145–155.

Block, Jack. A comparison between ipsative and normative ratings of personality. *J. abnorm. soc. Psychol.*, 1957, **54**, 50–54.

Block, Jack, & Peterson, Paul. Q-sort item analysis of a number of Strong Vocational Interest Blank Inventory Scales. *AFOERL tech. Memoranda* TM-55–9, 1955.

Blommers, Paul, & Lindquist, E. F. Rate of comprehension of reading; its measurement and its relation to comprehension. *J. educ. Psychol.*, 1944, **35**, 449–473.

Bloom, Benjamin S. (ed.). *Taxonomy of educational objectives, handbook I: Cognitive domain.* New York: Longmans, Green, 1956.

Blum, Gerald S. *The Blacky Pictures, manual of instructions.* New York: Psychological Corporation, 1950.

Bond, Elden A. *Tenth grade abilities and achievements.* New York: Teachers College, Columbia University, 1940.

Bordin, Edward S. Ethical responsibilities of instructors in testing courses. *Educ. psychol. Measmt*, 1951, **11**, 383–386.

Bordin, Edward S., & Bixler, Ray H. Test selection: a process of counseling. *Educ. psychol. Measmt*, 1946, **6**, 361–373.

Bradway, Katherine P., Thompson, Clare W., & Cravens, Richard B. Preschool IQs after 25 years. *J. educ. Psychol.*, 1958, **49**, 278–281.

Brickman, William W. Preparation for the Regents' Examination. *Sch. & Soc.*, 1946, **64**, 263.

Brogden, Hubert E. A new coefficient: application to biserial correlation and to estimation of selective efficiency. *Psychometrika*, 1949, **14**, 169–182.

Brogden, Hubert E. Increased efficiency of selection resulting from replacement of a single predictor with several differential predictors. *Educ. psychol. Measmt*, 1951, **11**, 173–196.

Brokaw, Leland D. Technical school validity of the Airman Activity Inventory. *AFPTRC Develpm. Rep.* 56–109, 1956.

Brown, Andrew W. The change in intelligence quotients in behavior problem children. *J. educ. Psychol.*, 1930, **21**, 341–350.

Brown, Clara M. et al. *Minnesota food score cards,* Princeton: Educational Testing Service, 1946.

Brown, Clarence W., & Ghiselli, Edwin E. Prediction of labor turnover by aptitude tests. *J. appl. Psychol.*, 1953, **37**, 9–12.

Brown, Ralph R. The time interval between test and retest in its relation to the constancy of the intelligence quotient. *J. educ. Psychol.*, 1933, **24**, 81–96.

Brownell, William A., & Moser, Harold E. Meaningful versus mechanical learning: a study in Grade III subtraction. *Duke Univer. Res. Stud. Educ.*, 1949, No. 8.

Bryant, Norman D. A factor analysis of the Report of Officer Effectiveness. *AFPTRC Res. Rep.* 56–77, 1956.

Burdock, Eugene I., Sutton, Samuel, & Zubin, Joseph. Personality and psychopathology. *J. abnorm. soc. Psychol.*, 1958, **56**, 18–30.

Buros, Oscar K. (ed.). *The 1940 mental measurements yearbook*. Highland Park, N.J.: The Mental Measurements Yearbook, 1941.

Buros, Oscar K. (ed.). *The third mental measurements yearbook*. New Brunswick, N.J.: Rutgers University Press, 1949.

Buros, Oscar K. (ed.). *The fourth mental measurements yearbook*. Highland Park, N.J.: Gryphon Press, 1953.

Buros, Oscar K. (ed.). *The fifth mental measurements yearbook*. Highland Park, N.J.: Gryphon Press, 1959.

Burt, Cyril. The inheritance of mental ability. *Amer. Psychologist*, 1958, 13, 1–15.

Burtt, Harold E. *Principles of employment psychology*. (2nd ed.) New York: Harper, 1942.

Byrd, Eugene. A study of validity and constancy of choice in a sociometric test. *Sociometry*, 1951, 14, 175–181.

Campbell, Donald T. A typology of tests, projective and otherwise. *J. consult. Psychol.*, 1957, 21, 207–210.

Canfield, A. A. Administering Form BB of the Kuder Preference Record, half length. *J. appl. Psychol.*, 1953, 37, 197–200.

Canning, L., & others. Permanence of vocational interests of high school boys. *J. educ. Psychol.*, 1941, 32, 481–494.

Cantoni, Louis J. Guidance: 4 students 10 years later. *Clearing House*, 1954, 28, 474–478.

Cantoni, Louis J. High school tests and measurements as predictors of occupational status. *J. appl. Psychol.*, 1955, 39, 253–255.

Carroll, John B. Use of the *Modern Language Aptitude Test* in secondary schools. Unpublished, 1959.

Carter, Launor F. (ed.). *Psychological Research on Navigation Training*. Washington: Government Printing Office, 1947.

Carter, Launor F., & Dudek, Frank J. The use of psychological techniques in measuring and critically analyzing navigators' flight performance. *Psychometrika*, 1947, 12, 31–42.

Cattell, R. B., & Stice, Glen F. *The psychodynamics of small groups*. Urbana: Laboratory of Personality Assessment and Group Behavior, 1953 (mimeographed).

Cattell, Raymond B. *Personality and motivation structure and measurement*. Yonkers: World Book, 1957.

Cavanaugh, Maxine C., & others. Prediction from the Cattell Infant Intelligence Scale. *J. consult. Psychol.*, 1957, 21, 33–37.

Cervin, Vladimir. Relationship of ascendant-submissive behavior in dyadic groups of human subjects to their emotional responsiveness. *J. abnorm. soc. Psychol.*, 1957, 54, 241–249.

Champney, Horace, & Marshall, Helen. Optimal refinement of the rating scale. *J. appl. Psychol.*, 1939, 23, 323–331.

Chapman, Loren J., & Campbell, Donald T. Response set in the F scale. *J. abnorm. soc. Psychol.*, 1957, 54, 129–132.

Christie, Richard, Havel, Joan, & Seidenberg, B. Is the F scale irreversible? *J. abnorm. soc. Psychol.*, 1958, 56, 143–159.

Clark, Kenneth E. *Differences in vocational interests of men in seven Navy rates*. Minneapolis: Department of Psychology, University of Minnesota, 1950 (mimeographed).

Clark, Kenneth E., & Gee, Helen H. Selecting items for interest inventory keys. *J. appl. Psychol.*, 1954, **38**, 12–17.

Coleman, William, & Cureton, Edward E. Intelligence and achievement: the "jangle fallacy" again. *Educ. psychol. Measmt*, 1954, **14**, 347–351.

Coleman, William, & Ward, Annie W. A comparison of Davis-Eells and Kuhlmann-Finch scores of children from high and low socio-economic status. *J. educ. Psychol.*, 1955, **46**, 463–469.

College Entrance Examination Board. *46th annual report of the executive secretary.* New York: CEEB, 1946.

Conrad, Herbert S. The validity of personality ratings of nursery-school children. *J. educ. Psychol.*, 1932, **23**, 671–680.

Conrad, Herbert S. Statistical analysis for the Mechanical Knowledge Test. Princeton: College Entrance Exam. Bd., 1944.

Conrad, Herbert S. *A statistical evaluation of the Basic Classification Test battery (Form 1).* OSRD Rep. 4636. Washington: Department of Commerce, 1946.

Conrad, Herbert S., & Satter, George A. *The use of test scores and Qualification Card ratings in predicting success in electrician's mate school.* Washington: Department of Commerce, 1945.

Cooperative Test Division. *Cooperative School and College Ability Tests, examiner's manual.* Princeton: Educational Testing Service, 1955.

Cottle, W. C. Card vs. booklet forms of the MMPI. *J. appl. Psychol.*, 1950a, **34**, 255–259.

Cottle, William C. A factorial study of the Multiphasic, Strong, Kuder, and Bell inventories using a population of adult males. *Psychometrika*, 1950b, **15**, 25–47.

Cox, Catharine M. *Genetic studies of genius. II. The early mental traits of three hundred geniuses.* Stanford: Stanford University Press, 1926.

Crandall, Vaughn. Induced frustration and punishment-reward expectancy in thematic apperception stories. *J. consult. Psychol.*, 1951, **15**, 400–404.

Cronbach, Lee J. The true-false test: a reply to Count Etoxinod. *Education*, 1941, **62**, 59–61.

Cronbach, Lee J. Response sets and test validity. *Educ. psychol. Measmt*, 1946, **6**, 475–494.

Cronbach, Lee J. A validation design for qualitative studies of personality. *J. consult. Psychol.*, 1948, **12**, 363–374.

Cronbach, Lee J. Statistical methods applied to Rorschach scores: a review. *Psychol. Bull.*, 1949, **46**, 393–429.

Cronbach, Lee J. Further evidence on response sets and test design. *Educ. psychol. Measmt*, 1950, **10**, 3–31.

Cronbach, Lee J. Les exigences de la validation des techniques projectives. *Rev. Psychol. appliquee*, 1955a, **5**, 245–253.

Cronbach, Lee J. Processes affecting scores on "understanding of others" and "assumed similarity." *Psychol. Bull.*, 1955b, **52**, 177–193.

Cronbach, Lee J. Assessment of individual differences. *Annu. Rev. Psychol.*, 1956, **7**, 173–196.

Cronbach, Lee J. The two disciplines of scientific psychology. *Amer. Psychologist*, 1957, **12**, 671–684.

Cronbach, Lee J., & Gleser, Goldine C. Review of *The study of behavior. Psychometrika*, 1954, **19**, 327–333.

Cronbach, Lee J., & Gleser, Goldine C. *Psychological tests and personnel decisions.* Urbana: University of Illinois Press, 1957.

Cronbach, Lee J., & Meehl, Paul E. Construct validity in psychological tests. *Psychol. Bull.*, 1955, **52**, 281–302.

Cronbach, Lee J., & Warrington, W. G. Time limit tests: estimating their reliability and degree of speeding. *Psychometrika*, 1951, **16**, 167–188.

Cronbach, Lee J., & Warrington, Willard G. Efficiency of multiple-choice tests as a function of the spread of item difficulties. *Psychometrika*, 1952, **17**, 127–147.

Crosby, R. C., & Winsor, A. L. The validity of students' estimates of their own interests. *J. appl. Psychol.*, 1941, **25**, 408–414.

Dana, Richard H. Clinical diagnosis and objective test scoring. *J. abnorm. soc. Psychol.*, 1955, **50**, 19–24.

Dana, Richard H. An application of objective TAT scoring. *J. proj. Tech.*, 1956, **20**, 159–163.

Daniel, Robert S., & Louttit, C. M. *Professional problems in psychology.* New York: Prentice-Hall, 1953.

Darcy, Natalie T. The effect of bilingualism upon the measurement of the intelligence of children of preschool age. *J. educ. Psychol.*, 1946, **37**, 21–44.

Darley, John G. Tested maladjustment related to clinically diagnosed maladjustment. *J. appl. Psychol.*, 1937, **21**, 632–642.

Darley, John G., & Haganah, Theda. *Vocational interest measurement: theory and practice.* Minneapolis: University of Minnesota Press, 1955.

Davenport, Beverly Fest. The semantic validity of TAT interpretations. *J. consult. Psychol.*, 1952, **16**, 171–175.

Davis, Allison. Socio-economic influences upon children's learning. *Understanding the Child*, 1951, **20**, 10–16.

Davis, Frederick B. *Utilizing human talent.* Washington: American Council on Education, 1947.

Davis, Paul C. A factor analysis of the Wechsler-Bellevue Scale. *Educ. psychol. Measmt*, 1956, **16**, 127–146.

Dear, Robert E. The effects of a program of intensive coaching on SAT scores. *ETS Res. Bull.* 58–5, 1958.

Dearborn, Walter F., & Rothney, John W. M. *Predicting the child's development.* New York: Sci-Art Publishers, 1941.

Deemer, W. L., Jr. *E.R.C. Stenographic Aptitude Test, manual.* Chicago: Science Research Associates, 1944.

Deri, Susan K. *The Szondi Test.* New York: Grune & Stratton, 1949.

Dewey, John. *Experience and education.* New York: Macmillan, 1938.

Dillon, H. J. *Early school leavers—a major educational problem.* New York: National Child Labor Committee, 1949.

Donahue, Wilma C., & others (eds.). *The measurement of student adjustment and achievement.* Ann Arbor: University of Michigan Press, 1949.

Doppelt, Jerome E., & Bennett, George K. A longitudinal study of the Differential Aptitude Tests. *Educ. psychol. Measmt*, 1951, **11**, 228–237.

Dressel, Paul L., & Schmid, John. *An evaluation of the tests for general educational development.* Washington: American Council on Education, 1951.

DuBois, Philip H. (ed.). *The classification program.* Washington: Government Printing Office, 1947.

Dudycha, George J. An objective study of punctuality in relation to personality and achievement. *Arch. Psychol.*, 1936, No. 204.

Duncan, Acheson J. Some comments on the Army General Classification Test. *J. appl. Psychol.*, 1947, **31**, 143–149.

Dunnette, Marvin D. Vocational interest differences among engineers employed in different functions. *J. appl. Psychol.*, 1957, **41**, 273–278.

Durrell, Donald D. *Improvement of basic reading abilities.* Yonkers: World Book, 1940.

Dvorak, Beatrice J. Occupational testing, the scientific approach to personnel selection. *The Labor Market,* July 1956, 8–14.

Eckelberry, R. H. Book review. *Educ. Res. Bull.*, 1947, **26**, 138–139.

Edwards, Allen L. *The social desirability variable in personality research.* New York: Dryden, 1957.

Eells, Kenneth. *Social status in intelligence-test items.* Unpublished doctor's thesis, University of Chicago, 1948.

Eells, Kenneth, & others. *Intelligence and cultural differences.* Chicago: University of Chicago Press, 1951.

Escalona, Sybille. The use of infant tests for predictive purposes. *Bull. Menninger Clin.*, 1950, **14**, 117–128.

Estes, Stanley G., & Horn, Daniel. Interest patterns as related to fields of concentration among engineering students. *J. Psychol.*, 1939, **7**, 29–36.

Ethical standards of psychologists. Washington: American Psychological Association, 1953.

Etoxinod, Count Sussicran. How to checkmate certain vicious consequences of true-false tests. *Education,* 1940, **61**, 223–227.

Ewart, Edwin, & others. A factor analysis of an industrial merit rating scale. *J. appl. Psychol.*, 1941, **25**, 481–486.

Eysenck, H. J. *Uses and abuses of psychology.* London: Penguin, 1953.

Fahmy, M. *Initial exploring of the Shilluk intelligence.* Cairo: Dar Misr Printing Co., 1954.

Feder, D. D., & Baer, Opal L. A comparison of test records and clinical evaluations of personality adjustment. *J. educ. Psychol.*, 1941, **32**, 133–144.

Feifel, Herman. Qualitative differences in the vocabulary response of normals and abnormals. *Genet. Psychol. Monogr.*, 1949, **39**, 151–206.

Ferguson, Henry H. Incentives and an intelligence test. *Australian J. Psychol. Phil.*, 1937, **15**, 39–53.

Finch, Frank H. Enrollment increases and changes in the mental level of the high school population. *Appl. Psychol. Monogr.*, 1946, No. 10.

Fisher, Jerome, Gonda, T. A., & Little, K. B. The Rorschach and central nervous system pathology: a cross-validation study. *Amer. J. Psychiat.*, 1954, **7**, 487–492.

Fisher, Seymour, & Fisher, Rhoda. A test of certain assumptions regarding figure drawing analysis. *J. abnorm. soc. Psychol.*, 1950, **45**, 727–732.

Fitts, Paul M. German applied psychology during World War II. *Amer. Psychologist,* 1946, **1**, 141–161.

Flanagan, John C. *Factor analysis in the study of personality.* Stanford: Stanford University Press, 1935.

Flanagan, John C. The critical incidents technique. *Psychol. Bull.*, 1954, **51**, 327–358.

Flanagan, John C. The development of an index of examinee motivation. *Educ. psychol. Measmt,* 1955, **15**, 144–151.

Fleishman, Edwin A. Testing for psychomotor abilities by means of apparatus tests. *Psychol. Bull.*, 1953, **50**, 241–262.

Fleishman, Edwin A. Dimensional analysis of psychomotor abilities. *J. exp. Psychol.*, 1954, **48**, 437–454.

Fleishman, Edwin A. Psychomotor selection tests: research and application in the United States Air Force. *Personnel Psychol.*, 1956, **9**, 449–468.

Fleishman, Edwin A. A comparative study of aptitude patterns in unskilled and skilled motor performances. *J. appl. Psychol.*, 1957, **41**, 263–272.

Fleishman, Edwin A., & Hempel, Walter E., Jr. Changes in factor structure of a complex psychomotor test as a function of practice. *Psychometrika*, 1954a, **19**, 239–252.

Fleishman, Edwin A., & Hempel, Walter E., Jr. A factor analysis of dexterity tests. *Personnel Psychol.*, 1954b, **7**, 15–32.

Fleishman, Edwin A., & Hempel, Walter E., Jr. Factorial analysis of complex psychomotor performance and related skills. *J. appl. Psychol.*, 1956, **40**, 96–104.

Ford, Adelbert, & others. *The sonar pitch-memory test: a report on design standards.* San Diego: University of California Division of War Research, 1944.

Fowler, William L. A comparative analysis of pupil performance on conventional and culture-controlled mental tests. *Yearb. nat. Council on Measurements Used in Education*, 1957, **14**, 8–19.

Frandsen, Arden N., & Higginson, Jay B. The Stanford-Binet and the Wechsler Intelligence Scale for Children. *J. consult. Psychol.*, 1951, **15**, 236–238.

Frandsen, Arden N., McCullough, Betty R., & Stone, D. R. Serial versus consecutive order administration of the Stanford-Binet Intelligence Scales. *J. consult. Psychol.*, 1950, **14**, 316–320.

Frank, Irving H. Psychological testimony in a courtroom. *Amer. Psychologist*, 1956, **11**, 50–51.

Frank, Lawrence K. Projective methods for the study of personality. *J. Psychol.*, 1939, **8**, 389–413.

Frank, Lawrence K. *Projective methods.* Springfield, Ill.: C. C. Thomas, 1948.

Frederiksen, Norman, & Melville, Donald S. Differential predictability in the use of test scores. *Educ. psychol. Measmt*, 1954, **14**, 647–656.

Frederiksen, Norman, & Satter, G. A. The construction and validation of an arithmetical computation test. *Educ. psychol. Measmt*, 1953, **13**, 209–227.

French, Elizabeth G. Interrelation among some measures of rigidity under stress and nonstress conditions. *J. abnorm. soc. Psychol.*, 1955, **51**, 114–118.

French, Elizabeth G., & Thomas, Francis H. The relation of achievement motivation to problem-solving effectiveness. *J. abnorm. soc. Psychol.*, 1958, **56**, 45–48.

French, John W. Validation of new item types against four-year academic criteria. *J. educ. Psychol.*, 1958, **49**, 67–76.

Fricke, Benno G. Subtle and obvious test items and response set. *J. consult. Psychol.*, 1957, **21**, 250–252.

Furst, Edward J. The effect of the organization of learning experiences upon the organization of learning outcomes. *J. exp. Educ.*, 1950, **18**, 215–228, 343–352.

Gage, N. L., & Cronbach, Lee J. Conceptual and methodological problems in interpersonal perception. *Psychol. Rev.*, 1955, **62**, 411–422.

Gage, N. L., Leavitt, George S., & Stone, George C. The psychological meaning of acquiescence set for authoritarianism. *J. abnorm. soc. Psychol.*, 1957, **55**, 98–103.

Gallagher, James J. Normality and projective techniques. *J. abnorm. soc. Psychol.*, 1955, **50**, 259–264.

Garry, Ralph. Individual differences in ability to fake vocational interests. *J. appl. Psychol.*, 1953, **37**, 33–37.

Gaw, Frances. A study of performance tests. *Brit. J. Psychol.*, 1925, **15**, 374–392.

Gee, Helen Hofer, & Cowles, John T. (eds.). *The appraisal of applicants for medical schools.* Evanston, Ill.: Association of American Medical Colleges, 1957.

Ghiselli, Edwin E. The measurement of occupational aptitude. *Univer. Calif. Publ. Psychol.*, 1955, **8** (2), 101–216.

Ghiselli, Edwin E., & Barthol, Richard P. The validity of personality inventories in the selection of employees. *J. appl. Psychol.*, 1953, **37**, 18–20.

Gibson, James J. (ed.). *Motion picture testing and research.* Washington: Government Printing Office, 1947.

Gobetz, Wallace. A quantification, standardization, and validation of the Bender-Gestalt test on normal and neurotic adults. *Psychol. Monogr.*, 1953, **67**, No. 6.

Goldner, Ralph H. Individual differences in whole-part approach and flexibility-rigidity in problem solving. *Psychol. Monogr.*, 1957, **71**, No. 21.

Goodenough, Florence L. Some special problems of nature-nurture research. *Yearb. nat. Soc. Stud. of Educ.*, 1940, **39**, Part I, 367–384.

Gordon, Leonard V. *Gordon Personal Profile, manual.* Yonkers: World Book, 1953.

Gottschaldt, Kurt. Über den Einfluss der Erfahrung auf die Wahrnehmung von Figuren. I: Über den Einfluss gehäufter Einprägung von Figuren auf ihre Sichtbarkeit in umfassenden Konfigurationen. *Psychol. Forsch.*, 1926, **8**, 261–317.

Gough, Harrison G. *Manual, California Psychological Inventory.* Palo Alto: Consulting Psychologists Press, 1957.

Gough, Harrison G. An assessment study of Air Force officers. Part IV: Predictability of a composite criterion of officer effectiveness. *WADC Technical Report* 58–91 (IV), Wright Air Development Center, 1958.

Gough, Harrison G., & Krauss, Irving. As assessment study of Air Force officers. Part II: Description of the assessed sample. *WADC Technical Report* 58–91 (II), Wright Air Development Center, 1958.

Grayson, Harry M., & Tolman, Ruth S. A semantic study of concepts of clinical psychologists and psychiatrists. *J. abnorm. soc. Psychol.*, 1950, **45**, 216–231.

Greene, Edward B. *Measurements of human behavior.* (Rev. ed.) New York: Odyssey, 1952.

Griffiths, Ruth. *The abilities of babies.* London: University of London Press, 1954.

Gronlund, Norman E. *Sociometry in the classroom.* New York: Harper, 1959.

Guide to the use of the General Aptitude Test Battery. Washington: Government Printing Office, 1958.

Guilford, J. P. (ed.). *Printed classification tests.* Washington: Government Printing Office, 1947.

Guilford, J. P., *Fundamental statistics in psychology and education.* (3rd ed.) New York: McGraw-Hill, 1956.

Guilford, J. P. A revised structure of intellect. *Reports from the Psychological Laboratory of the University of Southern California*, 1957, No. 19.

Guilford, J. P., & others. A factor analysis study of human interests. *Psychol. Monogr.*, 1954, **68**, No. 4.

Gulliksen, Harold. Intrinsic validity. *Amer. Psychologist*, 1950a, **5**, 511–517.

Gulliksen, Harold. *Theory of mental tests.* New York: Wiley, 1950b.

Guthrie, G. M. Six MMPI diagnostic profile patterns. *J. Psychol.*, 1950, **30**, 317–323.

Guttman, Louis. The determinacy of factor-score matrices with implications for five other basic problems of common-factor theory. *Brit. J. statist. Psychol.*, 1955, **8**, 65–81.

Haganah, Theda. *A normative study of the revised Strong Vocational Interest Blank for Men.* Doctoral dissertation, University of Minnesota, 1953.

Hall, Julia C. Correlation of a modified form of Raven's Progressive Matrices

(1938) with the Wechsler Adult Intelligence Scale. *J. consult. Psychol.*, 1957, 21, 23–28.

Hall, William E., & Robinson, Francis P. An analytical approach to the study of reading skills. *J. educ. Psychol.*, 1945, 36, 429–442.

Halstead, Ward C. Biological intelligence. *J. Pers.*, 1951, 20, 118–130.

Hanley, Charles. Deriving a measure of test-taking defensiveness. *J. consult. Psychol.*, 1957, 21, 391–397.

Harding, F. D., Jr. Tests as selectors of language students. *Modern Language J.*, 1958, 42, 120–122.

Harlow, H. F. The formation of learning sets. *Psychol. Rev.*, 1949, 56, 51–65.

Harper, Edwin A. Discrimination between matched schizophrenics and normals by the Wechsler-Bellevue Scale. *J. consult. Psychol.*, 1950, 14, 351–357.

Harris, D. Factors affecting college grades: a review of the literature. *Psychol. Bull.*, 1940, 37, 125–166.

Harris, Daniel H. Questionnaire and interview in neuropsychiatric screening. *J. appl. Psychol.*, 45, 30, 644–648.

Hartmann, A. A. An experimental examination of the Thematic Apperception Technique in clinical diagnosis. *Psychol. Monogr.*, 1949, 63, No. 8.

Hartshorne, Hugh, & May, Mark A. *Studies in deceit.* New York: Macmillan, 1928.

Hartshorne, Hugh, & May, Mark A. *Studies in service and self-control.* New York: Macmillan, 1929.

Hartshorne, Hugh, & May, Mark A. *Studies in the organization of character.* New York: Macmillan, 1930.

Hathaway, Starke R., & McKinley, J. C. A multiphasic personality schedule (Minnesota): III. The measurement of symptomatic depression. *J. Psychol.*, 1942, 14, 73–84.

Hathaway, Starke R., & Meehl, Paul E. *An atlas for the clinical use of the MMPI.* Minneapolis: University of Minnesota Press, 1951.

Hathaway, Starke R., & Monachesi, Elio D. (eds.). *Analyzing and predicting juvenile delinquency with the MMPI.* Minneapolis: University of Minnesota Press, 1953.

Havighurst, R. J., & Janke, Leota L. Relations between ability and social status in a midwestern community. *J. educ. Psychol.*, 1944, 35, 357–368; 1945, 36, 499–509.

Havighurst, R. J., & others. Environment and the Draw-a-Man Test: the performance of Indian children. *J. abnorm. soc. Psychol.*, 1946, 41, 50–63.

Hebb, D. O., & Williams, Kenneth. A method of rating animal intelligence. *J. gen. Psychol.*, 1946, 34, 59–65.

Helmstadter, Gerald C., & Ortmeyer, Dale H. Some techniques for determining the relative magnitude of speed and power components of a test. *Educ. psychol. Measmt*, 1953, 13, 280–287.

Hempel, W. E., Jr., & Fleishman, Edwin A. A factor analysis of physical proficiency and manipulative skill. *J. appl. Psychol.*, 1953, 39, 12–16.

Henry, William E. The Thematic Apperception technique in the study of culture-personality relations. *Genet. Psychol. Monogr.*, 1947, 35, 3–135.

Henry, William E. *The analysis of fantasy.* New York: Wiley, 1956.

Herbert, A. P. *Number nine.* New York: Doubleday, 1952.

Hertz, Marguerite R. Rorschach: twenty years after. *Psychol. Bull.*, 1942, 39, 529–572.

Herzberg, Frederick, & Bouton, Arthur. A further study of the stability of the Kuder Preference Record. *Educ. Psychol. Measmt,* 1954, **14,** 326–331.

Hewer, Vivian H. (ed.). *New perspectives in counseling.* Minneapolis: University of Minnesota Press, 1955.

Highland, Richard W., & Berkshire, James R. A methodological study of forced-choice performance ratings. *Res. Bull.* 51–9, HRRC, 1951.

Hilden, Arnold H., & Skeels, Harold M. A comparison of the Stanford-Binet Scale, the Kuhlmann-Anderson Group Test, the Arthur Point Scale of Performance, and the Unit Scales of Attainment. *J. exp. Educ.,* 1935, **4,** 214–230.

Hills, John R. Factor-analyzed abilities and success in college mathematics. *Educ. psychol. Measmt,* 1957, **17,** 615–622.

Hollingworth, H. L. *Judging human character.* New York: Appleton-Century, 1922.

Holmen, Milton G, Katter, Robert V., Jones, Ann M., & Richardson, Irving F. An assessment program for OCS applicants. *HumRRO tech. Rep.* 26, 1956.

Holt, Robert R. Clinical and statistical prediction: a reformulation and some new data. *J. abnorm. soc. Psychol.,* 1958, **56,** 1–13.

Holt, Robert R., & Luborsky, Lester. *Personality patterns of psychiatrists.* New York: Basic Books, 1958.

Holtzman, Wayne H., *The inkblot test.* Austin: University of Texas, 1958.

Holtzman, Wayne H., Iscoe, Ira, & Calvin, A. D. Rorschach color responses and manifest anxiety in college women. *J. consult. Psychol.,* 1954, **18,** 317–324.

Holtzman, W. H., & Sells, S. B. Prediction of flying success by clinical analysis of test protocols. *J. abnorm. soc. Psychol.,* 1954, **49,** 485–490.

Honzik, Marjorie P., Macfarlane, Jean W., & Allen, Lucile. The stability of mental test performance between two and eighteen years. *J. exp. Educ.,* 1948, **17,** 309–324.

Hooker, Evelyn. The adjustment of the male overt homosexual. *J. proj. Tech.,* 1957, **21,** 18–31.

Horn, Charles A., & Smith, Leo F. The Horn Art Aptitude Inventory. *J. appl. Psychol.,* 1945, **29,** 350–359.

Humphreys, Lloyd G., Buxton, C. E., & Taylor, H. R. Steadiness and rifle marksmanship. *J. appl. Psychol.,* 1936, **20,** 680–688.

Hunt, J. McV. (ed.). *Personality and the behavior disorders.* New York: Ronald, 1944.

Hunt, William A., & Stevenson, Iris. Psychological testing in military clinical psychology: II. Personality testing. *Psychol. Rev.,* 1946, **53,** 107–115.

Hutt, Max L. A clinical study of "consecutive" and "adaptive" testing with the Revised Stanford-Binet. *J. consult. Psychol.,* 1947, **11,** 93–103.

Identification and guidance of able students. Washington: American Association for the Advancement of Science, 1958.

Irvine, R. P. Critical flicker frequency for paretics and schizophrenics. *J. abnorm. soc. Psychol.,* 1954, **49,** 87–88.

Isaac, W., & Ruch, T. C. Evaluation of four activity techniques for monkeys. *Science,* 1956, **123,** 1170.

Jack, Lois M. An experimental study of ascendant behavior in preschool children. *Univer. Ia. Stud. Child Welf.,* 1934, **9,** No. 3.

Jackson, Douglas N., & Messick, Samuel. Content and style in personality assessment. *Psychol. Bull.,* 1958, **55,** 243–252.

Jenkins, William O. A review of leadership studies with particular reference to military problems. *Psychol. Bull.*, 1947, **44**, 54–79.

John, E. Roy. Contributions to the study of the problem-solving process. *Psychol. Monogr.*, 1957, **71**, No. 447.

Johnson, Ralph H., & Bond, Guy L. Reading ease of commonly used tests. *J. appl. Psychol.*, 1950, **34**, 319–324.

Jones, Harold E., & others. *Development in adolescence.* New York: Appleton-Century, 1943.

Jones, Margaret H., & Case, Harry W. The validation of a new aptitude examination for engineering students. *Educ. psychol. Measmt*, 1955, **15**, 502–508.

Jones, Vernon. A comparison of measures of honesty at early adolescence with honesty in adulthood—a follow-up study. *Amer. Psychologist*, 1946, **1**, 261.

Judd, C. H., & others. *Education as cultivation of the higher mental processes.* New York: Macmillan, 1936.

Keir, Gertrude. The progressive matrices as applied to school children. *Brit. J. statist. Psychol.*, 1949, **2**, 140–150.

Kelley, Truman L. Mental factors of no importance. *J. educ. Psychol.*, 1939, **30**, 139–142.

Kelly, E. Lowell. Consistency of the adult personality. *Amer. Psychologist*, 1955, **10**, 659–681.

Kelly, E. Lowell, & Fiske, Donald W. *The prediction of performance in clinical psychology.* Ann Arbor: University of Michigan Press, 1951.

Kelly, George A. (ed.). *New methods in applied psychology.* College Park: University of Maryland, 1947.

Kelly, George A. *The psychology of personal constructs.* Vol. I. New York: Norton, 1955.

Kent, Grace H. Suggestions for the next revision of the Binet-Simon Scale. *Psychol. Rec.*, 1937, **1**, 409–433.

Kirk, Barbara A. Test versus academic performance in malfunctioning students. *J. consult. Psychol.*, 1952, **16**, 213–216.

Kirk, Samuel A. *Early education of the mentally retarded.* Urbana: University of Illinois Press, 1958.

Klein, George S., & Schlesinger, Herbert J. Perceptual attitudes toward instability: I. Prediction of apparent movement experiences from Rorschach response. *J. Pers.*, 1951, **19**, 289–302.

Klopfer, Bruno, Ainsworth, Mary, Klopfer, Walter G., & Holt, Robert R. *Developments in the Rorschach technique. I. Technique and theory.* Yonkers: World Book, 1954.

Knauft, E. G. Test validity over a seventeen-year period. *J. appl. Psychol.*, 1955, **39**, 382–383.

Kohs, S. C. *Intelligence measurement.* New York: Macmillan, 1923.

Krathwohl, David R. Prediction of objective test behavior by means of the group Rorschach. *Amer. Psychologist*, 1953, **8**, 382–383.

Krugman, Judith L., & others. Pupil functioning on the Stanford-Binet and the Wechsler Intelligence Scale for Children. *J. consult. Psychol.*, 1951, **15**, 475–483.

Kunze, Bruno. Proben für die Zusammenarbeit von Menschen und deren Wechselwirkung. *Industr. Psychotech.*, 1931, **8**, 147–159.

Kurtz, Albert K. Recent research on the selection of life insurance salesmen. *J. appl. psychol.*, 1941, **25**, 11–17.

Langmuir, Irving. Science, common sense, and decency. *Science*, 1943, **97**, 1–7.

Laugier, H. (ed.). *L'analyse factorielle et ses applications.* Paris: Centre Nationale de la Recherche Scientifique, 1955.

Layton, Wilbur L. *Counseling use of the Strong Vocational Interest Blank.* Minneapolis: University of Minnesota Press, 1958.

Lennon, Roger T. A comparison of results of three intelligence tests. *Test Service Notebk.,* 1952, 11.

Lennon, Roger T. The test manual as a medium of communication. *Proceedings, 1953 Invitational Conference on Testing Problems.* Princeton: Educational Testing Service, 1954, pp. 90–94.

Lennon, Roger T., & Baxter, Brent. Predictable aspects of clerical work. *J. appl. Psychol.,* 1945, 29, 1–3.

Levitt, Eugene E. The water-jar Einstellung test as a measure of rigidity. *Psychol. Bull.,* 1956, 53, 347–370.

Levy, Leon H., & Orr, Thomas B. The social psychology of Rorschach validity research. *J. abnorm. soc. Psychol.,* 1959, 58, 79–83.

Lewis, Don. The learning function. *Amer. Psychologist,* 1946, 1, 260.

Lindahl, Lawrence G. Movement analysis as an industrial training method. *J. appl. Psychol.,* 1945, 29, 420–436.

Lindquist, E. F. The use of tests in accreditation of military experience and in the educational placement of war veterans. *Educ. Rec.,* 1944, 25, 357–376.

Lindquist, E. F. (ed.). *Educational measurement.* Washington: American Council on Education, 1951.

Lindquist, E. F. The Iowa electronic test processing equipment. *Proceedings, 1953 Invitational Conference on Testing Problems.* Princeton: Educational Testing Service, 1954, pp. 160–168.

Lindsley, Ogden R. Operant conditioning methods applied to research in chronic schizophrenia. *Psychiat. Res. Rep.,* 1956, 5, 118–139.

Lindzey, Gardner (ed.). *Handbook of social psychology.* Cambridge: Addison-Wesley, 1954.

Lindzey, Gardner. *Assessment of Human Motives.* New York: Rinehart, 1958.

Lindzey, Gardner, & Herman, Peter S. Thematic Apperception Test: a note on reliability and situational validity. *J. proj. Tech.,* 1955, 19, 36–42.

Linton, Harriet B. Dependence on external influence: correlates in perception, attitudes, and judgement. *J. abnorm. soc. Psychol.* 1955, 51, 502–507.

Lipsett, Laurence, & Wilson, James W. Do "suitable" interests and mental ability lead to job satisfaction? *Educ. psychol. Measmt,* 1954, 14, 373–380.

Longstaff, Howard P. Fakability of the Strong Interest Blank and the Kuder Preference Record. *J. appl. Psychol.,* 1948, 32, 360–369.

Lord, Edith. Experimentally induced variations in Rorschach performance. *Psychol. Monogr.,* 1950, 64, No. 10.

Lord, Frederic M. *A theory of test scores. Psychometr. Monogr.,* 1952, No. 7.

Lord, Frederic M. Speeded tests and power tests—an empirical study of validities. *ETS Res. Bull.* 53–12, 1953.

Lorge, Irving. Gen-Like: halo or reality. *Psychol. Bull.,* 1937, 34, 545–546.

Lorr, Maurice, Jenkins, Richard L., & O'Connor, James P. Factors descriptive of psychopathology and behavior of hospitalized psychotics. *J. abnorm. soc. Psychol.,* 1955, 50, 78–86.

Lorr, Maurice, & Rubinstein, Eli A. Factors descriptive of psychiatric outpatients. *J. abnorm. soc. Psychol.,* 1955, 51, 514–522.

Louttit, C. M., & Browne, C. G. The use of psychometric instruments in psychological clinics. *J. consult. Psychol.,* 1946, 34, 119–126.

Love, Mary I., & Beach, Sylvia. Performance of children on the Davis-Eells Games and other measures of ability. *J. consult. Psychol.*, 1957, **21**, 29–32.

Lowell, Frances E. A study of the variability of IQ's in retest. *J. appl. Psychol.*, 1941, **25**, 341–356.

Luborsky, Lester. Selecting psychiatric residents: survey of the Topeka research. *Bull. Menninger Clin.*, 1954, **18**, 252–259.

Luchins, Abraham S. Mechanization in problem solving. *Psychol. Monogr.*, 1942, **54**, No. 6.

Luchins, Abraham S. On recent usage of the Einstellung-effect at a test of rigidity. *J. consult. Psychol.*, 1951, 89–94.

McArthur, Charles. Long-term validity of the Strong interest test in two subcultures. *J. appl. Psychol.*, 1954, **38**, 346–353.

McArthur, Charles, & Stevens, Lucia Beth. The validation of expressed interests as compared with inventoried interests: a fourteen year follow-up. *J. appl. Psychol.*, 1955, **39**, 184–189.

MacArthur, R. S. An experimental investigation of persistence in secondary school boys. *Canad. J. Psychol.*, 1955, **8**, 42–55.

McCall, Raymond J. Face validity in the D scale of the MMPI. *J. clin. Psychol.*, 1958, **14**, 77–80.

McClelland, David C. (ed.). *Studies in motivation.* New York: Appleton-Century-Crofts, 1955.

McClelland, David C., & others. *The achievement motive.* New York: Appleton-Century-Crofts, 1953.

McClelland, David C., & others. *Talent and society.* New York: Van Nostrand, 1958.

Macfarlane, Jean W., Allen, Lucile, & Honzik, Marjorie P. *A developmental study of the behavior problems of normal children between twenty-one months and fourteen years.* Berkeley: University of California Press, 1954.

McHugh, Gelolo. Changes in IQ at the public school kindergarten level. *Psychol. Monogr.*, 1943, **55**, No. 2.

McKinley, J. C., Hathaway, Starke R., & Meehl, Paul E. The MMPI: VI. The K Scale. *J. consult. Psychol.*, 1948, **12**, 20–31.

MacKinnon, Donald W. An assessment study of Air Force officers. Part V: Summary and applications. *WADC Technical Report* 58–91 (V), Wright Air Development Center, 1958.

MacKinnon, Donald W., and others. An assessment study of Air Force officers. Part I: Design of the study and description of the variables. *WADC Technical Report* 58–91 (I), Wright Air Development Center, 1958.

McNemar, Quinn. On abbreviated Wechsler-Bellevue scales. *J. consult. Psychol.*, 1950, **14**, 79–81.

McNemar, Quinn. Book review. *J. abnorm. soc. Psychol.*, 1952, **47**, 857–860.

McPherson, Marion W. A method of objectively measuring shop performance. *J. appl. Psychol.*, 1945, **29**, 22–26.

Magaret, Ann, & Thompson, Clare W. Differential test responses of normal, superior, and mentally deficient subjects. *J. abnorm. soc. Psychol.*, 1950, **45**, 163–167.

Mallinson, George G., & Crumbine, William M. An investigation of the stability of interests of high school students. *J. educ. Res.*, 1952, **45**, 369–383.

Mandler, George, & Sarason, Seymour B. A study of anxiety and learning. *J. abnorm. soc. Psychol.*, 1952, **47**, 166–173.

Martin, Andrew W., & Weichers, James E. Raven's Colored Progressive Matrices and the Wechsler Intelligence Scale for Children. *J. consult. Psychol.*, 1954, 18, 143–144.

Maurer, Katherine M. *Intellectual status at maturity as a criterion for selecting items in preschool tests.* Minneapolis: University of Minnesota Press, 1946.

Mayer, Barbara A. Negativistic reactions of preschool children on the new revision of the Stanford-Binet. *J. genet. Psychol.*, 1935, 46, 311–334.

Mays, Russell J. Relationships between length of acquaintance and nature of trait rated and agreement between raters. AFPTRC *Res. Bull.* 54–55, 1954.

Meehl, Paul E. An investigation of a general normality or control factor in personality testing. *Psychol. Monogr.*, 1945, 59, No. 4.

Meehl, Paul E. MMPI: research results for counselors. Unpublished lecture, VA hospital, Fort Snelling, Minnesota, 1951.

Meehl, Paul E. *Clinical vs. statistical prediction.* Minneapolis: University of Minnesota Press, 1954.

Meehl, Paul E. Wanted—a good cookbook. *Amer. Psychologist,* 1956, 11, 263–272.

Meehl, Paul E., & Hathaway, Starke R. The K factor as a suppressor variable in the MMPI. *J. appl. Psychol.*, 1946, 30, 525–564.

Meehl, Paul E., & Rosen, Albert. Antecedent probability and the efficiency of psychometric signs, patterns or cutting scores. *Psychol. Bull.*, 1955, 52, 194–216.

Meier, Norman C. (ed.). Studies in the psychology of art. III. *Psychol. Monogr.*, 1939, 51, No. 5.

Meili, Richard. L'analyse de l'intelligence. *Arch. Psychol.*, 1946, 31, 1–64.

Meili, Richard. *Lehrbuch der psychologischen Diagnostik.* (3rd ed.) Bern: Huber, 1955.

Melton, Arthur W. (ed.). *Apparatus tests.* Washington: Government Printing Office, 1947.

Messick, Samuel, & Jackson, Douglas N. Authoritarianism or acquiescence in Bass's data. *J. abnorm. soc. Psychol.*, 1957, 54, 424–426.

Mettler, Fred A. (ed.). *Selective partial ablation of the frontal cortex.* New York: Hoeber, 1949.

Michael, William B., Zimmerman, Wayne S., & Guilford, J. P. An investigation of the spatial relations and visualization factors in two high school samples. *Educ. psychol. Measmt,* 1951, 11, 561–577.

Mitchell, Mildred B. The revised Stanford-Binet for university students. *J. educ. Res.*, 1943, 36, 507–511.

Monroe, W. S. (ed.). *Encyclopedia of educational research.* (2nd ed.) New York: Macmillan, 1941.

Moore, Herbert. *Experience with employment tests.* New York, Nat. industr. Conf. Bd, 1941.

Moreno, J. L. *Who Shall Survive?* Washington: Nervous and Mental Diseases Publishing Company, 1934.

Morgan, J. J. B. *Child psychology.* (4th ed.) New York: Rinehart, 1942.

Morgan, William J. *The O. S. S. and I.* New York: Norton, 1957.

Morsh, Joseph E., & Schmid, John, Jr. Supervisory judgment as a criterion of airman performance. *AFPTRC Develpm. Rep.* 56–56, 1956.

Mosier, C. I. Factors influencing the validity of a scholastic interest scale. *J. educ. Psychol.*, 1937, 28, 188–196.

Mosier, Charles I. A critical examination of the concepts of face validity. *Educ. psychol Measmt,* 1947, 7, 191–205.

Moursy, E. M. The hierarchical organization of cognitive levels. *Brit. J. Psychol., Statistical Section,* 1952, **5**, 151–180.

Mugaas, Hendrick D., & Hester, Ruport. The development of an equation for identifying the interests of carpenters. *Educ. psychol. Measmt,* 1952, **12**, 408–414.

Murphy, Gardner, & Likert, Rensis. *Public opinion and the individual.* New York: Harper, 1938.

Murray, David C. An investigation of the Rorschach white space response in an extratensive experience balance as a measure of outwardly directed opposition. *J. proj. Tech.,* 1957, **21**, 40–53.

Murray, Henry A., & others. *Explorations in personality.* New York: Oxford University Press, 1938.

Mussen, Paul, Sanford, Dean, & Rosenberg, Margery. Some further evidence on the validity of the WISC. *J. consult. Psychol.,* 1952, **16**, 410–412.

Mussen, Paul H., & Naylor, H. Kelly. The relationships between overt and fantasy aggression. *J. abnorm. soc. Psychol.,* 1954, **49**, 235–240.

Myers, Roger C., & Gifford, Elizabeth V. Measuring abnormal pattern on the Revised Stanford-Binet Scale (Form L). *J. ment. Sci.,* 1943, **89**, 92–101.

Navran, Leslie, & Stauffacher, James C. Social desirability as a factor in Edwards Personality Preference Schedule performance. *J. consult. Psychol.,* 1954, **18**, 442.

Newcomb, Theodore M. *The consistency of certain extrovert-introvert behavior patterns in 51 problem boys.* New York: Teachers College, Columbia University, 1929.

Newman, Frances B., & Jones, Harold E. The adolescent in social groups. *Appl. psychol. Monogr.,* 1946, No. 9.

Noll, Victor H. Relation of scores on Davis-Eells Test of General Intelligence to social status, school achievement, and other intelligence test results. *Amer. Psychologist,* 1958, **13**, 394.

Office of Strategic Services Assessment Staff. *Assessment of men.* New York: Rinehart, 1948.

Ombredane, A., Robaye, Francine, & Plumail, H. Résultats d'une application répétée du matrix-couleur à une population de Noirs Congolais. *Bull. Centre d'Études et Recherches Psychotech.,* 1956, **6**, 129–147.

Osburn, Hobart G., Lubin, Ardie, Loeffler, J. C. & Tye, V. M. The relative validity of forced choice and single stimulus self description items. *Educ. psychol. Measmt,* 1954, **14**, 407–417.

Osgood, Charles E., & Luria, Zella. A blind analysis of a case of multiple personality using the Semantic Differential. *J. abnorm. soc. Psychol.,* 1954, **49**, 579–591.

Osgood, Charles E., Suci, George J., & Tannenbaum, Percy H. *The measurement of meaning.* Urbana: University of Illinois Press, 1957.

Otis, Jay L. The prediction of success in power sewing machine operating. *J. appl. Psychol.,* 1938, **22**, 350–366.

Otis, Jay L. Psychological espionage. Unpublished address, American Psychological Association, 1957.

Palmer, James O. A dual approach to Rorschach validation: a methodological study. *Psychol. Monogr.,* 1951, **65**, No. 8.

Pascal, Gerald, & Suttell, Barbara J. *The Bender-Gestalt test: its quantification and validity for adults.* New York: Grune & Stratton, 1951.

Paterson, Donald G., & others. *Minnesota Mechanical Ability Tests,* Minneapolis: University of Minnesota Press, 1930.

Patterson, C. H. *The Wechsler-Bellevue scales: a guide for counselors.* Springfield, Ill.: C. C. Thomas, 1953.

Patterson, C. H. Predicting success in trade and vocational courses: review of the literature. *Educ. Psychol. Measmt,* 1956, **16**, 352–400.

Pemberton, Carol. The closure factors related to temperament. *J. Pers.,* 1952a, **21**, 159–175.

Pemberton, Carol. The closure factors related to other cognitive processes. *Psychometrika,* 1952b, **17**, 267–288.

Perry, Dallis K. Validities of three interest keys for U.S. Navy yeomen. *J. appl. Psychol.,* 1955, **39**, 134–138.

Personnel classification tests. War Department Technical Manual 12–260. Washington: War Department, 1946.

Peters, Henry N., & Jones, Francis D. Evaluation of group psychotherapy by means of performance tests. *J. consult. Psychol.,* 1951, **15**, 363–367.

Peters, R., & Campbell, Joel T. Diagnosis of training needs of B-29 mechanics from supervisory ratings and self-ratings. *AFPTRC tech. Memorandum* 55–12, 1955.

Peterson, Donald A. *Factor analysis of the new United States Navy Basic Classification Battery.* Princeton: College Entrance Examination Board, 1943.

Peterson, Joseph. *Early conceptions and tests of intelligence.* Yonkers: World Book, 1925.

Piaget, Jean. *The psychology of intelligence.* London: Kegan Paul, 1947.

Pieron, Henri, Pichot, Pierre, Faverge, J.-M., & Stoetzel, Jean. *Méthodologie psychotechnique.* Paris: Presses Universitaires, 1952.

Pierson, George A., & Jex, Frank B. Using the Cooperative Tests to predict success in engineering. *Educ. psychol. Measmt,* 1951, **11**, 397–402.

Pintner, Rudolf, & others. Supplementary guide for the Revised Stanford-Binet Scale (Form L). *Appl. Psychol. Monogr.,* 1944, No. 3.

Plant, Walter T. Mental ability scores of freshmen in a California state college. *Calif. J. educ. Res.,* 1958, **9**, 72–73.

Plant, Walter T., & Richardson, Harold. The IQ of the average college student. *J. counsel. Psychol.,* 1958, **5**, 229–231.

Pollaczek, P. P. A study of malingering on the CVS abbreviated individual intelligence scale. *J. clin. Psychol.,* 1952, **8**, 75–81.

Porteus, S. D. The validity of the Porteus maze. *J. educ. Psychol.,* 1939, **30**, 172–178.

Porteus, S. D. *The Porteus maze test and intelligence.* Palo Alto: Pacific Books, 1950.

Powell, Margaret. Comparisons of self-ratings, peer ratings, and expert ratings of personality adjustment. *Educ. psychol. Measmt,* 1948, **8**, 225–234.

Preston, Harley O. *The development of a procedure for evaluating officers in the United States Air Force.* Pittsburgh: American Institute for Research, 1948.

Rapaport, David. *Diagnostic psychological testing.* Vol. I. Chicago: Yearbook Publishers, 1945.

Raths, Louis. Basis for comprehensive evaluation. *Educ. Res. Bull.,* 1936, **15**, 220–224.

Reik, Theodore. *Listening with the third ear.* New York: Farrar, Straus, 1948.

Rice, J. M. The futility of the spelling grind. *Forum,* 1897, **23**, 163–172, 409–419.

Richardson, Marion W. Forced-choice performance reports: a modern merit-rating method. *Personnel*, 1949, **26**, 205–212.

Roe, Anne. *The making of a scientist.* New York: Dodd, Mead, 1952.

Roe, Anne. A psychological study of eminent psychologists and anthropologists, and a comparison with biological and physical scientists. *Psychol. Monogr.*, 1953, **67**, 50–51.

Roe, Anne. Early determinants of vocational choice. *J. counsel. Psychol.*, 1957, **4**, 212–217.

Roethlisberger, Fritz, and Dickson, W. J. *Management and the worker.* Cambridge: Harvard University Press, 1939.

Rogers, Carl R. *Test of Personality Adjustment, manual.* New York: Association Press, 1931.

Rogers, Carl R. *Counseling and psychotherapy.* Boston: Houghton Mifflin, 1942.

Rogers, Carl R. Psychometric tests and client-centered counseling. *Educ. psychol. Measmt*, 1946, **6**, 139–144.

Rorschach, Hermann. *Psychodiagnostics.* Paul Lemkau and Bernard Kronenberg, (trans.). (2nd ed.) Bern: Huber, 1942.

Rotter, Julian B., Rafferty, Janet E., & Schachtitz, Eva. Validation of the Rotter Incomplete Sentences Blank for college screening. *J. consult. Psychol.*, 1949, **13**, 348–356, 454.

Rulon, Phillip J. A semantic test of intelligence. *Proceedings, 1952 Invitational Conference on Testing Problems.* Princeton: Educational Testing Service, 1953, pp. 84–92.

Rulon, Phillip J., & Schweiker, Robert F. *Validation of a nonverbal test of military trainability.* Harvard University: Graduate School of Education, 1953.

Rust, Metta M. The effect of resistance on intelligence scores of young children. *Child Develpm. Monogr.*, 1931, No. 6.

Rust, Ralph M., & Ryan, F. J. The Strong Vocational Interest Blank and college achievement. *J. appl. Psychol.*, 1954, **38**, 341–345.

Ryan, T. A., & Johnson, B. R. Interest scores in the selection of salesmen and servicemen: occupational vs. ability-group scoring keys. *J. appl. Psychol.*, 1942, **26**, 543–562.

Samuels, Henry. The validity of personality-trait ratings based on projective techniques. *Psychol. Monogr.*, 1952, **66**, No. 5.

Sarason, Seymour B. *The clinical interaction with special reference to the Rorschach.* New York: Harper, 1954.

Sarason, Seymour B., Davidson, Kenneth, Lightbill, Frederick, & Waite, Richard. A test anxiety scale for children. *Child Develpm.*, 1958, **29**, 105–115.

Sarason, Seymour B., Mandler, George, & Craighill, P. G. The effect of differential instructions on anxiety and learning. *J. abnorm. soc. Psychol.*, 1952, **47**, 561–565.

Sarbin, T. R. A contribution to the study of actuarial and individual methods of prediction. *Amer. J. Sociol.*, 1943, **48**, 593–602.

Schafer, Roy. *The clinical application of psychological tests.* New York: International University Press, 1948.

Schafer, Roy. *Psychoanalytic interpretation in Rorschach testing.* New York: Grune & Stratton, 1954.

Seagoe, May V. An evaluation of certain intelligence tests. *J. appl. Psychol.*, 1934, **18**, 432–436.

Seashore, Harold G., & Ricks, James H., Jr. Norms must be relevant. *Test Serv. Bull. psychol. Corp.*, 1950, 39, 2–3.

Seeman, William. "Subtlety" in structured tests. *J. consult. Psychol.*, 1952, 16, 278–283.

Segel, David. Differential prediction of scholastic success. *Sch. & Soc.*, 1934, 39, 91–96.

Semans, H. H., Holy, T. C., & Dunigan, L. H. A study of the June 1955 graduates of public high school in certain California counties. *Calif. Sch.*, 1956, 27, 417–430.

Sessions, Frank Q. An analysis of the predictive value of the Pre-Engineering Ability Test. *J. appl. Psychol.*, 1955, 39, 119–122.

Shannon, Claude, & Weaver, Warren. *The mathematical theory of communication.* Urbana: University of Illinois Press, 1949.

Shapiro, Edna, Biber, Barbara, & Minuchin, Patricia. The Cartoon Situations Test. *J. proj. Tech.*, 1957, 21, 172–184.

Shneidman, Edwin S. (ed.). *Thematic test analysis.* New York: Grune & Stratton, 1951.

Siegel, Arthur I. Retest-reliability of a movie technique of test administrators' judgments of performance in process. *J. appl. Psychol.*, 1954, 38, 390–392.

Silverman, A. J., Cohen, S. I., Zuidema, G. D., & Lazar, C. S. Prediction of physiological stress tolerance from projective tests. *J. proj. Tech.*, 1957, 21, 189–193.

Silverman, Robert E. The Edwards Personal Preference Schedule and social desirability. *J. consult. Psychol.*, 1957, 21, 402–404.

Simpson, Ray H. The specific meanings of certain terms indicating different degrees of frequency. *Quart. J. Speech*, 1944, 30, 328–330.

Skinner, B. F. Teaching machines. *Science*, 1958, 128, 969–977.

Smith, Eugene R., Tyler, Ralph W., & others. *Appraising and recording student progress.* New York: Harper, 1942.

Soskin, William F. Bias in postdiction from projective tests. *J. abnorm. soc. Psychol.*, 1954, 49, 69–74.

Soskin, William F. The influence of four types of data on diagnostic conceptualization in psychological testing. *J. abnorm. soc. Psychol.*, 1959, 58, 69–78.

Spence, Kenneth W. A theory of emotionally based drive (D) and its relation to performance in simple learning situations. *Amer. Psychologist*, 1958, 13, 131–141.

Staff, Advisement and Guidance Service, Veterans Administration. The use of tests in the Veterans Administration counseling program. *Educ. psychol. Measmt*, 1946, 6, 17–23.

Staff, Division on Child Development, American Council on Education. *Helping teachers understand children.* Washington: American Council on Education, 1945.

Staff, Psychological Research Project (Pilot). Psychological research on pilot training in the A.A.F. *Amer. Psychologist*, 1946, 1, 7–16.

Standards of ethical behavior for psychologists. *Amer. Psychologist*, 1958, 13, 266–272.

Starch, Daniel, & Elliot, E. C. Reliability of grading high school work in English. *Sch. Rev.*, 1912, 20, 442–457.

Starch, Daniel, & Elliot, E. C. Reliability of grading high school work in mathematics. *Sch. Rev.*, 1913, 21, 254–259.

Statistical studies of selective service testing, 1951–1953. Princeton: Educational Testing Service, 1955.

Stead, William H., & others. *Occupational counseling techniques.* New York: American Book, 1940.

Stephenson, William. *The study of behavior.* Chicago: University of Chicago Press, 1953.

Stevens, S. S. (ed.). *Handbook of experimental psychology.* New York: Wiley, 1951.

Stewart, Naomi. AGCT scores of Army personnel grouped by occupation. *Occupations,* 1947, **26,** 5–41.

Stockford, Lee, & Bissell, H. W. Factors involved in establishing a merit rating scale. *Personnel,* 1949, **26,** 94–116.

Stoddard, George D. *The meaning of intelligence.* New York: Macmillan, 1943.

Stogdill, Emily L., & Thomas, Minnie E. The Bernreuter Personality Inventory as a measure of student adjustment. *J. soc. Psychol.,* 1938, **9,** 299–315.

Strauss, Alfred A. Enriching the interpretation of the Stanford-Binet test. *J. except. Child.,* 1941, **7,** 260–264.

Strong, Edward K., Jr. *Vocational interests of men and women.* Stanford: Stanford University Press, 1943.

Strong, Edward K., Jr. Vocational interests of accountants. *J. appl. Psychol.,* 1949, **33,** 474–481.

Strong, Edward K., Jr. *Vocational interests 18 years after college.* Minneapolis: University of Minnesota Press, 1955.

Strong, Edward K., Jr., & Tucker, Anthony C. The use of vocational interest scales in planning a medical career. *Psychol. Monogr.,* 1952, **66,** No. 9.

Stroud, J. B. Predictive value of obtained intelligence quotients of groups favored and unfavored in socio-economic status. *Elemen. Sch. J.* 1942, **43,** 97–104.

Stuit, Dewey B. (ed.). *Personnel research and test development in the Bureau of Naval Personnel.* Princeton: Princeton University Press, 1947.

Sullivan, P. L., & Welsh, G. S. A technique for objective configural analysis of MMPI profiles. *J. consult. Psychol.,* 1952, **16,** 383–388.

Sundberg, Norman D. The acceptability of "fake" versus "bona fide" personality test interpretations. *J. abnorm. soc. Psychol.,* 1955, **50,** 145–147.

Super, Donald E. (ed.). *The use of multifactor tests in guidance.* Washington: American Personnel and Guidance Association, 1958.

Swineford, Frances. Analysis of a personality trait. *J. educ. Psychol.,* 1941, **32,** 438–444.

Symonds, Percival M. *Diagnosing personality and conduct.* New York: Appleton-Century, 1931.

Taylor, Janet A. The relationship of anxiety to the conditioned eyelid response. *J. exp. Psychol.,* 1951, **41,** 81–92.

Technical recommendations for achievement tests. Washington: National Education Association, 1955.

Technical recommendations for psychological tests and diagnostic techniques. *Psychol. Bull.,* 1954, **51,** Supplement.

Terman, Lewis M., *The measurement of intelligence.* Boston: Houghton Mifflin, 1916.

Terman, Lewis M., & Oden, Melita H. *Genetic studies of genius. IV. The gifted child grows up.* Stanford: Stanford University Press, 1947.

Terman, Lewis M., & Oden, Melita H. *Genetic studies of genius. V. The gifted group at midlife.* Stanford: Stanford University Press, 1959.

Terman, Lewis M. The discovery and encouragement of exceptional talent. *Amer. Psychologist*, 1954, 9, 221–230.

Terman, Lewis M., & Merrill, Maud A. *Measuring intelligence.* Boston: Houghton Mifflin, 1937.

Terman, Lewis M., & Merrill, Maud A. *Measuring intelligence.* Boston: Houghton Mifflin, 1959.

Tharp, James B. A modern language test. *J. higher Educ.*, 1935, 6, 103–104.

Thigpen, Corbett H., & Cleckley, Hervey. A case of multiple personality. *J. abnorm. soc. Psychol.*, 1953, 49, 135–151.

Thigpen, Corbett H., & Cleckley, Hervey. *The three faces of Eve.* New York: McGraw-Hill, 1957.

Thomas, Dorothy S., & others. *Some new techniques for studying social behavior.* New York: Teachers College, Columbia University, 1929.

Thorndike, E. L. Intelligence and its measurement: a symposium. *J. educ. Psychol.*, 1921, 12, 124–127.

Thorndike, Robert L. *Personnel selection.* New York: Wiley, 1949.

Thorndike, Robert L., & Hagen, Elizabeth. *Measurement and evaluation in psychology and education.* New York: Wiley, 1955.

Thorndike, Robert L., & Stein, S. An evaluation of the attempts to measure social intelligence. *Psychol. Bull.*, 1937, 34, 275–285.

Thornton, George R. A factor analysis of tests designed to measure persistence. *Psychol. Monogr.*, 1939, 51, No. 3.

Thurstone, L. L. Primary mental abilities. *Psychometr. Monogr.*, 1938, No. 1.

Thurstone, L. L. *Multiple-factor analysis.* Chicago: University of Chicago Press, 1947.

Thurstone, L. L. Creative talent. *Proceedings, 1950 Invitational Conference on Testing Problems.* Princeton: Educational Testing Service, 1951, pp. 55–69.

Tiffin, Joseph. *Industrial psychology.* (3rd ed.) New York: Prentice-Hall, 1952.

Torrance, E. P., & Ziller, R. C. Risk and life experience development of a scale for measuring risk-taking tendencies. *AFPTRC Res. Rep.* 57–23, 1957.

Training Aids Section, Ninth Naval District Headquarters, Great Lakes, Ill. A comparative study of verbalized and projected pictorial tests in gunnery. Unpublished, 1945.

Traxler, Arthur E. *The nature and use of reading tests.* Chicago: Science Research Associates, 1941.

Traxler, Arthur E. The IBM test scoring machine: an evaluation. *Proceedings, 1953 Invitational Conference on Testing Problems.* Princeton: Educational Testing Service, 1954, pp. 139–146.

Treat, Katherine. Tests for garment machine operators. *Personnel J.*, 1929, 8, 19–28.

Triggs, Frances O. A study of the relation of Kuder Preference Record scores to various other measures. *Educ. psychol. Measmt*, 1943, 3, 341–354.

Tuddenham, Read D. Soldier intelligence in World Wars I and II. *Amer. Psychologist*, 1948, 3, 54–56.

Tupes, Ernest C. Psychometric characteristics of Officer Effectiveness Reports of OCS graduates. *AFPTRC Res. Bull.* 57–20, 1957a.

Tupes, Ernest C. Relationships between behavior trait ratings by peers and later officer performance of USAF Officer Candidate School graduates. *AFPTRC Res. Bull.* 57–125, 1957b.

Turnbull, W. W. Socio-economic status and predictive test scores. *Canad. J. Psychol.*, 1951, **5**, 145–149.

Tyler, Leona E. The relationship of interests to abilities and reputation among first-grade children. *Educ. psychol. Measmt,* 1951, **11**, 255–264.

Tyler, Leona E. The development of "vocational interests": the organization of likes and dislikes in ten-year-old children. *J. genet. Psychol.*, 1955, **86**, 33–44.

Tyler, Leona E. *The psychology of individual differences.* (2nd ed.) New York: Appleton-Century-Crofts, 1956.

Tyler, Ralph W. *Constructing achievement tests.* Columbus: Ohio State University, 1934.

Ullmann, Charles A. *Identification of maladjusted school children.* Washington: U.S. Public Health Service, 1952.

Underwood, Benton J., & Richardson, Jack. Some verbal materials for the study of concept formation. *Psychol. Bull.*, 1956, **53**, 84–95.

Unit on Evaluation. *Test scoring service and rental service.* Champaign, Ill.: University of Illinois, 1955.

Using the Iowa Tests of Educational Development for college planning. Chicago: Science Research Associates, 1957.

van Lennep, D. J. *The Four Picture Test.* (2nd ed.) The Hague: Nijhoff, 1958.

Vernon, Philip E. The significance of the Rorschach test. *Brit. J. med. Psychol.*, 1935, **15**, 199–217.

Vernon, Philip E. The validation of civil service selection board procedures. *Occup. Psychol.* 1950a, **24**, 75–95.

Vernon, Philip E. *The structure of human abilities.* London: Methuen, 1950b.

Vernon, Philip E. *The measurement of abilities.* London: University of London Press, 1956.

Vernon, Philip E., & Parry, John B. *Personnel selection in the British forces.* London: University of London Press, 1949.

Waehner, Trude S. Interpretation of spontaneous drawings and painting. *Genet. psychol. Monogr.*, 1946, **33**, 3–72.

Wechsler, David. *Wechsler Adult Intelligence Scale, manual.* New York: Psychological Corporation, 1955.

Wechsler, David. *The measurement and appraisal of adult intelligence.* (4th ed.) Baltimore: Williams & Wilkins, 1958.

Welsh, George S., & Dahlstrom, Grant W. *Basic readings on the MMPI in psychology and medicine.* Minneapolis: University of Minnesota Press, 1956.

Wesman, Alexander G. Separation of sex groups in test reporting. *J. educ. Psychol.*, 1949, **40**, 223–229.

Wesman, Alexander G. Faking personality test scores in a simulated employment situation. *J. appl. Psychol.*, 1952, **36**, 112–113.

Wherry, Robert J., & Fryer, Douglas H. Buddy ratings: popularity contest or leadership criterion. *Personnel Psychol.* 1949, **2**, 147–159.

Whyte, William H., Jr. *The organization man.* New York: Simon and Schuster, 1956.

Wiener, Daniel N. Subtle and obvious keys for the MMPI. *J. consult. Psychol.* 1948, **12**, 164–170.

Wiener, Daniel N. Empirical occupational groupings of Kuder Preference Record profiles. *Educ. psychol. Measmt,* 1951, 11, 272–279.

Wiener, Gerald. The effect of distrust on some aspects of intelligence test behavior. *J. consult. Psychol.,* 1957, 21, 127–130.

Wightwick, M. I. *Vocational interest patterns.* Teachers College Contributions to Education, 1945, No. 900.

Willemin, Louis P., Mellinger, John J., & Karcher, E. Kenneth, Jr. Identifying fighters for combat. *Personnel Res. Branch, tech. Res. Rep.* 1112, 1958.

Williamson, E. G. *How to counsel students.* New York: McGraw-Hill, 1939.

Wilson, Donald Powell. *My six convicts.* New York: Rinehart, 1951.

Wilson, James W., & Carpenter, Kenneth E. The need for restandardizing altered tests. *Amer. Psychologist,* 1948, 3, 172 f.

Wissler, Clark. *The correlation of mental and physical tests.* New York: Columbia University, 1901.

Witkin, H. A. The nature and importance of individual differences in perception. *J. Pers.,* 1949, 18, 145–170.

Witkin, H. A. Individual differences in ease of perception of embedded figures. *J. Pers.,* 1950, 19, 1–15.

Witkin, H. A., & others. *Perception and personality.* New York: Harper, 1949.

Wolfle, Dael. *America's resources of specialized talent.* New York: Harper, 1954.

Woodworth, Donald G., & MacKinnon, Donald W. The use of trait ratings in an assessment of 100 Air Force captains. *WADC Technical Note* 58–64, Wright Air Development Center, 1958.

Yates, Alfred, & others. Symposium of the effects of coaching and practice in intelligence tests. *Brit. J. educ. Psychol.,* 1953, 23, 147–162; 1954, 24, 1–8, 57–63.

Yates, Aubrey J. The validity of some psychological tests of brain damage. *Psychol. Bull.,* 1954, 51, 359–379.

Yoakum, Clarence S., & Yerkes, Robert M. *Army mental tests.* New York: Holt, 1920.

Index of Names

Index of Subjects

Institute of Personality Assessment and Research, 587
Institutional decisions, 284, 324–358
Intelligence, 160, 164, 244–246
  social, 319
    See also General Mental Ability
Intelligence quotient (IQ), 102, 170 ff.
  distribution, 171–173
  interpretation of, 173–174
  stability, 176–179
  as standard score, 171
Interaction recorder, 536
Interest inventories, 405–439
  interpretation, 428–434
  stability of scores, 418–419
  summary list, 437
Internal consistency, 141–142
Interpretation, dynamic, 455–456, 579–581, 592 ff.
  to subject, 431–434, 487
Intervals, equal, 71, 385–387
Intrinsic validity, 58
Introversion, tests of, 466–468
Inventory, *see* Personality; Interest
Iowa Tests of Basic Skills, 383
Iowa Tests of Educational Development (ITED), 383
Item form, 371
Items, selection of, 364–367, 406–408

Job analysis, 325–327
Job performance, prediction of, 116, 217, 225–228, 279–280, 281, 306, 312–314, 342, 485
Job replica, 304–306, 312–314
Job satisfaction, 420–425
Judgment, errors of, 346–348, 506–510

Kohs Block Design Test, 41–42, 82, 558–560
Kuder Preference Record, 412–417 ff., 437, 448, 450
Kuder Preference Record—Personal, 496
Kuder-Richardson formulas, 141
Kuhlmann-Anderson Test, 218–224, 230

Language, foreign, aptitude for, 320
Layman, appeal to, 142
Leaderless Group Discussion (LGD), 566–567
Leadership, assessment of, 118, 516, 520, 566–568, 582–589
Lee-Thorpe Occupational Interest Inventory, 438
Leiter International Performance Scale, 207
Length of test, 130–132
Lewerenz Test of Fundamental Abilities in Visual Art, 317
Lorge-Thorndike Intelligence Tests, 230

Machine, test-scoring, 67–69
Make-a-Picture-Story Test (MAPS), 574
Manifest Anxiety Scale, Taylor, 451, 469, 477, 495
Manual, 100, 144
Manual dexterity, *see* Dexterity
Mathematics, prediction of success, 278–279
Maximum performance, 29, 370
Maze test, 29, 55
Mean, 78–79
Mechanical comprehension, 251, 252, 281 ff., 341
    See also Bennett Test of Mechanical Comprehension
Median, 75
Medicine, selection and guidance, 338, 352, 429, 486
Meier Art Judgment Test, 317
Memory factor, 256
Mental ability, *see* General Mental ability; Special ability
Mental age, 168 ff.
Mental deficiency, 169, 173, 205
Mental Measurements Yearbook, 101
Merrill-Palmer Scale, 207
Metal Filing Worksample, 306
Metropolitan Achievement Tests, 384
Miller Analogies Test, 231, 584
Minnesota Clerical Aptitude Test, 306
Minnesota Counseling Inventory (MCI), 491, 496
Minnesota Multiphasic Personality Inventory (MMPI), 458, 468, 469–485, 584
  case interpretation, 472, 491
Minnesota Paper Form Board, 306, 340
Minnesota Preschool Scale, 183, 207
Minnesota Rate of Manipulation Test, 306, 361
Minnesota Spatial Relations Formboard, 273, 306, 340
Minnesota Vocational Interest Inventory, 438
Modern Language Aptitude Test, 321
Mooney Problem Check Lists, 487, 497
Motion-picture as testing medium, 393
Motivation of persons tested, 52–64, 441, 449, 549, 574
Multiple Aptitude Tests, 292
Multiple correlation, 339 ff.
Multiple cutoff, 342 ff.
Myers-Briggs Inventory, 469
Matrix test, 215 ff.

Navy personnel, prediction of success, 253, 344, 346, 361, 371, 480
Need for achievement, 572–574
Neurotic states, 478–485, 562
Nomination technique, 519
    See also Peer rating

VERMONT COLLEGE
MONTPELIER, VT.

WITHDRAWN

Date